Modern Legal Philosophy Series:

THE WORLD'S
LEGAL PHILOSOPHIES

BY
FRITZ BEROLZHEIMER
*President of the International Society of Legal and
Economic Philosophy at Berlin*

TRANSLATED FROM THE GERMAN BY
RACHEL SZOLD JASTROW
of Madison, Wisconsin

WITH AN INTRODUCTION BY
SIR JOHN MACDONELL
Professor of Comparative Law in University College, London
AND BY
ALBERT KOCOUREK
Lecturer on Jurisprudence in Northwestern University

THE LAWBOOK EXCHANGE, LTD.
Clark, New Jersey

ISBN-13: 9781584772552 (hardcover)
ISBN-13: 9781616190705 (paperback)

Lawbook Exchange edition 2010

The quality of this reprint is equivalent to the quality of the original work.

THE LAWBOOK EXCHANGE, LTD.
33 Terminal Avenue
Clark, New Jersey 07066-1321

Please see our website for a selection of our other publications and fine facsimile reprints of classic works of legal history:
www.lawbookexchange.com

Library of Congress Cataloging-in-Publication Data

Berolzheimer, Fritz, 1869-1920.
 [System der rechts- und Wirtschaftsphilosophie. 2, Kulturstufen der Rechts- und Wirtschaftsphilosophie. English]
 The World's legal philosophies / by Fritz Berolzheimer ; translated from the German by   Rachel Szold Jastrow ; with an introduction by Sir John Macdonell and by Albert Kocourek.
  p. cm.
 Originally published: New York : Macmillan, 1929. (Modern legal philosophy series ; 2)
 Includes bibliographical references and index.
 ISBN 1-58477-255-7 (cloth : alk. paper)
  1. Law--Philosophy. 2. Law--Philosophy--History. I. Title. II. Modern legal   philosophy series ; 2.

K230.B47 A37 2002
340'.1--dc21   2002025952

Printed in the United States of America on acid-free paper

Modern Legal Philosophy Series:

THE WORLD'S
LEGAL PHILOSOPHIES

BY
FRITZ BEROLZHEIMER
*President of the International Society of Legal and
Economic Philosophy at Berlin*

TRANSLATED FROM THE GERMAN BY
RACHEL SZOLD JASTROW
of Madison, Wisconsin

WITH AN INTRODUCTION BY
SIR JOHN MACDONELL
Professor of Comparative Law in University College, London
AND BY
ALBERT KOCOUREK
Lecturer on Jurisprudence in Northwestern University

New York
THE MACMILLAN COMPANY
1929
All rights reserved

PRINTED IN THE UNITED STATES OF AMERICA

COPYRIGHT, 1912,
BY THE MACMILLAN COMPANY.

Reprinted August, 1924.

PRINTED IN THE UNITED STATES OF AMERICA BY
THE BERWICK & SMITH CO.

EDITORIAL COMMITTEE OF THE ASSOCIATION OF AMERICAN LAW SCHOOLS

MORRIS R. COHEN, Professor of Philosophy, College of the City of New York.
JOSEPH H. DRAKE, Professor of Law, University of Michigan.
ALBERT KOCOUREK, Professor of Law, Northwestern University.
ERNEST G. LORENZEN, Professor of Law, Yale University.
FLOYD R. MECHEM, Professor of Law, University of Chicago.
ROSCOE POUND, Professor of Law, Harvard University.
ARTHUR W. SPENCER, Brookline, Mass.
JOHN H. WIGMORE, *Chairman*, Professor of Law, Northwestern University.

LIST OF TRANSLATORS

ADALBERT ALBRECHT, South Easton, Mass.
ERNEST BRUNCKEN, Washington, D. C.
JOSEPH P. CHAMBERLAIN, Columbia University.
WM. G. HASTINGS, Professor of Law, University of Nebraska.
ISAAC HUSIK, Professor of Philosophy, University of Pennsylvania.
RACHEL SZOLD JASTROW, Madison, Wis.
ALBERT KOCOUREK, Chicago, Ill. (of the Editorial Committee).
JOHN LISLE, Philadelphia, Pa. (of the Philadelphia Bar).
MARTHA MC. READ, Washington, D. C.
ETHEL FORBES SCOTT, Urbana, Ill.
JOHN SIMPSON, New York, N. Y. (of the New York Bar).

GENERAL INTRODUCTION TO THE SERIES

By the Editorial Committee

"Until either philosophers become kings," said Socrates, "or kings philosophers, States will never succeed in remedying their shortcomings." And if he was loath to give forth this view, because, as he admitted, it might "sink him beneath the waters of laughter and ridicule," so to-day among us it would doubtless resound in folly if we sought to apply it again in our own field of State life, and to assert that philosophers must become lawyers or lawyers philosophers, if our law is ever to be advanced into its perfect working.

And yet there is hope, as there is need, among us to-day, of some such transformation. Of course, history shows that there always have been cycles of legal progress, and that they have often been heralded and guided by philosophies. But particularly there is hope that our own people may be the generation now about to exemplify this.

There are several reasons for thinking our people apt thereto. But, without delaying over the grounds for such speculations, let us recall that as shrewd and good-natured an observer as De Tocqueville saw this in us. He admits that "in most of the operations of the mind, each American appeals to the individual exercise of his own understanding alone; therefore in no country in the civilized world is less attention paid to philosophy than in the United States." But, he adds, "the Americans are much more addicted to the use of general ideas than the English, and entertain a much

GENERAL INTRODUCTION

greater relish for them." And since philosophy is, after all, only the science of general ideas—analyzing, restating, and reconstructing concrete experience—we may well trust that (if ever we do go at it with a will) we shall discover in ourselves a taste and high capacity for it, and shall direct our powers as fruitfully upon law as we have done upon other fields.

Hitherto, to be sure, our own outlook on juristic learning has been insular. The value of the study of comparative law has only in recent years come to be recognized by us. Our juristic methods are still primitive, in that we seek to know only by our own experience, and pay no heed to the experience of others. Our historic bond with English law alone, and our consequent lack of recognition of the universal character of law as a generic institution, have prevented any wide contact with foreign literatures. While heedless of external help in the practical matter of legislation, we have been oblivious to the abstract nature of law. Philosophy of law has been to us almost a meaningless and alien phrase. "All philosophers are reducible in the end to two classes only: utilitarians and futilitarians," is the cynical epigram of a great wit of modern fiction.[1] And no doubt the philistines of our profession would echo this sarcasm.

And yet no country and no age have ever been free (whether conscious of the fact or not) from some drift of philosophic thought. "In each epoch of time," says M. Leroy, in a brilliant book of recent years, "there is current a certain type of philosophic doctrine—a philosophy deep-seated in each one of us, and observable clearly and consciously in the utterances of the day—alike in novels, newspapers, and speeches, and equally

[1] M. Dumaresq, in Mr. Paterson's "The Old Dance Master."

GENERAL INTRODUCTION

in town and country, workshop and counting-house." Without some fundamental basis of action, or theory of ends, all legislation and judicial interpretation are reduced to an anarchy of uncertainty. It is like mathematics without fundamental definitions and axioms. Amidst such conditions, no legal demonstration can be fixed, even for a moment. Social institutions, instead of being governed by the guidance of an intelligent free will, are thrown back to the blind determinism of the forces manifested in the natural sciences. Even the phenomenon of experimental legislation, which is peculiar to Anglo-American countries, cannot successfully ignore the necessity of having social ends.

The time is ripe for action in this field. To quote the statement of reasons given in the memorial presented at the annual meeting of the Association of American Law Schools in August, 1910:—

> The need of the series now proposed is so obvious as hardly to need advocacy. We are on the threshold of a long period of constructive readjustment and restatement of our law in almost every department. We come to the task, as a profession, almost wholly untrained in the technic of legal analysis and legal science in general. Neither we, nor any community, could expect anything but crude results without thorough preparation. Many teachers, and scores of students and practitioners, must first have become thoroughly familiar with the world's methods of juristic thought. As a first preparation for the coming years of that kind of activity, it is the part of wisdom first to familiarize ourselves with what has been done by the great modern thinkers abroad—to catch up with the general state of learning on the subject. After a season of this, we shall breed a family of well-equipped and original thinkers of our own. Our own law must, of course, be worked out ultimately by our own thinkers; but they must first be equipped with the state of learning in the world to date.
>
> How far from "unpractical" this field of thought and research really is has been illustrated very recently in the Federal Supreme Court, where the opposing opinions in a great case (*Kuhn* v. *Fair-*

GENERAL INTRODUCTION

mont Coal Co.) turned upon the respective conceptions of "law" in the abstract, and where Professor Gray's recent work on "The Nature and Sources of the Law" was quoted, and supplied direct material for judicial decision.

Acting upon this memorial, the following resolution was passed at that meeting:—

That a committee of five be appointed by the president, to arrange for the translation and publication of a series of continental masterworks on jurisprudence and philosophy of law.

The committee spent a year in collecting the material. Advice was sought from a score of masters in the leading universities of France, Germany, Italy, Spain, and elsewhere. The present series is the result of these labors.

In the selection of this series, the committee's purpose has been, not so much to cover the whole field of modern philosophy of law, as to exhibit faithfully and fairly all the modern viewpoints of any present importance. The older foundation-works of two generations ago are, with some exceptions, already accessible in English translation. But they have been long supplanted by the products of newer schools of thought which are offered in this series in their latest and most representative form. It is believed that the complete series will represent in compact form a collection of materials whose equal cannot be found at this time in any single foreign literature.

The committee has not sought to offer the final solution of any philosophical or juristic problems; nor to follow any preference for any particular theory or school of thought. Its chief purpose has been to present to English readers the most representative views of the most modern writers in jurisprudence and philosophy of law. The series shows a wide geographical representation; but the selection has not been centered on the

GENERAL INTRODUCTION

notion of giving equal recognition to all countries. Primarily, the desire has been to represent the various schools of thought; and, consistently with this, then to represent the different chief countries. This aim, however, has involved little difficulty; for Continental thought has lines of cleavage which make it easy to represent the leading schools and the leading nations at the same time.

To offer here an historical introduction, surveying the various schools of thought and the progress from past to present, was regarded by the committee as unnecessary. The volumes of Dr. Berolzheimer and Professor Miraglia amply serve this purpose; and the introductory chapter of the latter volume provides a short summary of the history of general philosophy, rapidly placing the reader in touch with the various schools and their standpoints. The series has been so arranged (in the numbered list fronting the title page) as to indicate that order of perusal which will be most suitable for those who desire to master the field progressively and fruitfully.

The committee takes great pleasure in acknowledging the important part rendered in the consummation of this project, by the publisher, the authors, and the translators. Without them this series manifestly would have been impossible.

To the publisher we are grateful for the hearty sponsorship of a kind of literature which is so important to the advancement of American legal science. And here the Committee desires also to express its indebtedness to Elbert H. Gary, Esq., of New York City, for his ample provision of materials for legal science in the Gary Library of Continental Law (in Northwestern University). In the researches of preparation for this Series, those materials were found indispensable.

The authors (or their representatives) have cordially granted the right of English translation, and have shown

GENERAL INTRODUCTION

a friendly interest in promoting our aims. The committee would be assuming too much to thank these learned writers on its own behalf, since the debt is one that we all owe.

The severe labor of this undertaking fell upon the translators. It required not only a none too common linguistic skill, but also a wide range of varied learning in fields little travelled. Whatever success may attend and whatever good may follow will in a peculiar way be attributable to the scholarly labors of the several translators.

The committee finds special satisfaction in having been able to assemble in a common purpose such an array of talent and learning; and it will feel that its own small contribution of this unified effort has been amply recompensed if this series will measurably help to improve and to refine our institutions for the administration of justice.

INTRODUCTION TO THE TRANSLATED VOLUME

By Albert Kocourek[1]

At this moment legal philosophy is split up in three important camps — the Neo-Kantians, the Neo-Hegelians, and the Positivists — and the contending parties are ranged in battle formation on the field of an unyielding triangular contest.

I. The Kantian system is essentially formal. The metaphysical problem of the nature of reality is subordinated to the inquiry into the validity of knowledge. Metaphysics, says Kant, is that science which takes upon itself the task of solving ultimate problems dogmatically and "without any previous investigation of the ability or inability of reason for such an undertaking."[2] Kant compared himself to Copernicus, and attempted a "complete revolution in the procedure of metaphysics after the example of the geometricians."[3] His system

---

[1] Lecturer on Jurisprudence in Northwestern University School of Law.

[2] "Critique of Pure Reason" (Meiklejohn's translation), London, 1893, Preface vii et seq., p. 5.

[3] "Critique," xxxi. "Time is the formal condition à priori of all phenomena whatsoever. Space as the pure form of external intuition is limited as a condition à priori to external phenomena alone" — "Critique," p. 30. "They are the two pure forms of all intuition and thereby make synthetical propositions à priori possible. But these sources of knowledge being merely conditions of our sensibility, do therefore, and as such, strictly determine their own range and purpose, in that they do not and cannot present objects

is an elaborate walled-in mechanism constructed of chilled steel set apart from a world about which nothing can be known. It has the rigorous motion of a mathematical demonstration and the absolute symmetry of an isosceles triangle. It is only natural that when Kant turned his attention to the law he should base it upon a formal principle, a categorical imperative. This principle is the pure self-determination of the rational will expressed in the formula "Act according to a maxim which may at the same time be applied as a general law."[1] It is at this point that Kant's dualism between a sensuous and a supersensuous world appears in its most prominent aspect. The theoretical reason breaks down to give place to the practical reason, in which freedom is a necessary postulate of faith for the activity of the rational will.[2]

The uniformity and the universality of the laws of nature are apparent to everyone, and the stability and necessity of mathematical propositions have appealed to the human mind from the beginning of philosophic thought. No illusion can be more spontaneous (and our author shows us that illusions are important in the progress of culture) than that there is a fixed external basis of measurement for the valuation of human acts; in other words, that there is a law higher, better, more ideal, or more just than positive law. This thought has paralleled the existence of law.[3]

as things in themselves, but are applicable to them solely in so far as they are considered as sensuous phenomena" — "Critique," p. 33. See *Windelband*, "A History of Philosophy" (Tuft's translation), N. Y., 1910, pp. 532 et seq., and *Paulsen*, "Introduction to Philosophy" (Thilly's translation), N. Y., 1907, pp. 389 et seq.

[1] "Metaphysische Anfangsgründe der Rechtslehre," p. 25.
[2] See *Windelband*, op. cit., p. 554.
[3] See *Bergbohm*, "Jurisprudenz und Rechtsphilosophie," i, Leipzig, 1892, p. 112.

INTRODUCTION xiii

Kant's system was not only an intellectual bombshell in the field of the mental sciences, but it also started important and far-reaching developments in the social sciences.[1] If persuasion is still necessary to show the importance of philosophies in the practical affairs of the world, that proof is readily found in the after-effects of Kant's ideas.[2] From the standpoint of the lawyer, perhaps the most important position arrived at by Kant is his atomistic conception of the State and law: the State is the sum-total of the number of individuals in it.[3] The purpose of the State is simply to afford legal protection to its members in an equal degree. Such a State is limited solely to a protective function, and in political economy gives the "laissez faire" principle.[4]

The Neo-Kantian school has attempted to humanize Kant. It has "sought a method of determining not the absolutely and eternally just but the just relatively and

---

[1] "Kant set everything into most animated motion in the camps of all the divisions of the intellectual army, and they all put themselves under his banner. His rationalism contained not only the germ of a new cultivation of the branches of jurisprudence for which philosophy is an indispensable basis, but even in the purely positive departments of the science, new creations were reared upon the foundation already laid." *Friedländer* (in "Outlines of the Science of Jurisprudence," translated by W. Hastie, Edinburgh, 1887, p. 262).

[2] Such persuasion as to legal philosophy is still desirable in this country according to Professor Pound, who says: "The present Anglo-American attitude toward the philosophy of law has its counterpart in the phase of juristic thought from which we have happily emerged in which it was fashionable for every dabbler in jurisprudence to have his fling at Austin." "The Scope and Purpose of Sociological Jurisprudence," *Harvard Law Review*, xxiv, no. 8, p. 607.

[3] *Berolzheimer*, "Für den Neuhegelianismus." (Archiv für Rechts- und Wirtschaftsphilosophie, Bd. III, Heft 2, p. 194.)

[4] See *Gareis*, "Introd. to the Science of Law," p. 223.

for the time being."[1] It does not propose the ancient doctrine of a system of fixed ideas which are intended to take the place of experience, but it still adheres to a formal principle, a fixed *standard* for human conduct — a "natural law with a variable content."[2] "The content of a rule of conduct is just when in its application it conforms to the social ideal."[3] This social ideal is a community of men having a (Kantian) free will. Stammler has substituted for Kant's conception of the highest good (which means a union of virtue and happiness) a concession to the materialism of Feuerbach, Marx, and Engels; but in so far as he gives primacy to the teleological rather than to the causal influence of the processes of economic life, he safely maintains the dualistic position of his great predecessor.[4]

The practical possibilities of this latest disguise of natural law (as Bergbohm would call it) are beyond question. It is adapted for a useful mission of presenting a tangible, readily understood, and attractive program for the juridical progress of tomorrow in the same manner that the Benthamic formula of happiness served as the theoretical basis of the legal development of yesterday.[5] In any event this new (if it can be so denominated) theory of justice will do much to fortify with respectability the rationalistic impulse which resides in every human breast; and it will at least temporarily rescue the doctrine of natural law from the bad eminence which it had attained before the late revival of juridical idealism.

[1] *Pound*, "The Scope and Purpose of Sociological Jurisprudence," II, *Harvard Law Review*, xxv, 2, 149–150.

[2] *Stammler*, "Die Lehre von dem Richtigen Rechte," Berlin 1902, pp. 137 et seq.

[3] *Stammler*, op. cit., p. 198.

[4] *Stammler*, "Wirtschaft und Recht," 2d ed., Leipzig 1905.

[5] Cf. *Maine*, "Ancient Law," London 1909, pp. 83–84.

INTRODUCTION

Yet, before a philosophical acceptance of a natural law with a historically changing content can be assured, this theory must justify itself on difficult ground. It will not be easy to see that form and content have any relation between themselves in a real world, and if they bear no such relation, then we are dealing with mere shadows. The alternative, of a relation as of genus and species, will present difficulties to the man with a logical turn of mind. If the concrete rules of law cannot be permanently fixed, then the generic rule itself must be subject to modification unless, of course, there is a difference of essence between a principle and a rule.[1]

II. The Neo-Hegelians — a name invented by Berolzheimer, who is one of the leaders of this school — adopt Hegel's concept of evolution but reject his dialectic process. According to Hegel, philosophy is "an inquisition into the rational and therefore the apprehension of the real and present. Hence it cannot be the exposition of a world beyond which is merely a castle in the air, having no existence except in the terror of a one-sided and empty formalism of thought."[2] The corner stone of the Hegelian system is the proposition, "What is rational is real, and what is real is rational." "The rational is synonymous with the Idea, because in realizing itself it passes into external existence. It thus

---

[1] In his latest book recently published ("Theorie der Rechtswissenschaft") Stammler makes clearer his philosophical position. In effect, our author, reviewing the book, says that it tries to make a compromise between the voluntarism of Schopenhauer and the formalism of Kant through the social welfare theory of Ihering, and the reviewer descriptively adds that Stammler's conception of the will ("wollen") is a body without head or feet ("Archiv für Rechts- und Wirtschaftsphilosophie" v, 2, 320).

[2] "Philosophy of Law" (Dyde's translation), London, 1896, xxvi.

appears in an endless wealth of forms, figures, and phenomena."[1]

It is a system of logical pantheism embracing all nature and history as a unified whole which unfolds as the self-development of Idea by logical necessity. The Idea or Spirit is objectified in Law, Morals, and the State. The subjective or absolute Spirit is found in art, religion, and science.

Hegel's concept of freedom is perhaps the most striking point of contact with the practical application of the law. Kant emphasized the freedom of the individual, and attempted to raise the principle of freedom to an universal principle. Hegel finds in the Kantian position antinomies and developments in which "the moral standpoint wanders aimlessly around without being able to find a way of escape from the mere abstract imperative"—"it lacks all organic feeling."[2] Freedom, says Hegel, is the substance of the Spirit;—not the will of individual men, but the general will of the Godly substance is the principle of Law, Morals, and the State.[3] The State is an ethical notion, but its full realization is found only in universal history.

From these metaphysical foundations (thus touched in most general outline) of the most imposing world-system in the history of philosophy—combining, as Windelband says, "the intellectual labors of two thousand years"—the school of legal philosophy of which Josef Kohler is the acknowledged head takes its essential groundwork.[4] According to Kohler, law is a cultural

[1] Op. cit. xxvii.
[2] Op. cit., p. 129.
[3] *Harms*, "Begriff, Formen, und Grundlegung der Rechtsphilosophie" (Leipzig 1889), pp. 67 et seq.
[4] "They [the Neo-Hegelians] may claim, not without reason, to be the heirs of what is best in the philosophical and historical schools of nineteenth-century Germany"—*Pound*, op. cit., in *Harvard Law Review*, xxv, 2, 155.

INTRODUCTION xvii

phenomenon.[1] It is, therefore, historical and relative, and not (as Hegel thought) the product of pure reason and logical unfoldment. Berolzheimer departs from Kohler, not in the foundations, but rather in the superstructure.

The two cardinal elements and working-ideas of Neo-Hegelianism are evolution and pantheism. There is constant transformation, and unity in diversity. Hegel's evolution differed from Darwin's in this, that it is a rational process and not simply mechanical.[2] Kohler has substituted for Hegel's rationalism the notion of Culture, unfolding, not with logical necessity, but yet governed by a transcendental principle.[3] "God does not make a reckoning every working-day." Progress therefore is not an unyielding dialectical process, but an empirical development with a fulness of life.[4] The logical principle is bound up in the world's history with much that is illogical.[5] Justice contends with injustice, and truth with error. Change is the relative manifestation of reason; and the cultural principle at the background of the multiplied activities of historical development leads progressively to man's increased dominion over the forces of nature. Man is not a mere placental mammal, as Haeckel asserts, but has the

[1] See *Kohler*, "Rechtsphilosophie und Universalrechtsgeschichte," in Holtzendorff Enz., 6th ed., Bd. i, pp. 1–69.

[2] See *Kohler*, "Moderne Rechtsprobleme," Leipzig 1907, sec. 3, p. 6.

[3] *Kohler*, loc. cit., p. 9. Cf. the critical essay on Kohler by Prof. *J. Castillejo y Duarte* in "Biblioteca de Derecho y de Ciencias Sociales," Madrid 1910.

[4] See in this connection the work of the Italian Neo-Hegelian, *Croce*, enlarged and translated into German under the title, "Lebendiges und Totes in Hegels Philosophie," Heidelberg 1909.

[5] *Kohler*, "Lehrbuch der Rechtsphilosophie," Berlin 1909, p. 13.

capacity of acquiring the attributes of godliness.[1] Thought and things are not, as in the Kantian system, poles apart, but are consubstantial; they are related as form and image.[2] Kohler places a strong emphasis on legal ethnology and universal history — Berolzheimer thinks too much emphasis.[3] Berolzheimer therefore also concludes that Kohler has perhaps made Culture too prominent, and that what he has felt with the intuition of the philosopher he has expressed rather with the skill of the artist than with the analytical and logical precision of the scientist.

In another important aspect, Berolzheimer again departs from Kohler — in the function of the human will. The Heraclitean notion that all things are in a flux of becoming, and that change is the essential attribute of being, Berolzheimer thinks excludes a practical mission to Kohler's philosophy of law. He therefore insists that legal philosophy is a branch of practical philosophy, having to do with human standards and requiring the interpenetration of the human will with the totality of forces which create the restless evolutionary chain.

The Hegelian doctrine therefore requires for its completion the idea that all culture, including legal culture, is an artificial force. This seems to be the principal point of separation between Kohler and Berolzheimer. Kohler's position seems to be quietistic,[4] at least teleologically, while Berolzheimer's point of view is active

---

[1] *Kohler*, "The Mission and Objects of Philosophy of Law," *Ill. Law Rev.*, v, 7, 426.

[2] "Lehrbuch," p. 9.

[3] "Die Deutsche Rechtsphilosophie im Zwanzigsten Jahrhundert" (1900–1906), in "Archiv f. R.- u. W. phil.," i, 1, 134.

[4] Kohler vigorously denies this: see "Moderne Rechtsprobleme," p. 17.

and practical. For him, philosophy of law is not merely an explanation of cultural phenomena, the possession of enlightened minds, the ideological counterpart which reflects but does not participate in the infinite multiplicity and variability of life, but is a tangible, objective and effective instrument which may be applied to the problems of human society. It should, however, be stated that the variance between these great leaders of Neo-Hegelianism on this important philosophical position may turn out to be apparent rather than actual, since neither writer has entered on the discussion of the point sufficiently to allow an absolute judgment.

III. The Positivist School displaces a metaphysics of things with a metaphysics of knowledge. According to Hume, one of the greatest of England's philosophers, "There is no knowledge of what things are and how they work: we can say only what we perceive by sensation, what arrangement in space and time and what relations of resemblance we experience between them."[1]

Hume's position reached its best applied formulation in Comte, for whom relativity is the only absolute principle. On its theoretical or epistemological side, Positivism changed into Kantian Criticism, while on the practical side, Positivism parallels in part the line of Neo-Hegelianism. For Comte, sociality is an original fact and is not connected with individuals. This postulate is one much admired by the Neo-Hegelians;[2] but the Positivists make society more important than the State, and this proposition the Neo-Hegelian does not admit.

[1] *Windelband*, op. cit., p. 478.
[2] Thus *Kohler*, "Vom Positivismus zum Neu-Hegelianismus," in "Archiv für Rechts- und Wirtschaftsphilosophie," iii, 2, 167.

The most recent and best known development of Positivism is expressed by the pragmatic philosophy,[1] "The test of amount of existence in a given object is, for pragmatism as for common sense, amount of resistance."[2]

If the Positivism of Comte was (as Kohler says) diluted materialism, it has at this day thoroughly dried out; it has become the philosophy which expresses the popular conception of the world, realistic empiricism. Thus Positivism rejects metaphysics, and looks with suspicion on ethics. Its methods are inductive and analytical; it proceeds upon the basis of the natural sciences in all departments of knowledge. The world is subjected to the test of scientific investigation by the aid of experience alone, and in the hands of such systematizers as Spencer an attempt is made to unify the results of this investigation in a single principle. It does not concern itself with the ultimate nature of things, holding them unknowable, and rests on mere description. It cuts into the dead body lying stark on the dissection table but it knows nothing of life.

This safely external and unimaginative method lends to Positivism both its weakness and its strength: its weakness, in that it is incapable of touching any of the ultimate problems of life; its strength, in that it never wanders out of the domain of lived truths. This school will find a place in this series in a work of the renowned Italian teacher, Icilio Vanni, and is brilliantly represented in this country in its sociological aspect by one of our profoundest juristic scholars, Roscoe Pound.

[1] Cf. *Dauriac*, "Positivisme et Pragmatisme," in "Revue Philosophique," xxxvi, 12, 584.

[2] *Dauriac*, "Le Pragmatisme et le Realisme," Rev. Ph. xxxvi, 10, 337 (Katherine Everett's summary in *The Philosophical Review*, xxi, 1, 119).

INTRODUCTION

Berolzneimer finds in the work of Stammler some things to commend, but he repels the assertions of the sociological school with the greatest vehemence, as fatalistic, teleological, and philosophically inert. It requires to be noticed, however, that the sociological school, through its adherents in the various departments of social science, has had a greater influence than the pure Hegelian philosophy in bringing about that very emancipation of the classes which Berolzheimer (annexing the group sociology of Gumplowicz) indicates as the greatest practical vocation of philosophy of law; and that it has been one of the strongest forces working with a practical program and a readily understood theory in the latter-day movement of the socialization of the law.

The Positivist claims a place in front of the stage of life. He relies for his understanding of the play on what comes to him in the way of representation. He deals with phenomena and not noumena. He does not know and assumes that he cannot know what goes on behind the scenes. The Kantian has a position back of the stage where in the midst of the mechanism of categories, analytic and synthetic judgments, and paralogisms of pure reason, he hears and sees with a foreign understanding, and concludes that the reality cannot be known. The Hegelian alone has the center of the stage and participates in the action. He is not troubled with the problem of reality. He knows that the play is governed both by the principles of unity and reason, but he inclines to the fatalistic view that the movement follows fixed laws of dramaturgy, that the unfoldment of the play is beyond his control. The position of both the Kantians and Hegelians has changed. The Kantian now assumes that the mechanical trappings of the stage may be used for various scenarios; and the Hegelian has come to believe that he may interpolate lines. The Positivist has, however, not changed his position; he is still a spectator, although a critical one.

In this enumeration of schools of philosophy of law the omission will be noted, of course, of some familiar and not unimportant theoretical viewpoints. This is because these standpoints are absorbed by one of the leading schools (and usually the Positivist School), or do not rise to the universality of a valid philosophy, or are wholly apart from a philosophy of law. Thus, ethnological and historical jurisprudence is only an auxiliary of philosophy of law; the psychological theory in its various aspects never rises above a method, a theory or a department of science; the biological theory seems to possess only an analogical and descriptive value; the theological view overshoots the mark of philosophy; the teleological notion is swallowed up by the Positivist School; the Natural Law standpoint is taken into account in the Neo-Kantian School in most of its recent variations, and in its eighteenth century form is discredited everywhere except in America; the purely ethical idea of law resolves itself into some other final or mediate theory; the last observation holds also for the types of the law of reason; the school of "free legal interpretation" rests either on a method or combines elsewhere — only once or twice has it risen to a philosophic attachment; and finally the imperative or political theory of law rests on nothing but the will of the lawgiver.

Berolzheimer's painstaking work, of which this book is the second volume, is the most important systematic contribution to philosophy of law since Lasson's "System der Rechtsphilosophie," published more than twenty years earlier. In this volume is presented everything of interest in the history of philosophy of law — so far at least as Germany has been concerned. The Germans are inclined to claim sufficiency unto themselves in any department of philosophy, and perhaps justly so; but the almost entire lack of consideration of modern philosophic thought in other countries, and particularly in Italy, will be quickly noted, and might be regarded as a defect not to be lightly excused in an author who has shown such immense reading, such sound legal and historical scholarship, and so masterly an execution of a most difficult labor. Taken even with its preponderant localization of treatment, and deducting for the fact that it carries a philosophy of its own which it seeks to impress on the reader at every point — even with these allowances, Berolzheimer's book is the most satisfactory treatise on the history of philosophy of law in any literature. The extent of the author's industry may be appreciated when it is seen that nearly seven hundred authors' names are entered in the original work, of which number about two hundred receive more or less extended notice. The original text is securely fortified by an impregnable defense of footnotes and arsenals of bibliographies. It was thought desirable in this translation to eliminate a large part of this reference apparatus.

"Since Kant," says the author, "the superstition has grown that clear and simple writing is not philosophical." This superstition is fairly demolished in the present original text, and the learned translator has adequately completed the work of destruction in this English rendering. If a comparison may be forgiven, we might say that the translator's English is better than the author's German.

No childbirth is so heavy with labor and pain as the childbirth of an idea. "It can hardly be realized," says Berolzheimer, "that a truth so near and so apparent as the reciprocity of economics and law should so tardily find a place in science, and that this truth is even yet combatted." For Berolzheimer, philosophy of law without an economic content is an empty vessel. A purely speculative philosophy of law based on categorical imperatives, intellectual abstractions, or a dialectical process leads to nothing in this world. Neo-Hegelianism certainly means idealism, but it is realistic idealism. It employs the methods of the laboratory sciences, and supplements their statistical and experimental results by the aid of comparative law and legal ethnology. The economic content of law of which Berolzheimer speaks is not, as he is careful to explain, the material conception of Marx, but includes all the factors bearing on social life. Law is the form, economics is the material. The economic associates are one with the citizens of the state; economic subjects are identical with legal subjects; and economic objects are the same as legal objects. Accordingly, he says, the idea of the just on its formal side is the object of philosophy of law, and the idea of the just on the material side is the object of economics.

Ethics, like law, is an artificial force; but it acts on social life by a different sanction. Politics is (as Berolzheimer has expressed it) the small change of philosophy of law. Philosophy of law alone is fruitful as the original source of political ideas.

In another place [1] Berolzheimer has made one of those interesting and illuminating generalizations suggestive of the genius of Maine to show the essential relativity of law. He outlines three evolutionary stages in the cultural progress of law and economics. The first is the period of the confusion of religion and law, in which society is a religious association. The second is the anethical stage, in which law breaks away entirely

[1] "Deutschland von Heute," Berlin, 1910.

from ethics. The classic example is the ancient Roman "jus civile." In the third step of evolution there is a synthesis of law and morals. Law is softened and refined by the ethical notion, which is fundamentally, as he tells us, nothing other than the humanitarian idea.

The present work exhibits the progressive steps in the development of this humanitarian thought in the law, based on economics; the whole modern period consisting of a variety of emancipation processes beginning with the separation of Church and State, following with the emancipation of the common people, and ending with the economic freedom of the Fourth Estate.

We are seriously concerned with the past because of our more serious concern for the future. The world now faces new economic problems of peculiar difficulty and urgency. Can anything be more stupid than our legal treatment of such questions as the tariff, the trusts, and the labor problem? In the words of the author, "The extent and variety of these problems point imperatively to a profounder, scientific preparatory labor which can only be furthered by a philosophy of law and economics."

INTRODUCTION TO THE TRANSLATED VOLUME

By Sir John Macdonell [1]

In Germany there is, and long has been, a vast literature treating, under the title "Philosophy of Law," of subjects which American and English lawyers rarely discuss. Our author propounds problems, debates, rejects or accepts solutions which for them have little interest; as to some of them, I might even say, no meaning. Only certain minds feel strongly the need of a complete conception including all phenomena in a particular region, a clear view of all the facts and their fusion into a whole.[2] Those who have been bred in the study of English law rarely experience this need, which has called forth the literature reviewed in this book. They do not inquire into the justification of coercion, discussed by Stammler and many other writers; enough for them that it exists. They do not examine the relations of economics to law; that question is for others. They do not deal with the proper province of the State; that also is outside their inquiries. I am tempted to say that English jurists begin at the point where many Continental jurists stop. For the former, philosophy

---

[1] Vice-chairman of The Society of Comparative Legislation, co-editor of the Journal of the Society of Comparative Legislation, Professor of Comparative Law in University College, University of London.

[2] "A systematic co-ordination of the several (social) phenomena under a comprehensive principle." *Stammler.*

is an intruder. They look with some suspicion upon Jurisprudence; they will not look beyond it, to the fundamental problems, discussed in these pages with great knowledge and wide outlook. That whole attitude has become untenable. In times such as these, of changes profoundly affecting all parts of law, it is essential to go back to principles; and he who would not be the mere "leguleius" must be the philosophic jurist.

As understood by many of the writers whom Dr. Berolzheimer reviews, the Philosophy of Law is not jurisprudence even in the widest sense of that term; it is not so in the view of Dr. Berolzheimer himself. It is not sociology or a part thereof; our author and others distinguish it therefrom; they show that sociology does not solve the chief problems with which they are concerned. It is not historical or comparative or ethnological jurisprudence. "The peculiarly important philosophic problem of the origin of law and Government, comparative law cannot be expected to solve, if for no other reason than that it ever finds the presence of law and Government as a pre-requisite for its study." The study of these subjects may be necessary preliminaries to a philosophy of law, but they are not identical with it. Nor is it Ethics, though according to some of the authors noticed in these pages, many of the problems of both are the same. It is not the psychological basis or origin of law; though that is discussed by Dr. Berolzheimer and many of the authors passed in review. Nor is this diversity wonderful. There being no agreement as to what is law, perhaps it is not surprising that writers are not at one as to what is the philosophy of law.

What then is the philosophy of law? The answers of the many authors who are passed in review in these pages, though very diverse, agree as to the vastness of the subject. "It is," says one answer, "an attempt to furnish the key to all the problems presented by legal phenomena" — which would embrace everything into which law enters. According to Krause, it is the science of law and the State in pure reason. According to Lasson it is "the doctrine of the realization of the idea of the good in human will." In the view of the latter, it is "a division of ethics." It touches economics; it deals with the province of the State. "Philosophy of law is the search of first and supreme principles, while general jurisprudence recognizes similarities of fact, of homonyms, and does not consider the reasons" (Miraglia). There are, no doubt, narrower definitions. Wundt in his "Philosophische Studien" classifying the sciences which deal with the products of human intelligence, places the philosophy of law along with Ethics, Æsthetics, and the Philosophy of Religion. According to Dahn, a writer of great acuteness, it is the rational and necessary element of law, which but for the ambiguous word "rational" closely corresponds to the ordinary definition of jurisprudence. The wider definitions, which predominate, bring us back to something like Ulpian's definition: "Jurisprudentia est divinarum atque humanarum rerum notitia justi atque injusti scientia." These fundamental questions are discussed by Dr. Berolzheimer in a work of remarkable learning, a striking example of the thorough and encyclopedic manner in which German investigators go to work; an impressive rebuke to those who neglect the labors of their predecessors and who are apt to confound with true discoveries what is novel to them only. I have before me as I write the works of Stahl, Krause, and Lasson, dealing with the Philosophy of Law. They are not comparable with this volume in point of research.

I should not, however, be stating my opinion with sincerity if I did not add a few qualifying words. Some of our author's criticisms seem to me to be defective; it could not be otherwise in so vast a review. Justice is not done to Hobbes, or Bentham, or Austin. Jurisprudence has been cleared by each of these writers, of ambiguities and false analogies. It is too little to say of Austin's contributions that "they consider the fundamental questions of legal science rather than those of legal philosophy." It is not without interest that some writers who have lately influenced jurisprudence in Germany have done so by adopting substantially the methods and conclusions of Austin; I have in view, in particular, Binding. His "fundamental idea," remarks Dr. Berolzheimer, "that the imperative norm forms the essence of law is a permanent contribution to legal philosophy," is a restatement of Austin's chief position. Full justice is not done (to name a very different writer) to Gans. I have found his history of inheritance full instruction. He had in no small degree the fine historic sense of his master, Hegel's power of discovering the great streams and movements of events. I take leave to question the statement: "It (Gans's book) had no influence upon the development of legal philosophy." Nor do I think that our author has accurately appreciated the value of Bachofen's teaching, or Ihering's; he has over-estimated the positive results of the inquiries of the former, and under-rated the merits of the latter. The evidence for the general existence of "Mutterrecht," does not, to say the least, increase; the influence of the "Geist des römischen Rechts" was never greater than now. It will seem to some that, though Ihering's legal philosophy is not the whole truth, it is an important part of it.

A further criticism may be added. There is in these

pages a mixture of many diverse things. Whatever be the definition of the Philosophy of Law, a fivefold task awaits the investigator: first, to trace the origin of law to its sources in human nature, whether the "appetitus socialis" of Grotius, or "desire of the communal life of man" of Wundt, or the pleasure in exercising power; in other words, to solve certain psychological questions; next, to connect law with the society and circumstances of the time in which it originates or exists; an inquiry of supreme importance if law be "the form into which substantive relations crystallize under the influence of economic conditions or of other elementary forces" (*Bosanquet*, "The Philosophic Theory of the State," p. 36); further to analyze the ultimate elements of law, for example, whether coercion is an essential element; further to state the laws (if there be such) of its growth; lastly to discriminate between ethics and law. Speaking frankly, I do not think that answers are to be found in these pages to all these questions, and the results, valuable though they are, of the inquiries, might have been more valuable if the various answers had been kept distinct.

One omission may be noted: our author has virtually nothing to say as to international law. And yet it must be included in any rational account of law, or reasons must be given for its omission. Nay, more, being one of the latest developments of law and outside most of the older definitions, it is of supreme interest to one who would trace the essentials of law and its growth.

I add one further observation suggested by the author. Mere accumulation of facts will not enable the investigator to solve these problems. But, if there is not to be much cobweb-spinning, he must know and keep in close contact with facts; he must at every step come back to them. Otherwise he will give us the "caput mortuum" of Scholasticism. Our author justly deplores the fact that "after Kant philosophy became in the main a specialty; and men wrote upon ethics without knowing humankind and on the philosophy of law without a thorough knowledge of law." The reader who has breathed the highly rarified air of the speculations in these pages, will derive pleasure and profit by turning from time to time to some highly concrete question of the law of landlord and tenant or the rights of parties to a negotiable instrument.

No two persons will extract the same results from this vast survey, beginning with the speculations of the Greek philosophers upon law and ending with the latest works on jurisprudence, economics, and sociology. I take leave to indicate these as in my view among the most important:

There is a constant or often renewed attempt to revive in a new form the conception of a natural law; of a "richtiges Recht," of a law to which legislation may or may not conform. Writer after writer discussed in these pages makes this attempt. They may mean thereby "natural laws favoring the interest of the race" (Ratzenhofer). They may speak of such a law as a theoretically just law under empirically conditioned circumstances — "a natural law with a variable content" (Stammler). They may say, "What is conformable to natural law represents the absolutely desirable" (Ratzenhofer). They may have us view "the necessary factors" in law as opposed to the accidental (Brentano). They may say with Schopenhauer: "The conceptions, wrong and right, as equivalent to injury and noninjury, are obviously independent of positive legislation and antecedent to it. There thus exists a pure ethical or natural law and a pure science of law independent from all statutes." Many agree in believing in a "lex naturalis" of some sort. It might be better to break with old associations and to annex this province in part to ethics and in part to politics; but inveterate usage, on the Continent at all events, terms it law. No one now supposes that there is a "lex æterna et universa" in the sense that certain laws are found everywhere and at all times; history and ethnological inquiries dispose of that assumption. Nor is it possible to evolve *a priori* from a few principles, as jurists of the seventeenth and eighteenth centuries conceived, a system of law. Criticising the shortcomings of Pufendorf's system, Leibnitz remarks that he should like to see a work in which would be found luminous and fruitful definitions; in which the conclusions would be deduced from some principles, logically and consecutively; in which the foundation of all actions and all proper exceptions should be established in an orderly fashion; nothing being forgotten, needed to enable those beginning the study of natural law to supply for themselves what was omitted and to decide by rules and principles all questions that present themselves. Few, if any, hope that this can be realized. In point of fact, the results obtained by the writers on natural law who have attempted this work fall far short of this; they have been meagre and dubious. But it is true — and this is brought out by several of the writers who are noticed in these pages — that at all times there exists a sense of justice which approves some kinds of legislation and condemns others. That sense of justice is in some societies and at certain times clearer and more exigent than at other times. "Just" and "unjust" are ambiguous words. They may mean no more than giving what the law awards. They may be used with a peculiar meaning in a theocratic state of society. The secularizing of jurisprudence has an effect upon their meaning. They are not the same thing for the Greek as for the Hebrew. But there is a sense in which justice is understood by all and at all times. It insists upon certain conditions. A law which condemned accused persons without hearing them; which took away property from one person and gave it to another chosen by mere caprice; which said that laws should be retrospective — such measures might be passed in conformity to statutory requirements; they would not be the less unjust. I borrow from Rümelin a remark as to this: "It (justice) is a universal critic; it makes increasing demands. Not content with 'Justitia' as understood by Roman law, which only sought to preserve to each his own, it strives that the rights and benefits which each should have, accord to his merits." That fact — the sense of justice everywhere present and always either growing or declining — is the second pillar of "natural law" as understood by modern jurists.

It has been said that "natural law" is the ghost of natural religion; it might be described as the embodiment or evolution of justice. To find a natural relation between certain conditions of society and certain moral ideals; to study the growth of the conception of justice and to ascertain the effects — that is the hope of many and is not unattainable. It is notable that the equivalent of "æquitas" and "naturalis ratio" reappears in modern Codes [1] Bentham, the enemy of natural law, as understood in the eighteenth century applied to all law the utility test; which is natural law in another form.

I note a fresh conclusion, which is, that society at any given time is a whole and of a piece; that there does exist a necessary relation between law at any time and

[1] See, for example, Article I of "Code Civil Suisse."

the existing society; that all law is relative to some existing society; that, though there is no absolute law suitable for all times and places, given certain economic conditions, certain forms of family, a certain ethical creed, there will be laws corresponding thereto. There is no escaping this necessity. A ruler may try to impose his will in capricious fashion. But everyone, even the ruler, is a child of his time and cannot overstep certain limits. (Bruns-Lenel Encyclopädie, I, 76) The law is not a robe or dress changeable at will; it is very part of the body social. Even the composers of Utopias are circumscribed and are the creatures of their circumstances. In the "Republic" and the "Laws" are imbedded much of the Athenian law of Plato's age. More and Campanella are unconsciously in their political romances thinking of their own time. All hangs together — law, ethics, religion, economics.

Again, I borrow from Rümelin a statement of this view: "Das es überhaupt eine Rechtsordnung giebt, dass die gesammte Staatsmaschine nicht still steht, sondern geht, dass die Räder ineinander greifen, ist nicht etwas Erzwingbares sondern etwas Thatsächliches" ("Reden," *Neue Folge*, 337). There is a social "Ordnung" and a "Rechtsordnung" corresponding thereto. One great advance has been to realize this necessary connection; while breaking with the idea of a universal and immutable natural law, to grasp the idea of law as constantly and necessarily changing in harmony with the changing national life. And that natural life is not a loose collection of fortuitous elements. "No contraction or 'Zusammenhang' of 'disjecta membra' will ever make a living whole. This is the truth that the whole eighteenth century fails to grasp and that the nineteenth has taught us to appreciate fully."[1]

[1] *Ward*, "The Realm of Ends," p. 120.

I state as a further result to be extracted from the elaborate review: In the opinion of the great majority of the authors considered, the functions of Government cannot be confined to the maintenance of peace and order. It is, and must be, an instrument of culture. It would seem as if with the decline of the power of the Church, the State were obliged to take over some of the interests which the former ought to guard. And so we have such expressions as that borrowed from Cohen ("Ethik des reinen Willens"): "Justice must be maintained as a guide to virtue; and its constant progress is possible only through the instrument of law and progress." (125.) Positive law is "a coercive effort towards Justice" (Stammler).

If humanity is to get a great lift upwards all must aid, including the representative of the will of all. The constant progress of justice is "possible only through the instrument of law and Government." "Laissez faire" is arrested development.

I note another conclusion to be deduced from the examination of the writings of the long list of authors, and especially the moderns. There is a new conception of liberty which it is the aim of law to carry out. Much has been written about political freedom; freedom to speak, write, meet, form associations, enter into contracts — in other words, protection against external pressure and freedom to do as one likes. It may mean also the minimum amount of interference comparable with each being free to do as he likes; regulations imposed upon all citizens in the interest of all.

But there is another conception of it as freedom for the development of all human faculties; freedom not merely from violence or tyranny and external pressure, but freedom from the pressure which checks, stunts and impoverishes the best in human nature; freedom which enables one to say, "We can do what we ought." There is the conception of the larger liberty, the higher liberty; the removal of all that stands in the way of the full development of man. Originating in philosophy, this conception has come to be recognized as one of the objects of law. "Law is," Kant said, "the aggregate of the conditions under which the arbitrary will of one individual may be combined with that of another under a general inclusive law of freedom." In such sentences as these is the starting point of a new conception of the province of the State and the functions of law. Certain writers — notably Hegel — have familiarized jurists with the conception of the State as realizing freedom. I cannot better express this idea than in the words of Durkheim: "Il se trouve que la liberté elle même est le produit d'une réglementation. Loin d'être une sorte d'antagonisme de l'action sociale, elle en resulte. Elle est si peu une propriété de l'état de nature qu'elle est au contraire une conquête de la société sur la nature."[1]

Yet another result: the secularization of law. Connected with religion in all primitive communities, in some most intimately connected therewith, it becomes more and more separated therefrom. "La religion embrasse une portion le plus en plus petite de la vie sociale. À l'origine elle s'étend à tout" (Durkheim). The supernatural sanctions of law decrease. Its chief support is the prevailing public opinion. The oracles become dumb, but conscience speaks, and where law is respected and jurisprudence is studied, speaks more and more clearly. Akin to this change is the separation of law and ethics; a process complete in certain branches of the former, but still in certain others (for example, in international law) not fully carried out.

[1] "De la Division du Travail Social," (1893), p. 433.

xxxviii   INTRODUCTION

I note a further conclusion of importance in view of the claims of sociology. No mere statement of facts, however general in terms, is sufficient; the element "ought" must be included; consequently sociology of itself is insufficient as a full philosophy of law; any theory which does not account for the ought, must be insufficient. The attempts of Ratzenhofer and others to found thereon a legal philosophy have failed. Ethics are not merely higher physics. Upon this subject our author justly remarks: "The definiteness of legal concepts gives way to the foggy confusion of social-political, social reformatory, and social ethical discussions, fertile in proposals that prove to be valueless and ineffective when philosophically tested. A return to legal and economic philosophy remains the sole scientific procedure." [1]

My last observation is this: There is a philosophy or spirit of law deeper than that of Montesquieu. He did much to get beneath the surface of law; to trace its roots and relationship; to show that mere legal analysis was imperfect; that the parts of national life were united to each other. His work has been continued and extended. "The generalities of Jurisprudence," it has been said, "are vitalized and completed by the work of the science of culture" (*Bosanquet*, "Philosophical Theory of the State," 41). Dr. Berolzheimer's work enables us to ascend to a height from which we can see law as an ever present part of an ever flowing stream.

[1] One of the latest attempts to reduce jurisprudence to a branch of sociology is made by M. Rolin ["Prolégomènes à la science du Droit" (1911)]: "La sociologie est l'étude des adaptations de l'homme à la vie en société. Le droit est une de ces adaptations, celle qui à pour but de combattre, par la contrainte, les effets ou les causes de certains *defauts d'adaptation, jugés intolérables*" (p. 4.) Expressed in words, the ethical element returns in the phrase italicized.

NOTICE OF THE AUTHOR'S LIFE AND WORKS

Fritz Berolzheimer, Jur. D., was born January 3, 1869. He is managing editor of the "Archiv für Rechts- und Wirtschaftsphilosophie" (now in the fifth volume), the world's leading journal of philosophy of law; president of the International Society of Legal and Economic Philosophy (Berlin); and joint-editor, with Dr. Paul Laband and six other eminent jurists, of the "Handbuch der Politik," now being issued (Rothschild, Berlin).

The present volume is the second of his five-volume work published by Beck at Munich (1904–1907) under the title "System der Rechts- und Wirtschaftsphilosophie." Volume I of this work (pp. xii, 327) is a philosophical introduction which treats the theory of knowledge; volume III (pp. xi, 370) deals with the philosophy of the State including the fundamental principles of politics; volume IV (pp. x, 335) deals with the philosophy of property and commercial transactions; and volume V (pp. ix, 280) treats the philosophy of crime and punishment. He is also author of "Rechtsphilosophische Studien (Munich, 1903); "Die Entgeltung im Strafrecht" (Munich, 1903); "Deutschland von Heute" (Berlin, 1909); "Die Gefahren einer Gefühlsjurisprudenz in der Gegenwart" (Berlin, 1911); and numerous smaller writings which have appeared in various German publications. He is one of the most active and best known of the Neo-Hegelians among legal philosophers, and has been one of the most efficient agents in the new German awakening of Philosophy of Law.

AUTHOR'S PREFACE

The present volume treats of the historical evolution of the philosophy of law and economics in their bearing upon contemporary interests and movements. The political and legal institutions of former periods are included only in so far as they show influence upon later developments. Avoiding the usual text-book account of the successive contributions to the philosophy of law, I have confined the presentation to that of the successive cultural stages in terms of their distinctive ideas, principles, conceptions, and doctrines, and of their practical issues and demands.[1] For this purpose the historical survey must go back further than the customary point of departure in ancient Greece, and include the legal and economic institutions of Egypt, Assyria, India, Judea, and Phœnicia, from which the theory and practice of the Græco-Roman legal philosophy were derived. The emphasis is to be placed not upon the doctrines, but upon the form and development of the legal principles which they illustrate. I have considered the philosophy of law not from without, as summarized in the presentations of writers on legal philosophy, but from within, as a natural and cultural product. While philosophers stimulate and lead their contemporaries, they are themselves products of the culture of their day; for they reflect the limitations of the available data and scientific

[1] Theoretical philosophy emphasizes in the historical survey the question: How shall the philosopher proceed? What shall be his method? But for the purposes of practical philosophy the chief question becomes: What results does he find? What is the outcome and the bearing of his conclusion?

knowledge, and follow current intellectual trends. Knowledge conditions the methods and range of facts and systems by means of which truth is extended; the stage of culture influences the general position, and the direction and mode of advance of practical philosophy. It is the intellectual attitudes, as they find expression from time to time, that have a larger importance for the philosophy of law and economics than have the doctrines and arguments of individual philosophers, whose chief value, indeed, lies in their service in presenting formulations of such general views. Moreover, theoretical principles are of secondary importance in comparison to the political embodiment, to which, in periods of agitation and progress, such philosophies aspire.

Such then is my task; and if, despite the valuable aid afforded by the efforts of my predecessors [1] in this field, it has proven to be a difficult one, the difficulties must serve to excuse the imperfections of my work. The emphasis, in the historical portions, of interpretations that bear out my general philosophical position, hardly needs justification. Law, government, morality, custom, and social regulation, are artificial forces registering accomplished advances in intellectual development; and the historical illustrations serve to support my views of the forces directing the philosophy of law and

[1] A commendable essay of this type is that of *Ahrens*, "Naturrecht," Vol. 1, sixth edition, Vienna 1870, pp. 13 seq. In this he gives a brief survey of Oriental civilization. But since his day new discoveries have brought forward notable information which must be utilized for its bearing upon legal philosophy. He contributes careful interpretations of Greek and Roman law; yet here likewise his expositions must be supplemented with reference to recent interests. Since *Lasson's* work in 1882 there has been no comprehensive survey of legal philosophy.

[A work bearing upon this field, but with closer reference to economics, is that of *Haney*. — Editor's Note.]

economics, as well as to survey the philosophical stages of development. If such development proves that the trend of civilization is towards the increase of human efficiency by establishing the artificial institutions of law, government, religion, ethics, and social organization, then the same inductive evidence applies to the interpretation of law and morality as equally artificial achievements; and the later volumes of this work may proceed deductively to apply this position to the institutions of law, the functions of economics, and the foundations of ethics.

The utilitarian attitude, as presented by Ihering, holds that progress is the issue of conscious rational and deliberate striving. The contrary is more nearly true. When we consider the larger cultural movements of ancient and modern times, we appreciate that the actual beliefs by means of which the masses are forced from their political conservatism, and won over to a new form of government, cannot be considered objectively valid. We observe that the reasons advanced in defense of the new movements and in opposition to tradition, whether in religion, in law, or in economics, are found in the light of later development to lack an objective basis. Yet such intellectual movements cannot accomplish their mission without the support of the real, though misinterpreted motives, which, in turn, often seek a false goal. History shows that the ends striven for and attained are not correctly formulated in consciousness; the alleged purpose and the achieved accomplishment are rarely the same. Indeed, one may even dignify this observation by making of it a principle of unconscious or disguised motivation.[1]

In the progressive development of law there may be

[1] *Kohler*, "Recht, Glaube, Sitte" (Grünh. Z., Vol. 19, 1892, pp. 561-612).

distinguished a foreground occupied by rhetorical accounts of the steps accomplished and the reforms proposed, and a more solid background of working forces that determine the real strength of the movement. Writers on the philosophy of law generally emphasize the former by giving an account of the contributions of the greater and lesser leaders; historians emphasize the latter in their descriptions of related cultural conditions. It is the second and more difficult task that must be undertaken by the student of the philosophy of law. Illusion and error may even serve a purpose in intellectual progress; and truth often comes to its own through the medium of fallacy. Yet such fallacies, common in periods of spiritual unrest, differ in trend and temper from consciously entertained deceptions. The latter are antagonistic to the interests of culture, while illusions [1] are conservative of cultural ends. This applies as well to government and to law; for it will be recalled that historically, political power, legal regulation, and customs were popularly conceived as expressions of the divine [2] will. The philosophy of law is ready to accept this as an historical fact, but finds the true meaning in the interpretation thereof.[3]

[1] For errors that have proven conducive to intellectual progress I shall use the technical term, *illusions*.

Although I discovered and developed this conception independently, it is by no means novel. In the preparation of this work I accidentally came upon the work of *Georg Adler*, "Die Bedeutung der Illusionen für Politik und soziales Leben," Jena 1904. Adler's priority of statement I gladly acknowledge.

[2] One is reminded of Nietzsche's phrase: "Philosophy does not suffice for the masses. They demand sanctity." "Der Fall Wagner," Part I, Vol. 8, Leipzig 1896, p. 14.

[3] *Dahn*, "Die Vernunft im Recht," p. 27: "In the consciousness of the people the legal norms appear in all manners of disguise." **Kohler** repeatedly refers to the same idea.

AUTHOR'S PREFACE

The latter portions of this volume present a survey of economic movements of modern, highly differentiated society. While approaching the problems objectively and without prejudice and partisanship, I assume a definite position in regard to current political questions and policies. The duty of an investigator, as I interpret it, is to set forth plainly what he considers sound and scientifically defensible, whether or not his subject bears upon the political contentions of the day. The stages of evolution of the law form the primary consideration, but the economic factors have not been overlooked; for legal progress is not limited to the formulation of laws, but embraces the economics and social institutions and movements which vitalize them. The reference to my political views may be justified by the fact that the great political questions and platforms are essentials of the philosophy of law. Philosophies become effective through their practical issues;[1] they form theoretical skirmishes in a political evolution or revolution;[2] they

---

[1] The work that gave *Grotius* his reputation was conceived and carried out primarily as a political treatise. The power of political documents to command attention appears in the reputation which *Montesquieu* achieved, while his contemporary, *Ferguson*, a man of no less distinction, received slight consideration. The former proposed fundamental political positions and the latter did not. Similarly *Marx* and *Lassalle* held the eager attention of the public, while those who were merely legal philosophers have been ignored and forgotten.

[2] There is an essential difference in the spirit of the ancient and of the modern legal philosophy. The Greek citizen-class, from which the most of the philosophers arose, was conscious of itself as an integral part of the civic city-state. It was therefore only through its opposition to every form of tyranny that the Greek economic philosophy had political importance. Apart from this, ancient legal philosophy, especially among the Greeks, was merely a legal appendix to ethics, as appears particularly in Plato's extreme emphasis of the communal spirit as opposed to an over-individualism.

accomplish their purpose as a political influence. The appearance of a new political view affects legal philosophy. The difference in attitude between law and politics is one of interest and, in turn, of scope; the broader view requires the larger field of vision. The subject-matter of the philosophy of law is government, and the law as organized; these are not finished constructions, but are in the process of growth. Accordingly philosophy, equally with politics, must be directed to the future.

Legal philosophy, though in part undesignedly, in the past has exerted a reforming influence upon politics,[1] and will maintain its position only in so far as it continues to exert it. The scientific standing of the philosophy of law was lost when vain dialectics were substituted for tangible results. The philosophy of law supplies practical jurisprudence with a special method whose power of analysis makes possible the solution of problems too complex for any less adequate instrument; to regain its proper status and esteem it must again assume this serviceable function, and not follow servilely the lead of practice. It may well begin with the inductive study of law and economics, but must proceed resolutely to its rightful philosophical function

It had no independent status and was more a theoretical philosophy of justice than a practical philosophy of law and government. It was only in the Middle Ages and under the pressure of the Church that there arose a longing for political freedom; under the influence of the intellectual emancipation following upon the Reformation there was inaugurated the great process of enfranchisement that found its consummation in our own day.

[1] The history of legal philosophy is essentially the history of the great political movements of liberation, of the emancipation of humanity. Ancient history closes with the advent and the Christian establishment of the humanitarian conception; modern times present the completion of the emancipation.

AUTHOR'S PREFACE xlvii

of providing the rational support, the directive guidance of theoretical insight.[1]

Legal philosophies and political doctrines are closely related. My own position reflects and supports the emphasis of "class interests," and accords to social and ethical principles the position of a corrective influence to counteract the unrestrained self-seeking, incident to a "laisser faire" policy.

Owing to the position of this volume as part of a projected series, I have supplied an Introduction in which, along with bibliographical references, I have presented the conception of legal philosophy, the method which it pursues, and its demarcation from allied disciplines. Literature, so far as it bears upon the philosophy of law, has been fully utilized; specific contributions to the philosophical aspects of law, sociology, and economics, are noted, but only the more important general works on philosophy and ethics are mentioned.

Munich, Easter, 1905.

---

[1] In the most notable philosophies of *Plato* and his disciples, as likewise of *Kant* and his school, reason plays a predominant part. But the ancient rational philosophy correctly interprets the nature of reason, while the modern does not. For Plato, as for Aristotle, reason is the capacity to interpret the nature of things. For Kant reason is pure experienceless thought. My own philosophy is neo-Platonic in that it regards reason as the capacity for knowledge based upon conceptions and ideas. This view involves a direct relation with the philosophy of knowledge as laid down in the Jewish-Christian religion. Man is a being endowed with the divine spirit, a being whose knowing and thinking, though dependent upon his material organization, is not restricted by it, but is capable of abstracting from the material embodiment, and has direct access to the infinite and to the possession of true ideas.

TABLE OF CONTENTS

INTRODUCTION

	Page
§ 1. Conception of the Philosophy of Law	1
§ 2. Literature of the Philosophy of Law	4
§ 3. Conception of the Philosophy of Economics	5
§ 4. Demarcation of the Philosophy of Law from Natural Law, General Jurisprudence, Comparative Law, and Legal Sociology	6
1: Philosophy of Law and "Natural Law"	6
2: Philosophy of Law and General Jurisprudence	9
3: Philosophy of Law and Comparative Law	12
4: Philosophy of Law and Legal Sociology	14
§ 5. Demarcation of the Philosophy of Economics from Political Economy, Social Economy, and Social Ethics	16
§ 6. The Method of the Philosophy of Law	17
§ 7. Law and Economics	20

CHAPTER I

ORIGINS OF ORIENTAL CIVILIZATION

§ 8. Ancient Egypt	25
§ 9. Babylonia and Assyria	32
1: Babylonian and Assyrian Civilization	32
2: The Code of Hammurabi	34
§ 10. The Vedic Aryans	37
§ 11. The Jewish State	40
§ 12. The Phœnicians	45

CONTENTS

CHAPTER II

THE ANCIENT COMMONWEALTH: GREEK CIVILIZATION

§ 13. The Greeks before Plato 46
    1: Fundamental Greek Conceptions 46
    2: Subjectivism and Objectivism 49
    3: The Pythagorean Philosophy 51
    4: The Philosophy of Heraclitus 55
    5: The Sophists 56
    6: The Socratic Philosophy 57

§ 14. Plato 60
    1: The Platonic Conception of Virtue and Justice . 60
    2: Plato's General Philosophy 63
    3: Practical Justice and Social Virtue 64
    4: The Ideal and the Real State 65
    5: The Influence of Plato 66

§ 15. Aristotle 67
    1: The Basis of Ethical Conduct 67
    2: The Greek Aristocrat 68
    3: Society and the State 70
    4: Justice and Equity 72
    5: The Origin of Civic Life 73

§ 16. The Post-Aristotelean Period 74
    1: The Cynics 74
    2: The Cyrenaics 75
    3: The Stoics 75
    4: The Epicureans 76
    5: The Sceptics 77
    6: The Neo-Platonists 77

CHAPTER III

THE CIVIC EMPIRE OF ANCIENT ROME AND THE MORALIZATION OF ROMAN LAW

§ 17. The Roman Peasant State: the "Jus Civile" 78
    1: Rights: Absence of Ethical Factors........... 78
    2: The "Paterfamilias" as the Center of Roman Law 80

§ 18. The Roman-Italian State: The Rejuvenation of Law through "Æquitas" 82

§ 19. The Roman Empire: Introduction of the Philosophy of Law through Cicero 87

§ 20. The Decline of the Ancient Empire: Christian Ethics 89

CONTENTS

CHAPTER IV
THE BONDAGE OF MEDIÆVALISM

§ 21.	The Spiritual Dominance of Rome (St. Augustine; Thomas Aquinas; The Doctrine of the Two Swords)	93
	1: The Church and Greek Philosophy	93
	2: The Philosophy of St. Augustine	94
	3: The Philosophy of Thomas Aquinas	98
	4: The Tenet of the Two Swords	101
§ 22.	Economic and Social Restrictions	103
	1: The Yeoman and the Citizen Class	103
	2: The Economic Influence of the Church	104
	3: The Crafts and Trades	106
§ 23.	More Liberal Trends of the Middle Ages	108
	1: Dante Alighieri	108
	2: William of Occam	108
	3: Marsilius of Padua and the Sovereignty of the People	109
	4: Nicholaus Cusanus	109
	5: The Writings of Niccolo Machiavelli	110

CHAPTER V
CIVIC EMANCIPATION: THE RISE AND DECLINE OF "NATURAL LAW"

§ 24.	The Reformation as a Stimulus to Individualism	113
§ 25.	Hugo Grotius	115
§ 26.	The Rebellion against Tyranny	118
§ 27.	Legal Philosophy of the Seventeenth Century	122
	1: Hobbes	122
	2: Pufendorf	124
	3: Spinoza	127
	4: Thomasius	132
§ 28.	Legal Philosophy in England	134
	1: Locke	134
	2: Bentham	137
	3: Mill; Austin	139
§ 29.	Legal Philosophy in France	141
	1: Montesquieu	141
	2: Rousseau	143
	3: Diderot	152
	4: Godwin	155

CONTENTS

§ 30.	Legal Philosophy in Germany	156
	1: Leibnitz	156
	2: Wolff	160
	3: Frederick the Great	162
§ 31.	Mercantilists and Physiocrats	165
	1: The System of Colbert	165
	2: Quesnay and other Physiocrats	167
§ 32.	The Classical Economists: Adam Smith; Ricardo	170
	1: Industrial Development: the Economics of Adam Smith	170
	2: Ricardo	174
	3: Say	178
	4: Malthus	178
§ 33.	Kant; Fichte; Schopenhauer	180
	1: Kant	180
	(a) The Historical Position of Kant	180
	(b) Kant's Ethics	181
	(c) Kant's Philosophy of Law	189
	(d) The Origin and the Purpose of the State	187
	(e) The Present Significance of Kant's Philosophy	188
	2: Fichte	192
	(a) The Position of Fichte	192
	(b) Fichte's Philosophy of Law	194
	(c) Fichte's Philosophy of Economics	198
	(d) Law and Culture	200
	(e) Fichte as a Statesman	201
	3: Schopenhauer	201
§ 34.	Schelling and the Historical School	204
	1: Schelling	204
	2: Other Representatives of the Historical School	211
§ 35.	Hegel and the Hegelians	215
	1: Hegel's Philosophy of Law	215
	2: Law and the Human Will	217
	3: Hegel's Dialectic	219
	4: Hegel's Conception of the State	223
	5: Fundamental Legal Ideas: Person, Property, Injury, and Crime	224
	6: A Critical Verdict of Hegel	228
	7: The Hegelians	232

CONTENTS

§ 36. Recent Systems of Legal Philosophy	233
1: Stahl	233
2: Trendelenburg	238
3: Krause	240
4: Ahrens	245
5: Herbart	248
6: Dahn	252
7: Lasson	255

CHAPTER VI
THE EMANCIPATION OF THE PROLETARIAT. ENCROACHMENT UPON THE PHILOSOPHY OF LAW BY ECONOMIC REALISM

§ 37. French Communism	260
1: Saint-Simon	260
2: Fourier	264
3: Louis Blanc	265
4: Communism, Anarchism, and Socialism	267
§ 38. German Socialism	269
1: Marx	269
2: Lassalle	274
3: Engels	276
4: Rodbertus	276
5: Bebel	278
6: Kautsky	279
7: Bernstein	280
8: A Survey of the Process of Emancipation	281
§ 39. Anarchism	287
1: Proudhon; the Older View	287
2: Stirner; Extreme Individualism	289
3: Krapotkin; the Communistic View	291
4: Bakunin; the Position of Violence	292
5: Tucker and Tolstoi; Moderate Anarchism	297
§ 40. Further Types of Socialism	298
1: Menger	298
2: Loria	303
3: Sombart	304

CHAPTER VII

The Sociological Reconstruction of Legal Philosophy

§ 41.	The Development of Sociology	308
	1: Comte and the Beginnings of Sociology	308
	2: Positivism and Sociology	313
	3: The Sociology of Spencer	317
§ 42.	Sociological and Social-ethical Extremists	323
	1: The Conception of "Society"	323
	2: Social Ethics	331
	3: Sociological Ideals	333
§ 43.	Social Utilitarianism	336
	1: Shaftesbury	336
	2: Ihering	337
§ 44.	The Sociological School	351
	1: Its Distinctive Position	351
	2: Its Precursors	352
	3: Gumplowicz	356
	4: Ratzenhofer	358
	5: Recent Representatives: Tönnies, Klöppel, Bergemann	365
	6: Critical Summary of the Sociological Position	368
	7: Applications of the Sociological Position	369
	(a) To Corporations	369
	(b) Penology	372
§ 45.	Realistic and Historical Trends in Political Economy and Sociology	375
§ 46.	The Theory of Norms	381
§ 47.	Ethnological Jurisprudence	387
§ 48.	The Reinstatement of Kant and Hegel; v. Hartmann	392
	1: Neo-Kantianism	392
	2: Neo-Hegelianism	422
	3: Hartmann	427
§ 49.	Psychological Aspects of Law and Economics	431
	1: The Psychological Basis	431
	2: Zitelmann	435
	3: Jellinek	435
	4: Criminal Psychology	442

CONTENTS

§ 50.	Recent Surveys of Fundamental Problems	446
	1: Merkel and his Followers	446
	2: Schmidt	450
	3: Paulsen	451
	4: Bauman	453
	5: Schuppe	454
§ 51.	The Influence of the Principles of Evolution	456
	1: Social Aristocracy; Nietzsche	456
	2: Evolutionary Monism; Haeckel	458
	3: Evolution and Socialism	461
§ 52.	Class and State	466

LIST OF JOURNALS, ETC., REFERRED TO IN NOTES

Grünhut's Zeitschrift für das Privat- und Öffentliche Recht der Gegenwart: *Grünh. Z.*
Zeitschrift für Vergleichende Rechtswissenschaft: *Z. f. v. Rechtsw.*
Hirth's Annalen des Deutschen Reichs: *Hirth's Ann.*
Beling's Strafrechtliche Abhandlungen: *Beling's Abh.*
Zeitschrift für die Gesammte Strafrechtswissenschaft: *Z. f. d. G. Str.*
Von Holtzendorff-Kohler, Enzyklopädie der Rechtswissenschaft: *Enzyklopädie.*
Schmoller's Jahrbuch: *Sch. Jahrb.*
Conrad's Jahrbuch: *Conrad's Jahrb.*
Braun's Archiv für Soziale Gestezgebung und Statistik: *Braun's Archiv.*
Avenarius, Vierteljahrsschrift für Wissenschaftliche Philosophie: *Avenarius.*

The World's Legal Philosophies

THE WORLD'S LEGAL PHILOSOPHIES

INTRODUCTION

CONCEPTION OF THE PHILOSOPHY OF LAW.—LITERATURE OF THE PHILOSOPHY OF LAW.—CONCEPTION OF THE PHILOSOPHY OF ECONOMICS.—DEMARCATION OF THE PHILOSOPHY OF LAW FROM "NATURAL LAW," GENERAL JURISPRUDENCE, COMPARATIVE LAW, AND LEGAL SOCIOLOGY: (1) PHILOSOPHY OF LAW AND "NATURAL LAW"; (2) PHILOSOPHY OF LAW AND GENERAL JURISPRUDENCE; (3) PHILOSOPHY OF LAW AND COMPARATIVE LAW; (4) PHILOSOPHY OF LAW AND LEGAL SOCIOLOGY.—DEMARCATION OF THE PHILOSOPHY OF ECONOMICS FROM POLITICAL ECONOMY, SOCIAL ECONOMY, AND SOCIAL ETHICS.—THE METHOD OF THE PHILOSOPHY OF LAW.—LAW AND ECONOMICS.

§ 1. *Conception of the Philosophy of Law.* The philosophy of law is the critical study of formulated law.[1] Leaving to practical jurisprudence the determination of what is lawful, the philosophy of law proposes the problem of the nature of the law itself. It is

---

[1] Parallel definitions are given by *Cicero*, "De legibus," I, 5: "Non ergo a prætoris edicto, ut plerique nunc, neque a duodecim tabulis, ut superiores, sed penitus ex intima philosophia hauriendam juris disciplinam putas." See also "De legibus," I, 4, at the end. Others interpret differently. *Hegel*, "Grundlinien der Philosophie des Rechts" (§ 1, p. 22), remarks: "The philosophy of law has for its subject the idea of law, the conception of law and its realization." *Stahl*, "Die Philosophie des Rechtes," Vol. 1, second edition, 1847, (p. 1): "The philosophy of law is the science of justice." See also *Stahl's* preface to the first edition, 1830, p. xi. *Geyer*, "Geschichte und System der Rechtsphilosophie in Grundzügen," Innsbruck, 1863, while not offering a definition, says: "Philosophy is the

a division of legal science, yet belongs equally to practical philosophy. The jurist considers the structure and function of law; the philosopher, its underlying principles and causes. The interest of the former is centered upon the content of the law; of the latter, upon

science that supplements all other sciences and brings them to completion" (p. 1); "The philosophy of law is a division of ethics" (p. 3); "The philosophy of law proposes an ideal which the actual order is to attain, not the law as actually prevailing" (p. 3). *Ahrens*, "Naturrecht," sixth edition, Vienna, — 1870 (Vol. 1, p. 1): "The philosophy of law or natural law is the science which derives the supreme principle or conception of law from the nature and destiny of man and of human society, and develops a system of legal principles for all the divisions of private and public law." *Ahrens*, "Cours de droit naturel," VIII, Leipzig, 1892 (Vol. I, p. 1): "The philosophy of law or natural law is the science that sets forth the first principles of law as conceived by reason and as based upon the nature of man considered in itself and in its relations with the universal order of things." What is thus characterized is not legal philosophy in general, but the legal philosophy of *Krause* and *Ahrens*. *Dahn*, "Über Werden und Wesen des Rechts" (II), in Z. f. v. Rechtsw., Vol. III, 1881, pp. 3 seq., § 6, designates the problem of the philosophy of law as that "of establishing the idea of law and the several products and manifestations of legal activity as a mode of manifestation of the absolute law. Legal philosophy thus attempts to determine and present the inherent logical element in the law." ("Rechtsphilosophischer Historismus.") See also *Dahn*, "Die Vernunft im Recht," Berlin, 1879, pp. 13–15. Also § 36. *Lasson*, "System der Rechtsphilosophie," Berlin and Leipzig, 1882 (pp. 1 and 10): "The philosophy of law is a division of ethics, and is the doctrine of the realization of the idea of the good in human will. . . . Ethics embraces in addition to the philosophy of law the co-ordinate divisions of the philosophy of customs, of moral philosophy or the doctrine of virtue, and the doctrine of morality or the moral personality. . . . The problem of the philosophy of law is to interpret existing law as an expression of reason and in its connection with other tendencies and phenomena of life." *Harms*, "Begriff, Formen, und Grundlegung der Rechtsphilosophie," edited by von Wiese, Leipzig, 1889 (p. 21): "Accordingly the philosophy of law is the science of the presuppositions and fundamental conceptions of an

"the spirit of the law."[1] The philosophy of law[2] stands in intimate relation to political science — to governmental, social, punitive, commercial, agricultural, and tariff regulations.[3] Politics considers how new legislative situa-

---

empirical study of law." *Bergbohm*, "Jurisprudenz und Rechtsphilosophie: Kritische Abhandlungen," Vol. 1, Leipzig, 1892 (p. 103): "We expect the philosophy of law to inform us as to the inner nature and ultimate basis of the law as it exists. It attempts to furnish the key to all the problems presented by legal phenomena." *J. Kohler*, "Enzyklopädie der Rechtswissenschaft," 1902 (p. 3): "The philosophy of law is a branch of the philosophy of humanity, that is, of that philosophy which is to determine the position of man and of human civilization in the world and in worldly activities. The expressions of human culture reach their highest point in philosophy in that they thus receive their interpretation as a part of the cosmos; the same is true of the law. The philosophy of law must envisage man as the bearer of culture; and as culture constantly advances, if man and the world are not to stagnate, the philosophy of law is the problem of interpreting law as a constantly developing evolutionary process." And again (p. 9): "We must place the results of the history of law in connection with the general history of culture; we must attempt to determine the significance of the history of culture in the cosmos, and further to determine the operation of legal institutions and of their history in the development of culture, and thus in the evolution of the cosmos. Only in this manner, as I conceive it, is a legal philosophy possible." *Eisler*, "Wörterbuch der Philosophischen Begriffe und Ausdrücke," Berlin, 1900 (p. 633): "The philosophy of law is the systematic study of the origin, content, and import of the conception of law in connection with the consideration of the principles of government."

[1] The term "spirit of the law" ("esprit des lois") appears first in the title of *Montesquieu's* well-known work. See below, § 29. *Ihering* (d. 1890) adopted it for his work, "Geist des Römischen Rechts auf den verschiedenen Stufen seiner Entwickelung."

[2] The philosophy of law is related to the encyclopedia of law which furnishes a systematic survey and arrangement of the material of law, and to general jurisprudence which presents a statement of the most important general legal principles and institutions as they occur in civilized communities.

[3] See below, § 4.

tions — such as those created by the telephone, the automobile, by arbitration, by colonial relations — may be met; it faces such problems as measures of immediate regulation — "de lege ferenda." The philosophy of law is concerned with the "ratio legis," with the general aspects of the end in view, and of the ideal conception of legislation. The two, however, are not sharply differentiated.

In courses and compendiums of law the philosophical aspects are commonly considered in connection with specific legislation: thus the philosophy of punishment is considered in connection with the laws of punishment, or as a criticism of the theory of punishment; the philosophy of government is treated in the study of the general principles of government. Political economy interprets the philosophy of government in connection with social theories and with politics as applied to the problems of society and government; ecclesiastical law has likewise philosophical problems to consider, such as the canonical proscription of interest, or the relation of Church and State; and similar legal problems enter into every comprehensive system of ethics.

Comparative law supplements the philosophy of law in so far as it proceeds beyond the collation of laws, and attempts to derive ethnologically general conceptions of law from the material which it collects ethnographically.[1]

§ 2. *Literature of the Philosophy of Law.*[2] The more important works upon the philosophy of law will be

---

[1] See below, § 4.

[2] For the less important works on "natural law" belonging to the early nineteenth century, see *Geyer*, "Geschichte und System der Rechtsphilosophie," pp. 60 seq; and *Warnkönig*, "Philosophiæ juris delineatio," Tübingen, 1855, Appendix: Bibliotheca philosophiæ juris et doctrinæ politicæ selecta.

mentioned in connection with the separate legal problems.[1]

§ 3. *Conception of the Philosophy of Economics.* While the science of law as an independent branch of knowledge is of great antiquity, economics as an independent science is relatively recent. Legal philosophy was well developed in early days, particularly among the Greeks and Romans, but a philosophy of economics still awaits formulation. The present renewal of interest in philosophical study and the growing attention to economic relations, owing to the increasing complexity of commercial life and the differentiation of class interests, furnish favorable conditions for a scientific study of the problems of economics. Recent contributions show a decided breadth of interest and philosophic insight, notably in the favorite field of sociology.

Law and economics are here presented in close affiliation, as form and content, as shell and kernel; yet, thus viewed, economics must not be confined to the study of the production, exchange, and consumption of human products, but should be extended to a general economics of cultural relations, comprising alike material and intellectual interests. The study of human industry leads to a philosophy of economics quite as readily as a study of legislation leads to a philosophy of law; it supplies the material setting, the content of legislation. Thus the philosophy of economics becomes the material or "content" aspect of the philosophy of law. The chief concern of the latter is the establishment of justice on the formal side, while the philosophy of economics relates to the same interests in their material aspects.

[1] [The author's partial bibliography of general systematic and historical works which appears in the original is omitted; the works are mentioned for the most part in later bibliographical footnotes. —Trans.]

§ 4. *Demarcation of the Philosophy of Law from Natural Law, General Jurisprudence, Comparative Law, and Legal Sociology.* 1: PHILOSOPHY OF LAW AND "NATURAL LAW." Philosophy of law was made equivalent to "natural law," "jus naturæ," by the Greeks and Romans, but more specifically by Grotius and his followers. The supporters of this position assume a natural law independent of statutory law — at times coincident with it, more often diverging from it, and representing an ideal just law. As conceived by this school, it is the purpose of the philosophy of law to establish natural law upon a philosophical basis, by deriving it deductively from fundamental principles.[1]

The historical school, anticipated by Hugo and founded by Savigny and Puchta under the influence of Schelling, was the first to break from the assumption of a natural law as something absolute, fixed, and unalterable.[2] It recognized as law, positive law alone; yet in discarding the principle of natural law, it did not reject the advances based thereupon.[3] No constructive

[1] *Stahl*, "Die Genesis der gegenwärtigen Rechtsphilosophie," 1830 (pp. 68 seq.): "The question as to how I recognize what is just and what is unjust implies the underlying question as to what makes justice and injustice. What is the nature of this distinction? What is the source of all obligation? The answer is thus decisive for ethics. Philosophy, which is limited to the recognition of the issues of reason can look for the source of this ethical element only in reason. Such is the character of 'natural law.'" See also pp. 70–77.

[2] See § 34. At present the doctrine of natural law has been generally discarded. Thus *Dahn*, "Über Werden und Wesen des Rechtes," Vol. II (Z. f. v. Rechtsw., 1881, Vol. III, p. 8, § 16): "As law is the peaceful regulation of a group of men there can be no natural law. What is held in common is the idea of law. The form which it takes is everywhere conditioned by national and historical circumstances."

[3] Consult *Bergbohm*, "Jurisprudenz und Rechtsphilosophie," Vol. 1, Introduction. Part I, "Das Naturrecht der Gegenwart." Leipzig,

principles were proposed in its place. The spirit of the times was inhospitable to philosophic study; the success of inductive methods in the natural sciences had discredited pure deduction. Accordingly an empirical position was taken, deriving law from historical considerations, primarily from Roman law, from the ensuing Germanic development, and from the later evolution upon these foundations. The older deductive system based upon "natural law" had lost its hold; but the modern philosophy of law had not yet appeared.

The need of a philosophical study of law became apparent with the questioning of the value of merely empirical results. For however valuable in extending the data of their several sciences may be the microscope of the bacteriologist, the retort of the chemist, the precise instruments of the physicist, the paleontological restorations of the geologist, and the exact findings of biologist, physiologist, and psychologist, they afford but an inadequate insight into the causes and relations involved; and a comprehensive view was sought that

1892. *Bergbohm's* work, though seriously criticized — especially by *Bernatzik* in Sch. Jahrb., 1896, XX, pp. 653 seq. — is most important despite its one-sided development. See also *Adolf Merkel*, "Über das Verhältnis der Rechtsphilosophie zur 'positiven' Rechtswissenschaft und zum allgemeinen Teil derselben." (Grünh. Z., 1874, Vol. 1, p. 1.) "Since legal philosophy, despite its officially pronounced death-warrant, has continued to survive in a transparent disguise and to exercise its influence quietly and, indeed, has extended it, it has become an object of embarrassment. Having supposed that it was happily disposed of, it is embarrassing to find that it must still be reckoned with." Concerning the influence of the doctrine of "natural law," upon the study and determination of fundamental economic conceptions in the manner of *v. Hermann's* "Staatswirthschaftliche Untersuchungen," second edition, 1870, see *Berolzheimer*: "Das Vermögen, juristische Festlegung einiger Wirtschaftsgrundbegriffe" (Hirth's Annalen, 1904, pp. 437 seq.). On "natural law" see also *Bonar*: "Philosophy and Political Economy," London, 1893, pp. 184–196 (Natural rights and law of nature).

should reflect the results of empirical science and yet pass beyond them. These tendencies influenced the philosophy of law. Historical research proved the limitations of its own data. Induction established the basic concepts (such as law, government, endeavor, causality, error, customary law) but could not account for them. There thus arose the need for more thorough fundamental principles.

There is a further important aspect of the philosophy of law — its constructive or synthetic side. It became necessary to establish the criteria of efficient legislation in general, and again specifically as applied to such laws as those of contract, of punishment, etc. Principles were needed rightly to judge the numerous proposed reforms and innovations brought forward on all sides; political policy appeared as a substitute for legal philosophy. The conception of justice, or at least of what satisfies the sense of justice, must ever remain the point of departure of the philosophy of law. Strictly interpreted legal philosophy is concerned with the problem of the analysis of justice — a problem recently considered by the Neo-Kantians, especially by Stammler. Such an inquiry does not disregard general jurisprudence or legal sociology, which are clearly of direct service to legal progress, and may indeed have a larger sphere of influence than belongs to a more theoretical pursuit. Legal philosophy likewise finds in general jurisprudence and in legal sociology important data for the successful pursuit of its problems, as well as significant illustrations of its principles; yet the method and interests of philosophy differentiate it from these related disciplines. The modern philosophy of law thus discards the conception of an original natural law,[1] and holds

[1] *Stahl*, "Die Philosophie des Rechtes," Vol. 1, 1830, p. 1. *Ahrens*, "Cours de droit naturel," Vol. 1, p. 5: "The philosophy of law is

fast to constituted law as conditioning the nature and origin of justice, in contrast to the older conception in which an ideal absolute law was set up as supreme, and positive law was made a derivative product. The modern view recognizes positive law alone,[1] but seeks to find in it and through it the permanent ideal concept of justice. The two thus present a common content but divergent attitudes.[2]

2: PHILOSOPHY OF LAW AND GENERAL JURISPRUDENCE. A recent movement advocates an abstract legal science in place of a philosophy of law. It is represented by Binding,[3] the founder of the "theory of norms," and by

the science of justice." "The philosophy of law sets forth the fundamental principles of law and determines the mannner in which human relations should be established in conformity with the idea of justice."

[1] *Bierling*, "Juristische Prinzipienlehre," Vol. 1, pp. 1 seq. The older natural law "attempted to determine not merely the general formal character of the law but also a certain general content growing out of human nature, and thus found its point of departure not merely in the study of actually existing laws, but as well in an inherent assumption of an ideal legal content, presumably underlying all positive law. Modern legal philosophy attempts to point out, in the problems which the human mind has had to solve, the special phases which belong to law, and to investigate what from this point of view may be regarded as generally applicable or as applicable under given conditions." Again (p. 5), "If it was an error of the theory of natural law to assume a certain though minimum content as determined once for all, it follows that the principles and conceptions which according to our view form the subject of juridical science can only be formal."

[2] *Bergbohm*, "Jurisprudenz, etc.," Vol. 1, p. 80: "Until some other assumption is made untenable for jurists and legal philosophers, it must continue to be emphasized that the characteristic of legal norms lies in their mode of operation. Whatever operates as a law, and only what thus operates, is law without exception."

[3] *Binding*, "Die Normen und ihre Übertretung. Eine Untersuchung über die rechtmässige Handlung und die Arten des Delikts." Vol. I, first edition, Leipzig, 1872, second edition, Leipzig, 1890; Vol. II, Leipzig, 1877. See also *Binding*, "Handbuch des Straf-

Bierling,[1] Adolf Merkel, and Jellinek.[2] Concerning the view that the philosophy of law is only general legal science, Merkel[3] remarks that "philosophy is an indispensable factor of the pursuit of science; to question whether philosophy is of importance for practical justice is to question its status as a science." Yet he proceeds: "To give the term philosophy of law a place conformable to its accredited usage requires that it be transferred to the abstract phases of legal science. This procedure would seem to be justified by tradition in

rechts," 1, Leipzig, 1885, pp. 155-222 (*Binding*, "Handbuch der deutschen Rechtswissenschaft," VII, 1, 1); *Binding*, "Grundriss des gemeinen deutschen Strafrechts," 1, fifth edition, Leipzig, 1897, pp. 58-72. A development of the theory of norms appears in *Thon*, "Rechtsnorm und subjectives Recht," Weimar, 1878. *M. E. Mayer*, "Rechtsnormen und Kulturnormen" (Beling's Abh. Vol. 50, 1903), influenced by *Kohler*, proposes to replace the "Rechtsnormen" by the richer and more vital "Kulturnormen." See also below, § 46.

[1] *Bierling*, "Zur Kritik der juristischen Grundbegriffe," 2 vols. Gotha, 1877, 1883. "Juristische Prinzipienlehre," 2 vols., Freiburg and Leipzig, 1894, 1898.

Upon the relation of the latter work to the former, Bierling thus comments ("Juristische Prinzipienlehre", Vol. 1, Preface, p. v): "This work is designed to present in systematic form a course of thought which I pursued in a different manner in my earlier and incomplete studies, 'Zur Kritik der juristischen Grundbegriffe.' The subject of the present book is thus in part identical with that of the former work." Concerning *Bierling*, see also § 46.

[2] *Jellinek*, "Die rechtliche Natur der Staatenverträge, Vienna. 1880. "Die Lehre von den Staatenverbindungen," Vienna, 1882. "Gesetz und Verordnung, Staatsrechtliche Untersuchungen auf rechtsgeschichtlicher und rechtsvergleichender Grundlage," Freiburg, i/B, 1887. "System der subjektiven öffentlichen Rechte," Freiburg, i/B, 1892.

[3] *Merkel*, "Über das Verhältnis der Rechtsphilosophie zur 'positiven' Rechtswissenschaft und zum allgemeinen Teil derselben." (Grünh. Z., Vol. 1, Vienna, 1874, pp. 1-10, 402-421).

DEMARCATION OF THE PHILOSOPHY 11

that such a science assumes the functions and meets the needs hitherto satisfied by the philosophy of law."[1] But abstract legal science yields merely basic juridical conceptions, and no more affords a philosophy of law than does general physiology afford a philosophy of nature; in both cases the constructive material is provided but nothing more.[2] The two disciplines differ both in content and in intent. Jurisprudence comprises fundamental legal conceptions apart from their specific concrete formulation; the philosophy of law applies

[1] *Paul Müller*, "Die Elemente der Rechtsbildung und des Rechts zur Grundlegung für die realistische Begründung des Rechts," Leipzig, 1877 (pp. 38 seq.). In this he brusquely eliminates philosophy from legal science. "The renewed attempts of philosophy to gain a direct and decisive influence upon legal science, or to undertake the foundation thereof, must be considered as an unwarranted presumption in the light of recent developments. A department of learning that itself lacks established principles can obviously not offer useful principles to other sciences. A department of learning whose own development rests upon uncertain ground can clearly not provide a serviceable basis for the teachings and the content of a legal science that is striving for an objective basis. It is better to have no foundations than to have poor ones." But in a later connection (p. 43), *Müller* says: "In an indirect way [that is, through the study of philosophical writings on the part of jurists] philosophy may exert an influence upon legal science and law but not by direct transference of its principles and the conclusions resulting therefrom." It thus appears that the legal philosopher is to be philosophically trained, but to what extent he is to make use of this training, Müller does not state.

[2] *Bierling*, "Juristische Prinzipienlehre" (Vol. 1, p. 1), aptly says: "The study of legal principles considers the systematic presentations of those legal conceptions and fundamental positions which are essentially — that is in their permanent nucleus — independent from the special peculiarities of any particular concrete expression of positive law." *Bierling* continues: "Here belong in the first place the conception of law itself and its necessary consequences; secondly, those conceptions and fundamental positions which are derived from the essentially uniform psychological nature of man as

to the field as a whole as well as to its divisions.[1] The jurist critically analyzes the fundamental conceptions within the field of jurisprudence and stops where the true work of the philosopher begins; that is, with the establishment of the relations between the juridical conceptions and the general philosophic systems in which they are comprised, and from which they are derived. Jurisprudence considers the formal constructive side of such conceptions; the philosophy of law considers their material basis and essential nature.

3: PHILOSOPHY OF LAW AND COMPARATIVE LAW. Under the leadership of Kohler the new and vigorous science of comparative law[2] has contributed the descriptive ethnographical data; and these in turn have been philosophically interpreted by Post and Kohler. Comparative law[3] proposes to further our insight into the nature of legal institutions and the spirit of their laws. It is vain to expect comparative[4] law to solve all the problems bearing upon the theory and practice of law. To this must be added that all these conceptions and fundamental positions with which the study of legal principles deals, or at any rate such as properly make up its subject-matter, are of merely formal nature."

[1] *Lingg's* definition of the nature and problems of legal philosophy is to be rejected for the reason that it does not specifically distinguish between legal philosophy and general legal science. *Lingg*, "Wesen und Aufgaben der Rechtsphilosophie" (Grünh. Z., Vol. 18, 1890, pp. 47, seq.): "Philosophy is the science of principles; legal philosophy is the study of the principles of law."

[2] See below, § 47. Also § 5.

[3] *Bekker*, "Über den Rechtsbegriff" (Z. f. v. Rechtsw., Vol. 1, 1878, p. 95), says: "That branch of legal science which we call the philosophical might properly be expected to advance the comparative study of law." In regard to *Schuppe's* view as against the comparative school, in "Die Methoden der Rechtsphilosophie" (Z. f. v. Rechtsw., Vol. V, 1884, pp. 209, 274), see below § 6.

[4] *Bernhöft*, "Über Zweck und Mittel der vergleichenden Rechtswissenschaft" (Z. f. v. Rechtsw., Vol. 1, p. 36), says: "Comparative law sets forth how peoples of a common origin have independently

DEMARCATION OF THE PHILOSOPHY

of legal philosophy. There is a tendency to overrate the value of the former for the latter.[1] Until vitalized by the force of philosophical principles, the most valuable materials are merely building-stones awaiting the design of the architect.[2][3]

4: PHILOSOPHY OF LAW AND LEGAL SOCIOLOGY. The philosophy of law and legal sociology supply standards both for the criticism of existing laws and for shaping future laws. The two are intimately related but do not coincide. "To judge the value of legislation is to test whether it furthers the purposes which the law pur-

developed the traditional legal conceptions; how a people modifies the institutions which it inherits according to its own views; and thus how, without any material connection, the legal systems of different nations develop according to common evolutionary principles. Briefly it attempts to discover the idea of law in the several legal systems."

[1] *Kohler*, in "Enzyklopädie," Vol. I, sixth edition, Leipzig and Berlin, 1902 (p. 14): "Without a general history of law there can be no adequate philosophy of law, just as without a general history there can be no philosophy of humanity, and without linguistics no philosophy of language." See also pp. 17-20.

[2] *Schuppe*, "Die Methoden der Rechtsphilosophie," (Z. f. v. Rechtsw., Vol. V, 1883, pp. 209-274).

[3] Such terms as "Allgemeines Staatsrecht" or "Allgemeine Staatslehre" are usually interpreted as the philosophy of government or a philosophic public law. Thus *Gumplowicz* calls the second edition of his philosophical public law "Allgemeines Staatsrecht." Accordingly this latter term refers to a body of knowledge that cannot be adequately presented merely by a comparative study of law. I cannot endorse the view expressed by *A. Affolter*, "Staat und Recht, Versuche über allgemeines Staatsrecht" (Hirth's Ann., Vol. 36, 1903, p. 51): "It cannot fail to be recognized that the essential content of what was, and still is taught as general public law ('Allgemeines Staatsrecht') is a comparative study of law; freed from the bias of natural law it becomes comparative public law ('Staatsrecht')." If one endorsed *Affolter's* view, the conclusion would be reached that "Allgemeines Staatsrecht" may and should omit the consideration of the philosophical questions concerning the

sues, or, more accurately, whether it is a serviceable means to the achievement of a justifiable end. It is the function of the philosophy of law to establish the fundamental postulates and purposes of law."[1] The assumption that the philosophy of law in its critical and reformatory aspects becomes one with legal sociology leads to the position developed by Ihering[2] in his "Zweck im Recht," wherein he holds that the end in view determines law, that all legislation serves social interests, and that the welfare of society is the chief and final purpose of law. The philosophy of law is thus resolved into the correct understanding of social welfare, and becomes one with the politics of law. This position, which gained prominence in the last quarter of the nineteenth century, is in a measure a re-formulation of eudemonism. It presents a one-sided and false interpretation of the scope of legal sociology, which, as applied to law, is by no means the same as that of philosophy of law. In the preface I have indicated their common ground and their relation to existing institutions, conceived not as fixed but as subject to constant development. Both disciplines must consider the interests of

origin and nature of the State and the position of the individual in the State; but this position would dismiss the most important questions.

Rehm, "Allgemeine Staatslehre" (pp. 1–8), considers the conception of his subject in detail. Agreeing with *Mohl* and *G. Meyer* he expresses the following view (p. 7): "'Allgemeine Staatslehre' is the study of government in general, of the State as a whole and not of its parts.'" This definition appears to me too broad and not sufficiently precise, for the subject also considers the divisions of the State, such as the distribution of authority within the State, the rights of freedom, of citizens, etc.

[1] *Liepmann*, "Die Rechtsphilosophie des Jean Jacques Rousseau," pp. 14–16.

[2] See below, § 43.

the future and direct opinion. Their chief difference lies in the relations which they emphasize and in the attitudes which they assume.[1] The philosophical aspect of law considers the broad and far-reaching policies somewhat after the manner of the great problems of finance; the political aspect considers the immediate and lesser interests, the smaller currency of everyday exchange. This difference of outlook inevitably induces an emphasis by the former of ideal theoretical considerations derived from the concept of law; and by the latter, of the concrete, more immediate practical purposes.[2] The relation of the philosophy of law — concerned with the mastery of its own problems — with legal sociology brings it about that legal philosophical doctrines, so far as they are directed to the shaping of policy for the future, have but a relative validity and not an absolute value; thus considered, the philosophy of law becomes the formulation of the economic tendencies of a given period.[3]

[1] *Kohler* (Enzyklopädie, pp. 15, 10) confirms this view of the relationship between the philosophy of law and legal sociology; he very correctly denies the identity of the two disciplines, and says: "The philosophy of law is related to 'Rechtspolitik' in that it gives the latter its proper warrant and foundation; in particular it shows the error of positivism in law." But he gives no sharp differentiation of the two disciplines. See also *Bluntschli*, "Allgemeine Staatslehre," Preface, p. v; *Rehm*, "Allgemeine Staatslehre" (pp. 8–10), whose definition applies to politics and not specifically to 'Rechtspolitik.' He says (p. 9): "Politics as a science is the science of politics as activity." *R. Schmidt*, "Allgemeine Staatslehre," Vol. 1, pp. 25–33; *Van Calker*, "Politik als Wissenschaft." Festrede, January 27, 1898, Strassburg, 1898, pp. 12-21.

[2] Legal sociology likewise extends into the philosophy of law as soon as it undertakes a thorough consideration of its principles. This appears in the recent writers on criminal sociology, especially *v. Liszt*. See below, § 44.

[3] One may further formulate the difference and the relation between the philosophy of law and legal sociology by saying that

§ 5. *Demarcation of the Philosophy of Economics from Political Economy, Social Economy, and Social Ethics.* The relation of the philosophical to the political aspect of economics is parallel to that which obtains in law. It is through the larger outlines of general principles and the formulation of postulates that political economy attains a philosophy of economics. Political economy has a near range, and regards the needs of the moment; the philosophy of economics deals with larger periods and more permanent interests; yet the boundaries of the one overlap those of the other.

Social economy is a subdivision of political economy, the latter being understood as extending beyond material economic interests to the inclusion of the cultural interests dependent upon economic conditions. It is "politics considered from a social point of view";[1] its material problems are included in political economy, and its philosophical problems in the philosophy of economics.

Social ethics is a subdivision of ethics, which in turn is a philosophical discipline intimately related in its applications to economics and law. From their combination there emerges the modern attitude, which in the interests of personal liberty tempers the strict requirements of the law by ethical considerations.

§ 6. *The Method of the Philosophy of Law.* Reflecting the influences of the development in general philosophy, the philosophy of law proceeds by no one method but shows several distinctive tendencies. From the Middle Ages on there appear in salient contrast the theological method of scholasticism; the Renaissance philosophy of "natural law" framed upon classical

---

the latter is the philosophy of the current situation, and that philosophy is a permanent politics.

[1] *Jastrow*, "Sozialpolitik und Verwaltungswissenschaft," Berlin, 1892, pp. 3–27.

models; the more speculative philosophy of "natural law," from Kant's critical idealism to the dialectics of Hegel; and the historical school, philosophically sponsored by Hegel's theory of development, established by Schelling, and juridically developed by Hugo, Savigny, and Puchta. The speculative tendency survives; and though the doctrine of natural law has been abandoned, the views of Kant and Hegel are still influential in general law.[1] The historical school prevails in private law.[2]

[1] *Bergbohm,* "Jurisprudenz und Rechtsphilosophie," Vol. 1; *Pachmann,* "Über die gegenwärtige Bewegung in der Rechtswissenschaft," an Address, Berlin, 1882. *Kohler,* "Rechtsgeschichte und Weltentwickelung," Z. f. v. Rechtsw., Vol. V, 1884, pp. 321–334; *Schuppe,* "Die Methoden der Rechtsphilosophie," Z. f. v. Rechtsw., Vol. V, 1884, pp. 209–274; *Lingg,* "Wesen und Aufgaben der Rechtsphilosophie," Grünh. Z., Vol. 18, pp. 42–63; *Jellinek,* "Das Recht des modernen Staates," Vol. I, Berlin, 1900, pp. 23–48; *Wundt,* "Logik," second edition, Vol. II, pp. 477–499, 533–588.

[2] The same holds of penology. See particularly *Richard Loening,* "Über geschichtliche und ungeschichtliche Behandlung des deutschen Strafrechts," an address delivered April 29, 1882, published in Z. f. d. g. Str., Vol. III, 1888, pp. 219–375. He strenuously contends against all forms of speculation and in favor of a purely historical treatment. "It is the problem of German penology, if it aims at a real understanding of the present criminal law and the several factors thereof, to place the study of its history in the foreground, and particularly to study the history of the essential part thereof upon which everything else depends, namely the subjective claims of punishment, the subjective justification attaching to violations of the law" (p. 228). "The objection is made to the historical method that it does not afford in ready and final form the ultimate and persistent bases of law that prevail independently of their historical expression, and overlooks that the implied demand is one nowhere available for human satisfaction. The historical method does not raise any such claim to supply absolute philosophical values. But what the historical method thus admittedly fails to provide is beyond the scope of any method, unless those who employ it had previously divested themselves of their human nature" (p. 239). "Present-day penology shows not alone a lack of the histor-

A newer movement is presented by the sociological[1] and comparative[2] school, which has largely invaded the field of criminal law and has influenced both the theory of punishment and of criminal reform. The compara-

ical method but of what is more serious, a lack of all definite and certain method; it is open to every manner of surmise. . . . The only means gradually to overcome the prevalent detachment from positive law, and gradually to restore the sympathy between it and science, seems to me to consist in a radical break with the scientific traditions of the preceding century. This must be done in two respects: first negatively, by an abandonment of all speculations and considerations 'de lege ferenda' that rest upon any other foundations than that of the positive law; and again positively by a thorough and unprejudiced study of the historical development of German criminology. . . . I may sum up the conclusion in these words: No penology except that founded upon existing positive law, and no science of positive law without historical foundation" (pp. 260–262). See also *R. Loening*, "Geschichte der strafrechtlichen Zurechnungslehre," Vol. 1, Jena, 1903, pp. ix, seq.

[1] See below, § 44, concerning criminal sociologists — the "positive" school of penology: *v. Liszt, Ferri* and others.

[2] See below, § 47. In "Die Methoden der Rechtsphilosophie" (Z. f. v. Rechtws., Vol. V, 1884, pp. 209–274), *Schuppe* treats the problem of the scope of comparative law in detail. His comments upon the comparative school are pertinent, although a fundamental error underlies his attitude. He says (p. 227): "After this psychological digression I return to the position which has been demonstrated. If it be the problem of the philosophy of law to determine the nature of law, to determine the factor by virtue of which an action or a circumstance is declared to be right or wrong, then the comparative method — if we mean thereby that we can only determine actions as right or wrong through comparison — most illogically assumes what is to be proven. There must always be some indication of the point to be established in order to ascertain what is pertinent to a comparison." The philosophy of law seeks the meaning of the nature of law; the comparative position believes it possible to determine it by comparing the various systems of positive law or a representative group thereof. The comparative study of law may be said to attempt to determine the nature of

METHOD OF PHILOSOPHY 19

tive method has also been profitably applied in the field of jurisprudence;[1] the influence of psychology and of other tendencies is apparent.

In such diversity of view we recognize a trait of a period of transition, which is likewise evidenced by the discontent with tradition, and by the many proposals for reform. Such profusion of doctrines is more disturbing than illuminating; and this is true in art and literature as well as in philosophy. Equally distinctive is the constructive weakness, the absence of originality in construction or presentation, wherein the older ideals may be incorporated and advanced. Yet above this diversity of effort and opinion there emerges a distinctive and newer idealism — an idealism loyal to the realities, and, in so far, a realistic idealism. The old idealism, that had spent its force towards the middle of the nineteenth century, failed by its lack of a sense of reality —

---

law as would a student of natural science who undertook to determine the nature of mammalia or of trees by comparing a sufficient number of species of mammals or trees, and finding their common characteristics. Comparative law looks upon positive law as its sole and complete means of study. The purpose of comparison is the discovery of essential or general common traits. Whether the purpose can be achieved by mere comparison is debatable; and I agree with *Schuppe* in maintaining the negative of the proposition; but the argument advanced by him seems to me untenable; yet his concluding observations may be endorsed. "It is hoped that the preceding considerations have made it clear that the philosophy of law, apart from experience and comparison, is a fiction; but that the insight cannot be attained directly as a result of comparison; that accordingly the mere volume and completeness of material is not indispensable, but that the main point is the thorough observation and analysis of the salient phenomena; and that such thorough observation and analysis do not discover the important distinctions by any method that may be taught, but is essentially a matter of individual endowment" (p. 267).

[1] See below, § 49.

a criticism as applicable to classicism in art and literature as to speculative philosophy. In accordance with the historical principle by which an extreme movement in one direction induces a reaction in the opposite direction, idealism was superseded by an equally uncompromising realism, a stern materialism of thought and deed. The sense of reality, once aroused, overreached itself to the exclusion of the theoretical and the constructive. Reality was limited to what the senses could perceive and the reason infer. Ideals were discarded as illusions. Theology was banished from the cosmic conception. Art and literature were invaded by naturalism, as was philosophy by empiricism. Similar influences replaced philosophy in the field of law by historical and ethnological research, and again by the economic materialism of Marx and his followers. With the inevitable reaction, idealism once more returned as a permanent factor in the view of nature and life. Nonetheless, the intervening period of materialism had itself served the purposes of culture, in that the reconstructed idealism, unlike its precursors, was not given to extravagant speculation, but took close account of realities. Neo-idealism developed an idealistic conception of human activity upon vital issues, avoiding both the one-sidedness of idealism and the self-sufficiency of realism. In the domain of law it rejected the principle of natural law as well as all extreme speculative tendencies, and interpreted the historical, ethnological, and economic data from a broader, more idealistic point of view.

§ 7. *Law and Economics.* During the dominance of the doctrine of natural law the sense for exact historical research remained dormant; yet deductive conclusions were not naïvely mistaken for historical truths, not even by so thorough-going a defender of "natural law" as Rousseau.¹ The advocates of "natural law" found the doctrine well-adapted to their political views and position; for apart from the fact that no other serviceable formula was available, it permitted the assumption of any number of prerogatives and privileges as natural rights lying within the scope of the primitive social compact, thus supporting the political positions which it was important to justify. When later, under the influence of Hegel and Schelling, the historical sense was aroused, the doctrine of natural rights, having served its economic and philosophic functions, declined. The study of history furnished the foundations for the political ideal of nationalism; next came the intermediate influence of economic materialism; and then was ushered in the present dominant sociological period in social and economic philosophy. Inasmuch as society is a worldwide and world-old institution, preceding government though developed by it, it remained for the comparative method to supply an all-embracing conception of its nature. Thus each period brought forward the legal and economic conceptions needed for the validation of its political views and positions. Each method in turn — the natural, the historical, and the comparative — incorporated the scientific advantages of its predecessors. The philosophical, the historical, and the comparative method must now be developed and applied to the modern State composed of free industrial classes. For such purposes a method reflecting the closely allied interests of law and economics is alone adequate.[2]

[1] "Contrat social," Vol. 1, 1: "Man is born free and everywhere he is in fetters. . . . How has this transformation come about? I do not know. What can justify it? This question I think I am able to solve."

[2] *Stammler*, "Wirthschaft und Recht nach der materialistischen Geschichtsauffassung. Eine sozialphilosophische Untersuchung." Leipzig, 1896; *Berolzheimer*, "Das Vermögen, juristische Festlegung

Economics and law considered as static phenomena are related as content and form; but both are subject to change — the one continuously, the other from time to time. In considering their development and interaction, it is well to recall that the materialistic conception of history has proved itself untenable. Economic movements do not of themselves change laws. The laboring classes in England would have continued to be oppressed, had not Karl Marx impressively portrayed their wretched condition. Ricardo had set forth that the "iron law of wages" must ever place a heavy burden upon these classes; and in India and China the coolies still remain contentedly adjusted to their condition. A spark is needed to light the powder. The material condition of the oppressed classes served to re-enforce the fervid appeal of high-minded reformers. Without the appeal to liberty and the enlightening influence of the Encyclopedists, the economic abuse on the part of the ruling classes, despite the oppressed condition of the masses, would not have brought on the French Revolution. Economic changes, particularly in a society in a wholesome, responsive condition, lead to legislative reconstruction. It is also true that law acts as an inhibitory force to check too rapidly assertive economic movements; yet changes in the law also react upon economic conditions and render them unstable. If we may conceive the evolutionary wave as formed of single stable points, then it would be true of each such point, statically considered, that economics and law at any given moment are one and the same.

einiger Wirtschaftsgrundbegriffe," Hirths Ann., 1904, pp. 437–453, 516–552, 592–606; *W. Ed. Biermann*, "Staat und Wirtschaft," Vol. 1, Berlin, 1905; *Lamprecht*, "Deutsches Wirtschaftsleben im Mittelalter," Vol. 1, 1, Leipzig, 1886 (Recht und Wirtschaft zur fränkischen Stammeszeit, pp. 3–60); especially "Die gegenseitigen Beziehungen von Recht und Wirtschaft," pp. 19–51. See also § 52.

LAW AND ECONOMICS

The conception of economics must not be a narrow one; it must not be applied solely to products together with their manufacture, distribution, and consumption; nor yet wholly be limited to the idealistic, spiritual, and cultural factors in society. Economics comprises both institutions and intellectual movements. It is somewhat surprising that so conspicuous a truth as the interaction of economics and law should have waited so long for recognition — a recognition by no means universal. Some of those who question it maintain the independence and self-sufficiency of law, while others maintain that of economics. The most distinguished representative of the former group is Binding, who holds that all law is by nature "imperative, a norm, a command." The norms are the result of regulation — of the supremacy of the State. The opposite view is represented by the materialists, who hold that economic conditions exclusively determine the development of history in general, and with it, that of law.

In reality law and economics are ever and everywhere complementary and mutually determinative, like form and content. The philosophy of law is furthered by a knowledge of its economic aspects; for without the vitalizing embodiment furnished by a living society, legal conceptions would be bare and dead. The alliance of economics with law gives economic values a firm hold[1] through legal enforcement; it is indispensable to the proper establishment of philosophical principles, which alone are capable of dispelling the inconsequent vagueness to which social, reformatory, and ethical teachings, when unsupported by a solid theoretical basis, are apt

---

On the method of economics see *Wundt*, "Logik," Vol. 11, pp. 499-533; and on the method of the social sciences, pp. 436-630.

[1] *Berolzheimer*, "Das Vermögen" (Hirth's Ann., 1904, pp. 437-448, 531-540, 601-606). See also § 45.

to degenerate. With the aid of this composite approach we reach the threshold of a comprehensive development of legal economics. The great struggle for emancipation begun in ancient times found its expression in the infusion of law with the ethical spirit, and closed with the emancipation of the fourth estate. The same ethico-legal spirit may serve as the foundation for a new alliance of law and economics, which shall similarly further the influence of each and their common purpose. Their joint pursuit will advance the recognition of the essential community of economics and law by providing the law with a basis adequate to meet progressive economic conditions.[1]

[1] See below, § 52.

CHAPTER I

THE ORIGINS OF ORIENTAL CIVILIZATION

ANCIENT EGYPT. — BABYLONIA AND ASSYRIA: (1) BABYLONIAN AND ASSYRIAN CIVILIZATION, (2) THE CODE OF HAMMURABI. — THE VEDIC ARYANS.— THE JEWISH STATE.— THE PHŒNICIANS.

§ 8. *Ancient Egypt.* The civilization of ancient Egypt influenced all later civilizations.[1] Greeks and Romans drew from it, and the Mosaic code was developed upon its soil. Certain Egyptian customs and views of an ethical or legal import are quite modern in suggestion, bringing to mind the austere spirit of Western Europe in the eighteenth century, or even the utilitarian attitude of our own day, rather than an established civilization upon the ancient and distant shores of the Nile. A defiant sphinx-like quality attaches to many phases of that ancient culture.

---

[1] The works of the French Egyptologist, *Eugène Revillout*, are especially important. "Cours de droit égyptien," Vol. I, Part 1; "L'état des personnes," Paris 1884; "Les Obligations en droit égyptien comparé aux autres droits de l'antiquité (suivies d'un appendice sur le droit de la Chaldée au XXIIIe et au VIe siècle avant J. C.)," Paris 1886. The appendix is by *Victor* and *Eugène Revillout*. "La propriété ses démembrements la possession et leurs transmissions en droit égyptien comparé aux autres droits de l'antiquité," Paris 1897; "La créance et le droit commercial dans l'antiquité," Paris 1897.

Revillout has made important original contributions, and has translated the legal records of ancient Egypt. These relate for the most part to the later Egyptian period, being written in the demotic script.

The meagerness of the sources of Egyptian philosophy makes it difficult to interpret the nature of institutions, whose outward form is described, but whose deeper import remains uncertain. Our knowledge thereof is derived from accounts of the daily life, from records of legal transactions, and from inscriptions upon tombs. The histories of ancient Egypt describing its customs and usages were prepared by foreigners, such as Herodotus and Diodorus Siculus, who naturally dwelt upon conditions contrasting with those of Greece or Rome; and who, moreover, accepted uncritically legends and traditions, which were, in turn, uncritically repeated by later writers.

Religion so dominated the culture of Egypt that its bearing upon the philosophy of law, though indirect, is illuminating.[1] In this religion may be distinguished the veneration of personified forces of nature, and the symbolic worship of animal life. Greek writers, not unlike modern Egyptologists, explain this worship by the belief in the transmigration of human souls into the bodies of animals. Yet it is difficult to maintain that the fear of injuring the soul of a departed fellow-man would account for the punishment by death of even the accidental killing of a sacred animal, and for the extreme resentment incident to such an offense. It may be urged that the spirit of Egyptian religion is more correctly interpreted by emphasizing the principle of energy, of life and generation and fertility, as divine. In this view animal life represents the divine forces conferring benefit upon man. The polytheistic worship is addressed to the supreme sun-god Rê, and to all other superhuman sources of energy and life; and the monuments dedicated

[1] *Wilkinson*, "The manners and customs of the ancient Egyptians," Vol. II, pp. 454–491, 509–515; Vol. III, particularly p. 353, also pp. 354–426, 427 seq.

to the gods, like the stupendous pyramids, by suggesting heroic efforts, become the mighty symbol of the divine order. Yet it must be admitted that the prominence of animal worship is difficult to explain. Historical considerations are helpful; and the Egyptian civilization, standing between primitive culture everywhere characterized by fetishism and an intimate regard for animal life, and the later, more anthropomorphic attitude of Greek thought, presents a transition embodying alike the older and the newer conceptions. It may further be suggested that the belief in transmigration was not the *cause* of animal worship but the *means* utilized by Egyptian ethics to enforce its ideals of self-restraint.

There is no systematic work bearing upon the ethics or law and political economy of the Egyptians. Their views must be inferred from their legislation, which contains a most comprehensive prescription for every detail of life — a minute policing and regulation that may well be called petty. Although the king was rated as the son of the most supreme, of the sun-god Rê, his functions were by no means those of a tyrant or despot, but his daily life was regulated to the minutest detail;[1] and such limitations illustrate the purpose of the establishment of a just sovereignty, which is to realize the conception of law through the perfect conduct of the subjects, to whom the king is an exemplar of virtue. The throne was hereditary; and the people were confined to rigid heredi-

[1] Compare *Diodorus*, Book 1, pp. 69–72. The care of the king's person was in charge of the highest nobles, in order that he might not be evilly influenced by his environment. His activities by day and night were precisely regulated. Even his food was regulated by law to avoid intemperance and drunkenness. In connection with every sacrificial act the practice of self-control, piety, mercy, and justice was enjoined. Upon the position of the king see Uhlemann, "Handbuch der ges. ägyptischen Altertumskunde," Vol. II, pp. 48–55.

tary occupations.[1] Questionable as may be the advantages or disadvantages of such extreme regulation, it was demanded by a legislation that accepted as its goal the maximum subjection of the will of the individual to legal prescription. In addition to the class of free citizens there were slaves. Slavery was looked upon as "the inevitable and direct issue of war." [2] Yet in progressive times, notably under the sovereignty of the

[1] The Egyptians did not acknowledge rigidly exclusive castes such as obtained in India; but the vocational classes, particularly the warriors and priests, were organized upon a caste basis. This, however, has been contested. See *Revillout*, "Cours de droit égyptien," Vol. I, pp. 131–150. "I regard it as useless to give here the concordant evidence of the ancients — Solon, Herodotus, Plato, Aristotle, Socrates, Diodorus, Dicæarchus, Strabo. All these authors, whether contemporary or later, distinctly record the existence of Egyptian castes and the inheritance of the same functions in the same families. They differ only in a more or less complete enumeration of these castes. Were they all mistaken? The opinion prevails among many Egyptologists that they were." (p. 131.) See particularly *Revillout*, "La propriété," etc., Paris 1897, Part 1, p. 56: "The Egyptian caste was a right of succession of sons from their father, and it was not, as in India, an absolute barrier placed upon the sons to prevent their leaving the status of their father."

The Egyptian priestly caste was, however, legally divided into several classes which were distinct, and membership in which was hereditary, so that a transfer from one class to another was not possible. See *Twesten*, "Die religiösen, politischen und sozialen Ideen der asiatischen Kulturvölker und der Ägypter," Vol. I, p. 355.

The Egyptian caste system, in contrast to that of India, depended "essentially upon the practical position that vocation was hereditary. The idea expressed in this inheritance of an occupation was that the calling, like every other possession, belonged not to the individual but to the family; that like a social office it was at once a privilege and a duty." *Twesten*, p. 371. See also *Uhlemann*, "Handbuch," etc.

[2] "A direct and enforced result of war." *Revillout*, "Cours," etc., 1, p. 62.

Pharaohs, slaves were humanely treated. They were permitted to marry; and if married, the union was not interfered with. They attained to positions of trust; as commercial agents, or as agricultural tenants, they enjoyed comparative independence. Herodotus mentions places of refuge for slaves, and modes of procedure for terminating the slave relation.[1]

The agriculture of a country depends primarily upon climatic conditions. The natural fertility of the soil of Egypt was further increased by a system of canals, and invited to the pursuit of agriculture, which was so highly esteemed that the care of the fields was made a public function.[2] The remarkable fertility of the soil made possible a rate of interest,[3] which, judged by our standards, would amount to usury, but which was justified by the conditions. The altruism of Egyptian civilization appears in the consideration of the economically and socially dependent. Humane provisions were made

---

[1] "It is by virtue of a religious rite that a slave maltreated by his master could terminate his sufferings." *Revillout*, "La créance," etc., p. 84; also p. 85. *Herodotus*, II, 113; *Revillout*, "Cours," etc., 1, pp. 61–114; "La créance," etc., pp. 84–86, 137–154, 155–178; *Pierret*, "Dictionnaire d'archéologie égyptienne," p. 211.

[2] *Revillout*, "La propriété," etc., pp. 49–72; *Pierret*, "Dictionnaire," etc., pp. 11–13. See also *Wilkinson*, "Manners," etc., Vol. IV, 1; *Revillout*, "La créance," etc., p. 125.

Only officials and the class of warriors were exempt from agricultural service, and even this privilege was at times not available. See *Revillout*, "Cours," etc., Vol. I, p. 130.

[3] The freedom of the people from pressing needs, due to the mild climatic conditions, was an additional factor. See *Wilkinson*, "Manners," etc., Vol. I, p. 312: "The necessary expenses of the Egyptians were remarkably small, less indeed than of any people, and the food of the poorer classes was of the cheapest and most simple kind." This condition persists almost unaltered to the present day. See "Description of Egypt," Vol. II, Part II, p. 408: "Frugality is the virtue of the inhabitants of Egypt."

in behalf of the debtor;[1] the position of woman[2] was in general on a par with that of man: as maiden, wife, or widow, she enjoyed full legal rights and freedom of action. The Code of Bocchoris[3] provided in the marriage contract for a general lien in the wife's behalf upon the available and future property of the husband. It stipulated that if the husband take an additional wife, he must convey the property to the oldest son by the first wife, investing him with a one-third interest as manager and partner. Polygamy seems thus never to have been legally abolished among the Egyptians. Under the Ptolemies the claims of the wife upon the property of the husband were restricted because of the prevalence of fictitious debts of the husband to the wife, which, through the rapid accumulation of interest, frequently led to bankruptcy. A tutelage ("quasi-tutelle"[4]) for the wife was established under Græco-Macedonian influence.

As already indicated, the ethics of the Egyptians was directed to the protection of the economically weaker classes.[5]

[1] The legal maximum rate of interest was thirty per cent. This high rate is explained by the fertility of the soil and presumably the correspondingly high profit of business enterprises. Interest beyond the double value of the capital was prohibited. See *Wilkinson*, "Manners," etc., Vol. I, pp. 310–312; *Revillout*, "Les Obligations," etc., pp. 44, 53, 65–89; "Cours," etc., Vol. I, p. 53.

[2] *Revillout*, "Cours," etc., Vol. I, pp. 52–54, 195–226; "La créance," etc., p. 6; *Pierret*, "Dictionnaire," etc., pp. 221 seq., 245 seq.; also *Uhlemann*, "Handbuch," Vol. II, pp. 272 seq.

[3] Bocchoris–Bak-en-ran-w; consult *Pierret*, "Dictionnaire," etc., p. 82.

[4] *Revillout*, "Cours," etc., Vol. I, p. 198.

[5] *Revillout*, "La créance," etc., pp. 3 seq.: The remarkable Egyptian code of morals "prohibited the abuse of authority, of social station, of the power attaching to a title, an honor, or a magistracy, prevented the doing of wrong to anyone, the abuse of the weak, or

In the Egyptian religion and morals the love of truth is a supreme duty;[1] truth and justice appear in indissoluble relation and are expressed by the same term "Ma," personified in the goddess Ma, who guides the dead to the judgment seat of Osiris.[2] Ancient Egyptian law absorbed its attitudes through a religious medium.[3]

the enrichment of one at the expense of another. These principles were diametrically the opposite of those which served as the basis of the constitution and law of the Roman people." See also pp. 55, 82–86, 102, 114, 202–214, 277. "In fact duty and charity were the two fundamental ideas that dominated Egyptian law and morality." (p. 82.)

[1] *Pierret*, "Dictionnaire," etc., pp. 561 seq; also *Revillout*, "Cours," etc., Vol. I, p. 43.

[2] *Pierret*, "Dictionnaire," etc., pp. 311 seq. The goddess of truth was "the daughter of Re" (Ma set Ra). See *Lepsius*, "Denkmäler aus Ägypten." Text by *Naville* (with the co-operation of *Bochardt* and *Sethe*). Vol. III, 1900, p. 181. *Leist*, "Græco-italische Rechtsgeschichte," Jena 1884, p. 573: "Truth, in the Egyptian conception, was the law, according to which verdicts were pronounced in the divine court of the dead, and approximately, in human courts. For this reason the presiding officer of the highest Egyptian tribunal wore suspended from his neck the badge of office called Truth, similar to the badge of office worn by the Jewish high priest." Also pp. 739 seq.

[3] *Revillout*, "Cours," etc., Vol. I, p. 43. "Diodorus Siculus informs us that the older Egyptian laws formed a code divided into eight books. Accordingly in the Egyptian law the religious conception and the written regulations were inseparable. Verdicts were rendered equally in the name of the code and in the name of the Gods. . . . Even in the contracts of sale at a relatively low period of culture — the originals of which have been preserved on papyrus with their attests and lists of witnesses — there frequently appears a religious oath in addition to the purely civil formalities." "In ancient Rome as in Egypt, religion and law were at the outset one and the same. The conservators of religious rules were also the conservators of legal rites." (p. 48.) See *Revillout*, "La créance," etc., pp. 84. 114.

The moral obligations of children towards their parents, their support when in need, and the veneration of ancestors, developed upon a religious foundation. Such obligations were considered as "duties not alone towards men but towards God."[1] This highly developed legislation and ethics naturally made Egyptian civilization the point of departure and the model for the economic institutions of Greece and Rome.

§ 9. *Babylonia and Assyria.* 1: BABYLONIAN AND ASSYRIAN CIVILIZATION. The civilization of Babylonia was presumably older than that of Egypt. Tradition places the origin of the human race in the vicinity of Babylon, where agriculture early drove out the nomadic shepherds; and this may be the symbolic meaning of the story of the killing of Abel, the shepherd, by Cain, the peasant. Babylonia reached a considerable economic and industrial development, but in military position was later excelled by Assyria, notable for the triumphs of its generals from Sardanapalus to Assarhaddon.

Conformably to the spirit of ancient civilizations, the king was revered; he was the high priest, the vicar of the divine upon earth. Slavery was a well-developed institution. The captive slaves were drafted for the building of palaces. In later periods a portion of the slaves attained a more independent position, becoming merchants and the creditors of freemen.[2] As evidenced by Babylonian tablets, women were qualified for trade

---

[1] *Revillout*, "La créance," etc., p. 215; also pp. 202–222. *Revillout*, "La propriété," etc., pp. 179 seq.

[2] *Kohler* and *Peiser*, "Aus dem babylonischen Rechtsleben," Vol. I, pp. 1–7; Vol. III, p. 8; Vol. IV, pp. 17 seq. *Revillout*, "Les obligations," etc., pp. 57–64. Also *Revillout*, "La créance," etc., pp. 137–178; "Les obligations," etc., appendix, pp. 367–370. On slavery in general, up to p. 373.

and business;[1] and married or unmarried were on occasion creditors and debtors, buyers and sellers, as well as bondsmen.[2] Yet along with these privileges, as a record of the thirteenth year of Nabuchudurusur shows, the sale of women had not been completely abolished.[3]

In Egypt the transfer of ownership was made at the time of sale, and required immediate payment; in Babylonia purchase was in the nature of a contract, and as in any other obligation, payment could be postponed as arranged.[4] This more advanced type of transaction makes it probable that while the Romans derived their "jus civile" from an Egyptian model, their prætorian and commercial law was derived from Babylonian sources.[5] The Chaldeans [6] were the first to develop trade by instituting specific commercial forms and facilities, marking the beginning of a political economy.[7] The modern word "capital," in the sense of a principal that

[1] *Kohler* and *Peiser*, "Aus dem babylonischen," etc., Vol. I, pp. 7–9; Vol. III, pp. 8, 10–16; Vol. IV, pp. 10–13. *Revillout*, "Les obligations," etc., appendix, pp. 318–321, 329–360, 367.

[2] *Revillout*, "La créance," etc., p. 6.

[3] *Kohler* and *Peiser*, "Aus dem babylonischen," etc., Vol. 1, p. 7. Also *Kohler* and *Peiser*, "Hammurabi's Gesetz," Vol. I, Leipzig 1904, p. 118.

[4] *Revillout*, "La créance," etc., p. ii.

[5] On the development of Babylonian commerce and commercial law see *Revillout*, "Les obligations," etc., appendix, pp. 374–530.

[6] Upon the meaning and development of the designation, Chaldean, see *Twesten*, "Die religiösen, politischen," etc., Vol. II, p. 416. At present Chaldean stands for the same as Babylonian.

[7] *Revillout*, "La créance," etc., p. 102, says: "Monetary science was the basis of Chaldean law; the principles of morality were the basis of the Egyptian law." Consult also pp. 55, 113, 114, 215–222, 277, 278–283.

bears interest, is of Chaldean origin — the Chaldean "Kakkadu" being rendered by the Roman "caput,"[1] a business term and not a legal one. The economic prosperity and the rich return of the soil made possible a high rate of interest, in Nineveh reaching a maximum of twenty-five per cent, thirty-three and one-third per cent, or even fifty per cent per annum,[2] according to the risk involved. Compound interest, prohibited in Egypt, was customary in Chaldea.[3]

The Assyrians were not unacquainted with the precepts of a progressive ethics. An inscription extolling the good works of the Assyrian king Sargon (722–705 B.C.) records his agricultural measures, his system of irrigation and dams, and his provision of repositories for grain, against famine; but mentions as well his sense of justice in allowing full value for all property condemned, in holding medicinal oil to the lowest price, in checking speculation in sesame and corn, and, in general, "in maintaining law and justice, protecting the helpless, and not oppressing the weak."[4]

2: THE CODE OF HAMMURABI.[5] Our knowledge of Babylonian and Assyrian civilization was markedly and unexpectedly enriched by the French excavations in Susa in 1901–1902, conducted by the archæologists, De Morgan and Scheil. They found and deciphered a tablet with the inscription of the Book of Laws of the sovereign Hammurabi, who reigned in Babylonia about 2250 B.C. This codex contains legislation concerning prosecution and punishment; concerning civil law,

---

[1] *Revillout*, "La créance," etc., pp. 56, 59. *Berolzheimer*, "Das Vermögen," etc., in Hirth's Ann., 1904, p. 596, note 2.

[2] *Revillout*, "La propriété," etc., p. 111.

[3] *Revillout*, "La créance," etc., p. 65.

[4] *Lyon*, "Keilinschriften Sargon's," pp. 31–51.

[5] *Robert Harper*, "Code of Hammurabi."

including family and inheritance law; a series of regulations corresponding to our commercial and industrial law; measures bearing upon water-rights, rights of pasturage, rights of tenure, also a public law, including sacramental enactments.[1] The resemblance of this code to the Mosaic legislation is so striking as to deprive the laws of Moses of their originality and claim to an inspired origin, but by no means of their comprehensive historical importance.[2] The interpretation of the Code of Hammurabi has been much disputed, but such discussion is hardly germane to our purpose. It appears to be a book of instruction for judges, or a book of information for the people, for laws are in constant need of formulation to become practically available. Furthermore, as originally promulgated, ancient laws were uniformly theocratic; but this code is distinctly not of such character. It does not set forth general precepts, but is a summary of practical measures. It contains the decisions of mooted points, thus suggesting an interpretation of the general laws — much in the spirit in which the Talmud serves as a commentary upon the Scriptural text. The Code of Hammurabi would thus not be an independent or exhaustive code, but an administrative version of a series of general enactments which have been lost.

While the Mosaic legislation presents many points of community and resemblance with the Babylonian legislation at the time of Hammurabi, it also shows essen-

[1] *Kohler-Peiser*, "Hammurabi's Gesetz," pp. 137–139, 174–188 seq. See also *David Heinrich Müller*, "Über die Gesetze Hammurabis." Lecture, March 23, 1904.

[2] Upon the relation between the Codex and the Bible see particularly *Müller*, "Über die Gesetze Hammurabi's," p. 45; *Oettli*, "Das Gesetz Hammurabi's und die Thora Israels," pp. 30–38, 35, 85 seq.; *Kohler-Peiser*, "Hammurabi's Gesetz," p. 126, note 2.

tial differences. That Jewish law, as also Jewish civilization in general, was influenced by Babylonian, as well as by Egyptian culture, may be regarded as established. The historical value of the Mosaic legislation is not thereby impaired; for it remains true that in many essential respects, notably in its social ethics, the Torah is pervaded by a humane spirit that appears but sporadically and imperfectly in the laws of Hammurabi.

§ 10. *The Vedic Aryans.* Our knowledge of the life, customs, and laws of the ancient people of India is derived from the Vedas.[1] The Vedic Aryans, at the time when their wanderings led them to the Indus and the Punjab, were a pastoral people, but were passing over to agriculture and permanent occupation. They lived in communal settlements;[2] their political organization may be considered as resembling that of the old Germanic peoples — as a group of independent tribes associated for pillage or defense. The government of the tribe, in turn composed of clans occupying different districts, was monarchical. The king as "sat-pati" held superior authority in war. There were assemblages of the people, of the village, the district, and the clan.[3]

[1] On the meaning of Veda see Vol. I, p. 1, note 2. The poets of the Indian Vedas lived about 3000 or 4000 years before Sâyana Akârya, who assembled the ancient commentaries upon the Rigveda. Sâyana Akârya lived about 1400 A.D.

[2] "Grāma," village, together with the cultivated and improved land attached to it. Its opposite is "Aranya," wilderness, which is uncultivated land, partly woodland. *Zimmer*, "Altindisches Leben," p. 141; *Leist*, "Alt-Arisches Jus gentium," pp. 31–44. Upon the economic life of the Aryans see *Zimmer*, "Alt-indisches," etc., pp. 221–235 (Cattle-raising); pp. 235–243 (Agriculture); 243–245 (The Chase); pp. 245–255 (Industry, etc.); pp. 255–260 (Commerce and Navigation).

[3] *Zimmer*, "Alt-ind.," etc., pp. 119 seq., 158 seq. *Kuhn*, "Zur ältesten Geschichte der indogermanischen Völker," in Weber's

While it is uncertain whether the castes of India existed in Vedic times,[1] it is well to bear in mind the four castes — the Brahmins,[2] the highest and the most privileged; the second, the military nobility or knights — both of these living at the expense of the third caste — the Vaisya or Arya, to which the mass of the people belonged; and the lowest, the Sudra, whose rights were limited to bare existence.[3] Though polygamy was legally sanctioned, monogamy was the rule; and upon the death of the head of the family the eldest son succeeded.[4]

Closely connected with the religious and philosophical views of the Aryans are certain fundamental positions in regard to the philosophy of law, which in turn became the antecedents of later legal and ethical developments among the Greeks and Romans. Foremost among these philosophical conceptions is "rita," which is at once the organized principle of the universe and the divine ordering of earthly life; as the former it regulates the appearance of sun and moon, of day and night, and embodies the unchangeable principle that pervades the succession of phenomena; as the latter it is affiliated with

"Indische Studien," Vol. I, pp. 321-363; 332: "Gopâ was originally the cowherd, later protector and guardian, — particularly as an appellation of the gods, — and finally the king."

[1] *Zimmer*, "Alt-ind.," etc. Upon the meaning and origin of the word *caste* see *Max Müller*, "Essays," Vol. II, "Beiträge zur vergleichenden Mythologie und Ethologie," pp. 265-315.

[2] Brāhmaná refers to the posterity of the wise and of the priestly bards (Brahmán). See *Weber*, "Über Haug's Aitareya-Brâhmana," in Weber's "Indische Studien," Vol. IX, 1865, p. 352; *Zimmer*, "Alt-ind.," p. 205.

[3] *Twesten*, "Die religiösen," etc., Vol. II, pp. 173-251; *Zimmer*, "Alt-ind,," etc., pp. 205-216.

[4] *Zimmer*, "Alt-ind.," etc., pp. 305-336; *Twesten*, "Die religiösen," etc., p. 292; *Bernhöft*, "Altindische Familienorganisation" (in Z. f. v. Rechtsw., Vol. IX, pp. 1-45), declares his belief that polyandry existed among the primitive Aryans.

purpose and human benefit, and is exemplified in the flow of the rivers which fertilize the fields; in the cattle useful to men; in the institutions of marriage, of the monarchical state, of the patriarchal home; and in man's sense of responsibility for his sins.

The derivative conceptions of "vrata," "dharma," "dhāma" (θέμις), "svadhā"[1] (ἔθος), represent special aspects of "rita"; thus "vrata" refers to any specialized embodiment of "rita"; "svadhā" to whatever is sanctioned by law, as custom or practice; "dhāma"[2] is the realized cosmos corresponding to "rita" as a conception; while "dharma" refers specifically to the moral function of rewarding good and punishing evil.

The last has special bearings upon legal and ethical rights and duties. Under its dominion the gods are honored and offered sacrifice, so that an equivalent reward may follow. As all law is subject to the divine regulation, so the State, the family, the social structure conforms to a ritual. "Dharma" thus acquires the several meanings of the just, or of the customary, or of conformity to standards and usage. Specifically "dharma" becomes the sum total of pious duties. The four commandments, together with five injunctions, form the core of Aryan ethics. The four commandments read: Thou shalt honor the gods; Thou shalt honor thy parents; Thou shalt honor thy country; Thou shalt honor the guest, especially when he stands in need of protection. To these are added the five

[1] *Leist*, "Græco-italische Rechtsgeschichte," Jena 1884, pp. 175 seq.; 187–199; 199–205; 221; "Alt-Arisches Jus civile," Part II, p. 6.

[2] *Leist*, "Græco-italische Rechtsgeschichte," pp. 197 seq.; 218; "Alt-Arisches Jus gentium," p. 573; "Alt-Arisches Jus civile," Part I, pp. 16–23. Also *Bluntschli's* article, "Recht, Rechtsbegriff im Deutschen Staatswörterbuch," in the German Dictionary. *Bluntschli* and *Brater*, Vol. VIII, pp. 483–485.

injunctions: Thou shalt keep thyself clean; Thou shalt hold thy senses in check, in particular, not violate; Thou shalt not kill; Thou shalt not steal; Thou shalt not lie.[1] Such commands are directed primarily to the holder of property, to the head of a family as its representative, who exercises the authority to judge and punish within the circle of the home.[2] Dharma thus acquires the meaning of what is just and customary in conduct.[3]

The explicit formulation of moral precepts is familiarly not a guarantee of moral practice; indeed the moral consciousness is commonly emphasized where temptation is strong and transgression common. While the Vedic writings extol the virtues of pure water and simple, wholesome living, the people were given to excesses; wealth was eagerly sought and highly prized,[4] and crimes due to avarice were common. Appeals were constantly made

[1] *Leist*, "Alt-Arisches Jus gentium," pp. 172–384; "Alt-Arisches Jus civile," Part I, pp. 16–23; 61–458.

[2] *Leist*, "Alt-Arisches Jus gentium," pp. 59–171; 385–567.

[3] *Benfey*, "Sanskrit English Dictionary," p. 432, gives eleven meanings to "dharma"—abbreviated form of "dharman"—virtue, merit, right, law, duty, justice, character, or quality, resemblance, sacrifice, personified justice; and as "yama", the judge of the dead. See also *Bernhöft*, "Über die Grundlagen der Rechtsentwickelung bei den indogermanischen Völkern" (Z. f. v. Rechtsw., Vol. II, p. 266). The following regulations of trade and industry from the Code of Manu are interesting, and aim to fix just prices: (p. 401) "The king shall set the price for purchase and sale of all commodities according to the place of origin and destination, the period during which they have been on the market, the profit of the seller, and the expenses of the purchaser." (p. 402) "Once in five days or in a fortnight, the king shall publish the price of commodities in the market." (p. 403) "Every scales and every weight shall be adjusted and shall be tested at intervals of six months." See *Jolly*, "Die juristischen Abschnitte aus dem Gesetzbuch des Manu," Z. f. v. Rechtsw., Vol. IV, p. 339.

[4] *Hirzel*, "Gleichnisse und Metaphern im Rigveda," pp. 406–408.

to the gods for protection against robbery and deceit, against slander and false witness.

Of interest to penology is the fact that the institution of outlawry, which is prominent in Germanic law, appears in Aryan law. The offender was excluded from communal privileges, and was forced to flee beyond the pale of jurisdiction. In cases of lesser transgression bodily punishment was applied. In difficult issues of law the gods were appealed to for a decision; and, as usual in ancient practice, civil, moral, and legal guilt were not differentiated.[1]

§ 11. *The Jewish State.*[2] The Mosaic dispensation is historically important, not alone because of the measures and institutions which it established among the Jewish people, but because of the extensive circula-

---

[1]*Zimmer*, "Altindisches," etc., pp. 272-276, 283-287; 177 seq.; p. 185; pp. 181-183. On page 181 he says: "The true conception of guilt is "rna": "rnavan," guilty and beset with guilt is the gambler (Rv. 10, 34, 10), who brings his family into misfortune and attempts to appropriate another's wealth under cover of the night. "Rna," guilty, is designated the thief "tāyu"; Rv. 6, 12, 5. "Rna" frequently has the special sense of debt in connection with loans.

[2] It is difficult to decide to what extent the Mosaic commonwealth may be described as a theocracy. The reference of the tribal dispensation, as well as of the behests of law, morality, and ritual to divine origin, the fact that the king, the leader in war, likewise exercised the highest priestly office, that the voice of God was heard in the words of the prophets advising and admonishing upon affairs of states — all this supports the theocratic interpretation. But it must be borne in mind that the spirit of the period and of the Oriental attitude, as well as the trend of the cultural stage through which the people of Israel were passing, were sympathetic with, if not conducive to allied views, particularly as bearing upon tribal and national protection and fortune. The insight of Moses as a lawgiver appears in his anticipation of the inevitable organization of his people under a kingdom, and his provisions for the onset of such a transformation as a just and legal consummation. Yet it is evident that the dominance of the monotheistic conception,

tion of Scriptural ideas. Moreover the fundamental features of Jewish institutions were ethical, and these ethical concepts in turn shaped the teachings of Christianity. That the Mosaic provisions were themselves influenced by the institutions of Egypt and Babylonia is evident, though the central and pervading conception of monotheism imbues them with a distinctive, and in large measure, theocratic [1] trend. By the Jews themselves the Mosaic dispensation was regarded as divinely inspired; the people of Israel were held to be the chosen people of God, and the several precepts were enforced by their promulgation as God's will and command. The dominance of the monotheistic [2] belief appears in its emphasis by Moses as the keynote of a national religion: [3] there is but one God and his name is Jahweh.[4]

exemplified in the peculiar mystery and sanctity attaching to the appellation of the deity, influenced the entire range of the political and economic prescriptions and gave the religious aspect of philosophical conceptions a commanding position in the intellectual and practical as well as in the religious life of the people. [Translator's note condensed from omitted portions of the text.]

[1] *Michaelis*, "Mosaisches Recht," Part I, §§ 35, 36. *Wellhausen*, "Prolegomena zur Geschichte Israels," Vol. I, pp. 435–451. "Die Theokratie als Idee und als Anstalt."

[2] *Twesten*, "Die religiösen," etc., Vol. II, p. 578: "We cannot regard the doctrine of the unity of God as a Mosaic creation for it is doubtless much older, but we may regard as Mosaic the plan to free this doctrine from the esoteric obscurity of the priests and to elevate it to the dominant religion of an entire people."

[3] Compare with *Renan*, "Geschichte des Volkes Israel," Vol. I, pp. 69–106.

[4] *Renan*, "Geschichte," etc., Vol. I, p. 101: "It was in all probability a foreign importation (though this is not significant) that Jahweh could arise in Egypt, while in Assyria, and particularly in the neighboring regions, Padan-Aram, of the Chaldeans, who were affected by Aramaic influence, the word Jahou or Jahweh seems to have been used as a designation of the divinity." This comment of Renan's is certainly not an explanation.

The limitation of Jewish ethics in social practice appears in that the precept, "Love thy neighbor as thyself," was applied primarily within the fold;[1] but when thus applied, it assumed the character of an obligatory assistance of those in need. The poor were cared for, but beggary was frowned upon. In a similar spirit the taking of interest was forbidden as usury, for it was the exploiting of another's need.[2]

The practical regulations of the Mosaic dispensation center about the economic status of an agricultural people.[3] Their practical prescriptions and proscriptions embody an underlying principle, at times carried to an extreme and semi-symbolic form. The purity of agricultural products and of animal strains was to be maintained. It was forbidden to sow with mixed seeds,[4] to mate different animal species, and even to wear a garment

---

[1] Leviticus XIX, 18. "Reg" is the neighbor in the sense of everyone "with whom I have any relation either good or bad"; thus including the relation of plaintiff and defendant. See *Michaelis*, "Mos.," etc., II, § 72, p. 16. He there (p. 15) attempts to explain, though unsuccessfully, why this provision is placed among the civic laws. The command of neighborly love is based upon the philosophical interpretation which I have given. For this reason it is directly related to the law.

[2] Deuteronomy XXIV, 13; Exodus XXII, 24; Leviticus XXV, 35-37; Psalms XV, 5; Ezekiel XVIII, 8, 13, 17; Deuteronomy XV, 7-11. See also *Michaelis*, "Mos.," etc., Part I, p. 20; Part III, §§ 152-156. The acceptance of interest from strangers was allowed; Deuteronomy XXIII, 21.

For the right of the poor to glean, see Leviticus XIX, 9, 10; Deuteronomy XXIV, 19, 20, 21; Ruth II, 2-19. In regard to the produce of the field in fallow years see Leviticus XXV, 5, 6; Deuteronomy XII, 5-12, 17, 19; XIV, 22-29; XVI, 10, 11; XXVI, 12, 13. See also *Oettli*, "Das Gesetz," etc., p. 88.

[3] *Michaelis*, "Mos.," etc., I, §§ 38-44.

[4] Deuteronomy XXII, 9, and Leviticus XIX, 19. *Michaelis*, IV, §§ 218, 219. Leviticus XIX, 19. *Michaelis* IV, § 220.

partly of linen and partly of wool. The Jewish race was to be kept pure[1]; sexual excesses were punished by stoning; debilitating luxuries were to be avoided; the daily life was to be kept clean. Offspring were looked upon as the blessing of God; to the first-born were reserved special privileges,[2] both in the religious and the economical institutions,[3] but the daughters were excluded from inheritance.[4]

Among the more special economic provisions the regulation of land tenure is characteristic. It is to be noted that the Mosaic dispensation applied to a people who were about to take possession of a land, free from the complications of ancestral rights or constituted privileges. The land was to be divided among the people of Israel by lot, thus preventing concentration of ownership in large estates; but all possession was conditioned by the institution of the year of Jubilee.[5] Once in fifty years the land reverted to the original owner,[6] so that in principle it was not the land that was sold but only its returns

---

[1] Leviticus XX, 18. *Michaelis*, V, § 271.

[2] *Michaelis*, "Mos.," etc., II, § 84. Deuteronomy XXI, 17. *Michaelis*, II, § 79. *Anders*, "Codex Hammurabi," §§ 165, 167. See above § 9, pp. 51 seq.

[3] Moses was unable to exterminate the prevalent polygamy. He so modified it that the abuses attaching to the practice were as far as possible minimized. See *Michaelis*, "Mos.," etc., II, §§ 94-97.

[4] They had no share in the father's house and were regarded as strangers. Genesis XXXI, 14, 15. Numbers XXVII, 2, 3, 4. Upon this point and its exceptions see *Michaelis*, "Mos.," etc., II, § 78. *Anders*, "Codex Hammurabi," §§ 180, 181, 183, 184. See above § 9, pp. 51 seq.

[5] From "Jobel," a musical instrument with which the fiftieth year was heralded on December 10th, or more correctly from "Jabal" (Syrian) to succeed; Jubal, succession. *Michaelis*, "Mos.," etc., II, p. 20, note *.

[6] Leviticus XXV.

until the next ensuing year of Jubilee.[1] Similarly once in seven years, by divine command, the land was to lie fallow;[2] and as among an agricultural people a debtor was dependent upon his crops to repay his loan, no payment was exacted during such sabbatical year.[3] The spirit of consideration thus inculcated extended to the humane care of animals,[4] to leniency towards the unfortunate, and to charity towards the dependent.[5] Though the agricultural pursuits of peace determined the economical regulation, the contingencies of war were prepared for. At stated periods a census of all the people was taken; and military service was exacted of all male adults above twenty years of age, the Levites alone being exempt. It is, however, but natural that, despite its ethical and cultural provisions, the Mosaic dispensation should reflect the dependence of Jewish civilization upon ancient tradition and usage. Thus slavery, though moderated in its exactions, was retained; and the purchase of wives, though not universal, was customary.[6] The right of retaliation for bodily injury and the institution of vengeance by the near of kin were likewise sanctioned;[7]

---

[1] Leviticus XXV, 14–16; Leviticus XXV, 23. According to the Egyptian model in which Pharaoh is the owner of the land, see Genesis XLVII, 20.

[2] Leviticus XXV, 1–8.

[3] Deuteronomy XV, 1, 2. *Michaelis*, "Mos.," etc., III, § 157.

[4] Deuteronomy XXII, 10; the prohibition of yoking an ox to an ass for ploughing; Deuteronomy XXV, 4; "Thou shalt not muzzle the ox when he treadeth out the corn." *Michaelis*, "Mos.," etc., Part II, § 130.

[5] *Oettli*, "Das Gesetz," etc., pp. 30–38; 35.

[6] Genesis XXIX, 15, 29; XXXIV, 12. Also Genesis XXXI, 15, 16. *Michaelis*, "Mos.," etc., II, §§ 85, 86.

[7] Exodus XXI, 23–27; Leviticus XXIV, 19, 20. Deuteronomy XIX, 19. *Michaelis*, "Mos.," etc., V, §§ 240–242.

though here again the spirit of equity is indicated by the establishment of places of refuge for unintentional murder.[1]

§ 12. *The Phœnicians.*[2] In older civilizations commerce was limited to within the country or to the adjoining territory. The rocky coast of Phœnicia gave little opportunity for agriculture or cattle raising, and the Phœnicians turned their energies to maritime trade,[3] serving the ancient world as the mediaries of international exchange, and laying the basis for a prosperous merchant-class, that, through the power of capital, was destined to overshadow that of the productive artisan. Therein lies the importance of the Phœnicians for the student of the philosophy of law and economics. Indirectly the great economic development following upon the enlargement of trade made necessary an extension of legal regulations; and this in turn culminated in the constitutional model of the Greek city-state, the "polis."

[1] Genesis IX, 5, 6; Exodus XXI, 12, 13, 14; Numbers XXXV; Deuteronomy XXIX, 1-10. *Michaelis*, "Mos.," etc., 7, II, §§ 131-137. Concerning the law of blood vengeance of the Egyptians and the Jews, see also *Leist*, "Græco," etc., note 29 to § 53, pp. 742-751.

[2] *Twesten*, "Die religiösen," etc., Vol. II, pp. 537-544.

[3] It is not known when the Phœnician voyages began; they were well established in the fifteenth century before Christ. Later the Phœnicians were repulsed by the Greeks. See *Eduard Meyer*, "Geschichte des Altertums," Vol. I, Stuttgart 1884, pp. 230, 311, 336 seq.

CHAPTER II
THE ANCIENT COMMONWEALTH: GREEK CIVILIZATION

THE GREEKS BEFORE PLATO: (1) FUNDAMENTAL GREEK CONCEPTIONS; (2) SUBJECTIVISM AND OBJECTIVISM; (3) THE PYTHAGOREAN PHILOSOPHY; (4) THE PHILOSOPHY OF HERACLITUS; (5) THE SOPHISTS; (6) THE SOCRATIC PHILOSOPHY.— PLATO: (1) THE PLATONIC CONCEPTION OF VIRTUE; (2) PRACTICAL JUSTICE AND SOCIAL VIRTUE; (3) THE IDEAL AND THE REAL STATE; (4) THE INFLUENCE OF PLATO.— ARISTOTLE: (1) THE BASIS OF ETHICAL CONDUCT; (2) THE GREEK ARISTOCRAT; (3) SOCIETY AND THE STATE; (4) JUSTICE AND EQUITY; (5) THE ORIGIN OF CIVIC LIFE.— THE POST-ARISTOTELEAN PERIOD: (1) THE CYNICS; (2) THE CYRENAICS; (3) THE STOICS; (4) THE EPICUREANS; (5) THE SCEPTICS; (6) THE NEO-PLATONISTS.

§ 13. *The Greeks before Plato.* 1: FUNDAMENTAL GREEK CONCEPTIONS. Philosophical conceptions were current in Greece before its philosophers formulated their views upon the nature of law and the origin and purpose of government. Among these *energy* or *nature*, as already noted in considering Egyptian culture, was the object of reverence. "Nature," or the "natural order" or "conformity to nature" is a philosophical conception; it bears upon the philosophy of law, and makes it pertinent to consider how it was conceived by the Greeks. "Φύσις" is the quality or disposition of nature, the essence of a person or thing, as derived from the conception of its growth, genesis, or development.[1] Accordingly φύσις

[1] *Vanicek*, "Griechisch-lateinisches etymologisches Wörterbuch," Vol. II, Leipzig 1877, pp. 640, 633.

is the order or constitution of nature — nature as a generating creative force, developing from the spontaneous energy inherent in material objects without the intervention of human artificial agencies. Nature is natural energy. What the Vedic Aryans expressed as "rita" became "φύσις" to the Greeks.[1] While the ancient Aryans made it a distinctively religious or divine quality, the Greeks, with their analytic insight, recognized it as the underlying basis of natural growth, as energy.

To the Aryan "dhama" there corresponds the Greek "θέμις." In the Greek conception, Themis, as a phase of the natural order, comprises the fact of sex and generation, marriage, and the filial relation. These were conceived as divinely established, as in general a divine decree underlies all that is expressed in Themis. It was by virtue of the revelation by Zeus in Dodona, and by the oracle of the Delphic Apollo through which the "θέμιστες" of Zeus were proclaimed, that Themis became the possession of mankind. The earthly representatives of Themis are the "Dicaspoloi" in the Agora. The protection of the stranger likewise falls to the province of Themis.[2]

Co-ordinate with Themis, the humane and worldly Dike exercises influence upon Greek law and practice. Dike, deified as a daughter of Zeus, holds sway in the Agora, and secures for the litigants a lawful and just procedure in civil as well as in criminal cases. To her is accorded the like divine authority that belongs to Themis; and

[1] See, above, § 10.
[2] See *Leist*, "Græco-ital.," etc., pp. 205–211, 211–216, 662, and the references there found. Also *Vanicek*, "Griechisch.," etc., Vol. I, p. 377; *Curtius*, "Grundzüge der griechischen Etymologie," fifth edition, Leipzig 1879, p. 254; *Bernhöft*, "Über die Grundlagen der Rechtsentwickelung bei den indogermanischen Völkern," Z. f. v. Rechtsw., Vol. II, p. 283; *Leist*, "Alt-Arisches Jus civile," Part I, p. 90; Part II, pp. 4, 56, 87.

Zeus supports her plea whenever she approaches his throne in behalf of clemency.[1]

Hybris[2] appears as the source of all evil; it is the rebellion of men against the gods, presumption, the overstepping of the limits set to human conduct, whence arises the rebellious mood and the resulting wrongdoing.

The Erinyes,[3] prompt and ready to reprove, and the Eumenides to reward, stand as the protectors of the eternal order of things; they are the forces of nature and life personified in feminine form. In conjunction with the ancient Greek conception of spiritual atonement, the expiation of a threatened or accomplished dishonor, there arises the duty of vengeance. Such pious

---

[1] *Leist*, "Græco," etc., pp. 211, 508–515, 662; *Curtius*, "Grundzüge," etc., p. 134; *Vanicek*, "Griechisch," etc., pp. 328 seq.

[2] Upon Hybris see *Curtius*, "Grundzüge," etc., p. 540; *Leist*, "Alt-Arisches Jus civile," p. 95; *Hildenbrand*, "Geschichte und System der Rechts- und Staatsphilosophie," I, p. 63. *Lassalle*, "Die Philosophie Herakleitos des Dunklen von Ephesos," Berlin 1858, Vol. II, pp. 445 seq.

[3] *Plutarch*, "Isis et Osiris," c. 48. *K. O. Müller*, "Aeschylos' Eumeniden," pp. 126–151. *Hildenbrand*, "Geschichte," etc., I, p. 63. *Leist*, "Græco," etc., pp. 286–423. *Curtius*, "Grundzüge," etc., p. 344. *Schœmann*, "Griechische Altertümer," Vol. II, pp. 337–354. *Pfleiderer*, "Religionsphilosophie auf geschichtlicher Grundlage," second edition, Vol. II; "Genetisch-speculative Religionsphilosophie," Berlin 1884, p. 500. *Rohde*, "Psyche," I, pp. 259–277; II, pp. 101, 405. *Bachofen*, "Das Mutterrecht. Eine Untersuchung über die Gynaikokratie der alten Welt nach ihrer religiosen und rechtlichen Natur," Stuttgart 1861, §§ 25–29, pp. 44–58: (p. 51) " Ἐρινύς is thus the name of the divinity residing upon the earth. The Erinyes are the powerful forces within the earth, — children of the night. They bring forth all life in the dark depths of matter. What the earth brings forth in its growths is their gift, their generation. Men and animals they nourish; they make the fruit of the womb prosper. If they are displeased then all decays, the fruit of the earth, the offspring of men and animals."

obligation towards a murdered kinsman was recognized by the Greeks, especially by the Athenians. The Erinyes were pictured as relentlessly pursuing their victim, and became the active personification of a guilty conscience.

According to Homer, Nemesis[1] is the displeasure which the disobedience of Themis calls forth; according to Aristotle,[2] Nemesis is the spirit of resentment against good fortune. Nemesis thus becomes a retributive justice equalizing the fortunes of men.

2: SUBJECTIVISM AND OBJECTIVISM. While the thought-processes of primitive man are primarily perceptive, civilized man conceives the world in terms of ideas. Early cultures stand closer to the thought-habits of primitive man; in them the perceptual view of things dominates while the conceptual attitude is yet to be developed. To the contrast of perception and conception as applied to the sensory apprehension of the material world, there corresponds the like contrast of feeling and thought as applied to the cultivation of the beautiful, the moral, and the just. At the lower cultural levels commendation proceeds upon an instinctive feeling, and the socially and traditionally acceptable; while civilized man judges and determines the beautiful, the ethical, and the just, by the aid of reason and philosophy.[3] Yet in a last analysis all ideas growing out of a knowledge of the material world are derived from experience, and, in so far, from perceptions; for otherwise they would be illusory, with-

[1] Upon Nemesis see *Schelling*, "Philosophie der Mythologie." Collected works, II, 2, p. 143. *Bernhöft*, "Über die Grundlagen," etc., Z. f. v. Rechtsw, II, p. 284.

[2] *Aristotle*, Rhet. IX (Sylb. 80, 7): εἰ γάρ ἐστι τὸ νεμεσᾶν λευπεῖσθαι ἐπὶ τῷ φαινομένῳ ἀναξίως εὐπραγεῖν.

[3] Compare pp. 178–215 in Vol. I of *Berolzheimer*, "System der Rechts- und Wirtschaftsphilosophie" ("Kritik des Erkenntnisinhaltes").

out real foundation. Practical philosophy, despite its intellectualistic setting, proceeds upon an empirical and impressionistic foundation. In a more advanced civilization the conceptual aspect of things, distinctive of an enlightened attitude, predominates; and the strong emotional factor, prevalent in a less developed civilization, declines. In all primitive stages of culture, ethical and legal values are established under conditions dominated by the emotional attitude, and practical philosophy appears in religious guise — a stage of development observable in Greek thought.

When in Greece the educated classes freed themselves from traditional religion, and natural philosophy was developed, the fundamental conceptions of ethics and law, which until then were enforced by religion, were no longer secure; and a different foundation was sought. Philosophy, by thus realizing the alternative either of assuming the possibility of an objective standard of conduct or of approaching the inquiry wholly without prejudice, was confronted by the fundamental problem of the existence of an objective criterion of right and wrong.

Continuously from their Greek beginnings the two trends persist, though with shifting import and application. The contrast involved may be described as that of idealism and realism, or of dogmatism and scepticism. Yet all such appellations are misleading by reason of the very different philosophical implications which the terms now carry; they increase rather than remove confusion. The terms "objectivism" and "subjectivism" seem preferable. Objectivism holds in general that an objective standard of right action exists; subjectivism, that there is no such standard, but that right action is determined by human choice.

Of the distinctive changes that objectivism and subjectivism have undergone in the history of the philosophy of law, the following may be noted: in Greek philosophy the problem appeared as the question whether right action was ordained by nature or by human enactment; in the mediæval attitude it appeared as the expression of the divine spirit through the medium of the dogma of the Catholic Church, and subjectivism became equivalent to impiety or heresy; in the doctrine of Natural Law objectivism claimed to have found a principle of right action and of natural right; in the modern philosophy of law the idealistic position becomes objective, and assumes the existence of an inherent conception of right ("Rechtsidee"), while realism stands for the position that might is right.

The Greek statement of the distinction between what is ordained by nature or by custom, "$\phi\acute{\upsilon}\sigma\epsilon\iota - \nu\acute{o}\mu\omega$ $\delta\acute{\iota}\kappa\alpha\iota o\nu$,"[1] fails to indicate the most general bearing of the problem, and in the first member of the alternative (Nature) somewhat anticipated the solution. For in this alternative the objective basis of right action is made equivalent to that which is ordained in and expressed through the natural order of things. In support of the assumption of an ideal or standard of right action, the objectivist position must be able to refer to an admittedly or presumably conclusive principle. This is found in the sense of right as part of the psychological endowment of human nature. While variously expressed at different periods, this is its common and consistent, though at times but vaguely recognized, basis.[2]

3: THE PYTHAGOREAN PHILOSOPHY. Objectivism finds its first development in PYTHAGORAS[3] (about 582–500

---

[1] See below, § 16. Also *Ahrens*, "Naturrecht," p. 36.

[2] This belongs to the sentiments; "Erkenntnisgefühl." See Vol I of *Berolzheimer*, "System," etc., pp. 310–317.

[3] *Ritter*, "Geschichte der pythagoreischen Philosophie," Hamburg 1826, particularly pp. 87 seq.

B.C.) as a direct issue of the Pythagorean philosophy of numbers. Like all symbolic systems, the symbolism of number is open to attack. While in the symbolic philosophy itself the ascribed quality is understood to be a mere symbol, yet it leads the symbolist to accept the appearance for the reality, and thus makes the prototype or analogy the real essence that adequately accounts for the thing itself.[1] Again the disciples, if not the founder of a symbolic system, drift to fanciful analogies, and arbitrarily combine wholly unrelated conceptions on the basis of a superficial relation or resemblance. Both faults are found in the Pythagoreans; the first in Pythagoras himself and the other in his followers. For example, there are assumed to be *ten* virtues corresponding to the *ten* celestial spheres.

Yet the valuable and significant part of the Pythagorean doctrine is found not in its symbolism but in its treatment of justice. For the first time an attempt is made to establish an objective justice in the spirit of that conception. Pythagoras calls justice the "equal multiple of itself." This phrase is transmitted through Aristotle, "ἀριθμὸς ἰσάκις ἴσος."[2] It is regularly referred to as the square number.[3] Hegel interprets it by saying that "justice is called the 'equal multiple (or power) of itself' in that it ever retains a like quality. So

---

[1] Upon the Egyptian influence upon Greek philosophy, especially upon the Pythagorean, see *Wilkinson*, "The manners and customs of the ancient Egyptians," Vol. II, pp. 491–510; also *Bachofen*, "Das Mutterrecht." Upon the Indian influence on the Pythagorean philosophy, especially the belief in the transmigration of the soul, see *L. v. Schroeder*, "Pythagoras und die Inder. Eine Untersuchung über Herkunft und Abstammung der pythagoreischen Lehren," Leipzig 1884.

[2] *Aristotle*, "Magna Moralia," I, 1, 6.

[3] *S. Hildenbrand*, "Geschichte und System der Rechts- und Staatsphilosophie," I, p. 55.

justice was determined by that number which, itself even, when multiplied by itself, remained even (equal)."[1] From Aristotle we learn that the Pythagoreans considered reparation or retribution, "Τὸ ἀντιπεπονθός," the absolute objective justice;[2] and thus the "doubly equal number" is interpreted as retribution.[3] Erdmann, in support of the Pythagorean procedure but without a detailed elucidation of the phrase, "ἀριθμὸς ἰσάκις ἴσος," comments: "That for which Aristotle criticized the Pythagoreans, namely, their mathematical formula of justice, is to be commended as consistent; even their designation of "ἀριθμὸς ἰσάκις ἴσος" is intelligible when it is recalled that they conceived justice as retributive."[4]

I confess that these interpretations impress me much as the splendor of the king's apparel appeared to the naïve lad in Andersen's fairy tale: where all the rest gazed and admired, he could see only the naked fact. Accepting "ἀριθμὸς ἰσάκις ἴσος" as "the square number," one is met by the obvious fact that there is no such thing as *the* square number; there is not a single or unique square number, but innumerable ones: 1, 4, 9, 16, 25, etc. Nor is it likely that the series as a whole is referred to. Hegel's interpretation, "A number itself when multiplied by itself remains even (equal)," is not apposite. For in the first place "equal" is not the same as "even"; and secondly, *every* even number when multiplied by itself remains even. Therefore, if the meaning had been, "The number which, itself even, when multiplied by itself, remains even," it would have been enough

---

[1] "Vorlesungen über die Geschichte der Philosophie," I, Collected Works 13, p. 273.

[2] *Aristotle*, "Ethic. Nicom.," V, 5 (8), 1: "δοκεῖ δέ τισι τὸ ἀντιπεπονθὸς εἶναι ἁπλῶς δίκαιον, ὥσπερ οἱ Πυθαγορείοι ἔφασαν.

[3] *Ritter*, "Geschichte der pythagoreischen Philosophie," p. 88.

[4] *Erdmann*, "Grundriss der Geschichte der Philosophie," I, p. 33.

to say "even numbers." Moreover "ἀριθμὸς ἰσάκις ἴσος" does not mean "multiplied by itself" (or a square number), but literally means "equally equal," or, more freely and clearly translated, "an equal multiple of itself." But equal multiples of themselves are all numbers whose factors are all the same and are present an equal number of times with the digit itself; or simply, the powers of a number equal to the number. Thus the second power of two, $2 \times 2 = 4$; the third power of three, $3 \times 3 \times 3 = 27$; the fourth power of four, $4 \times 4 \times 4 \times 4 = 256$, etc.

As noted, justice is not to be symbolized by a series of numbers but by a specific number; accordingly but one of the series is to be selected as its symbol, and this may well be the number four. In the first place the Pythagorean philosophy of numbers is confined chiefly to the digits, 1 to 10. And the number 10 itself, "deka," is derived from "four" in that $10 = 1+2+3+4$. Again "four" answers to the definition, an "equal multiple of itself,"[1] that is, the power whose exponent (2) is the same as its base (2). The "ἀριθμὸς ἰσάκις ἴσος" is thus presumably four, that is, not *any* square number, but specifically the square of 2.

In the Pythagorean philosophy retribution indicates the spirit of justice and is not restricted to punishment.[2] The word is not used in the sense ordinarily conveyed

---

[1] *Passow*, "Handwörterbuch der griechischen Sprache," Vol. I, Part 2. This view of mine is not new but its establishment may be so. *L. v. Schröder*, in "Pythagoras und die Inder," actually observes, but without proof (p. 80): "Four is the symbol of justice"; (p. 81): "They (the Pythagoreans) said that justice consisted in the equally equal or the square number, because it returns like for like, and they designated four, being the first square number, or nine, as the first uneven square number, justice."

[2] See the admirable exposition in *Hildenbrand*, "Geschichte," etc., p. 56.

§ 13] GREEKS BEFORE PLATO 55

in penology, but means the fixing of an equivalent reparation.¹ This conception, however, bears upon an important view of justice, or the concept of right, which reappears repeatedly in the historical survey of the philosophy of law. In addition the Pythagorean school is notable for the formulation of a practical ethical regulation of life, and along with Aristotle,² for its advancement of ethical principles.

4: THE PHILOSOPHY OF HERACLITUS. The Pythagorean position would favor an objective basis of justice in so far as an objectively expressed justice would imply its objective establishment, and thus its independence of human convention. On the other hand a philosophy that sceptically questions the reality of the world itself would, if consistent, deny the objective basis of justice. In this respect the philosophy of HERACLITUS,³ the Obscure (about 535–475 B.C.), is not consistent. His philosophical position is indicated in the formula, πάντα ῥεῖ.

According to him nothing is real; there is only a becoming and a decaying; nothing is abiding and real except change itself. Thus mutability is made real, while the reality of the world is denied.

In a sense the philosophical position of Heraclitus reappears in the dominant trend of later nineteenth century thought. For the philosophy of evolution, expressed idealistically by Schelling and Hegel,⁴ and real-

¹ See *Berolzheimer*, "Die Entgeltung im Strafrechte," Munich 1903, pp. 14–16, 30–39, 86, 129, 131–133, 135, 141 seq., 153–158, 167 seq., 177 seq., 191 seq., 203–205, 261, 318 seq., 433, 440, 446 seq., 449, 454, 458 seq., 472, 478–480, 488 seq., 491, 508–518.

² "Magna Moralia," I, 1.

³ On Heraclitus consult *Lassalle*, "Die Philosophie Herakleitos des Dunklen von Ephesos," 2 vols., Berlin 1858. *Hildenbrand*, "Geschichte," etc., I, pp. 62–66.

⁴ See below, §§ 34, 35, 48 (Kohler). The Hegelian *Lassalle* places the following citation from Hegel as the motto of his work upon

istically by Spencer and Darwin,¹ is founded upon a denial of fixed points of arrest in the natural world. If carried to its logical conclusion — and this applies to the philosophy of law — this position becomes pure nihilism (negation).² There are no fixed points of arrest, but only constant and endless evolutionary series; not a being but only a becoming. Either the evolutionary position remains consistent and puts an end to philosophy, or abandons consistency at one point or another, and in that case denies its own validity. Heraclitus chooses the second course. He accepts an eternal order protected by the Erinyes against the aggressiveness of the individual. Between the individual and the universal there obtains a harmony by virtue of which the individual derives his vitality from the universal; and conversely, by what he yields, strengthens the organic force of the whole. Yet this sound and vitalizing thought is quite positivistic in trend, and is opposed to the doctrine of flux, "πάντα ῥεῖ"; impiety, "ὕβρις," is the violation of this established harmony through the aggressive attitude of the individual, and thus becomes the supreme offense ethically as well as legally.³

5: THE SOPHISTS.⁴ As affecting the philosophy of law, subjectivism reaches emphatic and explicit develop-

Heraclitus: "In Heraclitus the philosophical idea first appears in its speculative form. . . . Here we are upon safe ground; there is no proposition of Heraclitus that I have not incorporated into my logic."

¹ See below, §§ 41, 51.

² "Physically, logically, and ethically, being has lost its value for Heraclitus." *Lassalle*, "Die Philosophie," etc., Vol. II, pp. 437 seq.

³ *Lassalle*, "Die Philosophie," etc., Vol. II (pp. 427 seq.), pp. 445 seq. Hildenbrand, "Geschichte," etc., p. 63.

⁴ Consult *Plato's* "Protagoras," and *Plato's* "Gorgias." *Hildenbrand*, "Geschichte," etc., I, pp. 66–80.

ment in the Sophists. They were the exponents of the intellectualism of their day. Sophistry is but the reflex of the spirit of transition. The belief in and reverence for the gods, as of the customs based thereupon, were disappearing, while the newer philosophic positions had not yet matured. Such transitional periods commonly present the marks of a dissolution; they reveal a lack of fundamental and reliable principles to support the spiritual outlook; all objective standards seem to be questioned. This is philosophically formulated in the fundamental position of PROTAGORAS (481?-411 B.C.) that "man is the measure of all things."[1] The practical man loses all objective ethical criteria to guide his conduct. The individual posits his own personality as a final purpose, and his personal advantage as the goal of endeavor. Each may do as he pleases; might alone prescribes limitations and makes right. The right of the stronger prevails. There is no objective justice, but right is determined arbitrarily by human enactment.[2]

6: THE SOCRATIC PHILOSOPHY. The extreme subjectivism of Sophistry had replaced objective principles by an eclecticism; and through such lack of positive standards the incentive to the practical appreciation of ethical factors was wanting. SOCRATES (469–399 B.C.) found philosophy and ethics in a condition at once chaotic and complacent; in this period of decline he appeared as the great teacher. By his life and teachings he pointed out a new guide for conduct, and established

[1] *Plato*, "Theætetos," p. 152. "Φησὶ γάρ που, πάντων χρημάτων μέτρον ἄνθρωπον εἶναι, τῶν μὲν ὄντων ὡς ἔστι, τῶν δὲ μὴ ὄντων ὡς οὐκ ἔστιν." "Diog. Laert.," IX, 51.

[2] *Aristotle*, Sophist. elench. 12. Callicles in *Plato*, "Gorgias," 482. Polus in *Plato*, "Gorgias," 470. Thrasymachus in *Plato*, "De Republica," I, 338. *Plato*, "Gorgias," pp. 482 seq. "Theætetos," p. 167. "De legib.," X, 889.

a path of virtue for the masses. He was the exponent of popular education, or, as we have altered but not improved the phrase, of social pedagogics. This aspect of the Socratic attitude must be clearly recognized, for it holds the key to his method as well as to his general philosophy. It accounts for the seemingly strange principle of his practical philosophy that "virtue is teachable."[1]

The same supreme value which the founders of religions placed upon faith, this philosophic reformer placed upon wisdom, and for a like reason: that it may become the source and support of life. The doctrine that virtue may be taught is not to be interpreted as an abstract theorem, but as a practical postulate; man must learn virtue, and it may be learned because it is teachable. The philosopher makes his appeal to the understanding and to insight, while the founder of a religion appeals to the emotions and to faith. When the ethical commandments of the ancient gods had been destroyed, Socrates proclaimed new ones, but the people had first to be taught to read the new message. He therefore preached to them upon the text: "Learn the virtue which we teach you." He replaced passive resignation by active endeavor, and substituted a consistent system for the confusion of the teachings of the Sophists. According to Socrates, virtue is not determined by the subjectivism of the individual. It is true that the ethical basis remains subjective in form, but the subjective consensus of the community replaces individual judgment.

---

[1] *Xenophon*, "Memorabilia," III, 9, 4: "Ἔφη δὲ καὶ τὴν δικαιοσύνην καὶ τὴν ἄλλην πᾶσαν ἀρετὴν σοφίαν εἶναι. Aristotle: "Eth. Nicom.," VI, 13: "Σωκράτης μὲν οὖν λόγους, τὰς ἀρετὰς ᾤετο εἶναι, ἐπιστήμας γὰρ εἶναι πάσας." "Magna Moralia," I, 1, "(Σωκράτης) τὰς ἀρετὰς ἐπιστήμας ἐποίαι." *Aristotle*, "Eth. Nicom.," III, 11; VII, 3.

Socrates could find no available conception of virtue. The religious positions had failed, and the teachings of the Sophists had yielded no positive construction. So he proceeded to establish virtue with reference to a normal type, the nature of which he derived empirically. He followed the same procedure in ethics which the Romans pursued in the philosophy of law. They assumed a normal man, who became the "bonus" (or "diligens") "paterfamilias," the Roman citizen performing his civic duties. Socrates set up the ethically normal man as an exemplar; and such he found in the Greek citizen. Socrates could not reach an absolute determination and definition of the good. Its basis, as among the Sophists, remained subjective, but in place of the arbitrary subjectivity of the individual, there appears the quasi-objective judgment of all good citizens, exemplified in the type of the virtuous citizen. Self-knowledge becomes the most important instrument of personal education. By comparing his own character with that of the normal, the individual is to find the incentive to overcome his faults and shortcomings. The laws of the State determine right action and represent what is right. The unwritten and universal divine decrees determine morality and lie beyond the sphere of law. He is just who obeys the laws of the State; the virtue of justice is a matter of wisdom — as is all virtue — and thus presupposes a knowledge of the reason for obedience to the laws of the State. Such obedience is not to be taken for granted, but is the result of reflection. The prerequisite of all government is self-government; the end of government is the welfare of the citizens; and the best government is that by laws.[1]

[1] *Xenophon*, "Memorabilia," II, 1; IV, 4, 5 seq.; 12: "Φημὶ γὰρ ἐγὼ τὸ νόμινον δίκαιον εἶναι," IV, 15; IV, 14; III, 9, 5; II, 1, 1 seq.; III, 2, 1 seq.; IV, 6, 12.

§ 14. *Plato*. 1: THE PLATONIC CONCEPTION OF VIRTUE AND JUSTICE. The influence of Socrates persisted after his death; through PLATO (429–348 B. C.), pre-eminent among his pupils, his doctrines became the common possession of the intellectual world. In the philosophy of Plato, Greek thought reached its culmination. He stands as the aristocrat among the philosophers of ancient days, an elect spirit of surpassing greatness. In his works Greek civilization finds its purest philosophical expression. The center of Greek culture was man, yet not man unqualified, but the noble man — man æsthetically considered. The notable unity of Greek culture appears in the selection of its noblest exemplar as the central subject of art, of philosophy, and of practical life. To the Greeks the subject of art was not man literally and realistically represented, with spot and blemish, disfigured by wrinkles and lines, worn by the cares and trials of life, but man æsthetically idealized — an abstraction of his realistic counterpart, man in the form he might assume were he to lead a godlike existence. Similarly, philosophy considered the ideal type of a moral man, not the average man, imperfect and tainted, bearing the marks of a restless struggle for existence and of a life of constant toil. Morality in the Greek view of life became equivalent to nobility of disposition.

Unless this attitude be clearly grasped, it is impossible to enter into the spirit of Platonism, or sympathetically to understand and reproduce its deeper content, however readily one may construe and repeat the statements of Plato's ethics or of his social philosophy. It would have been wholly impossible for Plato to conceive of a social philosophy devoted to the welfare of the artisan class as its central interest. Any such treatment would have impressed him as belonging to the crude uncultivated phases of human life, which only the modern drama has accepted as worthy of presentation.

To the elect of the ancient Greeks the central interest of their culture was the noble man. The entire Platonic ethics and the social and legal philosophy derived therefrom grew around this conception. The noble man was likewise the moral man. Morality is the active virtue of a refined character. Therefore the cardinal virtue is "σωφροσύνη," which is not to be interpreted as a plebeian sort of prudence, but as the aristocratic virtue of a poised self-sufficiency. It comprises all virtues, moderation in all things — the "æqua mens" of Horace,[1] including, as the prime virtue, justice. But virtue is not a natural inheritance; it must be acquired through moral education, training of character, and strengthening of the will. Education in virtue is accomplished primarily through the State; hence the close association of ethics and social philosophy, and hence the characteristic Greek view of the effacement of the individual in the interests of the State.

From these positions there follows the distinctive Platonic conception of the relation between virtue and justice, and between ethics and law. The foundation of the practical life is virtue or morality, and the basis of philosophical principles is an ethical one. The virtuous man is equally the just man. Justice becomes significant as a derivative of virtue. Legal and social philosophy is likewise based upon ethics, of which, in turn, the philosophy of law is a subdivision.

The origin and development of Plato's ethics disclose its social limitations. It cannot become universal and

[1] In the conception of Augustine: "Illa (scil. virtus), quæ Græce σωφροσύνη Latine temperantia nominatur, quâ carnales frenantur libidines, ne in quæque flagitia mentem consentientem trahant." *Augustine*, "De civitate Dei," lib. XIX, c. 4.

embrace all mankind, as does the ethics of Christianity; for the practice of Platonic virtue is the moral code of the noble man, and thus presupposes a certain measure of personal and economic independence. It is a prerogative of the Greek citizen, of the nobility of the Greek State; hence the contempt for manual labor, for according to the Greek view, common labor does not ennoble but alienates man from ethical ideals and diminishes his capacity to aspire to virtue. Plato approved of slavery unreservedly, finding it a necessary condition for the maintenance of the proper status of the citizen. The presence of an efficient slave class was necessary to the economic welfare of the State, and to the release of the citizen from manual and menial service. Thus in the maritime and industrial states there was a large slave class; in Corinth, 460,000; in Aegina, 470,000; in Attica (according to the census of 309 B.C.) 400,000.[1] It was thus made possible for the many prosperous citizens to devote themselves unrestrictedly to art, science, and culture.

The obligation of the individual to fulfill his highest duty — the practice of virtue — cannot adequately be met in and through the State alone. The State must indeed retire to give play to the free spontaneous activities of its citizens; these do not grow out of the laws enacted by the State, which secure the enforcement of rights and the preservation of liberty. In contrast to governmental regulation, the ideal of independent and spontaneous development of the members of the commonwealth gains in significance; through this ideal there was eventually established a conception of society destined to overshadow the importance of the State itself.

[1] *Gilbert*, "Handbuch der griechischen Staatsaltertümer," I, pp. 163, 287–292.

2: PLATO'S GENERAL PHILOSOPHY. From the consideration of Plato's ethics and philosophy of law in their relation to Greek culture, we may turn to the correlation of his ethics with his general philosophy. His ethics stand in close connection with his theory of knowledge. According to Plato [1] the real world, the absolute, the Kantian "thing in itself," is not the world as it appears to our perceptions. The true essence of things consists in ideas to be apprehended only directly through their phenomenal reflection. Ideas alone are real, eternal, and true. Man himself is real only in so far as he becomes the embodiment of the idea. The evolution of mortal man from his earthly condition to a higher plane of existence is graphically and pointedly portrayed in the following passage from Rohde,[2] who describes it as "a cleansing, by which the soul frees [3] itself from the distortion attaching to its earthly life, and restores the divine in man in its true light. Such purification makes the true philosopher immortal and divine while yet on earth;[4] in so far as he is able to move in the realm of rational knowledge and the understanding of the eternal, he shares in the life of the 'isles of the blessed.'[5] By laying aside all that is transient and mortal, he may

[1] Consult Vol. I of *Berolzheimer*, "System der Rechtswissenschaft," etc., pp. 8–10.

[2] "Psyche," second edition, Vol. II, pp. 285 seq.

[3] "Λύειν τὴν ψυχήν," of the body and of sensory perception: "Phædo," 83 A/B; 65 A; 67 D, "λύσις καὶ καθαρμός," of the soul through "φιλοσοφία"; "Phædo," 82 D; "λύσις καὶ ἴασις τῶν δεσμῶν," of the body, "καὶ τῆς ἀφροσύνης." "Rep.," 7, 515 C.

[4] "Θεῖος εἰς τὸ δυνατὸν ἀνθρώπῳ γίγνεται," the true philosopher; "Rep.," 6, 500 D. "ἀθάνατος"; "Symp.," 212 A.

[5] "Rep.," 6, 519 C; 540 B: "Τῆς τοῦ ὄντος θέας, οἵαν ἡδονὴν ἔχει, ἀδύνατον ἄλλῳ." "Rep.," 9, 582 C (compare "Phileb."): "γεγεῦσθαι πλὴν τῷ φιλοσόφῳ."

become more and more 'like unto the gods';[1] and upon the final release of his soul from earthly confines, he may more and more closely attain to the divine, the unseen, the pure, to the condition of an immortal, incorporeal soul, forever to dwell with others of his kind. But language, limited to the world of sense, becomes helpless to express this state.[2] A spiritual goal is thus indicated that lies out of relation to sense, or space, or time, in an eternal present, without past or future."[3]

3: PRACTICAL JUSTICE AND SOCIAL VIRTUE. In the derivation of the idea and practice of theoretical justice, Plato shows his dependence upon Socrates. Alcibiades, in the dialogue bearing his name, recognizes popular conviction, the collective sense of right, as the source of justice;[4] Anytos, in the dialogue "Meno," regards it as set by tradition;[5] Protagoras, in the dialogue "Protagoras," views it as a gift of Zeus conferred upon all citizens;[6] but Socrates is represented as holding that only the mediation of philosophy and the resulting knowledge can illuminate the nature of justice. Upon this is based the strange opinion of Plato that the philosopher should govern the State,[7] as though theoretical insight and practical ability were always combined.

Plato was not content to establish the principles of justice theoretically, but outlined their practical realization in the constitution of a just State. He stood for

[1] The flight, "ἐνθένδε ἐκεῖσε," induces "ὁμοίωσιν θεῷ κατὰ τὸ δυνατόν." "Theætet.," 176 B: "ὁμοιοῦσθαι θεῷ." "Rep.," 10, 613 A ("τῷ κατανοουμένῳ τὸ κατανοοῦν ἐξομοιῶσαι." "Tim.," 90 D).
[2] "Οὐ ῥᾴδιον δηλῶσαι." "Phæd.," 114 C.
[3] The "ἀίδιος οὐσία, τὸ ἔστι μόνον κατὰ τὸν ἀληθῆ λόγον προσήκει." "Tim.," 37 E.
[4] "Alcibiades," I 110 D.
[5] "Meno," 81 A.
[6] "Protagoras," 320.
[7] "Euthydemos," 291 A; "De Republ.," V, 473.

the true Greek culture as opposed to the decadent tendencies of his day. He repudiated the political doctrine of the Sophists that "might makes right," and recognized the need of order and reasonable regulation.[1] He considered lawlessness the greatest of evils; that the just man respects right and law;[2] that only by recognizing the dominion of law does man rise above the condition of the animal creation and reach a state of culture.[3] He held that the source of law lies in God and nature, and its essence is reason, and that the same is true of justice. Owing to the more complex formal relations involved, justice is more readily conceived in terms of the community than of the individual.[4] As the just service of the individual, "δικαιοσύνη ἀνδρός," consists in having each spiritual factor perform its function, so the just service of the State, "δικαιοσύνη πόλεως," requires that each class performs its proper work. As the Romans enunciated the "suum cuique tribuere," the rendering to each of his own, as a principle of justice, so Plato upon an ethical basis formulated a parallel duty of just conduct: "τὰ αὑτοῦ πράττειν," every man must do his part. "Σωφροσύνη," wisdom of action, which is the leading principle of virtue, becomes as well the criterion of justice as a social virtue.[5]

4: THE IDEAL AND THE REAL STATE. Plato set forth two conceptions of the State: the one as a legal institution, and the other as an ideal. The ideal State is a beautiful dream of the golden age which might be realized were the gods to descend to earth. It represents

---

[1] "De Republica," I, 351.
[2] "Gorgias," 470 seq., 477 seq., 504 seq.
[3] "De Legibus," IV, 716; IX, 874; X, 889.
[4] "De Republ.," II, 368; "De Leg.," III, 689 B, 702 A; VIII, 828 D; IV, 427 C seq., 433 D.
[5] "De Leg.," III, 696 D, E.

the imaginative ideals of Plato the poet, and not the real conditions to be considered by the constructive philosopher. The State as legally constituted is also an ideal, but an attainable one, and develops in response to political needs. The State as an institution of social betterment must strengthen and revitalize the cultural ideals of the people.

5: THE INFLUENCE OF PLATO. Plato's ethics and social philosophy brought the divine torch of enlightenment to mankind. Released from the bondage of the old religion, every man was to find the norm for the development of his character and conduct in himself. As the embodiment of the idea, as an emanation of the infinite through his own will and conduct, man, despite his frailty, may transcend his inferior self. In so far as he accepts the guidance of "σωφροσύνη," moderation, "æqua mens," he remains self-possessed, restrains his too eager impulses, his hasty resolves, and becomes the embodiment of the man of justice performing his duty and fulfilling his destiny. These two principles of Platonic ethics — "σωφροσύνη," as the regulating, restraining, negating principle, and "τὰ αὑτοῦ πράττειν," the active fulfillment of one's duty as the positive tenet — made possible an ethics free from a theological bias; and classical ethics, no less than classical art, became the model and exemplar for remote generations.

In contrast to the religious trend of the older civilizations (such as the Egyptian, the Jewish, and the early Greek), Plato's ethics was thoroughly humanitarian. The precepts of a religion addressed to its votaries alone was transformed into a philosophic appeal to all educated men. But even the genius of Plato could not transcend human limitations. In the restriction of ethical ideals to the privileged citizen, and again in the complete subjugation of the individual to the State, he shows that he is the product of his age. Christianity was the first to recognize and proclaim the universality of ethical law; and it remained for the more advanced position of later days to establish the freedom of the individual within the State.

§ 15. *Aristotle.* 1: THE BASIS OF ETHICAL CONDUCT. ARISTOTLE (384–320 B.C.) transferred Plato's social and political teachings from the Utopia of the poet's imagination to the prosaic world of daily life. His development of the Platonic philosophy was not always to its advantage; but his presentations have the merit of clearness and ready comprehensibility. The ethics of Aristotle — as presented in the "Nicomachean Ethics" and the "Magna Moralia" — follows Socrates and Plato, the modifications being more in form than in substance. Aristotle agrees with them in making the ethical end not one of extraneous utility, but an independent absolute good in itself. But while Socrates and Plato propose to educate man through instruction, Aristotle emphasizes the direct influence of motives. He sets forth that every human act is due to a purpose which finds a place in a graded series. The highest or final purpose is the rational perfection of man through the control of the intellect over the senses.[1] The concomitant issue of virtue is happiness, "Eudaimonia." The virtuous man is happy, but he does not aspire to virtue for the sake of happiness. Happiness is the correlative [2] of perfec-

---

[1] In the view that all human action has a general purpose, the Aristotelean ethics is psychologically faulty. It is not correct that all human acts are undertaken as a means to an end. Some are merely emotional or sentimental expressions, such as hate, love, duty, with no reference to purpose; and moral action is particularly of this emotional and not purposeful order. See *Berolzheimer*, "Rechtsphilosophische Studien," Munich 1903, pp. 143–148.

[2] *Lasson*, "System," etc., p. 56. "Ψυχῆς ἐνέργεια κατ' ἀρετήν." ("Eth. Nicom.," VII.)

tion.¹ Aristotle, in contrast to his predecessors, holds that knowledge has but slight influence upon character, which finds its determination in the will. The question whether Aristotle's freedom of the will implied the modern meaning of indeterminism has until recently been answered in the affirmative. In his valuable work on Aristotle, Loening has shown that Aristotle regarded the operation of the will as a definite psycho-mechanical process; yet the motives of the will remain purely psychic qualities. "Viewing man as a whole one may say that he himself determines his will, that he is himself the cause of his will, but only in the sense in which Aristotle looks upon man as the source of his own conduct and the cause of his acts." ² In its nature the will is ethically neutral; the ethical aspect appears through the development of character. Every man has the problem of transforming his natural character into a moral one. Such training of the will is accomplished through habit and through the co-operation of others. The State supplies the external medium and trains men to virtue. Thus Aristotle establishes the connection between ethics and social philosophy. The State is an institution for directing ethical aims towards the perfection of the individual while yet the individual remains completely subservient to the State.

2: THE GREEK ARISTOCRAT. In the Greek view the effacement of the individual in, and in behalf of the State, is not an undesirable issue but a necessary and natural relation. The State appears as an all-embracing organism,

---

¹ "Eth. Nicom.," I.

² *R. Loening*, "Geschichte der strafrechtlichen Zurechnungslehre," I, pp. 311, 130 seq., 273–318. *Loening* supports his expositions by numerous citations from the works of *Aristotle*. On this point, too, *John Stuart Mill* judges in a similar manner to *Aristotle*. See below, § 28, and note 18 in § 28.

the members of which are individual men, quite as the several human organs serve to compose the human organism. The presence of a social consciousness in the minds of the people is divinely ordained and provided; the law of nature similarly pervades and conditions philosophy. In the Aristotelean conception the State exists theoretically prior to its components, just as the whole exists prior to the parts. The State exists by virtue of natural law, and by virtue of the same law man is a social being, who can find his complete realization only in and through the State.[1] This close association of the individual with the State is explained by the fact that in the ethical and social philosophy of the Greeks the typical member of society is the citizen of the ruling class. Moreover society was compact, and emphasized the sense of solidarity, the community of origin and environment, in a manner not possible in modern countries subject to heterogeneous cultural conditions and a shifting population. To appreciate the strong civic spirit of the ancient Greek citizen in his city-state, one must have in mind the status of the select citizens or aristocracy in more modern parallels; such as the Hanseatic republics, or the free imperial cities of Frankfurt, Nuremberg, etc., or the provincial sovereignty in Switzerland. In these the citizens, inspired by an ardent local loyalty, rule and conduct the government. There is a strong solidarity and responsiveness between the individual and the community, between the Republic

[1] "Polit.," I, 1, 9: "Φανερὸν ὅτι φύσει ἡ πόλις ἐντὶ καὶ ὅτι ἄνθρωπος φύσει πολιτικὸν ζῷον." § 11: "Καὶ πρότερον δὴ φύσει πόλις ἢ ἕκαστος ἡμῶν ἐστίν. Τὸ γὰρ ὅλον πρότερον ἀναγκαῖον εἶναι τοῦ μέρους. Ἀναιρουμενου γὰρ τοῦ ὅλου οὐκ ἔσται ποῦς οὐδὲ χείρ. "De part. anim.," II, c. 1: "Τὰ γὰρ, ὕστερα τῇ γενέσαι πρότερα τὴν φύσιν ἐστί καὶ πρῶτον τὸ τῇ γενέσει τελευταῖον.

Compare with this the pertinent exposition by *Jellinek* in ' Allgemeine Staatslehre," pp. 282 seq.

and the citizen. A similarly constituted civic environment developed the sentiments and views of Greek social philosophy, as reflected in the expressions of their great philosophers, Plato and Aristotle. The individual felt himself so unhampered as a part of the whole, so intimately of the community in fibre and tissue, that he had no occasion or inducement to desire a moral or legal detachment from the State or withdrawal from its liberal rule.

In considering the origin of government, modern political philosophy is fond of referring to the Aristotelean dictum, "ἄνθρωπος πολιτικὸν ζῶον," "man is a social being." The "πολιτικὸν ζῶον" is commonly interpreted in the sense of a social being whose nature leads him to a socialized life; but this is misleading. The Aristotelean political economy is not applicable to large modern countries but to compact city-states and the civic spirit characteristic thereof. Moreover the "πολιτικόν" of Aristotle does not refer to the *social* nature of man, but to that quality by virtue of which man reaches his full cultural status only within the State. At best the association of "πολιτικόν" and "ζῶον" does not express a philosophical principle, but a natural consequence; and in turn not one applicable to all circumstances (including the slaves), but only to the ruling class whose lives are conditioned materially and intellectually by the State.

3: SOCIETY AND THE STATE. Aristotle's views concerning the constitution and administration of government are derived from Greek conditions, and stand in contrast with the modern treatment of legal problems in which economic questions are uppermost. In ancient Greece the political aspects prevailed. Its Republics were established in a thoroughly aristocratic spirit; while modern governments (monarchies included), are saturated with democratic tendencies. The economic questions were definitely settled for the educated Greek citizens by the conservatism of society. They were convinced that in every society there must be grades — masters and servants, the privileged and the unprivileged, the upper and the lower classes. The fully privileged citizen alone participated in the exercise of government and in all public functions. In the Greek view of life the extreme emphasis of class distinctions, the profound contempt for the class of artisans engaged in manual labor, and the approval of slavery,[1] are all due to the imperfect development of ethical ideas, which in pre-Christian times had not yet attained a general humanitarian application. But these harsh and severe views were due, for the most part, to the attitude and privileged position of the Greek citizen. In other respects Aristotle showed, as Plato had done before him, an adequate economic judgment[2] in his approval of private ownership, in his recognition of class interests, in his appreciation of the prosperous citizen as representing the sinews of the State.[3]

The economic situation was secure, but on the political side the Greek citizen was exposed to dangers. The menace to the welfare of the Greek State was not the problem of bread, but of political ambition — tyranny; the prevention of tyranny was to Aristotle the chief problem of statesmanship.

[1] "Polit.," III, 1, 4: "Μετέχειν κρίσεως καὶ ἀρχῆς," I, 13; III, 5; IV. 11; I, chaps. 3–7. Also *Hildenbrand*, "Geschichte," etc., pp. 395–406; *Wallon*, "Histoire d'esclavage dans l'antiquité," pp. 371–393. According to *Aristotle* slavery is just when it arises from so marked a difference between master and slave that the former appears as the regulating will and the latter as the material instrument; for then it is justified by nature.

[2] "Polit.," II, 2–7; IV, 11.

[3] On *Aristotle's* position as reflecting Greek culture, see "Polit.," I, 4, 7.

According to Aristotle there are three legitimate constitutional forms of government suitable to varying conditions: Monarchy, Aristocracy, and Polity; and three tyrannical kinds of government: Tyranny, Oligarchy, and Democracy.[1] The equitable government is that according to laws which limit the power of the governing; for the State is founded upon justice, and justice is its essence. Only on the basis of justice does the State fulfill its noble purpose, its ethical mission of fostering the perfection of its citizens.[2] The State must be founded upon right and not upon arbitrary power; law must prevail and the ruler but supplement the law wherever the latter fails to provide. By such measures the moral purpose of the State is attained: "τὸ ζῆν εὐδαιμόνως καὶ καλῶς," "a happy and beautiful life."[3]

4: JUSTICE AND EQUITY. Plato is the acknowledged master exponent of ethical principles; the leadership of Aristotle appears in his immortal masterpiece — the treatise on Justice. The Aristotelean principle that justice is equality is reached through the conception of virtue. As all virtue consists in moderation, so justice consists in the avoidance of too much or too little; the just is the equal. The equality of justice is partly an absolute direct equality, partly a relative equality. Absolute equality is expressed in the adjustments of private law as fairness, equity — a justice that compensates, offsets, or equalizes, "δίκαιον διορθωτικόν." Relative equality appears in a distributive justice, in the distribution of goods, "δίκαιον διανεμητικόν," according to the principle of relative standards; in the retribution which

[1] "Polit.," III, 6, 9; IV, 4, 8, 11. "Eth. Nicom.," VIII, 12.
[2] "Polit.," III, 17; V, 5-10; I, 2; I, 1 seq.; III, 9, 10; VII, 8. Also "Eth. Nicom.," III, 1, 7; II, 2; X, 10.
[3] According to "Polit.," III, 5, 13, the State is "ἡ τοῦ εὖ ζῆν κοινωνία."

the offender must make for his crime, as determined, not by an absolute standard of equality (thus opposing the principle of literal retaliation), but by the degree of guilt. The formula of absolute justice reads:—To every man let there be accorded the same; that of relative justice; to those on a par, let there be a parity of treatment, but for those unlike in circumstance there shall be unlike treatment, according to merit and service, according to worth or guilt.

Where formal justice would work material injustice, it must be supplemented by equity. The equitable is "ἐπιεικές," the just, which deviates from mere legality by becoming a corrective thereof through the mediation of standards resulting from the conception of justice. For while justice is of natural origin, law is due to enactment; it is changeable, and if defective, may be improved. Legal prescription, "νόμινον," and material justice, as alike issues of ethical precepts, should indeed coincide; but in reality, in any actual and imperfect legislation, they are likely to diverge. Where the provisions of the law, which must be general and adjusted to ordinary circumstances, "τὸ ὡς ἐπὶ τὸ πλέον," would result in an injustice, owing to the special circumstances of a particular case, the law is to be supplemented by equity, "ἐπανόρθωμα."[1]

5: THE ORIGIN OF CIVIC LIFE. Less distinctive are Aristotle's views of the evolution of the State and law; in them he substantially followed the Greek conception that life in cities was preceded by that of the village community. He derived the city or "polis" from a collection of villages, "κώμη,"[2] which in turn grew out of the individual house, "οἰκία" or homestead. The

[1] "Eth. Nicom.," V, 2, 10; 14; 1–3, 5, 9, 13. "Rhetor.," I, 10; 13, 15.
[2] "Pol.," I, 1. Leist, "Altarisches jus gentium," pp. 24–31.

salient point in this development, however, he over looked; for while the formation and extension of human groups is explained by the socializing spirit, the latter does not account for the origin of the State, or of communal right and government. According to Aristotle, law, like the State itself, is a product of the rational nature of man.[1] In this he likewise followed the Greek view which made human nature the central interest in art, as well as in philosophy. Human nature, quite too commonly held responsible for all sorts of qualities and conditions, can at best account for the social nature of customs, but hardly for the existence of the State and the evolution of law.[2]

§ 16. *The Post-Aristotelean Period.* 1: THE CYNICS. After Aristotle there ensued a period of decline in social and legal philosophy. Beginning with ANTISTHENES (b. 444 B. C.) a disciple of Gorgias, later a disciple and friend of Socrates, the Cynics make the virtue of the wise consist in the freedom from needs. They advocate a return to nature; they repudiate the results of civilization, such as government, marriage, property. In this reactionary attitude they anticipate the position of Rousseau or Tolstoi. Their merit lies in fostering the spiritual development of the less fortunate classes, who, in these views, found a philosophical consolation for their fate.

[1] "Eth. Nicom.," VIII, III, 15, 16; V, 10; X, 10, "Pol.," I, III, 6. This view of *Aristotle* became decisive for the philosophy of law and has been reinstated, though in my view falsely, particularly in modern times since the days of *Grotius*. See *Berolzheimer*, "Rechtsphilosophische Studien," pp. 149–151.

[2] See *Stammler*, "Wirtschaft und Recht," p. 535; also *Berolzheimer*, "Rechtsphil.," etc., pp. 150–152. Even if the Aristotelean explanation were correct, it would be merely causal and not philosophical. The origin of a phenomenon does not of itself provide its meaning and justification.

2: THE CYRENAICS. Prominent among the Cyrenaics is ARISTIPPUS (b. about 435 B.C.), who followed the teachings of the Sophists in favoring a hedonistic basis for conduct, and in holding that justice is the result not of nature but of enactment.[1] Another Cyrenaic, THEODORUS, carried this view to the extreme. He held that circumstances might justify the wise man in disregarding artificial statutes, and in committing theft, adultery, or sacrilege.[2]

3: THE STOICS. The Stoic school (founded by ZENO about 310 B.C.) was an outgrowth of the Cynic school, and had an important influence upon the Roman philosophy of law. The Stoic ethics proclaims the principle of natural living — of a life in harmony with the rational laws of nature. Such a life is in accord with reason and thereby with virtue. The Stoic sage is characterized by "$\dot{a}\tau a\rho a\xi i a$," a condition beyond the influence of fear and hope. He is the embodiment of "an individualistic self-sufficiency,"[3] standing for himself and by himself; he holds himself aloof from desire and action. If consistently applied, the Stoic principle would result in the paralysis and stagnation of economic life. The monistic position of the Stoics — meaning by this term their conception of the unity of law and natural reason — culminated in the social conception of cosmopolitanism. The Stoic ideal is a universal State. In its analysis of justice the Stoic philosophy holds that it is based not upon enactment but upon nature. The older formulation of the contrast of "$\phi\dot{\upsilon}\sigma\epsilon\iota\ \delta\acute{\iota}\kappa a\iota o\nu$" and "$\nu\acute{o}\mu\omega\ \delta\acute{\iota}\kappa a\iota o\nu$" is modified by the Stoics, for whom "$\nu\acute{o}\mu o s$" is equivalent to the rational law of the natural world, and who

---

[1] "Diog. Laert.," II, 93: "$M\eta\delta\acute{e}\nu\ \tau\epsilon\ \epsilon\tilde{\iota}\nu a\iota\ \phi\acute{\upsilon}\sigma\epsilon\iota\ \delta\acute{\iota}\kappa a\iota o\nu\ \mathring{\eta}\ \kappa a\lambda\grave{o}\nu\ \mathring{\eta}\ a\dot{\iota}\sigma\chi\rho\grave{o}\nu\ \dot{a}\lambda\lambda\grave{a}\ \nu\acute{o}\mu\omega\ \kappa a\grave{\iota}\ \check{\epsilon}\theta\epsilon\iota.$"

[2] "Diog. Laert.," II, 99.

[3] *Hildenbrand*, "Geschichte," etc., p. 507.

thus contrast "φύσει δίκαιον" with "θέσει δίκαιον."[1] The "φύσει δίκαιον" of the Stoics is not a principle of constituted law, but natural law as applied to life in its legal aspects.

4: THE EPICUREANS. EPICURUS (341–270 B.C.) taught the doctrine of the State contract. While Aristotle regarded men as members of an inclusive group, and derived the State from the affiliation of the several groups, Epicurus held that all men were originally individualistic and independent. The community thus arose not by a process of nature but by enactment, by voluntary association and contract. The purposes sought in such association, particularly the need of protection, formed the motive force inducing individuals to combine. Government and law were comprehensive contracts in the interest of security. Utility was the principle of human conduct, and happiness was its goal. Law became inefficient as soon as it no longer worked to advantage.[2]

This simple doctrine seems to illustrate the tendency for periods of philosophical decline to favor systems based upon an individual or social utilitarianism: witness Hobbes, Bentham, Ihering. The exponents of such views overlook the inconsistency of their psychology with history. Historically it is not the case that men federated by contract: and psychologically, man is not a coldly calculating machine regulated by utility, but an emotionally responsive being. Utilitarianism fails to account for government or law, not alone by reason of the many residual phenomena that refuse

[1] "Plutarch de Stoicorum repugnantibus" (Περὶ Στωικῶν ἐναντιωμάτων).
9. "Diog. Laert." VII, 128; "τὸ δίκαιον φασι φύσει εἶναι καὶ μὴ θέσει."

[2] "Diog. Laert.," X, 150. Compare with this "Diog. Laert.," X, 118; "Epicurus," κύριαι δόξει, 31–33; "Cicero de finibus," I, 13, 16.

to tally with this view, but because of the inherent difficulty of reaching an acceptable definition of utility.[1]

5: THE SCEPTICS. The Sceptics fell back upon the fallacies of the Sophists; their position was that of a rational resignation. They denied the existence of an inherent justice and based their denial mainly upon the evidence of the conflicting conceptions of law in different times and lands. From this they inferred the impossibility of a universal basis of right action.[2] TIMON (about 325–about 235 B.C.) maintained that in reality there is neither justice nor injustice and that men judge merely according to custom and tradition, "νόμῳ δὲ καὶ ἔθει." CARNEADES (214–129 B.C.) reasserted the doctrine that right is the expression of the power of the stronger. To deal justly is in his view to sacrifice personal advantage to an imaginary ideal. Obedience to the law of the State is based not upon a sense of justice but upon a shrewd policy that considers its own advantage.

6 THE NEO–PLATONISTS. The Neo-Platonists were the last representatives of Greek philosophy. Their philosophy was essentially mystic, and held that by withdrawal from the world of sense, men may come to know the divine upon earth through the understanding. The extreme transcendentalism of the Neo-Platonists, rejecting everything earthly, removes them from the field of social and legal philosophy. Their most notable representative was PLOTINUS, the Ascetic (204–269 A.D.).[3]

[1] *Berolzheimer*, "Die Entgeltung im Strafrechte," Munich 1903, pp. 180 seq. and "Rechtsphil.," etc., p. 147.

[2] *Zeller*, "Die Philosophie der Griechen," Part 3, Division 2, fourth edition, pp. 1–81. Scepticism likewise has found a disciple in modern times, namely, *Montaigne*. See *Rossbach*, "Die Perioden der Rechtsphilosophie," p. 45.

[3] Upon *Plotinus* see *Zeller*, "Die Philosophie," etc., pp. 500–734, 520–685.

CHAPTER III

THE CIVIC EMPIRE OF ANCIENT ROME AND THE MORALIZATION OF ROMAN LAW

THE ROMAN PEASANT STATE; THE "JUS CIVILE": (1) SUBJECTIVE RIGHT, ABSENCE OF ETHICAL FACTORS; (2) THE "PATERFAMILIAS" AS THE CENTER OF ROMAN LAW.— THE ROMAN-ITALIAN STATE: THE REJUVENATION OF LAW THROUGH "AEQUITAS."— THE ROMAN EMPIRE: INTRODUCTION OF THE PHILOSOPHY OF LAW THROUGH CICERO.— THE DECLINE OF THE ANCIENT EMPIRE: CHRISTIAN ETHICS.

§ 17. *The Roman Peasant State: the "Jus Civile."* 1: RIGHTS: ABSENCE OF ETHICAL FACTORS. The origin of the Roman Empire may be traced to the Roman peasant state. The life of the tiller of the soil was sturdy and rigorous, and his laws were of like tenor,— austere, rigid, and unyielding, severe in their provisions, and oppressive towards those falling under their authority. In the early stages of the development of law an explicit philosophy is lacking; hence the histories of the philosophy of law make slight mention of the early Roman period, which is characterized by the codification of the Twelve Tables (451–449 B.C.). But the character of the laws themselves inevitably reflects a philosophical conviction; and ancient Roman civil law is philosophically instructive by reason of its contrast to other periods and to our own attitudes. Such contrast serves to set in relief the progressive spirit of law and its historical development.

The distinctive mark of Roman law, as contrasted with later codes, lies in the complete absence of an ethical element; it illustrates the course of law antecedent to its association with ethics. By contrast it permits the modern student to realize the large dependence of legal principles upon ethical ones. Its advantage for such illustration lies in its thorough legal elaboration, its accredited standing, and, as noted, its freedom from the intrusion of ethical influences. An essential principle of law not yet permeated by the ethical idea, that is non-ethical or ethically indifferent, is the unconditionality or restrictedness of rights. Such apparently obvious positions as that all rights involve a corresponding duty, and that there are no rights without legal restrictions, do not appear in the non-ethical periods of law; they are of ethical origin and the product of constructive ethics.

The absolutism of early Roman civil law appears throughout. The owner of the farm, the "paterfamilias," is absolute monarch in the domain of private law. He lords it over his possessions, and the "familia" is unconditionally subject to his control. To him belong "personæ in mancipio," "uxor in manu," "filii" and "filiæ familias," over whom he exercises the "jus vitæ ac necis"; and again the "res mancipi," with which he may deal and dispose according to his pleasure. Property is not restricted by social considerations. There is no formulated law of the family — which is ever the issue of ethical factors — but only an undefined prerogative of the head of the household. Equally absolute is the law of indebtedness; the debtor who falls in arrears assumes an unconditional liability ("nexum"), even to the forfeiture of liberty and life.[1] There is

---

[1] XII, tab. III, 1-4; 6.

likewise no law of inheritance [1] in the modern sense. The "familia" continues in unbroken succession, the aggregate property and rights of the deceased pass on as a whole, and there are no personal claims of the individual members of the family.

The non-ethical character of Roman civil law appears likewise in the constitution of the family, which is not determined by the ethical concept of a natural relationship, but is conceived from the legal point of view that only juristically relevant facts establish or dissolve it. Hence the restriction of kinship to the agnates, and hence the possibility of an artificial kinship through "arrogation," as well as of dissolution of kinship through juristic acts.

The legal principles of early Roman law are in general terms; they take no consideration of the particular circumstances of a case, and provide for no concession in view thereof.

2: THE "PATERFAMILIAS" AS THE CENTER OF ROMAN LAW. To speak of early Roman law as non-ethical describes it negatively, as unaffected by ethical considerations, as purely legal. Yet it presents a positive side. It was rigorous; it regulated the life of the Roman citizen in the interests of the conservation of vigor. The early Romans were a yeomanry, and their laws were designed to support the yeomanry in undiminished vigor. The ancient Aryan householder, as the center of domestic life, was the upholder of a cult and of the ethical relations to which it gave rise. In contrast, the Roman view of the head of the family was primarily a legal one. He represented the center of private individual authority. The early Roman State was built upon

[1] L. 62 D. de R. J. 50, 17; L. 24 D. de V. S. 50, 16; L. 37 D. de adqu. her. 29, 2.

the "familia" as the artificial unit of authority; its foundation was not the individual, but the "familia" represented by the "paterfamilias"; to him all legislation was directed and from him it emanated.

The status of the "paterfamilias" was important for constructive legal development. Law secured order, and order furthered efficiency. The fundamental necessity of order in human life led to the search for a regulative principle; and this the Romans found in and through the central position occupied by the "bonus, diligens paterfamilias," the ideal type of the Roman citizen. The "paterfamilias" was the point of concentration of the legal provisions, the nucleus from which emanated the several divisions of the law. By setting the question, "How shall the ideal Roman citizen think and act?" the basis for the development of law and legislation was attained. The model Roman citizen furnished the constructive basis of law.

The power and authority of law as embodied in laws, and especially as realized in personal prerogative, was clearly present to the Roman mind. This may be inferred from the evidence — in part accredited as historical and in part circumstantial — that in the primitive Roman conception of law the acquisition of personal rights was not a matter of arbitrary assumption, but was established, either by means of a mutual agreement or contract, or by a unilateral act such as a testamentary disposition. Consequently in the olden times private claims could be established only under the same conditions as validated law, namely, by consent of the popular assembly. Vestiges of this original form of the subjective or personal right are to be found in the ancient Roman ceremonial of calling to witness — a requirement not easily accounted for on any other ground.[1] The underlying idea is that the collective interests of the State suffer through the litigation of private individuals, which accordingly require the consent of the community. In more developed and established communities such litigation but slightly affects the welfare of the State; and the consent thereto became a notification through the popular assembly, and was ultimately reduced to the merely formal presence of witnesses, who stand as the survival of the assembly of the people.

§18. *The Roman-Italian State: the Rejuvenation of Law through "Æquitas."* In temper the Greeks were artistic and philosophical, the Romans practical and constructive. The legal system of the Romans furnishes a brilliant example of unerring practical insight and notable constructive talent. The common opinion that the Romans contributed little to the philosophy of law is erroneous, and may be due to the exclusive consideration of Roman works upon legal philosophy. These, it is true, do not present any markedly original ideas; philosophizing was not a strong point with the Romans. Yet the contributions of their legal authorities should not be considered to the exclusion of the evidence supplied by the law itself; the true spirit of Roman philosophy and culture is reflected in the monument which Roman civilization has erected in the system of Roman law. The Romans contributed a classic and enduring model for the philosophy of law, quite as clearly as the Greeks supplied the prototype of ethical views. The two special contributions due to Roman legislation and practice are, in the first period, the establishment of the "bonus (diligens) paterfamilias" as the standard relation

[1] A more detailed exposition is found in *Berolzheimer*, "Rechtsphil.," etc., pp. 19–23. [See *Maine*, "Ancient Law," London 1909, on the Calatary will in Roman law, p. 210. — Editor's Note.]

for the development of private and criminal law; and, in the second period, the "jus æquum," as embodying law conformably to the principle of equity.

The principle of "æquitas" was expressed in the words: "summum jus summa injuria." Aristotle had already found that the stern conception of legal right must yield to considerations of equity. In Roman law such concessions were extended; and the older rigid legislation was encroached upon by the spirit of "æquitas." The Roman yeoman right became a law of universal scope; the foundations of this development were laid in the Roman-Italian period.

The renaissance of Roman law was accomplished practically by means of the prætorian edict, and theoretically through the philosophical principle of "Ratio," ("ratum").[1] It meant to the Romans what the Egyptians figured as "Ra," natural energy deified, or the ancient Aryans as "Rita," the regulative principle of the world and nature.[2] "Ratio" is not identical with the spirit of national law; for the latter is variously influenced by local and personal relations, by economic conditions, and by historical events. For this reason the Roman jurists speak of "ratio" in the sense of the Aryan "rita" as "naturalis ratio"; side by side therewith was the national Roman law reflecting its popular origin [3] as "civilis ratio." Thus to the Romans "naturalis ratio" was not equivalent to the sum total of the sentiments and consciousness of right action common

---

[1] See the bibliography noted by *Leist*, "Græco-ital.," etc., p. 199, note a, and p. 221, note f.

[2] See the confirmatory passages noted by *Leist*, "Græco-ital.," etc., p. 199. Note particularly *Cicero*, "De natura Deorum," 2, 16, 20, 37: "Tusculanarum disputationum libri quinque," 5, 24; In Verrem 2, 2, 52; Seneca, epist., 66; see also below, § 19.

[3] *Leist*, "Græco-ital.," etc., p. 609.

to all men, but signified the objective and external order of nature.[1] Yet such order must serve as the basis of just laws; and, following the Stoic argument, the legal construction based upon "ratio" becomes the artificial counterpart of the cosmic order.

The practical operation of "æquitas" belongs to the history of law. As to its conception and nature three views may be noted. The older view is that the quality of equity consists in the detailed consideration of the individual circumstances of a concrete case. Yet this most common application of "æquitas" does not adequately suggest its sphere of operation or its nature. For instance, it is due to the conception of "æquitas" that the principle of the "cognate" (maternal) relationship was established alongside and eventually in place of the "agnate" (paternal) relationship and succession. This may not be historically verifiable because the "æquitas" as applied to inheritance was not formulated as a legal institution but prevailed as a prætorian "bonorum possessio."

The view represented by Voigt is that the principle of equity would apply to new laws and legal regulations so long as these represent merely the positions of their proposers and have not yet become a constituent part of formulated law. In this sense "æquitas" in each period would be the most progressive expression of a developing legal consciousness. There would be several varieties thereof: a popular "æquitas," representing the demands growing out of the development of such consciousness in the people, and a scientific "æquitas," corresponding to similar demands due to the development of conceptions among scholars and legal practitioners. The distinction might also be made between

[1] *Leist*, "Græco-ital.," etc., pp. 664-668. (Opposed to *Savigny*, and in later days to *Bernhöft*.)

general and special "æquitas," according as it was applied to the entire field, or pertained only to a particular division of the subject. Voigt's interpretation of "æquitas" gives no objective definition of its nature, but merely indicates the subjective influences affecting its development. Nor is it the case that maturing legal convictions, under all conditions, times, and places, find representation in "æquitas." It applies historically to the growing consciousness and general development of the legal sense in the Roman evolution of law; but this is not a philosophical interpretation, and sheds no light upon the nature of "æquitas."[1]

The third view is that "æquitas" represents a "practical concession as the directive principle of a progressive legal development which finds itself in opposition to the strict civil law.[2] This view may be endorsed, but requires to be amended. "Æquitas" is the expression in Voigt's sense of a progressive legal attitude; but philosophically its significance lies not in its furtherance of a growing theoretical position, but in its introduction of the principle of practical justice into the province of law. This view must be supplemented by the consideration of the origin of the objective factors by virtue of which practical justice prevailed over formal justice. This objective factor was supplied by ethics. Ethics was first introduced in Roman law through the encroachment of "æquitas" upon the older severer conception of legal right. It may be that the introduction of "æquitas" came by way of the growing relations of the Romans with foreign peoples; but its formal legal introduction was due to the authority of the prætors.

[1] *Hildenbrand*, "Geschichte," etc., says (p. 624): "It was not 'æquitas' because it was commanded by the spirit of the times, but was approved by that spirit because it was 'æquitas.'"

[2] *Hildenbrand*, "Geschichte," etc., p. 624.

The subjective factor was the growing legal consciousness; but its objective ground and support was the ethical conception. Summarizing the result in simple terms, one may speak of it as the recognition that laws exist for the sake of man; or in philosophical terms, as the introduction of the conception of humanity in Roman law. In the later development of the philosophy of law, "bonum" and "æquum" were co-ordinate, "jus est ars boni et æqui";[1] and the entire field of law, as indeed of culture in general, was pervaded by the spirit of equity.[2]

Early law recognizes only holders of rights and not men as legal subjects. The subject of early Roman law was not the man as such, but merely the "persona." Man came into legal existence when he stepped upon the stage of the law and assumed the artificial rôle or mask of the "persona."[3] Accordingly the Roman citizen was alone prominently considered as a subject of law, and the paternal, "agnate," relationship was supreme. Early law recognized only legal transactions; conduct and its material consequences were non-existent for the law so long as they did not come under the formal requirements of legal provisions; but the reconstructed law reflected the principle: "Nemo cum damno alterius locupletior fieri debet."[4] Through this means legal

[1] I, 1, pr. D. I, 1; and § 1 eod.: "Justitiam . . . colimus et *boni et æqui* notitiam profitemur, æquum ab iniquo separantes." [See, in this connection, *Maine*, "Ancient Law" (Chapt. iii, Law of Nature and Equity), p. 48; and Sir Frederick Pollock's notes at pp. 73, 77. — Editor's Note.]

[2] L. 90, D. L. 17; and I. 52 § 3 D. II, 14; I. 32 pr. D. XV, 1; I. 2 § 5 D. XXXIX, 3; I. 8 C. 3, 1.

[3] *Berolzheimer*, "Rechtsphil." etc., pp. 104 seq.

[4] Fr. 206 D. L., 17: "Jure naturæ æquum est, neminem cum alterius detrimento et injuria fieri locupletiorem." See also *Cicero*, "De officiis," II, 22 § 78: "Aequitas omnis tollitur, si habere suum cuique non licet."

procedure became more liberal on its formal side, and more just on its material side.

§ 19. *The Roman Empire: Introduction of the Philosophy of Law Through Cicero.* CICERO (106–43 B. C.) was the leading spirit in Roman legal philosophy. He holds this position not by reason of his command of original and fundamental ideas, but as the intermediary of the traditional philosophy of Greece, which he made accessible to his generation and adapted to the conditions of Roman law. As an eclectic he drew from the several philosophies what appeared to him useful, and with literary skill fused their several contributions. His works bearing upon legal philosophy are the fragment, "Librorum de republica sex quæ supersunt"; and "De legibus libri tres" and "De officiis." In his method he was influenced by Aristotle, and in his position by the Stoic philosophers. To him the highest good was to live according to nature, "secundum naturam vivere";[1] the highest virtues were the Stoic ones of prudence, justice, magnanimity, and temperance — "prudentia," "justitia," "magnanimitas," "moderatio."[2]

The virtue of "justitia," which includes "beneficientia" or willingness to make sacrifices for communal interest — in modern phraseology, participation in the social consciousness — is practically set forth in true Roman fashion by enumerating the duties and standards resulting therefrom, such as to offend no one, "neminem læde," to live honestly, "honeste vive," to render to each his own,

---

[1] "De finibus bonorum et malorum," V, 9; III, 7, 26; IV, 10, 26; V, 9, 24, 26; "De officiis," III, 3, 13; I, 4, 14; I, 5, 14. "De finibus," V, 21, 58, 60; V, 23, 67. "De inventione," II, 53, 158, 160. "Tusculanarum disputationum" libri quinque, IV, 15, 45.

[2] "De off.," I, 4, 14, I, 7, 20-23; "De fin.," V, 23, 65, 67; "De inv.," II, 53, 160.

"suum cuique tribuere";[1] maxims that gained acceptance throughout the Roman empire. The basis of this philosophy of justice was the "naturalis ratio," the natural order as applied to ethics and law. Cicero uses a series of synonyms for this conception: "lex naturæ," "lex naturalis," "natura," "lex," "lex summa," "cœlestis," "divina et humana."[2][3][4] Law and government are not derived from arbitrary enactments of man but from objective factors, from the moral spirit inherent in the natural order.[5] The recognition of the "lex naturalis," which is "sapientia," leads to an insight into the connection of human affairs with divine decree: "rerum divinarum atque humanarum scientia."[6] In so far as practical conduct is infused with such knowledge, man is led to harmonize his activities with the "lex naturalis"; he confirms the "honestas," and exercises "justitia."[7] The law as applied consists of the "jus gentium," valid for all peoples, and of the "jus civile,"[8] which is conditioned by special local and temporal considerations.

Following the example of Aristotle, Cicero recognizes the principle of justice as that of equality; and likewise

---

[1] § 3. J. I, 1, and I, 10 § I, D. I, 1: "Juris præcepta sunt hæc: honeste vivere, alterum non lædere, suum cuique tribuere."

[2] "De leg.," I, 6; II, 24; I, 6; II, 4.

[3] "De off.," III, 6, 17; 5.

[4] "De natura deorum," I, 14.

[5] "De rep.," II, 1. "De leg.," II, 4.

[6] "De off.," I, 43, 153. Compare with this § 1, J. I, 1: "Jurisprudentia est divinarum atque humanarum rerum notitia, justi atque injusti scientia." On "naturalis and civilis ratio," see *B. W. Leist*, "Zivilistische Studien," I, pp. 76-99, and his sources, pp. 77 seq.; also IV, (Jena 1877,) pp. 1-13; 35-37; 56-60; 170-174; 174-176; 221 seq.

[7] "De off.," I, 4, 14; 155; III, 7, 17; II, 12; I, 17.

[8] "De republ.," III, 22; I, 32; 25; XXXII, 48.

makes the social impulse the incentive for the formation of the community, which in turn grows from its simplest form in the family to its more complex stages through the State up to the "societas hominum," the universal brotherhood of the Stoics, and the "societas hominum atque deorum," the cosmic commonwealth. The essential function of the State is to serve as the fountainhead of law, and as the welfare of the people, "quid est enim civitas nisi juris societas?"[1]

Seneca, the Stoic (3 B.C.–65 A.D.), was likewise influential in transferring the doctrine of human equality and liberty to the sphere of law and government.[2]

§ 20. *The Decline of the Ancient Empire: Christian Ethics.* The period of the decline of the Roman Empire witnessed the advancement of Christianity to an established national religion. Christianity displaced the Greek mythology, and through its ethics influenced the development of law, the organization of government, and the freest expansion of both. It is this cultural significance of Christian ethics that must first be considered. There is a certain analogy between the symbolic personifications revered as gods or as representatives of the divine idea, and the distinctive purposes of ethics. Primitive man made a fetish of some phase of inanimate nature or natural energy conceived as a symbol of the divine, such as the power of fire, or the vast, silent, mysterious majesty of the grove. At such a stage of culture explicit ethical ideals are lacking. The Egyptians in

---

[1] "De leg.," II, 4, 5; III, 12.

[2] "De beneficiis," I, III, chap. 20: "Errat, si quis existimat servitutem in totum hominem descendere: pars melior eius excepta est. Corpora obnoxia sunt, et adscripta dominis: mens quidem sui juris." "Opera omnia." T. II, Lipsiæ 1877, p. 154) Epistola XLVII: "Servi sunt? immo homines" ("Opera omnia," T. III, Lipsiæ 1878, p. 106).

turn held certain animals as sacred, and accorded them a greater ethical consideration than they gave to their own kind. Mosaic Judaism looked upon its God, if not exclusively, yet primarily, as the God of Israel; and Jewish ethics in general applied to the people of Israel alone.

The Greek ideal was the Hellenic aristocrat, cultivated spiritually and physically; and the gods were modeled upon this type. Greek ethics was aristocratic, like the Greek gods, who, in turn, were not free from the failings of polite Greek society. In contrast Christian monotheism aspired to universality. The God of the New Testament was proclaimed the Father and Protector of all, the Consolation and Support of the weak and the needy. Christian ethics embraced mankind in its totality, and made the individual a member of an enlightened fellowship, a spiritual being endowed with the potency of ideal conceptions. Ethics thus reached its highest expression. From the appearance of Christianity, mankind has endeavored to apply a universal humanitarian ethics to the practical problems of life, society and government. But the conception was limited to a Christian article of faith so long as the absence of temporal power deprived it of access to law and government. And therein lies the fundamental significance of the elevation of Christianity to an established religion within the Roman Empire.

Communists have ever contended that their teachings are the logical issue of Christianity; that Christian charity is realized in communism. This view is hardly in accord with historical fact. The social ethics of Christianity forms the last link in the chain of ancient moral systems, each in turn growing out of the religious views of the people and intimately bound up with them. Early ethical systems aim to hold self-seeking in check:

this is the basic principle of the sacrificial cult of primitive peoples, which is continued under the form of sacrifice to the gods from the abundance of temporal possessions. But the form of the sacrifice constantly changes, becoming ever more refined and spiritualized. The Israelitic cult made a step in advance by the abolition of human victims, as set forth in the story of Abraham's sacrifice. The spirit of Greek ethics appears in the condemnation of "Hybris," offensive to men and gods, in the vanquishing of an unbounded egoism, and in the myth of the Ring of Polycrates. Christian ethics spiritualized the entire sacrificial conception by transferring it from matter to spirit. It appeared in the precept of neighborly love, exercised not selfishly, or limited to one's own family, but as an expression of humanitarian sympathy. A universal ethics, embracing all humanity, required a world-empire for its development.

Considered theoretically, law and ethics are cultural forces that confer upon men an increased efficiency by introducing order into the communal life, by securing a sphere of action for the free will of the individual within the community, and by checking the overweening course of personal power—thus avoiding "Hybris," and setting limits to arbitrary authority. In this alliance ethics becomes a higher, more powerful force than law; for law ever requires the support of an efficient external organization to give it valid authority and enforcement. Ethics directly affects the training of human personality through moral motives without the intervention of external aid. Ethics is thus the more comprehensive cultural development.[1]

[1] Mechanically expressed, if ethics attains the same power or efficiency without additional means as law attains only with the instrument of legal compulsion, then is ethics more powerful in comparison with law by as much as the additional means increases the power.

The ethics of Christianity, compared with all preceding systems, assumes a higher cultural status and influence through its extension of salvation to all humanity and through its emancipation of the larger relations of human welfare.

CHAPTER IV

THE BONDAGE OF MEDIÆVALISM

THE SPIRITUAL DOMINANCE OF ROME: ST. AUGUSTINE, THOMAS AQUINAS, THE DOCTRINE OF THE "TWO SWORDS": (1) THE CHURCH AND GREEK PHILOSOPHY; (2) THE PHILOSOPHY OF ST. AUGUSTINE; (3) THE PHILOSOPHY OF THOMAS AQUINAS; (4) THE DOCTRINE OF THE "TWO SWORDS."— ECONOMIC AND SOCIAL RESTRICTIONS: (1) THE YEOMAN AND THE CITIZEN CLASS; (2) THE ECONOMIC INFLUENCE OF THE CHURCH; (3) THE CRAFTS AND TRADES.— THE LIBERALIZING TRENDS OF THE MIDDLE AGES: (1) DANTE; (2) WILLIAM OF OCCAM; (3) MARSILIUS OF PADUA AND THE SOVEREIGNTY OF THE PEOPLE; (4) NICHOLAUS CUSANUS; (5) MACCHIAVELLI.

§ 21. *The Spiritual Dominance of Rome (St. Augustine; Thomas Aquinas; The Doctrine of the Two Swords).* 1: THE CHURCH AND GREEK PHILOSOPHY. After the destruction of the Roman Empire the domination of Rome became stronger than ever; the ancient empire had held sway over the bodies of men; the empire of the Church dominated their souls. The mediæval attitude towards the law was centered upon the position to be assumed by the faithful towards the material interests of the State, which was ruled by law and devoted to industrial pursuits. Such position was not determined on the basis of comprehensive philosophic principles. Mediæval learning was not concerned with the interpretation and justification of the complex economic world of affairs, but with the adjustment of existing institutions to the purposes of an all-embracing Church; hence its philosophy of law was a philosophy of compromise. The Church doctrine, as expressed in the Scriptures, supplied one of the factors necessary for such construction; the other, the philosophy of earthly order and economy, was likewise accepted from established sources. Ancient Greece offered such an harmonious system; the only serious choice was that between Plato and Aristotle, and the decision was not difficult to reach. If the purpose sought in Greek philosophy was the loftiest expression of eternal truth, Plato would unhesitatingly be recognized as its chief exponent; if the object was a practical philosophic construction adequate to the needs of life, then Aristotle would inspire greater confidence. And thus the Aristotelean doctrines were accepted by, or rather welded to, the ecclesiastical system. The requisite amalgamation was accomplished in the main by the important activities of two leaders: Augustine [1] in the early period, and Thomas Aquinas [2] in the later period of the Middle Ages.

2: THE PHILOSOPHY OF ST. AUGUSTINE. The fundamental doctrine of AUGUSTINE (353–430) was that the Church has unconditional sovereignty over the State.

---

[1] "De civitate Dei," libri XXII. I cite from the edition issued by Teubner of Leipzig, in two volumes, 1877.

[2] Summa theologiæ prima secundæ qu. 90–97, secunda secundæ qu. 57–80, 120, 122 (edition Lugduni 1677). "De regimine principum," libri IV, 1509 (Books I and II by Thomas, the rest by Ptolemæus Lucensis). I have before me two editions, — "Divi Thomæ Aquinatis, Tomus XVII complectens opuscula omnia, Antverpiæ 1612, Opusculum XX, De regimine principum ad regem Cypri" (pp. 161–193); and, "Divi Thomæ Aquinatis opera, editio altera Veneta, Tomus 19 complectens opusc. theolog. Venetiis 1754, Opusc. XX. De regimine principum ad regem Cypri" (pp. 524–619). In some editions this work is published under the title of "De rebuspublicis et principum institutione," libri IV; for instance, in the Lugduni Batavorum edition, 1602.

§ 21] SPIRITUAL DOMINANCE OF ROME

The Church secures eternal salvation; the State but temporal protection. Yet Church and State are both conceived as "civitas," corresponding to the Greek "πόλις," though the term "civitas" is to be understood metaphorically or even metaphysically ("mystice").[1] Subordinate to the "civitas Dei" ("cælestis") is the "civitas terrena." At the end of time the "civitas Dei" will alone prevail, and the "civitas terrena" will be dissolved. The State is justified as a necessary means of keeping peace on earth; for this reason the laws of the State must be obeyed. While Augustine thus justifies the existence of the State, yet in certain passages he rejects and renounces it. These several statements of Augustine are not in reality contradictory.[2] The spirit of mediæval teaching justifies the State so far as it favored the service of the Church, but otherwise was opposed to it. A Christian State was pleasing to God, but a heathen State was the work of Satan.

Augustine's doctrine of evil is characteristic. According to him evil is not substance,[3] but the dissolution of substance, the withdrawal of good, "privatio et corruptio boni." It thus consists in the lack of character; its nature is wholly negative or privative.[4] In this con-

[1] See "De civ. D.," XV, chap. I; XIX, chap. 11. *Stahl*, in "Die Geschichte der Rechtsphilosophie" (p. 46), renders the expression "mysticum" by the word "symbolic." See also *Reuter*, "Augustinische Studien," pp. 128, 131.

[2] *Geyer*, "Geschichte und System der Rechtsphilosophie in Grundzügen," p. 25. Only the second conception is given by *Mohl*, "Die Geschichte und Literatur der Staatswissenschaften," p. 225.

[3] For example see *Augustine*, "De continentia," 21 ("Corpus scriptorum ecclesiasticorum latinorum," Vol. XL, sect. V, Part III, Pragæ, Vindobonæ, Lipsiæ 1900, p. 166): "ibi omnibus erit clarum atque perspicuum, quod nunc a fidelibus multis creditur, a paucis intelligitur, *malum non esse substantiam.*"

[4] "De civitate Dei," XIX, 13. See *Scipio*, "Des Aurelius Augustinus Metaphysik," pp. 80–69.

ception Augustine proves himself more successful than Spinoza, whose pantheism could not completely reconcile the antagonism of evil with the purposes of culture. Augustine also anticipates the Hegelian conception that only what is rational is real: injustice is not real, but the mere negation of justice.

The most important place in Augustine's philosophy of law is occupied by the doctrine of "Pax."[1] "Pax" is not peace, but that which brings peace, the blissful, sacred order.[2] Every organism and every part thereof has its own objective assigned order: the body, in relation to its parts and members, "pax corporis"; the unreasoning creation in the regulation of their instincts, "pax animæ in rationalis"; rational beings in the harmony between their activities and knowledge, "pax animæ rationalis ordinata cognitionis actionisque consensio"; and so on. In like manner there is a principle of order for the State, namely, "ordinata imperandi atque obœdiendi concordia civium"; and no less so for the "cælestis civitas," namely, "ordinatissima," minutely regulated; "et concordissima," in complete accord, "societas fruendi Deo et invicem in Deo."[3]

The concept of "Pax," which forms the immortal contribution of Augustine, became an essential part of mediæval philosophy. What Augustine sets forth as "Pax" appears to have been a possession of all cultures. We may recall that to the Vedic Aryans the central philosophic conception of organized nature was "rita," which included the natural and the human order. A

[1] Compare with this *Scipio*, "Des Aurelius," etc., pp. 44 seq.; and *Bernheim*, "Politische Begriffe des Mittelalters im Lichte der Anschauungen Augustins," pp. 3–6, 13 seq.

[2] "De civ. D.," lib. XIX, chap. 13: "pax omnium rerum tranquillitas ordinis."

[3] "De civ. D.," lib. XIX, chap. 13, introduction.

closely related conception was "dhama."[1] The Greeks, by emphasizing the creative energy, made of "rita," "φύσις," and of "dhama," "θέμις."[2] The Romans, through the Greeks, derived from "rita" their central conception "ratum," "ratio," "naturalis ratio";[3] and Augustine christianized "rita" into "Pax." Order is the universal bond[4] that holds the world together; order assigns a place to all created things; it is a directive and distributive justice.[5] Order is universally sought and esteemed. The opponents of order are not opposed to the principle; they renounce the existing order of things but not order itself.[6]

"Pax" acquires a special significance for ethics. It becomes the regulating principle which as "σωφροσύνη" protects man from "ὕβρις," from an overweening egoism. It sets limits to individual assertion and makes man a concordant member of the cosmos — at peace with himself and with God, protecting him from earthly misfortune and securing his salvation.[7] "Pax" is the supreme source of energy from which civilization

---

[1] See above § 10.

[2] See above, § 13.

[3] See above, §§ 10, 18, 19.

[4] "De pace universali, quæ inter quaslibet perturbationes privari non potest lege naturæ." The heading of chapter 13, Book 19.

[5] "Ordo est parium dispariumque rerum sua cuique loca tribuens dispositio." "De civ. D.," lib. XIX, chap. 13. One is reminded of the Roman, "Justitia est constans et perpetua voluntas jus suum cuique tribuens" (pr. Inst. I, 1). But this is merely an expression of "ordo" in general — the application of "ordo" to distributive justice.

[6] "De civ. D.," lib. XIX, chap. 12: "Nam et illi qui pacem, in qua sunt, perturbari volunt, non pacem oderunt, sed eam pro arbitrio suo cupiunt commutari. Non ergo ut sit pax nolunt, sed ut ea sit quam volunt."

[7] "De civ. D.," lib. XIX, chaps. 4, 10, 11, 13, 14; lib. XXI, chap. 25.

proceeds; as the earthly order, it proceeds from the cultivation of law; as the harmony of man's spiritual life and his physical activity, it becomes the goal of ethical cultivation. Thus Augustine, despite his theology, his religious dependence, and his narrow dogmatism, shows a deep and comprehensive recognition of the philosophical basis of law.

3: THE PHILOSOPHY OF THOMAS AQUINAS. The legal philosophy of the Middle Ages culminated in THOMAS AQUINAS (1228–1274), who presented and defended the Catholic position with extraordinary keenness and insight. He begins with a dualistic principle; he conceives the principle of evil as the temptation by the devil, and the principle of good as God. God inclines men to good by fostering knowledge through law, and by strengthening their will by his mercy.[1] Hence the nature of law must be understood. Accepting the position of Augustine, Aquinas assumes a "summa ratio," a "lex æterna," derived from the divine reason, and expressed in the principle of temporal rule. From the absolute rule of God arises natural law, "lex naturalis." The latter may appear superfluous: "Sufficienter enim homo gubernatur per legem æternam." In reality Aquinas recognizes natural law, from which men and States without a "lex scripta" derive the knowledge of good and evil. The "lex naturalis" is the "participatio" of mankind in the "lex æterna," by virtue of which men, despite the limitations of human knowledge through the fall of man, derive the distinction of good and evil, "secundum quam bonum et malum discernunt."[2] In addition to the law of the divine regulation

[1] II, 1 qu. 90: "Principium . . . exterius ad malum inclinans est diabolus. . . . Principium . . . exterius movens ad bonum est Deus, qui et nos instruit per legem, et juvat per gratiam."

[2] II, 1 qu. 91, art. 1; qu. 93. II, 1 qu. 91, art. 2. II, 1 qu. 91, art. 2, conclus.; qu. 94, arts. 2 and 3.

of the world, the "lex æterna," and of the natural law, the "lex naturalis," there is a third, a positive law, the "lex quædam ab hominibus inventa." Positive law carries out in detail the principles of natural law.[1] The purpose of the law is the perfection of man, "homines facere bonos." The master should rule justly, "bene imperare"; and the subject's primary duty is to be justly obedient,[2] "subditorum propria virtus." Positive law should be founded upon justice: should be in harmony with morality, "legem . . . honestam"; adapted to what is feasible, "possibilem"; concordant with the natural order, "secundum naturam"; considerate of local tradition, "secundum patriæ consuetudinem"; responsive to condition and circumstance, "necessariam"; useful and concise, meeting public needs.[3] It must consider the imperfection of humanity, and must define the range of forbidden conduct more narrowly than do the precepts of ethics. The law specifies only the more serious offenses, "non . . . omnia vitia cohibere, sed graviora tantum," that menace human society, and from which most men are able to refrain, "a quibis possibile est majorem partem multitudinis abstinere."[4]

Aquinas sets forth the distinction between what is moral and what the law forbids and punishes. As the Roman jurists found the norm or central point of their system, to which all enactments converged in the "bonus paterfamilias," so Aquinas finds in the average nature of man the limitations of legal restraint. He is thus the first philosopher to establish an appropriate penological

[1] "Secundum quam (in other words, of the positive law) disponunter quæ in lege naturæ continentur," II, 1 qu. 91, art. 3. See also II, 1 qu. 93, arts. 3 and 6, qu. 95, art. 2.
[2] II, 1 qu. 92.
[3] II, 1 qu. 95, art. 3. Also qu. 96, art. 1; II, 2 qu. 57.
[4] II, 1 qu. 96, art. 2.

principle, and correctly to determine its application. He recognizes custom as a source of law, but limits its domain.[1] Positive law should be modified only for sufficient grounds, either by reason of necessity or of notable benefit; for otherwise the harm, the insecurity brought about by constant change of the law, would outweigh the advantage.[2]

Justice, which Aquinas defines in conformity with its place in Roman jurisprudence,[3] is one of the four cardinal virtues, "temperantia, prudentia, fortitudo, justitia."[4] Justice is either "justitia generalis" or "justitia particularis." "Justitia generalis" comprises all earthly virtues.[5] "Justitia particularis"[6] is divided into "justitia commutativa," and "distributiva."[7] The principle, "medium," by means of which "justitia particularis" finds application is, in agreement with Aristotle, "æqualitas."[8] From "justitia commutativa" arises the obligation of restitution to prevent unwarranted acquisition.[9] "Æqualitas justitiæ" becomes superior to the prescriptions of the positive law

---

[1] II, 1 qu. 97, art. 3.

[2] II, 1 qu. 97, art. 2.

[3] II, 2 qu. 58, art. 1, conclus. See also pr. Inst. I, 1.

[4] II, 2 qu. 58, art. 3, § 3, and conclus.

[5] II, 2 qu. 58, arts. 3, 5, 6.

[6] II, 2 qu. 58, arts. 7, 8.

[7] II, 2 qu. 61.

[8] II, 2 qu. 58, art. X: "Æquale autem est realiter medium inter majus et minus." In distributive justice the application of justice proceeds by geometrical proportions, in commutative by arithmetical. II, 2 qu. 61, art. 2. See also *Baumann,* "Die Staatslehre des h. Thomas von Aquino," pp. 190–192.

[9] II, 2 qu. 62.

through "æquitas,"[1] "supplendo ex recta ratione, quod verbis scriptarum legum deest." The right of punishment is considered casuistically and indeterminately in respect to the several theories of punishment. Usury, "usura," is denounced on the ordinary scholastic ground; "cum pecuniæ usus sit illius consumptio ac destructio, injustum et illicitum est pro eius usu aliquid accipere."[2]

4: THE DOCTRINE OF THE TWO SWORDS. In the later mediæval conception of the State, two opposed influences meet: the vigorous Roman Empire of the Cæsars, conserved in the Roman-German Empire, as the bearer of the older culture through which the authority of the Pope was established, confronts the Catholic Church which had usurped control of all temporal power. The Church found its philosophic support in Augustine's doctrine of the "civitas terrena"; while the Aristotelean philosophy favored a more restricted conception of ecclesiastical rule. It was agreed that temporal and spiritual power are alike conferred by God, but there arose a violent conflict of opinion and doctrine as to whether the temporal sword is conferred upon the ruler directly by God or through the mediacy of the Pope. Upon this question Guelphs and Ghibellines were divided; and the old Saxon law took the side of the temporal power in opposition to the old Suabian law.

The doctrine of the "two swords" typifies the most important political issue of mediævalism. Upon it W.

[1] II, qu. 120. "Epiikeia" of *Aristotle*.

[2] II, 2 qu. 78, art. 1, conclus. See also *Berolzheimer*, "Das Vermögen (Hirth's Ann., 1904, pp. 601 seq.). *Baumann*, "Die Staatsl.," etc., pp. 196-203. *Aug. Oncken*, "Geschichte der Nationalökonomie," I, pp. 132-135.

Grimm comments:[1] "Christ bade his disciples buy a sword, and when they brought two, he said, 'It is enough.' Who would have thought that the biassed interpretation of these simple words, in which no unprejudiced mind could suspect covert allusion, should for centuries serve to justify the rival claims of the two greatest of earthly powers!" The doctrine of the two swords is a clear confirmation of the importance of "illusion" in the practical or applied philosophy of law, which is politics. A formal reasoning, in itself untenable, is used to support a political view in reality growing out of very different considerations. The Church party did not limit itself to the fictitious establishment of its position; and it welcomed the pseudo-Isidorian forgery in support of its claims.

In the work "De regimine principum," Aquinas sets forth the conception that the State is the product of human needs and of the social nature of man. It is justified in the interests of worldly virtue and general welfare and would have existed regardless of the fall of man. Monarchy is the best form of government; it affords the largest security against tyranny. There is no right of rebellion against the ruler; but the omnipotence of the Church stands superior to the State. The State serves finite purposes; the Church ministers to the soul, to morality, to eternal salvation. All earthly kingdoms are subject to the Pope, and all rulers are vassals of the Church.[2]

Among the representatives of this doctrine, Augustinus Triumphis (1243–1328) may be mentioned. He sets forth the reasons why the power of the Pope alone

---

[1] Preface to *Vridanke's* "Bescheidenheit," Göttingen 1834, p. LVII. See also pp. LVII–LXII.

[2] "De regimine principum," lib. I, chaps. 1, 2, 5, 6, 8, 14; lib. II, chap. 9; lib. III, chaps. 1–7; lib. IV, chap. 3.

is derived from God; while the temporal power is conferred upon the earthly rulers through the Pope: "in ministerium."[1] This position is also distinctly presented by Peter de Andlo.[2]

§ 22. *Economic and Social Restrictions.* 1: THE YEOMAN AND THE CITIZEN CLASS. Characteristic of the internal political structure of the mediæval State was the class system and its economic bondage. The resulting stratification of society affected the entire range of human relations. The economic organization of the Middle Ages was comprehensive, constituting at once a legal, an economic, and a social bond. Any member of a corporate guild was provided for; but at the same time he was much more essentially a member of the guild than he was his own master. In the course of events there resulted a shifting of power of the several classes within the State. Side by side with the feudally organized nobles and large proprietors, there appeared a new class — the middle class, as we should now call them—a third party, composed in part of the yeomanry, but mainly of citizens. The yeomen were essentially freemen who had advanced from a dependent to an independent class, from tenants to small farmers owning

[1] Principal work: "Summa de potestate papæ" (about 1320). The edition I refer to is "Summa Augustini de Ancona de potestate ecclesiastica," 1473. See also *Friedberg*, "Die mittelalterlichen Lehren über das Verhältnis von Staat und Kirche," pp. 93–110. *Lasson*, "System der Rechtsphilosophie," p. 81.

[2] *Petri de Andlo*, "De imperio Romano, regis et augusti creatione, inauguratione . . . libri duo; ad Fridericum III imp. scripti, Argentorati 1603." Characteristic are lib. I, chap. 1, and lib. II, chap. 9: "An maiestatis Imperialis auctoritas derivetur in Cæsarem immediate a Deo, vel illam accipiat ab eius vicario summo." See especially p. 107.

Consult also *Stahl*, "Geschichte der Rechtsphilosophie," pp. 57, 63; *Rehm*, "Geschichte der Staatsrechtswissenschaft," p. 204.

their own estates. Yet in many cases they remained within the dependent classes, and subject to the economic organization of the village community. The importance of the citizen class, however, steadily increased with the appearance and growth of a new economic condition, which brought about the transition from an economics based upon natural commodities to one based upon finance; or, inasmuch as these terms express merely the external medium of exchange, it is better to call the transition one from simple agriculture to agriculture combined with commerce and industry. The prosperity of the cities and the development of the citizen class to a powerful and wealthy class of the community followed upon the growth of industry and commerce.[1]

2: THE ECONOMIC INFLUENCE OF THE CHURCH. The spirit of the mediæval Church influenced all social strata. The Church of those days was Janus-faced, at once a tender protector and a cruel foe, an instrument of civilization and an obstacle to true progress, forbearing and likewise harshly intolerant. Those who acknowledged the power of the Church shared in its blessings; but a relentless persecution pursued those who, in large or small issues, questioned the prerogative of spiritual rule. The cultural influence of the mediæval Church was exercised through instruction in the schools of the monasteries, through the maintenance of libraries, ministrations to the sick, and aid to the poor. The cultural and ethical functions of the State, although a temporal service, were exercised by the Church. The

---

[1] v. *Inama-Sternegg*, "Deutsche Wirthschaftsgeschichte," III 2, p. 234: "The political economy of the German cities is dominated throughout by the idea that industry and trade can prosper only under local co-ordination and the legal regulation of the civic commonwealth."

Church suppressed every independent agitation hostile to the dominance of the priesthood over the emotional life; and thus apostasy, heresy, and schism became crimes. The papal excommunication outlawed and ruined its victims, inasmuch as its ban affected all economic and social ties. The papal power could bind or release; it could cancel even the oath of the vassal. Even the emperor, if under the ban, would be without rights — a helpless, detached stranger in his own country.

The Church adapted its measures to the coarse manners of the times. The lords and serfs of the Middle Ages enjoyed a superabundance of physical energy and strong nerves. The public infliction of punishments, cruel and disfiguring, seems to have been a gratifying spectacle to a sensation-loving populace; the surplus energies of the lords and their retinue were thus diverted. The Crusades became welcome outlets for the overflow of unemployed energy. Pillaging expeditions to the Orient took the place of the bouts of the knights and their followers, and enjoyed the papal favor as undertakings for the greater glory of God; through them the countries of central Europe became acquainted with the resources of the Orient. The spoils of war turned out to be valuable merchandise. Luxury increased and extended; precious stuffs, choice pearls, jewels and ornaments were highly prized. The Crusades gradually assumed the character of commercial raids; they became huge caravans bent upon spoliation.[1] Along with treasures, the plague made its disastrous entry into Europe.

---

[1] *Laurent*, "La féodalité et l'église," p. 630: "The feudal system recognized no other mission for society than warfare. For two centuries it found its ideal and immortal glory in an organized pillage of the Orient. The Crusades, which began as expressions of religious fervor, were in the end conducted in the commercial spirit and for the satisfaction of luxury."

When its devastations began to decimate the population, when want and failure of crops brought the discontent of the masses to a ferment, the resentment of the multitude was diverted; witches and conjurors were burned; Jews were persecuted, abused, and put to death, and their property, acquired by usury, plundered by the mob. The oriental raids were carried on at home.

3: THE CRAFTS AND TRADES. The economic activities of the city were directed by a corporate spirit. The city as a whole became an organized body divided into a group of minor corporations. The artisans of every craft were associated in guilds; and each guild formed a power in the community, bringing to its members at once influence and income, esteem and prosperity, while the independent craftsman had no standing.[1]

Politically organized industry was far more powerful than the growing commerce. Commerce was younger, enjoyed less esteem at home, and was largely in the hands of Jews. Furthermore the nature of commerce did not lend itself to so rigid an organization as the crafts. In commerce individuality was more prominent; and for this reason civic economics was mainly devoted to the interests of the crafts, and the nucleus of the new third party was formed by the crafts guilds. The merchants were enjoined to maintain a "justum prætium," a fair price. They were permitted to earn a livelihood for themselves and their families, but not to exploit the productive classes. A minutely organized police regulated the market to maintain a fair proportion between

---

[1] v. *Inama-Sternegg*, "Deutsche," etc., III, 1, p. 83: "Any artisan who did not acquire the right to belong to a guild was socially and economically debarred. As an industrial interloper or the like (in modern phraseology, 'scab,' German, 'Bönhase') he was not reckoned as a citizen. Indeed the toleration of his presence in the city was often in doubt."

service rendered and price demanded.[1] The organized trades flourished briskly while commerce grew but slowly, mainly by wholesale export of wine and fruits from the South to the North, and by exchange, at the great fairs, of the products of Orient and Occident.

While the powerful organization of the guilds represented the economic bonds within the community, the civic community became the economic unit as against foreign territories. The requirement of the artisan to join a guild was supplemented by a control of the market. This was of value at once for the purchaser and for the seller. "Just as the city producer had an exclusive market for his product within the city and seignorial limits, so the city consumer demanded within these limits an exclusive right of purchase as against outsiders." A consequence of such policy and of the resulting economic situation was that concessions and a fair market became valuable assets and definite objects of trade."

Economic advance in the Middle Ages was parallel with that of law and general culture. Civilization is ever homogeneous; the Church, the law, and industry jointly secured to loyal citizens an adequate livelihood, and gave them a share in the gay mediæval festivals, preserved to us in the pictorial representations of those times. It was only as a member of the corporate body and as a permanent part thereof that the individual made an impression. He enjoyed a recognized place in the community as a part of the whole, not as an independent personality. Reactionary agitations did not arise, or

---

[1] *Lamprecht,* "Deutsches Städteleben am Schluss des Mittelalters," p. 121; *Georg Adler,* "Der Kampf gegen den Zwischenhandel" ("Die Zukunft," 1896, Vol. 15), pp. 548 seq. *August Oncken,* "Geschichte der National-ökonomie, I, pp. 129–132. *R. Kaulla,* "Die Lehre vom gerechten Preis in der Scholastik." Z. f. d. ges. Staatsw., edited by Bücher, Vol. 60, 1904, pp. 579–602.

if they arose, were put down by the temporal or ecclesiastical authorities.

§ 23. *More Liberal Trends of the Middle Ages.* 1: DANTE ALIGHIERI (1265–1321)[1] was the philosopher-poet of romantic mediævalism. In "De Monarchia" he considered the establishment of a world empire, but made the Roman people the medium thereof, and looked to the emperor to renew the ancient Roman universal sovereignty.[2] The relation between Pope and Emperor was not that of sun and moon, nor was the doctrine of the two swords applicable. Constantine's *donation* [the supposed historical basis of the temporal power of the papacy] was likewise null and void. The emperor derived his authority from God and was thus not subject to the Pope.[3] Dante, loyal to the Catholic faith, was imbued with a modern attitude towards economic interests, though under the sway of the romantic appeal of the ancient Roman Empire.

2: WILLIAM OF OCCAM[4] (1270–1347) proceeds on the basis of "natural law." Before the existence of the State all property was communal. Natural law led humanity by way of contract to found the State; and thereby was created the authority of government. But

---

[1] On this period see *Zorn*, "Zur Geschichte des Verhältnisses von Staat und Kirche am Ausgange des Mittelalters," Preussische Jahrb., Vol. 45, 1880, pp. 439–470. *Prutz*, "Staatengeschichte des Abendlandes im deutschen Mittelalter von Karl dem Grossen bis auf Maximilian," Vol. 2, Berlin 1887.

[2] "De Monarchia," libs. I and II.

[3] "De Monarchia," lib. III: "Come l'officio del monarca, ovvero dell' impero, dipende immediatemente da Dio." It is similar in the edition of 1740: "Qualiter officium Monarchæ, sive Imperii dependet a Deo immediate."

[4] "Disputatio super prælatis ecclesiæ atque principibus terrarum commissa, temporibus Bonifacii VIII. pont. Rom. scripta sub forma *dialogi* inter clericum et militem (about 1303)."

the public rights are invested in the people as against the ruler; and theirs, too, are the Church rights as against the Pope. The temporal power is established through the people, yet its source rests with God since it is based upon accord with the divine order.

3: MARSILIUS OF PADUA AND THE SOVEREIGNTY OF THE PEOPLE. In collaboration with his friend, John Giandone, MARSILIUS OF PADUA (d. 1328) wrote the famous "Defensor Pacis." In it is advocated the doctrine of the sovereignty of the people. All political power is vested in the people; the ruler is chosen by them, and should he overstep the authority vested in him by the people, he may be deposed.[1] The Church is subject to the temporal authority and has no temporal powers.[2] The temporal power is derived from God; there is no authority superior to the "legislator humanus."[3]

LUPOLD VON BEBENBURG is another exponent of the doctrine of the sovereignty of the people. Hierynomus Balbus appraises critically the arguments for and against the independence of Emperor and Pope. He concludes that the papal and imperial sovereignty are collateral and independent, and extend over different spheres of influence. The imperial power is in reality conferred by election, the coronation being but a formality that confers no new rights.[4]

4: NICHOLAUS CUSANUS (1401–1464), whose chief work is the "Concordantia Catholica," takes an independent position. According to him the State is established by the voluntary subjection of individuals through con-

[1] I, chaps. 3, 4, 6, 9, 12, 15, 18.
[2] II, chaps. 8, 9, 13, 17, 20, 28.
[3] II, chap. 21.
[4] "De Coronatione," pp. 16–38; 38–46; 58–64, 68–71. It was also not necessary that the coronation should take place in Rome, de cor., pp. 71 seq.

sensus of action. The monarch is the representative of the collective will of the people. The Pope is urged to restore the temporal inheritance of St. Peter to the Emperor, and to place the Church under the powerful protection of temporal authority.

5: THE WRITINGS OF NICCOLO MACHIAVELLI (1469–1527) stand apart from those of his predecessors alike in form and content. In feeling and thought he no longer belongs to the Middle Ages, but is the issue of a different phase of culture; he belongs to the Renaissance, and must be judged and appreciated by its standards. He is the Colleoni of politics. In his "Prince" he portrays a ruler after the model of Cæsar Borgia, a monarch who acquires control over a servile State through bold intrigue and determination. Ethical motives are disregarded; whatever makes for power is permissible. In his portrayal of brute force, of self-seeking ambition pushing its way in the struggle for power, Machiavelli shows himself a brilliant writer and a master of expression.

The "Prince" was written to serve as a recommendation to Lorenzo de Medici. In this connection it was unfortunate that Machiavelli had previously expressed his views in his historical work upholding, on philosophical and political grounds, the constitution of the ancient Roman Republic as the model for all good government, and especially for the city-republics of Italy. To every critic of Machiavelli the inconsistency of these two positions is perplexing, and leads to wide diversities of opinion. A bourgeois morality, quite aside from time or place, would unreservedly condemn Machiavelli; for by its standards, talent would be of no avail if unsupported by good intentions. Machiavelli certainly exhibits an unparalleled lack of principle, a shocking frankness in expressing what others would hardly dare to think; yet the serious charge against him is his contemptible lack of principle in deserting one cause for another; and that for adventitious reasons. The historian comes to Machiavelli's rescue, and suggests that the salvation of Italy from the perils of the day seemed to Machiavelli to require the drastic measures of a temporary despotism. Thus considered the "Prince" becomes a patriotic document. The historian of culture looks upon Machiavelli as a classic expression of his times, as the morally emancipated man of the Renaissance for whom power and might were supreme, and in whom were combined notable failings. The student of the philosophy of law recognizes in him a reversion to ancient views in which the ethical ideal had not yet been awakened; he thus becomes representative of a transitional civilization that had freed itself from the shackles of the Church, but had not yet assumed the obligation of a humanitarian ethics.

CHAPTER V

CIVIC EMANCIPATION: AND THE RISE AND DECLINE OF "NATURAL LAW"

THE REFORMATION AS A STIMULUS TO INDIVIDUALITY.— GROTIUS.— THE REBELLION AGAINST TYRANNY.— LEGAL PHILOSOPHY OF THE SEVENTEENTH CENTURY: (1) HOBBES; (2) PUFENDORF; (3) SPINOZA; (4) THOMASIUS.— LEGAL PHILOSOPHY IN ENGLAND: (1) LOCKE; (2) BENTHAM; (3) MILL, AUSTIN.— LEGAL PHILOSOPHY IN FRANCE: (1) MONTESQUIEU; (2) ROUSSEAU; (3) DIDEROT; (4) GODWIN.— LEGAL PHILOSOPHY IN GERMANY: (1) LEIBNITZ; (2) WOLFF; (3) FREDERICK THE GREAT.— MERCANTILISTS AND PHYSIOCRATS: (1) THE SYSTEM OF COLBERT; (2) QUESNAY AND OTHER PHYSIOCRATS.— THE CLASSICAL ECONOMISTS: ADAM SMITH, RICARDO (1) INDUSTRIAL DEVELOPMENT, THE ECONOMICS OF ADAM SMITH; (2) RICARDO; (3) SAY; (4) MALTHUS.— KANT, FICHTE, SCHOPENHAUER: (1) KANT — (a) THE HISTORICAL POSITION OF KANT, (b) KANT'S ETHICS, (c) KANT'S PHILOSOPHY OF LAW, (d) THE ORIGIN AND THE PURPOSE OF THE STATE, (e) THE PRESENT SIGNIFICANCE OF KANT'S PHILOSOPHY; (2) FICHTE — (a) THE POSITION OF FICHTE, (b) FICHTE'S PHILOSOPHY OF LAW, (c) FICHTE'S PHILOSOPHY OF ECONOMICS, (d) LAW AND CULTURE, (e) FICHTE AS A STATESMAN; (3) SCHOPENHAUER.— SCHELLING AND THE HISTORICAL SCHOOL: (1) SCHELLING; (2) OTHER MEMBERS OF THE HISTORICAL SCHOOL.— HEGEL AND THE HEGELIANS: (1) HEGEL'S PHILOSOPHY OF LAW; (2) LAW AND THE HUMAN WILL; (3) HEGEL'S DIALECTIC; (4) HEGEL'S CONCEPTION OF THE STATE; (5) FUNDAMENTAL LEGAL IDEAS, PERSON, PROPERTY, INJURY, CRIME; (6) A CRITICAL VERDICT OF HEGEL; (7) THE HEGELIANS.— RECENT SYSTEMS OF LEGAL PHILOSOPHY: (1) STAHL; (2) TRENDELENBURG; (3) KRAUSE; (4) AHRENS; (5) HERBART; (6) DAHN; (7) LASSON.

§ 24. *The Reformation as a Stimulus to Individuality.* The interest of the historian of the Reformation is directed to the conditions that made possible so profound an intellectual readjustment; to such an interest the series of underlying changes are of prime importance. But for the philosopher the significant fact is the cultural mission of that intellectual awakening. The Reformation inaugurated not merely a new epoch, but the modern spirit itself as extending to and finding its culmination in our own day. The distinctive characteristic of the Middle Ages may be said to be the bondage, social and spiritual, of the individual; by contrast the period of the Reformation is characterized by the *emancipation* of classes and individuals. A survey of this process of emancipation, unique in history and extending over four centuries, discloses the limitations and inadequacy of the materialistic view of history; for it is ever a great idea that vitalizes and fertilizes the soil in which important economic changes mature. It must be conceded that circumstances — that is, the prevalent economic and cultural state of affairs — must be favorable to the growth of the new idea; but the decisive condition ever remains the creation and formulation of the attitude itself. Intellectually and spiritually the process of emancipation began with the Reformation; the French Revolution, proclaiming the rights of man, developed it formally; and its economic and social consummation was reserved for the social-ethical movement at the close of the nineteenth century.

In the sixteenth century the Teutonic spirit revolted against the yoke of Rome. It was by virtue of the popular appeal in Luther's language and teachings, and by virtue of the Germanic[1] spirit in his mental attitude,

[1] *Harnack*, "Das Wesen des Christentums," p. 177: "As the oriental phase of Christianity is called the Greek, and the mediæval

that he won adherents to the new cause. The tutelage of Rome was becoming oppressive, and the corruption and decadence of church officials were peculiarly objectionable to Teutonic feelings. The Roman faith was made to suffer for the faults of its priests. The weaknesses of the emperors brought on the destruction of the ancient Roman empire, and the sins of the popes that of the new.

In this connection attention may be called to the influence of "illusion" in history; for it seems to be the case that the issues of great historical movements are not the ends proposed, but the fulfillment of a cultural mission which they undesignedly serve. The deliberate purpose of the Reformation was the reform of religion — an end imperfectly attained in Teutonic countries, and hardly at all in those under Roman dominion. The cultural mission of the Reformation was to vitalize individual freedom, and this end was indeed first achieved by the Reformation. The Reformation broke the power of the Church by placing the individual in direct relation with God. Through Luther's translation of the Bible, the word of God was made available to the people; celibacy was abolished; the overweening dominance of the priests was swept aside; men were liberated from the oppression of the Church;[1] the dominion of the temporal power was restored.

occidental phase the Roman, so one may call the Protestant phase Germanic; and this despite Calvin, who indeed was a disciple of Luther and whose influence has been most permanent not among the Latin races but among the English, Scotch, and Dutch." See also *Laurent,* "La féodalité et l'église," p. 455: "As a man of action Zwingli is inferior to Luther, for the latter had that admirable sense that distinguishes practical men — the sense for the possible. Zwingli demanded of humanity more than it was able to give in the sixteenth century."

[1] *Harnack,* "Das Wesen des Christentums," p. 172. "Protestantism looks upon the Gospel as so simple, divine, and therefore truly

§ 25. *Hugo Grotius.* GROTIUS (1583–1645) may be regarded as the Descartes of legal philosophy. As the Cartesian "cogito ergo sum" became the point of departure of rationalistic philosophy, so the establishment of government and law upon reason made Hugo Grotius the founder of an independent and purely rationalistic system of natural law.[1] The conception of "natural law" was not wholly novel but appeared vaguely in the later Middle Ages. According to Grotius, "natural law" is unrelated to the will and existence of God;[2] for the State is a human institution and is based upon contract.[3] Law is a human creation and arises from the social impulse — as Aristotle[4] had indicated — and from

human, that it is most assured of acceptance when free to make its own appeal, and produces upon all essentially the same experiences and convictions." See also *Bergemann*, "Ethik als Kulturphilosophie," p. 199.

[1] On "natural law" in general see *Bergbohm*, "Jurisprudenz und Rechtsphilosophie," I; *Jellinek*, "Allgemeine Staatslehre," pp. 314–323; *Stammler*, "Wirthschaft und Recht," pp. 169–188; "Die Lehre von dem richtigen Rechte," pp. 93 seq.

[2] "De jure belli ac pacis." Proleg.: "Et hæc quidem quæ iam diximus, locum haberent (i.e., the existence and the compelling power of natural law) etiamsi daremus, quod sine summo scelere dari nequit, non esse Deum, aut non curari ab eo negotia humana." "De jure belli ac pacis," I, 1, 10: "Est autem jus naturale adeo immutabile, ut ne a Deo quidem mutari queat."

[3] 1, 4, 7 seq.: "Notandum est . . .homines . . . sponte adductos experimento infirmitatis familiarum segregum adversus violentiam, in societatem civilem coiisse."

[4] Grotius frequently refers to Aristotle, still more frequently to Cicero, and occasionally to Seneca. Grotius does not consistently adhere to the social impulse as the basis for the formation of the State. For example, in the following definition, which shows the direct influence of Cicero: "The State is a perfect association of free men, established for the benefits of law and the common welfare."

reason, that is, from the rational nature of man.[1] For Grotius the formal philosophical problem and end is to determine the source of the law of nations; for, as this is not due to positive legislation, its basis must be found in "natural law." The basis of the doctrine of "natural law" is that the origin of the State, and of all that is brought into being by the State, is due to contract. This assumption carries with it any and all political positions that one may desire to establish, and was frequently used to establish the sovereignty of the people.

In his science of justice Grotius makes a distinction between two orders of justice;[2] the one division of legal norms refers to legal relations of parity between equals, and the other to the legal relations of ruler and subject.[3] In judging the position of Grotius, we must bear in mind that his purpose was to prove that a law of nations exists. He was thus led to accept the postulate of "natural law," since there was no recognized positive law between nations. He attempted to prove his case by a study of the legal issues of war; which appeared in the very title of his work, "De Jure Belli ac Pacis." This approach influenced the character of his entire presentation. The problems of legal philosophy and of legal science were not considered in themselves, but in their bearing upon the legal aspects of war, its justification and its pro-

[1] Particularly I, 1, 10, 12.

[2] "De jure belli ac pacis," I, 1, 3: "Sicut autem societas alia est sine inæqualitate, ut inter fratres, cives, amicos, federatos: alia inæqualis . . . ut inter patrem et liberos . . .: ita justum aliud est ex æquo inter se viventium, aliud eius qui regit et qui regitur, qua tales sunt: quorum hoc jus Rectorium, illud Æquatorium . . . vocabimus."

[3] Upon the meaning given to punishment by Grotius ("malum passionis quod infligitur ob malum actionis"), see *Berolzheimer*, "Rechtsphil. Studien," pp. 86-92; and "Die Entgeltung im Strafrechte," pp. 130-133.

cedure. The plan pursued was first to determine what constitutes war, and then to consider the further question as to what constitutes law as thus applied.

It must not be inferred from the prominence of war as the basis of legal principle that Grotius derives the nature of law from its violation, that is, a positive concept from its infringement or negation.[1] Schopenhauer,[2] reflecting his antagonism to Hegel, repeatedly sets forth that wrong is the fundamental, primary, positive concept, and that the concept of right arises from it merely as the negation or absence of wrong; and he refers for support to "the first exposition of the concept as given by Hugo Grotius, the founder of philosophic jurisprudence: 'Jus hic nihil aliud, quam quod justum est, significat, idque negante magis sensu, quam aiente, ut jus sit, quod injustum non est.'"[3] But in Grotius this passage is immediately followed by the statement: "Est autem injustum quod naturæ societatis ratione utentium repugnat." If this expression occurred at the outset of a systematic work devoted to the philosophy of law, it would be fair to conclude that the author derived the concept of right from that of wrong. But in reality the statement, as it occurs in Grotius, forms the transition from the definition of the concept of war to the consideration of justice. According to Grotius "jus" has a threefold significance: first as "justum," that which is just; second as "qualitas moralis personæ competens ad aliquid juste habendum

---

[1] *Geyer*, "Geschichte und System der Rechtsphilosophie in Grundzügen," p. 31: "Grotius thus begins with the concept of right in the objective sense. He says, 'That is lawful which is not unlawful, that is unlawful which by its nature is contrary to the interests of reason and society.' Accordingly what makes rational and social relations impossible — such as conflict and strife — is wrong."

[2] See § 33, C.

[3] *Schopenhauer:* "Preisschrift über die Grundlage der Moral," Vol. 3, p. 598, § 17.

vel agendum," that is, legal right in the concrete sense, or claim; third as "lex," positive law, as constituted law. "Lex" must here be understood in its broadest sense as "rectum."[1] The "jus naturale" comes under the third meaning of "jus," and forms the decisive factor in the conception and nature of law. But the "jus naturale" Grotius derives from the social impulses of man. Whatever conforms to this social impulse is right; whatever opposes it is wrong. Wrong consists in that which disturbs or interferes with the natural and social harmony. Hence to Grotius the positive conception is the social unity or solidarity and the justice and law in accord with it. Injustice and wrong become the true negatives, and like all that deviates from the normal, their assertiveness makes them conspicuous just because they form a departure from the social harmony of life.

§ 26. *The Rebellion against Tyranny.* For three centuries the leaders of the movement of enlightenment growing out of the religious struggles in France and Scotland in the sixteenth century, who preached the right of active rebellion and even of assassination against tyrannical rulers, have borne the name of anti-monarchists ("monarchomachs").[2] The vogue of the appellation illustrates the ready acceptance of an apt phrase even by scholars. Yet it is somewhat misleading and fails to express the inherent nature of the movement. The hostility is directed not against the ruler but against the tyrant; so that anti-tyrannical ("tyrannomach") would be the more appropriate term. The monarch is

[1] Compare the use made by Pufendorf of the word "recte" ("De Jure Naturæ et Gentium," I, 1, 20).

[2] *Gierke*, "Johannes Althusius," Breslau 1880, p. 3, note 3, comments (the expression is derived from Guil. Barclaius (Barclay): "De regno et regali potestate adversus Buchananum, Brutum, Boucherium et reliquos *Monarchomachos*," libri sex, 1600.

distinguished from the tyrant; the tyrant is the ruler who oppresses the country and the people, the royal exploiter, the despot.[1] The Reformation made war upon the exclusive possession of men's souls by the Church; "tyrannomachs" made war upon the enslavement of men's bodies by their temporal masters; and in this aspect of the campaign lay its cultural mission.

Two parties appear among the representatives of the "tyrannomachs": the clerical or Jesuitical, eager to break the tyrannical autocracy in the interests of the Church; and the democratic, striving for the emancipation of the people. Both parties find support in the same authorities, partly in Scripture, and partly in human reason. By both the rights of the people are formulated substantially in the same terms, though their arguments differ in detail.

The central doctrine of the political philosophy of the "tyrannomachs" is the principle of the sovereignty of the people. While this idea was frequently advanced in ancient times, and was well developed in the Middle

[1] Thus Bodin, in "Les six livres de la République," in Book II, chap. III, devotes a chapter to "La monarchie Royale," and in chapter 4 considers in contrast thereto "La monarchie tyrannique"; this he defines (p. 211) as "a monarchy in which the monarch violates the laws of nature, abuses the liberty of free subjects as of his slaves, and the property of others as well as his own." (p. 212): "But the most marked distinction between the king and the tyrant is that the king obeys the laws of nature and the tyrant runs counter to them." See also pp. 212-218. In chapter 5 the question is discussed as to "whether it is legitimate to attack the person of the tyrant and after his death to annul and abrogate his ordinances." Althusius, in chapter 38, pp. 650 seq., of his "Politica," discusses some remedies against tyranny: "Tyranny is therefore contrary to a right and just administration." p. 651: "A tyrant therefore is one who by violating his oath of faith and religion attacks and breaks the ties and foundations of the body-politic." On pp. 652-658, the several kinds of tyranny are then distinguished.

Ages, its use to further political revolution, and as a text from which to preach the destruction of tyrants, was reserved for more modern times. The religious foundation of the doctrine, characteristic of mediævalism, is retained; yet at the same time it is supplemented by arguments derived from the newer doctrine of "natural law." The two tendencies unite in this transitional period: the Bible is referred to for support, but the appeal is to reason; the evidence of faith gradually recedes, and that of theoretical principle comes forward.

It will not be necessary to present the views of the several "tyrannomachs." The important men of the period, in addition to Junius Brutus, were Bodin and Althusius. Gierke[1] regards Althusius as the direct precursor of Rousseau, and thus makes him an indirect influence in bringing on the French Revolution; but this view has been contested. JUNIUS BRUTUS,[2] in his "Vindiciæ contra Tyrannos," discusses the right of resistance against tyrants, and defends it on the basis of casuistic and comprehensive arguments. The service of BODIN (1530–1597) for philosophy lies in his analysis of the conception of sovereignty as the distinctive characteristic of the State. To him "sovereignty is the highest, most permanent, unlimited, and hence in-

---

[1] *Gierke*, "Johannes Althusius," p. 76, regards Althusius as the founder of the theory of the social contract. In opposition thereto, see *Jellinek*, "Allgemeine Staatslehre," p. 183. *Liepmann*, "Die Rechtsphilosophie des Jean Jacques Rousseau," p. 22, holds that Rousseau showed clearly the influence of Althusius.

[2] Junius Brutus was formerly regarded as the pseudonym of Hubert Languet. It is now held that the author of the "Vindiciæ contra Tyrannos" is Du Plessis-Mornay. The proof of this was furnished by *Lossen*, "Die Vindiciæ contra Tyrannos des angeblichen Stephanus Junius Brutus," Munich 1887, Sitzungsberichte der bayer. Akademie der Wissenschaften, 1887, 2, pp. 215–242.

§ 26] REBELLION AGAINST TYRANNY 121

divisible power, comprising the entire State, and permeating all its functions. Such functions are the power of making laws without being bound by laws; the right to declare war; the deliverance of juridical decisions as a last resort; and the right of pardon, taxation, coinage. The power of the State is limitless, and thus not divisible."[1] Bodin properly emphasizes the close connection between public and private authority. He makes the existence of personal rights the basis of the power of the State: "Il n'y a point de chose publique s'il n'y a quelque chose de propre."[2]

In the systematic discussion of the theory of State and society by ALTHUSIUS (1557-1638), he distinguishes between the contract of alliance, by which a community is formed, and the contract of sovereignty, which forms the foundation of public authority and of the coercive nature of law.[3] The latter has the quality of a public decree. The people, like every associated group, "universitas," has the right to place at its head executives and to confer upon them full authority while yet limiting it. When the people exercise such privilege, the representatives whom they nominate under this contract of sovereignty become merely administrators of the governmental authority belonging to the community.[4] It is only by virtue of such a public commission of the authority, which belongs wholly to the people, that a legitimate government and regulation

---

[1] *Stintzing*, "Geschichte der deutschen Rechtswissenschaft," 1884, II, pp. 34 seq. *Bodin*, I, 10: "Des Vrayes Marques de la Souveraineté." Five essential traits ("marques") of sovereignty are there portrayed.

[2] I, 1.

[3] "Politica," chaps. I, 5, 10, 18.

[4] "Politica," chap. 18, §§ 1–14.

can be maintained.¹ The government should never become absolute, but always be limited by consideration for the people, the true supreme and authoritative master.² By this means, will the sovereignty of the people be strictly conserved, and their privileges maintained.

§ 27. *Legal Philosophy of the Seventeenth Century.* 1: HOBBES. The evidence of men's distrust of one another is everywhere apparent. Though at peace with their neighbors, countries guard their frontiers and cities by troops, walls, gates, and sentinels; even in the interior, where law and justice prevail and punishment awaits evil-doers, the citizens go about armed. While States and individuals thus show their fear and distrust, their theories, contradicting their actions, refuse to admit fear as the motive of human conduct. "Studio contradicendi aliis, contradicunt sibimet ipsis . . ." are the words of Hobbes (1588–1679) addressed to the reader in the preface to his "De Cive." The establishment of government cannot be derived from the social nature of man. The motive that has brought men together socially must be sought in their practical intercourse.³ Each individual regards his own interest and advantage; and self-interest alone is responsible for social institutions.⁴

¹ "Politica," chap. 18, §§ 15–31, 84, 104, 123 seq., and chap. 19 § 2 seq.; chap. 38, §§ 121–129.

² "Politica," chap. 18, §§ 28–46, 105, 106; chap. 19, § 2 seq.; chap. 38, §§ 121 seq., 128–130.

³ "De Cive," I, 2: "Quo . . . consilio homines congregentur, ex iis cognoscitur quæ faciunt congregati."

⁴ "De Cive," I, 2: "Omnis igitur societas vel commodi causa, vel gloriæ, hoc est, sui, non sociorum amore contrahitur. . . . Statuendum igitur est, originem magnarum et diuturnarum societatum non a mutua hominum benevolentia, sed a mutuo metu exstitisse."

Upon "Fear as Protection," *Leonardo da Vinci* has thus expressed himself: "As enmity is a menace to life, so fear is a security."

Life is the choicest of all possessions, and to minister to its needs is the chief purpose of man;[1] hence the general prerequisite of all self-seeking activity is protection and security, "pax quærenda."[2] This fundamental requisite, due to fear, leads mankind from the troublous state of nature, in which every man preys upon the other, "homo homine lupus," and every man's hand is raised against his neighbor, "bellum omnium contra omnes," up to the civic state, whose central function is to provide security by keeping faith, "pacta servanda præstanda."[3]

The State does not deprive the individual of his natural freedom, but merely relieves the terrors and anxieties incident to savagery; it maintains a comprehensive police system. Yet in so holding Hobbes overlooks the fact that the State, while notably lessening the uncertainties of primitive conditions, introduces other artificial perils of legally regulated intercourse. Hobbes' philosophy of law reflects his personal view of life. His deep distrust of human nature is increased by a keen observation of human frailties and susceptibilities. He particularly scores envy and vanity: whatever one man has or

---

"Leonardo da Vinci der Denker, Forscher und Poët," *Marie Herzfeld*, Leipzig 1904, p. 120.

See also "Leviathan," chap. 13 (De religione): "Atque hinc fortasse erat, quod veterum Poëtarum aliquis, *Deos primos a Timore factos esse dixerit.*"

[1] "De Cive," I, 7: "Neque enim *Juris* nomine aliud significatur quam libertas, quam quisque habet facultatibus naturalibus secundum rectam rationem utendi. Itaque *Juris* naturalis fundamentum primum est, *ut quisque vitam et membra sua quantum potest* tueatur."

"Leviathan," chap. 13: "Passiones quibus homines ad pacem perduci possunt, sunt Metus, præsertim vero Metus Mortis violentæ."

[2] "De Cive," I, 15; II, 2; III, 31; "Leviathan," chaps. 13, 14.

[3] "Leviathan," chap. 15; "Le Corps Politique," I, chap. 3, 1.

strives for, the rest covet;[1] "Ubi enim non præcessit Pactum, ibi Jus nullum est translatum, sed omnia omnium sunt."[2] Such a conception of government and law leaves no place for the reserved rights of the citizen. The State is an institution for protection, and exercises its protective functions as completely as power is concentrated in its hands. Accordingly, all privileges and powers must be transferred to the State by contract; for the State must rule absolutely and, like the Leviathan, encompass all living things. Such is the demand of despotism exercised in the interests of subjects whose welfare is the conscientious concern of the ruler.[3]

2: PUFENDORF. Hobbes marks a step backward in the history of civic emancipation. SAMUEL VON PUFENDORF[4] (1623–1694) aims to combine the views of Hobbes and Grotius, yet inclines to the position of the former. According to Grotius the social impulse urges men to socialize their condition, to found a State and to develop law; according to Hobbes it is fear of mutual extermination that drives men from the troublous primitive condition to the security of civic order. Pufendorf analyses man's natural disposition or nature, and finds a strong natural egoism antagonizing his social impulses;[5] hence the social impulse cannot be accepted unreservedly as giving rise to the State,[6] especially as man is equally endowed with ant-social inclinations: "in

[1] "De Cive," I, 6; I, 2.
[2] "Leviathan," chap. 15.
[3] "De Cive," chaps. 10 seq. "Le Corps Politique," I, chap. 2; II, chap. 9.
[4] "De Jure Naturæ et Gentium," libri octo, 1672. "De Officio Hominis et Civis," 1693. Also works noted by *E. Landsberg*, "Geschichte der deutschen Rechtswissenschaft," III, p. 19.
[5] "De Jure Naturæ et Gentium," I, VII, chap. 1, § 2.
[6] "De Jure Nat.," I, VII, chap. 1, § 3.

homine multa sunt vitia, civilem societatem perturbantia."[1] Nor is necessity an adequate ground for the formation of the State;[2] it is the helplessness of man, his exposure to the manifold perils of primitive conditions, and his desire to avoid future ills, that constitute the decisive factor.[3] In place of Hobbes' motive of fear, Pufendorf advances concern for the future.[4] While Hobbes regards the State as an instrument of protection, Pufendorf regards it as a preventive alliance; the distinction, however, is not a radical one. Yet Pufendorf shows a sociological insight absent in his followers; for, contrary to the usual presentation of the doctrine of "natural law," the foundation of the State is not derived by Pufendorf from the action of the individual, but from the family, the "patres familias," uniting together.[5] While following Hobbes in his view of the origin of "natural law," Pufendorf is opposed to him in other matters. He regards the State as the result of a series of contracts; such as a contract of alliance in the interests of socialization; and a contract for the constitution of the State, which in turn consists of the

---

[1] "De Jure Naturæ," I, VII, chap. 1, § 4: To the "avaritia," "superbia," "crudelitas," "Deorum negligentia," "ambitio," mentioned by Sallust, Pufendorf adds, "Ineradicable remembrance of an injury suffered, and fierce vengeance" ("Accedit vivacissima injuriarum memoria et vindictæ ardor").

[2] "De Jure Nat.," I, VII, chap. 1, § 6.

[3] "De Jure Nat.," I, VII, chap. 1, § 7: "Genuina igitur, et princeps causa, quare patresfamilias, deserta naturali libertate, ad civitates constituendas descenderint, fuit, ut præsidia sibi circumponerent contra mala, quæ homini ab homine imminent."

[4] "De Jure Nat.," I, VII, chap. 1, § 7: "Conspirant nobiscum, qui causam civitatum *metum* statuunt; per quem hautquidquam intelligitur perturbatio trepidantis et consternati animi, sed quævis præcautio futuri mali." See also De Jure Nat.," I, VII, chap. 2, §§ 1–5.

[5] "De Jure Nat.," I, VII, chap. 1, §§ 6–12.

contract for the constitutional form of government; and again the contract providing for the subjection of the governed to the governing classes.[1] The last, according to Pufendorf, is not a one-sided contract, investing the State with all the rights of the individual, but a mutual contract; it insists equally upon the duty of the governing classes to care for the common weal, and thus constitutes a moderate absolutism.[2]

Pufendorf's ethics is essentially theological; the will of God determines what is good and what is bad.[3] Pufendorf's relation to Grotius, as represented in his exposition of the doctrines of natural law, was similar to that, in a later period, of Wolff to Leibnitz. He developed the system for which Grotius laid the foundations; but in his hands Grotius' philosophy of law lost through his utilitarian[4] and theological[5] tendencies. As is commonly true of conventional and superficial expositions, Pufendorf's philosophy of law, despite its lesser originality, found popular favor and maintained its vogue for nearly a century.

[1] "De Jure Nat.," I, VII, chap. 2, §§ 4–13.
It may here be noted that the distinction made by Rousseau between "la volonté générale" and "la volonté de tous" is found in Pufendorf, "De Jure Naturæ," VII, 2, 8: "What therefore the individual citizens desire, that the people as such does not desire; and what the individual citizens do, is not to be regarded as the action of the people; and vice versa."

[2] "De Jure Nat.," VII, 2, 8 seq.; "De Officio Hominis et Civis," I, II, chap. 11, § 3; "Generalis lex summorum imperantium est hæc: *Salus populi suprema lex esto.*"

[3] "De Jure Nat.," I, 1, chap. 6, § 9; "De Offic. Hom. et Civis," I, 1, chap. 2, §§ 1–5. See also *Zimmermann*, "Das Rechtsprinzip bei Leibniz," Vienna 1852, p. 3.

[4] "De Jure Nat.," I, II, chap. 3, §§ 14, 15.

[5] "De Jure Nat.," 1, I, chap. 6, §§ 9–11: 1, II, chap. 3, §§ 19, 20. "De Offic. Hom. et Civis," 1, I, chap. 2, §§ 1–5.

§ 27] THE SEVENTEENTH CENTURY 127

3: SPINOZA. SPINOZA[1] (1632-1677) contributed a notable doctrine to metaphysics, but also a fundamental philosophical error. He stands out as a defiant rocky headland, suggestive of power, but wholly aloof from human interests. His distinctive philosophic contribution is the conception of *pantheism*. Schelling put in the place of a realistic pantheism an idealistic one; Goethe returned to the pantheistic position; while to Hegel, pantheism resolved itself in universal reason. Pantheism still forms the keynote of the modern opposition to realism.

The fundamental error of Spinoza's system is his unremitting adherence to pantheism carried to the consideration of the details of the physical world and of human action and purpose. Pantheism may be accepted as a point of departure and as a goal, but is not to be insisted upon in the procedure of scientific investigation. Human knowledge begins where the conception of a chaos giving way to cosmos through a pantheistic intervention, is abandoned, and is replaced by the gradual differentiation of the realms of knowledge.[2] The pantheistic view discloses each individual object, not as independent, but as an indispensable part of the cosmos. The scientific attitude postulates the detachment of objects from their meanings, and attempts their explanation and interpretation, not in terms of an ultimate purpose, "sub specie æternitas," but in terms of their specific nature, "principium individuationis."[3] By rea-

[1] Spinoza's works are: "Tractatus theologico-politicus," 1670. "Tractatus politicus," a fragment, 1678, published after Spinoza's death. "Ethica ordine geometrico demonstrata," 1677. (I cite from the edition: *Benedicti de Spinoza opera* quotquot reperta sunt recognoverunt van Vloten et Land, I, Hagae 1882.

[2] *Berolzheimer*, "System der Rechts-und Wirtschaftsphilosophie," Vol. I, pp. 131-135, and pp. 23-29.

[3] *Berolzheimer*, "System," etc., Vol. I, pp. 307 seq.

son of his insistent adherence to the pantheistic principle, Spinoza reaches a fatalistic determinism; a legal philosophy and a science of politics are made impossible, and attain an apparent reality by sacrifice of consistency.

God is substance and there is no other substance than God; all that is real rests in God.[1] Accordingly Spinoza's view requires the world and its phenomena, including man and his operations, to be conceived as parts of nature; he inevitably takes a position opposed to the rationalistic philosophy which preceded and followed him. In other philosophies man was set apart as a phenomenon by himself; and nature was conceived as an independent reality on the one hand, and man, with his desires, aims, and considerations, equally self-sufficient, on the other. The relation was conceived as though man were the absolute master of his actions, and as though his presence would disturb the order of nature rather than be subjected to it as part to whole.[2] This detachment of man from nature, and self-sufficient view of human activity, has at times led philosophers to disown or to slight human impulses and emotions, "affectus," instead of attempting an interpretation of their true meaning. It is clearly a part of the problem of philosophy to respect human passions and to give them a place in a philosophical system.[3]

As a fact human desire and action are partly determined by emotion, and partly by reason. In so far as man is swayed by emotion he becomes a slave; and in so far

---

[1] "Ethica," p. I, props. 11, 14, 15.

[2] "Ethica," p. III preface: "Nam hominem Naturæ ordinem magis perturbare quam sequi, ipsumque in suas actiones absolutam habere potentiam nec aliunde quam a se ipso determinari credunt."

Compare with this "Ethica," p. IV appendix, chaps. VII and I.

[3] "Ethica," p. III preface.

as he is guided by reason he becomes free.¹ In his ethical view Spinoza thus anticipates Kant; but the development of his ethics suggests Aristotle and the Stoics. While his insistence upon the ethical value of knowledge is at once Socratic and Aristotelean, his adherence to the equanimity conferred by wisdom is Stoic. Spinoza distinguishes three orders of knowledge:² the highest refers and reduces everything temporal and individual to God. As the mind of man considers human existence and activity "sub æternitas specie," and gains insight into the connection of every individual phenomenon with the system of the universe, the stronger becomes his conviction of the absolute inevitableness of events, and the greater is the power which his will acquires over his passions; the more deeply he feels himself at one with the cosmos, the firmer his inalienable love of God prevails over the vicissitudes of life.³ The free moral man entertains no depressing ideas of death; he is upright, and sympathetic with his neighbors; he is free from the desires of passion, and is thus superior to the ideas of good and evil.⁴ Significant in Spinoza's pan-

---

¹ "Eth.," p. IV: "*De servitute humana* seu de affectuum viribus"; "Eth.," p. V: "De potentia intellectus, seu *de libertate humana.*" We here note the same ethical consideration which later made Kant's ethics famous. Kant posits as an ethical fundamental principle that man should develop his natural character into a moral one; the natural character is not free, the moral character is free. Spinoza as a determinist refrains from a moral sermon and is content with establishing the correct data: the man who is shaped by his passions, impulses, and desires, is their slave; the man who is guided by reason is free, is master of himself. See also "Eth.," p. V preface; p. IV, props. 63, 67, 68, and the demonstrations pertaining thereto.

² *Berolzheimer*, "System," etc., Vol. I, pp. 28 seq.

³ "Eth.," p. V props. 14-16, 22-33; p. IV, appendix, cap. IV, p. II, prop. 44, cor. 2.

⁴ "Eth.," p. V, props. 63, 67, 68, 71, 72.

theism is his view of the identity of the favoring desire, "virtus," and capacity, "potestas"; the placing on a par of the conceptions, perfection, reality, and conduct, in which conduct is identical with activity.[1]

Carried to a consistent conclusion, Spinoza's ethics would hardly lead to a political organization; it might lead to solipsism (subjective idealism) or autarchy (self-sufficiency), to a passionless life of contemplation, to a Stoic worldly wisdom, or to the detachment more recently advocated by Stirner. But Spinoza was confronted by the fact of political life as legally organized, and attempted to solve the problem of bringing the State and law under his pantheistic system, though naturally with some violence to these conceptions.

Rationalistic philosophers assume a "natural law" which they derive, not objectively from a consideration of nature, but anthropocentrically from the rational or social nature of man, from certain of his qualities, or from the complex of human traits, dispositions, and considerations. Spinoza, however, proceeds from a "natural law" derived from objective nature, from the constitution of the universe: "Per jus......Naturæ intelligo ipsas Naturæ leges seu regulas, secundum quas omnia fiunt, hoc est ipsam Naturæ potentiam."[2][3]

---

[1] "Eth.," p. V, prop. 40, demonstrat.; compare with this, "Eth.," p. IV, prop. 54.

[2] "Tractatus Politicus," chap. 2, § 4. *Stahl*, "Die Genesis der gegenwärtigen Rechtsphilosophie," p. 63, is wrong when he states that "the later philosophers carry through definite, rationalistic systems. Spinoza has established the canon of rationalism."

[3] In this foundation of "Naturrecht" Spinoza appears as a pure Stoic, but the consistent adherence to Stoicism proves to be untenable. He therefore finds a way out to convention, advantage, and epicureanism. It is thus not correct to regard Spinoza simply as an Epicurean, as does *W. Ed. Biermann*, "Staat und Wirthschaft," I, pp. 7, 9. For Spinoza, epicureanism is a necessary makeshift, a departure from his own system, an inconsistency.

The study of nature teaches us that every creature lives according to the laws of its kind. Fish are designed to swim, and the larger ones to swallow the smaller ones. In like manner man needs a sphere for the exercise of his powers; and whatever man can achieve and accomplish, whether for good or for evil, is his natural right. Whatever happens, takes place by virtue of the laws of nature, and accordingly by a natural right. Everyone has "a supreme right to all that he can achieve." Whatever happens is right and in accord with right, for there is no wrong; the wrong would be the impossible. So far Spinoza is consistent; and his consistency leaves no place for natural right. Right is might; there is no order of right separable from the order of nature; everyone may do what he can do, and that alone is forbidden which nature makes objectively impossible— in reality, nothing whatever.[1]

Drawing upon Epicurus and Hobbes, Spinoza finds a way out of this tangle. Utility, which demands the choice of the lesser evil, leads mankind from an intolerable subjection to nature, to convention. The State and the law are results of conventional association,[2] and are determined and justified wholly by the utility which apparently they secure. As, however, no legally constituted law follows from natural law — not even Hobbes' principle that "Pacta esse præstanda" — utility becomes the sole test, not alone for the establishment, but as well for the validity and maintenance of

[1] "Tract. Theol.-Pol.," chap. 16; "Tract. Pol.," chap. II, §§ 40 seq.; "Tract. Theol.-Pol.," chap. XVI: "Ex quibus sequitur, Jus et Institutum Naturæ, sub quo omnes nascuntur, et maxima ex parte vivunt, nihil, nisi quod nemo cupit et quod nemo potest, prohibere."

[2] For this Spinoza uses the phrases: "In unum conspirare"; "pacisci"; "omne jus potestatem transferre."

State and law.[1] Accordingly the government must provide for the common welfare, for otherwise there would be danger of revolution and destruction of the State; government is the sole surety against tyranny and absolutism.[2] As will readily be understood, this doctrine exercised no influence upon political conditions. As compared with the absolutism of Hobbes, Spinoza's view of the State presents a point of advance in his emphasis that a tyrannical absolutism carries the seed of its own destruction; and in his further emphasis that no one can relinquish his own human dignity; for which reason authority should not and cannot be transferred to the governing authorities.[3]

4: THOMASIUS. The secularizing of legal philosophy, undertaken by Grotius, was completed by THOMASIUS[4] (1655–1728), a leader[5] in the intellectual Renaissance, and a popularizer of scientific learning. Utilitarianism

[1] "Tract. Theol.-Pol," chap. 16; chap. II, §§ 4 seq. See also "Eth.," p. IV, props. (20), (38), 40, 73 (append., chaps. 15, 16). In "Tract. Pol.," VI, I, III, 9, the constitutional agreement falls into the background. See *Menzel*, "Wandlungen in der Staatslehre Spinoza," Festschrift der Rechts-und Staatswissenschaftlichen Fakultät der Universität Wien für Unger, Stuttgart 1898, pp. 57, 59–63, 83–85. The explanations made by Menzel are somewhat extreme. The change is of no essential importance, as the entire politics of Spinoza, as indicated in the text, is not derived organically from his philosophy, but is merely attached to it on the basis of Hobbes' principle of utility.

[2] "Tract. Pol.," chap. 4, § 6; "Tract. Theol.-Pol," chap. 16.

[3] "Tract. Theol," chap. 17.

[4] "Fundamenta Juris Naturæ et Gentium," 1705. "Institutiones. Jurisprudentiæ Divinæ," Francofurti et Lipsiæ, 1688. The first work furnishes a good standard for judging the philosophical and legal standing and importance of Thomasius.

[5] Whether and how far Thomasius, with reference to his later works, was influenced by the study of Locke (see following pages) cannot be definitely determined.

is his ethical[1] principle, yet does not occupy a notable position in the development of his legal philosophy. He divides law, "rectum," into three kinds: justice, "justum," morality, "honestum," and propriety, "decorum."[2] The distinction is based upon the nature of justice, which is made to consist in its external relation, not in the inner disposition, and may accordingly be forcibly executed. The "lex positiva divina," as a prescription that cannot be imposed, falls beyond the pale of the law. There is a natural law[3] and a positive law.[4] The foundations of natural law Thomasius, like Pufendorf, derives from a divine decree. But according to Thomasius, natural laws are not issued by God as commands, "ut legislator despoticus," but as a wise admonition, "ut Pater, Consiliarius, Doctor,"[5] addressed to the heart.[6]

[1] "Fundam. Jur. Nat. et Gent.," I, 1, chap. 6, §§ 21 seq.; chap. 4, § 38. L. I, chap. 6, § 21; "Norma universalis quarumvis actionum et fundamentalis propositio juris naturæ et gentium late sic dicti est: Facienda esse, quæ vitam hominum reddunt et maxime diuturnam et felicissimam; et evitanda, quæ vitam reddunt infelicem et mortem accelerant."

[2] "Fundam. Jur. Nat. et Gent.," I, 1, chap. 6, §§ 32–43, 64, 66, 74, 75; I, 1, chap. 4, §§ 89–91; I, 1, chap. 5, § 47. Thomasius, in his "Bericht von den künftigen Thomasischen Collegiis und Schriften," renders "honestum," by the German "Ehrbarkeit," and "decorum," by "Wohlanständigkeit." *Lasson*, "System der Rechtsphilosophie," p. 74, translates "decorum," "das Schickliche"; *E. Landsberg*, "Geschichte der deutschen Rechtswissenschaft," p. 93, chooses the word "Anstand" for "decorum."

[3] Which Thomasius derives from "ex sensu communi," as likewise he designates his chief work, "Fundam. Jur. Nat. et Gent. ex Sensu Communi Deducta."

[4] "Fundam. Jur. Nat. et Gent.," I, 1, chap. 4, §§ 54 seq., 77–83.

[5] "Fund.," etc., I, 1, chap. 5, §§ 51, 52.

[6] "Fund.," etc., I, 1, chap. 6, § 15.

In contrast to Hobbes, Thomasius takes the position that, in themselves, contracts have no binding force.[1] He assumes innate rights [2] and also innate duties, "obligatio connata."[3] As instances of the former he mentions "libertas, communio primæva"; and of acquired rights, "imperium, dominium."[4] He proposes a formula of justice, which reads, "Do not to another what you would not have another do to you."[5] This principle is notable for the reason that Kant derived from it his categorical imperative.[6] Whether this dictum has any further claims to consideration will be examined in the survey of the Kantian philosophy. The principle appears as an ethical precept in the early Jewish-Christian writings. In the Book of Tobit (IV, 15) it is written, "Do that to no man which thou hatest"; and again in St. Matthew (VII, 12), "All things therefore whatsoever ye would that men should do unto you, even so do ye also unto them: for this is the law and the prophets"; and again in St. Luke (VI, 31), "And as ye would that men should do to you, do ye also to them likewise."

§ 28. *Legal Philosophy in England.* 1: LOCKE.[7] In LOCKE's (1632–1704) theory of knowledge, sensation

---

[1] "Fund.," I, 1, chap. 4, § 98: "Pactum non obligat immediate sed mediante et præsupposito consilio et imperio juris naturæ et positivæ." § 99; I, 1, chap. V, § 27: "Jam notatum fuit, pactum per se non obligare, ergo nec potest per se jus aut producere, aut confirmare."

[2] "Fund.," etc., I, 1, chap. 5, §§ 11, 12, 14, 27.

[3] "Fund.," etc., I, 1, chap. 5, §§ 13, 14.

[4] "Fund.," etc., I, 1, chap. 5, § 12.

[5] "Fund.," etc., I, 1, chaps. 6, 42; "(scil. primum principium) Justi: Quod tibi non vis fieri, alteri ne feceris."

[6] "Act only according to such maxims as would enable you to will that they may become universal laws." "Grundlegung zur Metaphysik der Sitten." "Collected Works," edition in 10 volumes, Vol. 4, Leipzig 1838, p. 43.

[7] *Berolzheimer*, "System," etc., Vol. 1, pp. 29–33.

or experience is made the source of all knowledge; hence his philosophy of law and economics[1] proceeds upon an empirical and not upon a rationalistic basis. In contrast to the preceding systems of "natural law," his procedure shows an essential advance, in that he derives the condition antecedent to the State from the study of the State as constituted, and eliminates therefrom whatever is presumably the result of the development of the State itself and of the several institutions within the State. This procedure is suggestive of the Biblical account of the creation. Locke reaches the following conclusions: Inasmuch as in the state of nature it appears that creatures of the same kind and of the same stage of development are born to like privileges and equipped for the enjoyment of like capacities, are free and equal without the one being subject to the other, it follows that privilege or rule must have been due to explicit assertion and direct establishment.[2] According to Locke, property exists in the state of nature. God gave man dominion over the earth and endowed him with reason, which he was to use to his advantage and to the improvement of his manner of life. God gave the world to men as a common right. This was not a communal grant such as would apply to the common land of a province or community, but constituted a special type of ownership. The world was a common possession; and everyone could acquire property through labor and through occupation. To

[1] *Locke*, "Two Treatises on Government," 1680. I cite from the tenth edition of Locke's works, Vol. 5, London 1801. "Two Treatises of Government." Book I, "Of Government," is of a polemical nature, against Robert Filmer and his disciples; Book II, "Of Civil Government," contains Locke's system of the philosophy of state.

[2] "Two Treatises," Book II, chap. 2.

whatever degree anyone could make property serviceable, his possession extended.[1] The condition antecedent to the State discloses a primitive form of the acquisition of right. In such condition there exists freedom, and on the basis of individual control over possessions, ownership. So long as the natural condition persists, everyone is free; freedom, however, does not mean license, but independence, and as such belongs to all. To make possible the independence of all, the assertiveness of each individual must be restricted. Accordingly no one must so abuse his liberty as to "destroy himself," or "harm another in his life, health, liberty, or property." In order to avoid or check such injury, "everyone has a right to punish the transgressors of that law to such a degree as may hinder its violation."[2]

In a state of nature, in which as yet there is no barter and trade, legal relations lack security — a guaranty which only the State can secure by the enforcement of law. The desire to acquire such regulated security leads to the establishment of the State. Consequently there would be no object in having individuals sacrifice more of their liberty and assign more of their rights to the State than is necessary to secure the governmental

[1] "Two Treatises," Book II, chap. 5. The same conception is found in *Bluntschli*, "Allgemeine Staatslehre," sixth edition, revised by *R. Loening*, Stuttgart 1886, p. 287: "Private property, that is, the control by the individual of material things, is as old as man himself. When the first men gathered fruit from the trees, and used it as food, they consciously exercised a dominion over it; that is, they took it as their property. When they chose a cave and prepared a regular, though transient abode, they also took possession of it; when they covered their nakedness with leaves and threw the skin of an animal over their body, they again acquired property. *Property was not created by the State.*"

[2] "Two Treat.," Book II, chap. 2.

guaranty of right. In the contract with the State, men assign only the power to punish, the right of legislation and legal jurisdiction; and assign these only so far as they may be requisite to secure individual freedom and private ownership. The State thus serves the interests of the common welfare; and the sphere of its authority does not extend beyond this service.[1] The authority of the government is derived from the people. They make the laws and are the supreme power. The monarch is only the executive. Unjust laws are not binding. If the authority of the monarch be abused, it may be repealed.[2]

There are two traits appearing in Locke's philosophy of government and law that are characteristic of the English attitude and mode of thinking in regard to the relation of the individual to the State — an attitude that has found a more pronounced expression in English legislation than in any other. The one is the high regard for individual liberty, and the other the respect for individual property. Locke's philosophy seems to anticipate the constitutional State ("Rechtsstaat"), and specifically, the English constitutional State, the Manchester State ("laissez faire" State). The high regard for personal liberty[3] which appears in Locke is a conspicuous trait of the English national character; and no less so is the vigorous defense of private property. In the construction and in the conclusions of his position, Locke proves himself a thorough representative of his national civilization. His ideas crystallize the attitude and temperament of the English mind.

2: BENTHAM. As Pufendorf popularized the utilitarianism of Grotius, and Wolff that of Leibnitz, so a

[1] "Two Treat.," Book II, chaps. 11, 14, 18, 19.
[2] "Two Treat.," Book II, chaps. 9, 11, 12, 15.
[3] "Two Treat.," Book I, chap. 1, and Book II, chaps. 2, 6, 8, 9.

century later Jeremy Bentham[1] supplemented Locke. And as the mass of mankind hold to the fallacy that man dwells upon the earth for his own happiness, Bentham's doctrine of "the greatest happiness of the greatest number" attained a popularity not accorded to the sterner views of Locke. BENTHAM (1748–1832) champions an epicurean, individual type of utilitarianism.[2] He reduces the principle to the simple formula of the maximum summation of happiness — the greatest happiness[3] of the greatest number. He combines a clear insight with balance. He regards man not as a cultural product, but as an automatic calculating machine, mechanically registering the advantages and disadvantages of every action; pleasures and pains[4] are entered

[1] *Bentham's* chief legal philosophical work I consulted in the French edition published by his scholar *Dumont:* "Traités de Législation Civile et Pénale," 3 vols., Paris 1802. The new editions, London 1858 and 1871, were not accessible to me.

[2] "Traités de Législation," I, chap. 1, begins: "The public good should be the object of the legislator; general utility should furnish the basis of his arguments"; in regard to utility, he says (p. 13), that it "expresses the property or tendency of a thing to prevent some evil or to procure some good. Evil is pain, or the cause of pain; good is pleasure, or the cause of pleasure."

[3] Vol. I, chap. 12, p. 98: "Morality in general is the art of directing the actions of men so as to produce the greatest possible sum of good. Legislation should have the same object." In the following citations the limits between morality and law are developed. "Of two opposite methods of action, do you desire to know which should have the preference? Calculate their effects for good and evil, and prefer that which promises the greater sum of good" (Vol. I, chap. 13, p. 140). "He who adopts the *principle of utility* esteems virtue to be good only on account of the pleasures which result from it; and vice is an evil only because of the pains which it produces." (Vol. I, chap. 1, p. 4.)

[4] Bentham thus deduces a penological principle: Actions which by their nature presumably or actually do more harm than good are forbidden by legislation; an action thus forbidden is called a crime;

and the balance brought forward.[1] But in fact a human being is neither a calculating machine nor a walking ledger; he is a thinking organism. The human mind is too complex and its motives too profound to be reduced to a simple formula. Bentham ignores the true ethical impulses in human nature unaffected by utility and unrelated to prospective pleasure or pain.[2] Bentham's influence may be due, in large measure, to the fact that he brought into ethics the embodiment of the Anglo-Saxon practical sense.

3: MILL; AUSTIN. The doctrines of Bentham were developed by JOHN STUART MILL[3] (1806–1873). Utilitarianism remains the leading principle, yet Mill's position is utilitarian only in its fundamental formula that

and to render the prohibition effective, punishment must be imposed. Preventive measures against crime are assigned a large place. Vol. I, chap. II, p. 89, and Vol. III, pp. 1–158. It is also notable that the conception of property is affected by the utilitarian view. "Property is merely the basis of expectation, the expectation deriving certain advantages from the thing possessed by virtue of the relations established in regard to it." Vol. II, p. 33.

[1] Bentham's work, "Panopticon, or the Inspection House," 3 vols., 1791, stands for reform of punishment. Postscript, Parts I, II, London 1791. "Panopticon" or the "Inspection House," written 1787, Dublin 1791. Compare with this "Traité de Législation," Vol. III, pp. 209–272. The German cellular prisons (at Moabit, Nuremberg, etc.) were built upon the construction of the Panopticon system first proposed by Bentham.

[2] From Bentham's point of view the opinion of a modern satirist would be correct, namely, that sin is an emotional expression for bad business.

[3] Among J. S. Mill's works it is not those dealing with political economy — "Essays on some Unsettled Questions of Political Economy," first edition, 1844; "Principles of Political Economy," first edition, 1848 — that are most to be considered, but particularly "On Liberty," second edition, London 1859, "Considerations on Representative Government," 1861; "Utilitarianism," second edit., London 1864; "System of Inductive and Deductive Logic," 2 vols.

morality consists in the furtherance of the happiness of all sentient beings.[1] For Mill, man is not a calculating biped, but a being endowed with an ethical nature. This appears first in his emphasis of the fact that the sympathetic qualities of man, the contacts of man and man, are not exclusively determined by considerations of utility, but as well by emotional factors which find their origin in unconscious human impulses;[2] and again in his view that man has the power to modify and refine his character. Human actions are determined, but not inevitably and minutely. The will is free in so far as man has the power to regulate desire by ideas and motives, and so direct the will to accepted proper ends. Human character is thus recognized as something growing, developing, as amenable to the moral motives of self-culture.[3] The conclusions drawn by Mill from his psychological analysis lead in practice to the abandon-

[1] "Utilitarianism," chap. 2 ("What Utilitarianism is"), pp. 9 seq.: "The creed which accepts as the foundation of morals utility or the greatest happiness principle, holds that actions are right in proportion as they tend to promote happiness, wrong as they tend to produce the reverse of happiness. By happiness is intended pleasure, and the absence of pain; by unhappiness, pain, and the privation of pleasure. . . . Some kinds of pleasure are more desirable than others."

[2] "Utilitarianism," chap. 3, pp. 39–51, chap. 5, pp. 62 seq.

[3] "Utilitarianism," pp. 59–61. "Will, the active phenomenon, is a different thing from desire, the state of passive sensibility." "Correctly conceived, the doctrine called Philosophical Necessity is simply this: that, given the motives which are present to an individual's mind, and given likewise the character and disposition of the individual, the manner in which he will act may be unerringly inferred." ("Logic," p. 522.) "He has, to a certain extent, a power to alter his character. . . . His character is formed by his circumstances . . .; but his own desire to mould it in a particular way, is one of those circumstances, and by no means one of the least influential." ("Logic," p. 524.)

ment of utilitarianism. In his essay, "On Liberty," Mill considers the limits of the authority of society over the individual, and outlines the sphere of freedom for the several portions of the community. In his "Considerations on Representative Government,"[1] he attempts to establish representation as the best form of government, and sets forth its nature and development.[2]

JOHN AUSTIN[3] (d. 1859) was the founder of the English analytical school of jurisprudence, to which, so far as he may be considered a jurist, John Stuart Mill also belonged. The contributions of this school are characterized by clearness and precision of thought; however, they consider the fundamental questions of legal science rather than those of legal philosophy.[4]

§ 29. *Legal Philosophy in France.* 1: MONTESQUIEU. MONTESQUIEU[5] (Baron de la Brède, 1689–1755) is the most striking example, in the history of legal philosophy,

[1] Chap. 3: "That the ideally best form of government is representative government."

[2] On *Mill's* "Law of Causation," see *Berolzheimer*, "System," etc., Vol. I, pp. 133–135, 237 seq., 252. See also *Berolzheimer*, "Die Entgeltung im Strafrechte," pp. 40–109, 350–352, and the literature there cited; and also *Berolzheimer*, "Rechtsphil. Studien," pp. 1–14.

[3] His chief works are: "Lectures on Jurisprudence or the Philosophy of Positive Law" (fourth edit. rev. & ed. by Rob. Campbell, London 1873), fifth edition, rev. & ed. by Rob. Campbell, 2 vols., London 1885.

[4] For a list of the most important of these writings see *Bergbohm*, "Jurisprudenz und Rechtswissenschaft," Leipzig 1892, p. 14, note.

[5] "L'Esprit des Loix," 1748; new edit., Amsterdam 1755. My citations are from this later edition.

The term "Esprit des Loix" *Montesquieu* interprets as "the several relations which the law may have with various interests." These relations he proposes to study; particularly the relation of the laws "with the nature and principle of every form of government." (Book I, chap. 3.)

of the fact that the formulators of fundamental political principles exert a more decisive influence than do the most eminent theorists. In a last analysis, Montesquieu's ideas go back to Aristotle, but are decidedly modified by the example of English legislation as interpreted in France. He demands a threefold division of authority in the State, "puissance législative, exécutive, et de juger,"[1] and holds that these safeguard political liberty. Such a division of authority preserves the dynamic balance of power, automatically checks abuse, and makes impossible the imperiling of civil liberty.[2] This system,

[1] "Esprit," etc., Book XI, chap. 6 ("De la Constitution d'Angleterre").

[2] "The political liberty of a citizen consists in that peacefulness of mind arising from the feeling of security; and to have this freedom the government must be such that no citizen shall fear another." (Book XV, chap. 6.) Montesquieu then sets forth that such security against abuse of political power and against tyranny can be established only by a proper division of authority. For Montesquieu the general purpose of government is to secure political freedom. "In order that authority shall not be abused, matters must be so arranged that one authority shall check another." (Book XI, chap. 5.)

The advantage of political freedom is set forth in Book XIX, chap. 27; compare also Book XXVI, chap. 15. "These first laws (political) gave men their liberty." See also Sorel, as cited above, pp. 102, 103. In regard to the foundation of the State, Montesquieu follows the principle of "natural law." "I have not derived my principles from my prejudices but from the nature of things." (Preface, p. iv.) In speaking of the laws of nature (Book I, chap. 2) he says: "Fundamentally these laws are natural ones and are so called because they are derived wholly from the constitution of our nature. To understand them one must consider man in a condition antecedent to the establishment of society. The laws of nature will be those which he acquired in that state." (See also Book I, chap. 3.)

Montesquieu refers to the influence of climate upon legislation, especially in its bearing upon political freedom. The title of Book XVII reads: "The relation of the laws of political slavery to the

§ 29] LEGAL PHILOSOPHY IN FRANCE 143

however, is barren in that it is negative and makes the protection of the citizen against tyranny [1] the sole basis of government. Furthermore such protection is to be secured mechanically, as though governors, officials, judges, and administrative officers were machines, and laws and ordinances were physical instruments. The success of his system shows how in the progress of politics an argument resting upon an "illusory" basis may exert an influence, when the political end which such faulty reasoning supports, is approved.

2: ROUSSEAU. Opinions differ widely as to the value of ROUSSEAU's [2] (1712–1778) position, as well as to its sources and influence. His peculiar mind and temperament must be taken into account. His personality, character, and genius suggest a comparison with Schopenhauer. Both show the querulous hesitant temperament of the neurasthenic, with its favorable as well as unfavorable influence upon intellectual development; both display brilliance of thought, expressed in clear, terse, artistic form; in both the larger and smaller irritations of life were confronted morosely, with a self-centered egotism; witness Schopenhauer's celibacy, and Rous-

nature of the climate." In Book XIX, chap. 27, he says: "I do not say that the climate has produced a large share of the laws, customs, and manners of this nation, but I say that its manners and customs may well have a decided bearing on its laws."

[1] *Stahl*, "Die Genesis der gegenwärtigen Rechtsphilosophie," p. 218. *Geyer*, "Geschichte und System der Rechtsphilosophie in Grundzügen," p. 47. *R. v. Mohl*, "Die Geschichte und Literatur der Staatswissenschaften," Vol. III, p. 387; while recognizing *Montesquieu, Mohl* says: "The world would have been saved many a false step and disaster if he had not brought the doctrine of the distribution of authority into a long-enduring predominance."

[2] I cite from the edition of his works that lies before me: "Oeuvres Complètes," 13 volumes, Paris, Hachette, 1884–1887 (Vol. XIII contains the analytical table of his complete works).

seau's abandonment of his children to a foundling asylum, and their common advocacy of detachment from life. But while Schopenhauer proclaimed disdain for life as the ultimate aim of a practical philosophy, Rousseau — like Tolstoi in our own day — rejected the claims of civilization, and advocated return to nature as the complete salvation. But the "nature" of Rousseau, under the shelter of which salvation and re-creation are to be found, is not at all the nature of things as they are. Rousseau's imaginary retreat is not to nature wild, savage and turbulent, but to nature in rosy coloring, a Watteau-like, peaceful, calm, pastoral idyll. While Schopenhauer's negation of life is modeled upon the Buddhistic "nirvana," Rousseau proposes the abandonment of the struggle for life, and the withdrawal from every manifestation of energy, from the daily toil, from self-assertion, and from one's individual advancement above his fellow-men. By annihilating self-interest, the inequality of men, which is the greatest of all evils, is to be removed.

The prize offered by the Academy of Dijon was the occasion for Rousseau's diatribe against the economic and legal inequality of human fortunes. The thesis proposed by the Academy was, "What is the origin of the inequality of men? Can it be justified, 'autorisée,' by the law of nature, 'la loi naturelle' "? In Rousseau's reply, "Discours sur l'origine de l'inégalité parmi les hommes" (1775), he argues that the physical inequality of men is determined by nature, but that their political inequality, "inégalité morale ou politique," if not due to convention, "le consentement des hommes," has at all events been legalized by it, "autorisée." Primitive man in his savage state was acquainted with but one instrument for all service — his own body. There were no considerations of good and evil, for as yet morality and duty were unknown. Now how, from such a state of savagery, did a civil State arise? "The man who first enclosed a bit of ground and gave notice by saying, 'This is mine,' and found people simple enough to believe him, was the true founder of civil society." "Le premier qui ayant enclos un terrain s'avisa de dire *Ceci est a moi*, et trouvé des gens assez simples pour le croire, fut le vrai fondateur de la société civile." So long as men were content to live, each on the product of his own labors, "tant qu'ils ne s'appliquèrent qu'à des ouvrages qu'un seul pouvoit faire," they remained free, healthy, kindly, and happy; but as soon as one man needed the aid of another, human equality disappeared; the rights of property became established, and work became a task. The use of metals and the cultivation of the soil revolutionized man's lot: "For the poet it is gold and silver that have civilized men and destroyed humanity, but for the philosopher iron and wheat have effected this"; "Pour le poëte, c'est l'or et l'argent; mais pour le philosophe, ce sont le fer et le blé qui ont civilisé les hommes et perdue le genre humain." These inventions were succeeded by others. The multitude of desires and needs created the master and the slave: the man of wealth required the labor of another, the poor man, his assistance. Three stages of increasing inequality were brought about through the legal establishment of private ownership, through the institution of government, "l'institution de la magistrature," and through the change of legal power into arbitrary rule, "changement du pouvoir légitime en pouvoir arbitraire." The first stage produced wealth and poverty; the second, rulers and subjects; and the third, masters and slaves. These fundamental considerations form the approach of Rousseau's philosophical masterpiece, "Du Contrat Social, ou Principe du Droit Politique." A further point, strangely and constantly neglected by critics, but which is important in any appreciation of Rousseau as a writer on social institutions and on the philosophy of law, is the *radical change* that took place in his development.[1] The Rousseau of the "Contrat Social" and the Rousseau of the "Discours" are altogether different persons. The latter is a supreme idealist preaching a return to nature.[2] Rousseau could not have composed the "Contrat Social" in the spirit of the "Discours," for the "Discours" pursued to its logical and practical consequences could

[1] Even *Liepmann*, who interprets *Rousseau* with insight, has failed to observe this. He, along with Stammler, first drew attention to the fact that Rousseau — who, in the theme set by the Academy for the "Discours" followed in "traditional lines"(*Liepmann*, "Die Rechtsphilosophie des Jean Jacques Rousseau," p. 65) — distinctly discarded the historical approach in the "Contrat Social." It was through Liepmann's emphasis of this point that my attention was called to the change of front in Rousseau's viewpoint.

It would be of interest, but does not fall within the compass of my survey, to show, in regard to the other works of Rousseau, a like contrast between the dualism of his idealistic social philosophy in his first period, and the objective position of the later period.

[2] Upon the "Discours sur les Arts et les Sciences," and the "Discours sur L'Inégalité parmi les Hommes," the opinion of *Maugras*, "Voltaire et J. J. Rousseau," is apt. He says (p. 39): "Voltaire was the most brilliant incarnation of his times. The civilization, the art, the science that Rousseau considered as the bane of society, Voltaire regarded as its source of illumination."

The opinion of Frederick the Great upon the Rousseau of the "Discours" is given in a letter to Lord Marischal — "Oeuvres de Frédéric le Grand," Berlin, Rod. Decker, 20 vols., pp. 288, 289, and mentioned by *Du Bois-Reymond*, "Friedrich II und Jean-Jacques Rousseau," Paris 1886, p. 337. "I consider that true philosophy consists in condemning abuse without interfering with use. One must be able to dispense with everything yet not give up one's claim to anything. It is ridiculous to preach that all are equal and that therefore we must live as do the savages, without laws, without society, and without police; that the fine arts have been harmful to morals, and other equally vain paradoxes."

lead to no positive construction; it is a negation of law, of government, and of civilization. A mind such as Rousseau's would at once have perceived this inconsequence when confronted with the attempt to evolve a philosophy of law and government. As a fact he broke radically with his former position, of which the following well-known citation gives evidence: "Man is born free, yet everywhere lives in fetters. In so far as he believes himself master of others, he is more enslaved than they. How does this change of status come about? That I need not consider. But what has legitimized it? This I believe I have set forth." "L'homme est né libre, et partout il est dans les fers. Tel se croit le maître des autres, qui ne laissent pas d'être plus esclave qu'eux. Comment ce changement s'est-il fait? Je l'ignore. Qu'est-ce qui peut le rendre légitime? Je crois pouvoir résoudre cette question."

This passage of the "Contrat Social" Liepmann [1] makes the focus of his defense of Rousseau's philosophy. He maintains that Rousseau thus states that he is not claiming an historical warrant for his social philosophy, but is merely engaged with its philosophic interpretation. This may be conceded; and if Rousseau had not also written the "Discours," Liepmann's argument might stand. But Rousseau has actually presented an historical evolution of the State, of law, and of society, describing how, in his opinion, law and the State arose. What then is the reason for the rejection of the historical basis which he had earlier framed? In his work on Rousseau — presumbly written under the influence of Stammler — Haymann [2] calls attention to the fact that

[1] "Die Rechtsphilosophie des Jean Jacques Rousseau," pp. 95–105. *Stammler*, too, notes the changed problem in "Die Theorie des Anarchismus," p. 14.

[2] This work is dedicated to *Stammler*.

Rousseau admits the historical position in other passages of the "Contrat Social" itself.[1]

The phrase "Je l'ignore," at the beginning of the "Contrat Social," cannot be interpreted to mean, "I recognize no historical development," but "I do not accept any"; it becomes a disavowal of the historical solution which Rousseau in his earlier writings had given. This change of opinion is accounted for by supposing that Rousseau, as he gradually elaborated and clarified his opinions in the course of writing the "Contrat Social," had reached the conclusion that a legal and social philosophy could not be established on the basis of the "Discours." Through the topic proposed for its prize by the Academy, Rousseau's attention was directed specifically to the problem of political inequality; and government and law were not then taken into consideration. Meanwhile Rousseau had turned to the general philosophic problems among which he considered prominently the conception of the nature of political liberty. In his view of liberty Rousseau shows the influence of the classic conception and of the "tyrannomachy," enmity to tyrants, derived therefrom. Liberty is the absence of tyranny; it is not lawlessness or license; it is the condition of complete obedience to the law, and of complete

---

[1] *Haymann*, "Jean Jacques Rousseau's Sozialphilosophie," p. 3. The significance Haymann attaches to "Je l'ignore," namely, that it is as if Rousseau were to say that at the very climax of his system he wished to have nothing to do with the historical development; that as a legal philosopher he knew nothing about it and had no obligation to consider it, that the present considerations need not make any assumptions in regard to those fundamentally different branches of knowledge; — this view is merely a forced explanation for lack of a better, and does not hold. For Rousseau rejects the historical evolutionary method and justification not only at this point of the "Contrat Social," but discards herein in general the historical presentation laid down in the "Discours."

absence of any rulership outside of law. In order that liberty shall exist, the law itself must be the product of liberty; not of the self-interested authority of a tyrant,[1] but the product of a common will,—in his own words "volonté générale," in contrast to the will of the collective individuals, "volonté de tous,"—thus expressing the sovereignty of the people.[2]

"L'homme est né libre, et partout il est dans les fers." To the exposition of this complete change of opinion the first book of the "Contrat Social" is devoted. Neither the social order nor the law is due to nature. Might never can make right. Hence the legality of right must be based upon convention.[3] The central problem which the "Contrat Social" attempts to solve is the determination of a communal bond, "trouver une forme d'association," that shall protect and secure the social service of the person and property of every citizen, and yet leave the individual, through his association with his fellow-men, "s'unissent à tous," subject to himself alone, and as free as ever. Every infraction of the social compact, "pacte social," would invalidate or destroy this contract. In case he were thereby to lose the regulated liberty resulting from the compact, and for the sake of which he gave up his natural liberty, each party to the contract would resume his former rights and regain his natural liberty.[4]

[1] "Contrat Social," I, 8.

[2] "Contrat Social," II, 1; II, 6; "Emile,"I, 5; "Lettre 6me de la montagne" ("Oeuvres" III, p. 203). See the citations used by *Haymann*, "J. J. Rousseau's," etc., p. 41, note 3, and pp. 85 seq.

[3] "Contrat Social," I, 2, 4. "The regulative character of the law is of a *conventional* type." *Liepmann*, "Die Rechtsphil.," etc., p. 101.

[4] "Contrat Social," I, 6. As a fact it is the complete enslavement and deprivation of rights of the individual as against the State which Rousseau, following ancient examples, advocates.

The nature of Rousseau's social compact may be thus rendered: each individual subjects his person and his operations to the superior control of the common will, "volonté générale," and in so far each becomes an indissoluble member of the whole. Such association replaces the individual contracting party by a legal corporate personality, "corps moral et collectif," termed the State when in a static condition, "quand il est passif," and the sovereign, as a political power, "quand il est actif," and authority, "puissance," with reference to the subjects, "en le comparant à ses semblables." The subjects of the State collectively are called the people. They are to be called citizens in so far as they have a share in political power, "comme participant à l'autorité souveraine." They are to be called subjects as subject to the laws of the State. These distinctions are drawn in accordance with the specified relations, but the terms are not always precisely used.[1]

The welfare of the people is the most important end of government. It is to be secured by carrying out the communal will in all respects.[2] The law, to justify its existence, must serve common interests.[3] The demands of the law should coincide with those of utility.[4] Government is to equalize the more pronounced inequalities of fortune, "l'extrême inégalité des fortunes," but must not do so by despoiling the wealthy to build homes

Rousseau's conception of freedom is the freedom of the community as against tyranny, but along with it an enslavement of the individual as against the community — a situation suggestive of modern socialism. See also *Maugras*, "Voltaire," etc., p. 176.

[1] "Contrat Social," I, 6.
[2] "Contrat Social," II, 11; "Économie Politique" ("Oeuvres," III), p. 283.
[3] "Lettre 6me de la montagne," p. 203.
[4] "Contrat Social," Introduction.

for the poor, but through preventive measures.¹ The most suitable forms of government are democracy for small States, aristocracy for those of medium size, and monarchy for large ones.²

A critical estimate of Rousseau cannot claim that his writings have directly advanced the theory of government and the philosophy of law,³ but rather that they were of far-reaching influence in supplying the basis of political positions. In this respect the "Discours" must be considered apart from the "Contrat Social." In content the former is far superior, but the influence of the latter was decidedly greater. The answer to the question whether Rousseau is to be looked upon as the precursor and intellectual sponsor of the fanatical struggle for liberty of the French Revolution will depend upon whether one has in mind the Rousseau of the "Discours" or the Rousseau of the "Contrat Social." With equal justice it may be answered in the affirmative or in the negative. If we consider Rousseau, the philosopher of the "Contrat Social," the answer must be "no,"⁴ for therein he does not advocate absolute political equality; if we consider the Rousseau of the "Discours," the answer must be "yes," for the outspoken singleness of purpose of the "Discours" was a suitable medium to influence the minds of the masses. The masses are ever led by striking phrases, by smooth and simple formulæ; and the lure of universal equality completely served its political purpose.

[1] "Économie Politique," pp. 290, 291; "Contrat Social," II, 11.
[2] "Contrat Social," III, 2, 3.
[3] Indirectly, however, in that *Rousseau* had a decided influence upon *Kant's* views of the State. See below, § 33.
[4] *Jellinek*, "Die Erklärung der Menschen und Bürgerrechte (Ein Beitrag zur modernen Verfassungsgeschichte)," *Jellinek-Meyer*, "Staats-und Völkerrechtliche Abhandlungen," Vol. I, Part 3, Leipzig 1895, pp. 4–6.

3: DIDEROT. The career of DIDEROT[1] (1713–1784) as a publicist formed an essential factor in the antecedents of the French Revolution. His influence was exerted partly through the popularity of his philosophic writings, but mainly through the Encyclopedia [2] which he edited. The former, sceptical in tone, at first assumed a deistic position, but later an explicitly atheistical one;[3] the latter assembled the destructive elements in the intellectual undermining of the leading minds of France. Diderot's strength lay in destructive rather than in constructive criticism. His style was brilliant and attractive. He adapted freely the moral philosophy of Shaftesbury;[4] he contributed some passages to Rousseau's "Discours sur l'inégalité;[5] and he commented upon Beccaria's "Dei Delitti e delle Pene";[6] his own views of punishment, expressed in regard to the divine exercise of punitive judgment, support the theory of

[1] "Oeuvres Complètes" de *Diderot*, 20 vols. Assézat and Tourneux, Paris, 1875–1877.

[2] "Encyclopédie, ou Dictionnaire Raisonné des Sciences, des Arts et des Métiers," Paris, 1751–1767, 17 vols., besides two vols. of illustrations.

[3] "Pensées Philosophiques" ("Oeuvres Complètes," I, pp. 123–170); "La Promenade du Sceptique ou les Allées" ("Oeuv.," pp. 171–257); "De la Suffisance de la Religion Naturelle" ("Oeuv.," pp. 259–273); "Lettre sur les Aveugles, à L'Usage de ceux qui Voient," and "Lettre sur les Sourds et Muets."

[4] "Principes de la Philosophie Morale ou Essai sur la Mérite de la Vertu," par Mylord S. (Shaftesbury), translated from the English. ("Oeuv.," I, pp. 3–121.)

[5] "Oeuv.," IV, pp. 100–104: "Morceau de Diderot inséré dans le discours sur l'inégalité des conditions parmi les hommes de J. J. Rousseau" (1754).

[6] "Oeuv.," IV: "Des Délits et des Peines," pp. 51–69 (pp. 53–60, Letter of Ramsay's on Beccaria's work); pp. 60–63, "Des Recherches sur le Style," by Beccaria; pp. 63–69; notes by Diderot on the treatment of offenses and punishments.

general prevention.[1] In his "Code de la Nature" he advocates, in a somewhat transcendental form, the Stoic[2] principle of living according to nature. His "Principes de Politique des Souverains"[3] contains maxims and aphorisms, with frequent classical allusions — the whole, at times suggestive of Machiavelli's "Prince" — that form a compilation of political principles for absolute[4] monarchs. Diderot makes no attempt to conceal his opinion of such rulers, and gives to one of his maxims the title "Maxime détestable," to another, "Perfidie abominable," and to a third, "Un rôle perfide et vil." While Diderot thus expounds the best principles for absolutism, he at the same time

[1] "Pensées Philosophiques," III, with reference to divine punishment. "What relation is there between the offender and the offense, and what between the offense and the punishment? Just a mass of absurdities and cruelties." "Oeuv.," chap. I, p. 165. "La Promenade du Sceptique" ("Oeuv.," I, p. 213), speaking of divine punishment he says: *"One cannot say that punishment occurs for the sake of example,* for there is no one whom punishment can intimidate. If our sovereigns inflict punishment it is in the hope of deterring those who may be tempted to imitate the culprit."

[2] "Oeuv.," IV, pp. 107–117: "Abrégé du code de la nature extrait du système de la nature du baron d'Holbach." (P. 116): "The morality of nature is the only religion which the interpreter of nature offers to his fellow-citizens. The friend of man can never be the friend of the gods. (P. 117): "Oh nature! sovereign of all beings, and you, adorable daughters, Virtue, Reason, Truth! may you ever be our only divinities; to you is due all the worship and homage of the earth. Then show us, oh Nature, what man shall do to obtain that good fortune which you desire for him. May the beneficent fires of Virtue inspire him, may Reason guide his uncertain steps in the paths of life, may the Torch of Truth light his way! Oh helpful deities, combine your power to support our hearts, banish from your minds error, malice, trouble; and let knowledge, goodness, and serenity, reign in their place."

[3] "Oeuv.," II, Paris 1875, pp. 461–502.

[4] "Oeuv.," II, p. 461, note 1.

expresses a severe disapproval of the absolutist program, and indicates its weakness.[1] Further excursions into

[1] "Look upon all ambitious persons as your born enemies.... The most dangerous are the high and mighty, the poor, and those in debt, who have all to gain and nothing to lose by a revolution." II; In *Diderot* there follows a citation from *Tacitus'* "Annals," Book XIV, chap. LVII. "Sulla inops, unde præcipua audacia." Compare with this, *Shakespeare*, "Julius Cæsar," 1, 2, Cæsar on Cassius.

"It is easy to obtain justice in small affairs; for that seems to confer the right to infringe with impunity in big affairs: "Maxime Détestable," III.

"When you are plotting against your sovereign, place a spy in his service." XVII.

"To make citizens of slaves is a very good thing, but it would have been better not to have had any slaves." XXXIII.

"Always put the name of the senate before your own (*Ex senatusconsulto, et auctoritate Cæsaris*). It will matter little if there is no senate." XXXV.

"Let it be agreed that the laws are made for all, for the sovereign as well as for the people; but do not believe it." XLI.

"Always respect the laws that do not trouble you, but trouble others. It is still better to respect all the laws." XLIV.

"Liberate the slaves when you need their testimony against a master whom you want to ruin." XLVI.

"Whatever is respected in a monarchy alone is merely a patent of slavery." LIX.

"Whoever is not master of a soldier controls nothing." LXV.

"For yourself you want slaves; the nation needs free men." LXXIX.

"Satire and complaint should be permitted; suppressed hatred is more dangerous than open hatred." LXXXVI.

"Sacrifice all for the military." XCI.

"Let there be no ministers abroad, only spies." XCVII.

"Let there be no ministers at home, but clerks." XCVIII.

"Be the first soldier of the army." CI.

"My subjects are only slaves under a more honorable name." CV.

"A king is neither father, son, brother, kin, husband, nor friend. What is he then? He is a king, even when he sleeps." CXXX.

"In the State there is but one refuge for evil doers — the palace of the king." CLXXIV.

"Let him persuade his subjects that the evil done unto them is for their good." CLXXXIV.

politics are to be found in his "Réfutation suivie de l'ouvrage d'Helvétius intitulé l'homme."[1]

4: GODWIN. The most important of the works of WILLIAM GODWIN[2] (1756–1836) is his "Enquiry concerning Political Justice and its Influence on Morals and Happiness." In this work Godwin appears as an advocate and defender of political liberty[3] and equality[4] before the law. The work also contains ethical studies and opinions[5] concerning certain legal issues, such as those involved in suicide, duelling, etc.[6] Godwin conceives the community as built up of individual components.[7] He attempts to establish as a political ideal an anarchistic state of society in which the power of the State shall be abolished, and in which there shall be no property in the sense of legal title. An equal distribution of property, with due consideration of equity, shall replace property legally secured and unequally divided. The principle guiding the measures of society and applicable to the distribution of property is that of the good of the community. Godwin believed that such anarchistic state of society could be brought about by convincing men of the necessity of abolishing

[1] *Diderot*, "Oeuvres Complètes," II, pp. 275-456. Particularly pp. 380-382, 388-390, 419, 442, 443-450.

[2] 1793, translated also in German. I cite from the second edit. 2 vols., London, 1796.

[3] See particularly Vol. I, pp. 96-105. "The real enemies of liberty in any country are not the people, but those higher orders who find their imaginery profit in a contrary system" (p. 105); pp. 249-306, "Of resistance, revolutions, tyrannicide"; Vol. II, pp. 1-207.

[4] Vol. I, pp. 144-148.

[5] Vol. I, Book IV, chap. X. "Of self-love and benevolence"; p. 425, "On the origin of benevolence."

[6] Vol. I, Book II, chap. 2, beginning.

[7] Vol. I, p. 137: "Society is nothing more than an aggregation of individuals."

the State and the law in the interest of the common good, in which view Godwin differs from the true anarchists and approaches the position of the Utopians. And indeed, upon the founders of anarchy, Proudhon and his successors, Godwin exercised no influence. It may be added that his wife, Mary Wollstonecraft (1759–1797) was the author of the "Vindication of the Rights of Women,"[1] a work in the interests of the feminist movement, the trend of which reflects the agitations of the French Revolution.

§ 30. *Legal Philosophy in Germany.* 1: LEIBNITZ. The legal philosophy of LEIBNITZ (1646–1716) is built upon the model of Roman law, yet with suggestions of Greek influence. In Roman law the interest is focussed upon the "paterfamilias"; Leibnitz similarly emphasizes the position of the "vir bonus." By this is meant the average man endowed with due reason, "sapiens," and in a cultured state, "qui amat omnes, quantum ratio permittit." The virtue with which the "vir bonus" is endowed, the φιλανθρωπία of the Greeks, is "justitia."[2] But "amare" signifies "felicitate alterius delectari," or "felicitatem alienam asciscere in suam." Accordingly, Leibnitz's "vir bonus" comprises the "social" man of Grotius; but ethically the concept goes beyond it. "Jus" is "quædam potentia moralis," while "obligatio" is "necessitas moralis"; but for the

---

[1] London 1792; German translation by *Salzmann*, 1793, 2 vols. In regard to the authoress see *Helen Zimmern*, "Mary Wollstonecraft," "Deutsche Rundschau," Vol. 60, Berlin 1889, pp. 247–259.

[2] Therefore "justitia" is "charitas sapientis, hoc est sequentem sapientiæ dictata." "De notionibus juris et justitiæ," Leibnitz, edited by J. E. Erdmann, Berlin 1840, p. 118. See also "Definitiones Ethicæ," Erdmann, edit. p. 670: "*Justi* scientiam voco seu ejus quod viro bono possibile est," "scientiam *officiorum* voco seu ejus quod viro bono impossibile et necessarium, id est ommissu impossibile est." *Mollat*, "Rechtsphilosophisches aus Leibnizens un-

"vir bonus," "moralis" and "naturalis"[1] are one. Here the "jus naturæ" has its origin; it appears in three stages, "gradus": "jus strictum" as referring to "justitia commutativa"; "æquitas," with regard to "justitia distributiva"; and "pietas (vel probitas)," applicable to "justitia universalis." From these are developed the three fundamental legal injunctions: "neminem lædere," "suum cuique tribuere," and "honeste (vel potius pie) vivere."[2] In contrast to Pufendorf, Leibnitz secularizes ethics and associates it intimately with law. The wise man is the just man. Justice leads to neighborly love as well as to personal happiness,[3] and happiness is a "constant state of pleasure."[4] As applied to

gedruckten Schriften," Leipzig 1885, appendix, p. 85. See also "Brief an Conring" (Gerhardt edition, I, p. 160): "homo prudens debet semper agere quod justum est."

[1] "De Notionibus Juris et Justitiæ," Erdmann edition, p. 118.

[2] "De notionibus Juris et Justitiæ," pp. 119, 120. "Initium institutionum juris perpetui," *Mollat*, "Rechtsphil.," etc., p. 6; "De tribus juris naturæ et gentium gradibus," *Mollat*, pp. 13–21.

[3] "Definitiones Ethicæ," Erdmann edition, p. 670: "Justitia est caritas sapientis. Caritas est benevolentia generalis. . . . Quisquis est sapiens, amat omnes. . . . Omnis sapiens multis prodest. Omnis sapiens Deo amico est. Omnis Dei amicus est felix. Quo quis sapientior hoc felicior in potentia pari. Omnis sapiens est justus. Omnis justus est felix." ("Sapientia," so often emphasized by Leibnitz, originates with Cicero.) "Wisdom is merely the science of happiness that teaches us how to achieve happiness." "Von der Glückseligkeit," Erdmann edit., p. 671. "Justitia est caritas sapientis." "De Justitia," 1; *Mollat*, "Rechtsphil.," etc., p. 36. "*Caritas est habitus amandi omnes seu benevolentia universalis suis tamen gradibus pro ratione objecti discreta.*" "De Justitia," 3; *Mollat*, "Rechtsphil.," etc., p. 37. "Quia Deus existit, ideo sapienti licet liberrime exercere caritatem." "De Justitia," 8; *Mollat*, "Rechtsphil.," etc., p. 40. "Et tanto quisque magi *justus* est, quanto magis delectatur communi bono. . . ." "Initium institutionum juris perpetui," *Mollat*, "Rechtsphil.," etc., p. 3.

[4] "Von der Glückseligkeit," Erdmann edit., p. 671.

the principles of human conduct the will of God and human reason coincide.[1] Leibnitz's definition of human justice is far more subtle than that of Thomasius: "Justus ea voluntate præditus erit, qualem omnes eius esse vellent, qui ipsos regit."[2] His formulation of "æquitas"[3] approaches that of Thomasius for justice: "Quod tibi non vis fieri, aut quod tibi vis fieri, neque aliis facito aut negato."[4] Yet Leibnitz holds to the utilitarian principle of the happiness of the greatest number: "Summa juris regula est: quicquid publice utile est, illud faciendum est."[5] In contrast to Spinoza's stern principle of causality, Leibnitz emphasizes the teleological factor. Yet he is far from being a utilitarian in the ordinary sense. He distinguishes between justice, which in his view belongs to ethics, and politics, for which the test of utility is decisive: "Scientia . . . Juris naturæ . . . Ethica est, de justo, . . . Politica

[1] "Voluntas Dei easdem quas sapientia nobis agendi regulas præscribit." "De Justitia," 7; *Mollat*, "Rechtsphil.," etc., p. 39. "It is a weakness to rejoice in the misfortune of another, and it is a virtue to rejoice in the good fortune of another. This principle means that God himself acts according to justice and would be blameable if he would act otherwise, although he has nothing to fear or to hope from the issue. This principle applies also to men." "Axiomes ou principes du droit"; *Mollat*, "Rechtsphil.," etc., p. 54. See also "Méditation sur la notion commune de la justice"; *Mollat*, "Rechtsphil.," etc., pp. 56–81 on p. 62, "Justice is merely that which conforms to wisdom and mercy combined."

[2] "Initium institutionum juris perpetui"; *Mollat*, "Rechtsphil.," etc., p. 3.

[3] "The principle of equity, or what amounts to the same, equality"; "the rule of equity or equality." "Méditation sur la notion commune de la justice"; *Mollat*, "Rechtsphil.," etc., p. 70.

[4] "Méditation sur la notion de la justice"; *Mollat*, "Rechtsphil.," etc., p. 70.

[5] *Mollat*, "Rechtsphil.," etc., appendix II, p. 86.

est, de utili . . ." [1] Three motives, "principia," impel man to right action, "ad juste agendum": the familiar self-interest, "utilitas propria"; altruism on the basis of sympathetic emotion, "sensus humanitatis atque honesti"; and religion, "religio." [2] The freedom of the will is defined by Leibnitz as the spontaneous activity of a rational being.

Under the pseudonym, Cæsarinus Furstenerius, Leibnitz wrote the "Tractatus de jure suprematus, ac legationum principum Germaniæ." [3] The author as a Christian and patriot advocates a political ideal of an imperial world-monarchy. The leading ideas of the work are thus summarized: [4] (1) "Imperatorem atque imperium in orbe Christiano non tantum dignitatis prærogativam habere, sed et jus Advocati Ecclesiæ Universalis, eoque nomine quandam potestatem extra Imperii quoque ditiones sese extendentem"; (2) "Electores recte æquiparari Regibus"; (3) "Non debere negari Electoribus ac principibus Imperii primariis quod conceditur principibus Italis quos non minus Imperio nostro obnoxios obstrictosque esse constat." [5]

[1] I, "Brief an Conring" (Gerhardt edit., I, p. 159).
[2] *Mollat*, "Rechtsphil.," etc., appendix V, pp. 95, 96.
[3] First edit., 1677. This is reprinted in Klopp's Edit., Vol. 4, pp. 9–305. See also "Leibnitii ad Cæsarini Furstenerii de suprematu librum explicandum atque defendendum opuscula," Klopp, Vol. 4, pp. 309-363; *Hartmann*, "Leibniz als Jurist und Rechtsphilosoph" (Festgabe der Tübinger Juristenfakultät für Ihering, August 2, 1892), pp. 51-60.
[4] "De Cæsarino Furstenerio judicium," Klopp, Vol. 4, pp. 324, 325. Also "Tractatus," chaps. XXXI–XXXVI. See also "Brief von Leibniz an Hobbes," July 13-22, 1670 (Gerhardt edit., I, p. 83): "Cum Deus sit omnium Monarcha communis."
[5] In the letter to Conring of Jan. 3, 1678, Leibnitz expresses himself approvingly of the book, the authorship of which he does not acknowledge. "Multa alia in illo libello non contemnenda animadverto; sunt tamen et alia crepera non nihil et dubitationi ob-

Leibnitz makes the freedom of the will equivalent to the spontaneous expression of a being endowed with reason.[1]

2: WOLFF. The influence of Leibnitz's philosophy of law and government was due to the form given it by CHRISTIAN WOLFF (1679–1754). His great work on natural law [2] appeared in nine large volumes; but he also published in his "Institutionen"[3] a summary of this tediously diffuse treatise. Wolff's philosophy of law is closely connected with his ethics.[4] The primary ethical principle is the highest earthly good. "As nature makes it incumbent upon men to perfect themselves [5] and their condition, and to avoid whatever detracts from such perfection,[6] there arises the precept, as a rule of nature, to do that which makes for the improvement of one's self and one's condition, and to avoid that which makes against it."[7] This moral principle he regards as applying to all practical life, including the province of

noxia (!)," and he emphasizes, "Mihi in hoc libello illud in primis placet, quod monstrat Principes nostros nihilo inferiores habendos Principibus Italiæ" (Gerhardt edit.), I, pp. 188 seq.

[1] "Libertas est spontaneitas intelligentis, itaque, quod spontaneum est in bruto vel alia substantia intellectus experte, id in homine vel in alia substantia intelligente, altius assurgit et liberum appellatur." "De libertate," Erdmann edit., p. 669.

[2] "Jus naturæ methodo scientifica pertractatum," 1740–1749.

[3] *Institutiones juris naturæ et gentium,* "in quibus ex ipsa hominis natura continuo nexu omnes obligationes et jura omnia deducuntur." Halæ Magdeburgicæ 1754.

[4] Wolff, *"Vernünftige Gedanken* von der Menschen Tun und Lassen, zur Beförderung ihrer Glückseligkeit den Liebhabern der Wahrheit mitgeteilt." Fifth edit., Frankfurt and Leipzig, 1736.

[5] "Vernünftige," etc., preface, p. 1: "Unhappy times are the fruit of vice, and happy times the fruit of virtue. Both statements are established in present deed."

[6] "Vernünftige," etc., pp. 78–116.

[7] "Vernünftige," etc., p. 16, § 19. Also §§ 12, 17.

§ 30] LEGAL PHILOSOPHY IN GERMANY 161

law. "Natural law" thus arises upon an ethical basis, and specifically from the sense of duty. The command of nature, "Perfect thyself," "Perfice te ipsum," is at once a direction for physical and moral self-development and the fundamental principle of justice.[1] Duties are divided into those towards ourselves, towards our fellow-men, and towards God.[2] But a duty also involves a right; and man may claim respect for these rights because the right is involved in the duty,[3] and indeed is an issue thereof. Hence human duties have their correlatives in inherent and inalienable human rights.[4] Compulsory duties fall to the province of law and justice.[5] The principle is "quod jure tuo tibi non vis fieri ab altero, id nec alteri faciendum esse, et quod jure vis fieri, id alteri quoque faciendum." [6]

The State arises from contract,[7] its object is to promote peace, security, and the self-sufficiency of all its members, "sufficientia;" and to grant abundantly, "abundantia," the satisfaction of the needs and conveniences of life. The common weal, "salus civitatis," rests upon the enjoyment of a contented life of peace and security.[8] This conception of self-content introduces an unexpected idyllic flavor into the philosophy of law. The practical importance of Wolff's philosophy is due to its acceptance as a philosophic foundation of an enlightened absolutism, pervaded by the spirit of ethical discipline and a closely regulated paternalism.

[1] See "Jus Naturæ," P. I., §§ 173, 609; "Institutiones," etc., § 36.
[2] "Institutiones," P. I., chaps. IV, V, VI.
[3] "Jus Naturæ," P. I., §§ 170, 608 seq.; "Institutiones," P. I., chaps. IV, V, VI.
[4] "Jus Naturæ," P. I., §§ 23 seq., 64, 72; chaps. II, III, IV.
[5] "Inst.," P. I., chaps. III seq.
[6] "Inst.," P. I., chap. III, § 73.
[7] "Inst," §§ 972 and 836.
[8] "Inst.," §§ 972 and 836, 87, 837.

The emancipation of the third estate was brought about by three distinct factors; as the demand of revolutionary violence, sponsored philosophically by Rousseau in his "Discours"; as the free concession of monarchs concerned in the welfare of their subjects, brought about by Wolff's philosophy; and in compliance with the demands of justice as theoretically formulated by Kant in his conception of the legally constituted State. These three factors — arbitrary injustice, benevolence, and an ethical sense of justice — formed the psychological motives which led to the establishment of the liberty and rights of the third estate, and to the recognition in modern times of an independent citizen-class.

3: FREDERICK THE GREAT. Frederick the Great (1712–1786) has left his impress upon legal philosophy through his writings, through the principles which he applied as a ruler, and through the code of the common law of Prussia compiled at his instigation. In the "Antimachiavel (1739),"[1] Frederick combats Machiavelli's "Il Principe." As a criticism it fails of its purpose in that Frederick shows no appreciation of the Italian author as a distinctive type of the Renaissance; but his philosophic grasp of governmental institutions is clearly shown. He expresses his firm opposition to the self-centered attitudes held by the princes of his time. His own position is summed up in his familiar saying that "the prince is not the absolute ruler of his people but its

---

[1] This is printed in French in the "Oeuvres de Frédéric le Grand," Vol. VIII, Berlin 1848, pp. 59–162: "L'Antimachiavel ou examen du prince de Machiavel"; and with this, pp. 163–299 "Refutation du prince de Machiavel." One edition, Amstelædami 1743, is edited in Latin by Johannes Fridericus Behrendt, and is dedicated to Frederick the Great. Its title is "Anti-Machiavellus, sive specimen disquisitionum ad principem Machiavelli."

foremost servant";[1] the prince is the protector of justice.[2] [3] The same thought, that the welfare of the State does not turn upon the interests and desires of its ruler, but upon the consideration of an organically united people, pervades his earlier work: "Considérations sur l'état du corps politique de l'Europe," as well as his later works: "Miroir des princes"[4] (1744), "Mémoires pour servir à l'histoire de la maison de Brandebourg"[5] (1751), and the "Essai sur les formes du gouvernement et sur les devoirs des souverains"[6] (1777). He became an exemplar to princes by replacing the inconsiderate self-seeking of the absolute ruler

[1] "It is true that the sovereign, far from being the absolute master of the people who are under his rule, is but their foremost servant." "Oeuvres," Vol. VIII, pp. 65 seq., "Antimachiavellus," cap. I: "Rex tantum abest, ut pleni arbitrii dominus sit populorum dictioni suæ subjectorum, ut primi tantum *magistratus* locum tueatur."

[2] "One may then say that it is justice that should be made the chief concern of the sovereign; it is the welfare of the people that should determine what he is to prefer above all other interests." "Oeuvres," Vol. VIII, p. 65. "Antimachiavellus," chap. I: "In justitia igitur administranda maxima Principiis cura versatur, commoda ergo, quibus præest, populorum, omnibus aliis utilitatum rationibus præferet."

[3] "Mémoires de Brandebourg," "Oeuvres," Vol. I, p. 123: "A prince is the first servant and the first magistrate of the State."

[4] "Miroir des princes ou instruction du roi pour le jeune duc Charles-Eugène de Würtemberg," "Oeuvres," Vol. IX, Berlin 1848, pp. 1-7.

[5] I am using the edition in three volumes, Berlin 1846. The "Mémoires" also appear in Vol. I of the "Oeuvres de Fréderic le Grand," Berlin 1846. Their contents are mainly cultural and historical.

[6] "Oeuvres," Vol. IX, pp. 193–210; particularly pp. 199-201; pp. 200 seq.: "The prince is to the society which he governs what the head is to the body; he should see, think, and act for the whole community in order to secure all available advantage."

by the ideal of a monarch inspired by a consciousness of the important duties of his exalted position. His political views are in harmony with his general system of ethics, from which doubtless they arose. In his "Épître au maréchal Keith" he sets forth that the pre-eminent value of virtue lies in its disinterested exercise and not in its extraneous advantage.[1]

Frederick did not stop at theory but exemplified his principles in his actions. His reign was dignified throughout by the fundamental purpose to strengthen Prussia. He was able by means of necessary wars to make Prussia a respected figure in the European concert of nations. In his internal policy he carried forward various governmental measures, pursuing them with extraordinary energy. He promoted the development of the economic and intellectual resources of the country, maintained justice and order, increased the comfort of his subjects, and improved and extended their productive activities. Frederick became the first successful defender of the form of government not very happily styled "enlightened despotism or absolutism" — for the despot ever remains the tyrannical ruler, while Frederick was an absolutist cherishing the interests of his people. He had a care for freedom of thought and conscience, and encouraged a more enlightened view of political offenses. He became the sponsor for the intellectual culture of his day.

The Prussian code, "Landrecht," which was completed and introduced (1794) after Frederick's death, was the first attempt to combine the principles of Roman law with the Teutonic legal attitude, and served as a model for later efforts. Despite its spirit of benevolent paternalism and its somewhat needless argumentative exposition, the Prussian code is a notable contribution to

[1] "Oeuvres," Vol. X, Berlin 1894, pp. 194–203.

legislation in that it is permeated with the spirit of justice. It is a law considerate of conditions, awarding to each his due, and inspired with that spirit of freedom of conscience[1] that leaves to the individual ample scope for social and intellectual initiative. The Prussian code practically solved the avowed purpose of providing "good and fair laws, clearly and definitely drawn." It is an organic document, inspired by a singleness of purpose. Its language is clear, simple, and intelligible, very different from the technical phraseology of modern German law. Owing to these advantages of content and form, the principles and definitions of the Prussian "Landrecht" entered into the consciousness of the people. The code formed a legislation for the people, while the present German Civil Code ("Das Bürgerliche Gesetzbuch") will ever remain the special property of jurists.

§ 31. *Mercantilists and Physiocrats.* 1: THE SYSTEM OF COLBERT. From the time when political economy began to be a science to the days of Smith and Ricardo, its classical representatives, the various systems exhibit errors and misleading deductions in detail as well as in general theoretical and practical issues. But they had the advantage over the economic science of today in recognizing that the prosperity of economic relations depends upon property;[2] that the subject of economics is national wealth; and that national economics must accept the national welfare as its first and chief concern. The misleading, artificial and false notion that human needs furnish the basis for a science of economics first appeared towards the end of the nineteenth and the

[1] Freedom of conscience is specifically guaranteed by the Prussian "Landrecht," Vol. II, Tit. 11, §§ 30 seq.; Tit. 12, §§ 10, 11. See also Vol. I, Tit. 4, § 9.

[2] See *Berolzheimer*, "Das Vermögen," Hirth's Ann. 1904, pp. 437–441.

beginning of the twentieth century, a period of feeble philosophic insight and misapplied constructive effort.

So far back as the mercantile system associated with the name of Colbert — which prevailed from the sixteenth to the end of the eighteenth century — the leading question was that of national welfare; and the increase of the assets of the people was regarded as the worthiest purpose of economics. Accordingly an attempt was made to determine the fundamental factors of prosperity. In those days men proceeded not upon scientific or theoretical arguments, but upon a consideration of practical ends. Princes needed money to carry on wars and to meet the luxury of extravagant courts. For the mercantile system national prosperity was equivalent to a full treasury for State and Court; and the primary problem, as likewise the worthiest object of economics, was to bring prosperity and gold to the country. Out of this need grew the protection of those days — a favoring of trade and of the productive industries, and likewise the restrictive policy, the interdiction of exportation of raw materials and precious metals. The economic life was not conceived as that of a living organism but as a mighty reservoir to supply the public and private expenditures of the rulers.

The principles of this political policy were not theoretically taught but practically followed. Of the literary contributions, the so-called "political testaments," of which there are three, should be mentioned; one is attributed to CARDINAL RICHELIEU (1585-1642); another to COLBERT (1619-1683); and a third to LOUVOIS (1641-1691).[1] The genuineness of the first is disputed; the

---

[1] "Testament politique du Cardinal-duc de Richelieu," 1688. The edition before me is the eighth, in two volumes, The Hague 1740.

"Testament politique de Jean Baptiste Colbert," The Hague 1693.

§ 31] MERCANTILISTS AND PHYSIOCRATS 167

other two were composed by SANDRAS DE COURTILZ,[1] and are more in the nature of questionable historical sketches than of political works.[2] In the ninth chapter of the "testament," attributed to Colbert, the ruler is urged to win the regard of his subjects;[3] but the precept leads to no notable consequences.

2: QUESNAY AND OTHER PHYSIOCRATS. The physiocrats,[4] particularly QUESNAY (1694–1774), the founder of this school, transferred the position of the Stoics to the theory of economic forces. Just as Spinoza, in so far as he is consistent, applied the laws of nature to the conduct of men and to "natural law," just as more recently Gumplowicz looked upon the individual as coming under the dominion of objective laws, so Quesnay believed in natural laws, by virtue of which the economic conditions and changes were definitely determined. Such a naturalistic conception tends to favor fatalism and determinism and a policy of resignation. For if material laws constitute the decisive factors affecting the growth and nature of human effort, the individual becomes the helpless and impotent plaything of natural

"Testament politique du Marquis de Louvois," 1693. The edition I am using is Cologne 1695; in that Part I, pp. 1–381, give a purely historical exposition.

[1] *R. v. Mohl*, "Die Geschichte und Literatur der Staatswissenschaften," 3 vols., p. 405.

[2] *Colbert's* "Testament" bears in the very title the remark: "Testament pol. . . . in which appears all the events of the reign of Louis le grand up to the year 1684. With remarks on the government of the kingdom." The first six chapters are historical, and the others contain not much else.

[3] Chapter IX treats of the love which the monarch owes to his subjects (and also of taxes!). See p. 444: "A prince should seek to reign in the hearts of his subjects rather than to subdue their wills by the fear of his authority."

[4] See *Turgot's* chief work, "Réflexions sur la Formation et la Distribution des Richesses."

forces, — a passive instrument of a universal natural order. Quesnay, however, used the assumption of an all-conditioning "natural law" as an incentive to effort, as a means for establishing an intellectual ideal and for determining the measures which shall advance men towards that ideal. This aspect of the physiocratic system favors the suspicion that their "natural" economics was something different from what its literal interpretation seemed to indicate; and such is really the case. The basis of the physiocratic position is negation. It is primarily a protest against the system of protection and trade restriction of the mercantilists. For the correct comprehension of this system an introductory consideration is necessary. Quesnay's doctrine holds that the effort of rulers and their officials to regulate the economic life according to their standards are futile and pernicious, for no human interference can permanently and enduringly influence the operation of natural laws and the prescribed order and relation of economic forces. Instead of attempting to correct such natural laws, the proper goal is to place economics in harmony with them; thereby will the "ordre naturelle" be achieved. Such a condition would be the most favorable, for it would be in accord with "natural law."[1] Thus interpreted, the physiocratic doctrine becomes an economic declaration of independence directed against the protective and exclusive dominance of self-seeking monarchical rule.[2]

The doctrine of the dominance of natural law in human affairs is the "illusion" by means of which the

---

[1] "The physical laws which constitute the natural order most advantageous for the human race and which confirm the natural law of all men." . . . *Quesnay*, "Oeuvres," by A. Oncken, p. 645.

[2] *Bauer*, "Zur Entstehung der Physiokratie," emphasizes that the views of the physiocrats "grew upon the soil of the Revolution."

economic freedom of the citizens or subjects, as against the authority of the monarch, was first explicitly realized. From this follows the fundamental position of the physiocrats that the State should in no manner interfere with economic life, but should permit freedom of unrestrained competition: "The natural safeguard of business lies in the free and unrestrained competition that secures for every people the largest possible number of buyers and sellers, and the most advantageous price for its sales and purchases." "La police naturelle du commerce est donc la concurrence libre et immense, qui procure à chaque nation le plus grand nombre possible d'acheteurs et de vendeurs, pour lui assurer le pris le plus avantageux dans ses ventes et dans ses achats."[1] In general the State should limit its activity to the protection of the country from external attack, and to the security of law within its borders. The watchword of the physiocrats is contained in the phrase of MIRABEAU (1715–1789): "Laissez faire et laissez passer."[2] Agriculture[3] was conceived to be the root of national

[1] *Quesnay*, "Oeuvres," by A. Oncken, p. 656.

[2] *Oncken*, "Geschichte der Nationalökonomie," I, p. 404. *Mirabeau*, "L'ami des Hommes," III, chaps. 3 and 5. In the latter the removal of restrictions is demanded by reason of justice and utility (pp. 218 seq., 290–292). The principle of justice is that formulated by Thomasius: "Do not to another what you would not have another do unto you" (p. 218).

The Physiocrats believed that the course of trade was best left to organize itself, and, too optimistically, considered that self-interest and justice were in most cases identical. *J. Bonar,* "Philosophy and Political Economy," p. 145.

[3] *Quesnay*, Article "Fermiers," Extrait de l'Encyclopédie (*Quesnay*, "Oeuvres par Oncken," p. 159): "Farmers are those who establish and give value to the wealth of the country and who procure the most essential and valuable resources for the maintenance of the State."

wealth:[1] "La terre est l'unique source des richesses"; the cultivation of the soil must accordingly be relieved of all burdens and taxes. The attempts of TURGOT (1727–1781) at legislative reform in the direction of the physiocratic position failed by reason of the opposition of the French ruling classes. It was in China[2] that Quesnay thought to have found a model State incorporating the physiocratic views; and therefore he looked upon despotism as it existed in the Chinese Empire as the ideal government. It was because of such views that his political influence during the period of the French Revolution was lessened;[3] in England, however, his views found favor.

§ 32. *The Classical Economists: Adam Smith: Ricardo.* 1: INDUSTRIAL DEVELOPMENT: THE ECONOMICS OF ADAM SMITH. The mercantile system looked upon the monarch as the central point of governmental interest;

Art. "Grains" (pp. 193-249). Included therein are "Maximes de Gouvernement Économique"; pp. 233 seq. Industrial labor does not increase wealth (p. 233). The wealth of the tillers of the soil create the wealth of civilization (p. 235). See also pp. 299-304, 305 seq., 379-383, 384-395.

Industry is never productive. See "L'ordre Naturel et Essentiel des Sociétés Politiques" (in regard to the author of this work see below, note 13), Vol. II, chaps. 52, 53.

[1] *Quesnay*, "Oeuvres," p. 337. Also *Mirabeau*, "L'ami des Hommes," I, chaps. 1, 3, 5, 8. One must increase the fertility of agriculture in order to extend the population. "L'ami des Hommes," I, chaps. 1, 2. Also II, chap. VIII, p. 577.

[2] "Despotisme de la Chine" (*Quesnay*, "Oeuvres par Oncken," pp. 563-660). The work of *Mercier de la Rivière*, which was influenced by Quesnay or upon which he collaborated, is of like tendency. See also *Elster* in "Handwörterbuch der Staatswissenschaften," Vol. II, pp. 717 seq. "L'ordre Naturel et Essentiel des Sociétés Politiques." (Anonymous, 2 vols., London 1767.) See especially Vol. I, chaps. 9-12.

[3] *Bauer*, "Zur Entstehung," etc., p. 157, note 2, gives the opinions of Diderot and the Encyclopedists.

accordingly the wealth of the nation was dependent upon the national exchequer. The physiocrats attempted to assimilate human activity to the type of a depersonalized nature; for them the most important occupation was that closest to nature. National prosperity was accordingly made dependent upon agriculture. In England particularly, there emerged a new productive class, the industrial class, whose status was greatly developed and transformed through the introduction of machinery. ADAM SMITH (1723–1790)[1] became its prophet, and Ricardo its most notable advocate. According to Adam Smith, labor is the basis for the satisfaction of human needs and for supplying the necessaries and conveniences of life;[2] and free industrial competition becomes the fundamental economic principle.

It may be that unconsciously the political or partisan attitude of the student eventually shapes his economic position. To realize the exceptional significance for

[1] *Adam Smith's* well-known work is "An inquiry into the nature and causes of the *Wealth of Nations*" (5 books), 4 vols., 1776. I cite from the fourth edition, Basle 1801. Lectures on justice, police, revenue, and arms. Delivered in the University of Glasgow by Adam Smith. Reported by a student in 1763 and edited by Edwin Cannan, Oxford 1896. (See Article, "Adam Smith," in Handwörterbuch der Staatswissenschaften, Vol. 6, p. 756.)

[2] "Wealth of Nations," Vol. I, p. 1. "The annual labor of every nation is the fund which originally supplies it with all the necessaries and conveniences of life which it annually consumes, and which consist always either in the immediate produce of that labor, or in what is purchased with that produce from other nations."

Hence the importance of studying the organization of labor and the best division of labor to increase productivity. See "Wealth of Nations," Book I, chaps. 1–3, and "Lectures by Adam Smith," edited by Cannan, pp. 161–173.

A further source of national wealth is thrift. See *Skarzynski*, "Adam Smith als Moral Philosoph," etc., Berlin 1878, p. 372, where he particularly emphasizes this source of national wealth.

economic philosophy of Adam Smith and Ricardo, it is necessary to appreciate how enormously the economic influence of industry has been extended and developed since their day, and to appreciate further that the intervening political development has been one vast economic struggle. The conflict is twofold: the struggle of industrial capital for supremacy and recognition in law and economics, and the economic emancipation of the industrial laborer.

The interests of the rapidly developing industries of England were directed not alone to the provision of the needs of home consumption, but also to the extension and conquest of a world-market. For this there was needed the protection of the State against hostile attacks, and a guaranty of peace and of the trade and commerce that flourish under peace. There was needed also a legal protection from within; for the free circulation of industrial products requires a prompt and certain justice. There were needed cheap provisions for the masses; for the smaller the expenditure upon which the laborer can supply his livelihood, the lower, other things being equal, may his wages be maintained, and the more favorable will be the competitive industrial condition; hence the corn tax, which raised the price of bread, was abolished. Finally there was needed freedom of contract to place the capitalists in the position of vantage as against the economically weak laborer. Such, in outline, are the essential positions upon which the advocates of free trade since the days of Adam Smith base their economic demands. The free traders demand a State of negative legal function, "Rechtsstaat," so that industrial interests may flourish. The anti-protectionist views of the physiocrats supported the political policies demanded by English industrialism. In view of Adam Smith's personal acquaintance with Quesnay, it is possible that he was influenced by the physiocrats; it may, however, be that he derived his economic position directly from the "natural law" of the preceding school;[1] yet the question has but an historic interest. In reality Adam Smith's doctrine of economic freedom of opportunity formed a new protectionism in behalf of working capital, especially of industry, including trade. While previously, prohibition or restriction of trade sought the economic protection of privileged industrial classes, industrial freedom was now to be made further serviceable by protecting class interests. This principle of the classical school was fundamental and distinctive; and its importance is not altered by the fact that Adam Smith regarded a protective tariff as justified [2] under certain conditions. The protection of industry, and of working capital in particular, under the plea of industrial freedom, was not a pure and undisguised expression of class interest, but was made to assume the illusory form of a plea for justice. According to Adam Smith and his school, the economic freedom that makes possible free competition is a fundamental and natural right. "All systems either of preference or of restraint, therefore, being thus completely taken away, the obvious and simple system of natural liberty establishes itself of its own accord. Every man, so long as he does not violate the laws of justice, is left perfectly free to pursue his own interest in his own way, and to bring both his industry and capital into competition with those of any other man, or order of men."[3]

[1] *Hasbach*, "Untersuchungen über Adam Smith," p. 207, and (in connection with *Hasbach*) *W. Ed. Bierman*, "Staat und Wirthschaft," p. 61.

[2] Book IV, chap. 2. See also *Schüller*, "Die klassische Nationalökonomie und ihre Gegner," pp. 59 seq.; and *W. Ed. Bierman*, "Staat," etc., pp. 64 seq., 75.

[3] "Wealth of Nations," Book IV, chap. 9 (Vol. 3, p. 308), and in other places.

174 CIVIC EMANCIPATION [Ch. V

2: RICARDO. The formulation of the principle of industrial freedom as one of justice is emphasized by RICARDO[1] (1772–1823). In his theoretical views and economic position[2] he agrees entirely with Adam Smith, and advances the same arguments. He, too, stands for the economic liberty of the individual and for non-interference of the State in the affairs of economics. His importance consists in his position as a pioneer in establishing an economic order on the basis of natural law. The advocates of natural law had assumed its existence, and on this assumption had founded what to them seemed a just model State. In a similar spirit Ricardo, as an economic philosopher, undertakes to outline a natural economic order and to determine the natural laws of economics, which were also to be the laws of justice. Ricardo represented the economic philosophy of natural law *par excellence*; Adam Smith prepared the foundations therefor, but it remained for Ricardo to complete the structure.

[1] *Schmoller*, "Die Gerechtigkeit in der Volkswirthschaft," 1880 (first appearance in Schmoller's "Jahrbuch") Vol. V, 1881, p. 19; and reprinted in Schmoller "Zur Sozial-und Gewerbepolitik der Gegenwart" (Reden und Aufsätze), Leipzig, 1890, p. 205. He aptly says:

"No one was more convinced than Adam Smith, Turgot, and some of their true disciples, that the reforms which they demanded would bring about a more absolutely just distribution of property. The faith in the justice of their demands was the strong point of the economics of 'natural law.' It is as a logical consequence of 'natural freedom and justice' that Adam Smith demanded free trade and unrestricted commerce. Free individual competition. . . . is presented by Ricardo, the most distinguished disciple of Adam Smith, as a demand of justice towards all working men." See also *Berolzheimer* in "Hirth's Annalen," 1904, p. 523.

[2] His chief work is "Principles of Political Economy and Taxation." The edition from which I cite is "The works of David Ricardo" by *McCulloch*, London 1846. (See the introduction by the editor on Ricardo's life and writings, pp. XV–XXXIII.)

An attempt to trace the complex economic life back to a relatively small group of economic laws, and to combine in a simple formula the intricate relations involved, cannot cover all concrete situations. Reality presents an indefinite number of grades and shades. This intricacy of actual relations Ricardo did not ignore. On the basis of his commercial experience he had occasion to confirm what he well knew, that the natural value and price of every article of economic trade were subject to large fluctuations. But Ricardo's method was not to determine statistically the average of the actual fluctuations in value, and to establish an ideal average of the just range of prices. On the contrary he undertook in a purely deductive fashion to determine their natural values. His procedure suggests that of the physicist, who does not determine the law of gravity empirically, nor questions the correctness of the law which he deduces, because in the actual phenomena, the law of gravity in consequence of friction does not strictly apply. Every fluctuation of the market price, as compared with the natural value and price, is based upon the effect of supply and demand. Under fluctuating conditions the market price varies above the natural price, according to the relation of current demand and supply. If conditions were steady, and supply and demand remained in a state of balance, then the market price would coincide with the natural price and value.[1] By reason of competition the market price ever tends to approximate to the natural value. In the determination of these natural values Ricardo proceeds upon Adam Smith's principle that only labor produces value. Accordingly labor, that is, the average quantity and quality of labor expended upon an object, determines the value

[1] "Principles," chap. IV.

of economic commodities.¹ The central doctrine of Ricardo's system is his theory of value, which forms the introduction to his "Principles." Adam Smith had taught that a distinction should be made between the "value in use" and the "value in exchange." Apart from objects that cannot be duplicated at pleasure, and to which their rarity lends value — notably works of art — and which form but a small portion of the articles of exchange, and considering only such products as may be indefinitely reproduced, it follows that the value of every useful article of every kind of wares, and "of every commodity or the quantity of any other commodity for which it will exchange," will be determined by the amount of labor necessary for the production of such article without regard to the scale of wages paid for its production.² As part of the labor involved in the production of an article must be considered not alone the labor expended directly upon that article, but also a *pro rata* charge upon the tools, machinery, and manufacturing plant used in its production.³ The natural value of commodities, in so far as machinery is involved, will be influenced by the fixed and working capital and by the permanence of such fixed capital.⁴ Accordingly the cost of production determines the natural value of every commodity, and in this general law of value Ricardo includes the value of labor. The natural value of labor thus consists in the cost of production of the labor itself, that is, in the cost of the necessary maintenance of the laborer and his family.

[1] *"Labour is the foundation of the value of commodities,* of the exchangeable value of all things. This is Ricardo's guiding principle." See "Principles," chap. I, p. 10; chap. IV, p. 47.

[2] "Principles," chap. I, § 1.

[3] "Principles," chap. I, § 3.

[4] "Principles," chap. I, §§ 4, 5.

The natural wage is the equivalent of the minimum cost of livelihood of the laborer necessary for the proper enjoyment of his life and provision for his family.[1] Owing to the law of supply and demand, the market value in Ricardo's opinion can never permanently rise above, or fall below the natural value in terms of labor; and this for the reason that every long-continued increase of the market value of labor above the natural value of labor will result in an increased size of the family, and later an increase in the supply of labor; and on the other hand, any permanent lowering of the market value of labor below the natural price will decimate the ranks of the laborer, and result in a lowered supply of the commodity, labor, and consequently an increase in the market price thereof. This iron wage-law, "eherne Lohngesetz," condemns the laborer permanently to a bare existence wage, to a slavery under productive capital. This explicit and definite fixation of the natural wage, and the resulting legitimized exclusion of the great mass of the people from the good things of life, has been decidedly influential in awakening the class consciousness of the proletariat, in leading laborers to form organizations, so that they may successfully demand their just share of the profits of their labor. Indeed the position of Adam Smith and Ricardo, that labor alone produces value, supports the position of the socialists in their demand for an adequate compensation for the wage earner. In the development of his economic

---

[1] In his essay on *Ricardo* in the "Hand. der Staatswis.," *Diehl* notes that Ricardo does not regard the natural wage as the physiological minimum of existence and has not carried out "the ironbound" law of wages consistently. However, the introduction of machinery resulted, for quite a time, in limiting the development of the wages of the industrial laborer to a minimum existence wage. Practice went even beyond theory.

theory, Ricardo endorses Bentham's utilitarian philosophy of which he became an adherent. The position that the self-interest of the individual coincided with the general welfare was for him an indisputable doctrine. The economic philosophy of Ricardo is a utilitarian bourgeois philosophy reduced to simple terms.

3: SAY. J. B. SAY[1] (1767–1832) cannot be regarded as the author of an influential and original economic theory. His relation to his eminent predecessors, Adam Smith and Ricardo, is similar to that of Lasalle to Marx. Say popularized the teachings of the English free trade school and introduced them into France. In a measure opposed to his English predecessors, Say repeatedly emphasizes that the desire for gain is not the exclusive motive to be considered in the economics of human affairs.

4: MALTHUS. The name of MALTHUS[2] (1766–1834) is associated with an important factor in the growth of population — a factor furthermore entailing grievous consequences. The chief work of Malthus, "An Essay on the Principle of Population," contains the important statement that population has a tendency to increase more rapidly than the means of subsistence necessary to its maintenance. This is the Malthusian law.[3]

[1] Say's chief works are: *Traité D'Économie Politique*, ou Simple Exposition de la Manière dont se Forment, se Distribuent et se Consomment les Richesses," 3 vols., first edition, Paris 1880. I cite from the fifth edit., Paris 1826. "Catéchisme D'Économie Politique." "Cours Complet D'Économie Politique," 6 vols., Paris 1828-29.

[2] On the principles of the Malthusian law in *Adam Smith* see *Skarzynski*, "Adam Smith als Moralphilosoph und Schöpfer der National-ökonomie." Berlin 1878, pp. 362-364.

[3] "Supposing the present population equal to a thousand millions, the human species would increase as the numbers 1, 2, 4, 8, 16, 32, 64, 128, 256, and subsistence as 1, 2, 3, 4, 5, 6, 7, 8, 9." (Bk. I, chap. II, p. 15.)

Moral restraint, as well as vice and poverty, are the factors which will equalize the increase of population and adjust it to the available means of subsistence.[1]

It is as an application of this idea that the Neo-Malthusians advocate the restriction of the family — the so-called "two-child" policy — and in several countries, notably in France, this has checked the increase of the population to such an extent as is likely in the course of time to be momentous for the manning of those countries for defense. The teachings of Malthus are also responsible for the misleading doctrines which for a considerable time sought to check the increase of the population in the interest of public welfare.

Malthus represents a transition from the classic school to the modern social-ethical movement, in that he emphasizes altruism in economic policy as an equalizing and mitigating measure. He recognizes the hardships and injuries that arise from the operation of economic self-interest, and studies the mutual relations of self-interest and altruism.[2] He belongs to the new movement in national economics for the additional reason that he pursues his investigations upon an historical and empirical foundation.

[1] In Book I, chap. II (pp. 33, 34), Malthus presents the following propositions: "1. Population is necessarily limited by the means of subsistence; 2. Population invariably increases where the means of subsistence increase, unless prevented by some very powerful and obvious checks; 3. These checks, and the checks which repress the superior power of population, and keep its effects on a level with the means of subsistence, are all resolvable into moral restraint, vice, and misery." Malthus repeats this principle literally in Book II, chap. XIII, Vol. II, p. 216, in the last chapter of his historical considerations.

[2] "An Essay on the Principles of Population," Book IV, chap. X, "Of the Direction of our Charity." Also Bk. IV, chap. I, "Of Moral Restraint."

§ 33. *Kant, Fichte, Schopenhauer.* 1: KANT. (*a*) The Historical Position of Kant. In the consideration of KANT's [1] (1724–1804) philosophy of law and ethics a distinction must be made between the material content and the form — meaning by the latter the course and the procedure by means of which the result is constructively obtained. In its content, Kant's philosophy of law is influenced by Thomasius, Leibnitz, and, despite Kant's antagonism to Wolff's hedonism, by Wolff himself. In its form, Kant's practical philosophy is affiliated with the position of "natural law," and the interpretation derived therefrom, and bears traces of the distinctive Kantian method as embodied in the "Critique of Pure Reason." Kant's ethics is but a secularization of the ethics of Christianity, which, indeed, is hardly improved by his formulation. In developing his practical philosophy, Kant incorporated Thomasius' [2] philosophy of law, including his definition of justice; he also built upon the "vir bonus" of Leibnitz — characterized as "sapiens" and "justus." He was antagonistic to the hedonism of Wolff and to the utilitarianism of Hobbes; for these doctrines seemed to him too insecure, and the emotion of happiness too subjective and intangible, to afford a durable basis for an ethical system. In thus definitely holding aloof from the hedonistic principle, Kant's ethics and legal

---

[1] The following works of *Kant* are here pertinent: "Idee zu einer allgemeinen Geschichte in weltbürgerlicher Absicht, "1784. "Grundlegung zur Metaphysik der Sitten," 1785. "Kritik der Praktischen Vernunft," 1788. "Ueber den Gemeinspruch: Das mag in der Theorie richtig sein, taugt aber nicht für die Praxis," 1793, II. "Vom Verhältnis der Theorie zur Praxis im Staatsrecht," "Zum ewigen Frieden," 1795. "Metaphysische Anfangsgründe der Rechtslehre," 1797. I cite from the edition in 10 vols, Vols. 4, 5, Leipzig 1838.

[2] See above.

philosophy pursued a course diametrically opposed to that of Wolff; ethics regained its objective foundation, and was released from an inadequate psychological motive — the pursuit of happiness. Kant returned to the older view that the essence of ethics lies in sacrifice — a view developed by Christianity in the spiritual form of the altruistic sentiment of neighborly love;[1] and he interprets disinterestedness as a moral duty. In his philosophy of government Kant rejected the theories of popular welfare and paternalism, and emphasized the function of the State as an institution of law and justice. In these considerations he showed the influence of Rousseau.

(b) Kant's Ethics. The "Grundlegung der Metaphysik der Sitten" aims to define morals in so large a philosophic sense as to include the concept of law.[2] The "vir bonus" served Leibnitz as his point of departure; similarly Kant begins with "what alone may be considered unreservedly good," namely, good will or intent. This good will, "though with reservations and limitations," is expressed in the concept that "occupies a foremost place in the judgment of conduct, and conditions all relations" — the concept of duty. Actions acquire moral value only when they arise, not from inclination, but from a sense of obligation. An action performed for an ulterior purpose, or in response to selfish impulse, cannot be called moral. Moral value may be ascribed only to actions resulting "from the conception of a self-sufficient law." Such direction of the will towards the good, determined through appreciation of the nature of principle or law, is possible only to "rational beings."[3] But what is the nature of the principle itself? "As I

---

[1] See above, § 20.
[2] "Grundlegung zur Metaphysik der Sitten," Vol. 4, p. 8.
[3] "Grundlegung," pp. 10, 11, 14, 16, 19, 20, 28.

have deprived the will of all impulses which it might have obtained through dependence upon a specific law, there is nothing left but the one motive of loyalty to law itself. This, indeed, is the only proper motive for the will to act upon; in other words, I should never so act that I cannot will that my rule of conduct may become a universal law." [1]

The conception of a principle that determines the will is called by Kant "a command" or a "formal command," which implies that the principle thus conceived is, as to its content, an *imperative*. The imperatives are of two kinds; the hypothetical imperative presents the necessity of an act as a means towards a desired end; "the categorical imperative is that which presents an act as of itself objectively necessary,[2] without reference to any ulterior end." This categorical imperative refers only to the form and to the principle in virtue of which the act results; it is the imperative of the moral.[3] As the categorical imperative comprises "in addition to the law, the obligation that the rule of conduct shall be in accord with the law, while the law involves no limiting condition, there remains nothing beyond the law in general to which the rule of conduct shall conform." The term "maxim," or rule of conduct, represents the subjective principle of action and is to be distinguished from the objective principle, which the practical law specifies. Hence the conception of the categorical imperative involves its content; and this reads: "Act so that your rule of conduct permits you to desire that it may become a universal law." [4]

[1] "Grundlegung," p. 20. "Act according to a principle which may also serve as a general law." ("Metaphysische," etc. "Collected Works," 5, p. 25.)
[2] "Grundlegung," p. 35.
[3] "Grundlegung," p. 38.
[4] "Grundlegung," p. 43.

If such categorical imperative is to govern the human will, there must exist a supreme principle which is a "purpose unto itself," and thus constitutes an objective principle for the will, and accordingly may become a universal practical law. The basis of this principle lies in itself, and constitutes the self-sufficient character of the rational nature. "The rational nature is a purpose unto itself." Pursuant to this rational basis man considers his own existence; hence the action upon principle becomes the subjective principle of human action. By virtue of the same basis every other rational creature forms the conception of its own existence. The principle thus becomes at once an objective one, from which "as the supreme practical principle we should be able to derive all the laws of the will." The practical imperative therefore reads: "Act so that you treat humanity, whether expressed in your own person, or in the person of another, ever as an end, never merely as a means."[1] In other words, respect yourself and your neighbor as a rational being, as one amenable to culture. Here may be detected the germ of the "Kulturstaat," as outlined by Fichte, and elaborated by Hegel.

In Kant's view the categorical imperative becomes valid only on the assumption of human freedom. The autonomy of the will is the supreme principle of morality; it is that "quality which makes the will a law unto itself," independent of the nature of the objects of its desire. Hence the principle of autonomy is "never to choose otherwise than that the rule of conduct of your choice may likewise be willed as a general law."[2] To be autonomous the human will must be free. "The conception of freedom is the key to the understanding

[1] "Grundlegung," pp. 52 seq.
[2] "Metaphysische," etc., pp. 57, 66.

of the autonomy of the will." [1] "The difference between the laws of nature, to which the will is subject, and a nature subject to a will, consists in the fact that in the latter case objects must be the causes of the concepts determining the will, while in the former the will is the cause of the objects, the causal relation thereof being resident in the capacity for pure reason, which, on that account, may also be called a practical reason." [2] In other words, by virtue of the rational will, man is master of himself, a free man, free.

Kant thus determines the relation between the law of morality and free will. The existence of the moral law — which has but one meaning if men are capable of pursuing it — leads to the inference of the free will; for freedom is the material assumption of the moral law. "Freedom is the basis of man-made moral law, and the latter becomes the means of knowing freedom." [3] The freedom of the will cannot be inferred or established theoretically, but is a practical inference from the very existence of the moral law.

(c) Kant's Philosophy of Law. Law is "the aggregate of the conditions under which the arbitrary will of one individual may be combined with that of another under a general inclusive law of freedom." [4] Law in contrast to morality thus refers to external practical affairs. Accordingly the general principle of justice reads: "So conduct your affairs that the free use of your will is compatible under a general law with the freedom of everyone else." [5]

[1] "Metaphys.," etc., pp. 73-93.
[2] "Kritik der praktischen Vernunft," "Collected Works," IV, p. 149.
[3] *Falckenberg*, "Geschichte der neueren Philosophie," fifth edit., p. 342.
[4] "Metaphys.," etc., "Complete Works," V, p. 30.
[5] "Metaphys.," etc., p. 31.

According to Kant a State is "an association of men under a system of laws."[1] Were it not for their distinctive phraseology, Kant's expressions[2] on the origin of the State would read like the words of Rousseau: "The action whereby the people constitute themselves into a State, but in reality form only the conception thereof — the conception determining how the conformity to law shall be thought of — is the original contract. By such contract, each and all of the people give up their external freedom in order to resume it again as members of a common body — of the people considered as a State. It is not proper to say that the individual for a purpose has sacrificed to the State a part of his inherent liberty, but that he has abandoned a crude lawless freedom, in order again to resume it unimpaired in a law-abiding dependence, in a legal condition — and this because such dependence originates from his own law-determining will." This in substance is Rousseau's "Social Contract."[3] But the difference between the position of "natural right" in Kant, and in pre-Kantians, consists in that in the legal philosophy of the former, the development from the pre-legal condition — a state of lawlessness, "status justitia vacuus,"— to the civic condition which the State brings about, is an issue of reason, a conception of the understanding.[4] A further merit of Kant is his rejection of Hobbes' view that in entering the State men give up all their rights.[5] This Spinoza had already set forth in his view that the free-

[1] "Metaphys.," etc., p. 145.
[2] "Metaphys.," etc., p. 148.
[3] See above, § 29.
[4] "Metaphys.," etc., pp. 144 seq.; "Vom Verhältnis der Theorie," etc., "Collected Works," V, p. 391.
[5] The essay "Vom Verhältnis," etc., bears in its title the words, "against Hobbes." "Collected Works," V, p. 382.

dom of man was necessary to his dignity and is inalienable. Kant solves the problem of legal coercion by holding that by the establishment of the State, human freedom is made secure. This again is the same problem which Rousseau had set himself in the "Contrat Social," and is essentially the same solution. Kant further agrees with Rousseau in regarding this solution as not historically but theoretically applicable.[1]

According to Kant the warrant of legal freedom of each member of the State is implicitly contained in the principle of law, and reaches a general expression in the law. In detail three *a priori* principles[2] form the basis of the legal condition: first, the freedom of every member of the community as a man; second, the equality of each with every other as a subject (as a consequence of this idea of equality, every citizen is eligible to any office, "to every rank of position in the commonwealth to which his talents, his industry, and his fortune may bring him," thus setting aside all hereditary privilege); third, the independence of each member in the State as a citizen. From this follows the right of serving as a legislator. Anyone having a right of vote in legislation becomes a citizen, "citoyen," "Staatsbürger.[3] The conception of the legal State, "Rechtsstaat," finds clear expression in these principles and is furthermore considered under legislation. "The only permanent constitution is that in which the law is supreme and depends

[1] In addition to what has been cited see also "Metaphys.," etc., p. 176: "It is futile to trace the historical origin of this governmental mechanism; that is, one cannot reach the period at which civil society begins."

[2] "These principles are not laws derived from the State as established, but laws determining how the establishment of the State, in accordance with the rational principles of objective human law, is alone possible." "Vom Verhältnis," etc., p. 383.

[3] "Vom Verhältnis," etc., pp. 383–391.

§ 33]   KANT, FICHTE, SCHOPENHAUER   187

on no individual person. The ultimate purpose of all public law is a condition of affairs in which each individual absolutely receives that to which he is entitled."[1]

In the controversy with Hobbes, Kant again distinctly opposes the principle of happiness, "which in fact does not amount to a definite principle," in these words: "The sovereign desires to make the people happy according to his own views, and becomes a despot. The people are unwilling to yield the universal claim to happiness and become rebellious."[2]

In his philosophy of punishment, Kant approves the theory of retribution. "Judicial punishment can never be merely a measure to further the good of another, either of the offender himself or of society, but must always be applied because the law has been violated." Kant distinctly rejects the view of punishment as a means to an end. "Punitive law represents a categorical imperative, and woe to him who pretends to find in the mazes of Hedonism an excuse for exemption from punishment on the ground of a larger advantage. For if justice fails there is no value in human life." "Even if civil society, with the consent of all its members, were to be dissolved, the last murderer confined in prison would first have to be executed."[3]

In the work, "Zum ewigen Frieden," Kant outlines and establishes the preliminary and definite provisions for a permanent peace among nations.[4]

(d) *The Origin and the Purpose of the State.* The philosophy of Kant presents a transition from the period of "natural law" to that of modern legal philosophy. According to the former position the State is established

[1] "Metaphys.," etc., p. 178.
[2] "Vom Verhältnis," etc., p. 397.
[3] "Metaphys.," etc. pp. 166–173.
[4] "Collected Works," IV, pp. 411–466.

by conscious intent. The constitution of the State is to be conceived in analogy with the foundation of an association. Individuals come together and for definite purposes found the State. This position Kant never wholly outgrew; yet his conception is far superior to that of the position of "natural law," in that he undertakes to prove that the State was founded not by human will but by the reason as immanent in human will, the establishment being a response to the demands of reason. The decisive motive thus becomes, not the material welfare which the State is to further, but the ideals and commands of practical reason. By assuming this position Kant solved, from the point of view of "natural law," three difficult and fundamental legal problems of philosophy. First: the foundation of the State appears as an objective necessity. The problem which Spinoza had formulated but failed to solve, namely, the objective conformity of the State and law to nature, is satisfactorily answered. Second: the establishment of legal coercion by the State, which for Rousseau was the decisive problem, Kant disposed of much as Rousseau had done. He concluded that freedom is not destroyed by the State, but is re-established therein, and elevated to true freedom. Third: through these steps the political life of the State is developed. The constitution and legislation of the State proceed not in response to the ends of utility or happiness, but to the idea of freedom. The State, inspired with the spirit of freedom, is one in which there is no form of despotism, but one in which legal rights are protected, "Rechtsstaat." Freedom becomes equivalent to the comprehensive dominion of law; so long as law prevails the dignity of man is secure.

(e) *The Present Significance of Kant's Philosophy.* The question arises as to the present significance of the Kantian philosophy. When a century hence the historian of civilization looks back to our time, he might readily conclude, in view of the many memorial volumes contributed at the beginning of the twentieth century to commemorate the centennial of Kant's philosophy, that we stood completely under the influence of Kant. Such an impression must be resolutely removed. Kant's greatness is limited to his day and generation. Viewed from our present position, Kant's metaphysics must be pronounced fundamentally false; his philosophy of law is that belonging to the outgrown position of the "Rechtsstaat"; his ethics is sound only in its formal trend, that is, in its rejection of Hedonism. The Kantian philosophy presents a dual aspect. It represents at once the beginning of a new era, but more especially the concluding moment, the last great uprising of rationalism in general philosophy, and of the doctrine of "natural law" in legal philosophy. The decline of "natural law," both in its mode of presentation and in its formal content, begins with Kant.

Up to his time philosophy employed the technical language of the scholar. The literature was in Latin or French; though the English wrote in their own language, German was not employed by the Germans. Leibnitz published only some scattered essays in German, and Wolff used the language for such writings as were addressed to a large circle of readers and were not conceived in a strictly scientific temper. Kant made the German language available for philosophy, but his German was not the language of the people, such as characterizes Luther's translation of the Bible. It was the language of the specialist, conceived in Latin, in a Latin style, and, through its abundance of technical terms, removed from the common comprehension. The important problem of post-Kantian philosophy should naturally have been to simplify the philosophic diction, to clarify it, and to

Teutonize it. This mission was accepted only by Schopenhauer, and by those following in his footsteps, such as von Hartmann, Dühring, and Nietzsche; for what, in contrast to the literary philosophy — "Salonsphilosophie" — of Schopenhauer, may be called the scientific tendency of the post-Kantian philosophy of Fichte, Hegel, and the Hegelians, is yet more difficult, abstruse, and artificial in expression. Since the days of Kant the unfortunate tradition has become legitimized in philosophic writings to use such involved language that the uninformed reader acquires a profound respect for the depth of the philosopher; and instead of gaining an impression of the unprofitableness of the philosophic author, he infers his own incapacity to follow so lofty a train of thought. From the days of Kant the fallacy has prevailed that it is not philosophical to write clearly and simply. Consider by way of contrast the pre-Kantian philosophy; when couched in Latin, the language is simple and clear; the French works are even elegant and spirited, and those in English are notably lucid. Until the days of Kant, philosophy was the common property of the educated classes and a source of inspiration for all science; since his day philosophy has become increasingly the specialty of a guild, and has lost in general significance.

These defects in form stand in close relation to the mode of logical procedure of philosophy from Kant to Hegel. Kant was presumably in earnest in attempting to exclude experience and the results of experience from philosophy. Pure or experienceless reason alone was considered adequate to yield philosophic knowledge. Inasmuch as in reality this postulate could not be carried through without condemning philosophy to a barren sterility, and confining it to mere elementary deductions, the results of experience are furtively introduced. They must disown their empirical character by appearing as rational products, by a transformation into the products of reason. This wearisome transformation and the artificial procedure which it necessitates find a welcome instrument in an artificial language; and the legacy of this linguistic artifice in large measure persists in modern philosophical writings, although the present-day philosopher has little need of such contrivances, except perhaps to conceal how meager or how unphilosophically simple is his stock of ideas.

We here reach an additional evidence of decline in much of the post-Kantian philosophy, and particularly in the ethics and the philosophy of law; though this applies with many exceptions, notably that of Hegel's construction of a universal science, upon an historical basis. Pre-Kantian philosophy in large measure derived its data from the rich mine of a many-sided life; it drew its resources from the inexhaustible font of experience. Philosophy was worldly wisdom. The accredited philosophers of the day were for the most part men notable in contemporary movements, responsive to the events of their time, and to the wealth of experience and manifold personal relations of a full life. Military leaders and statesmen, politicians and practical jurists, drew from the wealth of complex experience the positive data from which a philosophic interpretation might be derived. But after Kant, philosophy became, in the main, a specialty; and men wrote upon ethics without knowing human kind, and on the philosophy of law without a thorough knowledge of law; hence the detachment of philosophy from worldly widom and its scholastic development. In due course a reaction set in. A philosophic naturalism came forward, finding its support in the natural sciences, advocating an empiricism which recognized natural laws and natural products alone, and to which man was nothing more than a most delicately organized mechanism. A materialistic empiricism replaced philosophy, and ushered in a period, the conclusion of which we are now witnessing, but which is as yet not wholly superseded. We still suffer from the reaction which followed upon the dissolution of the doctrine of "natural law" and upon the post-Kantian decline of philosophy.

It would thus appear that Kant has slight significance for the present legal philosophy and particularly for economics, which is in large measure being replaced by a wholly practical sociology, with a program of social utilitarianism, seeking the welfare of society. This sociology follows Ihering in viewing the end sought as the purpose of the law. This "social welfare" philosophy is clearly unrelated to the position of Kant. It is in a measure a reinstatement of the position of Wolff, a reconstruction of his paternally regulated State, in which the social spirit of the law takes the place of the benevolence of the absolute monarch and his decrees. In so far as an independent philosophy of law is today recognized, it stands in diametrical opposition to the philosophy of Kant; for the latter is thoroughly rationalistic, *a priori*, based upon pure reason, while the former is inductive and empirical, and proceeds upon the data of history and comparative law.

2: FICHTE (1762–1814). (*a*) *The Position of Fichte.* In the development of Fichte's[1] practical philosophy two

[1] "Johann Gottlieb Fichte's Werke," published by *J. H. Fichte*, vols. 3, 4, 6, 7, Berlin 1845–1846. "Posthumous Works," published by *J. H. Fichte*, 2 vols., Bonn 1834. *"Zurückforderung der Denkfreiheit* von den Fürsten Europas, die sie bisher unterdrückten," Rede aus dem Jahre 1793. ("Collected Works," VI, pp. 3–35.) "Beitrag zur *Berichtigung der Urteile* des Publikums über die französische Revolution," 1793. ("Collected Works," VI, pp. 39–238.) *"Grundlage des Naturrechts* nach Prinzipien der Wissenschaftslehre," 1798.

§ 33] KANT, FICHTE, SCHOPENHAUER 193

periods are clearly distinguishable. In the first period, Fichte as a Kantian reasserts the "Rechtsstaat," the constitutional State, but shows the influence of Rousseau in providing a nullification clause in the civic contract. In the second period Fichte goes beyond the "Rechtsstaat" and regards the State and the members thereof not as fixed and unalterable, but as subject to evolution. Fichte advances from the conception of the State as the embodiment of law, "Rechtsstaat," to the State accepting the mission of culture, "Kulturstaat." In this he anticipates Hegel, and in his consideration of the human race in its entirety, and in its development, he foreshadows Schelling. Equally notable is Fichte's career as a statesman, the awakener of the German national consciousness. The transition from the first to the second period is marked by the formulation of the State of economic protection. Fichte undertakes an economic construction in which the factor of personal dignity, emphasized by Kant, shall be practically embodied in

("Collected Works," Vol. III, Part 2 A, "Zur Rechts- und Sittenlehre," Vol. I, p. 385.) "Das System der Sittenlehre nach den Prinzipien der Wissenschaftslehre," 1798, "Collected Works," IV (Part 2 A, Vol. 2, pp. 1–365). "Der geschlossene Handelsstaat. Ein philosophischer Entwurf als Anhang zur Rechtslehre und Probe einer künftig zu liefernden Politik," 1800. ("Collected Works," Vol. III (II, part A, Vol. I, pp. 388–513.) "Die Grundzüge des gengenwärtigen Zeitalters," 1804. ("Collected Works," Vol. VII, pp. 3–256.) "Reden an die deutsche Nation," 1808. ("Collected Works," VII, pp. 259–499.) "Anhang zu den Reden an die deutsche Nation," written in 1806, but never published independently. ("Collected Works," VII, pp. 503–516.) "Politische Fragmente aus den Jahren 1807, 1813. ("Collected Works," VII, 597–604.) "Das System der Rechtslehre in Vorlesungen," 1812. ("Posthumous Works," II, pp. 493–652.) "Die Staatslehre oder über das Verhältnis des Urstaats zum Vernunftreich in Vorlesungen," gehalten im Sommer, 1813, auf der Universität zu Berlin; published Berlin 1320. ("Collected Works," Vol. IV, pp. 367–600.)

the economic relations. The State must be so organized that each individual may be recognized as an economic factor. In the development of this conception Fichte falls into a strange Utopian socialism.

(b) *Fichte's Philosophy of Law.* FICHTE's "Grundlage des Naturrechts nach Prinzipien der Wissenschaftslehre" was written before the appearance of Kant's "Metaphysische Anfangsgründe der Rechtslehre," and in complete independence of the latter's views. Influenced by Rousseau, Fichte made human freedom central. "Every man is by nature free, and no one but he himself has the right to impose a law upon him." "Every man again becomes free as soon as he so desires, and has the right to withdraw from obligations which he has imposed upon himself." Such are the words in the "Beitrag zur Berichtigung der Urteile des Publikums über die französische Revolution."[1] Freedom and human dignity form the text of this address, in which is demanded "a restitution of the rights of free thought on the part of the rulers of Europe, by whom they had been refused." In speaking of the human conscience, Fichte calls it "the divine spark in human nature that elevates man above the brute creation, and makes him a citizen of the world, of which the first member is God. His conscience commands him directly and unconditionally to will one thing and not to will another — and this freely and of his own volition, without external compulsion." "To be able to think freely is the distinctive difference between the human and the animal mind." "Civil society" is based upon the free act of will of those participating in the common organization.

[1] "Collected Works," VI, pp. 262, 263. *Lasson* in "J. G. Fichte im Verhältnis zu Kirche und Staat," p. 167, comments as follows: "The dominant temper of this work may be most simply indicated by calling it Jacobin, while admitting the presence of other factors."

"Civil legislation becomes valid for the individual only in so far as he freely accepts it" — by what token is immaterial — and "thus freely imposes the law upon himself."[1]

In the "Grundlage des Naturrechts," the influence of Rousseau is in part obscured by the Kantian train of thought. In tracing the origin of the State and the law, and the State as embodying the law, Fichte proceeds upon the model supplied by Kant. The purpose of the conception of law is to provide an association between free individuals. The law must be so formulated that in principle each member of society may be conceived as restricting his external freedom by the exercise of an inner freedom so that all may likewise be free. Hence the obligation to restrict one's individual freedom by reference to the concept of the freedom[2] of all others with whom relations are maintained. Yet this postulate merely sets forth the condition under which alone the State and law are possible. The existence of a law-abiding community depends upon the mutual restraint of the freedom of the component individuals. But this condition of itself is not adequate to the establishment of the State. Its necessity[3] is not yet proven. Such necessity is a postulate of the practical reason. "If reason is to be realized in the world of experience, then it must first be made possible for several rational

---

[1] "Collected Works," VI, pp. 11–13.

[2] "Collected Works," III, pp. 9–11, 17–56, 89. "The deduced relation between rational beings through which each limits his freedom by the consideration of making possible the freedom of others, provided that others likewise will restrict their freedom, may be called the legal relation; and the formula thus enunciated is the principle of law." p. 52.

[3] "Up to this point no absolute reason has been advanced why anyone should accept the legal formula as the law of his own will and action."

beings to live together."[1] Consistently with Fichte's theoretical philosophy,[2] law becomes a condition of individual self-consciousness. The individual cannot become conscious of himself without at the same time positing the existence of other rational beings. For Fichte, as for Kant, law, and through it the State, is the direct product of reason. In contrast to the materialistic conception, the civil contract, by means of which the State is instituted, has no decisive significance. Strictly speaking, it is of formal, not substantive, consequence; it is not constitutive, but declaratory. The civil contract need not necessarily be agreed to; any manner of recognition of the State, even the consent of silence, is sufficient.

The maintenance of law and the State are dependent upon an almighty superhuman will loyal to the principle of law. There must be assumed "a will which becomes an actual power infallibly when it resolves to realize law."[3] There must be a guaranty that within the State no injustice shall fall upon any member thereof. Such guaranty must be absolute, and cannot be resident in any human authority. The absolute efficiency of the guaranty can be secured only by having the law, which is the embodiment of right, automatically make the community sensitive to any arbitrary action, to any injustice to an individual. For this purpose Fichte, following Rousseau, would so organize the State that the civil contract may be nullified. The relation must be so constituted that every injustice, however minute, against an individual shall also, and by the same token, become an injustice against all; that every form of

[1] "Collected Works," III, p. 92.
[2] *Berolzheimer*, "System," etc., Vol. I, pp. 74–89, particularly pp. 87–89.
[3] "Collected Works," III, pp. 92–106.

violation of the civil contract shall, by that very fact, nullify it, and by the very mechanism of the law shall justice be automatically secured.[1]

In theory this automatism of the law is beautifully conceived. To Fichte the State becomes so complete and balanced a construction that any disturbance, however slight, of its equilibrium would bring disaster; and assuredly all would be zealously mindful of the law lest the State be endangered. Viewed practically in consideration of governments and laws as they are, the notion becomes an absurdity in which Fichte's extreme idealism and his insistent pursuit of an idea, once assumed to be correct, have here, as elsewhere, imposed upon his judgment.

The superiority of Fichte's view to the doctrine of natural law consists in his clear recognition of the non-existence of any law antecedent to or outside of the State — that accordingly the assumption of "natural law," of a primitive or original law, serves only as a scientific hypothesis. "There are no primitive or inalienable human rights. Man acquires rights only as a member of a community. Primitive right ('Urrecht') is thus a mere fiction required by science."[2] Thus conceived, the primitive right is, in accord with Kant, the respect of personality, in deference to which man never becomes morally a means, but must be regarded and dealt with as an end. Fichte thus formulates primitive right: "It is the absolute right of the individual to be but a cause or agent,[3] 'Urasache' [that is, not an effect], in the world of experience." As, strictly speaking, outside of the State there is no law, so equally there is no universal citizenship. It is true that Fichte assumes it, but he

[1] "Collected Works," III, pp. 106-111, 120-149, 150-187.
[2] "Collected Works," III, p. 112.
[3] "Collected Works," III, p. 113.

makes of it merely the shadow of a right, limited to the privilege of moving about and asserting one's personality. "The right of the world-citizen consists in the right to walk about freely on earth, and to establish legal associations."[1]

Fichte distinguishes between what is legal and what is moral. The requirements of the law are limited to what is legal; the mechanism of the law, through the right of nullification in the civil contract, makes it incumbent upon the will to desire only what is loyal to the principle of law, and thus automatically supplies the place of a well-disposed will.[2]

In his "System of Ethics according to the Principles of Science," Fichte makes it a moral and conscientious duty of each one to associate himself with others in the State.[3] He makes law, not a self-sufficient product existing for its own sake, but a means towards the moral education of man. The legally constituted State is a matter of necessity. It is in and through the law that men are arrayed against one another, for government itself involves a certain mistrust. In order that the moral ideal may properly contribute to the improvement of man, the State dominated by mere legality must be transformed into the State dominated by rationality. The highest phase of the evolution would be a "community of saints," in which State and Church might be dispensed with as no longer necessary.[4]

(c) *Fichte's Philosophy of Economics.* In his work on "The Closed Commercial State," Fichte develops his economic philosophy. Of its fundamental principles the first is found in Fichte's philosophy of property,

---

[1] "Collected Works," III, p. 384.
[2] "Collected Works," III, pp. 140–142.
[3] "Collected Works," IV, pp. 206 seq., 238 seq.
[4] "System der Sittenlehre," "Collected Works," IV, pp. 238–241.

in his "Grundlage des Naturrechts." He there assumes that the general civil contract contains a contract of guaranty of property, and in addition, a guaranty of protection. Each man stakes his entire possessions as a pledge that he will not infringe upon the property of others; but the absolute inalienable possession of all men consists in their ability to live by their labor. If anyone cannot earn a livelihood by his labor, then, in his case, the property contract is broken, and he is no longer bound thereby; it becomes void, and with it, the general civil contract is set aside.[1]

A second fundamental principle arises from the transfer to the economic field of Kant's doctrine of the dignity of the individual; thus transferred, it follows in an economic respect that every man must be regarded as a self-sufficient individual, as a personal end. It must further be noted that in Fichte's time the liberal agitation arising in France was spreading throughout Europe, and that the ideas of the French Revolution deeply impressed him, as appears in his writings and in the influence of Rousseau upon his philosophy.

Upon these principles Fichte developed his economic philosophy. The essential postulate of the closed commercial State is that the State must guarantee everyone the right of existence. "The purpose of human activity is to enable one to live; and all who have been granted life by nature have the same claim to this privilege. The division of rights must thus first be so arranged that all may be able to exist. Live and let live!"[2] Fichte, however, does not confine himself to this postulate, but sets forth as a desirable end an equal division of the means of subsistence among all members of

---

[1] "Grundlage des Naturrechts," "Collected Works," III, pp. 195 seq., 210 seq.

[2] "Der Geschlossene Handelsstaat," "Collected Works," III, p. 402.

the industrial State.¹ His proposals for carrying out these ideals are so wholly impracticable, so little worthy of discussion, so ill-suited to bring about the desired results, that their further presentation may be omitted.²

(d) *Law and Culture.* In his later contributions to the philosophy of law, Fichte goes beyond the conception of the legally regulated State, and, in a measure, anticipates the views which Schelling and Hegel emphasized and developed. The legally regulated State exists for the benefit of the individual. Fichte's command of the historical spirit led him to see that the center of interest and development was not the individual but the human race as a whole. In his "Grundzüge des Gegenwärtigen Zeitalters," it is the race and not the individual that appears as the object of the State. The State is no longer conceived as static but as a member of an evolutionary series and at once the issue thereof; the "Rechtsstaat" becomes the "Kulturstaat";³ the interests of culture outweigh the importance of law. Historically conceived, evil is presented as the converse of that which makes for right.⁴ In his "System der Rechtslehre," law appears as the necessary condition of morality, and the State becomes a means to secure freedom. Its final purpose is morality; which, achieved,

¹ "Der Geschlossene Handelsstaat," "Collected Works," III, pp. 402 seq.

² "Der Geschlossene Handelsstaat," "Collected Works," III, pp. 408 seq.

³ "Die Grundzüge des Gegenwärtigen Zeitalters," "Collected Works," VII, p. 143–170, 187 seq., 221.

⁴ "Die Staatslehre," "Collected Works," IV, pp. 431–496, 497–600. "The extension of the dominion of reason over nature advances by degrees; this dominion must be attained up to a certain point by a co-operative effort and from such a point further progress is possible to a yet greater conquest, and to a clear conception of purpose on the part of the human race." (p. 585.)

in so far tends to make law superfluous and to bring about its own dissolution.¹

(*e*) Fichte as a Statesman. In his "Reden an die Deutsche Nation," Fichte appears as a statesman. He pleads for an efficient training and conscious pursuit of character to build up a new generation that shall be of the nation and for the nation. He pleads for a national Germanic consciousness that shall discard all narrow limitations within German lands so that there may arise a unified Germany composed of sturdy men. "I speak for Germany and of Germans, and I decline to recognize, indeed, I ignore and repudiate, all dissensions and factions which unfortunate events have for centuries produced among those in reality forming a single nation." ² In these addresses he proved himself an enthusiastic patriot, proclaiming the German national spirit, and an effective champion in the contest for German national development — as the protagonist of a German empire and German nation. These addresses form his enduring monument; in them appears the greatness of the man as a patriot and as a spiritual leader of his people.

3: SCHOPENHAUER. The importance of SCHOPENHAUER (1788–1860) as a philosopher is at present apt to be overrated; however, his treatment of the freedom of the will ³ must be considered in its bearing on the philosophy of law, especially because it has recently, and to my mind falsely, been regarded as of large in-

---

[1] "Das System der Rechtslehre in Vorlesungen," "Posthumous Collected Works," II, pp. 499 seq., 515 seq., 540–542.

[2] "Reden an die Deutsche Nation," "Collected Works," VII, p. 266.

[3] "Preisschrift über die Freiheit des Willens. Die beiden Grundprobleme der Ethik," second edit., pp. 11 seq. (Schopenhauer's Works in six vols., Grisebach edit., Vol. III, pp. 391 seq.) See also *Berolzheimer*, "Die Entgeltung im Strafrechte," pp. 40–48, 78, 97 seq.

fluence upon the theories of punishment.[1] Schopenhauer adapted and, as he thought, demonstrated Kant's doctrine that the will is not free in the world of experience, and is free only in the world of intellect.[2] The sense of responsibility, according to Schopenhauer, finds its roots in character: "Operari sequitur esse." The intellectually free will is reflected in character. Schopenhauer liked to be regarded as a disciple of Kant; as, however, he upheld the absolute unalterability of character, he placed himself in diametric opposition to a principle of Kant's ethics, which postulates the transformation of the will or character from the natural to the moral will. In his prize essay "Über die Grundlage der Moral," Schopenhauer takes Kant's ethics as his point of departure; but influenced by Buddhism, he accepts the doctrine of resignation, the negation of the will to live, and pessimism.[3] Schopenhauer's paradox that injustice is the positive conception as opposed to justice was doubtless directed against his successful contemporary, Hegel, who regarded injustice as the mere negation of justice. "Injustice or wrong consists in the injury of another; hence the conception of wrong is positive, and is antecedent to that of right, which is its negative, and merely refers to such actions as one may practice without injuring others; that is, without committing wrong."[4] The existence of a natural law

---

[1] *Berolzheimer*, "Die Entgeltung," etc., pp. 100–109.

[2] "Die beiden Grundprobleme," etc., pp. 483 seq.

[3] *Schopenhauer*, "Die Welt als Wille und Vorstellung," Vol. I, Book 4 ("Der Welt als Wille zweite Betrachtung: bei erreichter Selbsterkenntnis Bejahung und Verneinung des Willens zum Leben"), and Vol. II, Book 4 (supplements to Book 4 of the first volume).

A supplement to both of these writings is found in the essay "Zur Ethik," chap. VIII, Vol. II of "Paralipomena." *

[4] "Preisschrift über die Grundlage der Moral," § 17. (Grisebach edition, Vol. III, p. 598.)

* Grisebach edition, Vol. V, pp. 205-246.

[§ 33] KANT, FICHTE, SCHOPENHAUER 203

is thus presented by Schopenhauer. "The conceptions wrong and right, as equivalent to injury and non-injury, to which latter also belongs prevention of injury, are obviously independent of positive legislation, and antecedent to it. There thus exists a pure ethical law, or natural law, and a pure science of law independent of all statutes."[1] With reference to punishment he advocates a position combining the view that it is inflicted in fulfillment of the law ("Bewährungstheorie") with the view that its purpose is the prevention of crime.[2]

See also *Schopenhauer,* "Die Welt als Wille, etc.," Vol. I, Book 4, § 62, p. 400. (Grisebach edition, Vol. I, pp. 437 seq.) "Parergı und Paralipomena," Vol. II, chap. 9, "Zur Rechtslehre und Politik" (Grisebach edition, Vol. V, pp. 247 seq.). See also *Ed. v. Hartmann,* "Phänomenologie des sittlichen Bewusstseins," Berlin 1879, pp. 506–512; *Berolzheimer,* "Die Entgeltung im Strafrechte," p. 231. At one point Schopenhauer refers to a passage in Grotius which, however, he wrongly interprets. See above.

[1] "Preisschrift über die Grundlage der Moral," § 17 (Grisebach edition), Vol. III, p. 598.
See also *Schopenhauer,* "Die Welt als Wille," etc., Vol. I, Book IV, § 62, Grisebach edition, Vol. I, p. 440.

[2] "On the other hand it is certain that apart from the State there is no right of punishment. All right to punishment is based upon the positive law alone, which *before* the offense has determined a punishment for it, the threat of which, as a counter-motive, is intended to outweigh all possible motives for the offense. This positive law is to be regarded as sanctioned and recognized by all the citizens of the State. . . . Consequently the immediate *purpose of punishment* is, in the particular case, the *fulfillment of the law as a contract.* But the one purpose of the *law* is *deterrence* from the infringement of the rights of others. It is in order that every one may be protected from suffering wrong that men have combined to form a State. . . . Thus the law and the fulfillment of it, the punishment, are essentially directed to the *future,* not to the *past.* This distinguishes *punishment* from *revenge;* for the motives which instigate the latter are solely concerned with what has happened, and thus with the past as such." ("Die Welt als Wille und Vorstellung." Haldane's translation, Vol. I, p. 448.)

§ 34. *Schelling and the Historical School.* 1: SCHELLING.[1] Schelling's (1775–1854) influence upon the philosophy of law lies in the foundation which his contributions supplied for the historical school, representing the definitive break with the position of "natural law." Yet Schelling's importance for the philosophy of law is not confined to his doctrines bearing especially upon this field. His work, "Die neue Deduktion des Naturrechts,"[2] consists of a series of principles and brief considerations which in the main present, in an altered form,[3] Kant's and Fichte's legal philosophy; it reflects Schelling's extreme idealism, yet contains many suggestive passages bearing upon the nature of law. "Exist in the highest sense of the word; cease to be a mere appearance; strive to become a real being: such is the supreme demand of practical philosophy."[4] To be such a real being, or "absolutely free," man must strive untrammeled, and be independent of any power other than his own autonomy.[5] Autonomy as experi-

[1] The writings of Schelling here pertinent are: "Neue Deduktion des Naturrechts," 1795, "Collected Works," Part I, Vol. I, Stuttgart and Augsburg 1856, pp. 245–280. "Ueber die Methode des akademischen Studiums," Tübingen 1803, second edition, Stuttgart and Tübingen 1813. "System des transzendentalen Idealismus," Tübingen 1800. "Philosophische Untersuchungen über das Wesen der menschlichen Freiheit und die damit zusammenhängenden Gegenstände," 1809, "Col. Works," Part I, Vol. 7, 1860, pp. 331–416. "Einleitung in die Philosophie der Mythologie," 5. Vorlesung, "Col. Works," Part II, Vol. I, pp. 94–118.

[2] Schelling himself designates in an appendix his "Neue Deduktion des Naturrechts," as aphorisms. He had in prospect a commentary thereon. "Collected Works," Part I, Vol. I, p. 280.

[3] Corresponding to Schelling's general philosophy of his first period which in content is essentially Fichtean. See *Berolzheimer,* "System," etc., Vol. I, pp. 89–92.

[4] "Neue Deduktion," etc., § 3.

[5] "Neue Deduktion," etc., §§ 4–8.

enced is life or the active causality of the subject.[1] The expression of the subject is restricted by the physical antagonism of nature and also by other subjects in the moral world.[2] It is the problem of ethics to maintain the freedom of each through the freedom of all. "The individual will is limited by the general will only in that it becomes absolute through such restriction";[3] and it is absolute only " in that it is restricted by the limitation of the general will." According to Schelling, "the supreme command of ethics is to conduct yourself in such manner that your will may become absolute will, that the whole moral world — that is, the world of intellectual individuals — can will your action in content and form. ' So conduct yourself that through your action no rational being is made a mere object, but always a co-operative subject."[4] In their highest stages ethics and law coincide. "Ethics solves the problem of the absolute will in that it makes the individual will identical with the general will; the science of law solves the problem in that it makes the general will identical with the individual will. Were each completely to solve its respective problem, they would cease to be opposed sciences."[5] For the rest, law and ethics are distinct: the ethical is subject to the command of duty; the legal is what is authorized. In developing the nature of law on this basis, Schelling rightly recognized that law constitutes the primary warrant. "Whatever is theoretically possible I have the power to do; whatever is practically possible I may do; what I may do corresponds with what is right, as the term is ordinarily

---

[1] "Neue Deduktion," etc., § 9.
[2] "Neue Deduktion," etc., §§ 10-24.
[3] "Neue Deduktion," etc., § 44, §§ 30-44.
[4] "Neue Deduktion," etc., § 45.
[5] "Neue Deduktion," etc., § 72.

used; and the practical possibility by means of which anything becomes right is what is meant by law."[1]

He further distinguishes between the content and form of the permissible, the lawful. The content of the permissible, or the content of law, is the law as sanctioning; that is, the authorization which is created by the law for the conduct of the individual. But the law is at the same time a limiting force, or a restricting norm;[2] and this fundamental function of the law Schelling terms the form of the permissible or of the legal. Every rightly permissible action is, according to Schelling, at first a general permission, and secondly, also a limited permission.[3] This general permission furnishes the content of the law; the limitation or restriction within a given realm of what is permitted is the form of the law. Thus the content of legally permitted action is limited by the law. "The content of the law is determined by the form of the law and not *vice versa*.[4]

Schelling distinguishes the individual from the general will;[5] the former corresponds to what in his, and Fichte's theoretical philosophy, becomes the ego; the general will corresponds to the absolute.[6]

The most direct principle of the law enunciates that "you may do anything whereby you express the content of your will in so far as it is conditioned by the

---

[1] "Neue Deduktion," etc., § 65.

[2] "Neue Deduktion," etc., §§ 77, 78, 79, and so on.

[3] Schelling's expression is as follows ("Neue Deduktion," § 78): "Ich *darf* überhaupt, und ich darf *etwas*." "I am permitted to act, and I am permitted to act in a specific way." One may thus distinguish between the content and the form of the permission.

[4] "Neue Deduktion," etc., §§ 79 with 77.

[5] "Neue Deduktion," §§ 79 seq.

[6] *Berolzheimer*, "System," etc., Vol. I, pp. 85–92; *Schelling*, "System des Transzendentalen Idealismus," pp. 80 seq.

form thereof."[1] All problems of legal philosophy are concerned with the possibility of expressing the form of the will,[2] and must be derived from the contrast of the form to the content of the will. The analysis of the chief legal principles yields the following: "The right of moral freedom in contrast to the general will, that is, the complete right of the individual will with reference to law-abiding as well as law-defying actions on their content side; right in contrast to the individual will, that is, the right of formal equality, or the right of the self-assertion of the ego, — the right to express one's own individuality in opposition to that of any other; right in contrast to will in general, that is, the right to the world of experience, to things and objects in general, or natural right in the narrower sense."[3] Schelling follows Kant[4] in not assuming the freedom of the will in the world of experience, and in holding it not valid for that world, but only for the intelligent subject or ego, which for Schelling is the world of reason. "Free action follows directly from the intelligent factor in man."[5]

In the fifth lecture of the "Einleitung in die Philosophie der Mythologie," Schelling raises the question as to the origin of races. Such a question would be made superfluous either by the assumption that "races have always existed," or by the opposite assumption that "races originated spontaneously." According to Schelling only the second is worthy of discussion, and would

[1] "Neue Deduktion," § 88.
[2] "Neue Deduktion," §§ 91 seq.
[3] "Idealism first placed he doctrine of freedom in the realm in which alone it is intelligible." "Philosophische Untersuchungen über das Wesen der Menschlichen Freiheit," etc., "Collected Works," I, Vol. 7, p. 383.
[4] "Untersuchungen," etc., "Collected Works," I, Vol. 7, p. 384.
[5] "Neue Deduktion," § 140; also §§ 96-109, 110-140.

imply that races spontaneously arose from the constant increase of generations. But this assumption will not hold; for by such process there would arise only tribes, and not races.[1] The essential criterion of the diversity of races is that the different races represent heterogeneous divisions of humanity. But the decisive factors in the origin of such diversity could only have been 'internal causes, that is, causes spontaneously arising within a homogeneous humanity." [2]

Schelling's views on the study of history and jurisprudence — the association of the two being significant — form the subject of a lecture in his "Vorlesungen über die Methode des Akademischen Studiums." It is commonly assumed that the events of nature are necessarily fixed, but that this does not apply to human history. History merely repeats and copies nature in the ideal; to nature in the real world there corresponds history in the ideal.[3] History may be considered either empirically, or from the point of view of the absolute, in which latter case events are presented as the mere appearance of the absolute. The empirical treatment of history may proceed either pragmatically, or by mere determination of facts — historical research, which includes but one part of historical science. The pragmatic method in history sets forth the historical material "in a special, not a general aspect," whereby the universality of history is destroyed. History as a science consists in the synthesis of facts with ideas so that facts become the expression of ideas. Such

---

[1] "Collected Works," Part II, Vol. I, p. 94.

[2] "Collected Works," II, I, pp. 95 seq.

[3] "Vorlesungen über die Methode des Akad.," etc., pp. 213 seq. "If pure substance ("an sich") could be recognized in both (that is, in nature and in history), we would see pictured before us what is ideal in history to be real in nature."

phase of history is not philosophy, because philosophy "holds aloof from reality and is wholly ideal while history, though pertaining to the world of reality, must also remain ideal." This preferred method of treating history, "the third and absolute point of view of history," is the historical art.[1]

The practical sciences, including the science of law, are distinguished from philosophy by their empirical content, "by the historical factor." Only such phases of the historical part of jurisprudence fall within the field of science, "as constitute a statement of ideas. Thus it is not that phase which is finite in nature, as are all forms of laws, that depends solely upon the external machinery of the State. The latter comprises most of what is at present taught as the science of law, and in which the spirit of public affairs but very sparingly persists." [2]

A type of study that is not merely pragmatic, but artistic and historical, is applicable to the form of public life; for such life "presents necessary issues and may be conceived according to its particular conditions as the opposition of the incoming to the outgoing forms." Private life, however, including private law, is detached from the public phases thereof, and in such detachment retains so little of absoluteness "as in nature attaches to the existence of individual bodies and their particular relations to one another."[3] In this statement, which goes somewhat beyond his purpose, Schelling expresses an important thought. The modern development of law, from the Renaissance to the last quarter of the nineteenth century, under the favorable influence of an individual-

---

[1] "Vorlesungen," etc., pp. 214–224; "System des transz. Idealismus," p. 420.

[2] "Vorlesungen," etc., pp. 226 seq.

[3] "Vorlesungen," etc., pp. 228 seq.

istic view of natural law, has tended to separate private from public law, so that each seems to maintain an independent existence in the State. It is only under the influence of socialism that there has appeared an intimate association of public and private law, and likewise a permeation of private law with the spirit of social ethics. Yet this is but a transitional stage, and one of the foremost problems of every future philosophy of law will consist in reinstating the philosophical connection between private and public law. According to my view of legal philosophy the common issue of the two realms is determined by the possibility of such distribution of force within the State that the artificial legal position of vantage of the individual through his status in private law shall at the same time increase the position of vantage of the State. The modern attainment of individual freedom thus appears safeguarded as against the community, and at the same time there is established the intimate association of public and private law, and the elevation of private rights from their significance to the individual to a matter of interest to the political community, to the State. According to Schelling legal science deserves the name only in so far as it is open to an historical and not merely pragmatic study, that is, in so far as it may be set forth in its legal determination as a component of the absolute, as the expression of a supreme idea.[1]

In nature the absolute exists in itself, "an sich"; in history it exists for a purpose, "für sich"; it becomes objective. The issues of history are thus parts of the organism of the absolute. Inasmuch as all objects are products of the mind, and unconscious mind is an unconsciously realizing purpose, all objects appear as parts of a progressive organization whose highest aim is free-

[1] "Vorlesungen," etc., pp. 227-229.

dom. The State is likewise an organic construction — like man, an organism within the cosmic organism.[1] Schelling conceives the philosophy of law not as an issue of natural law already attained, and in course of development, thus at once breaking with the naturalistic point of view and establishing the foundations for the historical school of law.[2] The idea of the perfect State will be achieved "whenever the particular and the general form an absolute unity, whenever all that is necessarily free and all that freely occurs also necessarily occurs." The State must be primarily conceived as a realized organization.[3]

2: OTHER REPRESENTATIVES OF THE HISTORICAL SCHOOL. Under the stimulus of Herder's[4] ideas upon historical[5]

[1] "System des Transz. Ideal.," especially pp. 322-451, 593-597; also "Phil. Unters. über das Wesen der Menschl. Freiheit," "Collected Works," I, I, pp. 382-387.

[2] "System des Transz. Ideal.," p. 232: "The first effort of every one who desires to attain a free understanding of the positive science of law and government must be to acquire, by means of philosophy and history, a vital view of the modern world and of the forms of public life which it demands. One can hardly foresee what means of culture may be available in this science if it could be treated in an independent spirit, free from any bearing upon practice."

[3] "Vorlesungen," etc., pp. 229, 234; "System des Transz. Idealismus," pp. 411 seq., 422 seq.

Jurisprudence is therefore not a part of ethics, nor indeed of any practical science, but is a purely theoretical discipline "which serves the function for freedom which mechanics serves for motion, in that it merely deductively sets forth the natural mechanism under which free beings may be thought of in interaction — a mechanism which doubtless can be attained only through freedom and to which nature contributes nothing." "System des Transc. Ideal.," p. 406.

[4] *Herder*, "Ideen zur Philosophie der Geschichte der Menschheit," Riga and Leipzig, 1785-1792, Part I, pp. 294 seq. 312 seq.; Part II, pp. 189 seq., 301 seq.

[5] On the historical school in general see *Stahl*, "Geschichte der Rechtsphilosophie," pp. 563-582. *Geyer*, "Geschichte und System

development, Hugo (1768–1844) rejected "natural law," became the founder of the historical school, and foreshadowed the organic conception of the genesis of law and government. Hugo interprets the philosophy of positive law to be the "rational conception of what may be legally right."[1] Metaphysical deductions are pertinent only on their formal side; the content must be derived from experience and history.[2]

These views, which reflect Schelling's philosophy, attain their most distinctive and characteristic development in the brilliant jurist, Savigny[3] (1779–1861), and in Puchta[4] (1798–1846); and likewise in Niebuhr and Eichhorn. Savigny and Puchta made a thorough study of the origin and development of positive law. Savigny held that in primitive conditions civil rights are as characteristic of the status of a people as are their language, their customs, their constitution. Such phenomena are not detached results, but "appear only as one of several expressions and activities of a people, which are really one, and become separate only in our

der Rechtsphilosophie in Grundzügen," pp. 96–99. *Ahrens*, "Naturrecht," I, pp. 169–178. *Lasson*, "System der Rechtsphilosophie," pp. 18 seq.

[1] "Lehrbuch eines Zivilistischen Kursus," Vol. I, containing the juridical Encyclopedia, Berlin 1799, 4th edit., 1811, 2 vols. "Lehrbuch des Naturrechts als einer Philosophie des positiven Rechts," Berlin 1799.

[2] "Lehrbuch des Naturrechts," §§ 48, 52, 53. Also "Lehrbuch des Naturrechts," § 123. "Enzyklopädie," 4th edit., §§ 20, 21.

[3] "Vom Beruf unsrer Zeit für Gesetzgebung und Rechtswissenschaft," 3d edit., Heidelberg 1840, pp. 8–15 ("Entstehung des positiven Rechts"). "System des heutigen Römischen Rechts," Vol. I, Berlin 1840, pp. XIII–XVI, 13–18 ("Allgemeine Entstehung des Rechts").

[4] "Das Gewohnheitsrecht," I, Erlangen 1828, pp. 133–143 ("Entstehung des Rechts überhaupt. Kursus der Institutionen"). Vol. I, Leipzig 1841, pp. 23–27, 35–37.

study thereof. What binds them together in a whole is the common conviction of a people, the same sense of inner compulsion that excludes any thought of an accidental or arbitrary origin."[1] Law, like language, stands in organic connection with the nature or character of a people and evolves with the people. "Law grows as the people grow, develops with the people, and declines when the people lose individuality."[2] As summarized by Savigny, "Law arises according to what the prevalent, though not quite pertinent phrase calls 'customary law,' that is, it is first produced by custom and popular belief, and then re-enforced by jurisprudence. Throughout it is the result of inner, silently working forces, not of the arbitrary will of a law-giver."[3] According to Savigny, positive law may also be called popular law because it lives in the common consciousness of the people; but it there prevails, not as abstract regulation, but as "the living conception of legal institutions in their organic connection."[4]

Quite similarly Puchta presents law as the expression of a popular spirit, as the result of popular activity, which "legally establishes not the individual as such, nor as a member of the family, but as a member of the people — the legal function thus belonging exclusively to the people." In this respect law is set off against moral conviction, which may be entertained by the individual, the family, or the people. The entire body of the law is a national possession and a national product; and the conviction of the people is its source.[5]

[1] "Vom Beruf unsrer Zeit," etc., p. 8.
[2] "Vom Beruf," etc., p. 11.
[3] "Vom Beruf," etc., pp. 13 seq.
[4] "System," I, pp. 14, 16. "Kursus der Institutionen," p. 35.
[5] "Das Gewohnheitsrecht," I, pp. 138 seq., 141-143. "Kursus der Institutionen," pp. 24, 29, 35.

Harms[1] (1819–1880) may be mentioned as a later adherent of this "organic" theory of law,[2] by reason of his view that "popular law, due to custom, is further developed by the legislation of the State, by experience, and by the reactions of consciousness and will. The several stages of law present the same relation as obtain elsewhere in historical development, between the natural issues of habit and the rational processes of consciousness and will."

The historical conception has superseded the naturalistic or purely speculative position so far as concerns the principles or systems of law, but not in their scientific application. Bekker[3] points out that Savigny's system of natural law "still retains a small reserved area" where "natural law" persists; for he continues to construct his system deductively, and derives many of his positions "from the nature of things." Similarly Bergbohm observes that the conception of natural law was but officially driven out of legal science, and under a disguised name has continued to exert a directive influence. Yet he goes a little too far in his view that such terms as the "sense of justice" ("Rechtsgefühl") and the idea of right ("Rechtsidee") and similar permanent and necessary terms of legal philosophy should be rejected as metaphysical or naturalistic conceptions.[4]

[1] "Begriff, Formen, und Grundlegung der Rechtsphilosophie," pp. 126–134.

[2] "Begriff," etc., p. 134.

[3] "Über den Streit der Historischen und der Philosophischen Rechtsschule," Akad. Rede, Heidelberg 1886, p. 19.

[4] "Jurisprudenz und Rechtsphilosophie," Leipzig 1892, p. IX, 109–552. ("Das Naturrecht der Gegenwart.") *Stammler:* "Über die Methode der Geschichtlichen Rechtstheorie," Halle a/S 1888, pp. 28–48, undertakes to prove that the historical theory of law has not superseded "natural law."

The historical treatment of law, which nowadays under the influence of the historical school in legal science and philosophy has become the dominant one, is applied to penal philosophy by R. Löning, who emphasizes that an adequate treatment of the philosophical problems is possible only on the basis of a comprehensive historical study.[1] On the other hand, Jacques Stern, in a recent contribution,[2] pleads for the recognition of rational law ("Vernunftsrecht"), side by side with positive law.[3]

§ 35. *Hegel and the Hegelians.* 1: HEGEL'S PHILOSOPHY OF LAW. In the preface[4] to his philosophy of law Hegel[5] (1770–1831) has well expressed the purpose of the philosophic statesman, which is, not to construct an

[1] "Über Geschichtliche und Ungeschichtliche Behandlung des Strafrechts," in "Z. f. ges. Strafr.," Vol. III, 1883, pp. 219–375.

[2] "Rechtsphilosophie und Rechtswissenschaft," Berlin 1904.

[3] To the law of reason and as well to positive law belong the conception or idea of law, the general legal conceptions (legal principles and institutions), and the general legal conceptions adopted by legislation (legal principles and institutions). On the other hand the law of reason in contrast to the old natural law is not to include specific legal principles. But where is the point of division? In this respect the laws of civilized countries more or less diverge on the basis of fundamental questions. So far as this is not the case it is due to the historical fact of the common influence of Roman law.

Stern thus defines the law of reason: "The law of reason is the conception which strives to be realized as the idea of law and does so not under the moral point of view of a subjective attitude but under the objective point of view of purpose considered as an ordering principle and as justice protected by the moral reliability of coercion."

This definition will scarcely gain for Stern favor for a new model law, however limited it may be to general considerations.

[4] "Grundlinien," etc., pp. 18 seq.

[5] *"Grundlinien der Philosophie des Rechts,* oder Naturrecht und Staatswissenschaft im Grundrisse," "Collected Works," Vol. 8, Berlin 1833.

ideal State, nor to inform the government how it should be conducted, but to set forth how a comprehension of the nature of the State shall be acquired, how it shall be critically interpreted. In the Hegelian philosophy this postulate assumes a characteristic form; — to know the State is to prove its rationality. "To understand that which exists is the problem of philosophy; for whatever exists is reason."[1] Heretofore the State and law had been conceived as established and stable. Schelling emphasized the developmental factor in law; law itself was fixed, and it was only the laws — the legal system — that were subject to change. Hegel showed that government and law were to be conceived as plastic, as in the course of evolution. He approached philosophy as an historian, and as a philosopher of history he was confronted with the philosophy of government. It was his philosophy of history as applied to law and government that became his philosophy of law.

The subject of evolution is the human will, which at the beginning of the historical development is subjective, and in successive stages reaches an objective status. The subjective will is the arbitrary, non-moral will of the individual; the objective will is the moral collective will.[2] Morality, however, is freedom, and not merely freedom as a conception, but a realized freedom — and moreover freedom, not merely as existing in the world, but as the content of the world and of the human mind.[3]

[1] "Grundlinien," etc., p. 19.

[2] "Grundlinien," etc., §§ 1–33; particularly 4, 7, 11, 22, 29, 33.

[3] "Grundlinien," etc., § 142, p. 210. "Morality is the idea of freedom, of the conception of freedom as attained through self-consciousness in relation to the world as presented, and to nature." With this compare "Grundlinien," etc. § 129, p. 171: "The good is the idea conceived as the unity of the will, and of the particular will in which the abstract right, as well as welfare and subjectivity of the will and

Morality is the world with freedom established — freedom of the community as well as of the individual. Through morality or realized freedom the individual transcends his accidental or individual existence and becomes a part of the whole, so that his individual detachment is absorbed and dissolved in the whole. But through this process the individual persists in his true nature, in his real ego. His true nature thereby becomes realized. In this dissolution of the individual in the community lies "the absolute final purpose" of the world.[1] The history of the world is the process of the emancipation of humanity. Humanity is forcibly led to freedom in the State and through the State. In Asiatic States the individual is wholly without freedom; in the State of the Greeks and Romans he is partly free; in modern States he is quite free.

2: LAW AND THE HUMAN WILL. In Hegel, as in Kant and Fichte, government and law find their justification not in any external grounds but because they are "the absolute demands of the practical reason."[2] The source of law is the will, and the will is free. To will, means the capacity to reach a free decision.[3] Freedom constitutes the substance and determination of the will.[4] The subjective will which exists antecedent to the State is only free in itself; it is a natural or immediate will, being immediate because only direct impulses form efficient and determining motives, such as instincts, desires, dispositions. While in the Hegelian panthe-

the circumstance of objective being, are conceived as independent; while yet in their nature contained and containing. It is freedom realized, the absolute final purpose of the world."

[1] "Grundlinien," etc., § 129; see previous note 5.
[2] *Lasson*, "System der Rechtsphilosophie," p. 104.
[3] Hegel might have referred to the etymology, which derives "Wollen" from "Wählen."
[4] *Hegel*, "Grundlinien," etc., § 4.

istic system this form of will must also be rational, yet its rationality is relative. The will as antecedent to the State has indeed a content derived from "the rationality of the will," but is "not yet rational in form." Form and content are as yet distinct. It is rational in regard to the willing subject, but it is not yet wholly rational with reference to the community. It is "a will finite in itself."[1] The will transcends its limitation through the "purification of the instincts"; it achieves universality and becomes the absolutely rational or moral will, "in that it contains within itself universality as the infinite form of its content and purpose. It becomes the free will, the true idea, not only in itself but also for itself."[2] The will thus elevated from the natural to the moral state is absolutely free. It is a will existing in and for itself. It is infinite, real, rational. It exists and has reality. Such existence of the free will is guaranteed by the law;[3] fundamentally the law is but the realization of the free will, and by virtue thereof is itself real. "The law is holy because it is the realization of the absolute conception of self-conscious freedom."[4]

"A legal system is the realm of realized freedom."[5] The structure of the law will vary according to the stage of evolution which the process of the emancipation of the will in humanity has attained. The several stages of the evolution of the will correspond to the several stages of the development of freedom, and concur with the several periods of legislation. The higher the stage

---

[1] "Grundlinien," etc., § 11.

[2] "Grundlinien," etc., § 21, also §§ 19, 20, 22.

[3] "Grundlinien," etc., § 29: "This which is being in general, the being of a free will, is law."

[4] "Grundlinien," etc., § 30.

[5] See above.

that the will has obtained in its development, the richer and more adequate is its legal counterpart.[1] Thus Hegel demonstrates the rationality of law, and brings the fact of constantly changing legal construction under his universally rationalized system. This position forms a distinctive break with the doctrine of natural law. Natural law recognizes only a model law. Hegel shows the rationality of the law to be one which, though varying in its changeable forms, presents each successive legal construction as rational in that it corresponds to a definite stage of evolution of the will.

3: HEGEL'S DIALECTIC. This comprehensive and fundamental position of the Hegelian philosophy of government and law is not presented and deduced by Hegel in the manner of my exposition. His presentation contains mannerisms that seem to be inevitable accompaniments of the dialectic method.

Hegel is the last great rationalist. The "Cogito" of Descartes, with which rationalism made its appearance in modern philosophy, has in Hegel become an impersonal thinking, — "Es denkt." The Hegelian reason appears "as an absolute, subjectless, universal reason. It is pure thought, that is, without a thought of object. It is self-sufficient thought, 'substantielles,' that is, without a thinking subject. It is thought containing in itself its own laws which the philosopher but discovers by his dialectical method; while thought derives, creates, produces from within itself, the conception which it bears and which constitutes its nature."

The cosmic evolutionary process, and the form which

---

[1] *Hegel*, "Grundlinien," etc., § 30: "The formalism of law, however, (and later of duty), arises from the difference in the development of the conception of freedom as against the more formal, that is, the more abstract, and therefore the more limited law; there is a sphere or stage of the mind which attains a yet higher law in which it carries to definition and reality the further factors contained in the idea."

it assumes in government and law, are, according to Hegel, not objective processes but rational or logical ones. It is pure impersonal thought which in Hegel's idealistic pantheism comprises the world in itself. The problem of the legal philosopher is not to derive the process of development from the empirical world, but to determine the laws of pure thought, to comprehend pure thought in its dialectic process of evolution. Philosophical or true knowledge finds "in the concept alone the basis of its nature."[1] The philosopher must trace to their source the dialectic movements of the conception; and these are "pure autonomous movements which one might call souls, were it not that the conception thereof indicates something superior."[2] The general forms and determinations of pure or objectless thought, which contains thought in itself without being directed to an object, are the conceptions of being, not-being, quality, quantity, cause, action, etc. They are, to speak figuratively, the members by means of which pure thought moves. Pure thought, however, requires a method of progression. This method is an oscillation. The concept posits itself constituting "the abstract moment," and at once goes over to its opposite and thus dissolves itself, constituting "the dialectic moment." But out of such affirmation, which is also denial, being the concept of an object and of its opposite, arises a third, — the unity of these mutual dissolutions as the truth of both, constituting "the speculative or positive rational moment." The dialectic method serves not merely for analysis but to make possible a synthetic construction.[3]

[1] *Hegel*, "Phänomenologie des Geistes," "Collected Works," II, pp. 6 seq.

[2] "Phänomenologie," p. 46.

[3] "Grundlinien," § 31, with "Enzyklopädie," I, §§ 61–78 "(Collected Works," VI). See in this connection *Berolzheimer*, "System," Vol. I, pp. 99–103, and the references there found.

No one any longer believes in the legitimacy of this dialectic method, and a harsh judgment might pronounce it self-deception or worse. It is indeed a futile procedure; for in reality, the dialectician puts into the dialectic mill so much of experience and of the material resulting from a non-dialectical consideration, that the desired result eventually emerges. Hegel's dialectic is the consistent elaboration of Kant's rationalism with a Fichtean tone; and it is easy to make Hegel responsible for the sins of others. Yet the dialectic contains a profound truth, which is, however, different from what Hegel had in mind. It is the fact that objects come into full consciousness as independent realities only through their opposites. Such conceptions as beauty, brightness, greatness, attain a meaning in the world of experience through the concomitant consciousness of their opposites — ugliness, dullness, smallness. Whoever has not experienced sorrow and unhappiness may be in a fortunate position, but the consciousness of happiness is not his. All things are limited by their opposites and thus come to consciousness. Objects and their opposites are detached and fixed only in our conceptions. If we suppose the human capacity for knowledge to disappear, then all differentiation disappears, and there remains chaos and complete vagueness. To know means to differentiate. The world, as it is reflected in the human mind, is in fact a product of human differentiation — the positing of objects in human conception, each object revealing nothing in itself, and being crystallized and unified only through its opposite. But the recognition of this reciprocity in the realm of concepts is incapable of serving for the construction of a practical philosophy;[1] it can lead only to viewing the actual world as an absolute vagueness, as chaos, as the undif-

[1] *Berolzheimer*, "System," Vol. I, pp. 222–226.

ferentiated. It must then be noted that in the Hegelian theory of knowledge the stages of evolution do not constitute realities, but are merely emanations of the concept of pure thought or logical processes. Paulsen[1] aptly says that the Hegelian philosophy is a "philosophy that attempts nothing short of a reconstruction of the world of thought. Indeed the creation finds its true consummation only in such thought; without it the world remained a mere blind fact, though in itself a rational one. It finds illumination in speculative philosophy; there it recognizes itself as what it is, as a unified existent system of thought."

According to Hegel the evolution of the human mind shows six stages: consciousness, self-consciousness, reason, spirit, religion, and absolute knowledge.[2] The development of "the idea of the free will existing in and for itself," presents three stages. In the first the will is direct or immediate; to this there corresponds the sphere of abstract or formal law. The second stage shows "the will turned back into itself," "as a subjective individuality contrasted with the universal". Here the idea is divided, and exists in separate elements. This is the sphere of morality.[3] The third stage is the unity and truth of both previous abstract moments, — the realization of the idea of the good, — "the idea of morality in its independent general existence. "an und für sich." Law, ethics, and morality are the three stages in the development of the objective mind.

[1] "Immanuel Kant. Sein Leben und seine Lehre," second and third edit., Stuttgart 1899, pp. 389 seq. (I was not able to consult the fourth edit.)

[2] "Phänomenologie," pp. 73 seq.; see also *Berolzheimer*, "System," Vol. I, pp. 103 seq.

[3] In Hegel the term "Moralität" is given a special meaning apart from morality as "Sittlichkeit."

Together they constitute the objective mind; in them the mind achieves objectivity. The moral substance — "Substanz," likewise shows three stages: the natural spirit, the family; the civil society, or spirit in its dual existence and mere appearance; the State, the complete unity of the individual and the universal.[1]

4: HEGEL'S CONCEPTION OF THE STATE. Through the mediacy of civil society — not in the sociological sense of a primary association between family and State [2] — the State is shaped to a career of noble destiny.[3] The State is the supreme expression of morality. "It is the realization of the moral ideal, of the moral spirit, of the will, self-revealing, self-conscious, efficient, thinking and knowing, and carrying its knowledge into action."[4] This abstract form of expression seems strange because it is phrased in the language of the Hegelian philosophy; it involves a double meaning, the two factors of different import. Translated from his language to the vernacular, Hegel's definition implies: first, that the State is the complete development of morality; and second, that

[1] "Grundlinien," § 33.

[2] *Hegel*, "Grundlinien," § 182, p. 246: "Civil society expresses the difference that arises between the family and the State, even though in the course of evolution the resultant becomes the development of the State itself. For the distinction presupposes the existence of the State as an independent institution. The creation of a civil society is characteristic of the modern world which overcomes all the limitations of the idea."

[3] The principles of civil society are determined by Hegel as follows ("Grundlinien," § 182, p. 246): "The concrete person, who for himself is a particular purpose, an aggregate of needs, and a mixture of natural necessity and free will, is the sole principle of civil society. But the particular person is considered in relation to others of like status, so that each becomes valid and satisfied and his being mediated only through the rest, and as well, is realized only through the form of the universal, which is the other principle."

[4] "Grundlinien," § 257, p. 312.

the State ever meets the problems of culture as they are present to the consciousness of a given period. Hegel thus disposes of the seeming contradiction — applicable to the State as to law — that the State represents absolute reason in its supreme development while the activities of the governmental functions are decidedly varied at different times and stages of development. The State is the supreme form of reason or the rational, while yet it is not something fixed but ever in the process of formation. This conception places Hegel in advance of Kant and allies him to the world of present thought. For Hegel the State is no longer the constitutional State, "Rechtsstaat," but the State ready to accept the mission of culture, "Kulturstaat." Yet Hegel's conception of the State cannot be accepted. For, to begin with, the State is not the embodiment of morality. Hegel's assumption that it is so, recalls the Greek view of life. Greek idealism regarded the State as an ethical institution, but the modern conception is characterized by its detachment of law from the "ethos," the moral disposition of the community, by the separation of the State from spiritual community. Again, Hegel has no appreciation, indeed no suspicion, of the true nature of the State as the original source of law, and thus of its artificial legal status. Hegel's philosophy of law, despite the eccentricity of his system and its manifold errors, reveals the greatness of the man. His views are thoughtfully elaborated and bear the impress of his personality. He is not content to repeat the views of others, but infuses every detail with a vital individual spirit, with a reflex of his own thought.

5: FUNDAMENTAL LEGAL IDEAS: PERSON, PROPERTY, INJURY, AND CRIME. Hegel's comments upon the relation and difference between the laws of nature and of positive law may be cited by way of further contributions bearing upon fundamental legal ideas.[1] The former are absolute, and it is only our knowledge of their mode of working that is capable of extension. Positive laws are "established, instituted by man. With these conscience may conflict or accord."[2] In studying the nature of wrong Hegel comments upon a phase but little regarded, which he calls "unpremeditated wrong,"[3] "unbefangenes Unrecht," that condition or action which is objectively unwarranted, without, however, involving blame; an objective wrong without subjective guilt.[4] Of more importance is Hegel's doctrine of "the person."[5] Law transforms men into persons. The law does not deal with men as subjects, but rather the subjects of the law are always persons. This apt observation applies to Roman law. The owner of a legal right is not the man as man, but the man as a member of the legal organization — "the persona." Hegel's doctrine of "the person" is applied in his theory of the State. It there leads to the conception of the State as a personality in the legal sense. The State has a personality as a complete concrete realization of the will, as the manifestation of reason realized in the will. The sovereignty therefore belongs to the State and not to the people. The personality of the State is realized as

[1] Hegel's view is set forth by *A. Affolter*, "Naturgesetze und Rechtsgesetze," Munich 1904.

[2] "Grundlinien," p. 8, note.

[3] *Hegel*, "Grundlinien," pp. 128–130. For this Lasson uses the term "Schuldloses Unrecht," "blameless wrong." ("System der Rechtsphilosophie," § 44.)

[4] *Berolzheimer*, "Die Entgeltung im Strafrechte," pp. 119, 166, 168.

[5] *Berolzheimer*, "Rechtsphil. Studien," pp. 104–113. The fundamental principle of law ("Das Rechtsgebot"), according to Hegel, reads ("Grundlinien," § 36): "Be a person and respect others as persons."

a person in the monarch. The State is an organism; that is, an idea developed to its differentiations. The State exists as a concrete individual State, derived from a particular folk-spirit, as the outcome of the self-consciousness of a people, and particularly of its religious convictions. The State is "the real and organic spirit of a people" and is further extended by the relation "of particular folk-spirits to the higher development in a universal spirit of absolute reason of which law is the supreme expression." [1]

Hegel's doctrine of "the person" is peculiarly important in private law; and in this field there has not been accorded to him an adequate appreciation. His train of thought may be thus reproduced: Through law a human being attains the dignity of a person. This attribute of a person is expressed in property. Property is the legally artificial cloak under whose protection the power of man is extended through the State and law above his natural status. Just as other cultural factors show their beneficial effect by increasing human efficiency, so law stimulates and increases the artificial efficiency of each individual and of the community. "The word 'Vermögen' is etymologically related to 'vermögen'; that which one can do is his property. In the course of development there was derived from this general conception of capacity a narrower one, and 'vermögen,' in the narrower economic and legal sense means what anyone as a legal subject may do. It has thus been transferred to a legal economic sense. In its nature the State is the embodiment of legal power internally and externally. At the same time the State would be an empty concept, a shadowy essence, were it not that this concept of legal authority is brought to expression by investing the State with a material reality.

[1] "Grundlinien," pp. 312 seq.

This material investiture is made effective by property. The conception of private property thus also confers legal and economic power upon the State; and in this fundamental constructive significance, and in this alone, lies the justification of private ownership and property."[1]

I must at once add that this interpretation of the meaning of "vermögen," as quoted above, will in vain be sought in Hegel. The quotation, although taken from one of my own earlier writings, is substantially contained in Hegel's view of the philosophy of private ownership, and in the recognition of ownership or property as representing the legal economic efficiency of the individual. In the resulting support of the State by the individual, lies the justification of ownership and private property. The reason why this interpretation of Hegel's views on property has not been hitherto advanced may be due to the fact that the recognition of property as an economically efficient factor has not hitherto been adequately established. There may be another and more important reason; it may be due to the fact that Hegel does not speak of property, "Vermögen," which includes both real rights and obligations, but of ownership, "Eigentum." Ownership is the legal term for the right to material things, and is thus but a sub-division of one's property, "Vermögen." Fully to appreciate Hegel's presentation of property the word "Eigentum," which he employs, must not be understood in the legal sense, but must be replaced by the economic term, property, "Vermögen."[2] There will thus be introduced a pertinent meaning into Hegel's exposition. "The free will, in order not to remain abstract, must proceed to secure an existence; and the perceptible embodiment of such existence are things;

[1] *Berolzheimer*, "Das Vermögen," 1904, p. 519.
[2] *Berolzheimer*, "Das Vermögen," pp. 440 seq., 546 seq.

that is, external objects. This first form of freedom is what we may call ownership, 'Eigentum,' the sphere of formal and abstract law, to which belong equally ownership in its indirect form of agreement, and the right to regard the infringement of ownership as a punishable crime."[1] The following passage is apposite: "The person must attain an outer sphere for freedom in order to exist as an idea."[2] And later, in regard to agreement:[3] "Ownership, of which the aspect of existence or externality is no longer merely an object, but contains within itself the factor of a will, arises through agreement; and agreement is a procedure by which the contradiction is both presented and mediated, that I, as a self-existent owner, standing apart from the wills of others, am and remain such, in so far as I cease to be an owner by making my will identical with others." The infraction of the law in general, and crime in particular, are externally something positive, but are in themselves negative. The inherent negative character of wrong appears in that the right persists despite the infringement, and in that the infringement, in its negative character, is overcome and removed by the punishment. Punishment is thus the negation of the negation of right — a just retribution, the establishment of the equilibrium[4] of the State which the criminal has disturbed; it is a logical postulate.[5]

6: A Critical Verdict on Hegel. A definitive judgment upon Hegel's philosophy of government and law is not summarily to be reached. It seems the irony of

[1] *Hegel*, "Grundlinien," p. 70.

[2] "Grundlinien," pp. 78, 78–114 (influence of Fichte).

[3] "Grundlinien," pp. 114 seq., 114–126.

[4] *Berolzheimer*, "Die Entgeltung im Strafrechte," p. 32 and other places.

[5] *Hegel*, "Grundlinien," pp. 126–147.

fate that his own phrase of the identity of opposites applies to Hegel himself. While recognizing his supreme intuition, his keen philosophic sense, and his originality — which places him well above Kant, who in many ways still clings to the fetters of the traditional — one cannot disguise the fact that his dialectic method at times advances conclusions and opinions that come close to nonsense, and are, at the least, conspicuously inconsequential. If Kant's idealistic philosophy may be said to have dwelt in a magic garden, then Hegel's is suggestive of the intricate paths of a maze. It is easy to understand why the estimates of Hegel have varied from one extreme to another, from fanatic enthusiasm to absolute contempt, and even to the consideration of his philosophy and dialectic as a hair-splitting topsy-turvydom. Recently—notably through the influence of Kuno Fischer and Kohler—Hegel has again been recognized as a star of the first magnitude in the philosophical firmament. But the grounds for this appreciation are not the same as formerly obtained. The keenness of his speculations, the breadth of his ideas, and the cogency of his dialectic argument and treatment of the historical material as a whole, were the qualities of Hegel's philosophy that brought reputation to its author. His philosophy was admired for its art, its deductive perfection, its ingenuity of construction, and its proportion of execution. Today it is the baroque style of his philosophic architecture that repels. It is the intrinsic value of his thought that forms the basis of the modern appreciation. When the massive walls of the Hegelian structure are removed, and the bare skeleton, the iron framework, stands revealed, — or, to drop the figure, the shrewd observations and the astute opinions upon issues large and small which reflect his historical sense, — it is the latter that represent the enduring value of his philosophy. It is only in style that Hegel is baroque; to a generation that has advanced beyond naturalism, he is distinctly modern in content.[1]

The evolutionary idea, dimly suggested by Heraclitus, attained its renaissance in the nineteenth century; not without precedent, it appeared in a dual aspect. In its realistic formulation it led to the doctrine of evolution as expressed in natural science, represented by Goethe, Lamarck, Darwin, Spencer, and Häckel; its idealistic formulation appears in Schelling, Hegel, and Kohler. It is Hegel's greatest merit as a political philosopher to have replaced the "Rechtsstaat" by the "Kulturstaat," to have accomplished the affiliation of law with culture, and to have established the justification of the several evolutionary stages of law and government.

It has frequently been noted, more commonly by way of adverse criticism, that Hegel's philosophy of law and government was directed to the theoretical justification of the Prussian State of his day. In a measure such is the case. Just as Rousseau in his "Discours" afforded a philosophic foundation for the French Revolution; as Wolff became the theoretical representative of enlightened absolutism, and Kant the apologist of the State as a legal institution; as Fichte, the statesman, and Schelling, the romanticist, aroused the German national spirit; so Hegel's philosophy of law sounded the keynote for the intellectuals of the rejuvenated and awakened Prussian State. The environment, the spiritual temper, from which Hegel's philosophy of law emerged, was likewise the culture to which the Prussian State owed its growth and consummation in the recognition of the State as the supreme representative

[1] The resurrection of Hegel appears in such a contribution as Kohler's "Philosophy of Law."

of moral force and strength — the recognition that the State is designed and called to fill a mission of culture, and to fill it in such manner that the State shall not exist for the individual, nor yet the individual for the State, but that State and citizens shall enter in common the service of a definite cultural ideal, whereby the community and the members thereof shall advance, each according to his capacity, the progress of man. Simply expressed, Hegel conceived the State as the bearer of culture, and thus supplied the theoretical foundation of the "Kulturstaat," which was accepted as the ideal of the newly awakened Prussia.[1]

The weakness of Hegel's position is that attaching to the doctrine of universal flux. In a system in which everything is set forth as in course of evolution, there are lacking fixed points of attachment in the eternal stream. As an historian Hegel may retrospectively divide the stream of phenomena into periods; but as a political philosopher he fails to find a basis for government and law. The position of vantage accruing to the community and the individual through government and law, the vitality of the law, is a truth momentarily revealed in Hegel's philosophy of ownership; but no sooner does it appear than it again is lost. For this truth contrasts sharply with Hegel's entire position in so far as his philosophy divests government and law of reality, and reduces them to a mere emanation of an abstract dialectic movement. As a legal philosopher Hegel advanced many significant truths; but his abstract train of thought brought him, in many respects, in direct contradiction with the facts of the law and its evolution. However, taken all in all, Hegel was one of the greatest men that the philosophy of any age pro-

[1] Compare with former divisions of this section.

duced — great in his achievements, and great in his defects.

7: THE HEGELIANS. Of the three groups into which we may divide the Hegelians, we mention first the scientific group. It was their purpose to develop the system which Hegel had outlined and which was indeed but the framework of a comprehensive philosophical construction. Foremost in this group are Gans, and Lassalle, the author of "Das System der Erworbenen Rechte."[1] It may be noted that Hegel's philosophy of law bears the title of "Outlines"; Lassalle looked upon it as such, and regarded the mission of the younger Hegelians to be "to carry the project to its completion, to prepare a philosophy of private law, and to trace the development of the actual institutions connected therewith."[2] GANS[3] (1798–1839) endeavored to carry forward Hegel's philosophy of law. He undertook a comprehensive work, "Das Römische Erbrecht," in which he traced the historical development of the law of inheritance. In it the wide learning of its author, and his complete absorption and comprehension of the intricate system of Hegel's

---

[1] "*Das System der Erworbenen Rechte.* Eine Versöhnung des Positiven Rechts und der Rechtsphilosophie." Part I: "Die Theorie der Erworbenen *Rechte und die Kollision der Gesetze*, unter besonderer Berücksichtigung des Römischen, Französischen und Preussischen Rechts dargestellt." Part II, Divisions 1 and 2. "Das Wesen des Römischen und Germanischen Erbrechts in historisch-philosophischer Entwickelung. Unter besonderer Berücksichtigung des Römischen, Französischen und Preussischen Rechts dargestellt." (*Ferdinand Lassalle,* "Collected Works." Only edition published by Erich Blum, 4, 5 vols., Leipzig 1901.) I, preface, p. xi.

[2] "Das System der Erworbenen Rechte,"

[3] *Eduard Gans,* "*Das Römische Erbrecht* in seiner Stellung zu vor- und nachrömischem. Eine Abhandlung der Universalrechtsgeschichte," Vol. I, Berlin 1824, "*Das Erbrecht in weltgeschichtlicher Entwickelung.* Eine Abhandlung der Universalrechtsgeschichte," Vol. II, Berlin 1825. Four volumes have appeared.

philosophy, appears. It had, however, no influence upon the development of legal philosophy. Lassalle's work[1] attracted considerable attention, by reason not of its philosophical but of its political importance, due to its excursions into politics.

Although Stahl conducted a controversy against Hegel's pantheism, his philosophy of law and government may be regarded as a theological variation of Hegel's system, reflecting also the influence of Schelling. (For Stahl's position consult § 36.)

The economic philosophy of Karl Marx, and that of his pupil, Lassalle, may be regarded as the materialistic aspect of Hegel's philosophy, taking its mode of demonstration from Hegel's dialectic method.[2]

§ 36. *Recent Systems of Legal Philosophy.* 1: STAHL. The majority of orthodox legal philosophers attempted to show that a philosophy of law based upon ecclesiastical foundations was rational, and thus freed it from its religious forms and limitations. By a converse procedure J. STAHL[3] (1802–1861) divested the philosophy of law and government of its rationalistic foundations and reconstructed it upon a Protestant Christian basis. Whether Stahl has any claim to recognition as a scientific contributor to the philosophy of government and law, or whether he is to be dismissed as a partisan, is an open question. It is but fair that

[1] *Lassalle*, "System," I, pp. (157) 164 seq., 180–186, 279 seq., 361–386; Part II, Division 2, pp. 593–596.

[2] See below, § 38.

[3] "Die Philosophie des Rechts" Vol. 1 (third edit., Heidelberg 1856). "Geschichte der Rechtsphilosophie," 2 vols. "Rechts- und Staatslehre auf der Grundlage Christlicher Weltanschauung," Part 1, containing the general laws and private law (third edit., 1854); Part 2, "Die Staatslehre und die Prinzipien des Staatsrechts" (third edit., 1856). Vol. 2, Part 1, alone was accessible to me in the third edit., for the rest I cite from the second edition.

he be judged by the intellectual standards of his day. Rationalism, though not superseded, was on the decline. From the days of Descartes to those of the three great luminaries, Kant, Fichte, and Hegel, the mainstay of German philosophy had been the position that reason, or experienceless thought, yields genuine truth and philosophic knowledge. English empiricism was unable to assert itself, owing partly to its tendency to dissipate into a shallow utilitarianism. Though in his first period Schelling was bound by the rationalism and idealism of Kant and Fichte, it was through his influence that rationalism began to decline; and Hegel himself, the greatest of rationalists, who traced dialectically the growth of pure subjectless and objectless thought of a de-personalized agent, through his recognition of evolutionary doctrines, helped to dig the grave of rationalism. Stahl carried forward the program outlined by Schelling and Hegel for a withdrawal from the philosophy of reason. As an opponent of rationalism he sought a different basis for his philosophy of law and government. Had Stahl lived a few decades later, it is probable that he would have followed the prevalent tendency and would have become an empiricist, a sensationalist upon an evolutionary basis. But Stahl lived in a period in which the only scientifically approved philosophical method was that of a pure deductive derivation of principles as conclusions of a supreme, unquestioned major premise. As Stahl abandoned the dogma of reason, he had no choice but to accept the dogma of faith; his philosophy of law represents the Protestant counterpart of the Catholic philosophy of Schelling's later period.

An unprejudiced view of the great rationalistic systems of Kant, Fichte, and Hegel discloses that in fact empirical types of knowledge were forced into the rationalistic mould. Had those great minds not first had recourse to experience, and transferred the material thus inductively obtained to deductive premises, they would have been blocked at the outset, and would have failed to find a transition from pure reason to the realities of law and government. Critical idealism may be described as an ambitious philosophical edifice set with noble columns, which, however, carry no burden; indeed they have only the form of supports, while actually ornaments suggestive of the vagaries of the baroque period. Stahl's theological deductions likewise carry no burden; the true supports of his view were supplied by Hegel and Schelling.

Schelling took over pantheism from Spinoza; but instead of the dogmatic pantheism of the latter, he advanced a critical pantheism. Spinoza's pantheism is thorough-going; to him the world is the emanation and consists of universal substance. Schelling's pantheism went through the stages of the critical idealism of Kant and Fichte, and assumed a critical form. The world, or the absolute, became the mere accident of a rational ego. The philosophy of Spinoza and that of Schelling favored the doctrine of identity; that is, they assumed the identity or unity of subject and object. But Spinoza placed such unity in the absolute object, while Schelling placed it in the absolute subject. Stahl once more endowed pantheism with a personal God, and yet occasionally fell back upon a rationalistic basis. For Stahl reason, though not the source, is yet the means of recognizing justice; accordingly, the material content of law reaches human consciousness [1] through reason.

Law and custom, according to Stahl, are derived from the will of God. Ethics is objective or communal custom, "ethos," in so far as the divine design applies to

[1] Vol. II, Part 1, pp. XVIII–XXV, 7–69, 233–238 (opposed to this, p. 241).

the human race as a whole; ethics is morality or subjective custom ("ethos") in so far as the individual may be said to be formed in the image of God.[1] This dual aspect of the "ethos" reflects the position of Greek national ethics.

The interest of the maintenance of the objective existence of the moral world requires an external and enforcing temporal power, which is the law[2] — a law enforced against all opposition. "The divine order as applied to the human race must maintain human society through the human order which it establishes, and which imposes its authority upon all individuals; and such order is the law." The law becomes realized in the State;[3] it arises in the consciousness of the people,[4] but in the last analysis "it is the power of the divine order which creates law and endows it with its dignity."[5] "Criminal law is a retributive justice, and is designed to establish the realm or the glory of the moral power through the destruction or suffering of those who oppose it."[6]

While private law is based upon the idea of personality, public law is based upon the idea of a moral and intellectual realm. The idea of such a moral realm is the supreme ethical conception, and pervades every relation of human condition; it is its "universal and absolute purpose," "$\tau\epsilon\lambda os$." Its perfect realization lies, according to the Christian religion, in the hereafter, in the king-

[1] Vol. II, Part 1, pp. 70 seq., particularly 76-79.

[2] Vol. II, Part I, pp. 191 seq., 192.

[3] Vol. II, Part 1, p. 210.

[4] Vol. II, Part 1, pp. 233-238.

[5] Vol. II, Part 1, p. 241.

[6] Vol. II, Part 1, p. 165. The right of the State to punish is but objective, just as the moral dominion of the State is in general but objective.

dom of God. But even upon earth the moral world is a moral realm; it but lacks a visible outward form.[1]

The supreme institution of public law, its institution *par excellence*, is the State. "The State is the perfect moral intellectual realm which men should establish upon earth." It is based upon the common character of the people, and not upon that of the individual. The State must be legally regulated, but not restricted to the function of the law; it must become a moral commonwealth. The State is accordingly a "realm of ideas and intelligent purposes, realized and to be realized, established in the moral order of the world of which men are the self-appointed servants." The consequence of this conception of the State as a moral intellectual realm is to make its chief purpose the perfection of human communal life, and pursuant thereto, the freedom and right of each individual. The efficiency of the State extends to all parts of the common life, which reduces to the view that the State must assume a mission of culture.

From the nature of the State as a moral realm it follows that it must exercise a moral authority over the people and "must become conscious of itself and of its power as a personal force; such is the purpose ("τέλος") of the temporal kingdom. It is established in order that there shall be dominion over men, personal, consistent, self-sustained, not of human origin, worthy, authoritative, regulative, sacred, awe-inspiring. The dominion of the State, and thus the State itself, becomes personal in its king." In an hereditary monarchy the esteem of the ruler rests "not alone upon a general command and decree of God, as is true of all supremacy, but at the same time upon a very special divine provision. This is

[1] Vol. II, Part 1 (second edit., 1846), pp. 1, seq.; pp. 12, 102–105, 106–109, 112–123, 208 seq.

the principle of legitimacy which is peculiar to the hereditary monarchy."¹ The nature of a kingdom involves the primacy and independence of authority, but does not involve the absoluteness thereof; such would be against the order of nature and against the inviolability of the kingdom. The sovereignty of the monarch is co-ordinate with that of the constitution, just as the supremacy of the people is co-ordinate with that of the estates. The constitution must not be 'ooked upon as the source of sanctity, but only as providing "the legal and moral ties which form its content." The principle of representation leads to the institution of representatives as against the estates, by virtue of which the representatives are not chosen from among special classes, but from the people, and are called to represent not the interests of the estates, but the general interests of the people.² It is upon these three principles — that of legitimacy, that of the constitution, and that of representation — that Stahl founds the Christian State. His position may be said to form the theoretical basis of the conservative party in Prussia.

2: TRENDELENBURG. ADOLF TRENDELENBURG³ (1802–1872) proposes to determine the underlying idea of

[1] Vol. II, Part 2, pp. 219, 220: "The divine right and legitimacy are thus diverse but related conceptions; the former implies that the authority by virtue of which the king rules is of divine origin, and the latter that his accession to the throne is likewise divine. *They form the Christian principle of the State.*"

[2] Vol. II, Part 2, pp. 221 seq.; 241, 238–247; 244; 314–321.

[3] "Naturrecht auf dem Grunde der Ethik," second edit., Leipzig 1868. *Lasson,* "System der Rechtsphilosophie," Berlin and Leipzig 1882 (p. 108), thus comments: "Trendelenburg attempts to derive his position from Aristotle, though not always very clearly; and at the same time takes account in part of the notable achievements of modern science; but despite many suggestive comments, he does not attain to a clear presentation of principles."

the law; by the idea he means "the conception in which is contained the final determination of the inner purpose." In agreement with Plato and Aristotle, and in contrast to the "modern separation of the juridical and ethical, of the legal and moral," Trendelenburg reaches the position that "the conception of law stands in an essential and intimate relation to the content of morality." Following Plato and Aristotle, he further determines the idea of ethics as the fulfillment of the idea of human nature, and finds the ethical problem in "the realization of man as man."[1] This idea is to be realized only in the community. "The strengthening of individuals and their affiliation as a whole" proceed hand in hand as the law of every ethical community. "The realization of the ideal in the communal man and in the individual" becomes the ethical principle. Through the association of duties and ethical privileges, as also of duty and law, Trendelenburg reaches the following conception of law: "The law in the moral community is the conception of such universal limitations of actions resulting in the maintenance and furtherance of the ethical whole and its parts. The ethics of an immanent teleology yields this concept of law and no other."[2]

Trendelenburg proceeds to consider the physical aspect of law, that is, its power of enforcement and its logic or method.[3] He continues with an "outline of legal relations on the principle," of a deductive construction of the entire field of law in the spirit of a teleological ethics. His view of the State is thus given: "I conceive

[1] "Naturrecht," pp. 6, 22, 94 seq. "Construed in a most general sense, ethics pertains to the larger domain, and law is derived from it."

[2] "Naturrecht," pp. 41 seq., 45, 48–70, 71–100, 123–160; historical, pp. 100–118.

[3] For the logical aspect in the origin of law see "Naturrecht," pp. 160–173; and for the application of the law, pp. 173–191.

of the State as a whole, which in turn falls into special divisions, and its distinctive trait is that of exercising supreme legislation from within and independence from without, thus protecting right by might." The idea of the State is "to realize universal man in the individual form of the people." The problem of the State is "ethically determined by the welfare of the parts through the whole and of the whole through the parts." It is therefore "the design of the State that man in the State, and man in the parts thereof, shall ever remain or become human." "It is therefore the object of all governmental regulation to embody a mutual relation of the parts to the whole, and the closest and most favorable unity of disposition, insight, and authority of which the actual conditions permit."[1]

3: KRAUSE. KARL CHR. FR. KRAUSE[2] (1781–1832) is associated with the transition from the position of natural law to the modern philosophical view of government and law.[3] He proceeds deductively, deriving them from "pure reason." While his point of view is fundamentally that of the adherents of "natural law," he recognizes the historical development in legal philosophy.

In developing his practical philosophy, Krause avoids

[1] "Naturrecht," pp. 192 seq., 325 seq., 348, 481–485.

[2] *Krause*, "Grundlage des Naturrechts, oder Philosophischer Grundriss des Ideals des Rechts," Part I, Jena and Leipzig 1803. *Mollat* edited a second edition of Parts I and 2 (new material) from the posthumous manuscript, Leipzig 1890. I cite from this edition. *Krause*, "Das Urbild der Menschheit," Dresden 1811. "Abriss des Systems der Philosophie des Rechtes oder des Naturrechtes," Göttingen 1828. *"Lebenslehre* oder Philosophie der Geschichte zur Begründung der Lebenskunstwissenschaft." Vorlesungen (at the University of Göttingen, 1828–1829), first edit., 1843, Karl Hermann v. Leonhardi, second edit., P. Hohlfeld and August Wünsche, Leipzig 1904.

[3] "Abriss des Systems, pp. 1 seq., 8.

the danger attaching to a consistent pantheism, namely, the non-recognition of the personality of the individual man. In Spinoza's philosophy, God alone is substance, and all phenomena are attributes of substance. Like Spinoza, Krause assumes an all-pervasive omnipresent substance which he calls being — "Wesen"; the individual phenomena and the individuals, however, are not mere attributes, but likewise share in this quality of being; they are beings, and God is the original Being — "Urwesen." Krause calls this philosophical conception Panentheism, the doctrine of all in God. It differs from the Jewish-Christian position only in the pantheistic conception of the divine being. Krause's philosophy forms an advance upon Spinoza, a position the more readily attainable through the reconstruction of Spinoza's pantheism in a subjective form in Schelling's philosophy of identity; it there became a critical pantheism operative in the intellectual subjective world. The later development of his doctrine likewise shows the influence of Spinoza. Spinoza came to the conclusion that whatever occurs is fundamentally a natural process, and that accordingly all human action is right because it is a constituent part thereof. Wrong would be what none would attain and none desire. The practical untenability of this conclusion leads Spinoza to a breach with his own system, and to an affiliation with the utilitarianism of Hobbes. Reflecting the influence of the Stoics, and likewise of Hegel, Krause approaches the problem by assuming that every individual has a destiny, and that it is the purpose of the individual, as of the community, to attempt to fulfill such mission, to assume a place in the constitution of the world, and to assert it.[1] Every individual is thus an infinite problem for

[1] "Grundlage des Naturrechts,"I, pp. 23-34, with the note on p. 21. "Abriss des Systems," pp. 12-42.

knowledge as for conduct. The individual cannot fully attain his destiny, but must strive for it as an ideal. This ideal is to recognize the law of the world and to enforce it. The criterion, the medium of knowledge, by which the individual is put into accord with his destiny, is conscience. The voice of conscience is revealed as "the longing of love." Love is conditioned by the knowledge of the human value of others. Love leads to the recognition of other individualities, and elevates man above extreme self-assertion.[1] The nature of God is revealed as the bounty of God. In His endless bounty lies "the one good, the one highest possession." The realization of this good is therefore "the one law of life of every finite rational being — the destiny of life."[2]

In his "Grundlage des Naturrechts," Krause approaches the problem of law essentially upon the position of Fichte. Law is a postulate of reason, and thus "refers to the establishment of the external conditions of reason which exist, and which should be maintained independently of the freedom of the will and of natural forces." "The law thus seeks to make freedom a natural force and issue, without, however, destroying such freedom." There are as many types of rights as there are ideals of reason; a right to wisdom, religion, love, art, and, as a means of attaining a rational ideal, "a right to the maintenance of a bodily personality and to the inherent conception of earthly utility." Furthermore, "as law is to be independent of the bad or good intent, there is also the right of coercion," and for the enforcement of authority, a right of punishment, and

[1] "Grundlage des Naturrechts," I, pp. 34–39. "Das Urbild der Menschheit," pp. 100–126. "Abriss des Systems, " pp. 61–63. "Lebenslehre, pp. 90–98.

[2] "Abriss des Systems," pp. 36 seq.

consequently, "the right of supervision and correction of all individuals." In principle all enjoy the same legal rights. Law and morality are correlated and directed to the same end. Law is "a condition of morality."[1]

In his "Abriss des Systems der Philosophie des Rechts," Krause describes law as a definite and necessary relation of life, which must and should be established through free will and action as a definite possession and a definite good. Consequently "the one law of morality contains within itself the definite law to establish that relation to life which is right." Here law appears as a subordinate content of the moral law. The law is accordingly "an organic whole, a structure or organism of a timeless condition of the life of the absolute reason; or the absolute limitation of reason." Krause's term, "timeless," in reality implies the opposite of its literal meaning. Timeless means unlimited in time, that is, "in regard to time, quite free."

"Humanity, in so far as it realizes, lives, or individually establishes the law, becomes the legally regulated State of humanity, 'Menschheit-Rechtsstaat;' or the State of humanity, 'der Menschheitsstaat;' or simply the State without further connotation."[2] Krause looks upon the State, as upon law, as an organism. This conception, which he derived from Schelling, he develops, particularly in his "Urbild der Menschheit"[3] (1811),

[1] "Grundlage des Naturrechts,"I, pp. 43, 44-48.

[2] "Abriss des Systems," pp. 5, 8, 46 seq., 154-177, 177 seq.

[3] Pp. 99-100, 295-304, & 327 seq. "Independence and harmonious interaction form the fundamental principles of the structure of the world, of life and beauty." ("Das Urbild der Menschheit," p. 90): "Accordingly the relation in which all creatures are placed with one another must be so conditioned that all participating in the relation may yet persist therein with the retention of their peculiar nature; and that in and through such relation the harmony, for the sake of which the relation is constituted, is maintained

and in his biological work, "Lebenslehre."[1] In the latter he reaches a pertinent and clear conception of the nature of law, namely, that the norm of primary assent or authorization has but secondary application as a limiting norm for human action.[2]

The "Naturrecht"[3] of Ahrens, published simultaneously in German and French, incorporated Krause's philosophy of law, elaborated and improved it, and gained for it a wider circle of readers. Krause failed to gain this popularity because of his peculiar terminology which made the approach to his philosophy difficult, and perhaps also because of the unjust fate by virtue of which the discovery of a new truth seems commonly to be credited, not to the discoverer, but to his successor. In addition to Ahrens, RÖDER is to be mentioned as a disciple of Krause.

in conformity with the peculiar nature of the participants and of the eternal laws of the world. In every such relation all the participants therein must prosper and flourish each in itself and all in harmony furthered by God. As the harmony of all creatures of the world is one, so also must all the relations thereof and the several resultant individual harmonies be concordant within the one great harmony of universal life in God." ("Das Urbild der Menschheit," p. 91.)

[1] "Lebenslehre," pp. 82–90, upon the organic nature of law. (p. 85): "The law itself is one, the one temporally free condition of the unified life of God." The organic nature of the State is discussed on pp. 183–213.

[2] "Lebenslehre," pp. 189 seq.

[3] "Naturrecht oder Philosophie des Rechts und des Staates. Auf dem Grund des ethischen Zusammenflusses von Recht und Kultur," 2 vols., sixth edit., Vienna 1870–1871 (the last edition is in German). "Cours de Droit Naturel ou de Philosophie du droit," 2 vols. eighth edit., Leipzig, reissued after the death of the author upon the basis of the sixth edition, but thoroughly revised and supplemented by the theory of public law and of international law. In the French edition the historical portion up to the close of the Middle Ages has been omitted.

4: AHRENS. Following the example of Plato and Cicero, AHRENS (1808–1874) derived law from the inner nature of man; for law belongs to those ideas or conceptions of the human consciousness that involve obligation, and thus could not have been derived from experience. The law becomes operative in consciousness as a guiding principle in accord with which one may critically judge the existing conditions and seek their improvement. The idea of the good, the moral, and the just, constitute the content of the common moral law. The idea of good is the most general, and comprises that of the moral and the just. For everything is good "which is in accord with the rational nature of man and his perfection, and thus is worthy to be striven for. Morality and law are rooted in the nature of man; they are worthy to be striven for, and form the essential values of human life." Morality and law differ in that morality refers to the motives of actions, and law to the actions themselves, to the objective relations of life, which are for the most part property relations. Accordingly law is a "norm which regulates the use of freedom in accordance with the relations of human life and property."

The quality that elevates man above other beings is personality. Man alone is a person; and the criterion of personality is reason. It is through reason that the mind recognizes laws, and that thinking, feeling, and willing are elevated to the realm of the absolute, and the will becomes free will. Reason is the capacity of indefinite improvement. "Through the infinite power and disposition of God, all men are equal. Every man by possibility of endowment is humanity. Every man should therefore attempt to bring to ever more complete realization the idea and the ideal of humanity." Krause makes the good ("Das Gute") equal to goods ("Das

Gut"); similarly Ahrens makes "Gut" (possession) "everything essential to man and worthy of human effort—everything that is in accord with true human needs — that is serviceable to the effort for perfection." Ethics is the science of that which is good and of its realization through the free will. It is divided into the doctrine of values ("Güter"), and its two offshoots, morality and law. The good or the supreme good is the complete development of the divine in human nature in every direction in which life may contribute to the kingdom of God; that is, to a kingdom of all that is good in the human, modeled upon the divine. Without sacrifice of its unity, the supreme good divides into the several goods which attain this quality through the personality; it includes such as are inherent in the fundamental relations in which man stands towards the order of his life and being. These personal values are life, health, dignity, honor, liberty, together with such relations as become objects of practical endeavor by virtue of thinking, feeling, and willing. The values of the second order, or cultural values, express the trait of humanity, the susceptibility to human culture upon a divine model. They include religion, science, fine and applied art — the latter a combination of science and art — as well as education, morality, and law.

The more precise formulation of law involves an appreciation of the realm in which property is realized. These realms, according to Krause and Ahrens, are the realm of personality and the realm of property. The realm of personality comprises life in all essential aspects; and the stages thereof are individual personality, marriage and the family, the community, the race or the union of races into a nation or State, and finally, "the federation of peoples which nations are destined to form." The domain of property regulation and of culture is characterized by the dominant pursuit of a special purpose. Law is the regulative principle of personal and proprietary interests. Law is the organic ordering principle applied to the various relations of life. The legal relations are merely relations of property in so far as these are considered from their legal side. Every legal realm and institution must be developed from a uniform principle. Law and morality seek to realize the good. They differ in that law is chiefly directed to outer and enforcible transactions, — to the legality of the transaction — while morality is directed to the intent or disposition. Morality includes a more extensive domain is so far as what is legally prescribed or forbidden is also ethically prescribed or forbidden. Morality demands an ethical motive for right action, demands that it shall be done "with pure motives for the sake of the right itself, as a part of the human and divine order without coercion or penalty."[1] Law and justice in the last analysis depend upon God.[2] The relation of the idea of law, the true expression of justice and material law to positive or formal law, is expressed in the requirement of justice that all law shall be in accord with right. The subject, or the medium of the law, is man "as one who, by virtue of his rational quality, is an end to himself, and who can utilize material things as a means for his life's purpose." The object or content of law is whatever may be made serviceable to rational purposes.[3]

In the second volume of the "Naturrecht," the legal relations bearing upon the theory of values are further

[1] "Naturrecht," I, pp. 223–283, 297–316 ("Cours de droit naturel," I, pp. 158–167, with note I, p. 158).

[2] "Naturrecht," I, pp. 316–322, 221 seq. Ahrens distinctly rejects Hegel's pantheism. "Naturrecht," I, p. 187

[3] "Naturrecht," I, 322–337, 348–351.

developed and for the most part in the modern spirit; yet there is no real progress, no tangible result; indeed, essentially, nothing is added. Law and its institutions are set forth as available and useful; in brief the philosophy of law follows the science of law, instead of illuminating critically the content of the law and of attempting its further development as a contribution to civilization.

As Dahn properly notes,[1] the legal philosophy of *Krause* and *Ahrens* is based upon an equivocal use of terms, in that the good ("bonum, ἀγαθόν") is also property, "das Gut," and in that property is likewise viewed and valued as the good. The merit of his legal philosophy lies in the first place in its development and elaboration of the Hegelian "Kulturstaat," and again in the emphasis of the relative independence of the several realms of law — the realms of legal authority, which, since Ahrens, and on the basis of his terms, have been called "Rechtsgüter," (legally protected interests). By this means fixed points were established in the general field of government and law, with due consideration of the part played by the individual in the State.[2]

5: HERBART. The practical philosophy of HERBART (1776–1841) is founded upon his doctrine of ideas.[3] The moral ideas are the ideas of inner freedom, of per-

[1] "Zur Rechtsphilosophie," pp. 368 seq.

[2] *Berolzheimer*, "Die Entgeltung im Strafrechte," pp. 162–168; 'Rechtsphilosophische Studien," pp. 100–103.

[3] *Herbart*, "Allgemeine Praktische Philosophie," "Collected Works," Hartenstein edit., 8 vols., Leipzig 1851, pp. 3–212. "Analytische Beleuchtung des Naturrechts und der Moral," "Collected Works," 8, pp. 215–405. "Aphorismen zur Praktischen Philosophie," "Collected Works," Hartenstein edit., vol. 9, Leipzig 1851, pp. 389–449. Of special interest also are "Über einige Beziehungen zwischen Psychologie und Staatswissenschaft," "Collected Works," 9, pp. 199–219. "Über die Unmöglichkeit persönliches Vertrauen

fection, of charity, of justice, of mercy. The ideas form exemplars for human conduct. They appeal to the human will, to the "stronger and the weaker wills, which are more or less well-developed copies of the ideas." "Strife offends," and hence the idea of disapproval.[1] "Unrewarded and unpunished deeds offend," hence the idea of equity demanding reward and punishment.[2] In Herbart the ideas of law and equity, and thus of the philosophy of law in general, assume a complete ethical form, and become a division of ethics. Herbart's ethics rests upon a psychological basis. It appeals to the will and is determined by the "moral sensibility."[3] From these primary ideas Herbart

im Staate durch künstliche Formen entbehrlich zu machen," "Collected Works," 9, pp. 221-240. "Zur Lehre von der Freiheit des menschlichen Willens," "Collected Works," 9, pp. 243-385.

[1] "Allgemeine Praktische Philosophie," pp. 33-60, p. 30, pp. 49, 71. *Herbart* thus shows an agreement with Schopenhauer's position which, in opposition to *Hegel*, recognizes the positive, and in principle, the more fundamental conception in the wrong, the right being its negation. In his "Analytische Beleuchtung des Naturrechts," § 55 ("Collected Works," 8, pp. 267 seq.), *Herbart* refers to *Grotius:* "Hugo Grotius shows that law must have originated from dissatisfaction of conflict, for he refutes the contention that advantage was the source of law, and restricts his entire dissertation to the consideration of war. . . . He had hardly need to say that strife displeases. This displeasure pervades his entire admirable work."

[2] "Allgemeine Praktische Philosophie," pp. 55, 53-60: "Justice and equity as traits of character must have been acquired in consequence of displeasure with strife and unpunished deeds." ("Analytische Beleuchtung," etc, § 136, "Collected Works," 8, p. 344.

[3] "Allgemeine," etc., "Collected Works," 8, pp. 3-24. Also "Analytische," etc., § 54, pp. 262-266. The five original ideas — of subjective freedom, of perfection, benevolence, right, and equity — are not to be derived from a single supreme idea. The contraction of these original ideas in the unity of the person gives rise to virtue. "Allgemeine," etc., p. 109.

develops the derivative ideas. "When one thinks of a number of persons assembled within a given area, the varied products of which invite and engage their attention, and when one offers each of these products to all of the candidates, the natural and expected result is that these persons, filled with desire, will quarrel; but such strife is to be avoided, and the means of avoiding it leads to the idea of a society dominated by law."[1]

"Strife may arise; this emergency requires either a compromise so that it may not arise, or a settlement so far as it has arisen." Concession, that is, a division of the contested property, may avoid strife.[2] Thus Herbart reaches the establishment of real rights through the principle of avoidance of conflict. "If, however, conflict has broken out, if actions contrary to law have been committed, the next step is to minimize the consequences thereof." The disapproval of unatoned deeds brings about punishment of the offender and the reward of good actions.[3] The administration of the community arises from benevolence. It seeks the "general good, that is, the highest possible amount of satisfaction for all." "Benevolence is not restricted to merit; it welcomes every sympathetic advance." A mutual spiritual sympathy binds the members of a community into a cultural unity. "When the individuals are animated by a single spirit, which no one feels as his exclusively, and to which no one feels alien, the situation may be regarded as that of a single soul

---

[1] P. 76. In some of his minor writings *Herbart* likewise notes that "the presupposition of a legal society is that each individual desires to avoid conflict." "Aphorismen," etc., p. 400.

[2] Pp. 78, 78-83.

[3] "Allgemeine," etc., pp. 83-90. "Analytische," etc., pp. 315-320. "Aphorismen," etc., p. 415.

that has its life in all of them collectively." Thus the community becomes a "spiritual community."[1]

"If society is to have a basis of continuity it requires an external bond." "The State is characterized by its coercive power." "Legal duties are emphasized by coercion." Inasmuch as not every association "considered in itself alone can establish an authority, and through such authority protect itself," it follows that "the entire country, affected as it may be by conflicting interests, should be governed by the same authority. Thus arises a State which comprises a number of smaller and differently disposed groups."[2] "The State is an association protected by authority; and its interests include the interests of all associations which have been formed, or will be formed, within its sphere of influence." "The three factors of the conception of the State are private will, institutions, and authority." "Private will establishes society." The institutions are those provisions "which would have to exist in society even though society were not formed into a State." The most important of such institutions are the laws.[3]

[1] Pp. 90-96, 96-101, 101-106. The statesman is not an educator, but "he may seek the common spirit wherever he finds it, particularly in the minor social relations." "Thereby the will of men transcends the ordinary selfishness and reaches a higher sphere in which a common endeavor is vitalized and justified." "Furthermore the statesman may have a concern for the largest and most general interests; thus men acquire respect for the totality." ("Analytische," etc., §§ 173, 174, p. 366.)

Politics and pedagogy are branches of the science of virtue. The education of the young is directed to the development of virtue, and for this end awakens a many-sided interest and the development of a stable character. ("Allgemeine," etc., pp. 143 seq.; "Analytische," etc., §§ 124 seq., 169-172.)

[2] Pp. 129; 77; 183; 130 seq.

[3] "Analytische," etc., § 177; "Col. Works," 8, pp. 367 seq. Also "Aphorismen," etc., "Col. Works," 9, p. 406.

AUGUST GEYER (1831–1885), in his clear and well-written compendium of the philosophy of law entitled "Geschichte und System der Rechtsphilosophie in Grundzügen," applied the philosophy of Herbart to legal science.[1]

6: DAHN. FELIX DAHN[2] (b. 1834) a disciple of Professor Prantl, presents an idealistic legal philosophy. To philosophize, he says, means to seek principles. The problem of the philosophy of law thus becomes "to express absolute law in the concept of law, and in the resulting legislation, as well as in the several phenomena of life. The philosophy of law must seek and prove the rational and necessary element of law."[3]

Just as language, family, art, and religion, so likewise are morality, law, and the State, characteristic of "human qualities," and such qualities are the phenomena in the life of peoples which appear "uniformly at all stages of culture, though with everchanging expressions." These qualities arise from an inner factor which "in its last analysis is inexplicable," namely, the rational character; and from an external source, the aggregate of the "historical conditions operative in space and time." Individual and social psychology reveal among the human qualities a tendency towards law and government, which are made manifest in the realization of law

[1] *Geyer*, "Die Lehre von der Notwehr, eine Strafrechtliche Abhandlung," Jena 1857, p. iv of the preface; pp. 8–18 outline the development of Herbart's philosophy of law.

[2] The writings of *Dahn* here pertinent are: *"Die Vernunft im Recht.* Grundlagen der Rechtsphilosophie," Berlin 1879 (which developed from a criticism of *Ihering's* "Zweck im Recht," Vol. I). "Über Wesen und Werden des Rechts," "Z. f. v. Rechtsw.," Vol. II, 1879, pp. 1–10; Vol. III, Stuttgart 1881, pp. 1–16 (a philosophy of law presented in theses).

[3] "Vom Wesen u. Werden des Rechts," §§ 1–6; "Die Vernunft im Recht," pp. 13 seq.

and government. The actual origin of law and government lies in physical necessity, which leads men to the use of natural resources, and to social co-operation. The ideal origin is "an inner logical necessity, the logical or rational need to bring the individual under the general; hence there result laws and the law. To bring about the complete realization of the idea of law, the State upholds the law, which in turn rests upon the strong idealistic impulse of patriotism.[1] Law thus becomes "a rational peaceful ordering of a community of men in their outward relations to one another and to things."[2] The State becomes "the communal expression of a unified people for the protection and fostering of law and culture."[3] The oldest form of law is that through usage — "the law as crystallized custom." Property arises through "the protection of possessions, even though detention has ceased through the acknowledgment of the ownership on the part of the community. Such acknowledgment also played a part in the law of the family, especially in regard to marriage and paternal authority, and thus transforms what were originally relations of material fact into legal relations.

Upon the origin of the State, and upon the relation of State and law, Dahn concludes that "the State arises neither through explicit nor implicit contract, nor through superhuman intervention, but instinctively from the kindred clan and the community. Its sources lie in the natural impulse towards law, and in racial gregariousness. The tendency towards government is the idealized form

---

[1] "Vom Wesen," etc., §§ 8, 9, 10, 11, 12.

[2] "Vom Wesen," etc., § 8, nos. 6, 13; "Die Vernunft," etc., p. 14.

[3] "Vom Wesen," etc., § 14. Dahn here advocates the "Kulturstaat" as against the "Rechtsstaat." "Zur Rechtsphilosophie," p. 335. "The State is both 'Rechtsstaat und Kulturstaat.'" ("Die Vernunft," etc., pp. 60, 60–64.)

of the trend towards nationality. The State does not create law but is its prerequisite; it is the setting that provides the secure establishment of the law. Historically the State is distinguished from the kindred association and community, not absolutely, but relatively; that is, through the greater emphasis of the national interests, of the more conscious external contrast, and practically through the larger number of common purposes."

According to Dahn, punishment, viewed objectively, is "the assertion by repression that maintains a rational peace against irrational attack." Ethics and law differ in principle. Morality is the idea of the good; it is the rational means of internal peace; while law is the rational means of external peace in the relations of men to one another. From this it follows that legal duties can be enforced, but that ethical commands cannot be enforced; and likewise that the disposition of the ethical spirit prevails above conformity of the law. "Under normal circumstances" every breach of the law is also a breach of morals.[1]

Dahn calls his position "Historism," or "the speculative development of the older historical school."[2] He presents a synthesis of Hegel and Schelling, a dialectic

[1] "Vom Wesen," etc., §§ 19, 34, 35, 36, 31, 18, and § 8, no. 5.

[2] "In the combination of 'Historism' with dialectical speculation, and along with a modest recognition of the relativity of all human knowledge, I perceive the future trend of all legal philosophy." In this statement *Dahn* attempts to avoid the error of the "historical school (of *Savigny*), which looked upon a nation merely as an association in which law arises and through which its character is determined, . . . whereas it is evident that the impulse towards law, and the conception of law, are realized by virtue of an ideal necessity and a real need, long before the appearance of the nation in the narrower affiliations of the family, the clan, the horde, the community." *Dahn,* "Die Vernunft," etc., p. 12.

or idealistic "Historism." According to Dahn, the philosophy of law is to be developed by the application of a philosophical method in combination with a comparative study of law. He denies the position of "natural law"; there is no ideal model law, for law is always the rational and peaceful ordering of the external relations of a particular and concrete human society.

7: LASSON. The position that ADOLF LASSON[1] (1832–) assumes is that of Hegel's "Kulturstaat." Like Dahn, he withdraws wholly from the doctrine of "natural law." He combines speculative considerations with historical study. In his view the problem of the philosophy of law is "to interpret the prevailing law in its inner nature and in its relation to other movements and phenomena of life."[2] Of the historical school he says, "To understand law and government scientifically means to understand their historical genesis, which justifies their necessary development and their organic connection with the soil on which they grew. The historical is likewise the rational method. Law can only be that which prevails, which lives and finds its source in human consciousness." Lasson defines law as the aggregate of the governmental prescriptions enforced by the State. Therefore law and the State are inseparable.

In developing his legal philosophy Lasson offers an analysis of man according to his bodily and mental nature, including a study of "human relations," and a consideration of "human interests." In the analysis of the human mind Lasson is led to assume a free will in Kant's sense. "The will is autonomous so

[1] "System der Rechtsphilosophie," Berlin and Leipzig 1882, p. 19.

[2] "System," etc., p. 10. *Lasson* conceived the philosophy of law as a division of ethics, as the science of the realization of the idea of good in the human will. (p. 1.)

far as it evolves its own law spontaneously from the form of its own rationality. That is good which corresponds to the practical reason, and that will is a good will which desires the good, and desires it for no other motive than because it is good. The good will that comes to be in permanent sympathy with the nature of the subject is the truly free will." "The elevation of the natural will from a natural to a free will proceeds by training the will, by education." The highest stage of the emancipation of the will is to be called morality only when it is directly allied to the holy will of God; but the objective organ of morality is the Church."[1] Among the human relations Lasson emphasizes the family and the people. The interests of men he divides into the material or economic individual interests and the social interests.[2]

Such is Lasson's view of the law, and of its relation to the "practical reason" and the "natural will." In this connection the will appears as "a variety of the rational will which is assumed to be still in the stage of the natural will, and is moved by impulses and desires to which reason is added at first merely as an external limiting and restricting influence." In a later connection he characterizes law as "the statutory order," and finally as a limiting norm, as "the limit of authority." The principles of law are justice and liberty.[3] Inasmuch as positive law is an external ordering of a more

[1] "System," etc., pp. 19, 21, 22, 113–161, 162–174, 174–192 154, 141–161, 159–161.

[2] "System," etc., p. 187: "The human community in so far as it affords the setting for the interplay of all interests which all individuals or groups thereof pursue may be called society, or more exactly civil society."

[3] "System," etc., pp. 193–198, 198–207, 207–215, 215–242, 242–282.

or less accidental historical character, justice becomes the adequate expression of the practical reason, and as compared with the law, is an "ideal demand" that never can be fully realized.

The supreme function of law consists in its service as at once the expression and the medium for the inner life and the spiritual growth of the people. As a reflection of the subconsciously active cultural forces of a particular national spirit, the law becomes an harmonious expression of the relation between the inner life and needs of the community and the outer forms of regulation of the life of the community. By this means law "attains its value and its high positive significance for the cultural life of nations. By obeying their own positive laws nations attain their freedom, and men living in communities acquire the warrant of their human dignity."

The State is "a human association possessing an organized supreme authority as the ultimate source of all coercion." To the State belong the people, the land, the sovereignty. The authority of the State and the coercion which it exercises are at the service of law. Hence there is no law without government, and government has for its purpose the maintenance of the law.[1] In its origin the State is at once a product of nature and a necessary result of the rational disposition of man.[2] In its origin the State is remote from the will of the people. "The sovereignty of the people is a meaningless term."[3] The State is the realized legal order and

---

[1] "System," etc., pp. 231, 242 seq., 283, 287.

[2] "System," etc., pp. 298–300. *Jellinek* accordingly regards *Lasson* as an advocate of the "psychological" theory of the origin of the State. (*Jellinek*, "Allgemeine Staatslehre," p. 195, note 1.)

[3] "System," etc., pp. 293–311.

its function is to make order real.[1] According to Lasson the activity of the State in the course of historical development shows a tendency to confine itself to the minimum sphere, to leave the largest play to the free activity of all forces, and to intervene as a restraining force only when the maintenance of the State is in any manner endangered. The view thus expressed without modification is hardly correct. The problems and the sphere of governmental functions in administration are of variable scope according to the general cultural trend of a particular people at a particular time. In reality the State exists always and only as a positive historical phenomenon. From the point of view of civilization the highest form of State is the national State, and in consideration of the civilizing influences of Christianity, it is proper to speak of a Christian State. The ideal purpose of government not always realized is the advancement of law towards material justice. "Justice in its application to the fundamental relations of the State offers the ideals of freedom and equality as the goal for such development."[2]

In Lasson's view international law has no true legal status; it is not "a true law of a formal and a positive character."[3]

Hegel proposed the conception of a wrong without dishonest intention, an objective violation in deed, or relation without subjective blame. Lasson adopts this conception and calls it blameless wrong. Justice re-es-

[1] *Lasson* does well to substitute the word "function" for that of "purpose" ("Zweck"); for the latter at once suggests a utilitarian conception as though the State existed for the purpose of serving certain interests. ("System," etc., pp. 310 seq., 313 seq.)

[2] "System," etc., pp. 310-350, 670-686, 350-368, 368-380.

[3] "System," etc., pp. 405, 394-407. See also *Berolzheimer*, "Rechtsphilosophische Studien," pp. 45 seq.

tablishes right when wrong has been committed. A notable passage in regard to property occurs in Lasson's philosophy of private law. He holds that the institution of property is not established through the utility which the possession of property provides. The supreme consideration in the regulation of property relations is justice. Justice, however, does not consist in the equal distribution of property. "To make men equal would be to invert nature and to invite destruction."[1]

[1] "System," etc., 484, 518, 518 seq., 598, 596, 592-615.

CHAPTER VI

THE EMANCIPATION OF THE PROLETARIAT: ENCROACHMENT UPON THE PHILOSOPHY OF LAW BY ECONOMIC REALISM

FRENCH COMMUNISM: (1) SAINT-SIMON; (2) FOURIER; (3) LOUIS BLANC; (4) COMMUNISM, ANARCHISM, AND SOCIALISM.— GERMAN SOCIALISM: (1) MARX; (2) LASSALLE; (3) ENGELS; (4) RODBERTUS; (5) BEBEL; (6) KAUTSKY; (7) BERNSTEIN; (8) A SURVEY OF THE PROCESS OF EMANCIPATION.— ANARCHISM: (1) PROUDHON, THE OLDER VIEW; (2) STIRNER, THE EXTREME INDIVIDUALISM; (3) KRAPOTKIN, THE COMMUNISTIC VIEW; (4) BAKUNIN, THE POSITION OF VIOLENCE; (5) TUCKER AND TOLSTOI, MODERATE ANARCHISM.— FURTHER TYPES OF SOCIALISM: (1) MENGER; (2) LORIA; (3) SOMBART.

§ 37. *French Communism.* 1: SAINT-SIMON. The significance of the writings of Count CLAUDE HENRI DE SAINT-SIMON [1] (1760–1825), and of communism lies less in the positive construction of the communistic doctrine than in the questioning of existing conditions and in

---

[1] The writings of Saint-Simon that are here pertinent are: "Organisateur," 1819–20. "Système Industriel," 1821–22. "Catéchisme des Industriels," 1822–23. "Nouveau Christianisme," 1825.

The writings, instructions, and letters of Saint-Simon and the Saint-Simonists are published together as "Oeuvres de Saint-Simon et d'Enfantin," second edition, 25 volumes, Paris 1865–1872. "Du Système Industriel" is in vols. XXI–XXIII (1869); "Nouveau Christianisme" is also in vol. XXIII, p. 97. "L'organisateur" (from November, 1819, to February, 1820) is in Vol. XX (1869). "Parabole Politique" is in vol. XX, pp. 17–26; Vol. I also contains the "Parabole."

the political movement of socialism, to which they gave rise. The object was the emancipation of the fourth estate — the liberation of the laboring class and particularly of the industrial laborer. While the emancipation of the third estate, the establishment of a free class of citizens, was essentially a political movement, and proceeded by overcoming the dominance of the Catholic Church, by abolishing the feudal system, and by giving all citizens a share in the government, the emancipation of the fourth estate was essentially an economic one. The issue in the former was primarily that of a political, in the latter, that of an economic, enfranchisement. The motive of the civic emancipation was the desire for power; the emancipation of labor, at least in its origins, grew out of the struggle for existence. The several political agitations, from the beginning of the sixteenth to the close of the eighteenth century, as likewise the uprising in the year 1848, aimed to secure a proper recognition of the citizen in the government. The purpose of the economic political movement that was inaugurated towards the close of the eighteenth century was to protect the proletariat from material and moral starvation; yet naturally this economic trend was not uniformly prominent in the several expressions of the movement.

The first issue of the "Organisateur" of Saint-Simon, 1819–1820, contains the "Parabole Politique," which gained him his acquittal in the Court of Assizes. This parable inaugurates a new era in presentation. The method there introduced is still followed in the literature dealing with the problems of government, society, law, economics, and history. It presents an issue upon which opinions are divided, namely, the use of the causal conception in political science. Saint-Simon's application of the conception differs from that later employed by Marx and others. He proceeds from the position that the political value of each class is determined by its productivity, its indispensability in the State and to the State. In his parable Saint-Simon speculates as to what might happen were France to lose its most valuable productive class — its scholars, artists, proprietors, manufacturers, merchants, etc.[1] — and were further to lose its capitalists, together with the royal family and the higher officials. The former contingency, he concludes, would really seriously affect France, which, by such a loss, would become "a body without a soul";[2] in the second case others would assume the vacated places.[3] Labor and talent are personally valuable; rank and money are without personal value.

Proceeding historically, Saint-Simon, in his "Catéchisme des Industriels," attempts to establish the industrial class as the true core of the community. In his view, "industry" implies labor, which provides the community with the means of satisfying its needs and desires. Ultimately everything depends upon industry, and for that reason everything must be done for industry. The most useful and valuable, as well as most numerous members of society, are those of the industrial class. In this class, however, the true industrial element, the laborers themselves, owing to their need of credit, are reduced to a secondary position, subservient to the

[1] "In all the three thousand most noted scholars, artists and artisans of France." "Oeuvres," I, 1865, pp. 83, 84; XX, pp. 17–19.

[2] "The nation would become a body without a soul as soon as these would be lost." "Oeuvres," I, p. 85; XX, pp. 19 seq.

[3] "But this loss of the thirty thousand distinguished and prominent individuals of the State would produce no disturbance except in a purely sensational relation, for it would result in no political injury to the State." "Oeuvres," I, pp. 85, 86; XX, p. 21.

property-owning class, the bankers. A worthy civilization demands a social reform which shall place the industrial class — the workers in the largest sense — in the position of vantage. This view Saint-Simon presents in his "Système Industriel." In "Nouveau Christianisme" he proposes the establishment of a new Christian community,[1] based upon the interests of the working classes; yet the work contains little that is positive in construction.

The leading principles of Saint-Simon's doctrine and of his school may be thus summarized:[2] "All social institutions should have for their object the amelioration of the moral, intellectual, and physical condition of the most numerous and the poorest class." "To each according to his capacity, to each capacity according to its achievements."

His doctrines were developed by his disciples, of whom the most important was ENFANTIN (1796–1864). After a period of success, extending to about 1831, the views of Saint-Simon fell into decline, and finally into

[1] "God has said: 'Men should behave towards one another as brothers.' This sublime principle contains all that is divine in the Christian religion." ("Nouveau Christianisme," "Oeuvres," XXIII, p. 108. Also pp. 159, 173.) It is from this principle that all institutions of the new Christian dispensation are to be derived ("Nouv. Christ.," "Oeuvres," XXIII, pp. 113, 173). "Religion must guide society towards the great end of improving as rapidly as possible the condition of the poorest class." ("Nouv. Christ.," "Oeuvres," XXIII, p. 117.)

Saint-Simon opposes Catholicism as well as Protestantism, because, and in so far as they both fail to give proper consideration to this principle. ("Nouv. Christ.," "Oeuvres," XXIII, pp. 116–191.)

[2] "Oeuvres," I, p. VII. See also "Nouv. Christ.," "Oeuvres," XXIII, p. 173: "Society must labor for the improvement of the moral and physical condition of the poorest class; society must be organized in a manner most suitable to attain this great end."

oblivion. This was due in part to the eccentricities of its advocates, particularly of Enfantin, and in part to dissensions among its leaders; but mainly to the inherent untenability of the doctrine itself. The most permanent contribution of Saint-Simon was the substitution of the conception of the State by that of society. It was from this that Comte derived the foundations for his Sociology.

2: FOURIER. FOURIER[1] (1777–1837) was a man of genius, rather given to romantic dreams for the future of society. By training he was a mathematician and physicist, which may account for his fondness for quantitative forms of expression. In his system the fundamental number is twelve. Man has twelve fundamental instincts or natural traits which, by various combinations, form the individual character. The social order of the future is to bring about the harmonious development of these natural traits. He divides the community into a number of economic groups. Every such group, "phalanx," was to comprise from 1800 to 2000 persons, was to be assigned about a square mile of land, and was to occupy a large communal edifice called "Le Phalenstère." Agriculture and industry were to be the pursuits followed. Four-twelfths of the income was to be applied to capital, five-twelfths to wages, and three-twelfths to talent.[2] Here again the number twelve plays a decisive part.

The importance of Fourier for the emancipation of the fourth estate lies in his advocacy of the right to work as a political demand — a position previously urged by Fichte on other grounds. Somewhat after the manner

[1] Fourier's chief works are "Traité de L'Association Domestique Agricole," 2 vols., 1822 (second edition, 1841); "Le Nouveau Monde Industriel et Sociétaire," 1829.

[2] "Le Nouveau Monde," etc., 1829, pp. 364 seq.

of the advocates of "natural law," Fourier assumes a natural state of affairs in which there are four fundamental economic rights. Society, in which the natural resources are already disposed of, must grant an equivalent for these rights. Without making any sharp distinction Fourier calls such equivalent the right to work or the right to a minimum existence,[1] and prophesies a period of "guaranteeism" in which every man will be guaranteed by society a minimum livelihood, and primarily, the right to work. These ideas were further developed by his pupils.

3: Louis Blanc. The most modern and the most reasonable of the communists is Louis Blanc[2] (1811–1882), and so far as concerns the practical influence of his efforts, he is likewise the most successful. The problem which particularly engaged his attention was that of the unemployed. It seems a justifiable demand, alike from the position of legal philosophy and of social ethics, that the State or the community shall protect all men from starvation. The poor and the incapacitated should be a concern for public care; but the assistance of those able to work becomes charity, and is immoral. It encourages parasitism, and saps the moral force of the beneficiaries and of the community. It is familiar that the mediæval Church did much to favor such demoralization. Assistance of this type should be temporary, the main need being to provide work — a function now exercised by communal and corporate

[1] In regard to the right to work see "Traité," etc., pp. 137 seq., 143. In regard to the right for a minimum wage see "Traité," etc., pp. 126, 135; "Le Nouveau Monde," etc., pp. 4, 12, 38, 42, 74, 185, 328, 333, 373, 420, 430.

[2] Apart from the manifold contributions to periodical literature and important historical works, Blanc is notable for his tractate, "Organisation du Travail," 1840. (I cite from the ninth edition, Paris, 1850.)

institutions. Insurance against unemployment is similarly helpful.

The duty of the State, growing out of its ethical nature, to provide work according to their capacity for those willing and able to work, appears in Louis Blanc, as in Fourier, as a natural demand, applicable without reservation. The question [1] whether competition serves to secure work to the poor he tests by the observation of economic conditions. Reflecting the influence of the Malthusian position, he concludes that competition of labor depresses wages below the minumum of existence, supplies the manufacturer with the cheapest labor — child labor — fails to provide the means of subsistence, and starves or pauperizes the laboring classes. In opposition to Adam Smith and Say, who regarded free competition as conducive to the welfare of the community and of the individual, Louis Blanc maintains that it reduces workmen to a condition of wretched poverty, and further maintains that it injures the citizen-class through the resulting cheapening of commodities. In another connection he sets forth that even political relations are undermined by free competition, which eventually will lead to a deadly conflict between France and England. He proposes to avoid the pernicious effect of unlimited freedom by going to the other extreme and establishing the right to labor by governmental aid, or, in communistic phrase, by the social organization of labor. Society is to establish public industrial work-shops and a public system of agricul-

---

[1] "Organisation du Travail," Book I, chap. II, pp. 26, 25–56. On p. 56 Blanc thus summarizes his position: "As statistics show, competition produces poverty. As statistics show, the poor are extremely prolific. As statistics show, the fecundity of the poor throws upon society the unfortunates who need work but cannot find it. Under these circumstances society has the alternative of killing off the poor or of supporting them — either brutality or folly."

ture, through which the several classes of labor are to be communistically organized. But other callings are also to be publicly provided for, such as the literary profession, which even in those days brought no golden profits.[1] It is familiar that after the "Revolution of February" an attempt was made to realize Blanc's ideas by establishing national labor centers, but, as was to be expected, this proved a failure.

4: COMMUNISM, ANARCHISM, AND SOCIALISM. Communism, which in the main was originated and developed in France, has traits in common with socialism and with the communistic trend of anarchism; yet each movement presents points of contrast. The three positions agree in what they reject. They decidedly and radically reject the existing legal order and the resulting economic situation. They diverge in the positive construction of their doctrines, in their view of the conditions which are to replace the existing state of affairs. However, this is not the essential difference; the distinctive criterion dividing communism, anarchism, and socialism, is, so to speak, the political subsoil upon which the three tendencies grow. The theoretical foundations serving the intellectual leaders of these several movements are but incidentally determined by the practical purposes sought.

Communists, anarchists, and socialists regard the present conditions of labor and industry as thoroughly unjust. Communism believes that labor and ability are at a disadvantage; it proposes radically to reform the economic situation without prejudice or favor. Everyone who is efficient shall be justly rewarded; no class shall be favored; the actual abuses and injustices in the distribution of property and income shall be

[1] "Organisation," etc. Book I, chaps. III, IV, V, Book II, chap. IV; Book III, chap. III.

abolished. In so urging, communism is politically neutral; it does not desire to favor or disfavor one class in the State at the expense of other classes or economic groups, but attempts by radical measures to bring about a thorough and permanent improvement.

Anarchism goes a step farther. It questions whether law and government, the economic order and capital, can ever produce satisfactory economic and political conditions. Anarchism does not regard the existing laws and economic order as the cause of the unsatisfactory state of affairs, but regards as such the existence of law itself, with its power of coercion, and the existence of capital, which is assumed to be its inseparable concomitant. While communism rejects the existing law, anarchism rejects law in general. It is opposed not only to the established law but to every form of legal coercion. It believes that the natural altruistic tendencies of men would come into unrestricted play, were law and government to be abolished.

In contrast to communism and anarchism, socialism, in the name of justice, represents the interests of the laboring classes. Socialism is judge and advocate in one. The income belongs by right to the one, and to him alone, who creates the productive value, who labors, and whose labor is productive. But labor alone is productive; hence, the laborer should receive the lion's share of the product of his labor. While anarchism desires to set aside law altogether, and thus dispense with the governmental institution, and while communism is politically indifferent, socialism represents the legal and economic philosophy of class-interests of the laborer. In place of the legal State, "Rechtsstaat," and the culture State, "Kulturstaat," socialism proposes a coercive State, "Zwangsstaat," in the interests of the laborer. Such a coercive State socialism calls society.

§ 38. *German Socialism*. 1: MARX. The founder of German socialism, the chief pillar of the socialistic doctrine, was the Hegelian, KARL MARX [1] (1818–1883). He proposed to apply philosophy to economic relations. His most permanent service was his formulation of the philosophy of history. Saint-Simon, in the "Parabole Politique," applied the principle of causality to the community in the State; Marx applied it to the method of history. He regarded the decisive factors of historical development as the economic [2] ones; the factors that

[1] Marx's chief work is "Das Kapital. Kritik der Politischen Ökonomie," fourth edition, edited by *Friedrich Engels*. Vol. I, Book I, "Der Produktionsprozess des Kapitals," Hamburg 1890. Vol. II, Book II, "Der Zirkulationsprozess des Kapitals," second edition, Hamburg 1893. Vol. III, Part I, Book III, "Der Gesammtprozess der Kapitalistischen Produktion," chaps. 1–28, Hamburg, 1894. Vol. III, Part II, Book III, chaps. 29–52. Hamburg 1894, incomplete. A preliminary work, "Zur Kritik der Politischen Ökonomie," Berlin 1859, is likewise of great importance.

Marx, "Theorien über den Mehrwert," published by *K. Kautsky*, from the manuscript material of "Zur Kritik der Politischen Ökonomie." 1. "Die Anfänge der Theorie vom Mehrwert bis Adam Smith," Stuttgart 1905.

[2] See the summary ("Zur Kritik, d. pol. Ökonomie," preface, p. v): "The aggregate of conditions of production at any given stage of development of material resources constitutes the economic structure of society, the real basis upon which a legal and political superstructure is built, and to which correspond definite types of social consciousness. The manner of production of the needs of material existence, conditions the social, political, and intellectual mode of living. It is not the consciousness of man that conditions his being, but conversely his social life conditions the consciousness." That Marx was influenced by the materialism of the Hegelian *Feuerbach* is noted by *Masaryk*, "Die Philosophischen und Soziologischen Grundlagen des Marxismus," pp. 1–89, also pp. 92–101.

In this connection Marx has merely formulated more definitely the conception of history first put forward by Saint-Simon. Engels gave to this conception the name of "the material conception of history."

had been unduly ignored. New ideas are ever likely to receive a biassed and exaggerated consideration, and the socialistic position over-emphasized the material conception of history in terms of economic factors. In the last analysis the issue between the materialistic and idealistic conception of history depends upon the attitude assumed towards the problem of causality. If the cause be regarded as equivalent to the aggregate of the antecedent conditions, then, as is true of other efficient forces, the economic factors constitute the condition, but not the exclusive condition. If, however, the cause be regarded as equivalent to the distinctive and decisive condition, then the study of history shows that the idealistic conception is correct. Every progress, every real advance in the history of the emancipation of mankind, has been due to the initiative of leading minds. It is true that these find response on the part of their contemporaries only when the cultural conditions of a given period — which comprise the material as well as the intellectual factors — furnish a suitable atmosphere. Powder alone without a spark is powerless to produce an explosion.

It is not possible to summarize a work of eight hundred pages in a few sentences. I must be content to select from his "Capital" the gist of Marx's economic philosophy. A fundamental position in its development is his theory of Increment, which was not, as formerly held, original with Marx, but was borrowed from the English socialists, particularly from Thompson.[1] According to Marx the mechanism of exchange operates in such a manner that the producer receives gold (G) for his wares (W) and with the income produces new wares (W). In this process of exchange, represented

[1] *Anton Menger* "Das Recht auf den vollen Arbeitsertrag in Geschichtlicher Darstellung," p. 97, note 1, and pp. 39–58.

by the formula W–G–W, the W at the beginning is the same as the W at the end — the laborer has given and received equivalent values. If, however, the capitalist puts his gold (G) in circulation, buys wares (W), and again sells them, he is not content to receive an income equal to his original investment (G) — for in that event the whole transaction would have no meaning and be useless — but he always obtains a higher income (G1). In the process of exchange indicated by the formula G–W–G1, the increment of value consists in so much as G1 exceeds G. This increment, which the capitalist pockets, is unearned by him; it was the laborer who earned the increment, for only labor is productive.[1] Capitalists thus unjustly exploit labor. While the laborers are limited to the minimum wage, the capitalists amass great fortunes, until eventually a very small number of the exploiters are in turn dispossessed by the great mass of the exploited. This process of dispossession will spontaneously occur by virtue of natural development.[2] Under a socialistic régime society will con-

[1] "Das Kapital," Vol. I, pp. 59 seq.; Vol. II, pp. 1 seq.

[2] *Marx*, "Das Kapital, I, pp. 727 seq. ("Über die Geschichtliche Tendenz der Kapitalistischen Akkumulation"): "As soon as this process of transformation has sufficiently decomposed the old society from top to bottom, as soon as the laborers are turned into proletarians, their means of labor into capital, as soon as the capitalist mode of production stands on its own feet, then the further socialisation of labor and further transformation of the land and other means of production into socially exploited and, therefore, common means of production, as well as the further expropriation of private proprietors, takes a new form. That which is now to be expropriated is no longer the laborer working for himself, but the capitalist exploiting many laborers. This expropriation is accomplished by the action of the immanent laws of capitalistic production itself, by the centralization of capital. . . . Centralization of the means of production and socialization of labor at last reach a point where they become incompatible with their capitalist

duct manufacture and justly apportion the distribution of the proceeds.[1]

As already noted, according to the Marxian philosophy of history, the economic status at any given period is decisive for the form which society assumes, that is, for the material content of government and law, or its economics. Economic relations always produce two distinct classes in the community, the exploiters and the exploited. It is the purpose of the socialistic order of society to replace this perpetual conflict and enslavement of the economically weak by order and justice. The community is to regulate production and give to each his due. "The goal of development would be the complete unity of the State and society."[2] In place of a formal legal equality there shall be a material economic justice; and this is possible only in that supreme

integument. This integument is burst asunder. The knell of capitalist private property sounds. The expropriators are expropriated." (Moore's translations, p. 788.)

[1] *W. Ed. Biermann* ("Staat und Wirthschaft," pp. 107–125, Vol. I) opposes the view expressed by *Anton Menger* and others that the position of *Marx* favors a strong State control. *Biermann* urges that *Marx* looked upon the State as a great brutal expression and not as the assertion of authority. This interpretation of Biermann is not justified. It seems to me that Biermann does not observe the peculiar terminology of socialism. Marx regards the State as a capitalistic, brutal expression of power, but regards socially organized society as a just economic order. Yet what the Marxians call society is in truth the State, in that their society exercises the coercive power of the State, and determines the legal economic order. This social, or more properly, governmental order, as the socialists advocate it, ascribes to the State a comprehensive and omnipotent sphere as against the dependent individual, such as has not been advocated since ancient times.

Moreover Lassalle ("Arbeiterprogram," pp. 40–42) clearly and explicitly speaks of the State and of its problem as the emancipation of the working classes.

[2] *Jellinek*, "Allgemeine Staatslehre," p. 81.

and comprehensive socialistically organized form of government, which is called society.

The doctrine of Marx, holding to the position of the classic school of economics that only labor produces wealth [1] — and for the Marxians only the labor of the laboring classes is regarded as productive — has been thoroughly and definitely refuted, not only by science, but by the actual development of affairs. The importance of Marxism lies in the fact that through its agitation the emancipation of the laboring classes was stimulated and accomplished. It was the outrageous spectacle of the harsh exploitation of the laborers by the manufacturers — particularly in England — through excessive hours of labor, through starvation wages, through the truck system and the sweating system, and through overwork of women and children, that aroused the protest of Marx. The abolition of this slavelike treatment of the laboring classes has been accomplished by the socialistic movement, which grew out of the work of Marx, and which has extended to all civilized countries. The formal goal of Marxism was a socialistic coercive State that should control and regulate the production and distribution of income; and the result actually accomplished is the enfranchisement of the wage-earner.

The communistic manifesto of the year 1848, issued jointly by Marx and Friedrich Engels, had large political influence. Of Marx's minor writings of the earlier period may be mentioned "Zur Kritik der Hegel'schen Rechtsphilosophie," of the year 1843. The conclusion of the dialectic development of the economic revolution

[1] This principle is incorporated in the party platform. For example, see the Program of the socialistic labor party of Germany, May 1875, I: "Labor is the source of all wealth and of all culture." Reprinted in Conrad's "Jahrb.," 3d series, I, p. 235.

is thus described:[1] "The proletariat begins to assert itself in Germany through the invasion of the industrial movement; for it is not poverty of natural origin but poverty artificially created, that makes the proletariat. If the proletariat heralds the dissolution of the present social system, it is but delivering the secret of its own being, for it is in fact the dissolution of the social order. If the proletariat demands the abolition of private ownership, then it but elevates to a principle of society what society has already accepted as its principle, what without its aid has been embodied in society as a negative result."

2: LASSALLE. FERDINAND LASSALLE[2] (1825–1864), a political agitator and brilliant orator, introduced the Marxian ideas among the laboring classes in Germany. He emphasized the political side of socialism, and directed attention to the economic and political representation of the interests of the laborer.[3] From the philosophical point of view he gives the socialistic conception of the State a greater definiteness of expression. He does not use the confusing expression, "society," when he speaks of the State, but calls it the State. He opposes the con-

---

[1] "Collected Works," published by Mehring, Vol. I, pp. 397 seq.

[2] The political writings of *Lassalle* are edited by *Erich Blum*, Leipzig 1899. Of special import are "Arbeiterprogram," Zürich 1863. (Blum's edition, I, pp. 156–200.) "Offenes Antwortschreiben an das Zentral-Komite zur Berufung eines Allgemeinen Deutschen Arbeiter-Kongresses zu Leipzig," Zürich 1863 (pp. 1–39). "Macht und Recht, Offenes Sendschreiben," 1863. (pp. 101–106.) "Arbeiter-Lesebuch." (II, pp. 59–144.) A survey of the writings of *Lassalle* is found in the "Handwörterbuch der Staatswissenschaften," second edition, Vol. V, pp. 530 seq.

[3] "Offenes Antwortschreiben," p. 7 (Blum's edition, I, p. 7), 36 seq. (Blum's ed., I, p. 37). "Arbeiterprogram," pp. 32 seq. (Blum's ed., I, pp. 195 seq.), "Arbeiter-Lesebuch," Blum's ed., II, pp. 96, 110, 128, 139 seq.

ception of the Manchester school that assigns to the State the rôle of a night watchman,[1] and in opposition to the view of Adam Smith thus develops the socialistic conception of the State: "History is the struggle with nature, with misery, ignorance, poverty, helplessness, and slavery, to which the human race was subject at the beginning of history. The development of freedom is the story of the progressive conquest of this helplessness. To the State belongs the function of furthering the development of the human race to a state of freedom. It is the purpose of the State, through the alliance which it forms, to place the individual in such a position and to attain such purposes and such a stage of existence as individuals of themselves could not attain; to reach a position of culture, power and liberty which would be unattainable to them as individuals. It is the function of the State to bring the human race to a condition of positive progress, to realize the culture of which the human race is capable. It is the education and evolution of the human race to a state of freedom."[2]

Although with a socialistic trend, Lassalle presents the Hegelian "Kulturstaat" with a clearness of expression too often absent in socialists and sociologists alike.[3]

[1] This Manchester conception of the State is conceived of under the metaphor of "a night-watchman whose entire function is that of preventing robbery and burglary." ("Arbeiterprogram," p. 39.)

[2] "Arbeiterprogram," p. 40.

[3] In the Program of the socialistic party the State is identified in part, but in part only, with society. In the Program of the social-democratic party (August 1869), § 1 reads as follows: "The social-democratic labor party strives to establish a free State of the people." In the Program of May 1875, § 2, it is affirmed: "The socialistic labor party aims at a free State and a socialistic type of society." In § 1 it is further stated that "the total product of labor belongs to society, that is, to all parts thereof." What is meant by society, and what by the members of society, unless it be the State and the members of the State?

The State is explicitly described and is not masked under cover of society.

3: ENGELS. FR. ENGELS[1] (1820–1895), the friend and political associate of Marx, is known both as the editor of "Kapital" and as an independent writer. His chief works are "Ursprung der Familie, des Privat Eigentums und des Staats,"[2] and "Herr Dühring's Umwälzung der Wissenschaft."[3] In these he popularizes and develops the ideas of Marx. He thus defines the material conception of history: "The determining factor in history is the direct production and reproduction of life." This in turn proceeds in two ways; first, by the productions of the means of subsistence, — of clothing, dwellings, tools, — and again by the reproduction of the species. "The social institutions under which men live at a given historical period and in a given country are conditioned by both forms of production, by the stage of development of labor on the one hand, and that of the family on the other."[4] According to Engels the State is "a product of society at a given stage of evolution. It is a confession that such society stands at the moment in an insoluble contradiction with itself, is divided by irreconcilably opposed forces which it is powerless to control."

4: RODBERTUS. RODBERTUS–JAGETZOW (1805–1875) maintained the Marxian view of the theory of incre-

---

[1] In addition to the principal writings of Engels as above cited, there are considerable contributions in periodical form, including numerous essays in "Die Neue Zeit." For the earlier writings of Engels, see the collected edition of his publications dating from the years 1841–1847, arranged by Mehring.

[2] In connection with Lewis H. Morgan's "Forschungen," 1884, second edition, Stuttgart 1886.

[3] First edition, Leipzig 1878; second edition; Zürich 1885; third edition, Stuttgart 1894.

[4] "Der Ursprung der Familie," pp. iv, 135.

ment. He developed his theory independently of Marx, though both were indebted to previous socialists. His point of departure is the statement that all economic values, in contrast to natural values, cost labor and labor alone. Accordingly the time expended in labor affords an economic standard of value. Interest he interprets as the income from property without labor. The rent yielded by real estate is ground rent, and the rent yielded by capital is interest. Rodbertus assigns two reasons as the origins of rent — the economic reason is that under existing conditions labor yields a surplus above the minimum necessity of livelihood of the laborer; the second reason lies in the legal principle of interest, namely, the private ownership of land and capital. Rodbertus, like Marx, in the consistent development of his views, holds that all value depends upon labor, and thus regards the income from rent as the exploitation of labor and of the product of the labor of others. He ascribes the existence of poverty and industrial crises to the tendency of wages to decline.[1]

To remedy the existing social distress Rodbertus demands the introduction by the State of standard hours of work and of a standard output.[2] It is not his intention entirely to dispossess the capitalist of the increment of value. Incomes of ground rent and capital are in principle to remain, but the wages of labor are to be generally improved. Rodbertus is not a true socialist but a State socialist. The State is to conduct whatever

[1] "Soziale Briefe an v. Kirchmann."

[2] *Rodbertus*, "Der Normal-Arbeitstag," 1871 ("Kleine Schriften," pp. 337–359), particularly p. 338: "The normal working day of many hours must first be advanced to a working day of so much work; it must be standardized, not merely in terms of time but particularly in terms of labor." This is further considered on pp. 339 seq.

business is by nature public, and only by official delegation is business to be conducted by private capital, which in turn is to be operated from the public point of view.[1]

5: BEBEL. The work of BEBEL[2] (b. 1840), "Die Frau und der Sozialismus," is a popular scientific work dealing primarily with the social position of woman in the past, present, and future; it is at the same time a propagandum for the socialistic cause. The enormous success of this book — in 1904 it had reached its thirty-sixth and thirty-seventh edition — which attempted to enlist women in favor of socialism, is in large measure due to its effective treatment of social wrongs in the past and present. It is not free from exaggerations, and holds the "capitalistic order of society" responsible for evils that are inevitable. Bebel proclaims the emancipation of woman through the socialistic order:[3] "In the new society woman will be completely independent, socially and economically. She will be subject to no form of domination and exploitation. She will be mistress of her fate." Socially and legally, so far as sex does not involve necessary differences, woman is to be placed upon complete equality with man. Woman will be free in the choice of profession, in expenditure, as also in the choice of a mate. By his advocacy of free love he placed a weapon in the hands of the opponents of the socialistic doctrines,

[1] See particularly "Das Kapital" ("Literary Remains," II, pp. 77 seq.)"

[2] "Die Frau und der Sozialismus." Thirty to thirty-third edition (unaltered after the Jubilee edition), Stuttgart 1899–1902; thirty-sixth to thirty-seventh edition, unaltered after the thirty-fourth edition, Stuttgart 1904. (I cite from the twenty-seventh edition unaltered after the Jubilee edition, Stuttgart 1896.) The remaining writings of Bebel are far less important and less influential than this work.

[3] "Die Frau," etc., pp. 427 seq., 441–463, 464–470.

who were not disposed to find fault with his economic and social views.

Bebel discountenances the fear of over-population and the neo-Malthusian position. He offers some pertinent remarks upon "over-population of intelligence" which in Germany has produced "an uncommonly large number of proletariat scholars and artists" — "a strong proletariat in the so-called liberal professions." For these, despite their higher education, can find no satisfactory professional income, and are justly embittered; all of which leads inevitably to political radicalism.

6: KAUTSKY. KAUTSKY[1] (b. 1854) devotes his book, "Die Agrarfrage," to the interests of the rural laborer, the agriculturist and the independent farmer. He discusses in detail the social democratic politics of the agrarian position, and offers pertinent comments and proposals upon the public administration of schools, the care of the poor, the maintenance of roads, and the gratuitous conduct of lawsuits. The last is hardly likely to reduce the number of pettifogging lawsuits among farmers. To win over the independent farmer to the socialistic movement, Kautsky holds that the existence of the agricultural intermediary is necessary, quite apart from the parasitic intermediary; and that it is not part of the socialistic program to dispossess "the non-parasitic intermediary in agricultural business, who fills an important function in economic life."[2] "The farmer need have no concern for the welfare of his home. The socialistic régime will not fail to leave its influence

[1] His writings are "Die Agrarfrage. Eine Übersicht über die Tendenzen der modernen Landwirtschaft und die Agrarpolitik der Sozialdemokratie," Stuttgart 1899; and various essays and contributions in "Die Neue Zeit."

[2] "Die Agrarfrage," pp. 301 seq., 414–417, 417–420, 436–439, 440–451, 451.

upon it; but the changes which it will produce will be in the direction of sanitary and æsthetic improvements to the advantage of the rural homestead."

7: BERNSTEIN. EDUARD BERNSTEIN [1] (b. 1850) opposes the "theory of catastrophe," the view "that we are rapidly approaching a collapse of civil society, and that social democracy should shape its campaign by the prospect of such imminent social catastrophe, or adjust its actions to such contingency."[2] His book, "Die Voraussetzung des Sozialismus und die Aufgaben der Sozialdemokratie,"[3] a collection of his essays which, for the most part, appeared in the periodical, "Die Neue Zeit," is devoted to the presentation of a scientific basis of his position and his unqualified repudiation of the Marxian view. In his philosophy, as evidenced in this and other writings, he shows a leaning towards Kant,

---

[1] His writings are "Zur Theorie und Geschichte des Sozialismus," Berlin-Berne 1901. "Probleme des Sozialismus," "Die Neue Zeit," 1896–97, XV, Vol. I, pp. 164–171 (204–213), 303–313, 772–783; Vol. II, pp. 100–107, 138–143. "Der Kampf der Sozialdemokratie und die Revolution der Gesellschaft," "Die Neue Zeit," 1897–98, XVI, Vol. I, pp. 484–497, 548–557. "Kritisches Zwischenspiel," pp. 740–751. "Das Realistische und das Ideologische Moment im Sozialismus." ("Probleme des Sozialismus," second series, II A) "Die Neue Zeit," XVI, Vol. II, pp. 225–232, 388–395. ("Die Probleme des Sozialismus" are reprinted in "Zur Theorie und Geschichte des Sozialismus," pp. 167–286.)

[2] "Social democracy neither sanctions nor desires the prompt collapse of the present economic position as a result of a great sweeping industrial crisis." "Der Kampf der Sozialdemokratie und die Revolution," "Die Neue Zeit," XVI, Vol. I, p. 556. *Belfort-Bax,* "Der Sozialismus eines gewöhnlichen Menschenkindes gegenüber dem Sozialismus des Herrn Bernstein,'" Die Neue Zeit," XVI, I, pp. 824–829, contends against Bernstein in behalf of a future governmental "goal and movement."

[3] See likewise *Bernstein,* "Der Kampf," etc., pp. 406–416, the treatise, "Abwehr wider Kautsky's Schrift: Bernstein und das sozialdemokratische Programm," a rejoinder to Kautsky.

and may be regarded as a neo-Kantian emphasizing the idealistic factors in evolution as against an extreme materialism.[1]

8: A SURVEY OF THE PROCESS OF EMANCIPATION. At the present time the newer socialism seems to have receded from the main positions of Marx's socialism. It is not possible here to review the several varieties of socialism. Marx's theory of deterioration, "Verelendung," which is not in accord with the facts of development, was made the subject of a critical study by Julius Wolf. Basing his arguments upon the statistics of expenditure and income, upon those of poverty and crime, upon the inheritance tax and bank deposits, he proved that the middle classes were not being reduced to a proletariat.[2] It is only necessary to contemplate the economic life of the present with an intelligent understanding to detect, in the higher salaried positions in the large mercantile, industrial, insurance, and financial enterprises, the rise of a new middle class.

Were present-day socialism to accept as its scientific basis the doctrines of the Hegelian Marx, it would be burdened by an obsolete, devitalized heritage of the past, much as would be the present conservative party if it accepted as its theoretical foundation the philosophy of the Hegelian theologian, Stahl. Marx and Stahl represent a superseded point of view. Although the socialistic party, as likewise the conservative party, has

[1] See particularly, "Das Realistische und Ideologische Moment im Sozialismus," "Die Neue Zeit," XVI, 2, pp. 225-232, 388-395. Opposed thereto, see *Belfort-Bax*, "Synthetische contra Neumarxistische Geschichtsauffassung," "Die Neue Zeit," XV, I, pp. 171-177. "Kautsky, Bernstein und die Materialistische Geschichtsauffassung," "Die Neue Zeit" 1898-99, XVII, 2, pp. 4-16.

[2] *Julius Wolf*, "System der Sozialpolitik," Vol. I, "Grundlegung." "Sozialismus und Kapitalistische Gesellschaftsordnung," Stuttgart 1892.

acquired a more powerful position than it held when the philosophy of Hegel and the economics of Marx prevailed, its present influential position is presumably due to a very different and more practically significant political principle. Social democracy is the political expression of the laboring classes, who form an important economic constituency of the State, much as the "Bauernbund" and the conservative party represent the political position of the landholding constituency, and of the affiliated economic and social classes. As representing important economic interests, these several parties justly exercise a considerable power, and represent an essential group in the development of the modern "classstate"; it is this "Klassenstaat" that, as an ideal, is gaining the support of many intelligent socialistic leaders.[1] It appears in Bernstein's opposition to the theory of catastrophe, as also in Kautsky. "Whether it will be

---

[1] In the year 1880 the word "legal" was canceled from the Program of 1875. "Proceeding upon these principles the socialistic labor party of Germany aims to establish a free State and a socialistic society by means of legal measures." The striking out of this word assumed the importance of a political demonstration, of a protest against the socialist laws. (1878–1890.) In contrast, later proceedings of the party (Dresden 1904) clearly demonstrated that social democracy was rapidly becoming an efficient radical labor party on the basis of the present governmental and economic order, with slight consideration of an ideal future State. It is not surprising that in so large a party there should be marked divergences among the leaders — a more radical (Marxian) and a more civic tendency favoring revision. These differences have less practical importance, inasmuch as the leaders of a pure Marxism are influenced by considerations of party interest to hold rather tenderly to the Marxian position. Every religious or political party dealing with large masses of the people presents this tendency towards dogmatism. For the masses want simple slogans ("Schlagwörte") which they can use and do not easily relinquish. But it would be unfortunate, particularly in the interests of labor, to have social democracy become catholic.

possible to win the peasantry to the ranks of social democracy by advocating such an agragian policy may be doubted. Social democracy will ever remain in essence a proletarian, urban party, — a party of economic progress. In the conservative farmer, to whom city life is alien, and who holds fast to the patriarchal form of family, it will ever encounter a deeply rooted prejudice, and will never make the same appeal as that made by the agrarian party, which not only stands closer to his interests but is ready to promise larger advantage." A party of three million voters can obviously not be expected to change its political allegiance in a day. But careful attention to the views of the leaders in the socialistic camp convinces me that the withdrawal from revolutionary trends in favor of the interests of organized labor is slowly but steadily gaining. Social democracy has doubtless favored atheism and materialism; yet it deserves the credit of supplying the masses with an idealistic basis for their reflection and action; likewise is it to be remembered that nowadays, quite irrespectively of socialism, atheism and materialism are independently taking hold of large masses of the people. The great cultural importance of social democracy lies in its service to the masses of the laboring people, to whom it gave an intellectual stimulus, and whom it elevated to a higher spiritual level through the medium of political agitation. While Marx's "Capital" forms the cornerstone of socialism, the communistic manifesto,[1]

[1] The manifesto of the communist party published in February, 1848, London, printed in the office of the Comminists' League. Its motto is "Proletarians of all countries unite."

The manifesto begins with these words: "A specter is hovering over Europe, the specter of communism!" The emphasis of the document is placed upon the fact that the history of all previous society has been the history of class conflicts (p. 3), and that all previous society has been organized on the basis of the opposition

which he issued jointly with Engel in February, 1848, is far more significant for the emancipation of the fourth estate and for the cultural development of modern times. This manifesto was the general alarum which awakened the dispossessed — the slaves oppressed under the yoke of the capitalists — to a self-consciousness, to a class-consciousness, to a conscious solidarity. "Let the ruling classes tremble in view of the impending communist revolution. The working classes have nothing to lose but their chains. They have a world to win. Workingmen of all countries, unite!"[1] This appeal, which forms the closing words of the manifesto, brought into being the present German socialism. It contains the philosophical basis of the cultural movement which socialism introduced, the goal of which has now been reached — the emancipation of the fourth estate.

Herewith the series of the great recent movements for emancipation is completed. Since the close of the Middle Ages the watchword of the philosophy of law and economics has been "freedom." In earlier days the intellect was set free from the ban of the Catholic Church through the heroic efforts of Luther. Grotius released the law from its scholastic fetters; he brought rationalism to earth, and his contract theory contains the germ of the idea of popular sovereignty. In the same temper the "Tyrannomachs" led the fight against tyranny. In these efforts it was at times forgotten that freedom represents a cultural ideal and does not consist in the complete independence of all conditions, but in throw-

of the oppressors and the oppressed (p. 10). "When capital shall have been transformed into a capital that belongs in common to all members of society, it does not follow that personal property will have been transformed into social property. It is only the social character of the possession that is changed; it loses its class character" (p. 12).

[1] "Manifesto," p. 23.

ing off the yoke of slavery; license was mistaken for liberty. Such an extreme and extravagant conception of freedom assumed equality as a rightful demand on the basis of "natural law"; and by way of Rousseau's "Discours" and the destructive philosophy of the Encyclopedists, it led to the French Revolution. The aftermath of the Revolution, supported by the ethical philosophy of Wolff, brought about an enlightened absolutism. But the people, released from their fetters, exchanged them for leading strings. It was through Kant that the citizen was made to realize his right to freedom and equality; the great revolutionary philosopher was more radical than the provincial Robespierre. The latter was an extremest in action, but Kant was an extremist in thought. The issue of the French Revolution, as affecting freedom and equality, was destructive, nihilistic; Kant's philosophy was comprehensively synthetic. He erected a splendid edifice for freedom and equality — the "Rechtsstaat"; and its economic complement was contributed by the physiocrats and by Adam Smith. With these advances the process of emancipation, which brought law and government out of the bondage of the mediæval Church to the freedom of the modern world, would have been completed if it were the fact—as rationalism had naïvely assumed in the theory of contract — that the law was an independent institution. But the law is not something fixed, unalterable, and absolute; it is flexible and subject to change, as was recognized by Schelling and Hegel. The study of its fluctuations, which condition legal advance and legislative reforms, led to the science of economics. In Marx and Lassalle a period of economic materialism set in, and a new emancipation became necessary, because a new class had been awakened to a class-consciousness.

The emancipation at the close of the Middle Ages and at the beginning of modern times was directed by temporal interests against the spiritual aggrandisement of the popes and their subordinates. The emancipation of the legal philosophers, from the "Tyrannomachs" to Kant, was centered upon the people. But the people, the subjects, the ruled classes, were, or appeared to be, the citizens in the cities, and the independent farmers in the rural districts. The oppressors were the lords, the rulers, the ruling classes, together with the aristocracy of the feudal system. In the Kantian movement the people gained their freedom. But it appeared that such freedom was for the benefit only of the citizen class, — the property owners, the capitalists. The freedom and equality which the law guaranteed were legally and formally for the benefit of all, but actually and economically existed only for the property-owning classes. This disparity between formal legal freedom and economic enslavement became evident through the spread of a new form of production, that of machine labor. There thus arose a new great class which was enslaved by the very medium of the law itself, which was exploited by the class of citizens who themselves had just attained their own free development. There became necessary a still newer and last process of emancipation through economic measures.

Reviewing this order, there appeared, in succession, temporal freedom as against ecclesiastical bondage; the freedom of legal government as against tyrannical rule; the freedom of private law as against the economic enslavement of the citizen and the peasant; economic freedom as against the abuse of the capitalistic power of the middle class: thus the circle of the great emancipation was completed. The process of emancipation of ancient days was concluded by the formal legal moralization of private rights; the process of emancipation of modern times by their material and economic socialization.

§ 39. *Anarchism.* 1: Proudhon; the Older View. The position of anarchism is variously presented by its adherents. Their common points may be said to include the unconditional opposition to the State, to all authority and coercion, and a like opposition to capital, the presence of which makes the equal consideration of all a myth.[1] Their common, though negative purpose, is the abolition, indeed the destruction of government and of governmental control and authority. The second part of their program is to work for this end by the use of violence, inasmuch as at present those in authority will not yield peaceably. The anarchists are divided into two chief camps on the issue of the end to which endeavor is to be directed, and of the means to be employed in reaching it.

Yet if all compulsory enforcement is abolished, and if society is freed from capital, what then? What shall

[1] "According to the expression of an influential capitalist interested in the distribution of justice, the important point is to equalize opportunity for all who have to face the chances of life." (*Elisée Reclus*, "L'évolution, la révolution et l'idéal anarchique," third edition, Paris 1898. "Bibliothèque Sociologique," No. 19, p. 121.) The supreme power of capital is emphasized by anarchists on all sides. (*Reclus*, "L'évolution," etc., pp. 85-90, 201. "Money in the present state of society is the open sesame" (*Grave*, "La Société Future," p. 338). See also *Krapotkin*, "La Conquête du Pain," pp. 47-63, 93. Capital is the chief cause of crime. (*Grave*, "La Société Future," pp. 138-142.) *Mackay*, "Die Anarchisten," p. 267, says that "it may be shown that the crimes of the State produce crime." The argument in regard to the exploitation of the laboring classes on the part of the citizens, used by the socialisits, is often advanced by the anarchists. (*Grave*, "La Société Future," p. 24, "The citizen class has become parasitic; it lives at the expense of those who are busy at work, and is itself losing the power to produce."

be put in their place? Here opinions diverge. The older trend is in the main represented by Proudhon (1809–1865). In the name of justice[1] he discards law, government,[2] and property — the last by reason of its irrational and disturbing consequences.[3] For all he substitutes anarchy,[4] which is based upon the only valid law,[5] namely, that contracts must be kept.[6] Herein appears the influence of the doctrine of "natural law." His brilliant and eloquent presentations, his pertinent definitions and arguments, found favor, particularly as his views were flattering to the spirit of the times. His definition of business appealed directly to the masses, envious of the possessions of others. "The definition of business is familiar; it is the art of buying at three francs what is worth six, and of selling at six francs what is worth three." The universal acceptance of Proud-

[1] "De la Justice," I, pp. 182–185, new edition, second essay, pp. 86–91. p. 87: "Justice is the respect of human worth spontaneously exercised and mutually guaranteed for every person and for every situation and at whatever risk its defense entails." "Idée Générale," pp. 235, 342, 343.

[2] "Qu'est-ce que la Propriété," I, pp. 239–245 (p. 240): "A kingdom may be good when it is the only possible form of government, but it never can be legitimate." (p. 242): "The authority of man over man is in inverse ratio to his intellectual development." See in this connection, "De la Justice," new edition, I, fourth essay, pp. 13, 18, 108–110, 111–128, 134–143.

[3] "Qu'est-ce que la Propriété?" I, pp. 129–193.

[4] "Qu'est-ce que la Propriété?" I, p. 237. "I am an anarchist." (p. 242): "Anarchy, the absence of a master, of a sovereign, this is the form of government which we are approaching day by day."

[5] Idée Générale," pp. 149 seq., 235.

[6] "Idée Générale," pp. 343, 235: "In order that I may remain free there must be eliminated all that remains of the divine in the government of society, and the structure must be rebuilt upon the human idea of *contract*." Proudhon has in mind Rousseau, who, however, was not consistent in the development of his thought.

hon's phrase — though the idea is not originally his — that property is theft [1] is a telling example of the carrying power of neat phrases.

The older anarchism, beginning with Proudhon and including Bakunin, is but partly communistic or collectivistic. In contrast to the newer, thoroughly communistic anarchism, it is individualistic: that is, property as income, as possession, or as conferring advantage, is rejected; but property as ownership is retained and made accessible to all, though not under the legal title of ownership, but under the terms of a party to a contract.[2]

2: STIRNER: EXTREME INDIVIDUALISM. MAX STIRNER (1806–1856), a pseudonym for Kaspar Schmidt, is an individualist maintaining that everyone should stand on his own footing. He carries his individualistic views consistently to the extreme, and represents the purely atomistic position. The individual exists for his own sake alone; he must express his own activity, be allowed to live his individual life; he must be his own master, a State in himself, a man of nature. Stirner accepted and developed in an original manner the doctrine of

[1] "Qu'est-ce que la Propriété?" I, p. 233; pp. 2, 229–234.

[2] *Adler*, "Nord und Süd," p. 372; *Zenker*, "Der Anarchismus," pp. 26, 41, and others take the position that Proudhon did not unconditionally reject property. *Eltzbacher*, "Der Anarchismus," p. 70, opposes this view: "He (Proudhon) rejects property unconditionally without restriction of space or time. Indeed he looks upon it as a legal relation which is peculiarly adverse to justice." The entire content of "Qu'est-ce que la Propriété?" seems to support *Eltzbacher* in this contention; for this work is a constant tirade against property. *Eltzbacher* is however not correct in so far as Proudhon did not carry to its extreme consequences this antagonism to property. He rejects property, but reintroduces it in his anarchical system under another term. His private property becomes a share in the social goods in a contractual society. This is not property by name, but is so for all intents and purposes.

personal and economic freedom advanced by Adam Smith and Ricardo. He called attention to the fact that freedom is but a negative quality, the release from bondage, the removal of restraint. To supply a positive ideal, Stirner accepted the formula: "Be your own master, live for yourself, in accord with your own individuality."[1] Dispensing with its anarchistic setting, Nietzsche

[1] The unusual emphasis of individuality and of individual freedom, which it is held that the State and the present social order suppress, forms an important argument of the anarchists, including those belonging to the communist group. Thus *Grave*, "La Société Future," p. 155: "But if the individual is compelled to live in society it must not be hastily concluded that he must sacrifice himself in such association"; or again, p. 157: "For the anarchist, society has a reason to exist and develop only if it brings about an improved condition for man considered individually as well as collectively; if it contributes to his advancement and permits a larger extension of his powers without demanding any restrictions unfavorable to his personality other than such as already exist by virtue of the natural conditions of existence in the environment in which he finds himself."

Again, p. 166: "Hence society has no reason to exist except upon condition that those who form part of it find therein a greater development of their welfare and self-expression." See also *Reclus*, "L'évolution," etc., p. 121: "We claim everything, all that is possible to the development of our powers and our physical health in their fullest expression."

Mackay: "Die Anarchisten," p. 286: "The freedom of labor once achieved by the abolition of the State, which will then no longer monopolize money, paralyze credit, withdraw capital, check the circulation of goods, or in brief, shall no longer be able to control the affairs of the individual — when once this shall have become a fact, the sun of anarchy will have arisen"; and again, p. 281: "All forms of slavery had to be experienced. Peoples ever struggled in search of freedom, but found in every change the same lack of freedom. At last the truth was found that all outer forms involving coercion were to be rejected. Force began to decline."

The anarchistic dream of freedom is clearly set forth by *Mackay*, "Die Anarchisten," p. 122: "A condition of equal opportunity, for every free, independent, sovereign individual — whose sole

developed this extreme individualistic doctrine into the will to prevail,—"Wille zur Macht."

3: KRAPOTKIN: THE COMMUNISTIC VIEW. The counterpart of individualistic anarchism is to be found in communistic anarchism, which is advocated by the Russian Prince, PETER KRAPOTKIN (b. 1842). Considering that the individual man is powerless and helpless in the face of natural forces, it is evident that he needs social co-operation [1] to maintain himself, yet under the

demand upon society consists in claiming respect for his freedom, and whose sole self-imposed law is the respect for the freedom of others — such is the ideal of anarchy." *Grave* (as above, p. 306): "But if man cannot live in isolation, if he cannot overcome the obstacles imposed by the precarious conditions of existence in which he finds himself, it is clear that such association, if it is to endure, must be based upon the condition of perfect equality among the contracting parties"; and again (p. 400): "But we have also such a thirst for justice and liberty that we desire a society without judges, governors, and all those parasites that constitute the monstrous social organism with which humanity has been afflicted since the beginning of history." Upon the individualistic anarchism as opposed to communistic socialism, see *Mackay*, "Die Anarchisten," pp. 109-142.

[1] The communistic tendency is at present dominant. See *Grave*, "La Société Future," VII edit., Paris 1895 ("Bibliothèque Sociologique, No. 8), p. 147: "The anarchists know that man cannot live in isolation; they know that he must combine forces in order to obtain the maximum benefit; it is for this reason that they desire a society based upon solidarity and not upon conflict." Again, p. 149: "The purpose of the social state is to enable man to disengage himself from natural obstacles, is a means of extending the field of his activity, of developing his self-expression, of decidedly increasing his strength in overcoming difficulties." (p. 155): "Association is thus a human necessity. It is one of the indispensable conditions of man's intellectual development." (p. 166): "Hence society has no reason to exist except upon condition that those who form part of it find therein a greater development for their welfare and self-expression." See also *Krapotkin*, "La Conquête du Pain," pp. 21-29, 31-45.

condition of retaining his personal freedom. "Freedom is the absence of aggressive force or coercion." "The State is the power of might organized; its nature is violence and its privilege is robbery; its maintenance is due to the robbing of one for the benefit of another."[1]

Communistic anarchism and communistic socialism are closely related. It may be said that the two coincide economically and diverge politically. The anarchists provide a freer position of the individual as against the community, the communists desire organization without rule, without force, — organization, but not authority.[2] The communistic anarchists maintain that communism will lead to the prosperity of the community.[3]

4: BAKUNIN: THE POSITION OF VIOLENCE. The anarchists are agreed that only violence can lead to their

[1] *Mackay*, "Die Anarchisten," p. 111.

[2] *Grave*, "La Société Future," pp. 201-211. (p. 201): "What we understand by organization is the relation that comes to obtain between individuals associated in a common work in virtue of their interests; it is the mutual relations that arise from daily contact which all the members of a society are forced to have with one another." See also *Krapotkin*, "La Conquête du Pain," pp. 31-45, 213-234. (Does not this assume that harmony can ensue without the dominion of authority?)

[3] *Grave*, "La Société Future, pp. 51-56. p. 51: "True wealth is the most perfect adaptation of the world to our needs." (p. 53): "There are in Europe immense territories unproductive by reason of the aridity of the soil, and on the other hand rivers carrying to the sea not alone millions of cubic metres of water, but also fertilizing deposits taken from the soil in their course and encumbering navigation at their outlets."

Krapotkin, "La Conquête du Pain," preface by *Reclus*, p. vii: "The forces at our disposal should be applied not to useless or ineffective works but to the production of everything that is necessary to feed men, for their housing and use and comfort, and to the study of the sciences, and the cultivation of the arts." See also *Krapotkin*, "La Conquête du Pain, pp. 17 seq.

desired goal;[1] but as to how this violence is to be exercised, opinions differ. The scientific group, the theoretical socialists, advocate an international revolution as the radical solution without giving much thought as to how and when and where this revolution is to occur. This group is represented in the officially circulated literature of anarchism. The other party constitutes the "propagandists of action," the "terrorists," who, by intimidation and attacks upon crowned heads or other

[1] *Elisée Reclus*, "L'évolution, la révolution et l'idéal anarchique," pp. 147-154, argues against those who optimistically "hope that everything will come about by itself," that capital will yield only to force, that it spoils the character, that whoever comes into money or power realizes his authority. In concluding Reclus says (p. 289): "Let us not be self-deceived. We know that the final victory will cost much blood, labor, and suffering. The international organization of the oppressed will be counteracted by a similar organization of the oppressors."

Similarly *Grave*, "La Société Future," p. 85: "Revolution will be inevitable, for the privileged classes will never abdicate of their own accord." Again, p. 113: "There is a fatal stage to cross." That revolution can be effective only if it be international is emphasized by *Grave*, "La Société Future," pp. 61-70.

The necessity of expropriation by revolution is urged by *Krapotkin*, "La Conquête du Pain," pp. 21-26; see also the Preface by Reclus. (pp. 21 seq.): "But this problem will never be solved by way of legislation; that is an idle dream. There has been an evolution brought about in the mental attitude in the course of the last half century but it has been checked by the minority, that is, by the dominant classes; and having no outward embodiment, it must remove obstacles by force and establish itself by the violence of revolution." Godwin (see above, § 30) is not an advocate of force; and Tucker (see below) rejects the use of force for reasons of political policy.

Even women must take part in the revolution. "For the woman of the proletariat, legal marriage affords but illusory guaranties against the man who wishes to desert her and her children. The woman of the proletariat, like the laborer, can become free only by social revolution." *Grave*, "La Société Future," pp. 338 seq.

conspicuous figures in government and society, wish to force a change of social condition in accord with the anarchistic plans. The former advocate war, but the latter practise a guerilla warfare; the one present a program, the other deeds.[1]

Of considerable importance in the anarchistic movement, and particularly for the advocates of action, is the principle of agitation. Among the anarchistic agitators Bakunin[2] (1814–1876) is most promiment.

Many anarchists are moved by an emotional philanthropy, a deep sympathy with the distress and poverty under which large numbers suffer. Such conditions as obtain in the poorest London slums, with their squalor and degradation, are painted in lurid colors, and are regarded as standard, with the direct implication that society and government are responsible[3] for them. Like the socialists, the anarchists would like to banish poverty and misery from the world[4] and yet guarantee

[1] The majority of theorists seem, however, favorably disposed towards the terrorists. *Grave*, "La Société Future," pp. 393 seq.: "Force appeals to force, terror brings forth terror. It is not for us to judge those who agitate, many of whom pay by their life and their liberty for their errors, if they are in the wrong." See also *Mackay*, "Die Anarchisten," pp. 185–215, on the trial of the anarchists in Chicago.

[2] On Bakunin see *Zenker*, "Die Anarchisten," pp. 100–110. *Eltzbacher*, "Die Anarchisten," pp. 102–124. *Ludwig Stein*, "Die soziale Frage im Lichte der Philosophie," pp. 392 seq. *W. Ed. Biermann*, "Staat und Wirthschaft," I, p. 102.

[3] *Mackay*, "Die Anarchisten," pp. 143–184, 245–262.

[4] This idea constantly recurs in the projects of communistic writers, particularly in *Grave*, "La Société Future." See the above citations from this work. See also *Krapotkin*, "La Conquête du Pain," in general, and the Preface by Reclus, pp. vi seq.: "The title of the work, 'La Conquête du Pain,' should be understood in the largest sense; for man does not live by bread alone. We must be able to assure to all a complete satisfaction of their needs and enjoy-

freedom of conduct, a good income, and a maximum of happiness. If the anarchistic program were to be realized, the result would be a retrogression from the present high stage of culture to a much lower one. The influences of culture would be paralyzed and deprived of their sphere of operation. It would result in the worst form of demagogic rule, an appeal to the ineradicable vanity of men, in a futile rivalry for popular favor. No less deceptive are the measures that anarchy advocates. The baseness of a terrorism that, to establish its conception of humanity and the recognition of individuality, proceeds forcibly to destroy innocent individuals, hardly needs proof. Such vagaries of a morbid imagination correct themselves. The plea for a general international revolution amounts to massacre — and that not, as at present, restricted to a few conspicuous individuals.

It is a vain attempt of Reclus to divest the idea of revolution from its inherent terrors, and its accompanying horrors, by explaining that revolution is but an evolution on a large scale,[1] and differs from the latter only in the degree of evolutionary change. But the quantitative difference, here as elsewhere, conditions the qualitative one.[2] One might just as well say that the crop-destroying hail or the destructive cloudburst is but quantitatively different from a fruitful rain. Evolution is the unfoldment of energy,—is life; revolution is the destruction of energy,—is death. Finally, with reference

ments." On p. xiv is considered the reawakening of "a natural friendliness among men," "when there will be neither rich nor poor." See also pp. 15–29: "L'aisance pour tous"; as well as the ideals of the future considered from p. 65 to the end of the volume.

[1] "L'évolution, la révolution et l'idéal anarchique," pp. 3–5, 14–19. Also *Grave*, "La Société Future," inclines to minimize the importance of revolution, and notes that "social revolution proceeds by evolution."

[2] *Berolzheimer*, "System," Vol. I, pp. 216–221.

to its philosophical appreciation, it is not the consequence to which anarchism leads that is decisive, but the faultiness of its theoretical foundation. Anarchism proceeds upon a false conception of freedom. Freedom has been the purpose and goal of civilization for the last two thousand years. But the freedom thus sought, and at present substantially attained, is the emancipation from every type of slavery and oppression on the part of the State and the law. And the means whereby freedom has been secured is the legal absorption of the ethical principle, the recognition of the conception of humanity, the moralization of the law.

As against this result, the anarchists propose an absolute conception of freedom under which everyone shall be subject only to his own will; and in consistent pursuit of this idea, they naturally reject every form of coercion, of authority, of subjection.[1] As, however, the radical and absolute execution of this idea would lead the undisciplined will to reject all culture, and to the deterioration of humanity, — for anarchism, if consistent, would likewise abolish education, — the anarchist leaders, with the exception of Stirner, take refuge in some form of association which they term society, but which in reality would be tantamount to the dominance of the people,— a society that rejects all authority of the State and through the State, and replaces it by mob rule.[2] The anarchists take their

[1] *Proudhon,* "Qu'est-ce que la Propriété?" I, p. 244: "The landholder, the thief, the hero, the sovereign — for these all mean the same thing — *imposes his will as law,* and suffers no contradiction or check." (The italics are mine.)

[2] *Ludwig Stein* gives a pertinent refutation of anarchism in his essay "De L'autorité" (see above), wherein he shows that governmental control is an absolute necessity for bringing people to a state of civilization, and indeed represents the chief condition of culture. Thus on p. 7: "Authority is the indispensable school of the human

position upon the principle of pure might: Might is right.[1] If this holds, then the present wielders of authority might consistently resolve upon the forcible suppression of anarchistic agitation and expression, and their complete annihilation and destruction.

5: TUCKER AND TOLSTOI; MODERATE ANARCHISM. TUCKER[2] turns anarchism away from the position of self-assertion and utilitarianism. Nominally the law is to remain, but it is to be made so plastic that the courts, somewhat after the manner of the Roman prætor, will decide upon the applicability or inappropriateness of the law in concrete cases, according to the principle of justice. The anarchistic order of society is to be brought about by refusal of compliance, by passive resistance to the governmental laws on the part of those convinced of the truth of the new doctrine. Tucker does not reject terrorism in principle, but disavows it through considerations of prudence.

The Russian Count, LEO TOLSTOI (1828–1910), by

race." (p. 8): "The forms under which authority is exercised among a people become refined and perfected in direct ratio to their progress in civilization." (p. 14): "On the other hand we are forced to conclude that races that persist in their primitive anarchy are incapable of civilization. (p. 17): "The most solid reason for the necessity of authority is the evidence supplied by itself." (p. 18): "Authorities may change but authority persists," pp. 21, 23.

[1] *Reclus*, "L'évolution," etc., p. 206, puts the sentiment, "Let force rule," in the mouths of the opponents of anarchy, the defenders of the present régime. Similarly *Grave*, "La Société Future," p. 42: "You yourselves have said that victory belongs to the strong." See also pp. 25–42. *Mackay*, "Die Anarchisten," p. 267: "It was our purpose to show that the State was a privileged power and that force maintained it, that it was the State that converted the harmony of nature into the disharmony of coercion."

[2] *Tucker*, "Instead of a Book," pp. 25, 52, 60, 104, 158, 167, 312, 413, 427, 429.

the trend of his teachings belongs to the anarchists, but judged by the theoretical basis of his views he must be classed as a social moralist with a religious turn. His intense ethical and social sympathy and his romantic impressionism led him to take a stand against the State. He does not advocate the use of violence, but of passive resistance towards civic duties. In view of his later writings he has frequently been compared to Rousseau. The comparison is pertinent in so far as both advocate a return to nature; but while Rousseau as a rationalist presents the state of nature as desirable, Tolstoi accepts the primitive Christian religious attitude, the goal of which is the establishment of universal love. But Tolstoi, like Rousseau, is saturated with the extreme culture of his social environment. As a whole, the Russian people are not troubled by an excess of civilization; and like the rest of mankind they can well afford to strive for further culture. However highly one may estimate Tolstoi as an author, Tolstoi as a social philosopher may be dismissed without further notice.

§ 40. *Further Types of Socialism.* 1: MENGER. Of the writings of ANTON MENGER (b. 1841) there are to be considered, "Das Recht auf den vollen Arbeitsertrag,"[1] "Das Bürgerliche Recht und die besitzlosen Klassen,"[2] and "Die neue Staatslehre."[3] In the first Menger proposes "to consider the fundamental ideas of socialism

[1] "Das Recht auf den vollen Arbeitsertrag in geschichtlicher Darstellung," Stuttgart 1886, third edition, 1904. (I cite from the first edition.)

[2] Third edition, Tübingen 1904. I cite from the original which appeared in Braun's "Archiv für Soziale Gesetzgebung und Statistik," Vol. II, Tübingen 1889, pp. 1–73, 419–482; Vol. III, Tübingen 1890, pp. 57–74.

[3] First edition, 1902; second edition, Jena 1904.

from the legal side";[1] he presents the legal phases of socialistic doctrines historically.[2] His concluding consideration proposes the question: "What is the practical significance, for present-day movements, of the two new legal conceptions which, in the course of a century, have gradually been formed in the consciousness of the great laboring classes — that of the right to the entire proceeds of labor, and the right of existence? It is Menger's view that our social development is gradually approaching the realization of these demands. The communal duty of providing for the poor is an example, though a sad one, of a substitute for a right to existence. Compulsory education guarantees to an extent the intellectual training of minors. In regard to the right of existence, present legislation simply checks the worst forms of exploitation of the laborer; and these, in the main, only as concerns the industrial laborer. According to Menger the realization of the right to work, to which the prevalent political attitude is favorably disposed, might appropriately be a first step in the new economic order — a transition to the socialistic form of the State. Menger sets forth two legislative ends as particularly desirable and attainable. Legislation should take care not to establish any further forms of income without labor, and not to extend existing forms of such income. Yet more important is it that legislation should not forcibly transfer the ground rent or interest of capital from one class of the people to another. As an example of such measures may be cited the redemption of agricultural mortgages at the cost of the State; this would constitute a fundamental breach of the law in that the ground rent which would accrue in the cities would be taken away from them, and given by the State to the landholders.

[1] "Das Recht auf den vollen Arbeitsertrag," p. III
[2] Pp. 12-162, 163

In the second work, "Das Bürgerliche Recht und die besitzlosen Klassen," Menger criticizes, from the very interesting point of view of those without means, the outline of the civil law of the German Empire. This work was merely the forerunner of "Die neue Staatslehre;" for Menger was well aware that "the purpose and task of the author of the compendium was to prepare it upon the basis of private law," for which reason "every profitable criticism must consider the work with reference to the actual state of affairs."[1] He restricts himself to proposals for improvement within the province of private law. He sets forth that the compendium, which he criticized in his former work, follows, as do all compendiums for the use of the laity, the principle of private ownership, of freedom of contract, and of the right of inheritance. Yet current individualistic forms of treatment of property rights may also be considered socialistically. According to the socialistic views these three principles are converted into their opposites. The legal system of private right is psychologically based upon self-seeking; the socialistic, upon the communal impulses. Menger then undertakes in detail to socialize the conditions of property rights of the "Compendium," and to transform the content of legislation in the interests of the economically dependent classes.

In "Die Neue Staatslehre" Menger bases his socialistic teachings upon the legal foundation of a "popular labor state," "Arbeitsstaat." He sets up the socialistic legal order as against the modern "Kulturstaat," which everywhere bears the impress of the individualistic State. "The individualistic form of government may be termed the ruling and commanding State, or the State of authority, and the socialistic order of government may be termed the State of the working classes,

[1] Braun's "Archiv," Vol. II, p. 2.

or the popular Labor-State." Even in the latter State a certain amount of governmental force would be necessary, but a much smaller amount than obtains in the present State. "When the welfare of all shall actually become the purpose of our social institutions, and when the masses of the people through these institutions shall be educated to a higher degree of insight and of personal sacrifice, then it will be possible to leave far more to their initiative than we slaves of convention deem possible." The individualistic State, "the hereditary form of government, has developed with substantial uniformity in all countries on the basis of the military and political authority." To it Menger opposes the "socialistic or popular 'Labor-State'; and this, reduced to its most general formula, consists in making the individual interests of the masses of the people the chief concern of the government." He regards as of primary import the economic side of the people's interest, "the maintenance and fostering of individual life, the preservation of the species, and the security of life and health"; while such matters as political rights, participation in the government of the State, are assigned a secondary place as "means to an end."[1] For the masses the prime consideration is the question of bread. Menger does not allow that the State exists for itself, and considers only the ends for which the authorities work.[2] Right is might; legal questions are questions of might.[3] He

[1] "Neue Staatslehre," pp. 17, 15, 20 seq., 75–154 (93–198 of the first edition).
[2] "Neue Staatslehre," p. 157: "States as such have no purpose. It is only their rulers who have."
[3] "Neue Staatslehre," p. 164: "The legal order is the prevalent conception of the permanently recognized authorities in the land." "The sovereignty is the highest actual power in the State." Whoever is sovereign in the State takes his stand according to historical experience.

distinguishes four types of authority: first, the supreme authority in the State, the monarch and his family, or the administration in Republican States; they seek power and pomp; second, the nobility and the higher clergy, with their striving for preferment; third, the citizen and the farmer class, who are anxious to possess material goods and intellectual opportunity; fourth, the unpropertied classes of the people, who, in general, form the working classes. "Their interests coincide with the fundamental objects of life, and are thus directed to personal security, to the maintenance of a life worthy of a human being and to a regulated family life. Their energies go to secure the conditions of existence."[1]

Menger's views in regard to government and law are the most sensible that have been advanced from the socialistic standpoint. He divests socialism of its disguise — a service not gratefully accepted by the Marxians. He shows socialism in its true nature to be the emphatic, and deliberate, and likewise the partisan advocacy, of the interests of the working classes. Such advocacy looks upon the material and economic interests of labor as the center of governmental concern, and desires to make law and governmental institutions serviceable exclusively to the economic interests of the fourth estate.[2]

---

[1] "Neue Staatslehre," pp. 157-160.

[2] *Gumplowicz* pertinently refutes *Menger's* conclusions on the basis of the latter's acknowledged premises. He says ("Die soziologische Staatsidee," Graz 1892, p. 116): "The State is either 'the aggregate of permanently recognized authorities,' or it is not; if it be so, which even Menger recognizes, the inequality is inherent, for there can be relations of authority only where inequality prevails. Where perfect equality exists, there can be no relations of authority." The comment of Gumplowicz upon the economic value of the laboring classes is also pertinent. (*Ibid.* p. 46): "The laborers can at best organize a strike and thereby paralyze industry.

2: LORIA. LORIA[1] (b. 1857) approaches socialism and communism with a radical distrust of capital. Somewhat reminiscent of Rousseau, he makes the assumption of a condition of government in which all are free; it is cupidity that brings a proprietary class into existence. This supposition[2] is not put forward as an historical fact, but serves to express his view that morality, law, and political institutions grow upon an economic basis and are determined by economic relations. By virtue of the dynamic force of economic laws, the various forms of income lead men into class conflicts. In summarizing his position he advocates the replacement of the capitalistic order by an "equalizing and associative economics." The advantages of this form of society as against the capitalistically organized State are set forth in the following words: "In an equalizing and associative type of economy, the social organism, being in perfect equilibrium by virtue of its nature, will have no need of finding the guaranty of its permanence in perverting the expressions of human nature, which, if persisted in, are likely to repress the legitimate and moral development of men. In the economic stage morality will be the natural and spontaneous expression of the enlightened self-interest of man; law will be reduced to a guaranty to the pro-

but they cannot establish industries. They and their labors, though forming an integral part of the State, form but a part."

[1] "Les Bases Économiques de la Constitution Sociale," second edition, translated from the Italian by *A. Bouchard* ("Bibliothèque Historique et Politique"), Paris 1893. The first edition appeared in Italian in Turin 1886. The French edition was translated into German by *Karl Grünberg*, with the title, "Die wirthschaftlichen Grundlagen der herrschenden Gesellschaftsordnung," Freiburg i/B and Leipzig 1895. There is also an English translation.

[2] *Barth*, "Die Philosophie der Geschichte als Soziologie," Leipzig 1897, p. 336: "It is indeed peculiar that Loria presents not an historical but a constructive development of economics."

ducer of the proceeds of his labor, and there will be no need to have recourse to severe penalties to enforce its decrees. Finally, the political constitution will be the expression of the universal consensus and the aggregate of the institutions necessary to secure the collective welfare. The capitalistic spirit of these relations will give way to a social or humane attitude. Morality, law, and politics will still remain the associative institutions of society, but instead of being put to the service of one class and of their economic interests, these institutions will have for their end the advantages of all men and the realization of their highest destiny."[1]

3: SOMBART. WERNER SOMBART[2] (b. 1863) favors the materialistic conception of history. "Human history is either a struggle for food or a struggle for the feeding places of the earth." Every social class is the result of a particular type of production; the proletariat is the result of capitalistic production. "The history of the origin of the proletariat is accordingly the history of capitalism. Capital cannot exist develop without producing a proletariat." The modern social movement is an inevitable result. The important point is to plan the social conflict as a legal struggle, and to conduct it with propriety, and without malice.[3] In his chief work

[1] "Les Bases Économiques," pp. 9, 13–74, 77–122, 423, etc., pp. 125–392; pp. 423–430; pp. 424, 425.

[2] His chief work is "Der moderne Kapitalismus," 2 vols., Leipzig 1902. Vol. I, "Die Genesis des Kapitalismus," Vol. II, "Die Theorie der Kapitalistischen Entwickelung." Other works, "Sozialismus und soziale Bewegung im 19. Jahrhundert," Jena 1896. I cite from the fourth edition (the 18th to 23d thousand), Jena 1901. "Die Volkswirthschaft im neunzehnten Jahrhundert" (Schlenther, "Das neunzehnte Jahrhundert in Deutschlands Entwickelung," Vol. VII, Berlin 1903.)

[3] "Sozialismus und soziale Bewegung im 19. Jahrhundert," fourth edition, pp. 2, 1, 4, 96–100.

"Der moderne Kapitalismus," Sombart considers the alternative between a causal and a teleological procedure; he decides for the former. In the social sciences the consideration of historical development must furnish the clue to the immediate future development.

Since the decay of ancient culture there have been three great economic periods, — the peasant feudal order, the artisan order or industrial development, and the capitalistic order, characterized by the dominance of mercantile life. The first indications of the fourth period, that of a socialistic form of association, are now evident. The earlier portions of the work trace the course of development up to the point at which the capitalistic economics prevailed over previous systems and became the dominant influence.[1] These volumes set forth the organization of industry in the artisan group;[2] and at greater length, the rise of capitalistic production[3] and its further development. In considering the "modern reconstruction of economic life," Sombart observes that this renaissance is characterized by three factors: modern law, modern technology, and modern standards of living. Modern law is described as industrial freedom, or as the system of the individualistic legal order of free competition. The guiding principle of the new legal order is freedom of acquisition, or industrial freedom in the narrower sense; freedom of contractual association; of property; the transfer of ownership, of sale, and of the debtor relation; freedom of willing and general protection of legitimately acquired private rights. He believes that the importance of economic laws for the

[1] "Der moderne Kapitalismus," I, pp. XIII seq., XVI seq., XXXI seq.

[2] Book I: "Die Wirthschaft als Handwerk," pp. 75–192.

[3] Book II: "Die Genesis des modernen Kapitalismus," pp. 195 seq.

development of the several economic forms is overrated. The new technical methods were established through the application of machinery. Machinery increased the human output above the maximum attainable by any individual effort, and therein, and not in the saving of human labor, lay its essential advantage. The new methods appeared further in the application of science to technology through the replacement of empirical skill by rational or scientific procedure. The new standards of economic life appear in the increased cost of living, and in the increasing dominance of the factor of material productions over other interests. Towards the close of the work Sombart describes the rise of modern agriculture; the origin and character of the modern city; modern needs, and their extension, concentration and refinement; the consolidation and uniformity of expenditure in the cities; the wholesale expression of conformity, as in the demands of fashion; the transformation of the commercial market. He continues with the "theory of industrial competition." In the victory of the capitalistic industrial order over the artisan organization, the point at issue was not the opposition between business on a large or a small scale, but between the organization of manual labor and of capital. The latter proved the stronger; first in the competition for the quality of the products, and again in the competition of prices. The several factors in the competition for efficiency of production were, first, the attractiveness and appeal of the goods. The capitalistic enterprise was better able to meet the growing demand for wholesale production and prompt delivery. It could manufacture upon demand, and supply a fresh stock, always marketable, up-to-date, and attractive. Second, the quality of the product. Capitalistic enterprise, as opposed to hand labor, produced better, more durable, stylish, artistic, and uniform goods. It was the development of taste that deprived manual labor of its existence; for though the artist continues to serve his art, yet the form in which his service reaches the public is controlled by capitalistic enterprise. In the conflict of prices, likewise, capitalistic enterprise got the better of manual labor. Capitalistic superiority was able to assert itself despite sporadic checks and the hopes of the trades-unions.[1]

[1] "Der moderne Kapitalismus," Vol. II, pp. 25-89, 91-420, 421 seq., 430, 432-462, 463-539, 540 seq., 544-560.

CHAPTER VII

THE SOCIOLOGICAL RECONSTRUCTION OF LEGAL PHILOSOPHY

THE DEVELOPMENT OF SOCIOLOGY: (1) COMTE AND THE BEGINNINGS OF SOCIOLOGY; (2) POSITIVISM AND SOCIOLOGY; (3) THE SOCIOLOGY OF SPENCER. — SOCIOLOGICAL AND SOCIAL-ETHICAL EXTREMISTS: (1) THE CONCEPTION OF "SOCIETY"; (2) SOCIAL ETHICS; (3) SOCIOLOGICAL IDEALS. — SOCIAL UTILITARIANISM: (1) SHAFTESBURY; (2) IHERING. — THE SOCIOLOGICAL SCHOOL: (1) ITS DISTINCTIVE POSITION; (2) ITS PRECURSORS; (3) GUMPLOWICZ; (4) RATZENHOFER; (5) RECENT REPRESENTATIVES — TÖNNIES, KLÖPPEL, BERGEMANN; (6) CRITICAL SUMMARY OF THE SOCIOLOGICAL POSITION; (7) APPLICATIONS OF THE SOCIOLOGICAL POSITION: (a) CORPORATIONS; (b) PENOLOGY. — REALISTIC AND HISTORICAL TRENDS IN POLITICAL ECONOMY AND SOCIOLOGY. — THE THEORY OF NORMS. — ETHNOLOGICAL JURISPRUDENCE. — THE REINSTATEMENT OF KANT AND HEGEL: V. HARTMANN: (1) NEO-KANTIANISM; (2) NEO-HEGELIANISM; (3) THE PHILOSOPHY OF V. HARTMANN. — PSYCHOLOGICAL ASPECTS OF LAW AND ECONOMICS: (1) THE PSYCHOLOGICAL BASIS; (2) CRIMINAL PSYCHOLOGY. — RECENT SURVEYS OF FUNDAMENTAL PROBLEMS: (1) MERKEL AND HIS FOLLOWERS; (2) SCHMIDT; (3) PAULSEN; (4) BAUMANN; (5) SCHUPPE. — THE INFLUENCE OF THE PRINCIPLES OF EVOLUTION: (1) SOCIAL ARISTOCRACY — NIETZSCHE; (2) EVOLUTIONARY MONISM — HAECKEL; (3) EVOLUTION AND SOCIALISM; CLASS AND STATE.

§ 41. *The Development of Sociology.* 1. COMTE AND THE BEGINNINGS OF SOCIOLOGY. AUGUSTE COMTE[1] (1798–

[1] Comte's chief work is "Cours de Philosophie Positive," 6 vols., 1830–1842. Vols. IV, V, "Physique Sociale"; Vol VI contains the

1857) is the founder of a philosophy of experience which he calls positivism. It holds that knowledge is limited to the phenomenal world, to the relations of phenomena to one another, which are to be studied from the point of view of natural science or natural philosophy. From the same point of view it attempts to interpret the nature of government and to derive the phenomena of political life. But government and law are not amenable to this naturalistic treatment; accordingly Comte, accepting the term of Saint-Simon, makes the object of his study not the institutions of government and law, but society.

He distinguishes three stages of human development characterized by different philosophies and methods. The theological or "mythical" stage is the oldest; under its dominance every object is personified and made a fetish. It is succeeded by the metaphysical or abstract stage. The gods — or in the monotheistic system, God — are replaced by the concepts of the thinkers whose faith invests them with reality. The third and final stage is reached in the conception of a positive or scientific philosophy.[1] Its point of departure is the conviction that the ultimate nature of things is unknowable. Man can merely study phenomena and their mutual relations inductively; all knowledge is empirical and is based upon inductive reasoning; all scientific conclusions proceed from inductions; the law of causality, in the last analysis, is the result of an induction. Such approximate knowledge is adequate for human needs. Positive science is content to determine the laws of

complement of the social philosophy. I cite from the third edition, Paris 1869.

[1] "Cours," Vol. I, p. 8. *Comte* describes the three stages as "the theological or mythical, the metaphysical or abstract, the scientific or positive stage."

nature; it renounces the hope of an ultimate explanation, and stops with an understanding of the operations of laws of nature. In his philosophy Comte subjects the several sciences to a "positive" interpretation. Proceeding from the simpler fundamental sciences to the more complex, he considers Mathematics, Astronomy, Physics, Chemistry, Biology; the latter including the three main groups of the phenomena of organic life, of animal life, and of intellectual and moral life dependent upon the nervous system. The last of these groups should presumably include law and government; but in the positive philosophy these become the great independent discipline of sociology, or "physique sociale"; for, according to Comte, the nature of a science does not determine its method, but the method determines the science. It is because government and law are not amenable to the methods of natural science that the State is replaced by society, and law and economics by social life. Thus Comte became the founder of the new social science, calling it first Social Physics — "Physique Sociale," — and later Sociology — "Sociologie."[1] In time sociology encroached upon, and more or less absorbed, the philosophy of government and law.

Following the dissertation on method and the consideration of the relation of social physics to the other positive sciences, Comte treats of social statics and dynamics — the method again determining the nature of the conclusions. In his biology, environment is accorded the largest influence.[2] The nature and development

---

[1] "Cours," Vol. IV, p. 185. *Comte* uses the term "sociology" for his own original phrase, "physique sociale."

[2] "Cours," Vol. III (Biology), p. 209, note 1: "It will be superfluous, I hope, to justify the frequent use which I shall henceforth make in biology of the term 'environment' to designate briefly

of living creatures are determined by environment. Carrying this principle into sociology, the individual is made the resultant of his social conditions. Social statics treats of the nature and relations of social phenomena, which it presents as crystallized. Its fundamental law is that of organic dependence. The primary social unit is the family.[1] Social dynamics treats of the laws of genesis and normal development of social phenomena in their process of evolution. Comte applies the three stages — theological, metaphysical, and positive — to the phenomena of social life. Society is an organism which shows its stage of progress by the degree to which its higher activities prevail above the lower. If the entire social life were completely determined by natural law, and man were absolutely conditioned by his environment, then fatalism is inevitable. This is not Comte's conclusion. He seeks a mode of escape for social politics from the absolute determinism of nature. He holds that the development and perfection of the human species is the goal of all endeavor; and by this conception gives positivism a practical value.

No work of the nineteenth century had so ominous, not to say fatal, an influence upon the course of the political sciences as Comte's "Cours de Philosophie Positive," an influence at once socialistic and sociological. So far as concerns socialism it was comparatively easy to separate the chaff from the wheat and hold the scientific interests intact. But the science of government, including the philosophy of law, was ousted by sociology and is still suffering from the confusion and vagueness

and summarily, in particular not alone the medium in which the organism is immersed, but in general the sum total of external circumstances of whatever character necessary to the existence of each special organism."

[1] "Cours," Vol. IV, pp. 398 seq.

of thought thus induced. For "society" became an insistent concept, absorbing law, government, and economics, or relegating them to wholly subordinate positions. "Social welfare" was made the goal of development, though the term was not clearly and critically defined. It was left undetermined in what welfare consists, or what group of persons was referred to by the unassimilated aggregate, so diversely concerned in public welfare. Indeed from the nebulous background of sociological principles there emerges little more than an uncritical tendency towards democratic or demagogic hedonism.

Positivism, like the philosophy of Kant, accepts the impossibility of knowing the ultimate nature of things. It confines itself to the world of phenomena, is limited by experience, and proceeds by the method of natural science. Whatever transcends experience is rejected. Comte's positive philosophy is hardly a philosophy at all; and his sociology is not a philosophy of law, government, and society, but a collection of facts and descriptions of logical relations. He deals with mere empirical consequences, such as that from a follows b, and if there is no a, there is no b; and social philosophy as well as social ethics becomes the embodiment of a general mechanical fatalism. Events follow from a natural necessity. There is no place for ethical norms and moral obligations. The severe logicality of positivism may be adequate to the scientific breeding of dogs, but hardly to the education of human beings. Positivism leaves the individual without rules of conduct, and society without guides for its orderly development. Even Gumplowicz, though a supporter of sociology, admits that it leads to a fatalistic resignation alike in practice and in theory. Sociology does not solve, or try to solve, the fundamental problems of the philosophy of law and government; it merely evades them.

This radical defect is not due to the expositors of sociology, but is inherent in the sociological attitude. When sociology attempts to be more than a purely descriptive discipline dealing with its subject from the point of view of ethnology and race-psychology, and attempts to be a social philosophy serving as a philosophical basis for law and government, it fails by reason of an inappropriate method. Sociology as a social philosophy approaches the solution of the problems of law and government by the method of the natural sciences. Modern criticism would not tolerate an attempt to present natural philosophy from the legal point of view, would hardly approve the interpretation of the laws of nature from the point of view of the laws of justice. The converse procedure is not more commendable. Sociology proceeds from the concept of socialization in its most comprehensive aspect. Every form of associated group is considered — the State and its economic institutions form one of these groups, as a species of the genus society. Here we touch upon the basal misconception or evasion of sociology. For whether or not the State is more than a form of socialization is a fundamental question of the science of law and government. Positivism assumes it to be so; the difference between it and other forms of socialization lies merely in its distinctive position, its power of legal coercion. Consequently right is simply might. For the positivist this is an inevitable conclusion because it is an implicit presupposition; in the Kantian terminology, it is the positivist's analytic judgment. That is all there is to the positivist's legal philosophy: simply that right is might. Natural law prevails in the social sphere. Science may study laws, but men must yield to them.

2: POSITIVISM AND SOCIOLOGY. The objection to a sociological philosophy is not limited to the practical and personal one of its issue in fatalism; its fundamental position is misleading. Comte regarded himself as the first contributor to true science; but in reality the philosophical bases of positivism are quite uncritical. The most tangible, and presumably most certain fact of our environment, as revealed to our perceptions, is the nature of the world of objects, which Descartes proposed as the starting point of philosophical inquiry. For him the essence of matter was extension. This solution of the problem seemed too superficial to Leibnitz, who regarded the essence of matter as force or energy; in Spinoza's pantheism the problem lost its pertinence; Kant relied upon the efficiency of pure reason, space and time being considered *a priori* concepts, and space as antecedent to human experience and as a medium for the location of objects. Kant did not inquire critically as to the nature of objects, but only to what extent the conception of space belonged to pure reason; he concluded that the conception of space preceded experience, but that spatial content was a matter of experience. The question whether and how far knowledge can transcend experience, positivism relegates to the domain of faith, which deals with the world that lies beyond the province of science. But positivism is not thorough-going enough to examine seriously the nature of this external world of things. Since Leibnitz, no philosopher has given adequate attention to this primary and urgent problem of metaphysics and the theory of knowledge. The world of experience, the world as apprehended by our senses, appears primarily as composed of objects. Hence philosophy asks: What is an object? And if we begin with number as most certain and concrete, the question becomes: What is unity, the unity of experience? In the first volume of my work I presented a solution which may be inadequate, imperfect, perhaps even erroneous, but which is a serious and critical attempt. Positivism, like most other empirical systems of philosophy, passes lightly over the fundamental questions of the nature of the elementary facts of experience. But in the light of this problem, the inadequacy of the positivistic hypothesis is evident; and with the proof of its failure, the positivist social philosophy likewise crumbles, and its sociology falls to the level of a descriptive science, as little suited to replace a philosophy of law and government as is anthropology or biology or any other of the natural sciences dealing with man.

Positivism is uncritical, self-contradictory, and opposed to the facts of history. It attempts to derive all knowledge from experience, which it regards as the exclusive source of human knowledge. Yet the material of Comte's biology and sociology is not the world of experience as it actually is, but our interpretation of it, growing out of a false view of the law of causality. In Comte's biology the most important principle is that environment determines development. Every object is the result of the forces and factors to whose influence it is subjected; and this he applies to human associations. The nature and development of the individual is determined by the group to which he belongs. This view disregards the most fundamental fact of history — the emancipation of man. History shows a constant process of emancipation of man from the control of environment. At first helpless in the presence of the world of objects, man eventually conquers nature through the processes of culture. As development proceeds, the dependence upon natural endowment diminishes. Emotion replaces instinct, and reason replaces emotion; the organism acquires artificial capacities. As culture progresses, differentiations increase in refinement, human individuality becomes more marked and more assertive, and the influence of circumstances recedes. As illustrations of natural forces, the falling stone, the reactions of plants to stimuli, the response of animals to impulses and situations, and the rational behavior of man, are all on a par. But such a statement disregards the fact that in each step of this series the analogy weakens for the reason that the initiative of the subject constantly increases and the influence of the objective situation diminishes. Human history shows the same process, the constant growth and assertiveness of subjective spontaneity. Positivism is a naturalistic corollary of Spinoza's pantheism. In both systems the individuality is lost and absorbed, — in Spinoza, in the divine; in Comte, in the natural world.

Comte and the sociological school did not discover, but they adequately emphasized the fact that men have ever been associated in groups, and the further fact that the impulses towards the establishment of government and law originated not in the isolated individual but in the social group; and this forms their permanent contribution. Comte is the last of the writers who found it necessary to antagonize the view that the individual forms the objective point of "natural law," and that society is built upon an individualistic basis. The central position of the social unit is established, and Comte's share therein must be acknowledged. Beyond this but little of Comte's system will be retained. In course of time it will be recognized that the principle that social welfare is the determining motive in the development of government and law is but a revival of Wolff's position, in which the paternalism of benevolent law replaces the benevolent absolutism of the monarch, and an undisguised hedonism is replaced by the doctrine of social welfare.

3: THE SOCIOLOGY OF SPENCER. In the nineteenth century the theory of evolution was reconstructed deductively, inductively, and by combination of the two procedures, thus again indicating that method is secondary to the dominant intellectual trend. In his speculative philosophy Hegel employed the deductive method, and restated in modern phraseology the principle of the Heraclitean flux. Lamarck and Darwin studied the processes of evolution inductively. The combined method forms the basis of the system of HERBERT SPENCER (1820–1903). In the history of ideas an extreme movement in one direction is apt to induce a reaction in the other. The older philosophy was so intensely occupied with "being" that it disregarded "becoming"; contemporary philosophy everywhere detected growth and evolution, and fixed relations disappeared. This extreme assertiveness of the idea of evolution, and of an all-pervading evolutionary philosophy, has reacted disadvantageously upon the development of legal philosophy. It is overlooked that evolution itself consists of an infinite series of momentary points of arrest, and that the study of evolution must be supplemented by a consideration of the static moments embodied in governmental and economic institutions. For individuals realize themselves as static units, and their interests claim the available benefits of the protective institutions of government, of law, of ethics, and of civilization in general.

The "sociology" of Herbert Spencer is under obligations to Comte, yet is the direct issue of evolutionary principles.[1] It reflects the common failing of sociolog-

[1] For *Spencer's* principles of evolution see *Berolzheimer*, "System," Vol. I, pp. 124–128, especially pp. 127 seq. *Hensel*, "Hauptprobleme der Ethik," Leipzig 1903, pp. 17–42, gives a good exposition and criticism of the theory of evolution.

ical systems — that of regarding the State merely as a type of social alliance. In the first volume of his "Principles of Sociology," under the heading, "The Data of Sociology," Spencer brings together considerable ethnographical and anthropological material. Societies resemble individual organisms; they originate in small beginnings and, as they develop, become more and more complex in structure; the mutual dependence of the constituents of societies constantly increase, while society as a whole becomes more independent of the units of which it is composed. Yet the social organism presents large differences from individual organisms, and Spencer applies the term "superorganic"[1] to the evolution of society. The phenomena of social evolution are conditioned partly by the external influences acting on the "social aggregate," and partly by the character of its constituent parts. Both groups of evolutionary factors are subject to progressive variations. "While the *fear of the living* becomes the root of the political control, the *fear of the dead* becomes the root of the religious control."[2]

The second part of the work establishes the organic nature and functions of society.[3] The third part describes domestic institutions;[4] the fourth, ceremonial institutions; the fifth, political institutions, including those of the church, of the professions, and of the industries. Thus government and law are completely

[1] Ch. I.

[2] Ch. 27, § 209, p. 521.

[3] "Sociology," Part II, "The Inductions of Sociology." Appleton edition, 1890. This biological conception of society is stated by *Spencer* in "Social Statics" and again in "The Social Organism," and in the "Study of Sociology" (chap. XIV).

[4] Under the title, "The Domestic Relations."

incorporated in sociology, and are considered merely as sociological factors.

In the chapter on "Political Organization in General," Spencer concludes that "political organization [is] to be understood as that part of social organization which consciously carries on directive and restraining functions for public ends." An important principle appears in the political differentiation of men and women; what was originally a "domestic relation between the sexes passes into a political relation, such that men and women become in militant groups the ruling class and the subject class; so does the relation between master and slave, originally a domestic one, pass into a political one as fast as, by habitual war, the making of slaves becomes general. It is with the formation of a slave class that there begins that political differentiation between the regulating structures and the sustaining structures, which continues throughout all higher forms of social evolution." In short, masters and slaves are necessary factors in political society. Neglecting the small nomadic groups, class differentiations still persist and go back to the beginnings of social life. A study of the "political forms and forces" reveals three essential factors in the community: a small group of the powerful, a large group of the weak, and one individual, — the chieftain, the ruler, — emerging by reason of his superiority from the ranks of the powerful. "In its primitive form, then, political power is the feeling of the community acting through an agency which it has either informally or formally established." History furthermore shows the force of conservatism whereby "a government is in the main but an agency which works the force of public feeling, present and past." To a large extent the ruler is the instrument executing the will of the dead past. Spencer emphasizes the decisive influence of the feeling of the community or of its dominant classes in developing and maintaining power, so that "in its widest acceptation the feeling of the community is the sole source of political power," at least in those communities which are not under foreign domination. The position of the ruler rests upon superior ability, usually combined with courage.[1] In later parts of his work Spencer analyzes, or rather describes, the political forms and forces; the representative bodies, the ministries, the local governing agencies; military systems; judicial and executive systems. But these descriptive studies yield little of value for the philosophy of law and government.

"Law, whether written or unwritten, formulates the rule of the dead over the living." This dominance of the past results from the belief in Animism; it leads to regulation and law; and the law, by virtue of its supposedly sacred origin, attains its inviolable and permanent character.[2] "Such being the origin and nature of laws, it becomes manifest that the cardinal injunction must be obedience." It is thus by an ethnological approach that Spencer reaches Binding's "Theory of Norms." Law arises from four sources: "inherited usages which have a quasi-religious sanction"; "special injunctions of deceased leaders, which have a more distinct religious sanction"; "the will of the predominant man," either by reason of ability or power; and "aggregate opinion." At a later stage, laws are differentiated into sacred and secular; again into laws designed to uphold the authority of the heads, and "those which, directly and irrespective of authority, conduce to social welfare." As laws change in form, the sentiments which

---

[1] "Sociology," Part V, chap. VI: "Political heads — chiefs, kings," etc.
[2] Part V, chap. XIV, treats of the laws.

they arouse in the community likewise change. With such changes the theory of legal sanction also changes; in a theocratic State the laws are regarded as the emanation of the divine will; in States in which an absolute form of government in centered in the hands of a single person or of a few, the source of the law is the will of the rulers. As progress is made towards popular government, it becomes more generally agreed that the ultimate sanction of the law is the popular will. Yet the last view is but a transitional stage towards the view which Spencer defends, namely, "that the source of legal obligation is the *consensus* of individual interests itself, and not the will of the majority determined by their opinion concerning it, which may or may not be right." Already, even in legal theory, especially as expounded by French jurists, natural law or law of nature is recognized as a source of formulated law: the admission being thereby made that, primarily certain individual claims, and secondarily the social welfare furthered by enforcing such claims, furnish a warrant for law, anteceding political authority and its enactments. Already in the qualification of common law by equity, which avowedly proceeds upon the law of "*honesty* and *reason* and of *nations*," "there is involved the presupposition that as similarly constituted beings, men have certain rights in common, maintenance of which, while directly advantageous to them individually, indirectly benefits the community; and that thus the decisions based on equity have a sanction independent alike of customary law and parliamentary resolves."

Spencer thus assumes that "natural law" becomes operative when "natural law" as a principle has been superseded and is but occasionally referred to; furthermore he holds that law is based on the "consensus of individual interests" — in a measure a strange conclusion, as it conflicts with the sociological doctrine of class differentiation. It is a sad commentary upon the inevitable result of making the philosophy of law an appendix to sociology,[1] that nothing more notable than this is reached in the chief work of a pre-eminently great thinker writing at the end of the nineteenth century.

Spencer's sociological bias affects unfavorably his treatment of property. He does not distinguish between private possession and private ownership, and uses the two terms indiscriminately. Both Spencer's insight into human nature and his evolutionary principles dispose him unfavorably towards socialism. "While the doctrines of the socialists are evidently not consoling biologically, they are at the same time psychologically absurd. They assume an impossible intellectual endowment." According to Spencer socialism would bring about a compulsory association in which "the directors would pursue personal advantage with undiminished self-seeking," just as is done in the present State by the employers, and there would be "no strong union of free laborers to oppose them," — a condition undesirable in the interests of the laborer and from the point of view of evolution.[2]

Spencer transfers a valuable observation from the field of biology to that of sociology: "Social evolution in the distant future, as social evolution in the past, must submit to leave many lower forms untouched, as it develops step by step new forms of society." The

---

[1] *Spencer* himself speaks of the legal philosophical basis which he sets forth in § 534 as "a somewhat parenthetical discussion." (§ 535.)

[2] "From Freedom to Bondage," p. 15, in "Introduction to Thomas Mackay": "A Plea for Liberty," N. Y. 1891. (German ed. by Bode, p. 17.) "Metamorphosis is the universal law exemplified throughout the Heavens and on the Earth: especially throughout the organic world; and above all in the animal division of it."

fact that rudimentary vestiges of lower stages of culture survive in higher stages shows clearly the falsity of a utilitarian philosophy of law and government as well as of a utilitarian ethics. Law, government, ethics, society are cultural phenomena whose function it is to increase human efficiency. The stronger presupposes the weaker element; along with the powerful there must always be the weaker. The weaker represents the waning survivals from earlier stages.[1]

§ 42. *Sociological and Social-ethical Extremists.* 1: THE CONCEPTION OF "SOCIETY." Current scientific phrases are but vaguely understood by the majority, have a definite meaning to a small minority, and are correctly grasped only by the select few. In the period following the Middle Ages the phrases "sovereignty of the people," "liberty," "reason," were current; they represented a composite of vagueness, error, and truth. Since Saint-Simon, "society" has enjoyed a similar vogue. As used by Saint-Simon, the term was a proper substitution for State, for it was his purpose to establish an earthly kingdom governed by neighborly love, without legal coercion, and consequently without a State. He defines society as a communal association organized without legal or governmental coercion. The term "society" is likewise justified when applied to the ideal community by communistic anarchists, who believe that with the abolition of government, law and capital, men would regain their natural innate good will which the State has corrupted. But the use of the term by the socialists,

[1] In regard to these rudimentary organs in the human organism which in the biological, and partly in the social sense, are no longer useful but harmful, see *Metchnikoff*, "Studien über die Natur des Menschen. Eine Optimistische Philosophie." Authorized edition from the French. Introduction by *Wilhelm Ostwald*, Leipzig 1904. Pp. 3-177 ("Die Disharmonien der Natur des Menschen"). Metchnikoff is a professor in the Pasteur Institute at Paris.

as applied to their prospective State, is false, for the socialistic State is not a free State but a Leviathan. They propose to regulate production and consumption by law, and use the term "society" as a demagogic device; for the proposal to abolish the present form of the State sounds more inviting if the proposed substitute does not bear the name of State. Sociologists use the term "society" for all types of human association, including the State as a social group; and they use the term "sociology" as equivalent to political science in other than its formal legal aspects. The term "society" is thus used to designate very differently constituted groups; it is applied to the associations peculiar to an age antecedent to the establishment of the State, and to the State itself after its establishment and development as a society regulated by law. If the affiliations within the horde or tribe, out of which the State was formed, are to be called society, then such early types of society must not be used interchangeably for society as a constituent of the State. In current usage society stands indiscriminately for pre-governmental affiliations, for the community as shaped by law and government, for the several independent associative groups within the State, and for them collectively. The evolution of society is constructed by tracing the stages of growth from the pre-governmental groups to the State as at present constituted. That is a convenient mode of avoiding the fundamental problems of law and government: the State is simply set down as a differentiated highly developed form of society as compared with the pre-governmental social groups. This looseness of usage is paralleled and still further favored by the elastic meaning attached to the term, "social ethics."

In view of the violence thus done to the concept of "society," it seems necessary to assign to it its proper meaning. ROBERT V. MOHL[1] (1799–1875) was the first to undertake a critical analysis[2] of "society." He concludes:[3] "It has thus been set forth that these affiliations based on community of interest are distinctive, and not to be confused or compared with the products of individual interests, nor with a corporate relation to the State; they require a distinctive term, and the term 'society' fulfills the need. Social affiliations or organizations are accordingly the separate associations that severally develop from a given set of interests, whether formally or informally organized; and social conditions are the results of such association, as they affect the participants directly, and all others indirectly. Society thus becomes a comprehensive concept embracing the combined social institutions of a given region, such as of a State or a country." This view correctly represents society as the spontaneous expression of human interests, not in response to law or coercion, but by individuals or by associations independent of governmental direction.

LORENZ V. STEIN (1815–1890) contributed to the study of the nature of society. He held that "if society is

[1] The conception of civil society in Hegel has no relation to the ambitious modern conception. See above.

These comments of *Ahrens* ("Naturrecht," sixth edition, Vol. II, pp. 253–262) are not important.

[2] "Die Geschichte und Literatur der Staatswissenschaften," I, pp. 72–110. See also *Bluntschli*, "Über die neuen Begründungen der Gesellschaft und des Gesellschaftsrechtes" ("Überschau der Deutschen Gesetzgebung und Rechtswissenschaft," Vol. III, Munich 1856, pp. 247–251). *v. Treitschke*, "Die Gesellschaftswissenschaft. Ein kritischer Versuch," Leipzig 1859, pp. 65 seq. According to *Treitschke* the State is unified organized society (pp. 87 and 81–84). *Gumplowicz*, "Allgemeines Staatsrecht," Innsbruck 1897, pp. 176–178. *Jellinek*, "Allgemeine Staatslehre," pp. 81 seq.

[3] "Die Geschichte und Literatur," etc., pp. 100 seq.

in fact something more than an unorganized and accidental aggregate, and is an independent and distinctive expression of human interests, then it will be possible to fix upon a single and unified definition combining its varied issues; such a dominant concept is that of 'society.'" "Every association of men is in a sense a society; all societies, however different, must contain a common factor."[1] "The social order as shaped by the distribution of human problems and advantages, safeguarded by the law, and secured in perpetuity by property and the family, constitutes human society."[2] "Through modern society the quantity and quality of the most desirable aids to life, as well as the advantages of life, have been made available and perfected to an unprecedented measure, and nations have been made wealthy and free beyond anything known in the past. But the distribution of the possessions of wealth and of liberty is not determined by the principle of the highest development of the individual, but is regulated by the law which controls the use of capital in enterprises; namely, that the social order rests upon the supremacy of capital over labor without capital."[3] In another connection[4] he says: "In addition to the

[1] "Der Sozialismus und Kommunismus des heutigen Frankreichs," second edition, p. 15. The first part of the book bears the subtitle: "Die Gesellschaft und das Proletariat."
Compare with Stein's interpretation of the concept of society *Gumplowicz*, "Allgemeines Staatsrecht," pp. 176, 182–185. *Jellinek*, "Allgemeine Staatslehre," p. 81.

[2] "Der Sozialismus," etc. p. 23.

[3] "Der Sozialismus," etc., pp. 38 seq.

[4] In his work on the social movement in France: "Von 1789 bis auf unsere Tage," 3 vols. Leipzig 1850. Vol. I: "Der Begriff der Gesellschaft und die soziale Geschichte der französischen Revolution bis zum Jahre 1830."

direct action and expression of the State there is a life of the State." This life is "society." [1]

The objects of ownership, and consequently ownership itself, are of three kinds: landed property, money, and industrial wealth, or so-called standing or fixed capital. These in turn may be subdivided. "Among the well-to-do the *kind* of wealth affects the sphere of the individual's activity; the *amount* of wealth affects his station." Labor presents similar distinctions; "even more than wealth it forces the individual to accommodate himself to its demands; and the kind of labor conditions the type of personal development." The mode of living as conditioned by material possessions in turn conditions the general range and manner of life, and is perpetuated through the family from one generation to another. "This organic unity of life conditioned by the distribution of wealth, mediated by the organization of labor, sustained by human needs, and fixed by legal institutions and family tradition, is human society." In v. Stein's exposition the conception [2] of society shows the modern tendency unduly to extend its meaning, and to include the functions of government and law and national economics. In the works [3] of R. GNEIST (1816–1895), the celebrated writer on public law, the sphere of society is considered. "French precedent gives the term 'society' the meaning of the relation of

[1] "Der Begriff der Gesellschaft und die Gesetze ihrer Bewegung· Einleitung zur Geschichte der sozialen Bewegung Frankreichs seit 1789." Of special import are pp. XXIV–XXVIII.

[2] "Die Volkswirthschaftslehre," second edition, Vienna 1878, pp. 458 seq.

[3] "Self-government Kommunalverfassung und Verwaltungsgerichte in England," third edition, Berlin 1871, pp. 879 seq.; "Der Rechtsstaat und die Verwaltungsgerichte in Deutschland," second edition, Berlin 1879, pp. 1 seq. See also *Gumplowicz*, "Allgemeines Staatsrecht," p. 185.

man to material possessions, and gives the term 'social relations' the meaning of the aggregate of men's relations to one another. Amid all the complexities of social organization, two principles may be adhered to: the one, that, since every kind of wealth results in the dependence of those who are without it, those who have it will do all in their power to establish and continue such dependence; the other, that the dependent will equally endeavor to diminish and, if possible, to do away with such dependence. The clash of class interests can be adjusted only through State regulation. Hence society and the State are permanently opposed. The State, especially in its service as a communal self-government, serves to unite [1] the interests of society." [2]

Following v. Stein and Gneist some contemporary writers conceive society as an organism, as the body social, as an independent reality; [3] but others, such as Gumplowicz,[4] recognize the presence of varied interests

[1] "Self-government," pp. 880, 881; "Der Rechtsstaat," p. 10.

[2] For Tönnies and Klöppel see below, § 44. See also the article by Gothein in "Handwörterbuch der Staatswissenschaften" on "Gesellschaft und Gesellschaftswissenschaft," Vol. IV, pp. 200-216; for the concept of society, 200-203.

[3] The organic and superorganic conception of society is set forth by *Schäffle, Worms, Giddings* ("The Principles of Sociology," New York 1896, pp. 420), and others. See below, § 44. See also *Zenker*, "Die Gesellschaft," 2 vols., Berlin 1903, pp. 27-80. (pp. 36-52 are upon the "objective existence of social structures.")

[4] *Gumplowicz*, "Grundriss der Soziologie," Vienna 1885, p. 139: "If one considers the aggregate of the several groups, circles, classes, and occupations that reach their development in the State, and their mutual actions and reactions, one may give to this totality the general name of society, in contrast to the State. In this sense society is not something different from the State but the State itself from another point of view. In the narrower and stricter sense society refers to every one of such groups that is distinctive

as represented by those interested, but do not regard such interests as independent of the State and State interests, though admittedly the two are occasionally divergent, nor as justifying their consideration as a distinctive organic unity.

If it were only a matter of substituting another word for a vague or unjustifiable concept, the opposition to the extreme extension of the term "society" would be a mere academic effort. The question of terms is of slight importance; writers on government and economics may, if they choose, call the interests of political economy those of "society," or use any other preferred expression. But it is a different matter when the misleading term leads to a false theoretical construction. In my somewhat heretical opinion such is the fact; and I shall venture to state briefly my objections to the prevailing view of "society." That a notable change of material conditions has taken place as a result of the increase of working capital and of the exploitation of the laboring classes consequent upon the introduction of machinery, is clear; but that such change invalidates legal procedures and principles of government is yet to be shown. It is far more likely that the present reconstruction of economics will prove to be a stage of transition, which, in due course, will furnish a theoretical support for the improvement of the lot of a class whose legal and political status has been unduly neglected. It is a further objection to the prevalent interpretation of sociology that its procedure was modeled upon that of the natural sciences. A philosophy of government and law which, judged by the spirit of its procedure, may be applied

by virtue of its common interest or interests. In brief, it is a group held together by one or more interests." See also *Gumplowicz*, "Soziologie und Politik," Leipzig 1892, pp. 49–66, 72–75. "Allgemeines Staatsrecht," pp. 170–198. See also below, § 44.

biology, or ethnology, or indeed anything but philosophy, may properly be viewed with suspicion.

Government, law, and ethics have a place among the distinctive factors of culture. We may call the affiliations of men as they existed before government was instituted, society, — the term thus standing for the social alliances of men in uncivilized and semi-civilized stages, — but to call human alliances existing under the State and the rule of law one species of this same genus, and the forms of animal society yet another, is to adopt a zoölogical or biological procedure, and not a philosophical one. To consider society organized under government and pre-governmental society as contrasted but not co-ordinate, is no more pertinent than to classify man as a species of the genus animal or mammal; for the purposes of the natural history of man this is legitimate, but not for the philosophical interpretation of culture. The student of government or law can no more assume that man is merely a more highly organized animal, without running the risk of reaching strange conclusions, than can the historian of civilization or the moralist. If we except the reactionaries, such as Rousseau in his earlier period, and Stirner, and perhaps Tolstoi, and the strenuous Nietzsche, legal philosophers are agreed that the pre-governmental condition demands consideration merely as an evolutionary stage in the historical development of government, of law, of ethics, of civilization. Quite independently of the question of desirability, the conditions as organized within the State, and those that prevailed where no government existed, cannot be regarded as of parallel status. It is equally idle to construct a new legal dispensation based on the assumed claims of social welfare. State, law, economics, and society must be conceived and interpreted as cultural developments according to the standards of our existing civilization, and not according to those of another world, which, however preferable, is unreal and visionary. In the world as it is, government and law give the setting and conditions for economic operations. The residual phenomena, representing society and social interests, are the aggregate of the situations, associations, and activities, directed to freely developing interests, the manifold operations and relations of all citizens, apart from those fostered and maintained by governmental or legal organization. Subtract from the collective activity of a community under governmental organization the direct issues secured and conditioned by the law, and the rest is society.[1] The weaknesses of sociology are doubtless those of a youthful science. In older views and conditions, the interests and service of social organizations had been neglected; it is natural that a movement aiming to assert the value of these social interests should in its enthusiasm overshoot the mark.

2: SOCIAL ETHICS. The practical bearing of the sociological attitude finds expression in what is commonly known as "social ethics." The principle of economic materialism, and particularly of socialism, drew the attention of central Europe to the question whether, in fact, formal equality before the law resulted in economic justice. There was much evidence that a rigid adherence to a formal legal equality, and the unrestricted pursuit of commerce, had resulted in the oppression and exploitation by unscrupulous capitalists of the economically weaker classes, the industrial laborer, and of the economically weaker individuals subject to the exactions of the

[1] See the admirable account of *Jellinek*, "Allgemeine Staatslehre," pp. 84–89. *Jellinek* is one of the few economic philosophers who recognize the extreme and ambitious conception of society, advanced by the sociologists.

stronger. The situation induced a powerful movement in the direction of social reform; in Germany it brought about the labor insurance laws (inaugurated through the initiative of Bismarck by the imperial messages of Nov. 17, 1881, and April 14, 1883), as well as other reforms of industrial legislation for the protection of the laborer. The commendable purposes of social reform may be said to consist of the economic liberation through legal reforms of the economically dependent classes, and the infusion of the law with the ethical spirit, by framing laws to prevent the exploitation of the economically dependent.[1] Every friend of progress will regard with sympathy all efforts in behalf of the economically weaker classes and individuals, and every attempt to check the exploitation that takes shelter under the law. But the thoughtful student views with misgiving the brand of practical philosophy now in vogue and its dire possibilities. The words "social reform" and "social ethics" are bandied about by all sorts and conditions of men; and even the intelligent among them, including political economists and officers and administrators of the law, connect no definite notion with these terms which, indeed, seem to stand for a tendency to favor the man without property and without means, especially if he belongs to the laboring classes, as against the economically stronger capitalist; and to do so only

[1] See the account of the recent movement in behalf of political welfare in *Van der Borght*, "Grundzüge der Sozialpolitik" (*Frankenstein-Heckel*, "Hand- und Lehrbuch der Staatswissenschaft," I, 15), Leipzig 1904 (Part II: "Arbeiter-Wohlfahrtspolitik," pp. 87–445; Part IV: "Wohlfahrtspolitik in Bezug auf sonstige Personen in unselbständiger Arbeitsstellung," pp. 483–519). Bibliography, pp. 520–566. See also in "Handwörterbuch der Staatswissenschaften," second edition, Vol. II, pp. 921–923, 930–939, the article "Bismarck" (by H. Dietzel), the division "Sozialpolitik," and Vol. VI, pp. 828–848, the article "Sozialkonservative Bestrebungen" (by G. Uhlhorn).

because he is the under dog. He is to be favored in legislation, in judicial decisions, in administration, in business, in contracts, and in daily intercourse. The sound principle of social ethics, that the law must afford protection against economic enslavement or exploitation, is to be made over into a feeble and indefensible principle of social compassion, a principle the more willingly enforced as it is exercised at another's expense. Neither in theory nor in practice can this extreme application of the social-ethical attitude be justified. Its acceptance is due to an unwarranted extension of the conception of society, and as well to the lack of clear views of political economy among those not affected by the socialistic movement. It may be referred to the extension of the spirit of romanticism into political economy, swayed by an emotional antagonism to capital. Its purposes are as uncertain as its foundations; and the outcome of this social-ethical sentimentality cannot be viewed with complacency.[1]

3: SOCIOLOGICAL IDEALS. The comprehensive and thorough survey of LUDWIG STEIN [2] (b. 1859), "Die Soziale Frage im Lichte der Philosophie," graphically presents, with a wealth of illustrative material, the views on sociological questions of philosophers and economists from the earliest times up to the present day. Stein represents a social optimism.[3] Optimism cannot be justified on the principle of hedonism. "Any balance

[1] See below, § 45.
[2] The following works of Ludwig Stein are here pertinent: "Die soziale Frage im Lichte der Philosophie," Stuttgart 1897, second edition, 1903. "An der Wende des Jahrhunderts. Versuch einer Kulturphilosophie," Freiburg i/B 1899. "Der soziale Optimismus," Jena 1905.
[3] "Die soziale Frage," etc., Lecture 41: "Der soziale Optimismus," pp. 563-584. Stein, "Der soziale Optimismus," pp. 1-27, 126-154, 218-238.

struck between pleasure and displeasure is illusory."[1] Optimism is not to be demonstrated logically; the optimistic tendency is "the great pledge of future joys, a κτῆμα εἰς ἀεί, an inalienable possession of mankind."[2] The movement of human ideas as revealed by the comparative study of history is spiral; it advances at once forward and upward. "The evolutionary optimism, which is characteristic of Hegel, no less than of Leibnitz before him, and of Eduard v. Hartmann after him, projects the movement of ideas not as a circle but as a spiral." To social optimism the alternative between the individual or the race is not final; neither the extreme individualism of Nietzsche, nor the extreme communistic view of life, will hold good.[3]

The moralist cannot escape the question: Are there any ultimate purposes? Why should we lead a moral life? In order to be happy. How shall we be moral? By recognizing the connection between the cosmos and human destiny, between the world of nature and the world of spirit. "The insight into this connection imbues man with strength to curb his selfish impulses, to refine his instincts, and thereby to eliminate every vestige of his original predatory nature." The goal of evolution is the refinement of the human type.[4] The goal of external politics is to make our civilization prevail universally;[5] this will become realized through a world federation, while the goal of internal politics

[1] "Die soziale Frage," pp. 563–570.

[2] "An der Wende des Jahrhunderts," pp. 336–347, 211, 212–230. "Die soziale Frage," pp. 563–584.

[3] "An der Wende des Jahrhunderts," pp. 233, 270 seq., 240, 233–241.

[4] "Die soziale Frage," pp. 583 seq.

[5] "An der Wende," etc., pp. 391 seq. "Die soziale Frage," pp. 562 seq.

is to bring about a reign of peace through unceasing social effort.[1]

PAUL BERGMANN's "Ethik als Kulturphilosophie"[2] presents substantially the same views as Stein, but returns to Kant for support of the fundamental basis. The supreme injunction is thus expressed: "On all occasions do your individual and social duty"; or expressing the two separately: "Always act in complete accord with yourself as a moral personality"; and, "Always place yourself at the service of the community to which you belong."[3] The object of morality is the completest realization of the ideal of culture,[4] the participation in, and furtherance of the progress of civilization.

VAN CALKER[5] (b. 1864) makes human perfection the guide of political endeavor. He bases it on the sense of evidence — "Gefühl der Evidenz"— the innate trend which makes the idea of perfectibility appear as a commendable aim. This ethical principle should be applied in penology;[6] the penal law should be made to conform to the standard of a just retribution. Van Calker's principle of perfection has been applied to penology by Netter.[7]

[1] "An der Wende," etc., pp. 392 seq., 410 seq. "Die soziale Frage," pp. 551-562, 457-496, 496 seq.
[2] Leipzig 1904, especially pp. 274-475.
[3] "Ethik als Kulturphilosophie," pp. 474 seq.
[4] See below, § 44.
[5] "Politik als Wissenschaft," Address of January 27, 1898, Strassburg 1898, pp. 16-21, 37, 20.
[6] S. van Calker, "Strafrecht und Ethik," Leipzig 1897, pp. 12-16, 16-22. Also Berolzheimer, "Die Entgeltung im Strafrechte," pp. 99 seq.
[7] "Das Prinzip der Vervollkommnung als Grundlage der Strafrechtsform," Berlin 1900, especially pp. 346 seq. Pp. 253-260 contain the historical presentation of the principle of perfection. On v. Calker's influence see pp. 355 and preface, p. VI.

§ 43. *Social Utilitarianism.* 1: SHAFTESBURY. SHAFTESBURY [1] (1671–1713), the English moralist, bases his ethics on the following considerations: "Every creature [has] a private good and interest of his own," what Diderot calls "un intérêt privé, un bien-être qui lui est propre," representing the satisfaction of his desires as determined by his nature. If the natural expressions of inclination, emotion, or passion are thwarted, it reacts disturbingly upon the welfare of the organism; and if the untoward status of its emotional life reacts to the disadvantage of other beings, the result is likewise unfavorable to the general welfare. If the same disturbed emotional state affects the vital interests both of the being primarily concerned and of others who cross his path, and if the favorable regulation of his natural disposition would serve his own welfare and that of others, then the favorable interest of others coincides with concern for his own welfare, and private interest is in harmony with morality.[2] Accordingly virtue not only leads to the happiness of the virtuous but likewise to the welfare of the community. Vices make the individual unhappy and weaken the bond that attaches him to the community.[3]

[1] *Shaftesbury,* "An inquiry concerning Virtue and Merit," 1699. I cite from the collected works of *Shaftesbury,* "Characteristics of Men, Manners, Opinions, Times, with a Collection of Letters," Vol. II, Basle 1790; translated into French by *Diderot* under the title "Principes de la Philosophie Morale ou Essai sur le Mérite de la Vertu, par Mylord S." . . . (Shaftesbury). A German translation from the French bears the title "Über Verdienst und Tugend, ein Versuch von Shaftesbury," Leipzig 1780.

[2] Book II, Part II, § 1.

[3] Book II, Part II, § 1: "How unfortunate must it be for a creature, whose dependence on society is greater than any others, to lose that natural affection by which he is prompted to the good and interest of his species and community? . . . For whoever is unsociable, and voluntarily shuns society or commerce with the world, must of necessity be morose and ill-natured."

Briefly, vices are anti-social impulses. Shaftesbury traces vices to three sources: to weak and defective natural affections; to the predominance of private interests; or to the fact that the natural affections tend neither to the special interest of the individual nor to the general welfare of the species.[1] Vice disturbs individual well-being as well as the welfare of the community; while the social inclinations, or the communal feeling which is inherent in human nature, form the source of ethical values.

This same emphasis upon the concurrence of private with communal welfare appears in the social philosophy of Ihering; he, however, does not assign the decisive part to the ethical sentiment and its practical expression, but to the self-centered impulses which are directed to personal welfare and at the same time further the welfare of the community.

2: IHERING. IHERING's [2] (1818–1892) chief work, "Der Zweck im Recht," was preceded by the "Geist

See Book II, Part II, § 2, beginning with the words: "We are now to prove, that by having the self-passions too intense or strong, a creature becomes miserable." This is then proven by various illustrations.

[1] Book II, Part II, § 3. Shaftesbury, as he notes at the end of the section, proposes to establish the following thesis: —

I. "That to have the natural, kindly, or generous affections strong and powerful towards the good of the public, is to have the chief means and power of self-enjoyment," and "That to want them, is certain misery and ill."

II. "That to have the private or self-affections too strong, or beyond their degree of subordinacy to the kindly and natural, is also miserable."

III. And, "That to have the unnatural affections, viz., such as are neither founded on the interest of the kind, or public, nor of the private person or creature himself, is to be miserable in the highest degree."

[2] The works here pertinent are "Zweck im Recht," 1 vol., third edition, Leipzig 1893; Vol. II, second edition, 1886, third edition,

des Römischen Rechts,"[1] which formed a notable contribution to the study of Roman law, and of its historical and philosophical evolution. Though neither work was completed, the earlier work may be regarded as finding its complement in the later, which begins by considering the nature of human conduct. The law of causality, which acts mechanically in the natural world, when applied to the human will becomes a psychological law. A stone falls because, deprived of its support, it must fall. "Human conduct is determined not by a 'because' but by a 'for,' by a purpose to be effected; the 'for' is as indispensable for the will as is the 'because' for the stone. The stone cannot move without a cause; no more can the will operate without a purpose." Hence the law of causality, as applied to the human will, becomes the psychological law of purpose, "Zweck-gesetz." The purpose is the motivating incentive of the human will. The will does not act without a purpose; to act, and to act as a means to an end, are one and the same.

The direction of desire exclusively to self-interest is called egoism. Such self-seeking is incompatible with larger ends, but is utilized by these ends in that they "enlist it in their service by paying it the wages which it demands." The larger interests secure the co-operation of the individual by interesting him in their purposes. Every phase of human life — government, society,

1898. (The third edition, from which I cite, was published by *v. Ehrenberg* after the author's death.) Fourth edition (the first in popular form), 2 vols., Leipzig 1905.

"Der Kampf ums Recht," fifteenth edition, Vienna 1903. (I cite from the thirteenth edition, Vienna 1897.)

[1] "Geist des Römischen Rechts auf den Verschiedenen Stufen seiner Entwickelung," Part I, fifth edition, Leipzig 1894; Part II, Division I, fifth edition, Leipzig 1894; Part II, Division II, fifth edition, Leipzig 1899; Part III, Division I, fourth edition, Leipzig 1888.

commerce, and business — depends upon the interrelation of individual purposes with the interests of others. If there is no concurrence of selfish individual interests with the general purpose, it must be brought about artificially. In all human intercourse, including that of social life, the "lever of interest" may be brought to bear upon those unaffected as well as those directly affected. The same is true of communal purposes, among which organized purposes are of the greatest practical importance; that is, purposes which have an adequate instrument in a permanent and regulated association of those interested. Organized purposes reach their highest expression in the State; the characteristic of such purposes is their extensive utilization of the law. In some cases the law acts as a direct mechanical coercion — as the attachment of property of a debtor; in others it acts indirectly as a psychological coercion — as by the threat of a penalty or legal disability. Psychological coercion is indirect; it appeals to the interest of the individual will which is subjected to the influences of the law.

Human purposes are either individual or communal, that is, social. The purposes "emanating from and acting upon the individual" are the selfish ones. They are of three kinds — the assertion of the physical, of the economic, and of the legal self; or briefly, the assertion of the individual or the ego. The purposes of the communal life, including the objects of the State, are the social ones. The activities of the individual in the furtherance of these communal purposes are appropriately called "social." The individual is stimulated to social conduct by an appeal to two kinds of impulses: first, by an appeal to self-interest — "The means which the State and society employ to enlist the individual in their service are reward and punishment," — and second, by an appeal to the ethical self, that is, "to the ethical feeling in regard to the purpose of man's existence, the conviction that his life is to be lived not for himself alone but for the service of mankind." The ethical nature can alone account for self-denial.

The individual's place in the world will be determined by his attitude towards the three following propositions, which reflect his loyalty to public spirit and to law: *I exist for myself:* or, *The world exists for me:* or, *I exist for the world.* The egoistic or individual self-assertion leads to concern for physical well-being. To provide for more than the needs of the moment, men accumulate the means of subsistence for future use. This gives rise to the amassing of property as a form of economic self-assertion. To safeguard life and property, law is instituted. "Without law there is no security of life and property." It is not logical consistency but practical purposes that lead from law to government. The law affects every phase of individual life. The maintenance of the position which the law secures is legal self-assertion. It concerns life, honor, property, family, and public rights.

Next to the demands of self-assertion, life must be viewed "as it concerns others or society"; all civilization depends upon making the individual serviceable to the communal purposes. No man exists for himself alone but for the sake of all. "As each individual existence is due to others, so likewise he exists for others, whether with his intent or not." It is by virtue of the influence which the individual exerts beyond the limits of his own existence that the progress of human culture becomes possible; the legal aspect of the influence upon posterity takes the form of inheritance. "Society is the realization of the position that every man exists for the world, and the world exists for every man."

Theoretically society in part overlaps the sphere of the State, "but in part only, that is, to the extent to which the needs of society require the coercive power of the State." Legal coercion serves the subsidiary purpose of protecting the social order from injury. Geographically the sphere of society is not limited by the boundaries of the State. Society has the quality of personality, though the law cannot accord it the legal status of a person. "Yet society should not be denied personal value because it may not serve legally as a person."

Social mechanics, "the levers of the social movement," are the means whereby society makes the individual subservient to its purposes. Of such social levers, two — reward and coercion — appeal to self-interest; and two are ethical — the sense of duty and sympathy. Trade may be regarded as an organized means of "satisfying human needs by the lever of reward." The needs supply the motive, the reward is the means, and the organization of the relation between the two constitutes trade. Trade is not carried on upon the basis of benevolence. When we are told that in ancient Rome the intellectual professions were practised without compensation, this means only that the service was not paid for directly. The compensation came in an ideal form by way of honor, respect, popularity, influence, power; the reward was not economic but moral; but there was a compensation. For the fundamental principle of trade is "quid pro quo." "The expression 'contract of exchange,' 'Tauschvertrag,' which legally is confined to the barter of one article for another, applies to whatever has value." The fact that our needs differ leads to exchange; the fact that they are in part the same, leads to co-operation, when the purpose sought exceeds the power of the individual, or can be attained more economically by co-operation. The legal correlative of this is "Sozietätsvertrag," partnership agreement. The reward of a contract is determined by the relative value of the individual interests of the contracting parties. "The point of equilibrium at which the interests of the parties balance is the equivalent or price agreed upon. The equivalent represents the embodiment of the idea of justice in trade." The social regulation of self-interest is accomplished by competition. When social regulation of private interest fails, possibly by reason of a temporary monopoly, individual interest is nonetheless regulated by "a consideration for the future"; as, for example, the consideration that future business interests might be compromised by exploiting a momentary advantage. But when both these regulations of private interest fail, and the contract in question threatens to give an undue advantage to one party, the law enters as a preventive or adjusting agent in the form of legal taxes, restriction of the rate of interest, penalty for usury. But the action of the law alone is commonly inadequate. Equitable compensation is determined and insured through a standard in consideration of the general conditions affecting a given occupation. Pay is not determined by the individual services alone, but compensation depends upon the status of the occupation for instance, the preparation which it requires, and the trouble and expense which it involves. Organized trade finds a means of economic compensation through credit, particularly commercial credit. There are honorary compensations, such as office and reputation, as well as material ones. Under the social organization, compensation is expressed through trade, and coercion through the State and law. Coercion is either mechanical or psychological. "According to the purpose sought, that is, whether it is negative or positive, coercion is propelling or compelling. The former aims to prohibit, and the latter to ensure a given action. Self-defense propels, self-help compels." Law is governmental coercion organized; side by side with it there is an unorganized "social form of coercion",— the moral. To settle differences by establishing a "modus vivendi" binding upon both parties, to restrain power within limits, is the function of law. In the early establishment of the social order the might that prevails plays a great part. In tracing the influence of might in the beginnings of social order, Ihering remarks: "We cannot rely upon history, which tells us nothing concerning this point, but must accept purpose as our guide. The study of purpose will show how, in order to prevail, human ends depend upon might." In a regulated state of society propelling coercion becomes operative in the form of the right and duty of defense, and again as self-defense; and in ancient systems of law, in taking the law in your own hands. Compulsive coercion, as legally expressed, appears in the authority of the father over his family, and in contracts of ever increasing scope. Purposes so regulated can become effective only through the coercive organization of the law. Such legal coercion is indispensable; the important point, however, is not whether it is indispensable, but whether it is successful. The social organization of force, concentrated in the law, is effective only when "the balance of power is transferred to the side of the law." This result is attained through association, "Sozietät," which is the "automatic mechanism of power, measured in terms of law." But socialization through associations of all sorts would not suffice to guarantee the complete success of legal coercion. That requires the coercive power of the State. "The State is society exercising coercion." The State is "the organization of social coercion." The cultivation of the law is the "vital function" of the State; and legal coercion is the "absolute monopoly" of the State. The external quality of law is force; its inner quality is its normalizing power. Law makes for order and equality. The practical aim of justice is to establish equality. Moreover, the aim of material justice, that is, justice viewed primarily as the moral duty of the legislator, is to establish inner or subjective equality, the balance of merit and reward, or punishment and guilt. The fundamental object of formal justice, which primarily means law practically administered, is to establish outer equality; that is, uniform application to all cases of an established rule of action. But equality before the law is not an object in itself. It is desirable only because such equality is a condition for the welfare of society. The inner guaranty of justice is the sense of right; the outer guaranty is the administration of the law.

Norms or rules of action and coercion are thus the factors of the law. But these are formal only, and decide nothing as to the content of the law, which is determined by its purpose; hence the law must regulate the social conditions. This accounts for the constantly shifting character of the legal content, which varies with social conditions and is subject to constant change. The purpose of law is to secure the conditions which society demands. From the point of view of content, therefore, law is the form in which the coercive power of the State attains and secures the conditions requisite for the social life. In intent this is ever the purpose of the law; naturally the lawmaker may err in the choice of the means, as the physician in the choice of a remedy.

The fundamental conditions of existence of society are the preservation and propagation of the species, labor, and trade. Normally these coincide with the fundamental conditions of existence of the individual; in so far as they tend to conflict, it is the province of the law to intervene. Ihering extends this view to other realms of the law, and attempts to show that the impelling motive of legal forms is the welfare of society, the securing of the conditions of existence, in which process he emphasizes the subjective intent as a factor of the law.[1]

Crime has been defined as an act subject to public punishment, or an act that breaks the law. But this is merely an external definition. Ihering tries to find the underlying principle that makes an action subject to punishment, or the legislative principle defining crime. "The purpose of the penal law is no different from that of any other law: to secure the conditions of existence of society. It employs a distinctive means, which is punishment, in the pursuit of this object. And why?" The reason cannot lie in the non-observance of the law, for not all kinds of non-observance of the law result in punishment. Crime is a menace to the conditions of existence of society which legislation recognizes as preventable only through punishment. The menace is not that of the specific action but the abstract menace inherent in all that type of action. The problem of legislative regulation of punishment thus becomes a problem in social politics. The decisive principle is that "punishment must be applied in all cases in which society cannot do without it." The more valuable the social advantage, the more severe must be the punishment for its injury. "The scale of punishment measures the

[1] "Der Zweck im Recht," I, pp. 3–25; 32–40; 40–46; 47–61; 67; 62–76, especially pp. 65, 73; 77–92; 81; 92; 89; 192 seq.; 93–97; 97; 100–115; 115–120, especially pp. 123 seq.; 124–127, 208–225; 131–140, 133 seq., 135, 136, 137, 231 seq.; 140–156; 156–181; 181–193, 194–208; 193 seq., 234–258; especially 234–236, 245, 248, 258; 258–262; 262–264; 264–270; 270–291; 291 seq.; 296, 291–307; 309, 307–312; 318, 312–320; 320–329; 329 seq.; 352–369; 369; 379 seq.; 435 seq.; 443; 445–450, 449; 453 seq.; 485. Ihering considers criminology under the title "Crime" in Vol. I, pp. 483–504.

value of social possessions." In assigning penalties there must be considered not only the objective factor of the menace to social possession, but the subjective factor of the danger attaching to the criminal disposition, to the actual commission of crime; such factors as intent or negligence; crimes of passion or premeditated crimes; conspiracy; organizing criminal gangs. Ihering classifies crimes according to the nature of the object menaced, such as crimes affecting the person — injury to life, body, or health; crimes affecting economic conditions, such as crimes affecting property; moral relations, such as attacks upon honor, family; crimes affecting the State, such as threaten its existence, its economic position, or its ideal purposes, whether through its official representatives or through the citizens whose co-operation the State requires, such as defiance of the authorities, refusal to serve as juror or witness, resistance to, or neglect of, civic duties, etc.; crimes affecting society in its material welfare, such as threaten the security of life through devastation by fire or flood; or again as affecting society in its economic relations, such as threaten the security of trade, for example, counterfeiting and forgery; and thirdly, crimes as affecting society in its ideal relations, as threatening the moral and religious foundations; for example, perjury, and offenses against religion or morality.

The net outcome is that law is the realization of the conditions required by the body social in a liberal sense of that term, and as secured by governmental force: all this from the point of view of society. Society, however, is merely the sum of individuals, and the question arises whether the individual's welfare is secured along with the welfare of society. The price which the individual pays in order to participate in the privileges of the law represents "the legal pressure upon the individual." The individual has legal obligations of several kinds towards the community. To begin with, he furthers all social ends by bearing his share of the taxes. "The taxes tell what society costs in bare cash." In addition there is personal service, as in the army, or on juries, and submission to police and penal regulations. But these do not include all the occasions on which society interferes with the legal privileges of the individual. Society has established restrictions which the individual must accept in the interest of the community. These include the duty of providing for children, and the limiting of the exercise of the right to participate in, or withdraw from educational privileges. What applies to the family applies no less to property. Did not private interest suffice to ensure systematic cultivation of the soil, and the construction of buildings by the owners of land, society would have to establish these as legal duties. The many legal restrictions of individual rights prove the falsity of "the individualistic theory of property," which regards property from the point of view of the individual, and the correctness of the "social theory of property," which regards it from the point of view of social interests. All private rights have a social bearing; though their immediate purpose may be the safeguarding of individual interests, they nevertheless are influenced by social considerations. However, the interference of society with the individual as an organized restraint must have its limits; and this makes the problem of governmental control of individual freedom. Such limits must ever remain elastic. As the purposes of society grow in comprehensiveness, the conceptions of the individual's obligations towards society will expand. The welfare of the individual is never a purpose in itself, but ever a means for securing social welfare; therefore when an individual is forced to an action conducive to his happiness, it is not done in his own interests but in the interest of society. The relation between the authority of the State and the freedom of the individual cannot be determined "by an abstract theoretical formula but by practical considerations."

The claims which the law makes upon the individual, have as their correlative the services of the State in behalf of the individual. The State affords protection against encroachments from without and from within — the protection of the law — and establishes public institutions in the interest of society. The balance between the social claims made, and the social services rendered, is merely a theoretical matter; in reality the interests of the individual and society are one. In the law the individual finds a means of defense and assertion. Nevertheless legal coercion becomes necessary for two reasons: first, because of inadequate insight, for not everyone recognizes the concurrence of his personal interest with that of society, — "law may be defined as the combination of the wise and the far-seeing against the short-sighted"); second, because of the inherent divergence of private and public interest. This divergence is at once the source of the strength of the law and of its weakness: of its weakness, because of the more intimate hold of private interest upon the individual; of its strength, because the common interest combines all against each partisan of special interests. While thus insisting upon the social indispensability of coercion, Ihering observes that society cannot adequately coerce. Crimes occur despite it. The social measures of reward and coercion are not adequate and require the complementary pressure of morality.[1]

[1] I, pp. 485–487; 490 seq.; 492; 494 seq.; 495–504; 511 seq.; 512–515; 516–536, 526 seq., 532, 534 seq.; 536 seq.; 545 seq; 550 seq.; 551–559; 560–568; 570.

The second portion of the work is devoted to morality. In order to attain an insight into the nature of ethics, Ihering draws upon the evidence of language, in which, however, he relies too much upon contemporary usage to the neglect of the early stages and growth of language. His etymological argument leads him from morality, "Sittlichkeit," to custom, "Sitte," which in turn leads to a study of custom. His thesis is that morality finds its source in social utilitarianism.[1] Morality and law have but a relative validity, depending at every stage upon the existent needs of society.

In his popular work, "Der Kampf um's Recht," Ihering contends that the aim of law is peace, and the way to secure peace is through war. Law is ever the result of struggle. The issue in legal contentions is not the particular case but the "ideal purpose or principle at issue, the assertion of the individual or of his sense of justice." Hence to fight for one's rights is a duty. "Every man is a champion of the law in the interests of society."[2]

Ihering carries his readers by the convincing quality of his style. It is his mode of viewing and of dealing with the philosophical aspects of legal problems, together with his emphasis of purpose as a pervading principle, that accounts for his wide influence upon writers, upon the sociological penologists most of all.[3] Yet his theory is psychologically faulty. It is not the case that all human conduct comes under the law of purpose. It is true that all action involves the contemplation of a purpose; yet a considerable share of human actions are not actually done with a view to a purpose; the consciousness of the end, and the striving for it, are not the

[1] II, pp. 20-57, 241 seq.; 177-241.
[2] "Der Kampf um's Recht," pp. 1; 18; 20; 52
[3] See below, § 44.

decisive and determining psychological factors of the action; but the action arises from an emotional condition, and this emotional factor is decisive — all of which is particularly true of moral actions.[1] Nor is Ihering's view justified by history. A consideration of the historical evolution of law shows that actions, carried out without conscious reference to a purpose, play an important part therein; and that frequently the intention and the accomplishment diverge.

The fundamental fallacy of Ihering's legal philosophy, which is fundamental enough to undermine his ambitious construction, is inherent in his basal assumption. Considerations of purpose and use cannot serve to define the nature of law, government, or morality; and this, first, because these concepts represent nothing objective. What must be determined is the objective nature of law and government, how their objective forms may be justified. But the concepts, *purpose*, and *use*, have meaning only with reference to a human subject. If we take away from purpose the purpose-conceiving individual, or from use its beneficiary, nothing remains. In the second place, even though thus regarded as subjective factors, *purpose* and *use* do not afford an insight into law and economics; by their nature they look to the direct result, the immediate effect. If a law — and the same is true of the action of an individual — seeks a purpose or use, it considers and influences only the immediate or slightly remote consequences; and if it succeeds, it has a temporary, never a durable effect. Furthermore purpose and use have not the same field of operation as law and government. Acting for an end makes for constant endeavor and complete satisfaction. If it were the nature of law and government and ethics to realize purposes, they would either fail

[1] *Berolzheimer*, "Rechtsphilosophische Studien," pp. 146-148.

of their ends, that is, not conform to their purpose (in which case Ihering's theory would be deprived of its basis), or they would actually attain their purposes, in which case the regulation of life by law would involve, that under the dominion of law, and with the acceptance of ethics, wrong and crime could not exist. Government and ethics would preclude rebellion against governmental authority or commission of crime, etc. Law, politics, and government, viewed with reference to ends, are ever imperfect; there are always unassimilated remnants. But any interpretation of law and government that pretends to be a real solution must be all comprehensive. My own position urges that this condition is fulfilled in the theory of forces, the view that government, law, and morality are cultural forces. Along with force there must be weakness, just as light involves shade. Purpose is economical; force in its abundance is extravagant and implies a surplus.

Welfare, use, happiness, do not give the cardinal directions to human ends and endeavors. Happiness rarely finds its home among the upper levels of human attainment; it abides at the lower levels. The poet may proclaim an idyllic peace, but the evolution of human culture is dramatic, full of stress and strain.

§ 44. *The Sociological School.* 1: Its Distinctive Position. The sociological school that developed upon the basis of the doctrines of Comte and Spencer makes man primarily and distinctively a social being, a member of a composite community. Its position stands in direct contrast to the individualistic trend, which attained its marked development in the seventeenth and eighteenth centuries. For Hobbes, Rousseau, and other adherents of "natural law," the fundamental problem was this: What disposes men collectively to form a State, and subject themselves to governmental coercion? The sociologists frame, or rather answer the question from a different standpoint. They reply: the State is not formed by the combination of individuals, but at the outset men are naturally united in larger or smaller groups. Like many types among the higher animals, primitive men formed a gregarious band. It is the merit of sociology to have established this generally accepted view of prehistoric life and to have appreciated its significance.

A further distinction of sociology — though this is limited to Gumplowicz and his followers — relates to the manner in which the State presumably arose. It is held that the means by which the larger collective associations in primitive culture were maintained, up to the point of their consolidation into a State, were those of conflict — a struggle and rivalry for power. Such an antagonism between two groups, as hordes, tribes, or the social aggregates leading to the relation of master and servant, forms the underlying situation leading to government. Such antagonism may be more or less pronounced; the exploitation of the enslaved by the dominant class may be regulated by law, or it may be the result of social and economic circumstances; at all events there remains a more or less sharply defined dualism, separating the State into strata, and this fact is emphasized by the sociologic theory of the formation of the State. The individual is represented as withdrawing in favor of the class and as completely absorbed by it, intellectually, socially, and politically.

2: ITS PRECURSORS. Gumplowicz regards FERGUSON (1723–1816) as the forerunner of the sociological school. In 1767 Ferguson published "An Essay on the History of Civil Society," [1] which has received greater attention

[1] "An Essay on the History of Civil Society." I cite from the third edition, London 1768.

in recent times than it obtained upon its appearance. Ferguson's claim to a position in the sociological school is based upon his conclusion that men have always been associated in groups; that even before a State was established they did not live in isolation but were socialized.[1] As evidence he adduces the accounts of travelers in American and other contemporary accounts of conditions among primitive peoples.[2] He further points out that by virtue of a fundamental trait,[3] struggle leads to progress; for danger makes men combine, and struggle promotes the interests of culture.[4] He also refers to

[1] See *Ferguson*, "History of Civil Society," Part I. "Of the general Characteristics of Human Nature," § 1. "Of the question relating to the State of Nature," pp. 1–16. p. 6: "Mankind are to be taken in groups, as they have always subsisted." § 3. "Of the principles of Union among Mankind," pp. 26–31. p. 26: "Mankind have always wandered or settled, agreed or quarreled, in troops and companies. The cause of their assembling, whatever it be, is the principle of their alliance or union." p. 27: "Man is born in society," says Montesquieu, "and there he remains. The charms that detain him are known to be manifold."

[2] "History of Civil Society," Part II. "Of the History of Rude Nations." § 2: "Of Rude Nations prior to the Establishment of Property," pp. 133–157. See also § 3: "Of Rude Nations under the Impressions of Property and Interest," pp. 158–177.

[3] "Hist. of Civil Society," Part I, § 4. "Of the Principles of War and Dissension." p. 33: "Mankind . . . appear to have in their minds the seeds of animosity, and to embrace the occasions of mutual opposition, with alacrity and pleasure."

[4] "Hist. of Civil Society," Part I, § 4, pp. 32–41. p. 39: "Without the rivalship of nations, and the practice of war, civil society could scarcely have found an object, or a form. Mankind might have traded without any formal convention, but they cannot be safe without a national concert. The necessity of a public defense has given rise to many departments of state, and the intellectual talents of men have found their busiest scene in wielding their national forces."

the trait later emphasized by Gumplowicz,[1] namely, the complete moral subjection of the individual to his group.

Although SCHLEIERMACHER's[2] (1768–1834) philosophy and ethics differ from that of the sociological school, he must be mentioned in this connection by reason of his psychological treatment[3] and his acceptance of the primitive horde[4] as the element which led to the establishment of the State. He held that this occurred whenever the antagonism between ruler and subjects became manifest.[5] The State arose whenever custom passed into law and made justice possible.[6]

ALBERT E. F. v. SCHÄFFLE[7] (1831–1903) is the author of a comprehensive system[8] of general sociology which

[1] *Gumplowicz*, "Die Soziologische Staatsidee," Graz 1892, p. 68. I have not been able to deduce this principle from Ferguson's work, at least not explicitly.

[2] "Die Lehre vom Staat," "Col. Works," Part III. "Zur Philosophie," 8 vols. Literary remains. "Zur Philosophie," 6 vols., Berlin 1845, published by Chr. A. Brandis. The book is complete, but the manuscript is not perfected for publication; it is in the form of detailed sketches and notes for lectures on the subject.

[3] "Die Lehre vom Staat," p. 2: "These lectures are regarded as wholly physiological; their purport is to consider the nature of the State as living and the several functions in their mutual relations."

[4] "Die Lehre vom Staat," p. 3, note **: "The race is earlier than the State." See also pp. 2–4, 7–10.

[5] "Die Lehre vom Staat," p. 3: "The contrast of ruler and subject. Wherever that obtains there is government, and vice versa."

[6] "Die Lehre vom Staat," pp. 8 seq.: "Let us place side by side the last stage where there is as yet no State, and the first stage at which the State comes into being, and ask what is the change. The transformation is merely the explicit expression of custom as law, and thus a transition from an unconscious to a conscious state of community." See also the fourth lecture, pp. 6 seq., the subject of which is that "the State exists only to guarantee law."

[7] Austrian "Minister of Commerce" in 1871.

[8] For his writings see "Handwörterbuch der Staatswissenschaften," second edition, 6 vols., pp. 507 seq., and Schäffle's work itself, "Aus meinem Leben," Berlin 1905, Vol. II, pp. 244–247.

he describes as "a philosophy of the several social sciences in so far as such a system may at present be attempted." In addition his work contains a special system of sociology.[1]

Schäffle portrays the body social as a more complex, more highly developed and differentiated organism, the nature and variety and activities of which are to be traced by analogy with the natural characteristics of animal and plant life. He calls it a hyperorganism in view of the complexity of its organization through government and law, which transcend the natural and spontaneous group-formations.[2] The social affiliations are by structure and functions superorganic. In carrying out in detail this analogy, he sets forth "likenesses and differences between organic and social bodies."[3] Thus the family becomes "a fundamental physiological trait of the social body,"[4] supported by "primary association." The several gregarious and communal associations instituted by society are treated as "social tissues," or social histology, and so on.

Schäffle's ambitious project was not worth the effort. His painstaking analogies are after all merely analogies, comparisons, and figures of speech. To call society a

[1] See *Schäffle*, "Neue Beiträge zur Grundlegung der Soziologie," Z. f. d. g. Staatsw., Vol. LX, 1904, pp. 103-204. Also Vol. LIX, 1903, pp. 294 seq., 479 seq. (in Schäffle's essay: "Die Notwendigkeit exakt entwickelungsgeschichtlicher Erklärung und exakt entwickelungsgeschichtlicher Behandlung unserer Landwirtschaftsbedrängnis," pp. 255-340, 476-552).

[2] "Bau und Leben des sozialen Körpers," Vol. I, p. 1.

[3] "Bau und Leben," I, pp. 8-18, 18-23; 26-85; 86-124, 124-137.

[4] "Avenarius Vierteljahrschrift für wissenschaftliche Philosophie," Vol. II, 1878, pp. 38-67; p. 53: "Law without authority cannot exist. Law which has not the power to maintain itself cannot be permanently esteemed and therefore cannot endure. Law and custom must be looked upon as forces, as living powers."

"hyperorganism" adds nothing to our knowledge of society, nor does it in any way increase our sociological insight. The same criticism applies to Schäffle's essay on "Law and Custom, Considered as a Sociological Expansion of Artificial Selection," though the essay is valuable for its recognition of law and custom as social forces.

3: GUMPLOWICZ. Among the foremost leaders of the sociological school is Gumplowicz[1] (1838–1910). He commands a large range of illustrative material with which he enriches the principles of sociology, and sets forth their bearing with exceptional clearness and effectiveness. His style is at once vigorous and engaging, and appeals to the literary sense. This talent, and the individuality of his position — somewhat withdrawing him from the dominant sympathies of German investigators — may account for his immoderate indulgence in controversy.

According to Gumplowicz the State "is a social phenomenon due to the natural action of social factors, and whose development is dependent upon their further operations."[2] The essential characteristics of the State

[1] The works of Gumplowicz here pertinent are: "Rasse und Staat, Eine Untersuchung über das Gesetz der Staatenbildung," Vienna 1875. This smaller volume contains the nucleus of the legal economic views of Gumplowicz. See especially pp. 6-8, 13-15, 26, 30, 50. "Der Rassenkampf, Soziologische Untersuchungen," Innsbruck 1882 (translated into French by Charles Baye, Paris 1893, "La Lutte des Races," and into Spanish, "La Lucha de Razas," Madrid 1894), "Grundriss der Soziologie," Vienna 1885. "Philosophisches Staatsrecht" (in the second edition the title was changed to "Allgemeines Staatsrecht," Innsbruck 1897). "Die soziologische Staatsidee," Festschrift der k. k. Karl-Franzens-Universität zur Jahresfeier am November 15, 1892. Graz 1892. "Soziologie und Politik," Leipzig 1892. "Geschichte der Staatstheorien," Innsbruck 1905 (pp. 434-436, 446-491, 559 seq.).

[2] "Grundriss der Soziologie," p. 113.

are the same as those enumerated by Schleiermacher: "Rulers or a ruling class and subjects; the governing authorities and the governed classes: these are the eternal, unchangeable, fixed factors of the State. There never was, nor does there now exist, a State without this antagonism."[1][2] The nature of the State is expressed as "a division of labor made and maintained by coercion among a number of social elements organically united into a whole. The development of this composite unit proceeds by a struggle among its constituents for the purpose of determining their relative powers — the issue in each case being expressed in law and statutes."[3]

The constructive factor of the State and of its evolution is not the individual nor the family, but the social group involving the dualism of the ruler and the ruled. "The elements of the State are not human atoms, nor family cells, but human groups or races; in them the State originates, and through them it continues. Those who emerge from the struggle as victors, form the ruling classes; the conquered and subjugated form the laboring and serving classes."[4]

Gumplowicz does not favor the socialistic principle which becomes operative as class conflict, but gives a sociological interpretation to the struggle of races which anthropology reveals. In so doing he was influenced by the anthropological investigations of Count Gobineau,[5] and may have drawn a suggestion from the racial

[1] "Allgemeines Staatsrecht," pp. 33 seq.; see also "Rasse und Staat," pp. 6–8, 13–15, 26, 30, 50.

[2] *Gumplowicz*, "Grundriss der Soziologie," pp. 115 seq. and 127.

[3] "Die soziologische Staatsidee," p. 55.

[4] "Allgemeines Staatsrecht," p. 116. See particularly pp. 110–136; "Grundriss der Soziologie," pp. 115 seq., 127–135.

[5] *Gobineau*, "Essai sur l'Inégalité des Races Humaines," 4 vols., first edition, Paris 1853–1855.

factions in Austria. He thus makes sociology the study of the "interactions of social groups, which obey natural laws as unalterable as those controlling the movements of the sun and planets. . . . Sociology is not concerned with judgments of value."[1] For "individual actions are based not upon physiological but upon social motives. The influence of environment always and in all situations determines the action of the individual."[2]

4: RATZENHOFER. GUSTAV RATZENHOFER's (d. 1904) work, "Die Soziologische Erkenntnis,"[3] is based upon that of Gumplowicz. He holds that when[4] "two communities become one, the victorious tribe annihilates the conquered, not objectively, but politically, so far as concerns its existence as an independent social factor. . . . Despite this subjection, the conquered tribe continues its social life; in the reorganized community it constitutes a lower stratum of society, and social inequality becomes established. The subjugated group becomes a slave, or at least, a laboring class; and the conquerors assume a privileged position. This relation between the dominant and the subject class is the external expression of the communal bond. . . .Through the

In "Der Rassenkampf," p. 38, note 1, Gumplowicz mentions that he was influenced by Gobineau's essay, and makes a long citation therefrom, with the conclusion, "Let us compare not men but groups."

[1] *Gumplowicz*, "Soziologie und Politik," pp. 54, 53–57, 67–100, 89, 89–95. See also *Gumplowicz*, "Die soziologische Staatsidee," pp. 40, 56.

[2] It is not possible within the compass of this work to refer to the extremely voluminous literature of sociology. It will be sufficient to mention the more important works.

[3] "Positive Philosophie des sozialen Lebens," Leipzig 1898.

[4] "Die soziologische Erkenntnis," pp. 156–164.

inequality thus resulting, law replaces custom as a regulative force."[1]

Ratzenhofer's "Positive Ethik, die Verwirklichung des Sittlich-Seinsollenden," a philosophy of "monistic positivism,"[2][3] regards ethics sociologically, and transfers the principles of sociology to ethics. "A significant, though formal requisite of ethical interpretation" is the proposition "that moral obligation is derived from the evolution of primitive might, that immorality is a disturbance of such evolution, and that the ethical will reflects the inherent spirit of such evolution." This is the Stoic "living according to nature," restated in terms of modern evolution.

The ethical sense originates in the tribal feeling which transfers "the individual's effort to develop his individuality to a community of kin." The essence of the ethical sense is "renunciation exercised by the individual in favor of the species." Evil is what is useful to the individual and harmful to the community, and good is what is beneficial to all. The ethical principle demands the "development from what is useful to the individual to what is useful to the community."

According to positive ethics based upon human nature, the source of morality is not the will but the development of inherent natural interest. Self-interest presents the following varieties: physiological interests directed towards the end of normal physical development; racial interests arising from the family relation, and directed

[1] "Die soziologische Erkenntnis," pp. 157 seq.

[2] His other works are: "Wesen und Zweck der Politik." Part of the "Soziologie und Grundlage der Staatswissenschaften," 3 vols., Leipzig 1893. (Preliminary to "Soziologische Erkenntnis.") "Der Positive Monismus und das einheitliche Prinzip aller Erscheinungen," Leipzig 1899. (Preliminary to "Positive Ethik.")

[3] "Positive Ethik," Leipzig 1901.

towards the maintenance and perpetuation of the species; individual interests or self-interest, by the extension of the physiological; social interests, by the extension of the racial interests, including all manner of communal interests reflected in social institutions; transcendental interests, which arise through the idealistic expansion of individual and social interests, and through which the individual "feels himself consciously at one with the enduring primal motive force."

Each of these five spheres of interest is further developed in its ethical aspects. Sociology teaches that individual and social prosperity depends upon adaptation to natural processes, among which Ratzenhofer includes the facts of sociological evolution. These must direct the expressions of the will. The desirable and the moral are thus prefigured in the nature of the primal force. "Virtues, whether individual or social, express limitations within the sphere of the will exercised under natural laws." Christian ethics disregards the ethical sense of the individual as directed towards himself; utilitarianism disregards it as directed towards others, and ignores the social requirements. Neither tendency can harmonize the several interests. "The harmony of interests is based upon the interests of the individual directed towards his bodily, intellectual, and moral improvement, and upon racial interests directed towards the common purposes of social institutions. Of these the individual is a part, and in their behalf he is ready to bring larger sacrifices according as they make a closer racial and cultural appeal; these, in turn, he forms into a transcendental interest, thereby feeling his participation in the laws of the primal force." Ratzenhofer finds the most durable guaranty of a harmony of interests in the moral and intellectual concordance of the motives inspiring ideals. The monistic position, based upon a positive knowledge of nature in its ethical bearing, furthers a harmony of interests and collective purposes.

Every expression of the will is guided by a moral norm, which in the concrete is prescribed by natural laws favoring the interests of the race. "What is conformable to natural law represents the absolutely desirable, and what is collectively beneficial to mankind represents the morally desirable, which coincides with human purposes as ordained by nature." In addition to the morally desirable there is the relatively desirable, that is, "the moral norm which is acknowledged as collectively beneficial at a given stage of intellectual development and as established by custom and reason." The relatively desirable represents the current stage of morality "since it is not possible, and indeed harmful, and therefore immoral, to attempt to short-circuit stages of development. Every period and every people has its morality; and radically to depart therefrom may produce moral results as undesirable as would departure from the laws of nature." Conscience represents the ethical force of man. The appeal of the relatively desirable to human endowment awakens "moral suggestions; and these, in so far as they contain the rudiments of an ethical principle, lead to the moral sense or conscience. Conscience is a product of the development of innate interest, and asserts itself as soon as racial interests show signs of social interest." Conscience gives rise to the sense of responsibility as exercised towards one's own affairs, or towards others; and from it arises the appearance of free action. Conscience is to be developed by the education of the young, and the enlightenment of the mature. Conscience is the ethical regulator in all relations of life; in personal service, in the relation of the sexes, in business, in politics, in science, and in art. It is developed in school and through the moralizing influence of labor. The expressions of conscience are the virtues.

Side by side with the moral qualities of the individual are those due to social organization. Sociology teaches that men adapt the expression of their desires to a general purpose. "The social organization thus acquires an active will which is more than the aggregate of individual wills, and is indeed the resultant of the forces of the constituent wills." "This distinction between the social will and the will of the individual has induced many writers to speak of a 'folk-soul,' and to accept a racial psychology, — such acceptance in some cases being inspired by hostility to sociology, and by a desire to replace sociology, which is slowly attaining a proper scientific insight, by something novel and barely intelligible." This criticism of Ratzenhofer's is not merely unjust but is based upon a serious error. The distinction between the will of society and the aggregate of individual wills is neither new nor a contribution of sociology. Rousseau spoke of a "volonté générale," and a "volonté de tous"; and racial psychology is older than Gumplowicz. Indeed the first volume of the "Zeitschrift für Völkerpsychologie und Sprachwissenschaft" appeared in 1859-60.

The origin of the social will according to Ratzenhofer lies not in the spontaneous conscious processes of the individual, but in external influences, — alike in the prevailing purposes and expressions of one's fellow men, and in prevalent conditions. Social virtues are such as family feeling, racial and national consciousness, the latter growing into patriotism. Social consciousness represents the consummation of a complete morality. However strong his communal sense, every man, in following the precepts of positive ethics, must retain his legitimate personal interests, and protect them while yet bringing them into accord with the communal interests.

Viewed historically, the sociological characteristic of ethical development is thus expressed: "Through the struggle to gain favorable conditions of life, mankind rises from a mere instinctive expression of the social nature to an individualization of interest as yet without a conscience, but making morality necessary; in turn conscience is awakened and directs self-interest into social channels, and — the conditions of life having been satisfied — makes possible the reign of morality by subjecting vices to an ideal moral control." To make a nation successful in a struggle for existence there is no better way than to accept the aims and purposes which positive ethics recognizes as morally desirable.[1]

Ratzenhofer's sociological ethics aims to show that social utilitarianism is in accord with nature and natural law. As to the practical value of his sociological position as endorsed by Gumplowicz, a few objections may be noted. Positive ethics, as every form of utilitarianism, fails to find a proper support in the facts; it is likewise inconsistent with sociological principles. For such principles, holding that social evolution proceeds according to natural laws, would lead to fatalism, resignation, the acknowledgment of human impotence in the presence of the mighty forces of nature; in which case it is futile to enlarge upon what may be ethically desirable. Spinoza was unable to construct an ethics upon the Stoic position, and found a way out by recourse to individual utilitarianism. Similarly Ratzenhofer, in an attempt to construct an ethical system, draws upon a social utilitarianism, and reaches a compromise which

[1] "Positive Ethik," pp. 34, 60 seq.; 36; 51; 66; 67; 68-113; 113-115; 116-121; 121-128; 128-131; 138-211, 231-291; 212-223, 223-230; 292 seq.; 304-318, 304, 309, 317; 327, 333.

is hardly a philosophic solution; thus again showing the failure of sociology to hold consistently to its fundamental principle of accordance with natural law.[1]

[1] Of the most recent contributions to sociology the following may be referred to: The writings of *Alb. Herm. Post*, for which see § 47; those of *G. Tarde*, § 49; of *Adolf Bastian*, whose contributions are mainly ethnological, serving to illustrate the descriptive data; of *Paul v. Lilienfeld*, whose position is similar to that of *Schäffle*; of *Gustave le Bon*, who applies to sociology the principles of psychology and mental evolution; of *Letourneau*, who emphasizes the comparative study of social organization in animal societies and among primitive peoples; of *Roberty*, who treats sociology philosophically; of *Lippert*, who approaches the subject with a special interest in the science of religion; of *Worms*, who considers society a distinctive organism; of *Giddings*, who regards society as a complexly organized expression of psychological forces, and says, on p. 420 of his "Principles of Sociology": "Certainly it is not a physical organism. Its parts, if parts it has, are physical relations. . . . A society is an *organization*, partly a product of unconscious evolution, partly a result of conscious planning. An organization is a complex of physical relations"; of *Ludwig Stein*, who has touched upon several phases of sociology as reflected in philosophy, in law, and in practical movements; of *Ernst Victor Zenker*, who traces the development of society from its most primitive stages to its most complex differentiation in the interests of a general philosophical interpretation; of *Coste*, who emphasizes the objective character of sociology, which finds its material in history and ethnology ("Society must be studied as though we formed no part in it, as though we were not men belonging to this planet"); of *Heinrich Schurtz*, who traces the fundamental forms which society assumes; of *Friedrich v. Baerenbach*, who presents a convenient survey of the sociological positions; of *Paul Barth*, who takes a sociological view of the history of culture, and of the phenomena of comparative psychology; of *Lester F. Ward*, who interprets the movements and forces of modern society as illustrations of comprehensive sociological principles. (See also bibliographical note in § 51.) As a bibliographical guide to these writers, reference may be made for *Le Bon* to his "L'Homme et les Sociétés, leurs Origines et leur Histoire." Part I: "L'Homme, Développement Physique et Intellectuel." Part II: "Les Sociétés, leurs Origines et leur Développement," Paris 1881 (particularly pp. 287–

5: RECENT REPRESENTATIVES: TÖNNIES, KLÖPPEL, BERGEMANN. The distinction of Ferd. Tönnies[1] rests upon his separation of the terms "community," "Gemeinschaft," and "society," "Gesellschaft," and upon his original development of these conceptions as expressions of the human will. Every contact of human wills has a mutual effect. In so far as each tends to support the other, they are affirmative, make for a "unity in the

317, 344-392); for *Letourneau,* "La Sociologie d'après l'Ethnographie," Paris 1880; for *Roberty,* "La Sociologie, Essai de Philosophie Sociologique, Paris 1881; for *Lippert,* Der Seelenkult in seinen Beziehungen zur althebräischen Religion," Berlin 1881; "Die Religionen der europäischen Kulturvölker, der Litauer, Slaven, Germanen, Griechen und Römer, in ihrem geschichtlichen Ursprung," Berlin 1881; "Allgemeine Geschichte des Priestertums," 1883, 1884; and, "Die Geschichte der Familie," Stuttgart 1884; for *Worms,* "Organisme et Société," Paris 1896 (particularly pp. 17-41); for *Giddings,* "Principles of Sociology," New York 1896; for *Ludwig Stein,* "Die soziale Frage im Lichte der Philosophie," second edition 1903, and, "Wesen und Aufgabe der Soziologie," an address at the third sociological congress in Paris, 1897; for *Zenker,* "Die Gesellschaft," Vol. I, 1899, Vol. II, 1903; for *Coste,* "Les Principes d'une Sociologie Objective," Paris 1899 (particularly pp. 26-51, 104-111); for *Heinrich Schurtz,* "Altersklassen und Männerbünde," Berlin 1902 (particularly pp. 173-189); for *Friedrich v. Baerenbach,* "Die Sozialwissenschaften," Leipzig 1882; for *Paul Barth,* "Die Philosophie der Geschichte als Soziologie," Leipzig 1897. A suitable introduction to the study of sociology is that by *R. Eisler,* "Soziologie. Die Lehre von der Entstehung und Entwickelung der menschlichen Gesellschaft," Leipzig 1903. In addition, the "Archiv für soziale Gesetzgebung und Statistik," Vol. I to XX; N. S. Vols. I and II, 1904-05, contains a survey of the social conditions of all lands. The first 18 volumes were edited by *Heinrich Braun,* and the later volumes by *Sombart, Max Weber,* and *Edgar Jaffé.*

[1] His chief works are: "Gemeinschaft und Gesellschaft. Abhandlung des Kommunismus und des Sozialismus als empirischer Kulturformen," Leipzig 1887. Also "Über die Grundtatsachen des sozialen Lebens" ("Ethisch-sozialwissenschaftliche Vortragskurse," published by the Swiss society for ethical culture, Vol. VII), Bern 1897.

plurality, or a plurality in the unity." The group resulting from this positive relation is called an association. "The relation itself, and hence the association, is to be regarded either as a real and organic life, which is characteristic of the community, or as an ideal and mechanical formation, which is the concept of society." A community is the primitive living together of men as conditioned by natural lines of kinship, — community of blood or propinquity, community of habitat. The communal relations extend from the home to the village, tribe, nation, and city. Within the city appear distinctive communal relations based upon community of worship, fraternal orders, the religious congregation, "Gemeinde," "the last being the supreme expression of the idea of community."

In comparison with community, society is an artificial and external product of civilization. "Society is an aggregate formed by convention and natural law, and is conceived as a composite of individuals bound by natural and artificial ties, whose wills and spheres of activity are variously related, and yet remain independent without reciprocal subjective influence." Society is the world of affairs, particularly of business, dealing with contract, trade, money, credit, etc. Society tends towards the world's markets and great cities.

For Tönnies the will or intent is the standard criterion differentiating between community and society. The will develops in two directions, either as a natural will, "the psychological equivalent of the human body or the principle of the unity of life," or as an artificial product, as "the issue of thought." The first of these phases he calls "Wesenwille," the will as it is by nature, the second, "Willkür," arbitrary will. The natural will spontaneously leads or disposes to community, while the arbitrary will leads to society. All social phenomena are derived either from the natural will or from the arbitrary will. The community expresses itself in law primarily as it affects the individual, "the self," or "subjective agent of the natural will," and as it affects possession, real estate, and the family. Society appears in law as it affects the person, that is, recognition of personality in the legal sense, as it affects assets, money, and rights of obligation. Whatever the human will produces, including the law, is at once natural and artificial. The trend of national development is towards an increasing social complexity.[1]

In his address, "Über die Grundtatsachen des sozialen Lebens," Tönnies makes marriage and property the fundamental facts of social life.

KLÖPPEL takes a most comprehensive view of society. "Every variety of communal association among men belongs to the relations comprised under the term "society." Society as constituted, or "natural society," represents "the totality of all relations of authority and dependence among men." The social struggle creates positions of vantage. The law intervenes to set limits to these positions of social vantage growing out of economic conditions. Historical development shows that the purpose of governmental authority is the establishment and maintenance of law and order for the promotion of public welfare.[2]

PAUL BERGEMANN may be classed among the sociologists by reason of his "Ethik und Kulturphilosophie,"[3] in which he represents the ethos as the resultant of the

[1] "Gemeinschaft und Gesellschaft," pp. 3; 9–45, 27, 284–287, 289 seq., 290–292; 46–95, 287–290; 99–194, 99 seq., 183, 206–209, 212 seq., 230; 212–217; 227 seq., 245 seq., 289 seq.

[2] "Staat und Gesellschaft," Gotha 1887, pp. 6; 9; 153 seq., 281 seq.

[3] Leipzig 1904, pp. 69–72.

rivalry between two classes. "Out of this struggle there emerges the moral 'pathos,' . . . and ultimately there prevails, as morality, as custom sanctioned by morals, the platform of the victorious party — whether liberal, adjusted to the newer conditions, or conservative of the older traditions."[1]

6: CRITICAL SUMMARY OF THE SOCIOLOGICAL POSITION. The meritorious service of the sociological school consists in its dispossession of the individualistic position of the older doctrines through its emphasis of the importance of the group, the class, the social solidarity. Nor is it fair to minimize this service, as Adolf Merkel and others have done, by objecting that the group or class is composed of individuals, and that these are the true agents of the processes which sociology ascribes to the group. The group as such represents a social point of vantage, — a surplus of power above that of the individuals composing the group. The correct emphasis of this fact remains to the credit of sociology. The serious fault of the sociological school, particularly as expounded by Gumplowicz, is its one-sidedness. This appears first in the complete absorption of the individual in the class. His position and efficiency as an individual, apart from his status as a member of the group, are completely ignored or denied. The individual is considered fatalistically, as determined by inherited or imposed influences; his spontaneity and initiative are not taken into consideration. Although sociology replaces the doctrine of natural law — according to which the State is composed of individuals all occupying a like position — by the correct view according to which mankind was always socialized, it nonetheless falls into an error analogous to that of the naturalistic conception. For while natural law regards the State as composed of

[1] "Ethik und Kulturphilosophie, p. 70. Also above, § 42.

units, Gumplowicz regards it as similarly composed of aggregates or groups; and the State becomes the conflict of groups. The independent existence of the State and of economics for their own ends disappears. Of the three, the individual, the group, and the State, Gumplowicz recognizes only the group. For socialism the economic group is everything, and the State and the individual are nothing; so with Gumplowicz, the individual and the State disappear in the ethnological group. In the second place, the State is slighted by the sociologist in that its functions are replaced by the so-called social functions, which in reality form a part of national and public life. Thirdly, the sociological school overemphasizes the factor of conflict in the rivalry of the several classes for supremacy and vantage. The factors of morality which antagonize conflict are not recognized and acknowledged in their true importance.[1] Man is made merely a more highly organized type of animal, and his desire for power, his most distinctive characteristic, the commanding importance of the ethical side of his nature, is disregarded.

The service of greatest practical value rendered by Gumplowicz is his emphasis, as against the levelling tendencies of modern social ethics, of the importance of classes, and of the tendency inherent in each class to assert itself in its conflict with other classes. His failure lies in the one-sided exaggeration of what, in its place, is a fundamental sociological truth.

7: APPLICATIONS OF THE SOCIOLOGICAL POSITION. (*a*) To Corporations. OTTO GIERKE's (b. 1841) "Genossenschaftstheorie" forms a corollary to sociology. While in appearance a contribution to the history of law, it is primarily a contribution to sociology from the

[1] They are regarded and considered only as supporting factors. See *Gumplowicz*, "Die soziologische Staatsidee," pp. 57 seq.

point of view of the professional jurist. His theory bears the same relation to the jurisprudence of his day as sociology bears to political economy based upon the individualistic position.[1] "What man is he owes to association among men." These introductory words express the thought which is elaborated into the central conception of Gierke's work.

The importance of association had been neglected except by BESELER[2] (1809–1888), a forerunner of Gierke. In German law the association has always been an important legal institution. Association falls under the generic type of the corporation; as opposed to a partnership, a corporation in the legal sense is based upon a permanent co-operation. Hereby the corporation acquires "a certain organic character which qualifies it to participate permanently in the life of the State and in the law." Corporations are of two kinds: they are either communities or associations. This is Beseler's fundamental principle,[3] and is the position developed by Gierke. In its narrow and technical sense an association according to Gierke is "any cor-

[1] In addition to "Das deutsche Genossenschaftsrecht," 3 vols., Berlin 1868, 1873, 1881, are to be noted: *Gierke*, "Die Genossenschaftstheorie und die Deutsche Rechtssprechung," Berlin 1887. "Das Wesen der menschlichen Verbände," an address of October 15, 1902, Leipzig 1902 (particularly pp. 7 seq.). "Die Grundbegriffe des Staatsrechts und die neuesten Staatsrechtstheorien" ("Z. f. d. g. Staatsw.," Vol. XXX, 1874, pp. 153–198, 265–335). "Über Laband's Staatsrecht und die deutsche Rechtswissenschaft" ("Sch. Jahrb." VII, Vol. IV, 1883, pp. 1–99, particularly pp. 29 seq.). See also *Berolzheimer*, "Rechtsphilosophische Studien," pp. 104–115, 111, note 2; 112, note 1.

[2] "Volksrecht und Juristenrecht," Leipzig 1843; especially "Das Recht der Genossenschaft," pp. 158–194; "Begriff und Arten der Genossenschaften," pp. 161–169. See also *Gierke*, "Das deutsche Genossenschaftsrecht," I, p. 5.

[3] *Beseler*, "Volksrecht und Juristenrecht," pp. 161 seq.

poration voluntarily formed, that is, an association that has independent legal personality." In a larger sense, communities[1] and the State[2] itself may be ranged under the term "association." But State and community are more than associations; their functions and nature go beyond those of an association.[3] "As against the 'persona ficta' the theory of association sets up the conception of a corporation which treats it as a real corporate personality; and this is the essence of the theory of association."[4] The human individual and the human community are true realities possessing a unity of nature.[5] To this doctrine are due the modern theories which oppose the assumption of a legal fiction in regard to juristic persons — a fiction surviving through inertia.

[1] "Das deutsche Genossenschaftsrecht," I, pp. 207 seq.

[2] *Gierke*, "Die Grundbegriffe," etc., Vol. XXX, pp. 304 seq.: "Among the social institutions of men the State is conspicuous. The essence of association within the State consists in its supreme power to carry out the general will. It represents the collective political life. Its essence is the general will; its manifestations, organized authority; its purpose, conscious action." Accordingly the State has "a real and peculiar nature" (p. 305). "The law of the State invests its personal representatives, and corporate law invests the personality of corporations, with the qualities derived from the nature of the State or of the corporation, which give such personal representation the value of a collective personality" (p. 321). *Gierke*, "Das Wesen der menschlichen Verbände," etc., p. 12: "The organic view regards the State and other associations as social organisms; it posits the existence of composite organisms (the parts of which are human beings) as above individual organisms." See also *Gierke*, "Laband's Staatsrecht und die deutsche Rechtswissenschaft," p. 31.

[3] *Gierke*, "Das deutsche Genossenschaftsrecht," I, p. 5.

[4] *Gierke*, "Die Genossenschaftstheorie und die deutsche Rechtsprechung," p. 5.

[5] "Die Grundbegriffe des Staatsrechts und die neuesten Staatstheorien" ("Z. f. d. g. Staatsw.," Vol. XXX, p. 301).

The law dealing with the individual has its co-ordinate counterpart in the law of association.[1] This law is social law when applied to the largest social interests, culminating in the law of the State. The two great varieties of social organizations in German law are associations and the foundations which form their complement. The theory of association is completed by the theory of foundations.

Gierke clarifies the legal character of associations in German law, and throws light, from more than a technical aspect, upon the importance of the social structures which are legally organized and co-ordinate with, as well as in part transcending, the status of the individual and his legal rights.

(b) *Penology.* The dominant tendency in criminology is sociological.[2] Ferri [3] (b. 1856) may be considered the founder of the sociological or positive criminology, and von Liszt [4] (b. 1851) its leading

[1] "Die Genossenschaftstheorie," etc., pp. 6 seq., 10, 10 seq.

[2] *v. Liszt,* "Lehrbuch des Deutschen Strafrechts," twelfth and thirteenth edition, Berlin 1903, pp. 65–88. *Auer,* "Soziales Strafrecht, Ein Prolog zur Strafrechtsreform." Munich 1903, pp. 1–8. *Berolzheimer,* "Die Entgeltung im Strafrechte," Munich 1903, pp. 136–145, 153–158, 446–480.

The sociological school, in the persons of its founders Ferri and Garofalo, took its origin from Lombroso's criminal anthropology. The anthropological phase of the subject, which considered the physical and psychological deviations of the criminal from the average man as its fundamental position and the basis for classification of criminals, has a further value for penological reform in so far as its conclusions are responsible for the recognition in legal procedure of states of diminished responsibility — a problem brought forward by the sociological criminologists.

[3] The chief works here pertinent are *Ferri,* "Das Verbrechen als soziale Erscheinung" (the German version by *Kurella*), "Bibliothek f. Sozialwissenschaften," Vol. VIII, Leipzig 1896.

[4] Articles to be specially noted are "Der Zweckgedanke im Strafrecht," "Z. f. d. g. Str.," Vol. III, 1883, pp. 1–47. "Die psycho-

exponent. Its most distinguished representatives are Prins (Brussels), G. A. van Hamel (Amsterdam), and von Liszt. These men are the founders of the "International Union of Criminal Law," which affords a opportunity for all interested in criminal sociology to unite in practical efforts with theoretical students interested in the administration of punishment. To the above names there should be added Finger[1] (b. 1858), von Lilienthal[2] (b. 1853), the psychiatrist Aschaffenburg,[3] Garofalo,[4] Sighele,[5] Karl Stooss[6] (b. 1849) and

ogischen Grundlagen der Kriminalpolitik, "Z. f. d. g. Str.," Vol. XVI, 1896, pp. 477–517. "Lehrbuch des Deutschen Strafrechts," pp. 65-88. v. Liszt is one of the founders and publishers of the "Zeitschrift für die gesamte Strafrechtswissenschaft."

[1] "Das Strafrecht" ("Kompendien des Österreichischen Rechtes," Vol. I), Berlin 1894, pp. 2–26. "Lehrbuch des Deutschen Strafrechts," Berlin 1904, pp. 1–45.

[2] "Der Stooss'sche Entwurf eines schweizerischen Strafgesetzbuchs" ("Z. f. g. Str.," Vol. XV, 1895, pp. 97–158, 250–356. *v. Lilienthal* is associate editor of this journal.

[3] "Die verminderte Zurechnungsfähigkeit," "Ärtzliche Sachverständige Zeitung," V, p. 397. "Alkoholgenuss und Verbrechen, eine Kriminalpsychologische Studie" ("Z. f. d. g. Str."), Vol. XX, pp. 80–100. "Das Verbrechen und seine Bekämpfung, Kriminalpsychologie für Mediziner, Juristen und Soziologen, ein Beitrag zur Reform der Strafgesetzgebung," Heidelberg 1903.

The "Monatschrift für Kriminalpsychologie und Strafrechtsreform," Vol. I, Heidelberg 1904–05, is edited by *Aschaffenburg*, assisted by *Alf. Klotz, v. Lilienthal* and *v. Liszt.*

[4] "Criminologia" ("Bibliotheca Anthropologico-Giuridica," Ser. I, Vol. II), 1885.

[5] "Psychologie der Massenverbrechen" (trans. by Kurella), Dresden and Leipzig 1897. See also below, § 49. For Tarde, see also § 49.

[6] "Vorentwurf zu Einem Schweizerischen Strafgesetzbuch." General Part: Prepared by *Karl Stooss* (translated at the same time by Alfred Gautier into French), Basle and Geneva 1893. "Motiv zu dem Vorentwurf des Schweizerischen Strafgesetzbuchs." General Part. *Karl Stooss*, Basle and Geneva 1893. The position of this

Lammasch[1] (b. 1853). This school considers crime as a social phenomenon, as an anti-social act that must be suppressed by society. The function of the law is to protect social interests. The penal law is the intensive protection of those interests that stand in peculiar need of protection, that is, of legally recognized property.

Doubtless the sociological position as applied to penology cannot be completely established;[2] and the discussions by penologists on the old and ever insoluble question of the freedom of the will — which is made necessary by the issue of determinism, and which has caused a sharp division in the ranks of criminologists[3] — recall the scholastic disputations. Nonetheless it is

project is given by Stooss (p. 84) in this statement: "A penal law accomplishes its purpose only when it proves effective in reducing crime."

Stooss, "Der Kampf gegen das Verbrechen," Lecture 1894. "Schweizerisches Strafgesetzbuch," Basle and Geneva 1894. Stooss is the editor of "Schweizerische Zeitschrift für Strafrecht."

[1] The works of *Lammasch* here pertinent are the following: "Kriminalpolitische Studien" ("Im Gerichtssaal," Vol. XLIV, 1891, pp. 147–248); and various smaller essays).

[2] Article II of the Constitution of the I. K. V. (International Union of Criminal Law) in a series of theses states the position of the society. The first thesis expresses the fundamental purpose: "The purpose of punishment is to make war upon crime as a social phenomenon." Punishment, however, is not the sole instrument in this movement. (Thesis 3.)

The statutes vary as recorded in the proceedings of the International Union (Vol. I, Berlin and Brussels 1889). See below § 47 for "Die Strafgesetzgebung der Gegenwart in Rechtsvergleichender Darstellung." *Kitzinger* gives an account of the workings of the International Union in "Die Internationale Kriminalistische Vereinigung. Betrachtungen über ihr Wesen und ihre Bisherige Wirksamkeit," Munich 1905.

[3] *Berolzheimer*, "Die Entgeltung im Strafrechte," pp. 40–109, 157, 351 seq., 437 seq., 441, and the bibliography there referred to. Also *Berolzheimer*, "Rechtsphilosophische Studien," pp. 10–14.

generally recognized that, especially in its practical proposals, this school represents the progressive party in penology.

§ 45. *Realistic and Historical Trends in Political Economy and Sociology.* Modern political economy depends for its material upon history, observation, and statistics; in other words, upon the empirical study of facts. This the survey of recent literature abundantly indicates. Confining the presentation to its chief representatives, we may mention as earliest Knies[1] (1821–1898), who distinctly takes the historical position; and L. Brentano[2] (b. 1844), who, commenting upon the failure of the classical school, concludes that "the only method is that of direct observation of economic phenomena." Accordingly, "special or practical economics must be emphasized, and the general or theoretical considerations must be assigned a subordinate place. Indeed there is no general economics. Any given economic relation is based either upon agriculture, or industry, or commerce, or

[1] *Knies,* "Die Politische Ökonomie vom Geschichtlichen Standpunkte," a new edition of "Politische Ökonomie vom Standpunkte der Geschichtlichen Methode," Braunschweig 1883, p. 23: "The historical development of political economy has up to the present been considered merely as a subject of historical investigation and presentation. . . . One must be prepared for the question, 'What purpose is served nowadays by tracing the historical evidence for the theoretical opinions, ends, and arguments of former ages,' since all such contributions have long since been superseded and are now regarded as negligible or unsound. . . . The complete reply to this objection will appear in due course. At the moment I note that the lack of consideration of the historical development of economic conditions, as well as of the principles of political economy, must affect disadvantageously the position and service of a science that is closely dependent upon an understanding of reality and which must conceive its purpose in an historical evolutionary spirit."

[2] *L. Brentano,* "Die Klassische Nationalökonomie." An address delivered April 17, 1888 (Leipzig 1888, pp. 20–28, 28 seq.).

trade, or service, or capital; and economic observations are possible only in these several fields. Hence the large number of studies in Germany in applied economics during the last decades. Theoretical economics has not been slighted, but the reconstruction of the science has required fresh material. Those who accept this position will naturally regard the historical study of economic development and the description of present economic conditions as of prime importance; and this not because concrete conditions are decisive, or because the theory of economics is to be replaced by its history, but because economics requires the same change of front which led the natural sciences to abandon *a priori* deductions in favor of an account of facts and processes." For Brentano notes in his address entitled "Ethik und Volkswirthschaft in der Geschichte,"[1] that the direct observation of concrete phenomena leads to an insight into "what in a given phenomenon is due to the inherent nature of things, and what to accidental circumstances." "All influence (of the State) upon the social life may be regarded as desirable and just, only in so far as it does not oppose the nature of things of which natural evolution is a part." Empiric observation leads to "a distinction between necessary factors and accidental circumstances."[2] Overlooking the fact that this view contains a suggestion of the Stoic or the physiocratic position in its assumption of a "recognized nature of things" and of "necessary factors," one may ask how shall the observer of economic development separate the essential from the accidental or abnormal? How can observation determine whether, and to what extent, socialism, or miners' strikes, or combinations, or trusts, or general strikes, are justified? A study

[1] November 28, 1901; second edition, Munich 1902.
[2] Pp. 33, 38.

of facts can merely determine facts, but does not afford a standard for a critical view of actual conditions nor a proper basis for reform. While Schmoller (b. 1838), the most distinguished political economist of the present day, endorses the point of view of the historical school,[1] Carl Menger[2] (b. 1840), and his Austrian associates, maintain that economics at present undervalues constructive analysis and precise determination of fundamental concepts; and this criticism is pertinent. The dominant school of political economy is not yet free from the fetters of economic empiricism. The collection and selection of material through historical and statistical study too completely absorb attention, and the fundamental theoretical problems are slighted. The conviction must sooner or later be reached that an extreme attention to the uninterpreted facts can result in no permanent advance. Such conviction would perhaps have been more promptly attained had not idealism entered the field of political economy through the dubious portal of social ethics.

The social-ethical formulation of political economy certainly does not provide a satisfactory substitute. If it holds to its own purposes,[3] social ethics in reality is applicable only to a limited field. If disposed as it is

[1] "Zur Methodologie der Staats- und Sozialwissenschaften" ("Sch Jahrb." Vol. V, Part IV, 1883, pp. 239–258); p. 247: The historical school represents "a return to a scientific conception of reality in place of vague abstractions lacking all reality."

[2] *Carl Menger*, "Untersuchungen über die Methode der Sozialwissenschaften und der Politischen Ökonomie insbesondere," Leipzig 1883; "Die Irrtümer des Historismus in der Deutschen Nationalökonomie," Vienna 1884. (This is a strongly personal reply to Schmoller's attack.) *Schüller*, "Die Klassische Nationalökonomie und ihre Gegner. Zur Geschichte der Nationalökonomie und Sozialpolitik seit A. Smith," Berlin 1895.

[3] See above, § 42.

at present to encroach upon the entire domain of law and economics, it is likely to obstruct a sound legal and economic philosophy, and to obscure and distort by vague phrases the fundamental principles of the philosophy of law and economics. For it is pertinent and important to consider that the social phenomena form but a section of the larger sphere of government and economics. The State is the source of law, and supplies the formal bond of the law which embraces and holds together the community. If the State were to disappear, law would likewise go, for it originates and develops only in and through the State; without it society would be nothing but a loosely bound aggregate. Economics represents the content aspect of government — the conditions under which law finds its application. It is the economic life that makes government and law something more than empty terms, and endows them with a vital meaning. If law were to disappear, then government and economics would likewise disappear both in form and substance, and what would remain would be society; or, expressing the same thought positively, social life consists of the free spontaneous expressions, activities, and operations of individuals and of their associations so far as these are not an outcome of the law. The members of the community in their spontaneous activities form society, and the part which society plays is thus limited. The importance of society lies in its supplementing of government and law in situations which the latter cannot and should not cover; and again, in the cultural preparation which it supplies, in the currents of interest which it starts, that in turn lead to changes in government and law.

However there are many good reasons why "society" should be assigned a large efficiency and scope, independent of whether we agree or not that the governmental functions shall likewise be considered as in part belonging to its domain. Such extension of its influence is favored by historical study, which shows that the State is not built up of single individuals but is composed of group formations representative of "society." Yet it is not to be overlooked that such communal groups as existed previous to the establishment of government and law, for which we use the term "society," are something wholly different from the "society" of the present day. Primitive conditions, it is true, furnish the factors necessary for the foundation of government and law. For primitive times, primitive society satisfied the needs which at present require the joint activities of government and society. The society of primitive times embraced the entire range of communal interests, while the "society" of the twentieth century represents such communal interests as are sustained apart from government and law. Pre-governmental society and society within an established State are wholly distinct.

The socialistic position favors the view of society as absorbing the State; it replaces the State as it now is by the State as it will come to be; yet such a State of the future is no longer a State in the technical sense, but the replacement of the State by "society." Socialism regards the State as a systematic economic and political oppression of the working classes by the minority of capitalists and ruling interests. In place of this autocracy based upon the arbitrary and unrestricted control by capital, it advocates the associative organization of manufactures and resources, the regulation of labor, and the fair distribution of wages. The whole of public economic life is to be comprehended in a sort of universal company, organized to control all public affairs; and such a company would be "society." Accordingly the socialistic State of the future, which socialism regards as a just State, by absorbing the State in "society," would replace capitalistic control, and establish a just law instead of class legislation. Thus society assumes its place in the philosophy of government as the supposed representative of a just economic order and organization — with the implication that government and law, as at present formulated, involve injustice. These socialistic views of justice make social ethics, social politics, social reform, the true expression of a righteous social order; they stand for the higher and the better, as against the unjust defective government and law of the present. This, however, is the converse of the true relation; instead of considering society as a division of the State, the State is made to appear as subordinate to society, and in addition, as an imperfect unregenerate institution.

Finally, the exaggerated importance attached to "society," and to "social ethics" resulting therefrom, is, in my humble opinion, due to the fact that too many non-jurists occupy themselves with the philosophy of government and law, and therefore are disposed to replace the definite, though complex and difficult conception of government and law, by the more elastic and vague one of society. "Society" is more readily managed; it is like a lay figure upon which any sort of garment may be neatly fitted. The definiteness of legal concepts gives way to the foggy confusion of social-political, social-reformatory, and social-ethical discussions, fertile in proposals that prove to be valueless and ineffective when philosophically tested. A return to legal and economic philosophy remains the sole scientific procedure.

This digression was necessary to make clear the weaknesses of social ethics. The classical political economy regarded too slightly the realities and was too much given to speculation; the historical-empirical school kept so closely to the facts that it slighted the theoretical foundations of economic principles. And though it is true that this school regarded the collection and ordering of its material as a preparatory procedure to supply the data for a later philosophical construction, it is much to be feared that if the material thus collected is all that is available, the construction will be indefinitely postponed. Like brick and mortar, facts need the well-devised plan of an architect; the plan cannot be derived from the building materials alone.

§ 46. *The Theory of Norms.* BINDING's (b. 1841) "theory of norms" is derived from criminal law and belongs primarily to general legal science.[1] It is, however, of import for the philosophy of law and government, in that it upholds governmental authority distinctively as the type of the legal imperative. Binding holds that what the criminal transgresses is not the particular statute applicable to his offense, but the underlying norm or principle which finds expression in such statute.[2] Criminal statutes are in the nature of imperatives or regulating principles, designed "to provide penal regulations and to determine their content . . . as affecting two classes of persons: those possessing the

---

[1] *Binding*, "Die Normen und ihre Übertretung. Eine Untersuchung über die Rechtmässige Handlung und die Arten des Delikts." Vol. I: "Normen und Strafgesetze" (1872), second edition, Leipzig 1890; Vol. II: "Schuld und Vorsatz," Leipzig 1877.

Binding, "Handbuch des Strafrechts," Vol. I. (*Binding*, "Handbuch der Deutschen Rechtswissenschaft," VII, I, 1) Leipzig 1885, pp. 155–222. "Grundriss des Gemeinen Deutschen Strafrechts," I, fifth edition, Leipzig 1897, pp. 58–72. (The sixth edition, Leipzig 1902, was not accessible to me.)

[2] "To be liable to punishment involves that the offender must have acted as set forth in" [that portion of the law which] "specifically characterizes punishable actions." "Normen," I, p. 4.

right of punishment [that is, the right of criminal sanction], and those against whom it is directed." Criminal laws attempt to "regulate . . . the relation between the State and the offender; and pertain primarily to the State as the maker of criminal laws, and secondly to the offender under such laws. . . . Criminal statutes include all legal principles which standardize the conditions of application, the nature and the consequences of violation, of the legally established duties of criminal law." It is the legal nature of these norms that Binding unfolds, and ably and effectively develops.

The governmental authority exercises a "right to exact conformity." Such authority is forcibly directed against those who do not "conform." As against the transgressor "the law that is transgressed takes the form of a right to coercion by reason of such transgression. The person of the one who disregards the law becomes forcibly subject to the power of the law, so that it may be felt and known which is master — the will of the law or the will of the individual. This subjection to coercion in behalf of the maintenance of the law, this enforced conformity, which is somewhat inaptly described as an enforced retribution or satisfaction, is public punishment as history discloses it." "The relation of [legal] norms to acts, is like that of a condition, and what is affected by the condition; the latter must be adapted to the former."[1]

Binding's theory of norms has gained more opponents than adherents.[2] The most notable criticism of his

[1] "Normen," I, pp. 19–21, 423–426; II, p. 54.

[2] *Adolf Merkel*, "Über Binding's Handbuch des Strafrechts," Vol. I ("Z. f. d. ges. Str.," Vol. VI, 1886, pp. 512 seq.). (*Merkel*, "Hinterlassene Fragmente und Ges. Abh.," II, 2, pp. 509–534): "Besprechung von K. Binding 'Die Normen und ihre Übertretung,'" second edition of Vol. I (*Merkel*, "Hinterlassene," etc., II, 2, pp.

position is that of Adolf Merkel. He and his followers not unjustly charge the theory with an extreme emphasis of the formal side.[1] While it is conceded that law is the result of governmental supremacy, this statement establishes merely an external criterion of the nature of government and law. The legislating State that formulates an enforcible law on the basis of unwritten norms does not assume the dictatorial position of the wielder of such power, setting up an individual will and pleasure against the will of subjects, and suppressing the expression of any rebellious will. The purpose of the State is not primarily to secure obedience to its supremacy, but to direct legislation toward the maintenance of individual rights. The legal order is intended not to restrict, but primarily, to maintain rights.

The problems of the philosophy of law and government cannot be mastered from the position of the theory

679–686). *v. Liszt*, "Rechtsgut und Handlungsbegriff im Binding-'schen Handbuche." ("Z. f. d. g. Str.," Vol. VI, pp. 670–672.) *Hugo Heinemann*, "Die Binding'sche Schuldlehre, ein Beitrag zu ihrer Widerlegung." ("Abh. des Kriminalistischen Seminars zu Marburg," edited by *v. Liszt*, Vol. I, Part IV) Freiburg i/B 1889. *v. Weinrich*, "Strafrecht und Kriminalpolitik. Ein Beitrag zur Kritik der Normentheorie und der Neuesten Reformbestrebungen." "Z. f. d. ges. Str.," Vol. XVII, 1897, pp. 779 seq. *Berolzheimer*, "Die Entgeltung im Strafrechte," pp. 126–129, 159–168, and the bibliography there noted.

Zitelmann, "Irrtum und Rechtsgeschäft," Leipzig 1879, p. 221, contests the imperative value of norms. Opposed to Zitelmann see *Heinemann*, "Die Binding'sche Schuldlehre," pp. 40 seq.

The function of the norms as a legal protection is considered in detail by *Oetker*, "Rechtsgüterschutz und Strafe" ("Z. f. d. g. Str.," Vol. XVII, pp. 493 seq.). See also *Oetker*, "Besprechung von Binding's Normen," Vol. I, second edition ("Z. f. ver. Rechtsw.," Vol. XVII, pp. 141–154).

[1] *Ihering*, "Der Zweck im Recht," I, p. 435: "Norms and coercion are purely formal factors that afford no knowledge as to the content of the law."

of norms; for this theory is misleading in that it sets up the law as an isolated institution. But Binding's fundamental idea that the imperative norm forms the essence of law is a permanent contribution to legal philosophy; for, though one-sided, the theory of norms is thoroughly sound on its own ground. So far as concerns the second of the two functions of the legal order — that of safeguarding rights and that of restricting license — the theory offers a satisfactory position.

THON[1] (b. 1839), in "Die Norm und die Rechtsfolgen ihrer Übertretung," pursues the study of norms in the spirit of Binding. Norms are imperatives. "The law of a community expresses its will; and such expression aims to regulate the conduct of those regarded as subject thereto. All laws are imperatives." The legal consequences of transgressing the norm likewise become "the introduction of new, or the abolition of existing imperatives." Accordingly "the aggregate law of a community is merely a complex of the imperatives which are bound up with one another in so far as the violation of one constitutes the assumption for the requirement to another." The norms are differentiated according to the purposes which legislation pursues in the establishment of its imperatives. One group comprises the norms to which is attached the legal consequence that anyone violating them is subject to punishment; the second group attempts so far as possible to make good a wrong, either by restitution[2] or compensation or security.

[1] "Rechtsnorm und Subjectives Recht. Untersuchungen zur Allgemeinen Rechtslehre," Weimar, 1878 p. 69; 1, 8, 7 seq., 69 seq.

[2] This is Thon's expression; what is meant is a consequent necessity of restitution through the legal order.

BIERLING[1] (b. 1841) modifies the theory of norms [2] by his view that "the constituent factor of law, and especially of the constituted law, is merely the acknowledgment on the part of those who share it as the norm of their social life." [3] "Accordingly legislation imposes nothing more than a duty because, and in so far as it is recognized as a binding social norm by the members of the State. An unconditioned general obligation towards the laws of the State can only exist because, and in so far as a general norm is acknowledged which shall be binding upon legislation; or in other words, in so far as a norm exists to which every act of legislation is subject or appears to be so." [4] "The funda-

[1] His works are: "Zur Kritik der Juristischen Grundbegriffe," I, II, Gotha 1877, 1883. Revised and enlarged under the title "Juristische Prinzipienlehre," 2 vols. Freiburg i/B and Leipzig 1894, Freiburg, Leipzig and Tübingen 1898.

[2] Bierling defines the limits of jurisprudence as against the philosophy of law as follows: "The science of juristic principles, in the sense here used, is limited to a definite part of the philosophical elaboration of law. It is limited to the determination of certain formal conceptions and principles, operative in legal practice, and more or less recognized in the several divisions of jurisprudence, and makes these the object of special investigation, seeking to establish the basis, the meaning, and the limits of their validity. All further questions connected with this position, that undertakes to interpret law in the narrower sense with reference to a general view of things, in other words, that attempts to show the place and the significance attaching to law in the collective order of the universe, — all questions of this kind, the science of jurisprudence leaves untouched. . . . But such problems constitute the peculiar domain of the philosophy of law."

[3] "Zur Kritik der Juristischen Grundbegriffe," I, p. 66. (p. 92): "That this living together [in the family] becomes a true living together, a true communal life only through the norms recognized by those participating therein." See pp. 121, 134 seq., 158; Vol. II, pp. 33 and Appendix B, pp. 351–364. See also below, p. 386, note 3.

[4] "Zur Kritik," etc., I, p. 138. Also "Juristische Prinzipienlehre," Vol. II, pp. 3–45: "Über die Entstehung, Auflösung und

mental point is to establish the imperative nature of law"; and to this the latter portion of "Die Juristische Grundbegriffe" is devoted. The conception of the permissible ("Dürfen") offers considerable difficulty in this treatment because it seems to stand in contradiction to the theory of norms. Bierling considers it as a mistake to derive the conception of duty, of what is enjoined or forbidden, from what is permitted. It is nearer the truth that "what is permitted or allowed, is simply what is not prohibited, or more correctly speaking, what does not stand in opposition to the requirements of the law."[1] "All law consists of norms, and whatever cannot be reduced to a norm does not in reality belong to the law."[2] The norm becomes a legal norm "by the acknowledgment thereof on the part of the members of the community as their communal norm." Legal acknowledgment is "an acknowledgment of the norms as communal, and as applying between one member of the community and another."[3] Hence the law is "whatever men who live together in any form of communal life mutually recognize as the norm and regulation of such communal living."[4]

Veränderung der Rechtsnormen und ihre Beziehung zur Entstehung und Aufhebung der Rechtsnormen."

[1] "Zur Kritik," etc., II, pp. 8, 18; I, p. 157; Vol. II, Appendix A pp. 307–350.

[2] "Juristische Prinzipienlehre," Vol. I, p. 30. On Norms, see pp. 30–40; for various kinds of legal norms, see pp. 71–144; for legal norms as the content of legal relations, see pp. 145–200.

[3] "Zur Kritik," etc., II, p. 33. See also the citation in note 10. Also "Juristische Prinzipienlehre," Vol. I, p. 19; Vol. II, p. 103, note 39, pp. 103–116.

[4] "Juristische Prinzipienlehre," I, p. 19. On restitution, see pp. 41–53. *Schuppe*, in "Die Methoden der Rechtsphilosophie" ("Z. f. v. Rechtsw.," Vol. V, p. 270), agrees with Bierling with the condition that the principle of acknowledgment requires to be perfected.

The work of MAX ERNST MEYER, entitled "Rechtsnormen und Kulturnormen,"[1] presents a happy combination of the legal philosophy of Kohler and Binding. Kohler, following Hegel, emphasizes the quality of the law as a cultural phenomenon, and the dependence of legislation upon the prevalent general culture.[2] M. E. Meyer sets these cultural norms, which thus become vitalized with a new content, in the place of legal norms. The objection to be urged against the theory of norms in its several formulations, from Binding to Meyer, is its one-sidedness, its view of the law merely as an imperative, as a restricting force; it recognizes the law merely as imposing obligation, while the phase of the law that acknowledges, confirms and safeguards is neglected. Yet the latter phase is really the essential one. For example, the nature of property does not consist in the fact that the encroachment thereon by another is forbidden, but in its conferring of right, in legally empowering the one justly entitled to it to use it, to enjoy it, and to dispose of it.

§ 47. *Ethnological Jurisprudence.* The study of foreign law as a basis for the improvement of legislation is not an innovation. The laws of ancient Egypt served as a model to other countries. In such service lies the origin of comparative law. Yet the study that is now called "comparative law," and the collation of laws for professional purposes, differ widely from these earlier essays. Comparative law is not exclusively or primarily directed to application, but pursues the theoretical purpose of finding a sounder foundation for,

---

[1] *"Beling's* Strafrechtliche Abhandlungen," Heft L, Breslau 1903.

[2] *v. Holtzendorff-Kohler's* "Enzyklopädie der Rechtswissenschaft," p. 6: "Cultural demands supply the ideal which the law of a given period attempts to meet. The law thus rests upon the basis of culture." See also below, § 48.

and a deeper insight into, the fundamental conceptions of law. Again, such comparison is systematic and comprehensive, aiming at universal principles. It is in these interests that a reference to the results of comparative law is here pertinent. By such systematic and comprehensive study the philosophy of law, as well as general legal science, has acquired a new method, comparable in value with that of comparative linguistic study to philology. Yet neither in philology nor in law can the comparative method be expected to provide a universal solution of problems. The peculiarly important philosophical problem of the origin of law and government, comparative law cannot be expected to solve, if for no other reason than that it ever finds the presence of law and government as a prerequisite for its study; similarly comparative philology cannot remove the obscurity attaching to the origin of language.

One of the founders and important contributors to the ethnological [1] study of law is J. J. BACHOFEN (1815–

[1] As a matter of terminology the division of the modern science of law treated in this section is in part ethnographical, in part ethnological, and in part both. Ethnography is the inductive and descriptive study and presentation of any group of facts from the life of peoples. Ethnology is the deductive, synthetic interpretation of ethnographical results; it is the synthetic elaboration and derivation of general laws of the life of peoples. See *S. Günther*, "Ziele, Richtpunkte und Methoden der Modernen Völkerkunde," Stuttgart 1904, pp. 11 seq.

Upon the import of comparative law see *Bernhöft*, "Über Zweck und Mittel der Vergleichenden Rechtswissenschaft ("Z. f. v. Rechtsw."), Vol. I, Stuttgart 1878, pp. 1–38. *Dahn*, "Vom Wesen und Werden des Rechts" ("Z. f. v. Rechtsw.", Vol. II, Introduction. "Die Rechtsvergleichung als Grundlage der Rechtsphilosophie," pp. 1–10. *Bernhöft*, "Über die Grundlagen der Rechtsentwickelung bei den Indogermanischen Völkern" ("Z. f. v. Rechtsw.," Vol. II, 1879, pp. (253–328), 254 seq. *Ernst Schuster* (London), "Die Praktische Bedeutung der Vergleichenden Rechtswissenschaft für das Familien-

1887), who is the author of "Das Mutterrecht," a study of matriarchal government in the ancient world in its religious and legal aspect (Stuttgart 1861). With patient industry this author gathers and correlates all forms of legal institutions and enactments that lead to the conclusions that a matriarchy, which assigns precedence in civilization as in domestic arrangements, to the child-bearing member of the family, (survivals of which may be found in most recent times,) preceded the patriarchical form of government, which gives precedence to the masculine factors in government, civilization, and law, and makes the father of the family the central authority. He finds such evidence in myths and sagas, in cults, in the accounts of ancient authors, and in the Greek drama.

Similarly directed is the other extensive work of Bachofen, 'Antiquarische Briefe," bearing particularly upon our knowledge of the ancient forms of relationship (2 vols., Strassburg 1880, 1886). There should likewise be mentioned Bachofen's "Die Sage von Tanaquil," a study of Orientalism in Rome and Italy. (Heidelberg 1870.) [1]

und Erbrecht" ("Jahrb. der inter. Vereinigung f. ver. Rechtsw. und Volkswirthschaftslehre," Vol. II, 1896, Berlin 1897, pp. 71–97.) For what follows see especially *Kohler*, "Enzyclopädie," pp. 14–20.

[1] See the comments on method by *Kohler* on J. J. Bachofen, "Die Sage von Tanaquil," and "Antiquarische Briefe," I–XXX, Strassburg 1880 ("Z. f. v. Rechtsw." IV), Stuttgart 1883, pp. 266–277 (pp. 275 seq.): "The proper path which ethnological jurisprudence must pursue is that of studying the several races by the aid of all material bearing upon law, and then proceed to further correlations, particularly to the treatment of myths and sagas from the point of view of legal ethnology. This procedure is more certain because observation yields more exact results than the study of dubious tradition which is never pure, but is ever affected in its uncertain course by biased editing. This method I propose to pursue in my work upon the legal relations of primitive peoples, and hope thus to establish the principle upon a firm basis."

J. KOHLER (b. 1849) is at present the recognized leader of the school for the comparative study of law. He is the author of numerous ethnographical and ethnological studies, and is associate editor of the "Zeitschrift für Vergleichende Rechtswissenschaft." In relation to our present topic his works that are of special importance are: "Shakespeare vor dem Forum der Jurisprudenz," Würzburg 1884; "Rechtsvergleichende Studien über Islamitische Rechte, das Recht der Berbern, das Chinesische Recht, und das Recht auf Ceylon," Berlin 1889; "Zur Urgeschichte der Ehe, Totemismus, Gruppenehe, Mutterrecht" ("Z. f. v. Rechtsw.," Vol. XII, pp. 187–353).[1] Kohler's ethnological position is more accurately set forth in his essay "Recht, Glaube, und Sitte," [2] and in Holtzendorff's "Enzyklopädie" [3] for which he prepared a new edition in 1904.

ALB. HERM. POST (d. 1895) was a notable representative of the ethnological school of law. In a series of writings he investigates the original form and appearance of law. His works are: "Das Naturgesetz des Rechts," an introduction to a philosophy of law on the basis of a modern empiric science, Bremen 1867; "Die Geschlechtsgenossenschaft der Urzeit und die Entstehung der Ehe," a contribution to a general comparative science of government and law, Oldenburg 1875; "Der Ursprung des Rechts," an introduction to a general comparative science of law, Oldenburg 1876; "Die Anfänge des Staats- und Rechtslebens," a contribution to general comparative history of government

---

[1] *Kohler*, "Rechtsenzyklopädie," p. 20, note 1, gives a partial list of Kohler's works.

[2] In Grünh., Z., Vol. 19, Vienna 1892, pp. 561–612.

[3] Pp. 14 seq., 17–20. See also *Kohler*, "Zur Ethnologischen Jurisprudenz, Rezensionsabhandlungen" ("Z. f. v. Rechtsw.," VI, pp. (407–429) 407.

and law, Oldenburg 1878; "Bausteine für eine Allgemeine Rechtswissenschaft auf Vergleichende Ethnologischer Basis," Vol. I, Oldenburg 1880 (see pp. 1–8 for the comparative method in law); Vol. II, 1881; "Die Grundlagen des Rechts und die Grundzüge seiner Entwickelungsgeschichte," suggestions for a general science of law upon a sociological basis, Oldenburg 1884; "Einleitung in das Studium der Ethnologischen Jurisprudenz," Oldenburg 1886; "Afrikanische Jurisprudenz," ethnological-juridical contributions to the science of indigenous law in Africa (two parts in one volume), Oldenburg and Leipzig 1887; "Studien zur Entwickelungsgeschichte des Familienrechtes," a contribution to a general comparative science of law on an ethnological basis, Oldenburg and Leipzig 1890; "Über die Aufgaben einer Allgemeinen Rechtswissenschaft," Oldenburg 1891.

In this field B. W. Leist (b. 1819) has contributed the following works: "Græco-italische Rechtsgeschichte," Jena 1884; "Alt-Arisches Jus Gentium," Jena 1889; "Alt-Arisches Jus Civile," Part I, Jena 1892; Part II, Jena 1896. He insisted that his works were not to be considered as belonging to comparative law but rather to the history of law, as the title "Arische Stammrechtsgeschichte" indicates.[1] Nonetheless he proceeds upon the comparative method. His studies of the legal conceptions of ancient India, Greece, and Rome, as bearing upon the government, civilization, and science of these peoples, have great merit; and their conclusions have been largely utilized in the first chapters of the present work.[2]

[1] "Alt-Arisches Jus Gentium," pp. 6–11.

[2] There may be added the contributions of *F. Meili*: "Die Neuen Aufgaben der Modernen Jurisprudenz" (1892); and the compendium entitled, "Institutionen der Vergleichenden Rechtswissenschaft"

§ 48. *The Reinstatement of Kant and Hegel: v. Hartmann.* 1: NEO-KANTIANISM. The neo-Kantians represent the position that the further development of the work of critical idealism and the independent advance of systematic philosophy will mutually further and condition one another.[1] Hermann Cohen [2] (b. 1842)

(1898); of Bernhöft: "Die Inschrift von Gortyn" (Stuttgart 1885); together with articles in the "Z. f. v. Rechtsw.," and in the "Jahrbuch der Intern. Ver. für verg. R.," of both of which he is co-editor; of *S. R. Steinmetz*: "Ethnologische Studien zur Ersten Entwickelung der Strafe," 2 vols. (Leyden 1894); "Bearbeitung des Fragebogens der Internationalen Vereinigung für Vergleichende Rechtswissenschaft und Volkswirtschaftslehre (Berlin 1903); of *Henry Sumner Maine*: "Ancient Law" (London 1861); "Lectures on the Early History of Institutions" (London 1875); "Dissertations on Early Law and Custom" (London 1883); of *Lewis H. Morgan*: "Systems of Consanguinity and Affinity of the Human Family" (Washington 1871); of *Friedrich Boden*: "Mutterrecht und Ehe im Altnordischen Recht" (Berlin and Leipzig 1904); of *Labriola*: "Del Concetto Teorico della Società Civile" (Rome 1901); "Revisione Critica delle piu Recenti Teorie su le Origini del Diritto" (Rome 1901).

The "Z. f. v. Rechtsw." (established 1878), and the "Jahrb. d. I. Ver. f. verg. Rechts. und Volksw." (established 1895), contain numerous articles upon various aspects of comparative law by Dargun, Friedrichs, Max Schmidt, and others. For penology a similar service is performed by "Die Strafgesetzgebung der Gegenwart in Rechtsvergleichender Darstellung," of which the first volume appeared in 1894, the second in 1899, and others of which are to follow.

The work of Ernst Neukamp, "Entwickelungsgeschichte des Rechts" (Berlin 1895), belongs in part to this group, but is distinctive by reason of his advocacy of an evolutionary trend in the development of legal systems. The comparative study is to afford the data from which the discovery of the actual laws of evolution are to be derived.

[1] *Cohen*, "Kant's Begründung der Ethik," preface, p. III. See also *Berolzheimer*, "System," Vol. I, pp. 128 seq.

[2] To be noted are: "Kant's Theorie der Erfahrung," Berlin 1871. "Kant's Begründung der Ethik," Berlin 1877. "System der Philosophie," Part I: "Logik der Reinen Erkenntnis," Berlin 1902 (pp.

may be termed the father of the movement; and associated with him are Natorp, Stammler, Eduard Bernstein. In Cohen's "Kant's Theorie der Erfahrung," he interprets Kant's views of purpose and idea, making the idea of cause that of purpose. Previous to Kant, the teleological position looked upon purpose or design as itself a creative force; but in Critical philosophy, purpose "enters only when causes have been exhausted; but the analysis of causes should in reality never cease. Purpose is the extension of cause." The categorical imperative was developed under the influence of this conception of purpose ("Zweck"), or means to an end. "The noumenon or essence of freedom is contained in the ethical principle that the moral character, the autonomous nature, is such purpose existing for its own sake, as a final purpose." Kant's principle of freedom is to be supplemented in the spirit of Kant by the statement: "I mean by freedom not an exemption from the law of causality, but an exemption from any intermediate mechanism or any purposive limitation."

"In the position that ethics is the study of duty, of things as they should be ('Sollen'), there is an ambiguity that confuses the conception of ethics." For science considers the actually existent, while ethics, according to this principle, is directed to that which should be. But appearances are deceptive. Ethics must establish the legitimacy of the moral ideal, must show the real nature of moral effort as it appears in human experience. A moral ideal is necessary to moral endeavor; hence ethics is concerned with moral endeavor.

172-175); Part II: "Ethik des Reinen Willens," Berlin 1904. For *H. Cohen* see *Ueberweg-Heinze*, "Grundriss," IV, pp. 219-221 (on p. 219 is a list of Cohen's writings).

The formulation of moral laws is to be derived from the conception of pure will. Pure will implies that the moral law is "excluded as an objective motive." If one were to posit pleasure or pain as the material condition of the will, then morality would not have an *a priori*, but an empirical foundation, and this would not lead to a moral law. "The form of general legislation considered as the sole condition of pure practical reason is the community of autonomous beings which is ever thought of and utilized 'as an end, never merely as a means.' The mere form of legislation in accordance with the general meaning of form as law, is the autonomy of the end; the *a priori* goal is found in the community. Thus the 'formal' *a priori* procedure finds so favorable a reality that the moral nature of the individual appears to be derived from that which is common to all moral natures. In the last analysis the moral law consists in the conception of such community." Upon this position Stammler develops his social philosophy. The idea of moral law is equivalent to the idea of humanity. "Both ideas are realized in the realization of humanity in man." Cohen further sets forth, in the spirit of Kant, how the moral law, with due allowance for human nature, may be practically and psychologically realized.[1]

In his "Ethik des Reinen Willens," Cohen elaborates and develops the conception of humanity. Man as a moral being is not man in the psychological sense, not man as a self-contained individual, but man as the conception of humanity, as a participator in immortality. The view that the State is the chief ethical expression of the moral consciousness suggests Hegel. "The State as a self-conscious expression is the unity of

[1] *Cohen*, "Kant's Theorie der Erfahrung," pp. 231–233. "Kant's Begründung der Ethik," pp. 233 seq., pp. 117 seq., pp. 154 seq., 163, 168, 172, 176, 198, 201, 273, 275 seq.

subject and object in the will."[1] The view that in the supremacy of the State the individual finds his exemplar suggests the Platonic position. Morality implies an ideal; there must ever remain a gap between the moral status of man and the moral idea in its complete purity. Hence government and law are neither dispensable nor replaceable. "Justice must be maintained as a guide to virtue; and its constant progress is possible only through the instrument of law and government." The State as it actually is, is the State of the estates and the ruling classes. It is not a State based upon justice. "The State as the instrument of justice is guided solely by moral consciousness. The authority which it acquires is directed to this end. The self-consciousness of the State is the self-consciousness of its members. Justice makes universal brotherhood the self-appointed purpose of mankind.[2]

Natorp's[3] (b. 1854) "Sozialpädagogik" considers the problem of the relations of education and society. He distinguishes three stages of conduct — instinct, will in the narrower sense, and rational will. Will is instinct concentrated; rational will is "the highest

[1] "Ethik des Reinen Willens," pp. 7, 21, 595; pp. 76, 231 seq., 241, 232. The State unites men "in an ideal unity of all." "This unity of a universality forms the State. The moral, and consequently, the political conception of the State, rests upon the unity formed by this totality." "The true conception of the State is embodied and vitalized in the conception of society." "The conception of the State is the ethical phase of the conception of culture." "The State alone presents the self-consciousness of man." "Ethik des Reinen Willens," pp. 76, 173, 241, 242.

[2] "Ethik des Reinen Willens," pp. 568, 270–306, 307 seq., 565, 582 seq., also 603.

[3] For Natorp see *Ueberweg-Heinze*, "Grundriss der Geschichte der Philosophie," Vol. IV, pp. 221 seq., where will be found a survey of Natorp's works. *Labriola*, "Revisione Critica Delle più Recenti Teorie su le Origini del Diritto," Roma 1901, p. 99.

concentration of practical capacity in general." As is true of the individual, so is it true of society which affects the individual, that "only by work and by discipline of the will, can there be progress toward the law of reason," "progress from a mere formal aggregation to a spiritual community," and progress from external rule, heteronomy, to self-rule, autonomy, in Kant's sense. The social instruments for the education of the will are the home and the school; and for adults, the education afforded by the communal life. Practice and study are the means of training the will. Ethics, æsthetics, and religion also have a share in its education.[1]

Introductory to the discussion of the methods of the education of the will, Natorp sets forth the foundations of ethics and social philosophy. The individual virtues are truth as the virtue of reason; courage or moral efficiency as the virtue of the will; purity or moderation as the virtue of instinct; and lastly justice as "the individual basis of social virtue."[2] The moral constitution of social life must exhibit a complete parallelism in its nature and operation to the individual life, and must equally comprise the three fundamental factors of human conduct. The individual virtues are equally social virtues; the love of truth is the dominance of conscience in the social order, the pervasion of the body social with a sense of truthfulness; courage is the condition of law and order; temperance is the complete harmonious regulation of the social instincts, that is, the organiza-

[1] "Sozialpädagogik," pp. 77; 54-96; 217-388; 99-214.

[2] "Under justice as an individual virtue I understand the aspect of all virtues belonging to the individual that bear upon the community; and the essence of such virtue is already completely contained in the relation that what morality requires is again required in a newer and larger sense by the interests of the community. The virtue thus transferred brings with it no distinctive content." "Sozialpädogogik," p. 135.

tion of labor and the enjoyment of the fruits of labor on a sound basis, "including a comprehensive organization upon the basis of equality and co-operation." Justice is the cardinal social virtue, embracing all the rest. Social justice is characterized as the widest application of command to render to each his own; in principle the maintenance of the same law for all, — a just participation on the part of each "in education, in the government, and in service, jointly, and in their inherent and established relation to one another."

Social regulation requires as a higher legal standard practical reason, and in the form of communal reason. The fundamental law of social development is "the law by virtue of which the ideal relation of the three factors of the social life become immutably one, valid and stable for a given period"; and this law becomes established by the "adjustment of the idea to experience." "The rational ordering of social life can be realized only by means of social regulation, which represents the formal will of social life. In its application this refers to industrial labor and its technical organization, but the progress of such technical procedure depends directly upon the progress of science." Social life requires the assumption that the laws of nature "in the last analysis must be one and the same, so far as they bear upon the issues of consciousness, because the root thereof lies in the fundamental laws of consciousness itself." Accepting Kant's method as an exemplar, we reach "the idea of a universally valid functional connection among the essential factors of social life — the connection resting upon a community of method, and designed ultimately to establish a comprehensive connection in the human consciousness between the laws to which ideas are subject and the general law of nature. For the two are inherently related by an original community of origin, and likewise appear in close connection in human consciousness. This connection is established by a systematic adaptation of natural properties to the purposes of social technology, making economics a part of governmental concern, and bringing both under the direction of practical reason, that is, of creative activity. Yet all this takes place with constant and conscious consideration of an orderly progress towards that solidarity which results from the supremacy of reason, which in turn determines its direction. This consummation furthers the interests of the individual and of his associations; it places in relation the several interests requiring correlation, while also serving the individual as a member of the community.[1]

Among the most important contributions to the modern philosophy of law are those of the neo-Kantian, Rudolf Stammler (b. 1856). Of his two chief works, the one, "Wirthschaft und Recht," furnishes the foundation of his social philosophy, and the other, "Die Lehre von dem Richtigen Rechte," contains a searching examination of the philosophy of law. Both are notable works; the latter particularly has failed to receive the appreciation which it deserves.[2]

Stammler was influenced in the direction of neo-Kantianism by Cohen, and Natorp. In "Wirthschaft und Recht" he develops a social philosophy as Kant might have done, had he undertaken the problem. Stammler holds the error of former systems of legal philosophy to have been the acceptance of law as the underlying principle. This is quite as misleading as would be the theoretical formulation of natural science upon the conception of gravity. "Wirthschaft," the economic life, Stammler likewise considers unsuitable as the point of departure;

[1] "Sozialpädagogik," pp. 202-214, 180, 182, 182 seq., 192, 200.
[2] See also his recent "Theorie der Rechtswissenschaft," 1911.—Ed.

it is the *social* life that constitutes the underlying problem, and with it we must begin.

The method of generalization upon historical data proves to be as inadequate as the comparative study of law; and a general legal science is equally unable to solve the fundamental problem of social philosophy.[1] The problem is the determination and analysis of the principles of social life, in which, as it is realized, law forms but one factor, though an important one. Instead of studying individual social phenomena the attempt must be made to establish "a systematic co-ordination of the several phenomena under a comprehensive principle." In other words, "the object of social philosophy is the ordering of the social life of man as such"; while the object of general legal science is "the determination of the common content of different legal systems." To obtain a clear view of the general conditions of social science a critical philosophical survey is necessary. The material conception of history is the first that seriously undertook to interpret the law-abiding character of the history of man. Social materialism attempts to explain the orderly development of human society on the basis of economic phenomena, yet does so inadequately because it fails to explain what "the economic relations really are."

Law, society, and economics. Rejecting Spencer's analogy of sociology to the natural sciences, Stammler holds that the social life of man is far more than a mere physical gregariousness. The significant difference between the two is the regulation of intercourse and communal life, which is of human (artificial) origin. Social life is thus an externally regulated living together

[1] "Wirthschaft und Recht," pp. 22, 7 seq., 8–11, 13, 15, 14, 17, 22–80, 78 seq., 245–263. The materialistic conception of history likewise stands without proof (pp. 624–633).

of men.[1] An external regulation of human intercourse is one which in spirit is quite independent of any individual motive to conform to it. In this, social regulation differs from ethical regulation.

Of the several meanings attached to the word *social*, two must at once be considered; first, *social* as applied to what is regulated from without, in contrast to human action considered as that of an isolated individual; and second, as regulated from without but conformably to human nature, "thus contrasting to an unnatural standardization of communal life." Two classes of social laws may be distinguished,— legal enactments, and the norms of propriety — custom, fashion, usage, — which Stammler includes under convention.[2] The distinction between these two classes of norms does not consist in the fact that the State makes the laws, and that social intercourse gives rise to conventions; the real distinction lies in "the spirit of the requirement in which the regulation concerned was formed." The law claims obedience as by compulsion; convention claims obedience by an appeal to the consent of those conforming to it.[3] Law and convention together constitute the form or external phases of social life.

The expression of social life is co-operation directed to the satisfaction of needs; such co-operation Stammler

[1] "Wirthschaft und Recht," pp. 83–88, 89 seq., 93 seq., 97 seq., 100, 101 seq., 104, 108, 111, 257, 259–263; p. 108: "Social life is a living together of men regulated by externally uniting norms." p. 257: "There is no other form of social association than that established by human rules."

[2] "Wirthschaft und Recht," pp. 105, 105 seq., 115–124, 122, 125 seq.

[3] The distinction is not an historical, but a logical one. In a formal sense law aims to prevail as a coercive measure, while conventional prescription has but an hypothetical validity. ("Wirthschaft und Recht," pp. 125–135, especially pp. 129, 132.)

calls social economics, and urges that it should be more fully conscious of its obligation to supply a scientific interpretation of the social life of man.[1] "A rule without application is vain; the conception of a social economics without consideration of the definite ordering of communal life is futile." Yet a theoretical consideration of formal principles is legitimate if held within bounds. The doctrine of natural law followed a false clue, for there is no such law that can be established *a priori* in terms of its positive content. Only such statutes may be considered to be natural laws as embody a theoretically just law under empirically conditioned circumstances, — "a natural law with variable content."[2] On the other hand the material of social life does not afford an underlying principle unless it is conceived in its general aspects. Social-economic study must proceed on the basis of definite external regulations. There are no self-sufficient principles of social economics.

The relation of law and social economics is by no means adequately characterized by the statement that the former exercises an influence upon the latter. Legal regulation and social economics are not related as cause and effect; "for this would imply that law and economics are independent and contrasted, which is not the case; socially considered they are two inherently related expressions of one and the same phenomenon." Law is not self-sufficient; every legal regulation implies the application to underlying social operations. "Laws represent the formal side of the one comprehensive object of social science, namely, social life." "From

[1] "Wirthschaft und Recht," pp. 136-162, especially pp. 137, 152 seq., 157, 158.
[2] "Wirthschaft und Recht," pp. 165, 165-188, especially pp. 184, 185.

the point of view of social science, there is always presented a definitely regulated co-operation directed to the satisfaction of human needs. Accordingly, social economics is not the effect of law as a cause; but objectively there is presented the one object of social consideration, namely, a definite situation of a social-economic type."[1] What we call an economic phenomenon is merely "a homogeneous composite of legal relations."

The philosophical issues: causality or teleology. Stammler's philosophical position is based upon a monistic conception. "Monism, as applied to social phenomena, seeks a unitary basis of causal relations in the solidarity of social life. The monistic view holds that the legal order and social economy are but form and content of one and the same phenomenon; and that all social movements, including the directive causes of changes in the law as they arise and become effective, are comprised in the one and the same orderly principle. Monism explains all social changes as "movements of the content of the social life." The interpretation of the social life requires the determination of a regulating principle; there are two available ones, — the principle of causality and that of purpose. "It is unfortunate that modern usage makes conformity to law and causality the same." One's own action or that of another may be considered "either as causally produced from without or as due to the agent." The latter case implies a purpose: "Purpose is an object to be effected; the conception of an object as something to be effected brings it within the sphere of the will." Will is not a force, but a direction of consciousness. It is not correct to speak (as does Ihering) of a psychological law of causality; for the

[1] "Wirthschaft und Recht," pp. 188–219, 220–228, 229–244, 229, 230, 231. See also the article "Recht" in "Handwörterbuch," Vol. VI, pp. 333–337.

law of purpose is not causal but teleological. Teleology is conformity to law in terms of desire. "A will which is exercised in the direction of an ideal, and accepts the universally valid point of view of purpose, is a good will; and its law of action (as Hermann Cohen aptly remarks), may be summarized in the precept: 'Let your actions be free.'"

Only such purpose is justified as makes for the unconditioned final goal of human endeavor; but there arises the difficulty of the application of purpose to human endeavor and activity, as concretely exemplified. Teleology seems to fail through "the irrevocableness of the law of causality." But this contradiction is apparent only, and is due to the false conception of free will. The freedom of the will must be understood in Kant's sense; it does not imply an exemption from the law of causality, but only the independence of the will from "the subjective content of the end to be attained. It is the regulation of desire; it is the thought of an unconditioned goal as the standard for the determination of purposes; it is the idea of an absolute final purpose which imparts to every individually sought end a unity and universality. It thus justifies the concretely chosen end: 'Think as though you were to act; this is the practical precept which the idea of freedom inculcates.'" But the conception of the good is derived from human experience; and there emerges an objective criterion of endeavor and conduct by the standard of an universal law of approved desire.

Social materialism, if it carried out its position consistently, would result in a teleological principle, which, in turn, convincingly refutes materialism. For materialism finds its only philosophical support in the mistaken supposition that there is no order in the social life except the irrevocable dominance of the law of cause and effect.

The fundamental orderliness of the social life refers only to the form or regulation thereof. The principle of such social order is a supreme unity of purpose, embracing all individual ends of the social order. Hence the law of such order can be found only in purpose. The point is to determine the supreme object of social life, to determine the answer to the problem: To what universal ends do men use the instrument of the social order? The principle of the social order must be one that considers the interests and purposes of those affected by social ties, and must be expressed with reference to those coming under its influence. We thus return to the two types of social regulation: to law, which exercises a coercion upon the individual, and to convention, which rests upon the consent of those conforming to it. By its nature, law attributes to itself the quality of compulsion; in the light of history this claim is properly made. Law, therefore, cannot be derived from the will of those subject to it. The question arises: How is the coercive character of law to be justified? Coercive dispositions, promulgated as law between man and man, may be justifiable, and thus become "legal measures of force"; or lack justification, and become "arbitrary measures." What is the basis of the distinction?

Stammler does not propose to answer this question *a priori*. His aim is to determine, from experience, in what connection the conception of law arises, and what are its essential criteria as differentiated from arbitrariness. The answer cannot be in terms of any particular content of social regulation, but must be in terms of the formal definition of law. He finds "the desired criterion in the determination of whether or not the commands have a mere personal bearing, and serve merely to express a personal caprice." The opposite of arbitrariness results "when the promulgator of the command is also bound by it. Both [ruler and subjects] must be bound by the same command; if such is not the case then there is sheer arbitrariness. There is no inviolable command, and thus no true law." If the spirit of the proposed norms implies that they are not binding upon those invested with the authority of establishing them, then such law is arbitrary; but if their spirit is such that until these proposed regulations are abrogated, no action in opposition thereto is permissible, then such law is just. Law raises the presumption of inviolability, therefore law is "in spirit, the inviolable coercive regulating of the communal life." [1]

The justification of legal coercion. Thus law is formally distinguished from arbitrary power as embodied in the form of laws; but the questions still remain: Why is this intermediary between free convention and arbitrary force necessary? Why should there be legal enforcement? The reply must consider mainly the underlying principle in law and not its incorporation in any set legislation; the problem must be considered as that of justifying legal coercion, of justifying the existence of law in general, and not of specific legislation, of justifying precisely what the anarchists regard as unjustifiable.

Such coercion cannot be based upon contract or the consent of those affected by it; for history shows that law demands the obedience of its subjects, without reference to their consent or to consideration of their wishes or desires. To put it briefly, the issue is "the

[1] "Wirthschaft und Recht," pp. 263–284, 264, 284–304, 305–345, 315, 324 seq., 349–356, 349, 351 seq., 354, 357–380, 369, 380–394, 381, 392, 395–448, 449–484, 485–523, 487 seq., 491, 496, 497 seq. See also article "Recht" in "Handwörterbuch der Staatswissenschaften," Vol. VI, pp. 327 seq.

right of law to exist,"[1] its justification. Convention likewise regulates social relations but does not require such justification. Its validity is conditioned by the will of those submitting to it. It says: Do thus and so if you please; but the law demands unconditional obedience.

The necessity of legal coercion must be proven. But necessity may be understood in two senses: the causal, or the teleological. The discussion of the question is readily affected by the philosophical error of conceiving necessity in the sense of causal necessity. In judging the attempts to establish a philosophical basis for legal coercion, one must distinguish between such as aim to prove it to be a causal consequence, and those that present it "as the indispensable means to a necessary end." The latter attempt a teleological justification of legal coercion, regarding the law either as a means to the maintenance of the human race or as a means to the interests of morality. The former justifications, which Stammler also called the dynamic, are variously expressed. Some justify legal coercion "by a recourse to a psychological cause, to the necessity of obeying certain commands." Such a social impulse — as suggested by the "ζῶον πολιτικόν" of Aristotle, or the "appetitus socialis" of Grotius — would explain merely the fact of socialization but not the coercive authority of the law in contrast to convention. Other dynamic theories urge that those who issue social regulations are impelled by natural causes, by irresistible influences, to invest their dispositions with the quality of legal commands. The evidence for such a view would not bear upon the principle of coercion, upon the coercive power as such, but only upon a given concrete law of one kind

[1] "Das Recht des Rechtes" is the last (the fifth) book of the work, (pp. 585 seq.)

or another. Finally, one may have recourse to the empirical fact that legal enforcement is as old as any record of human culture. But this fact does not provide a scientific foundation of legal coercion; and the question of justification of such coercion in the future— which is what the anarchists deny—remains unsolved.[1]

The teleological arguments are likewise various. Hobbes justifies coercion on the ground that without it there would be the danger of war of all against all. This is hardly in point; for the question at issue is not the justification of social regulation in general, but of the special quality of legal coercion as part of social regulation. The second type of teleological argument makes the law the necessary condition of morality; here again the legal order is incorrectly regarded as equivalent to the social order in general.

Convention makes its appeal to the individual. Those who conform to it, do so of their own accord. If social life were organized exclusively upon the basis of convention, it would affect only "certain men with certain qualifications." Hence convention does not account for the entire range of social life. "Convention alone cannot produce an orderly social life or even approximate it." Legal coercion alone has within it the capacity to regulate all phases of social life; and therein lies its justification — "as a necessary means to the establishment of the principle of order in the social life of man." [2]

---

[1] "Wirthschaft und Recht," pp. 524–533, 533–541, 541–547. See also article "Recht" in "Handwörterbuch," Vol. VI, pp. 330–333 (on p. 333: "Kritische," foundation of the coercive power of the law).

[2] "Wirthschaft und Recht," pp. 547–551, 551–571, 553, 554, 557. See also *Stammler*, "Die Theorie des Anarchismus," p. 43: "I base the legality of law in its formal phase upon the consideration that

Thus is legal coercion established; but this applies only to the justification of law in general. It determines nothing as to the content which the law is to express. Inasmuch as the spirit of the legal order consists in the attainment of a certain form of co-operation and mutual intercourse of men, the justification of its positive legal construction will be determined by "its success in finding in its material embodiment the right means to the right end of the social life of man." Such an objective end of social life must be a universal one. The requirement of universal validity as the absolute end cannot be met by any particular and more limited purpose. The ultimate goal of social existence turns upon "a formal idea which in unrestricted unity of purpose directs all subsidiary purposes; and from it alone every empirical variety of social purpose must derive its warrant."[1] Good will is the unconditional law of human intercourse applied to the social life; it results in "a community of free agents, and such community is the unconditional final purpose of social life." Legal enactments imposed from without must concur with the autonomous law governing the desires of the subjects as expressed from within — a conclusion that reflects the social philosophy of Rousseau,[2] Kant,

the legal organization is the only one open to all men without distinction of peculiar and accidental qualities.

"Organization means to unite under regulation. Such regulation of human intercourse is a means to an end, an instrument in the service of the pursuit of the ultimate purpose, the maximum perfection of man. Accordingly, only such regulation of human collective life can lay claim to a universal recognition which embraces comprehensively all men without regard to their subjective and individual peculiarities, and that alone is represented by the law. Yet in a bad law the legal coercion, considered in itself, appears to be well justified."

[1] "Wirthschaft und Recht," pp. 572 seq., 575.

[2] For this and the "inconsequence" of Rousseau see *Stammler*, "Wirthschaft und Recht," pp. 605 seq. See also above, §§ 29, 33

and Fichte. "The community of free agents, in the sense ascribed to the phrase, is admittedly merely an ideal, yet it forms the guide to experience." It is the regulative principle for the objective justification of social coercion.

Stammler is an opponent of social hedonism. He reaches a general interpretation of social ideals [1] by a different route. The thesis maintained is expressed in the statement that "the social ideal is a unitary formal idea which is to serve as the standard and guide for all empirical efforts in social life, by conformity to which any concrete desire, involving the retention or alteration of any legal enactment, is to be legitimately and objectively justified; but which itself never enters, and never can enter, as an empirical datum of social life as experienced."

Regulative principles: justice and morality. The next question concerns "the practical application of social ideals to existing society." In every social-economic order there are attempts to re-enforce or modify the existing situation. In judging such efforts, "a clear distinction must be drawn between the material phases of social purposes and the formal principle directing them." Three questions arise: What is the origin of social effort? When is it objectively justified? and, In what measures are the right means for the improvement of social conditions to be found? Social struggle and endeavor appear in connection with situations which develop under uniform conditions and affect collective interests. Such social efforts are justified as accord with the spirit of the social ideal, which is the spirit of a community of free agents. The right means

---

[1] "Wirthschaft und Recht," pp. 576, 584–588, 576–584, 588–613. See also article "Recht" in "Handwörterbuch," Vol. VI, pp. 340 seq.

for the improvement of social conditions "require such regulation of the social life as would bring the situations in which men live in accord with the ideal of a community of free agents."

The socialists of the type of Marx regard the communal distribution of the means of subsistence as a social necessity; but whether they mean a causal or a teleological necessity is not indicated. If it be causal it will in due course make its appearance; if it be teleological, then, according to the above principles, it is warranted only if it proves to be the right means, under actual existing conditions, to serve the social ideals of a community of free agents. A convincing proof that communism meets this requirement is as yet lacking.

Stammler emphasizes the comprehensiveness of the social ideal which his philosophy advocates. Social philosophy must "establish a fundamental regulative social principle in accordance with which minor concrete principles may be determined and applied." The social problem can never be solved, "for that would imply a realization of the social ideal." By its nature this ideal can never be absolutely attained but only approximately realized. The social philosopher will have solved his problem when he shall have furnished a social ideal which will guide the statesman in his political course.[1]

The problem of the philosophy of "natural law" was to establish a natural law, that is, an absolute just model law, *the* law *par excellence*. But the evidence of history makes against any such assumption. Stammler reinstated this fundamental problem of natural law, while yet avoiding the error of the older position. Stammler's problem in "Die Lehre von dem Richtigen Rechte" is not the determination of an absolute law,

[1] "Wirthschaft und Recht," pp. 588 seq., 613, 613-624, 614, 615, 616, 617, 624-633, 629, 634-640.

but of the absolute idea of law. After specifically noting that he is not an adherent of "natural law," he explains that his purpose "is not to supply an ideal code, but to consider the law as it has historically developed; not to determine the origin of law as though this could be evolved out of one's inner consciousness, but to subject every law within the range of experience to the test of investigation. The question of the specific mode of origin of law is not pertinent." Stammler's study of the justice inherent in law becomes a mode of procedure which, by "maintaining a self-consistency," prepares the way for the determination of the nature of a just law; the justness is that quality of a law, "which in a particular relation accords with the fundamental idea of law in general." The science that attempts such formulation is a formal one; that is, "it is a study, the results of which set the conditions for other knowledge."

What is the relation of constituted positive law to the "just law"? Positive law ever intends to be just or right but is not always so. In its tendency positive law "is a coercive effort towards justice." But there are unjust laws; there are even "consciously recognized unjust laws," that is, legal tolerance of relations or affairs that stand in contradiction to the idea of justice.[1]

In legal transactions and decisions there occur a series of expressions defining the just law, specifying the nature of the quality of justice. Among the Romans there are the terms "bonum et æquum," "bona fides," "æquitas," "jus naturale" or "naturalis ratio," "boni mores" or "mos," "benevolentia," "humanitas," "pudor," "pietas" or "officium pietatis," "justa causa," "arbitrium boni viri," "justitia." In the legal language

[1] [See below.]

of today, we have such terms as "good faith" in the performance of financial obligations, avoidance of "abuse of power" (in the family law of the BGB), "cogent ground" for the dissolution of a legal relation, "intelligent appreciation of the facts of the case" in the avoidance of declarations of intention, while the designation "good faith" expresses a legitimate alteration of an obligation which, as it is, is a binding obligation; the term "equity or fair appraisal" is applied when the point at issue is to find the limits of a given cause which can only be determined by equity.[1]

The content of just law cannot be derived from ethics. Moral teachings are directed to improve the disposition; the legal order is directed to the regulation of conduct. Yet this contrast is not decisive. It may be said that in regard to their material, the justice of law and morality bear upon the same domain; yet their problems and methods are different. This difference, however, is not an absolute one, for law, as well as morality, "is directed to what is right, and to influencing human desire, and thus must be subject to the same regulative principle." The moral law is based upon that conception of humanity whereby man is to be regarded as a rational being, as ever his own final purpose. The term moral has four meanings: first, as equivalent to all *right desires* of man in general, whether based on inclination or conduct, and in this sense the social question may be termed a moral one; secondly, as equivalent to moral in the sense of pure inclination, the "ethos"; thirdly, as equivalent to the *norm of conduct* thus objectified, representing the rule of justice — such a rule, for example, as that gifts expressing a recognition of a moral duty may not be recalled; fourthly, as equivalent to the right conduct

[1] "Die Lehre von dem Richtigen Rechte," pp. 38–44, especially pp. 40 seq.

in matters of sex; in this sense the term "offense against morality" is used. That the formulation of the just principle of law has its own problems is made clear by the fact that agitation for the correct regulation of social life is always necessary, however much the moral condition of men may improve. Moral relations cannot be maintained wholly by mutually accepted regulations among men. Political questions as such do not belong directly to the moral law but to the law of justice. The moral law has likewise its own problems, which are directed to the inner life. The idea of perfection in Christian ethics refers to the mental attitude.[1] But the distinction between the law of justice and morality is only one of direction of approach; their purposes must converge. The law of justice must be supplemented by the law of morality; and the law of morality, in order to be realized, requires the law of justice. "Justice without love is vain, and pity without just rule lacks discernment."[2]

Stammler proceeds to a critical examination of "natural law," the existence of which he denies.[3] Rousseau first made clear the detachment of natural law from human nature. There are no innate human rights; there is, however, a "limit to the power of tyranny, to the exercise of control by a legal sovereign." Yet this cannot be deduced from human nature, "but only from the idea of a justly ordered life. What may be established is not natural law, but only principles involved in the

[1] "Die Lehre von dem Richtigen Rechte," pp. 12, 93–121, 13–15, 8, 19–168, 21–27, 27–32, 268–270. Article "Recht" in "Handwörterbuch," Vol. VI, pp. 337 seq. See also *Berolzheimer*, "Die Entgeltung im Strafrechte," p. 165, note 2.

[2] "Die Lehre von dem Richtigen Rechte," pp. 51, 52–57, 60, 63 seq., 70–75, 72, 73, 74, 76–83, 80 seq., 84–92, 85, 87, 90.

[3] § 3, "Richtiges Recht und Naturrecht," pp. 93–121.

nature of law."[1] The object is to find a generally valid formal method by means of which the underlying content of law, though subject to a constant change, may be tested by the criterion of material justice. Mercy should be exercised only upon the basis of an inner justification and in the interests of material justice, or by reason of uncertainty, or to rectify the positive law, or in consideration of the consequences of applying the law. Mercy then becomes "the exercise of the law of justice without coercion, merely upon the basis of moral duty." But to thus exercise mercy presupposes the law of justice and the power of the moral will adequate to carry out what is recognized to be just. So the first requirement is to determine how the law of justice shall proceed. It must not be the expression of a natural sense of legal justice based on judicial decision; nor the legal consciousness of the folk-spirit; nor of popular sentiment, which may be right in intent but uncritical in its application; nor of the morality of special classes; nor of the personal judgment of the judge. Every legal regulation relates necessarily to an end to be effected, to a purpose; and the problem becomes that of finding the regulative principle of purpose: "to establish a generally valid method that enables one to divide the content of contemplated purposes into two classes, those of just and of unjust content." The principle to be applied to the purposes that determine conduct is not that of freedom and equality; for equality before the law implies merely

---

[1] "Die Lehre von dem Richtigen Rechte," pp. 93-98, 97 seq. Natural law incorrectly opposes positive law by the assumption of an *a priori* natural law. But all law arises from experience. The difference is based merely upon the mode of considering law; law is considered either as granted or is made part of a teleological series. (pp. 99-103, 117.)

the like treatment of one and all; nor is this principle that of welfare and happiness; but the true principle of the law of justice is the social ideal of the community of free agents. "The content of a norm of conduct is just when it conforms in a particular situation to the social ideal attitude."

Stammler attempts to determine the just law by developing the underlying principles. This cannot be done by "casual historical observation," nor empirically; the social ideal determines it and demands that the individual shall not be coerced in his legal relations to forego his recognized interests, and yet that each individual give evidence of his sense of community with his fellows. "While the one demand is directed to the consideration of the individual in his own right action, the other leads to the consideration of the social community and to participation in its affairs. Every one is called upon to bear his own burden; yet this does not contradict the injunction, that he shall bear the burden of another." From this there follow four principles of the law of justice. The two principles of respect are: "One's wishes must not arbitrarily interfere with the will of another," and, "Every legal demand can exist only in so far as he who is obliged remains one's equal." The two principles of participation are: "No one under legal obligation shall be arbitrarily excluded from common advantages," and "every legally assigned power is exclusive only in so far as the one excluded may still remain one's equal." These principles do not imply that by their means legal rules may be directly established; they merely set limitations. The historical development of law should fall within the limits set by these principles. In so far as it does so, it makes for a just law. So the material of justice is the law as history reveals it, the positive law in its transformations; but the form is the unity of the permanent element. The form conditions the content in the logical, not in the causal sense.

The extent to which the relations of life may be regulated through usage and custom, and not through legal force, is determined by the legal order itself. Regulation through mere custom or usage is legitimate so long as the conventional regulation of certain relations accords with the principles of the law of justice. The teachings of the theory of justice do not coincide with the social-ethical tendency in economics; for the latter affects directly the material of the social life, while the former bears upon the content of justice, and affects economics only through it.[1]

Applications: the mission of the law. Stammler next considers the means of establishing the law of justice. The two possible extremes would be either that the legislator shall himself determine the regulation, or that the legislator leave it to the individual "voluntarily to make his contributions to the maintenance and development of the social life." The extent to which the central regulation shall control, and how far the members of the community may set their own rules, cannot be laid down in general principles. Limitations can be set only in concrete cases, but ever with reference to the desired end of establishing a just law.[2]

[1] Pp. 116–121, 122–137, 137–141, 142–145, 146–168, 171–187, 187–191, 191–195, 196–200, 201–204, 204–208, 208–210, 211–213, 213–215, 216–234, 234–239, 239–244, 245–275.

[2] Pp. 245–252. Stammler places as the heading of this section "Einheitswirtschaft und Freie Beiträge" ("Individual Economy and Free Contributions"). I do not find this simile well chosen nor pertinent to the content. It reflects Stammler's deductive mode of treatment. The history of man is a continuous process of emancipation. The stage of civilization attained at any given moment furnishes the basis for the sphere of free action of the individual as

Just law is a law that tends to "determine in advance a justice that is generally applicable to future disputes," while merciful law leaves it "to the parties — the counsellor, the judge," to determine the proper solution in the individual case.[1] A further contrast is that of actual and formal law. The latter is established law, which, in order to strengthen the legal security, may depart in its application from the principles of justice. Such are the provisions relating to the public credit attaching to the land registry book; the statute of limitations; the rules of civil procedure.[2] Consciously unjust law Stammler calls the toleration by the law of unjustifiable conditions and actions. Analogy to supply omissions in the law has only a subsidiary place.[3]

While the principles of justice should lead deductively to its determination, "it is the problem of the ideal of the law of justice to make concessions" to the "status quo" by the consideration of "legal conditions set by the situation." The ideal of the law of justice must, how-

against the community. The important point is not how much the central authority and how much the individual contributes to social regulation, but how heavily the central authority bears upon the individual, or how much free play it leaves for the expression of individuality.

[1] Pp. 252-261. Stammler refers to the model set by Aristotle: "δικαιοσύνη-ἐπιείκεια". The German translation into "gelind" (lenient) is taken from Luther.

[2] Pp. 262-268. This point of Stammler's is to be commended. The conflict with the conception of law which may arise from the formal nature of law was formerly not sufficiently considered and elucidated by legal philosophy. See *Berolzheimer*, "Die Entgeltung im Strafrechte," pp. 189-191, 270-327. The formal prescription, and the proof, as well as the burden of proof or presumption, give rise to positive law which in an individual case may seem unjust.

[3] "Die Lehre von dem Richtigen Rechte," pp. 268-271. See also *Berolzheimer*, "Die Entgeltung im Strafrechte," pp. 165, 168, 495.

ever, not be itself empirically conditioned, but must be of general validity. It must accordingly effect "a correlation of the empirical material which shall be independent of the details thereof." Consequently "the ideal of justice" in its "formula and function" must be derived from the idea of just law.

"The model considered by the law of justice is that of a select community — the principle of selection itself determined by the just law"; such community is naturally not a reality but merely an aid to constructive thought.[1] One must put the hypothetical question: With whom shall I in thought ally myself in a select community? or, Whom shall I consider to be my neighbor? The reply varies and includes in one relation narrower, and in another, wider groups of persons of affiliated interests.

Under the phrase "Types of Performance," Stammler sets forth that the idea of a select community involves that every participant may demand of every other, consideration and participation. The principles of consideration and participation are thus maintained in the legal relations of a number of persons bound together by a common legal tie, and likewise in the relation of such persons to third persons. In its legal aspect the value of performance rendered must be determined; its value must be objectively stated. The formula proposed by Marx will not hold; for value "sets an independent standard apart from legal control." Value can be rightly determined only in accord with the principles of justice, as based on objective facts. When thus considered the law of justice will be available for practice.

[1] "Die Lehre von dem Richtigen Rechte," pp. 271-275, 276-280, 281-284, 285-291, 292-298, 311-598. Stammler's comments upon usury should be noted.

The part of Stammler's work that considers the practice of the principles of justice makes a first attempt to indicate how it may be applied. The subject is divided as follows: (1) The just administration of legal relations, including performance in good faith, the avoidance of abuse of family rights, performance under the formula "if it can be done," performance according to an equitable standard. (2) The limits of the freedom of contract. The theory of justice prescribes the chief limitations. (3) The duties of justice, that is, the legal duties obligatory upon the parties concerned, arising directly from the idea of the just law;[1] thus, performances in compliance with moral duty or the rules of social propriety, equitable compensation, intentional injuries contrary to good morals, acceptance of performances offensive to good morals. (4) The establishment of a just content of acts in the law. Under this head are considered the real will of the parties, a reasonable understanding of the facts, interpretation according to good faith supplementing incomplete contracts. (5) The termination of legal relations. Legal relations that are permanent, like marriage, or entered into for long periods, may under certain conditions be dissolved. The principles of the law of justice furnish directions for the legitimate circumstances.

The conclusion of the book is devoted to the mission of the theory of justice. The principles of justice are necessary "for uniformity in every social consideration." It is only through the principles of justice that sociology attains uniformity.[2] It alone makes possible an insight into the regulative principle of social history, which is

---

[1] "The question is . . . to what actions and restraint men are in justice bound without the necessity of a legal enactment forcibly demanding such compliance" (p. 247).

[2] Pp. 447–496, 497–553, 554–598, 601–627.

not causal, but teleological. The purpose of evolution is set by the conception of the community as a real and just co-operation, and can be realized only through the standards of justice.[1] This law forms the fundamental determining condition for social economics, and forms "one of the necessary stages" to a true philosophy.[2]

A critical view. Stammler's importance as a legal philosopher is not adequately recognized. Most writers decline to accept his theory of legal coercion or dispose of it with brief criticism. But such an attitude overlooks the importance of the correct statement of a problem, in which consists Stammler's special claim to consideration. He is the first since Rousseau seriously to consider the problem of the coercive power of the law. He may have been led to this by the position of anarchism, which denies the justification of coercion altogether, as well as by his radical modification of the material conception of history. Yet this is not important; every student is influenced by others, and frequently by those of opposite opinion. Stammler has clearly conceived and formulated the specific problems of the law. Even such luminaries as Aristotle and Grotius have so considered the problems of government and law that their solutions merely account for — and this imperfectly — the socialization of man, and do not analyze the nature of the legal association which the law establishes. Rousseau as well as Kant and Fichte considered the nature of law and government, but not from the inherently legal aspect of the problem, but from that of its counterpart, freedom. Their problem was not, How is legal coercion to be accounted for? but, What elements

---

[1] "Die Gesellschaftliche Entwickelungslehre." ("Die Lehre von dem Richtigen Rechte," pp. 607-620.)

[2] "Orthosophie." ("Die Lehre von dem richtigen Rechte," pp. 621-627, 626.)

of freedom must be conserved by the law in order that the law shall be justified? Stammler, with a subtle logic, analyzes the nature of legal coercion in itself, and independently of any particular form or content of the law. His solution is as follows: The coercive power of the law is justified by its necessity to the social life. The answer is in part inadequate and in part false; inadequate in that it is not unconditionally necessary that all humanity shall be socially united; and false, or rather no solution at all, in that the attempt to dispense with legal coercion is conceivable. Apart from his results, Stammler's method is open to criticism, for teleology involves a subjective or anthropocentric factor. Teleology recognizes law only in its subjective aspect, its value for humanity. But the true question relates to the objective nature of law, irrespective of the opinion of society. To my mind Stammler's deductive procedure unfavorably affects the value of his conclusions; nonetheless I regard them as not far removed from the correct result. Legal coercion is in fact a necessity, though a relative and not an absolute one. Like custom and morality it is a cultural necessity, because it artificially restores and increases that power which humanity has sacrificed in culture and through culture, that is, the natural exercise of impulses, lost or enfeebled in the course of civilization.

Stammler's conception of the relation between law and economics, though open to objection, is helpful. What he calls social life or social economics is substantially economics as the material content of law; but inasmuch as Stammler regards all social life as regulated by the law or by the conventional rules of custom, he fails to consider — which Jellinek and Gothein especially object to — the true social expressions, the spontaneous expressions of the members of the community, which are not determined by hard and fast conventional rules.

Stammler's studies are notable in the philosophy of law by reason of his restatement of the fundamental problem raised by "natural law," the problem of determining the principle of justice, the criterion of the legal ideal. His contributions enrich important problems in the general theory of law and economics. He reinstates the conceptions of the older philosophy of law and of historic legislations; he frequently refers in his applications of the principles of justice to what the Romans called "æquitas" or "naturalis ratio," and what the modern legislation of the German code terms equity or equitable standards, performance in good faith, etc., or to express it in a single phrase, the idea of a balanced, concordant law.

2: NEO-HEGELIANISM. J. KOHLER (b. 1849) is a neo-Hegelian, holding with Hegel that law is to be considered as a cultural phenomenon; but while Hegel regards a philosophy of law as the product of deduction, Kohler proceeds empirically, leaning upon history and ethnology; and this is a great step in advance. Kohler rejects the principle of hedonism. The sentiment with which he begins his work, "Recht, Glaube, und Sitte," reads: "The world does not exist for our pleasure."[1] The culture of a people determines the development and form of its laws. "The law of a people can be interpreted only in the light of its entire culture; which, in turn, is to be interpreted, as extending beyond the material economic factors, to include the ethical and religious views which the law reflects. Laws are not shaped consciously or unconsciously by considerations

[1] Grünh., Z., Vol. XIX, p. 561; also pp. 561–565, 609, 612, on which will be found views against utilitarianism and social eudemonism. See also the excellent presentation in the "Enzyklopädie," p. 10.

of utility. The general view of life influences the law, and from such composite cultural forces the law arose. The law establishes the channels through which the stream of culture flows, and the course and nature of the channels take their character from the cultural trends, which in large measure are sustained by the prevalent beliefs in regard to the spiritual life and the divine rule."[1] Kohler compares the religious origins of legal institutions and enactments and thus concludes:[2] "What I wish to set forth is that in the shaping of the law there have been operative very different forces than the pursuit of temporal welfare, very different efforts than those aiming at happiness. The religious attitude is responsible primarily for the majority of legal institutions; the law finds its sanction in the command of a higher realm. The origin of primitive law lies in animistic conceptions; but even after primitive beliefs have declined, and survive only in superstitions, the law retains its religious tenor; even when law is apparently non-religious in that it treats all religious communions upon an equal footing, it becomes not irreligious but

[1] Grünh., Z., Vol. XIX, p. 561. Also *Kohler*, "Zur Ethnologischen Jurisprudenz" ("Z. f. v. Rechtsw.," VI, p. 407): "Law is no dead product of the understanding but a living creation of human civilization which is firmly rooted in the mental soil prepared by religion, custom, and education, by faith, love, and individual efforts." "Rechtsgeschichte und Weltentwickelung" ("Z. f. v. Rechtsw.," V, pp. 328 seq.: "As in every cultural development so also in the development of law, the unconscious plays the largest part; inasmuch as the development does not proceed, or at least not notably, according to the desire and expectation of those participating therein. Evolution has its own organic laws. That there is an unconscious rationality in the history of civilization is the supreme principle supplied by the history of law." See also "Enzyklopädie," p. 6, § 3. "Recht als Kulturerscheinung." Also "Shakespeare vor dem Forum der Jurisprudenz," pp. 84 seq., 239.

[1] "Recht, Glaube und Sitte," p. 610.

religiously neutral as affecting the several religious confessions. The belief, arising from the deep conviction that the destiny of humanity is not determined by the goal of personal happiness, persists in the law. The law remains primarily moral and not merely hedonistic. The law has its ideals, as nations have their ideals; and it is these ideals and not the sense of utility that have brought forth legal institutions."

Kohler's position appears in his conception that "the process of the formation of the law can be understood only as part of the general development of a people. A history of law that disregards the racial element would be like a history of art that neglects the cultural forces from which the art-impulse and its expression were derived." "The philosophy of law must set forth how at every stage of development definite legal institutions have embodied the cultural ideals then maintained." [1]

The State is justified by the indispensable part that it plays in the development of culture; its existence is necessary because only an association of the governmental type can meet the needs of civilization." The Hegelian view makes the State a requirement of the rational nature of man and rejects the limitation of the State to the interests of law.[2] Historically the State appears first as a "Totem-State," the totems or clans growing out of the family, and further associated by

[1] "Recht, Glaube und Sitte," pp. 564, 611. "Enzyklopädie," § 8, pp. 14 seq.; p. 14: "Without a universal history of law there cannot be any adequate philosophy of law, just as without a universal history there can be no philosophy of humanity, and without linguistics, no philosophy of language. See also § 11, pp. 17-20.

[2] "Enzyklopädie," § 40, pp. 55-57. "Einführung in die Rechtswissenschaft," second edition, pp. 109-112. P. 110: "The State is a legal personality existing for the purpose of advancing through their inherent value the chief cultural efforts of men, within certain realms."

intermarriage; and the resulting alliances strengthened by a common headship. Common forays for pillage and booty led to their organization under a chief; and with the support of the priestly class, the chieftainship became a kingship. States based upon community of race were transformed by the addition of foreign elements into a State based upon territorial boundaries.

In the domain of family law, as in law in general, men at first formed a compact communal body; it is only in later stages that the individual emerges to a position of legal and moral self-assertion. In primitive times the family bond was that of religion, the emblem of the common totem being usually that of an animal form, and the totem itself maintained by restrictions of marriage alliances. The restriction of marriage under the totem was based upon a matriarchy, which in turn, as a consequence largely of the capture and sale of wives, gave way to a patriarchy, the process aided by the ruling position of the chief. Marriages restricted to the communal group step by step gave way to the freedom of individual marriage.[1]

Freedom of action may lead to wrongdoing; and wrongdoing to atonement. Punishment is justified as an atonement, which restores the individual who undergoes the punishment, through the atoning and purifying quality of pain, and through him the effect reacts upon humanity. "Humanity, which suffers through misdeed, is saved, and the poison which sin brings to men is counteracted by an antidote."[2] Law as retributive justice — a principle still operative — grows out of blood vengeance, the right of revenge. Punishment is not to be upheld for its effect upon the individual;

[1] "Enzyklopädie," § 38, pp. 51-54; § 39, pp. 54 seq.; §§ 17-23, pp. 27-34.
[2] "Das Wesen der Strafe," pp. 6-19, 9.

punishment must be strictly differentiated from compulsory educational and protective measures.[1]

Men began with a communal law, and the right of the individual was a much later issue; yet social institutions continue to restrain self-assertion and the personal exploitation of others. A return to a communal form of life and a communal economics is out of the question. The principle of individual right is firmly established. "So far as we can foresee, the ultimate goal of human evolution is not personal happiness, but the maximum development of culture, on the one hand towards the conquest of worldly power, and again towards the dominion of the spiritual life. Legal theory as well as legal practice, the philosophy, the history, the doctrine, and the art of law, are similarly indispensable as means to the comprehensive advancement of human destiny. The law partakes of the divine and as such will endure."[2]

Kohler's philosophy and its development upon the legal side is the most important, and perhaps the most valid contribution to legal philosophy since Hegel. His researches, ethnological and legal, may be said to have made possible the reinstatement of the philosophy of law as a worthy philosophical discipline. The modernization of the Hegelian philosophy, the presentation of the law as a cultural expression, is a most valuable and permanent service not as yet sufficiently appreciated. Certain of his critics comment disparagingly on his versatility, forgetting that broadness of view is a com-

[1] "Enzyklopädie," §§ 41–46, pp. 57–63; "Einführung in die Rechtswissenschaft," second edition, pp. 148–152.

[2] "Enzyklopädie," § 51, pp. 68 seq. ("Künftige Bildungen"). Also "Rechtsgeschichte und Weltentwickelung" ("Z. f. v. Rechtsw.," V, pp. 328–330; "Die Rechtsphilosophie des 20. Jahrhunderts" ("Deutsche Juristenzeitung"), 1904, pp. 29 seq.

mon sign of capacity. His position as a student of the historical and technical aspects of law has been more generally recognized then has his merit as a legal philosopher. It may be that the artistic and literary temper of his writings has detracted from the judgment of their scientific value; but the more important criticism relates to his view of legal and economic institutions, as constantly shifting, as lacking all points of arrest, which deprives his philosophy of practical application. We are part of an endless stream of development, involuntary instruments of a rational idea, in which we believe, but which we cannot direct. Instead of encouraging the efforts of the individual and of the community in their guidance of the ship of State towards the realization of a practical justice, instead of supporting a rational direction of the forces of evolution, instead of thus affording an effective objective goal of endeavor, philosophy invites the distracted pursuit of a constantly shifting purpose. If the philosophy of law is to be fruitful it must become a practical discipline, must provide norms of human action. The Hegelian view, as an expression of culture, must be supplemented by considering that the purpose of culture, including the cultural aspects of law and ethics, is to increase human efficiency.

3: HARTMANN. Ed. v. HARTMANN[1] (b. 1842) in his study of the moral consciousness observes the existence of a psuedo-morality which is egoistic, seeking individual happiness; and again, of an altruistic pseudo-morality

[1] The works of Ed. v. Hartmann to be noted are: "Phänomenologie des Sittlichen Bewusstseins. Prolegomena zu Jeder Künftigen Ethik," Berlin 1879. The second edition bears the title, "Das Sittliche Selbstbewusstsein. Eine Entwickelung Seiner Mannigfaltigen Gestalten in Ihrem Innerlichen Zusammenhang mit Besonderer Rücksicht auf Brennende Soziale und Kirchliche Fragen der Gegenwart." Selected works, 2 vols., Leipzig 1886. "Die Sozialen Kernfragen," Leipzig 1894. "Ethische Studien," Leipzig 1898.

represented by moral principles enforced by authority. The former is inconsistent with self-denial which sets the negative lower limit of ethical action; the latter derives its power from the authority of the head of the family, or of the State through its legislation, or of custom as unconscious morality, or of religion as expressive of God's will or that of the Church.

Moral principles can be derived only from the moral consciousness of the individual. "The attempt to bring about an action of subjective ethical value by the imposition of a foreign will is as misdirected as would be the increase of one's own rations for the purpose of adding to another's weight." If there be such a thing as true morality, it must grow out of the moral autonomy on the basis of the voice of conscience; yet conscience "is not a simple and original datum but a very complicated result of all the several impulses, feelings, opinions, prejudices, tastes, reasonings, etc., that participate in the formation of the ethical consciousness."

As motives of morality, or subjective moral principles, must be considered a series of factors which v. Hartmann groups according to their æsthetic, emotional, and rational foundations. Among the emotional motives of moral action are the moral principles of reciprocity and the social impulse. Dissenting from Kant's view, Hartmann regards the sense of duty merely as a tendency, as a decisive inclination, provided that the sense of duty is strong enough to lead to action. Among the rational motives of moral action are the principles of freedom and equality, including moral freedom. Here also belong righteousness and justice and equity. To bring about the general recognition of order, morality must be transformed into positive enactments; and from this necessity arises the legal order. Morality is older than the legal order in which it finds its issue.

It is false to regard the power of coercion as the criterion, differentiating law and morality; the distinction fails in that the enforcement may not always be realized; for crime may go undetected and injury may not have compensation. Coercion is not an essential element of the law. "It is not the physical coercion, but the right to exercise it, that is an integral part of the law, and it is a confusion of the two to accept physical coercion as the essential factor." The legal order reflects the expressions of the moral consciousness, in so far as these have become clearly realized and definite and amenable to formal regulation. Hence "the legal order ever lags a little behind the general level of the moral consciousness."

Law must have the support of might, but must never rest upon it. The position of "natural law" cannot be sustained; but we may accept as established its underlying ideas that the legal structure is not accidental but necessary, proceeding from a natural trend of human nature, and that the legal order requires guidance in its developmental advance.

Schopenhauer's view that wrong is the positive conception, and the conception of right is derived therefrom, will not hold. To the obligation of obedience on the part of the citizen subject to the law, there corresponds that of justice on the part of the judge as guardian of the law. Righteousness and justice are the dominant virtues of men. "Where women have influence, there favoritism obtains." The intervention of reason in supplement of the law constitutes equity. As ends of morality or objective moral principles there have been proposed social hedonism, evolution, "the moral principle of cultural development," and the moral order of the universe. The primitive basis of morality, or the moral principles, appear as the monistic principle which is equivalent to the essential unity of the individuals; as the religious moral principle which is equivalent to the identity with the absolute; as the absolute moral principle which is that of an absolute teleology or self-sufficiency; and as the moral principle of salvation which is the negative absolute hedonistic principle.

The moral consciousness finds its satisfaction in the absolute moral principle, according to which all moral ideas appear as strict logical consequences. The absolute moral principle is all-embracing. "It appears on the one hand as the real principle and basis of development of the subjective and objective moral order, as also of the moral instincts, ideas, and institutions; and on the other hand it is the conception of this real principle as the rational basis of all relative moral principles and of all moral problems." Through the absolute moral principle the identity of the individual with absolute being is secured. Yet the conviction is lacking that the absolute process is teleological. If the individual, on the basis of his identity with the absolute, accepts the absolute teleology, he does so in the expectation that the moral services of the individual will accrue to the benefit of the absolute. But this is the case only when the relative purpose furthered by the individual is a means to the absolute end, and when the absolute end also accrues to the benefit of the absolute. The first of these conditions is fulfilled "when the absolute becomes strictly logical and self-determining"; the second only when "the absolute purpose of the supreme unity is absolute and hedonistic, that is, when the super-moral end which all moral means serve, is the happiness of the absolute." The negative absolute hedonistic principle,[1] considered

[1] On the relation of Hartmann's ethics to eudemonism see *Hartmann*, "Ethische Studien," pp. 160-227.

as the absolute, is as follows: "The salvation of the absolute from its transcendental misery ('Unseligkeit') through the immanent toil of the world-process. It may be more briefly termed the moral principle of salvation, obviously only in the absolute sense."

This view combines the positions of Schopenhauer and Hegel. The individual as a corporeal being finds the salvation of which he is capable, spontaneously, in the course of nature, through death after the surcease of vital processes; the world finds its salvation "only through consummation of the world-process, that is, through the salvation of the absolute by means of the fulfillment of the world-purpose. Only through the construction of a moral world-order on the part of reasoning self-conscious individuals can the world-process be directed towards its goal; and only through an ultimate consciousness of the negative absolute hedonistic meaning of this purpose can the end itself be attained. Real being is the incarnation of divinity. The world-process is the history of the passion of the incarnated God and at the same time the path to the salvation of Him crucified in the flesh. But morality is co-operation in the reduction of this path of sorrow and salvation."[1]

§ 49. *Psychological Aspects of Law.* 1: THE PSYCHOLOGICAL BASIS. WILHELM WUNDT[2] (b. 1832) may

[1] The sources of these principles will readily be traced in the successive chapters of the "Phänomenologie des Sittlichen Bewusstseins."

[2] The works of Wundt to be noted in this connection are: "Logik," second edition, 2 vols., 2 parts, Stuttgart 1895, pp. 477–499, 533–588. "Ethik, Eine Untersuchung der Tatsachen und Gesetze des Sittlichen Lebens," 2 vols., third edition, Stuttgart 1903. "Völkerpsychologie, Eine Untersuchung der Entwickelungsgesetze von Sprache, Mythus und Sitte," Vol. I, "Die Sprache," Parts I and II, Leipzig 1900. (See *Berolzheimer*, "System," Vol. I, p. 118, note 23, and pp. 117 seq., for bibliography.)

be regarded as the most influential philosopher of the day. The experimental psychology which he emphasized forms the most important division of philosophy considered as a science of investigation and not merely of description. This dominant psychological trend may be called neo-Socratic in that it aims to establish philosophical truths by a study of the content of the human mind.

The origin of law is according to Wundt an issue of the psychology of races.[1] "Like language, myth and custom, law is not the issue of an arbitrary consensus, but is a natural product of consciousness firmly rooted in the emotions and desires arising from the communal life of man."[2] Wundt proposes as the formal definition of law "the aggregate of privileges and duties which the superior will of a community acknowledges as incumbent upon the individual members of such community and upon itself." There is no natural law, and law is ever a concrete positive law.[3] From the mode of the origin of law Wundt, in his "Logik," concludes that the law is not necessarily attached to the State. Law may rise in communities and in societies, indeed in every form of association[4] "that is capable of developing a communal will through a sufficient consensus of conceptions, efforts and interests." Law has external and internal characteristics; the former appear as expressions of the will, the latter relate to "the conform-

---

[1] *Wundt,* "Logik," second edition, Vol. II, Part II, pp. 533–542, 533, 543, 542–561.

[2] This was also the position of the historical school, though only as bearing upon communal interests. See above, § 34.

[3] "Logik," p. 542: "There is accordingly as little an abstract law as there is a universal speech or a universal custom."

[4] "Logik," II, 2, pp. 543, 545–559, 546, 553.

ability of the order instituted by the will as expressed in law, and the justice thereof."[1]

Wundt proceeds to construct an ethical system upon a psychological basis, by reference to the data of the moral consciousness and to historical consideration and criticism of moral philosophies.[2] His procedure is inductive but is not confined to a merely empirical study. Experience shows that moral conceptions vary widely and thus cannot be determined *a priori*. Yet moral development does not depend upon mere chance; it reveals an ethical aspiration, a striving toward a higher purpose. Moral conceptions are consistent issues of general culture. Side by side with the individual will exists the general will of the community. When such a collective will asserts itself, it is a real force; it comes to prevail above individual wills and develops a cultural efficiency, expressed in such social products as speech, custom, law, and morality. The formulated purpose and the one attained are often quite diverse. The purpose is generally more extensive than the conscious intent. This Wundt explains by the fact that the individuals are themselves representatives of a larger cultural movement; as such they have the ethical task of bringing their individual purposes into harmony with those of a general progress. Such evolution Wundt accepts as the true ethical goal,[3] which can be completely

---

[1] This factor of the will in the formulation of law is also emphasized by *Schuppe*, but the further development of his view is so bound up with his ethics that it cannot properly be considered in this connection. See below, § 50.

[2] The data of the moral life, that is, language and moral conceptions, religion and morality, custom and social life, the nature and cultural conditions of moral development. "Ethik," I, pp. 20–279, Vol. I, pp. 280 seq., is historical — the development of moral conceptions.

[3] "Ethik," II, pp. 27–30; pp. 31 seq. is on the racial psychological basis of this ethical theory.

realized, not in terms of the individual, but of the race. Considering that for "the life according to nature" of the Stoics there is substituted the injunction to shape the purposes of the will in accord with the development of culture, we may call the position a stoicism upon a racial-psychological basis.

The moral life includes the individual personality, society, the State, humanity. With regard to the ultimate moral purpose of the law, in terms of content, the objective law may be described "as the inclusive conception of all individual rights and duties, which the law, as expressing the general moral will, secures as a right. It secures them in its own behalf and in behalf of the individual wills subordinated to it in order to aid them in their pursuit of moral purposes; and it imposes them as a duty for the protection of such laws."[1]

Externally law and the legal order appear as "the operations of the will of the State, which, as such, have enforcing power over the individual wills and over all the more limited general wills, which belong to the community as legally instituted. Law embraces the purposes which the will of the State pursues and the regulation of the means by which such purposes are to be attained."[2] Wundt considers the functions of the State with reference to communal ownership and economics, to law as a common possession, to the social community, and to the cultural community. Punishment is the natural reaction of the general will against the attempted infringement on the part of the ill-disposed individual will against the general will. It is a special type of reaction, related to retribution and reformatory pur-

[1] "Ethik," II, pp. 224 seq., 208; on Justice, see pp. 209-211; on Equity, pp. 211 seq.

[2] "Ethik," II, p. 206. The definition is faulty in that the one unknown, will, is given as the explanation of the other unknown, law.

poses but not identical with them. The essential factors of punishment are discipline, atonement, and educational influences.[1]

2: ZITELMANN. ZITELMANN (b. 1852) contributes an important study of will, reason and consciousness. In his work, "Irrtum und Rechtsgeschäft,"[2] he concludes that "will is that operation of the mind which acts directly upon the motor nerves and thus causes a distinctive bodily movement. The will is in itself neither conscious nor unconscious; it becomes the one or the other according as it is accompanied by the perception of its content or not."[3] Zitelmann proceeds to study the relation of perception and will with regard to acts, the juristic act, "Rechtsgeschäft"; the relation of mistake to juristic acts in general; and the kinds of mistake in the several divisions of juristic acts in particular. The compass of this work does not make possible the further consideration of his suggestive treatment.

3: JELLINEK. GEORG JELLINEK[4] (1851-1911) is an important contributor to the philosophy of government.

[1] "Ethik," II, pp. 306–350, 144–157, 152–156.
[2] "Eine Psychologisch-Juristische Untersuchung," Leipzig 1879, pp. 34–79, 83 seq.
[3] "Irrtum und Rechtgeschäft," p. 79.
[4] The works of *Jellinek* here pertinent are: "Die Sozialethische Bedeutung von Recht, Unrecht und Strafe," Vienna 1878. "Die Rechtliche Natur der Staatenverträge," Vienna 1880. "Gesetz und Verordnung, Staatsrechtliche Untersuchungen auf Rechtsgeschichtlicher und Rechtsvergleichender Grundlage," Freiburg i/B 1887, pp. 189–225. "System der Subjectiven Öffentlichen Rechte," Freiburg i/B 1892. "Über Staatsfragmente," Heidelberg 1896, pp. 11 seq. "Das Recht des Modernen Staates," Vol. I, "Allgemeine Staatslehre," Berlin 1900, pp. 3–48, 96–101, 121–258, 302–341, 394–460, 544–572, 696–719, 725. See also *Ludwig Stein*, "Die soziale Frage im Lichte der Philosophie," second edition, pp. 411–415, for an estimate of Jellinek.

Without prejudice to other writers, his "Allgemeine Staatslehre" may be said to be the most illuminating of recent works in this field. He approaches the problems critically and is under no inclination to yield to the allurement of the social philosophy that in recent years has inveigled so many able minds.

The State is intimately bound up with all social phenomena, but is nonetheless a man-made institution; accordingly "the analogy between a communal State and animal societies rests upon a confusion of the necessary consequences of physical organization and instinctive psychological expressions with the operations of ethical forces." There are indeed animal societies, but no animal States. The conception of society implies the existence of independent institutions intermediate between the individual and the State. "Society, in the largest sense, refers to the totality of the psychological associations among men that find external expression. In this sense it is identical with a corporation, which consists of a large number of separate permanent or transitory relations between individuals. This conception, however, is so broad that it cannot be made the basis of profitable scientific study. The materials upon which modern sociology bases its conclusions are often but a deceptive cover for *a priori* constructions based upon inadequate inductions." Such a conception of society is valuable only as a corrective to biased theories of government.

In the narrower sense society denotes "the sum total of human associations, that is, of groups of men held together by some common factor." A hard and fast differentiation of State and society is not possible. The State is itself a form of social product, and at once the condition as well as the issue thereof. "No social group can be conceived as existing beyond the range of the State or without it. One may, therefore, question the validity of this conception of society, since a separation of State and society is possible only as an abstract conception." On the one hand all social groups are influenced directly and indirectly by the State; and on the other hand the State itself forms such groups. "To avoid confusion a third and still narrower conception of society must be proposed that shall include the social groups with the exception of the State." "It is a permanent merit of the socialists, and of those who have profited by their teachings,to have directed attention to the connection between the progress of the law and social movements. Yet science must protest against the attempt to explain the entire range of political problems upon a narrow socialistic basis." [1]

The State is often termed an historical necessity; but if the view is to be scientifically acceptable, the term necessity must be interpreted as a psychological one.[2]

---

[1] "Allgemeine Staatslehre," pp. 74–90, 74 seq., 84, 86 seq., 88 seq.

[2] In Jellinek's earlier writings the psychological moment centering about the *will* is conspicuous in his theory of the State, but in "Allgemeine Staatslehre" it is relatively subordinate. See *Jellinek*, "Die Rechtliche Natur der Staatenverträge," pp. 16 seq.; "System der Subjectiven Öffentlichen Rechte, p. 28: "The will of the State, which in this respect is but a special case of a collective person, is no figment, but exists by virtue of the same logical necessity by which associated permanent and unitary purposes, pursued co-operatively by groups of men, appear as an association or, as we may say, a unity. If such unitary personality be admitted in behalf of practical thought, it has also its own will, in so far as it is constant and single in purpose, coherent, and exercising its will in the fostering of its purposes. The same logical necessity through which we make unity of plurality appears in this constant active will directed to the attainment of its purposes as a distinctive will, not merely as the voluntary phase of a physical volition." See also "Gesetz und Verordnung," p. 190: "The State is a dominant organization supported by a powerful will."

The psychological view, foreshadowed by Aristotle — and in some respects the ethical view of society — includes the position of "natural law," which regarded certain human traits as directly responsible for the establishment of government.

Jellinek does not consider that this psychological and historical position justifies the exercise of coercion by the State. If the object of all society is civilization, its regulation, which means a permanent voluntary association of defense and offense, must likewise be recognized. Without some form, however defective, of legal order, there would be a state of war of all against all. The problem of government is substantially the same as that of law. Jellinek regards the position of Aristotle as most acceptable: man, improved by government, is a worthy creation, but unrestrained by law and order, he is far from being so. Government as such is thus justified, but not any special form of government, nor any special type of distribution of authority within the State. The philosophy of government must ever be directed to the State of the present and to the growing institutions of the immediate future. The State in its concrete development can only be justified by the ends which it accomplishes.

According to Jellinek the State is characterized by a unity of purpose. The social politics resulting from this conception must set forth the purposes by which the manifold interests combined in the State shall appear as one. "The existence of such purposes may be deduced from the incontestable psychological fact that the life of the State consists of an uninterrupted series of human actions, each of which is necessarily conditioned by a motive, and thus, by a purpose." The problem of the purposes of the State cannot be solved deductively. Even the demand that the purpose of the State shall be the realization of law, tells one nothing concerning the content of the law, and through it of the State's purpose. After a review of the several theories of purpose, Jellinek reaches the formulation of his theory of relative State purposes. A simple psychological reflection will show that the State cannot enforce what belongs to the inner life of man; therefore the sphere of the State includes only "collective human expressions. Such purposive collective human expressions belong distinctively to the State. They may be reduced to the three great categories, of protection, regulation, support. The greater the joint interests, the more does the State serve for their satisfaction; the more unified the purposive organization that is needed for its protection, the more completely does it become the concern of the State. Such solidarity is a dynamic force, differently expressed in the several spheres of communal development at different times and among different peoples. The detailed formulation of the principle must be adapted to the prevalent stage of culture."

Among the most important interests conducive to social solidarity is the development of individuality. Jellinek pertinently remarks that the "vague idea of furthering welfare yields no insight" as to the nature of the problems of the State. The final purpose of all governmental activity is to further the progressive development of the individual members of society and of the race. "As justified by its purpose, the State is a complex associative expression of a people. Its operations are designed and centralized; and its institutions utilize the activities of individuals, of the nation, of humanity. It possesses a dominating legal personality, and directs collective interests towards a progressive development." This conception of the State is a functional one: along with it must be considered the legal conception in which the State is the subject of law. Under the legal conception, the State is "the corporate expression of an established people with an autonomous sovereignty," or "an autonomous corporation exercising territorial sovereignty."[1] The factors of the State are its territory ("Staatsgebiet"), the people ("Staatsvolk"), and authority ("Staatsgewalt").[2] Sovereignty is "the negation of every subjection or restriction of the State through an alien power." The sovereign authority of the State is therefore "at once the independent and supreme authority." Sovereignty is no essential characteristic of the governmental authority.[3]

The question as to the origin of the State falls into two subsidiary problems: the historical beginning of governmental institutions, and the formation of new States within the existing governmental development. As to the former, only hypotheses are possible. The developed form of communal life, which we today designate "the State," is dependent upon permanence of settlement. Such permanence of settlement is closely

[1] "Allgemeine Staatslehre," pp. 195–204, 205–238, 209, 213, 224, 226 seq., 228, 235, 236, 237, 121–161, 149–151, 161. See also "System der Subjectiven Rechte," pp. 12–39, 13, 20, 26.

On the etymology and change of meaning of the word "State" see "Allgemeine Staatslehre," pp. 115–120.

[2] "Allgemeine Staatslehre," pp. 355–393. "Über Staatsfragmente," p. 12: "A state is accordingly a collectivity with its own sphere, its own subjects, and its own authority, which is either independent of any external authority, that is, sovereign, or is in some respects limited by the authority of a still higher sovereign State and is thus not sovereign. All three elements are necessary for the existence of the State; if any one is lacking then there is no State, but merely some form of organization subordinate to the State."

[3] "Allgemeine Staatslehre," pp. 394–460, 431 seq., 442 seq. Also "Gesetz und Verordnung," pp. 197–201, 201–205. See also note 18, above.

connected with the pursuit of agriculture; but the phases of its early stages of evolution are uncertain. The consolidation of human intercourse is aided by "a natural tendency of regulated uniformity of action." The incentives for the formation of the State are thus also the incentives for the formation of law.

The problem of law may be approached either through metaphysical speculation, that is, through its conception "as a force independent of man, and involved in the objective nature of phenomena"; or psychologically, that is, by its study as a subjective phenomenon of human expression. Jellinek adopts the second procedure. The law consists of regulations for human conduct. It is further to be distinguished from other norms, such as those of religion, morality and custom. Its specific character lies in the following characteristics of legal norms: "They are norms for the external relations of men to one another; norms that issue from a recognized external authority; and norms whose binding force is guaranteed through external authority." The essential characteristic of law is that it shall prevail; for this, it is necessary that its psychological efficiency be guaranteed. "The operation of a law is guaranteed when the motive power of its prescriptions is so re-enforced by social psychological influences, that the expectation is justified that the norms which the law enforces will be able to assert themselves as motives of conduct against the opposing individual motives."[1] If the term "State" is to be understood as the developed

[1] "Allgemeine Staatslehre," pp. 239-254, 241, 302-341, 302, 302 seq., 304. "Die Sozialethische Bedeutung von Recht, Unrecht und Strafe" (The social ethical meaning of right, wrong, and punishment), p. 116: "Acts, undertaken by society, and in a developed state of civilization, by the State, against the perpetrator of a wrong, through which the effects, injurious socially and psychologically, resulting from the wrong, are equalized, is punishment."

State in the modern sense, then law existed even before the State; but if the term implies the supreme and sovereign corporation of any period, then the law will find only in and through such dominant organization, the necessary external guaranty for the realization of legal norms. But the State is not the exclusive source of law; Jellinek maintains that even at the present time there are numerous associations independent of the State (such as the Church), that create laws; but this view may be questioned.[1]

George Simmel[2] (b. 1858), in his "Einleitung in die Moralwissenschaft," makes a careful analysis of the fundamental ethical conceptions from the psychological point of view. In his "Philosophie des Geldes"[3] the problem of values and the social and cultural significance of possession are considered in detail.[4]

4: CRIMINAL PSYCHOLOGY. GABRIEL TARDE[5] (b. 1843) holds that the psychological impulse, expressed

[1] "Allgemeine Staatslehre," pp. 320-331.

[2] Von Simmel: "Bemerkungen zu Sozial-Ethischen Problemen," Vol. 12, 1888, pp. 32-49. "Über Soziale Differenzierung, Soziologische und Psychologische Untersuchungen" (Schmoller's "Staats- und Sozialwissenschaftliche Forschungen," Vol. 10, Part I), Leipzig 1890. "Einleitung in die Moralwissenschaft, eine Kritik der Ethischen Grundbegriffe," 2 vols. Stuttgart and Berlin, 1892-1893. Anastatic reprint, Stuttgart 1904. "Philosophie des Geldes," Leipzig 1900. Kant, "16 Vorlesungen an der Berliner Universität," Leipzig 1904.

See *Ueberweg-Heinze*, "Grundriss der Geschichte der Philosophie," IV, p. 347, for an estimate of Simmel.

[3] "Philosophie des Geldes," pp. 3-87. The significance of money is to represent the economic relativity of things (pp. 82-87). In addition there is the material value of money (pp. 88-112).

[4] "Philosophie des Geldes," pp. 279-454, 455-554.

[5] The writings of Tarde here pertinent are: "Les Lois de l'Imitation. Étude Sociologique." Second edit., Paris 1895 ("Bibliothèque de Philosophie Contemporaine," 146). "La Logique Sociale ("Bibl.,"

in the law of imitation, is the important trait leading to social solidarity. He interprets rational behavior as psychological. He bases ethical and legal responsibility upon the sense of social similarity.[1] He was the first to emphasize and illustrate in detail the importance for the social life of conscious imitation and subconscious assimilation.[2] He aims to establish logic as a psychological phenomenon.[3] Tarde finds followers in Sighele, Aschaffenburg, Krause, and others.[4]

etc., 124), Paris 1895. "La Philosophie Pénale," eighth edit., Lyon-Paris 1904. (I cite from the 1900 edition, the one accessible to me.)

[1] "La Philosophie Pénale," pp. 83-213 (Chap. III: "Théorie de la Responsabilité," pp. 83-148; Chap. IV: "Théorie de la Irresponsabilité," pp. 149-213). See also *Berolzheimer*, "Die Entgeltung im Strafrechte," 92-97, 102, 206, 319.

[2] See particularly "Les Lois de l'Imitation," second edit. Chap. II, "Les Similitudes Sociales et l'Imitation (pp. 46-65); Chap. III, "Qu'est-ce qu'une Société?" (pp. 66-98); Chap. V, "Les Lois Logiques de l'Imitation (pp. 158-212); Chaps. VI & VII, "Les Influences Extra-Logiques" (pp. 213-266, 267-396). P. 73: "Hence arises this definition of the social group: a collection of individuals so far as they are disposed to imitate one another or in so far as without actual imitation they resemble one another and their common traits are older copies of the same model." P. 95: "Society is imitation; and imitation is a kind of somnambulism; such is the epitome of this chapter."

[3] "La Logique Sociale," Part I, Chap. I, "La Logique Individuelle," pp. 1-86. Chap. II, "L'esprit Social ("Logique Sociale Statique)," pp. 87-133. Chap. III, "La Série Historique des états Logiques ("Logique Sociale Dynamique"), pp. 135-150. Chap. IV, "Les Lois de l'Invention ("Logique Sociale Dynamique, suite"), pp. 151-223. Part II: "Applications; La Langue; La Religion; Le Coeur; l'Economie Politique; l'Art.

[4] For further references see *Wahlberg*, "Gesammelte Kleinere Schriften und Bruchstücke," Vol. II, Vienna 1877. "Die Moralstatistik und die Strafrechtliche Zurechnung," p. 295. *Havelock Ellis*, "Verbrecher und Verbrechen" (Kurella's translation), Leipzig 1894, pp. 310-315. *Hans Gross*, "Kriminalpsychologie," Graz 1898, pp. 566-569. *Lombroso*, "Die Ursachen und Bekämpfung

J. Mark Baldwin's "Social and Ethical Interpretations in Mental Development"[1] shows the influence of Tarde. The following is Barth's[2] comment upon it: "In the present work Baldwin develops the view that the psychological analogy, as already proposed by others, between the mental life of the individual and that of society, between the egoistic and altruistic actions, should also be made the problem of psychology. He maintains that external actions referring to persons, whether to one's own person or another's, spring from the thought of the self, from our conception of human personality in general; and that in our actions we are by no means always conscious of ourselves or whether the personality is our own or belongs to another." Such considerations affecting human action Baldwin calls sanctions,[3] which in turn are in part personal, in part

des Verbrechens," translated by *Kurella* and *Jentsch*, Berlin 1902, pp. 188 seq.

Scipio Sighele's "Psychologie des Auflaufs und der Massenverbrechen" (translated by Kurella: Dresden and Leipzig, 1897, especially pp. 41–106) is influenced by Tarde. For Aschaffenburg see above, § 44. The sociological school of penology emphasizes the study of criminal motives. See *A. Krauss*, "Die Psychologie des Verbrechens, ein Beitrag zur Erfahrungsseelenkunde," Tübingen 1884, and *Andreas Thomsen*, "Untersuchungen über den Begriff des Verbrechensmotivs," Munich 1902. See also the symposium, "Zur Psychologie der Gefangenschaft. Untersuchungshaft, Gefängnis- und Zuchthausstrafe Geschildert von Entlassenen," compiled by *Fritz Auer*, describing phases of prison life as portrayed by discharged prisoners. Munich 1905.

[1] "Social and Ethical Interpretations in Mental Development" (translated from the second English edition by *R. Ruedemann*, with a preface by *Paul Barth*, Leipzig 1900). Baldwin's other writings are not pertinent here.

[2] Preface to the German edition, p. x.

[3] "Das Soziale und Sittliche Leben," pp. 285 seq.

social.[1] "A sanction is any ground or reason which is adequate to initiate action, whether the action be conscious or not that this is the ground or reason of the resulting action."[2] Baldwin sets forth that man is frequently not fully aware of the motives of his actions, that he may even be deceived as to the motives; or that the unconscious exerts more or less important influence upon the content of the conceptions that serve as motives.[3]

Bearing upon the last consideration is Georg Adler's position in his "Bedeutung der Illusionen für Politik und Soziales Leben."[4] He sets forth that in politics and social movements, and notably in modern socialism, the cause assigned and the actual cause bringing about collective movements frequently diverge, and that fal-

---

[1] German edition, pp. 285-322, 322-354. The institutions through which these sanctions are expresssd are divided into four groups — natural sanctions, pedagogical and conventional sanctions, civil sanctions, ethical and religious sanctions.

[2] P. 288 (German edition); first English edition, p. 361.

[3] See especially pp. 285-289.

[4] Jena 1904. See also above, preface, p. XLII, Note 1. In this work Adler refers to his former writings in which he has developed this thought. The idea was first explicitly formulated by *Adler;* others had previously expressed the same general view. See *Schmoller*, "Die Gerechtigkeit in der Volkswirtschaft" (*Schmoller*, "Zur Sozial- und Gewerbepolitik der Gegenwart," Leipzig 1890, p. 205): "No great social or economic reform can overcome the inert opposition that it arouses by proof of its utility. It is only when what is demanded can be set forth as just, that the claim is vitalized and starts a movement. I have for years observed how and when the question of justice was introduced in public discussion and in economic publications, and I found that it occurs involuntarily in almost all cases." See also *Alex. Tille*, "Volksdienst," Berlin and Leipzig 1893, p. 110.

lacy and illusion exercise an important beneficial influence in the history of civilization.[1]

§ 50. *Recent Surveys of Fundamental Problems.* 1: MERKEL AND HIS FOLLOWERS. The writings of ADOLF MERKEL[2] (1836–1896) are notable for their wealth of pertinent observations and keen analysis. They present an idealism based upon an appreciation of actual conditions which gives promise of a fruitful development of the philosophy of law. Though not forming a system of legal philosophy, Merkel's writings are important for their thorough treatment of the fundamental problems of law and punishment.

There is an inherent human interest in the apportionment of what men deserve and what they secure. There is a deep-rooted conviction that in some manner fortune and merit must be brought into relation. This conviction permeates popular religious and moral conceptions; it gives rise to a popular proverbial philosophy. The demands of morality require a presumable connection between good or ill-fortune and the laws of compensation. In this sense of moral adjustment lies the source of the legal demand for retributive justice.[3]

[1] *Masaryk:* "Die Philosophischen und Soziologischen Grundlagen des Marxismus," Vienna 1899, p. 156, and *Eisler:* "Soziologie," Leipzig 1903, pp. 63 seq. (see above, § 44, p. 381), emphasize the psychological phase of social origins and relations. *Bergemann,* "Ethik als Kulturphilosophie," Leipzig 1904, pp. 367–475 (see above, §§ 44 and 42), considers the social-psychological factor in addition to the personal factor in the genesis of morality. *Karl Kniess* in "Der Kredit," Berlin 1876, p. 138, had already noted the "psychology of the masses" as a contributing social force.

[2] *Adolf Merkel,* "Hinterlassene Fragmente und Gesammelte Abhandlungen." Part I: "Fragmente zur Sozial Wissenschaft," Strassburg 1898. Part II, 1 and 2: "Gesammelte Abhandlungen aus dem Gebiet der Allgemeinen Rechtslehre und des Strafrechts," edited by *Rudolf Merkel,* Strassburg 1899.

[3] "Über Vergeltende Gerechtigkeit" ("Hinterlassene Fragm.."

The philosophy of law has to do only with positive law.[1] Law is "the standard which a community establishes with reference to the relation of its members to others and to itself, as well as to the expressions of its own activity." Law is the principle of order.[2] "A certain element of authority is inherent in all law. It is itself a form of authority to which certain superior qualities are attached." This applies as well to law as to rights. The conception of rights involves the actual power to exercise them. The starting-point of law is self-help; hence, so far as bears upon its efficiency, law depends upon the means of enforcement which the claimant is able to put into operation. In so far as this principle of self-help holds, "the success of rights in any given case depends upon the contest of power between the claimant and his adversary, and thus individual right and individual power are closely associated." This applies also to the acquisition of rights. The primitive mode of such acquisition seems to have been seizure; in primitive stages of legal development, the legal status of possession was substantially independent of the manner in which it was acquired.[3]

Progress in the forms of acquiring rights and of legal contests and standards was very gradual. Instead of the trial of strength between the litigants, a procedure of proof, presented to the constituted authority, was introduced; in the weighing of evidence "the distinctive

etc.), II, 1, pp. 1-14, 2, 3, 6. See also "Lehrbuch des Deutschen Strafrechts," pp. 9-29.

[1] "Über das Verhältnis der Rechtsphilosophie zur 'Positiven' Rechtswissenschaft und zum Allgemeinen Teil Derselben" ("Fragm.," etc., II, 1, pp. 291-323, 308 seq. See above; also *Merkel*, "Elemente der Allgemeinen Rechtslehre, §§ 12-14.

[2] "Elemente der Allgemeinen Rechtslehre," § 1.

[3] "Recht und Macht" ("Fragm.," etc., II, L, pp. 400-428, 403. See also "Elemente der Allgemeinen Rechtslehre," § 7.

position of legal authority appears with ever extending importance. The question of law comes to be more nearly a question of the better cause in view of the interests and considerations which have instituted the power of the law. The acknowledgment of a claim comes to have an equally legitimate bearing upon past and future interests. It involves an ethical judgment of the past circumstances which underlie the presented claim." In such development the contrast of status between the strong and the weak in the realm of the law is diminished. Indeed in many respects the law becomes the protection and defense of the weak and thus restores the balance of power. Were it possible to find a harmonizing principle applicable to all human interests, it would serve as the basis for a universally recognized law. But the law will never be able to satisfy all the several legitimate interests and attitudes and feelings, as well as the demands growing out of them. The law thus bears throughout "the character of a compromise." [1]

In his development of general jurisprudence Merkel approaches the position of the theory of norms. But in contrast to Binding, Merkel denies the autonomy of the law. "The law does not carry its purpose within itself," nor does it exist for the sake of the ethical satisfaction which arises from the operation of justice. Merkel, in common with Ihering, inclines to regard the end in view ("Zweck") as creating the law. The law is the organ of social interests. Law and the State arose together and had a common development. But the State could not create law, nor does the legal quality belong to all the expressions of the State. For "every

---

[1] "Recht und Macht," pp. 407–411, 410, 411–420, 411, seq., 420 seq., 420–422. See also "Elemente der Allgemeinen Rechtslehre," § 11: "Die Kompromissnatur des Rechts."

community which possesses the power to regulate independently the relations of its members to one another and to the State may establish its own laws." Whether it does so by virtue of governmental delegation is a question of fact. And on the other hand the State is not merely a legal institution. In this opinion Merkel has in mind the governmental operation of industrial institutions in the emergency of war.

The factors of the State are the State authority, the State territory, and, in the classical as well as in the modern State, the unlimited legal power of regulation within the sphere of the State. The State is the "organization of a community or the sum total of institutions by means of which the regulated activities of the common life of a people finds its realization." "Associations of various types" precede the State. The chief occasion leading to the formation of the State is war; it is through the suppression of feuds, or again in the interests of a common defense, and for the forcible subjection of a foreign tribe, that the State is established through the medium of war. With reference to the nature of the State, Merkel inclines to the organic evolutionary conception thereof, yet with due recognition of the free self-assertion of the individual.[1]

By retribution Merkel understands "a counteraction to offset evil or good transactions, which, as affecting their authors, bring about an equalization of the disproportion between the status of those involved actively and passively in the transaction."[2] He holds that as affecting punishment, retribution and the effect upon the individual, "Zweckstrafe," are not exclusive. The sources of the feeling of responsibility are based upon

[1] "Elemente der Allgemeinen Rechtslehre," §§ 4, 5, 39 seq., 2, 14, 15–17, 18, 19.
[2] "Lehrbuch des Strafrechts," p. 187.

the consciousness of being the cause of one's own acts, and likewise upon the traditional ethical conceptions of value which remain uninfluenced by the deterministic attitude which Merkel supports.[1]

Merkel's view of the philosophy of punishment is represented and developed by M. LIEPMANN.[2] Like Merkel[3] he sees no incompatibility between punishment as retribution and for its effect upon the individual ("Zweckstrafe"). The incompatibility would apply only as against a view which determined the treatment of criminals according to their menace to society. He likewise finds no incompatibility between retribution and determinism.[4]

The penological theory of social disapproval of VON BAR[5] (b. 1836) is likewise similar to the position of Merkel.

2: SCHMIDT. RICHARD SCHMIDT[6] (b. 1862) is the author of an "Allgemeine Staatslehre." The problem

[1] "Vergeltungsidee und Zweckgedanke im Strafrecht" ("Hinterlassene Fragm.," II, 2, pp. 687–723, 692, 710, 716–720. "Lehrbuch," pp. 72–78. See also *Berolzheimer*, "Die Entgeltung im Strafrechte," pp. 97–99, 103, 139.

[2] "Einleitung in das Strafrecht. Eine Kritik der Kriminalistischen Grundbegriffe," Berlin 1900. See also *Liepmann* ("Z. f. g. Str.," Vol. XVII, pp. 691 seq.). Also *Berolzheimer*, "Die Entgeltung im Strafrechte," pp. 99, 151 seq.

[3] "Einleitung in das Strafrecht," pp. 196–212: "Die Aufgaben der Strafe," p. 196.

[4] "Einleitung in das Strafrecht," pp. 197–204, 204.

[5] *v. Bar*, "Geschichte des Deutschen Strafrechts und der Strafrechtstheorien," Berlin 1882, pp. 311 seq., especially pp. 316, 323, 327; "Probleme des Strafrechtes," an address, Göttingen 1896. See also *Berolzheimer*, "Die Entgeltung im Strafrechte," pp. 151 seq.

[6] For his views on penology favoring the principle of general prevention, see *Rich. Schmidt*, "Die Aufgaben der Strafrechtspflege," Leipzig 1895. See also *Berolzheimer*, "Die Entgeltung im Strafrechte," pp. 155 seq.

of the origin of the State he regards as insoluble in so far as the attempt to trace a systematic evolution of the oldest forms of alliance has failed. But the problem as to the conditions which lead to the establishment of the State may be answered substantially as follows: "One may regard a governmental association as arising whenever a group of men, acting in the main as a body, dispose of their common interests based upon their communal life. The State is thus independent of the family and the clan." The functions of the State cannot be defined in explicit principles. The general problems of welfare fall but in subsidiary manner within the sphere of the activity of the State; the maintenance of security belongs to it primarily, and with the precedence of the State as against individuals and groups. The functions of the law are "the consolidation and regulation of human cultural interests as furthered by the intercourse of members of society."

The scientific study of the origin of the law has decided limitations; observation shows that the legal norms gradually emerge from "the primitive manifestations of men," and become differentiated from the norms of religion, custom and morality. It may be said that "the law as a whole is the average standard of legislation which, through the public guaranty of the State, becomes an established part of the morality and customs of the people."[1] Yet this need not apply to individual legislative acts.

3: PAULSEN. For present interests Paulsen's (b. 1846) "System der Ethik" is the most important of his writings.[2] To Paulsen, welfare is "the supreme good,

---

[1] "Allgemeine Staatslehre," Vol. I, pp. 116–121, 121–123, 122, 145–156, 167, 168, 170, 238 seq.

[2] "System der Ethik mit einem Umriss der Staats- und Gesellschaftslehre," 2 vols., sixth edition, Stuttgart 1903. (I cite from

the ultimate point of reference of all judgments of value of human relations, and at the same time the ultimate goal of the normal will." But wherein does welfare or the supreme good consist? Two views are possible, the hedonistic or the dynamic. "The former regards pleasure as the supreme good; the latter makes it an objective perfection of one's nature and of one's functional efficiency." Paulsen advocates a dynamic view of ethics. The most general formula of this position makes the goal of endeavor of every living being the normal development of its functional efficiency as determined by its nature. In agreement with Aristotle happiness or welfare appears as "the realization of all virtues and capacities, and particularly those of the highest types."

Paulsen assumes the freedom of the will essentially in the sense of Spinoza and Kant. "The freedom of man is the dominance of his rational nature, and the slavery of man is the dominance of his animal desires." The dynamic and teleological ethics of Paulsen may be termed a more thorough elaboration and refinement of social utilitarianism. Justice is a virtue and an ethical duty. The general formula of the duty of justice is when positively worded, "Observe and protect the law"; or in another version: "Do no wrong, and so far as lies in your power, do not permit wrong to be done." From the idea of the welfare of the community, there follows the duty of the community to provide for its self-preservation; and this justifies the application of legal coercion. The purpose of punishment is to maintain peace and security in the community.

The forms of the communal life are the family, socia-

the fifth edition, 1900.) Also "Einleitung in die Philosophie," eleventh and twelfth edition, Stuttgart 1904: "Philosophia Militans gegen Klerikalismus und Naturalismus," five essays, Berlin 1901.

bility, and friendship, the economic life and society, and the State. By society, Paulsen understands "the spontaneously arising organization of the people for economic purposes; the co-operative production of commodities and the exchange thereof form the chief object of its operations." The State is the organization of the people into a supreme unity of will, authority and law. The purpose of the State is to further the life interests of the people in their external relations, and the preservation of an inner peace; and in support of the free activity of the individual, the fostering of culture and of material welfare.[1]

4: BAUMANN. JOH. JULIUS BAUMANN[2] (b. 1837) regards the problem of the philosophy of law as the establishment of the ultimate principles comprised under the term law. This problem cannot be solved by a comparative study of law, for such comparison affords merely a formal conception of law. The object of the legal philosopher is to determine whether there exists a general equitable content of law, how such is formed, and for what reasons it is not everywhere the same.

"The institutions, which the free association of men with one another makes possible and necessary for the development of such communal life, constitute the law; or otherwise expressed, the law is the underlying conception of the demands between one man and another which are indispensable to freedom of intercourse."

[1] "System der Ethik," I, pp. 209-235, 235-269, 235, 253, 424-442, 442; II, 128-163, 128, 134, 134-139, 314-512, 512 seq., 323, 512-516.

[2] The writings of *Baumann* here pertinent are: "Sechs Vorträge aus dem Gebiete der Praktischen Philosophie," Leipzig 1874 (III, IV, and V, pp. 46-142). "Handbuch der Moral nebst Abriss der Rechtsphilosophie," Leipzig 1879. "Realwissenschaftliche Begründung der Moral, des Rechts und der Gotteslehre," Leipzig 1898.

All law has reference to the community. Baumann proceeds to consider the most important legal relations — such as those resulting from property, incorporeal ownership, contract, marriage, inheritance — which represent the more individualistic rights in which the individual is uppermost, together with those phases of the law in which the interests of society dominate. The State appears as the most general legal corporation; and its essential characteristics are a permanent purpose, fixed institutions, exemption from change in membership, and "the free activity of the individual or of particular groups of individuals, but ever within the law and thus in subordination to the whole." If in consideration of these attributes the State is termed an organism, care should be taken that the analogy produces no false impression. "The State must be conceived as composed of conscious and free men, and not as an organic natural product; for of the fundamental nature of organic processes — so far as they are not the results of mechanical laws — we know nothing, and tend to ascribe them by analogy to human action."[1]

5: SCHUPPE. From an ethical position W. SCHUPPE (b. 1836) concludes that "it is through their inner nature that men feel the need of communal life and are designed to live together." If ethical requirements were voluntarily met, if perfect insight and love prevailed, law and legislation would be superfluous. But as men are ever morally imperfect, government and law are necessary institutions.[2] "Law is the will which arises from the judgment of the concrete consciousness as such,"[3]

[1] "Handbuch der Moral," pp. 372, 374–391, 383, 392–423, 424–445, 426 seq.

[2] "Grundzüge der Ethik und Rechtsphilosophie," pp. 276, 276 seq., 382.

[3] "Die Spezifische Differenz im Begriffe des Rechts," pp. 194 seq. In this essay the distinction between law and ethics is upper-

in which the term concrete consciousness is the concrete ego of the individual man.¹ Schuppe says of his conception of law that it denotes "the inner incentive in all legal institutions, and does not present a bare formulation of the content, but makes the material realization dependent upon the actually existing factors; and thus there can be no ideal of law valid for all times."² A legal right is a power, and finds its necessary complement in duty.³ The State exists for cultural and economic interests.⁴

most. The essay, "Der Begriff des Rechts," which was inspired by *Zitelmann's* "Irrtum und Rechtsgeschäft," deals mainly with the will in its relation to the law.

¹ "Die Spezifische Differenz im Begriffe des Rechts," p. 168. See also "Der Begriff des Subjektiven Rechts," pp. 2 seq., 5–8, and "Das Gewohnheitsrecht," pp. 17 seq.

² "Die Spezifische Differenz im Begriffe des Rechts," pp. 195 seq.; See also "Das Gewohnheitsrecht," pp. 17–51.

³ "Grundzüge der Ethik," pp. 292–294. See also "Der Begriff des Subjektiven Rechts," pp. 8–10.

⁴ "Grundzüge der Ethik," pp. 202, 315 334, 384–389. P. 292: "A State as a legal institution and nothing else is an anomaly; for to desire and realize law in the narrower sense is possible and justifiable only by virtue of the desire to make real that which is the source of all law — namely, the cultural mission of the State." P. 315 In addition to its legal function the State has the positive purpose "of service to inherently ethical ends." P. 318: The ethical will is absolute and the governmental will but relative and dependent. P. 320: "The State stands for the furthering of the moral and intellectual perfection of each individual in material and spiritual relations; its interests extend to the highest spiritual as well as material values."

See also *Schuppe*, "Rechtswissenschaft und Rechtsphilosophie," p. 234: "The goal of the legal will is limited by the principles of equality and individual freedom, and as well by racial and national character, by historical vicissitudes and all such outer conditions of life as determine the trend of mental evolution, and also determine what in one situation or another will be regarded as desirable to welfare. The legal norms acquire their content through such external factors."

The problem of punishment is in the last analysis directed to the question of the justification of infliction of evil; it consists "in the contradiction between the universally recognized presence of immorality, together with the injustice of inflicting pain, and the widely disseminated and traditional sentiment which in particular cases, requires such infliction and does so with the appearance of justice and law." The infliction of pain appears as immoral by virtue of the command of neighborly love; and yet the position is relatively justified by which the personality should only be valued in terms of its actual accomplishment. It is not the law of morality, but a moral sense that demands the punishment of the offender. Freedom is a condition of responsibility. What deserves to be punished is the evil disposition.[1]

§ 51. *The Influence of the Principles of Evolution.* 1: SOCIAL ARISTOCRACY; NIETZSCHE. In his assertive period consequent upon emancipation from Schopenhauer, Friedrich Nietzsche (1844–1900) came to look upon the prevalent Christian morality as the gospel of the decline, decadence, and degradation of the individual. Against this slave or herd morality Nietzsche, under the influence of Stirner and of the theory of evolution, set up the morality of man as his own master, of the human ego standing upon its own footing. The self-assertion of the individual appears characteristically in a striving for power — "Wille zur Macht," the will to prevail.[2] The goal of ethical culture is a breeding

[1] "Grundzüge der Ethik," pp. 339–382, 349–361, 366 seq., 370, 376–378.

[2] "Wherever I found life there I found the will to prevail, and even in the will for service I found the will to be master. . . . And wherever there is sacrifice and service and affection there also is the will to be master. By devious paths the weaker creeps into the castle, and even into the heart of the more powerful and there

of a higher type of man, the creation of a superman.[1] At the close of the ultra-democratic nineteenth century, Nietzsche appeared as a prophet of social aristocracy.

Nietzsche misapprehends the nature of ethics; he regards Christian ethics from without, and not in its historical setting. His argument would read: Inasmuch as Christian ethics is the prevalent ethics and stands for asceticism, and as asceticism means the denial of the will to achieve power, which in turn is the suppression of individuality, it all results in the advocacy of slave or herd morality and in the checking of cultural progress. To this Nietzsche opposes his ethical ideal, the breeding of the superman, in whom will be represented a new morality, above the sphere of good and evil, which shall affirm the will to live and to achieve power — in brief, shall affirm the autonomy of the individual, through which shall result the larger human progress mediated by the breeding of the superman. In the prevailing ethics Nietzsche sees only the denial of life, a check to extreme individualism, and ignores the significance of ethics as a dominant cultural force. His emphasis of power is sound; but his narrow perspective gives it a false development, in that he regards ethical power as equivalent to austerity, and political force as equivalent to might. The evolution of history is against him.

steals power." "Also Sprach Zarathustra," p. 167. "Zur Genealogie der Moral," pp. 397 seq. "Der Wille zur Macht," pp. 265 seq. "Nachgelassene Werke," Part II, Vol. XII, pp. 101 seq.

[1] "Jenseits von Gut und Böse," pp. 233 seq. "Götzendämmerung," pp. 145 seq. "Also Sprach Zarathustra," pp. 16-18, 51, 72, 287-313. "Nachgelassene Werke," Part II, Vol. XI, p. 131, No. 418; Vol. XII, p. 188, No. 403; p. 205, No. 437; p. 209, No. 443.

ALEXANDER TILLE, in his popular scientific book, "Volksdienst,"[1] advocates the position of social aristocracy as against socialism. The motto, "A like wage for all," would be but a temporary solution for existing inequalities. "Natural selection is, so to speak, thoroughly aristocratic." "All selection is aristocratic, for no one chooses to perpetuate the worst." "Men, like animals, are by inheritance efficient or inefficient, but efficient and inefficient alike develop their working capacity through social means; and thus he who through his innate efficiency in the field of work produces more than another, may in a favorable sense be called a social aristocrat, and the condition, in which property, influence, and power are dependent wholly upon service, may be called a social aristocracy." Social aristocracy leads to a new rank, to the creation of estates of performance.

2: EVOLUTIONARY MONISM; HAECKEL. ERNST HAECKEL (b. 1834), the distinguished zoölogist and early protagonist of evolution, was largely influential in making Darwin's teachings available to Germany. In one of the later chapters of "Die Lebenswunder"[2] he applies the doctrine of monism to all realms of science, to physics, chemistry, mathematics, astronomy, geology, biology, anthropology, psychology, linguistics, history, medicine, psychiatry, hygiene, technology, pedagogy; furthermore to ethics, sociology, politics, jurisprudence, and theology. In the accompanying note[3] I have

[1] "Volksdienst." By a social aristocrat, Anonymous. Publisher, *Tille*, Berlin and Leipzig 1893, pp. 112 seq., 110–133, 134–153.

[2] Pp. 531 seq.

[3] The ethics of monism attempts to supplement the metaphysical foundations of morality by assuming a free will and an inherent moral consciousness on the basis of a physiological ethics, supported by the laws of biology in general, and of evolution in particular. "Die Lebenswunder," p. 548.

expressed almost literally Haeckel's position so far as it is here pertinent, in order that the reader may form an opinion of its value. Haeckel predicts a new future for the science of law as soon as legislation shall be exclusively guided by reason. This position does away entirely with natural law. A further condition to the salvation of the philosophy of law is the acceptance of determinism, which already dominates in the sociological

Sociology proceeds monistically by referring "the laws regulating society to the natural laws of heredity and selection." "While in social intercourse many educated men still hold to dualistic prejudices, how little truth and nature are 'valued in our refined and educated society?' How much deception and untruthfulness determines standards is shown conclusively by Max Nordau in his well-known book, 'Die Konventionellen der Kulturmenschheit'" (Die Lebenswunder, pp. 548 seq.).

Upon monistic politics Haeckel remarks ("Die Leben," p. 549): "Internal politics is regulated in civilized States by constitutions, and external politics by international relations. According to the monistic view, pure reason should determine issues in both fields; the mutual relations of citizens to each other and to the State should be regulated by the same ethical laws as prevail in the personal intercourse of one citizen with another. It is obvious that in modern civic life we are very far from having reached this ideal goal. External politics still shows the prevalence of brutal self-seeking. Every nation is thinking only of its own advantage and devotes the largest share of its resources to military equipment, while internal politics is for the most part under the dominion of the barbarous prejudices of the Middle Ages. Constitutional struggles are directed to a contest for power on the part of the government on the one hand, and of the mass of the people on the other. Parties are ranged in unprofitable strife; yet the vital issue is not as to the forms of government but as to whether reason prevails in their operations. Whether a constitution is that of a monarchy or that of a republic, whether aristocratic or democratic, is quite subordinate to the main issue, which is, whether, as a modern civilized country, it is spiritually or worldly minded. The question is whether it shall be ruled under the theocratic dominance of unreasoning dogma and clerical control or under the rational dominance of unreasonable laws and civil rights." ("Welträtsel," p. 11.)

school of penology. Speaking of desirable reforms in economics and law, Haeckel urges that legal science would be advanced by the study of biology. Biology, however, was introduced into the philosophy of society, government, and law in the nineteenth century, without contributing more than certain analogies to nature of rather doubtful value. Is it not plausible that familiarity with economic life will be more profitable for the jurist and

The postulate of monistic jurisprudence Haeckel finds wholly unsolved. He maintains that dualistic principles still prevail. "In this field likewise the dualism of Kant's practical reason still prevails with unfortunate consequences. The false conceptions of the immortality of the soul, of the freedom of the will, and of a personal God as lawgiver and supreme Judge, influence legislation and legal minds, and determine the views of lawyers as well as of statesmen. There are moreover many carefully conserved vestiges of mediæval superstition which modern legislation merely transforms. The powerful influence of religious prejudice and ecclesiastical dogma affects the situation unfavorably. We are constantly reading in newspapers of strange decisions of the higher and the lower courts which are amazing to any sound understanding. In this domain improvement will ensue only when jurists are thoroughly grounded in anthropology and psychology and understand the laws of life." ("Die Lebenswunder," p. 550.)

[n speaking of the harmony of monism, Haeckel in conclusion (p. 557) says that where "a fully consistent mode of thinking applies the highest principles to the totality of the cosmos — including the organic and the inorganic world — the opposition of theism and pantheism, of vitalism and mechanism, will dissolve, and the two views converge. But it must be admitted that consistent thought is a rare phenomenon." Haeckel then continues: "Of the reality of this reconciliation and dissolution of opposing views, I am more and more fully convinced. The insight is gaining ground that the dualism of Kant must gradually give way to the metaphysical monism of Goethe and the growing pantheistic trend of thought. In this consummation our ideals are by no means lost. On the contrary, an objective view of the world shows that ideals are deeply rooted in human nature. While we cultivate the world of ideals in art and poetry, and our emotional nature finds pleasure in their pursuit, we still retain the firm conviction that the world of reality

legal philosopher than a knowledge of biology? And one may ask, how is Haeckel's demand for the limitation of egoism in the relation of the States to one another, consistent with the struggle for existence and the theory of selection?

3: EVOLUTION AND SOCIALISM. Haeckel's proposal to apply the teachings of Darwinism to political economy

can only be truly known and become an object of science, by the purely rational exercise of experience and thought. 'Wahrheit und Dichtung' will unite in the complete harmony of monism."

That Haeckel's views have been the subject of decided protest is familiar. His somewhat contemptuous opposition and judgment of philosophical dualism and the sharp polemical tone of his writings has as usual brought about an equally keen retort, of which *Paulsen's* "Philosophia Militans" (pp. 179 seq.) may be cited as an example. In fact Haeckel is a fanatic, and fanaticism is always intolerant. If Haeckel were conversant with the history of philosophy, he would know that dualism and monism were opposed to one another long before Kant, and that in general views of the world, differences of position are more common and justifiable than in the exact sciences. Paulsen shows that the absolute certainty which Haeckel believes he possesses in regard to the solution of the "Riddle of Existence" was already claimed in the nineteenth century by Hegel in his philosophical system. "There is but a slight difference between the old and the new position. In Hegel's monism reality is conceived as reason, in Haeckel's monism it is conceived as unreason." "Philosophia Militans," p. 180: "Haeckel's true purpose, his ultimate goal, is suggested by the names of Bruno, Spinoza, Goethe. He strives to attain an outlook which shall present life, and mental life, not as something in reality external, foreign, and accidental, but as something inherently belonging to it, as the reverse, the inner side of its being. Haeckel really wishes to say that every closed system of material processes contains a system of spiritual processes; all things are by nature psychological. . . . This is Haeckel's real meaning, but he stops at the very approach in that he speaks of the souls of atoms and cells but has not the courage to follow the principle of analogy thus suggested and speak as well of earth-souls and world-souls." (*Paulsen*, "Philosophia Militans," pp. 189 seq.) The doctrine of universal souls was proposed by *Fechner* (See *Berolzheimer*, "System," Vol. I, pp. 119 seq.).

and sociology has been followed in various directions. The collection, "Natur und Staat," consists of prize essays [1] (edited by H. E. Ziegler, Conrad, and Haeckel) in competition upon the theme: "What may we learn from the principles of evolution with reference to the political development and legislation of States?"

MATZAT,[2] who follows Stammler in his mode of approach to the problems of law, explains the origin and maintenance of law as "an adjustment of objective conduct to a foreign will." Accordingly a legal relation is "a relation of mutual adjustment between two or more persons, in which a part of the conduct of the first party must be conditioned by the will of the second, and a part of the conduct of the second party by the will of the first." He defines the State as "a community of men in a legal relation in which a part of the conduct of all members thereof is conditioned by the will of the individual member, and a part of the conduct of the individual is conditioned by the will of all the members, such relation not being subject to alterations by any foreign will." The fundamental functions of the State are protection and the maintenance of the law. The

[1] These prize essays bear the following titles: *Heinrich Matzat*, "Philosophie der Anpassung," with special reference to law and the State; also an Introduction to the general work, "Natur und Staat," by *H. E. Ziegler*, Jena 1903. *A. Ruppin*, "Darwinismus und Sozialwissenschaft," Jena 1903. *Schallmeyer*, "Vererbung und Auslese im Lebenslauf der Völker," a sociological study on the basis of the newer biology, 1903. *Hesse*, "Natur und Gesellschaft," a critical investigation of the significance of the theory of descent for the social life, 1904. *Kurt Michaelis*, "Prinzipien der Natürlichen und Sozialen Entwickelungsgeschichte des Menschen," "Anthropological and Ethnological Studies," 1904. *A. Eleutheropulos*, "Soziologie," 1904. As announced in "Natur und Staat," Part I, Introduction, pp. 22-24, the remaining volumes are as yet unissued.

[2] "Philosophie der Anpassung," pp. **131-190**, 155, 169, 207, 205, 308, 309 seq., 303, 282-310, 308.

State may also assume other functions. To what extent it may proceed is determined by the principle of "adjustment." "The activity of the State is decreasing and must decrease, is so far as the restriction of individual thought and desire is involved (for example, in the religious domain). It increases and must increase so far as it bears upon the objective conduct of men." Such adjustment is the natural character of government. The lowest stage of adjustment consists in the elimination of conflict. "But conflict can be eliminated only by mutual adjustment of one's conduct to another's will, and another's conduct to one's own will, and thus by relations of adjustment which are legal relations."

ARTHUR RUPPIN, in his "Darwinismus und Sozialwissenschaft," studies the four principles of the theory of evolution — heredity, adaptation, natural selection, and sexual selection, — with reference to their application to the social life of men.[1]

H. E. ZIEGLER[2] attempts to show that socialism[3]

[1] Here belong some of the works mentioned in § 44, particularly *Lilienfeld;* also *Schäffle's* essay, "Über Recht und Sitte vom Standpunkt der Soziologischen Erweiterung der Zuchtwahltheorie," (in "Avenarius," II, 1878, pp. 38–67); *Otto Ammon's* "Die Gesellschaftsordnung und Ihre Natürliche Grundlagen," an outline of a social anthropology for the use of all educated persons interested in social problems, Jena 1895, third edition, Jena 1900; *Joh. Speck,* "Gesetz und Individuum. Ein Beitrag zur Individuellen und Sozialen Entwickelungsgeschichte des Menschen," Hanau 1904, pp. 112–143. This attempts to apply the theory of evolution, in the sense of Goethe's idealism or law of harmony, to the study of government and law.

[2] "Die Naturwissenschaft und die Sozialdemokratische Theorie, ihr Verhältnis Dargelegt auf Grund der Werke von Darwin und Bebel." This is also a contribution to the scientific criticism of the theories of current social democracy. Stuttgart 1893.

[3] In "Freie Wissenschaft und Freie Lehre," a reply to an address delivered in Munich by *Rudolf Virchow* on "Die Freiheit der Wis-

finds no support in Darwinism. He compares the several fields of natural science with the social democratic theory, particularly with regard to marriage, struggle for existence, property, and the State.

OTTO AMMON [1] also opposes socialism from the position of Darwinism. He emphasizes the social-aristocratic value of the several classes of society, which value, the socialistic régime would destroy.[2] "The existence of classes continues the work of natural selection in man and establishes a natural improvement of the species in Darwin's sense." The educated classes should oppose social democracy "because the dominance of the masses

senschaft im Modernen Staat," Stuttgart 1878, pp. 9–50, 51–69, Ernst Haeckel outlines the principles of the theory of evolution, and then replies to Virchow's attack upon the socialistic character of the doctrine of evolution, and particularly of the theory of selection. "Darwinism is anything but socialistic," is his contention (pp. 73, 70–77).

[1] "Der Darwinismus gegen die Sozialdemokratie. Anthropologische Plaudereien," Hamburg 1891. (A collection of short essays.) "Die Gesellschaftsordnung und Ihre Natürlichen Grundlagen, Entwurf einer Sozial-Anthropologie zum Gebrauch für alle Gebildeten, die Sich mit Sozialen Fragen Befassen," Jena 1895, second edition 1896 (third edition 1900). See also in this connection *Ferd. Tönnies*, "Jahresbericht über Erscheinungen der Soziologie aus den Jahren 1895 und 1896" ("Archiv für Systematische Philosophie"), Vol. IV, 1898, pp. 237–239.

[2] "Der Darwinismus," etc., p. 74: "Social division is a natural division based upon the Darwinian law of natural selection in the struggle for existence." P. 76: "If Darwin's doctrine is not an idle invention then the fourth estate can never attain leadership, and certainly not supremacy in human society, despite such endowments as they may have; and if the fourth estate were ever to triumph by means of applying their crude strength, the success would be but temporary." Pp. 97–102: "Panmixie as the opposite of natural selection." "Die Gesellschaftsordnung und Ihre Natürlichen Grundlagen," pp. 52–66, on the social mechanisms for the natural selection of individuals; pp. 90–96, 104–127, 156–163, 177–186, 363 seq., 370–390.

is irreconcilable with the natural principles of every order of society, and would lead to the destruction of all." "The law of natural selection is operative everywhere, for example, in the army, in official, commercial, and laboring classes." "The general conclusion is that a true social and national politics cannot issue from the masses, but only from the educated classes."[1] On the other hand, Enrico Ferri,[2] an Italian follower of Karl Marx, attempts to show that socialism is not inconsistent with Darwinism in that the law of the struggle for existence may also be operative, though weakened in force in the socialistic State. At best his arguments lead to the conclusion that there is no essential relation between socialism and Darwinism.

Under the title, "Natürliche Grundlagen des Rechts und der Politik," a contribution to the philosophical and critical appreciation of the theory of evolution,[3] L. Kuhlenbeck presents a condensed survey of the natural theory of descent of Lamarck, Goethe, Geoffroy, St. Hilaire, Darwin, Weismann and Haeckel. He accepts the theory of evolution, though not the materialism often associated with it. He applies biological laws to government and society, in the course of which he considers the history of the evolution of society and of the origin of the State in general, with special consideration of the racial, class, and caste elements in the State, and of the further development of special classes, such as the professions, the clergy, and the learned classes, etc. He considers the significance of racial

[1] "Die Gesellschaftsordnung," etc., pp. 94, 372, 377, 388.

[2] "Sozialismus und Moderne Wissenschaft" (German translation, Kurella), 1895, pp. 11, 27, 30, 35–37, 83. See also *Gumplowicz*, "Geschichte der Staatstheorien," pp. 496 seq.

[3] "Thüringische Verlags-Anstalt Eisenach und Leipzig" [1905], pp. 5–54, 57 seq., 170–222, 223 seq., 232.

stock as a factor of internal political development, and of such forces as tradition, social adjustment, and the bearing of biological laws upon individual fields of the law — such as trial procedure, punishment as a means of social selection, etc. Throughout, the treatment emphasizes the place of economic forces in the political careers of nations.

Kuhlenbeck is opposed alike to socialism with its ultra-democratic and retrogressive tendencies, and to the materialism represented by capitalistic interests. He advocates a social-aristocratic idealism, "a conscious social aristocracy that shall so regulate the struggle for existence, particularly the selection among nations, that a nobler type of mankind may emerge."

§ 52. *Class and State.* Viewing retrospectively the stages of development of legal philosophy from the close of the Middle Ages to the present, we observe a continuous process of emancipation gradually brought to completion. The Reformation achieved the liberation of State supremacy from the fetters of ecclesiastical dominance and the papal throne. The Tyrannomachs abolished the civic enslavement by an appeal to reason and to Scriptural faith — at once rationalistic and theological; later, through the mediation of the spirit of Rousseau and the Encyclopedists, the great French Revolution swept away despotism, and paved the way, in republics, for the rule of the middle classes, and in other governments, for the prosperity of the third estate under the beneficent régime of an enlightened absolutism. Of similar import were the efforts of Adam Smith in behalf of economic freedom, and of Kant in behalf of the "Rechtstaat," the State as the embodiment of law. Step by step the third estate reached the position of political supremacy and economic control under legal regulation of private interests, which, while formally proclaiming the freedom of the laboring classes, actually favored their economic subjection. At this juncture the fourth estate came to its own. The laboring classes agitated for an economic emancipation to be attained under the red badge of communism and socialism. In the closing quarter of the nineteenth century this last great act of emancipation was accomplished, and with its accomplishment we approach a new and far-reaching development.

The history of such movements never presents a radical break with the old and an immediate assimilation of the new; transitional conditions ever intervene in which the vestiges of the period meeting its decline, persist side by side — and at times in sharp contrast — with the first beginnings of the new. Nature never advances by leaps and bounds. Such a period of transition, in which the symptoms of the decline of the older and of the onset of the newer ideas are evident, still prevails.

The movement of emancipation of the last century was not limited to the liberation of the great classes that suffered most from mediæval oppression. When we observe that in the course of four centuries the temporal power was emancipated from the spiritual power, and the civic estates from despotism, and the laboring classes from the capitalistic yoke, we equally note that the emancipation was always that of classes as such. It is true that with the liberation of a given class the individual members thereof also were set free, but the movement was centered upon the overthrow of the class burden, leaving the individual within the class in complete dependence. A clear example thereof is afforded by the course of social democracy, which imposes upon its adherents a discipline of such severity, and demands of the individual such large sacrifices in behalf of class interests, as would make every form of governmental or capitalistic paternalism seem mild in comparison. The masses never really attained true freedom; they merely got rid of one burden to assume another. The change induced a feeling that the oppression was gone, but in reality it was only that the yoke had been shifted. The emancipation of the classes had yet to find its complement in the emancipation of the individual. The classes concerned form a mere collectivity of men, constituting not a political nor an economic, but merely a social class, sharing the same real or apparent restrictions.

Another phase of accomplished emancipation is that relating to the status of the Jews. This began in the last quarter of the eighteenth century, but was formally completed in Germany only by the enactment of 1848 and the imperial law of July 3, 1869, proclaiming the civic and political equality of all religious confessions.

At present the emancipation of woman is coming to the front. The claim seems a just one that such women as do not seek or find the possibility of marriage should have open to them a larger number of callings and intellectual opportunities. Under the influence of the feminist movement the legal position of the married woman has been decidedly improved in the German code. While the husband remains the acknowledged head of the family, the wife enjoys co-ordinate rights. She is protected against abuses of the husband's authority; and her rights [1] as a wife and a widow are safeguarded.[2]

---

[1] Particularly laws concerning education: "Parent's control" of §§ 1626, 1684 seq., of the BGB, instead of the "paternal" control derived from Roman law. See also §§ 1356 seq., 1365-1371.

[2] See, for instance, §§ 1357, Part II, 1391-1394, 1406 BGB.

The woman's movement likewise aims to improve the political status of women, demanding that they shall have like political rights with men. When thus comprehensively expressed, the demand cannot be conceded — and that for historical, political, and practical reasons: in the first place, because so tremendous a change as that from political absence of rights to political equality would violate every principle of historical evolution; secondly, because at present the granting of political rights to women, in view of the preponderance of the laboring classes, would mean an enormous strengthening of the political influence of these classes, which, as things are, is already unduly strong; finally, because the great majority of women have no interest in public affairs, and by virtue of their physiological and psychological endowment, and of their relations to the family, naturally have a larger inclination and understanding for family cares and the household than for questions of general interest. On the other hand it is not justifiable to exclude a woman pursuing a profession from political life, nor desirable to deny the feminine mind a participation in public affairs. Practicable proposals are more likely to be brought forward as soon as the general political development will have advanced from the present transitional stage to a clearer view of the situation.

An offshoot of the general "woman's movement" is that for the abolition of the "white slave" traffic. It may be admitted that every form of prostitution indicates a cultural retrogression. But for many reasons it seems difficult to avoid the toleration,[1] though not the official recognition, of prostitution. The "abolitionists" may well limit their war against prostitution to social in-

[1] *Berolzheimer*, "Die Entgeltung im Strafrechte," pp. 168, 495-500, and the bibliography on p. 483.

fluences, and in this way are likely to produce a wholesome effect. By advocating legislative regulation the movement has conducted a successful campaign against the "white slave" traffic.[1]

A further outcome of the movement for the emancipation of woman is the agitation for an improved social status for children born out of wedlock. It proceeds upon the humanitarian sentiment that condemns the social branding of these innocent victims; it also urges the practical consideration that, as experience shows, the mothers of illegitimate children, as well as the girls thus born, are frequently led into prostitution; while statistics show that illegitimate children furnish the largest percentage of criminals. In fact there seems no reason why illegitimate children in general, or at least in cases where the mother is faithful to one man, should not socially and legally be given such position as is now granted in general to the mother and her offspring. The words of the German code read: "An illegitimate child has, in relation to the mother and to the mother's relatives, the same legal status as a legitimate child." [2]

The great process of emancipation of the laboring classes is today substantially accomplished, but problems of detail remain. Social democracy has brought

[1] See § 48 of the laws of the German Empire upon emigration, June 9, 1897. See also *Berolzheimer*, "Die Entgeltung im Strafrechte," pp. 39, 483, 499, and the bibliography there cited.

[2] *Berolzheimer*, "Die Entgeltung im Strafrechte," p. 500. Also *Shakespeare*, King Lear I, 2: —

"Why brand they us
With base? with baseness? bastardy? base
Who, in the lusty stealth of nature, take
More composition and fierce quality
Than doth, within a dull, stale, tired bed,
Go to the creating a whole tribe of fops,
Got 'tween asleep and wake?"

to the polls a body of no less than three million voters. It requires a bugle blast to reach this enormous army of recruits. Among so many leaders dissensions are inevitable; yet, despite factions and the differences of the older and the newer social democracy, there is a practical unanimity of sentiment among its leaders. This applies not alone to Germany; the international character of socialism is now more marked than in the days of Marx and Lassalle. It has affected the economic interests of middle Europe and North America, and recently those of Russia. The socialistic labor party is strongly asserting itself in behalf of the establishment and extension of its economic and political position. The dream of a Utopia is giving way to the attainment of an effective direction of government, economics, and the law in the interests of the laboring classes. Organized labor is demanding and receiving a share in the government; in France it is represented by a member of the ministry; in Germany it has many representatives in the Reichtstag, and is represented as well in governmental and municipal counsels. In the United States, in England, in Belgium, France, Germany, powerful labor unions protect the economic interests of the laboring classes. Such legislation as insurance against accident, sickness, and incapacity, indicates the scope of the measures now adopted for the protection of labor. The same applies to laws for the improvement of the hygienic condition of the laboring classes, the erection of homes for workingmen in healthful locations, with proper sanitary equipment, of sanatoriums, and recreation homes. Sanitary conditions in factories and workshops are insisted upon. There are laws that prescribe safety devices to eliminate accidents; insurance laws that protect children, pregnant and nursing women; factory inspection that secures the observance of laws and ordinances and minimizes abuse; and if, despite these provisions, the laboring classes believe that they have occasion for dissatisfaction, they threaten or declare a strike or boycott, and do not hesitate to intimidate by demonstration and sympathetic strikes.

Reviewing this general state of affairs from an unprejudiced outlook, one may reach a critical estimate of the social democracy of the present. The State of the future — whether as a consummation of hope or of fear — is but a pretext, or at most, a point of appeal for agitation. Socialism is essentially the party of labor, strenuously representing the political interests of the laboring classes. The gains of socialism are due to its enlistment of the industrial workers and of the portions of the population socially and economically affiliated with them. It appeals to the agricultural laborers, to the overworked and underpaid employees. Socialism has become a significant political force as the platform of a radical party; as such it attracts bright and energetic leaders of the intellectual type, who would not be drawn to it as the representatives of labor interests.

These considerations suggest the future importance of socialism and the position which, in their own interests, the ruling classes must assume towards it. It will be conceded that mere labor is justified in advancing its special class interests with all legally legitimate and socially available measures. By so doing it advances the interests of civilization; it undertakes to complete the emancipation of the fourth estate, and to outline the proper status of the working classes in the State of the future, which will be organized on the basis of class interests. It is, however, a short-sighted view of affairs to interpret the position of social ethics and social reform, as is now commonly done by professional writers, as representing the special interests of labor alone. On the theoretical side economics, sociology, and political economy, and on the practical side legislation and administration, should understand the purposes and motives of the socialistic movement, and shape their policies accordingly. The socialism of today is the partisan representation of the class interests of the fourth estate, and of the wage earner in particular. As such it considers the legitimate class interests of labor; under these circumstances it is no less important that the professional and commercial classes shall be similarly represented and brought to efficient expression. The socialism of the laboring classes thus appears as at once the last stage of the great process of emancipation extending from the Middle Ages to the present, and as the forerunner of the new period of the modern class-State.

The differentiation of class interests is furthermore distinctly favored by the tendency towards centralization, as against free competition in industrial enterprise. While until recently manufacturers and dealers entered into a fierce competition with one another, they have learned, through the experience of the ruin of some of their number by excessive competition, that the common interests of the manufacturers of a given trade when centralized can secure the prosperity of all. There have thus developed selling agreements, pools, trusts, and various other consolidations of interests. Legislation cannot ignore these conditions. As I have elsewhere indicated,[1] legislation must face the problem "of

[1] *Berolzheimer*, "Zur Kartellfrage. Legislativpolitische Betrachtungen." Appendix: "Entwurf Eines Gesetzes betreffend die Kartellierungen" ("Juristische Vierteljahresschrift des Deutschen Juristenvereins"), Prague, 35 vols., N. S., 19 vols., Parts III and IV, Vienna 1903, pp. 97-149, 101.

finding a proper legal embodiment for these economic conditions, so that they shall no longer be forced to resort to subterfuges and irregular procedures to retain an appearance of conformity to the law. Legislation must likewise devise means to prevent abuse and exploitation on the part of the consolidation of interests."

It may not be amiss to observe that the organization of syndicates and other forms of consolidation forms a practical argument against the socialistic position of Marx and his followers in their views of the present form of the State. For socialism urges that a capitalistically organized society will never be able to regulate production; that periods of over-production will inevitably be followed by crises due to under-production; and that the socialistic order alone can properly regulate these interests. It has been shown that when the situation arises, the State, as at present organized, can successfully deal with the problem. As representatives of class interests there must further be considered the very influential landholding class, and again, the independent middle classes, which, since the rise of the great mercantile and industrial enterprises, have changed their character and been replaced by a new middle class, composed of the higher grade employees of the great industries, and of business men.

Recent legislation has considered the interests of special classes and passed laws in behalf of the members of one or another economic class. Labor has been represented in the legal recognition of its claims to a share in the organization of industry, and again in labor insurance laws. Special provisions for employers and laborers, as well as for clerks and apprentices, have been established in connection with courts devoted specifically to industrial and mercantile affairs. The

§ 52] CLASS AND STATE 475

restrictions of the privileges of the stock exchange,[1] laws for the prevention of unfair competition,[2] regulations for medical practitioners, and so on, are further examples of class legislation. In so far as these laws emphasize the affiliation of the members of particular callings, industries, or occupations, they serve to reenforce the stratification of society, and present examples of the influence of legislation upon social and economic phenomena.

Parallel to the development in law and economics, there proceeds a transformation of an intellectual order, which, in its effect upon religious belief, is especially noteworthy. This intellectual unrest, characteristic of our day, has produced an extraordinary upheaval of religious faith. All possible attitudes find their representatives. Leaders abound and disciples are few. The absence of uniform cultural standards is evident æsthetically in the many adaptations of the styles of former periods, and in the failure to originate an adequate style expressive of present needs. Out of this period of intellectual and moral disruption there is gradually emerging a new unity and solidarity. The psychological factor that is tending towards the formation of the "Klassenstaat," the class-State, is the disorganization of our culture, and the consequent desire for peace of mind and material stability. But there

[1] See § 10 of the laws of the Stock Exchange of June 22, 1896 (Börsen-Ehrengericht).

[2] There is a sharp conflict of opinion regarding the character of the law for the prevention of unfair competition, of May 27, 1896. 'The conception which I suggested and established is as follows: 'The regulations in regard to unfair competition constitute a disciplinary law for the trades within the scope of the adjective and substantive divisions of the common law." See also *Berolzheimer*, "Die Entgeltung im Strafrechte," pp. 213–217, 214; also p. 232, notes 6 and 9, for the references to my presentations in former writings.

can be no progress without struggle. The newer materialism or monism, an intolerance of a mediæval type, an enlightened tolerant Protestantism, and other related trends of an idealistic philosophy, are all competing for favor. To the observant student of civilization there will hardly be a doubt as to which of these tendencies represents an advance to the cultural achievement of the future.

CONCLUSION

The stages of the evolutionary series thus presented may be summarized as follows: the universal absolutism of the Church; the absolutism of the ruling nobility; enlightened absolutism; absolutism of the law; and the limited absolutism of the law. Here enters a new series, the first stages of a new evolution typified by the modern class-State, the "Klassenstaat." Though this finds its parallel in certain phases of mediæval and later conditions, yet, in contrast, the new classes are essentially economic in nature: they are free, and tend to express themselves in a free, spontaneous, not legally prescribed form of association.[1]

What the ultimate form of the class-State is to be, cannot be predicted. Prophecies in the field of economics are likely to be vain. But it is certain that the class-State, founded as it is upon an economic basis, must bring about political changes. The change of economic conditions must sooner or later involve a fundamental change of the law, and particularly of public law. Parliamentary representation of the people will pave the way for legislation in the interest of the new class interests. The answer to the great political problem

---

[1] What is decisive is not merely the pursuit, but the publication and emphasis of class interests, and the growing recognition of the validity of such endeavors.

as to which class will gain supremacy may perhaps read: The free economic classes as recognized by the law of the future.

It is a significant symptom that the proprietary and educated classes are asserting their rights. Such assertion, it may be hoped, will counteract the extreme democratization of social ethics, which threatens to make the interest of the lower classes equivalent to the welfare of the State, and in its ultimate consequences leads to the economic oppression of the upper classes, as clearly as the influence of Rome is aiming at the spiritual enslavement of the lower classes.

The original problem of legal philosophy, which Rousseau formulated and Kant accepted, was the manner of association of the community through law and government, both as an expression and as a guaranty of individual freedom. This problem now demands a restatement in consideration of altered economic conditions and intellectual outlook. Present-day interests sound a note of warning to the effect that the emancipation of the fourth estate must not result in an enslavement of the upper classes, must not permit the intellectual gains which European civilization has achieved since the days of the Reformation, to be placed at the mercy of the powers of darkness.

The legal representation of the legitimate interests of every economic class, and the legal guaranty of intellectual freedom, alone can secure for every class within the State, and for every individual within his class, the self-assertion, influence, and freedom which are necessary to the complete expression of each class and of its individual members as such. It is only by such means that a people can attain its efficient development and a position of influence in the commonwealth of nations.

INDEX

[The numbers refer to the pages.]

Absolutism, 132; 153.
Adler, Georg, xliv, note 1; 107, note; 445; 445, note 3.
Adler, Max, 289, note 2.
Affolter, 13, note 3; 225, note 1.
Ahrens, xlii, note 1; 2, note; 8, note; 51, note 1; 211, note 5; 244; 245-248; 325, note 1.
Althusius, Johannes, 118, note 2; 119, note; 120; 120, note 1; 121.
Ammon, Otto, 463, 464; 463, note 1.
Anarchism, 267 seq.; 287 seq.
    violence in, 292 seq.
Anders, 43, note 4.
Antisthenes, 74.
Aquinas, Thomas, 94; 94, note 2; 98-101; 98, notes 1, 2; 99, notes 1, 2, 3, 4; 100, notes 1-9; 101, note 1.
Aranya, 36, note 2.
Aristippus, 75.
Aristotle, 28, note 1; 49, note 2; 52, note 2; 53, note 2; 57, note 2; 67 seq.; 68, note 2; 71, note 3; 72, notes 1, 2, 3; 73, notes 1, 2; 74, notes 1, 2; 76; 94; 100; 101, note 1; 115; 142; 239; 417, note 1; 420.
    ethical concepts in, 67; 68.
    Greek institutions in, 68-72; 73.
    justice in, 72.
    philosophy of, 67 seq.
Aryans, Vedic. See Vedic Aryans.
Aschaffenburg, 373; 443; 444, note.
Association of American Law Schools, v.
Assyria. See Babylonia and Assyria.
Auer, Fritz, 372, note 2; 444, note.
Augustine triumphans, 102.

Augustine, St., 61, note; 94 seq.; 94, note 1; 95; 95, notes 1, 3, 4; 96, notes 2, 3; 97, notes 5, 6, 7.
Austin, John, xiii; 141; 141, note 3.
Babylonia, 33. See also Babylonia and Assyria.
Babylonia and Assyria, 32 seq.
Bachofen, 48, note 3; 52, note 1; 388-389.
Bakunin, 289; 292-294.
Baldwin, J. Mark, 444-445.
Bar, von, 450.
Barclay, 118, note 2.
Bärenbach, Friedrich von, 364, note.
Barth, Paul, 303, note 2; 364, note; 444; 444, note 1.
Bastian, 364, note.
Bauer, 168, note 2; 170, note 3.
Baumann, J. J., 101, note 2; 453-454.
Bebel, 278-279; 403, note 2.
Beccaria, 152.
Bekker, 12, note 3; 214.
Belfort-Bax, 280, note 2; 281, note 1.
Benfey, Th., 39, note 3.
Bentham, xiv; 76; 137-139; 138, notes 1, 2, 3, 4; 139, notes 1, 2.
Bergbohm, xii, note 3; xiv; 3, note; 6, note 3; 9, note 2; 17, note 1; 141, note 4; 214.
Bergemann, 114, note; 335; 367; 446, note 1.
Bernatzik, 7, note.
Bernheim, 96, note 1.
Bernhöft, 12, note 4; 37, note 4; 39, note 3; 47, note 2; 49, note 1; 84, note; 388, note; 392, note.
Bernstein, Eduard, 280; 282; 393.
Berolzheimer, vii; xiii, note 3; xv; xviii; xxi; xxii; xxiii; xxiv; xxxix; 7, note; 21, note 2;

[The numbers refer to the pages.]

Berolzheimer—(*continued*).
23, note 1; 34, note 1; 49, note 3; 51, note 2; 55, note 1; 63, note 1; 67, note 1; 74, notes 1, 2; 77, note 1; 82, note; 86, note 3; 101, note 2; 116, note 3; 127, notes 2, 3; 129, note 2; 134, note 7; 141, note 2; 165, note 2; 174, note 1; 196, note 2; 201, note 3; 202, note 1; 203, note 1; 204, note 3; 206, note 6; 220, note 3; 221, note; 222, note 2; 225, notes 4, 5; 227, notes 1, 2; 228, note 4; 248, note 2; 295, note 2; 317, note; 335, note 6; 350, note 1; 370, note 1; 372, note 2; 374, note 3; 383, note; 392, note 1; 417, notes 2, 3; 450, notes 1, 2, 5, 6; 461, note; 469, note; 470, notes 1, 2; 473, note; 475, note 2.

Beseler, 370; 370, note 1.
Bierling, 9, note 1; 10; 10, note 1; 11, note 2; 385–386, and notes.
Biermann, W. Ed., 22, note; 130, note 3; 173, note 2; 272, note 1; 294, note 2.
Binding, 9, note 3; 23; 320; 381–384; 387; 448.
Bismarck, 332.
Blanc, Louis, 265–267.
Blum, Erich, 274, note 2.
Bluntschli, 15, note 1; 38, note 2; 136, note 1; 325, note 2.
Bocchoris, 30. See also Code of.
Boden, Friedrich, 392, note.
Bodin, 119, note; 120; 121, note 1.
Bonar, J., 7, note; 169, note 2.
Borght, v. d., 332, note.
Bouchard, 303, note 1.
Brahmin, 37.
Braun, Heinrich, 365, note.
Brentano, L., 375.
Bruno, 461, note.
Buddhism, 202.
Cæsarinus, Furstenerius. See Leibnitz.

Calker, van, 15, note 1; 335; 335, note 7.
Capital, 270 seq.; 277.
and Labor. See Labor.
Caput, 34.
Carneades, 77.
Castes, 37, note 1.
in Egypt, 28, note 1.
in India, 37 seq.
Castillejo y Duarte, xvii, note 3.
Catholic Church, 51.
and Greek philosophy, 93; 94.
and State, 95–97; 102; 119.
doctrines of, 101 seq.
Pax, 96–98.
Two Swords, 101 — philosophy of 102.
St. Augustine, 94 seq.
Thomas Aquinas, 98 seq.
sovereignty in, 107 seq.
Chaldea, 33; 34. See also Babylonia and Assyria.
China, 22.
Christianity. See also Catholic Church.
ethical view of, 89–90.
Cicero, 1, note; 83, note 2; 86, note 4; 87–89; 87, notes 1, 2; 88, notes 1, 2, 3, 4, 5, 6; 89, notes 1, 2; 115, note 3.
Civic emancipation, 124 seq.; 162.
Code —
of Bocchoris, 30.
of Hammurabi, 34 seq. See also Hammurabi.
of Manu, 39, note 3.
Prussian, 164.
Codex Hammurabi. See Hammurabi.
Coercion. See Law, and Coercion.
Cohen, Hermann, 392–395; 392, notes 1, 2; 398; 403.
Colbert, 165; 166.
Communal will. See Community.
Communism, 260 seq;. 291 seq.
and anarchism, 267 seq.
and communists, 90.
and socialism, 267 seq.
French, 260 seq.

INDEX

[The numbers refer to the pages.]

Community —
    organization of, 365 seq.; 367.
Comte, xix; 308–316; 351.
Conrad, 462.
Corporation, 370 seq.
Coste, 364, note.
Crime. See Punishment.
Croce, xvii, note 4.
Crusades. See Economic organization and the Crusades.
Culture —
    conception of, xvii seq.
    stages of, xli; xlii.
Curtius, 48, notes 1, 2, 3.
Cynics, 74.
Cyrenaics, 75.
Dahn, xlii, note 3; 2, note; 6, note 2; 248; 252–255.
Dante, 108; 108, notes 2, 3.
Dargun, 392, note.
Darwin, xvii; 56; 230; 317; 458; 463, note 2; 464; 464, notes 1, 2; 465.
Dauriac, xx, notes 1, 2.
De Morgan, 34.
Descartes, 115; 234; 314.
De Tocqueville, iii.
Dhama, 38; 97.
Dharma, 38; 39.
Dialectics, 17.
    in Hegel, 219–223.
Dicaspoloi, 47.
Diderot, 152–155, and notes; 170, note 3; 336.
    his maxims, 154, note.
Diehl, 177, note.
Dietzel, 332, note.
Dike, 47.
Diodorus Siculus, 26; 27, note 1; 28, note 1; 31, note 3.
Diogenes Laërtius, 76, notes 1, 2.
Dodona, 47.
Du Bois-Reymond, 146, note 2.
Dühring, 190.
Dumont, 138, note 1.
Du Plessis-Mornay, 120, note 2.
Economic organization, 328 seq.
    and the church, 104–106.
    and the Crusades, 105.
    crafts and trades, 106–108.

Economic organization — (continued).
    influence of Jews upon, 106.
    in Middle Ages, 103 seq.
Economics —
    and industry, 172 seq.
    and law, 20 seq.; 399 seq.
    conception of, 23.
    classical, 170 seq.
    Egyptian, 27 seq.
    Mosaic, 43 seq.
    of labor. See Labor.
    philosophy of, 16; 375 seq.
    conception of, 5.
    in Fichte. See Fichte.
Egypt, 25 seq.
Eichhorn, 212.
Eisler, R., 3, note; 365, note; 446, note 1.
Eleutheropulus, 462, note 1.
Ellis, Havelock, 443, note 4.
Elster, 170, note 2.
Eltzbacher, 289, note 2; 294, note 2.
Emancipation, 281 seq.; 286; 315; 467 seq.
Enfantin, 263.
Engels, Fr., xiv; 269, note 1; 273; 276; 284.
Epicureans, 76.
Epicurus, 76; 131.
Erdmann, Joh. Ed., 53; 53, note 4.
Erinyes, 48; 49; 56.
Ethics, xxiv; xliii. See also Law, ethical concepts in.
    Egyptian, 26 seq.
    Greek, 47 seq.; 91.
    Kantian, 181–184.
    of the Vedic Aryans, 38 seq.
Ethos, 38.
Eumenides, 48.
Evolution, xvii; 456 seq.; 458 seq.; 461 seq.; 463 seq.
Exchange. See Supply and Demand.
Falckenberg, 184, note 3.
Fechner, 461, note.
Federal Supreme Court, v.
Ferguson, xlv, note 1; 352–354.
Ferri, 18, note 1; 372; 465.
Feudal system. See Economic organization.

INDEX

[The numbers refer to the pages.]

Feuerbach, xiv; 269, note 2.
Fichte, J. G., 183; 192–201, and notes; 221; 230; 234; 235; 264; 409; 420.
  philosophy of law of, 194–198.
  philosophy of economics of, 198–200.
Finger, 373.
Fischer, Kuno, 229.
Flux —
  Heraclitean, xviii.
Fourier, 264–265. See also Communism.
Fourth Estate, xxv.
Frankenstein, 332.
Frederick the Great, 146, note 2; 162–165, and notes.
Freedom, and Free Will, 194; 362.
  concept of, 218.
  in anarchism, 296.
  in Hegel, xvi; 218 seq
  in Kant, 183 seq.
Free Trade, 172; 178.
French Revolution, 22; 113; 152; 170; 199; 285; 466.
Friedberg, 103, note 1.
Friedländer, xiii, note 1.
Friedrichs, 392, note.
Gans, 232; 232, note 3.
Gareis, xiii, note 4.
Garofalo, 372, note 2; 373.
Gary, Elbert H., viii.
Geyer, 1, note; 4, note 2; 95, note 2; 117, note 1; 143, note 1; 211, note 5; 252; 252, note 1.
Ghibellines, 101.
Giddings, 364, note.
Gierke, 118, note 2; 120; 120, note 1; 369–372; 370, notes 1, 2; 371, notes.
Gilbert, G., 62, note.
Gneist, 327 seq.
Gobineau, 357, note 5.
Godwin, W., 155.
Goethe, 127; 230; 461, note; 465.
Gopa, 37, note 1.
Gothein, 328, note 2; 421.
Government, xliii.
  and liberty, 148, 149.
  and popular welfare, 150.
  and popular will, 150.

Government—(*continued*).
  in Egypt, 27.
  in India, 36.
  sovereign in, 121; 162-164; 187.
Grama, 36, note 2.
Grave, J., 287, note; 290, note; 291, note; 292, notes 2, 3; 293, notes 1, 2; 295, note 1; 297, note 1.
Gray, vi.
Greek Institutions. See Institutions, Greek.
Greek Law. See Law, Greek.
Greek Philosophy. See Philosophy, Greek.
Grimm, W., 102.
Gross, H., 443, note 4.
Grotius, Hugo, xlv, note 1; 6; 74, note 1; 115–118; 115, notes 2, 3, 4; 116, notes 1, 2, 3; 117, note 1; 126; 156; 284; 420.
Grünberg, 303, note 1.
Guelphs, 101.
Gumplowicz, xxi; 13, note 3; 167; 302, note 2; 312; 325, note 2; 326, note 1; 327, note 3; 328, note 4; 352; 354; 354, note 1; 356–358, and notes; 362; 363; 368; 369; 369, note; 465, note 2.
Günther, S., 388, note 1.
Haeckel, Ernst, xvii; 230; 458–462; 465.
Hamel, van, 373.
Hammurabi, 34, 35.
Haney, xlii, note 2.
Harms, xvi, note 3; 2, note; 214.
Harnack, 113, note; 114, note.
Harper, Robert, 34, note 5.
Hartmann, Ed. von, 190; 334; 427–431.
Hasbach, W., 173, note 1.
Haymann, F., 147; 148, note; 149, note 2.
Hegel, xv. seq.; 1; 1, note; 17; 52; 53; 55; 117; 127; 183; 190; 191; 215–232; 249, note 1; 254; 255; 258; 282; 285; 317; 334; 387; 422; 431; 461, note.

INDEX

[The numbers refer to the pages.]

Hegel—(*continued*).
  conception of the State, 223–224.
  critical verdict of, 228–232.
  dialectics of, 219–223.
  ethics of, 217–219.
  legal ideas, 224–228.
  philosophy of law, 215–217.
Hegelians, xxi, seq.; 215; 232–233.
Heinemann, 383, note.
Hensel, 317, note.
Heraclitus, 55; 56; 230.
  philosophy of, 55; 56.
Herbart, 248–251; 248, note 3; 249, notes 1, 2, 3; 250, note 1; 251, notes 1, 2, 3.
Herder, 211–213.
Hermann, Fr. B. W. von; 7, note.
Herodotus, 26; 28, note 1; 29, note 1.
Hesse, A., 462, note 1.
Hieronymus Balbus, 109.
Hildenbrand, 48, notes 2, 3; 52, note 3; 54, note 2; 55, note 3; 56, notes 2, 3; 71, note 1; 75, note 3; 85, notes 1, 2.
Hirzel, 39, note 4.
Historism, 254, 255. See also Law, Historical School of.
Hobbes, 76; 122–125; 131; 132; 180; 185; 241; 351.
Homer, 49.
Hugo, 6; 17; 212.
Hume, xix.
Hybris, 48; 91; 97.
Idealism, 50.
Ihering, von, v; xv, note 1; xliii; 3, note 1; 14; 76; 129; 337–351; 337, note 2; 345, note; 383, note 1; 448.
Illusion—
  principle of, xii; xliii; xliv, note 1; 102; 168; 445.
Inama-Sternegg, von, 104, note; 106, note.
India, 22.
Individualism, 289 seq.
Industry. See Labor.

Institutions—
  Greek, 67 seq.
    the aristocrat, 68–70.
    society, 70–72.
  Roman, 78 seq.
    paterfamilias, 80 seq.; 82.
    property in, 81.
    Roman-Italian State, 82 seq.
  Yeoman, 103.
Jaffé, Edgar, 365, note.
Jahweh, 41; 41, note 4.
Jastrow, I., 16, note 1.
Jellinek, 10; 10, note 2; 17, note 1; 69, note; 115, note 1; 120, note 1; 151, note 4; 257, note 2; 272, note 2; 325, note 2; 326, note 1; 331, note; 421; 435–442.
Jewish State. See Law, mosaic.
Jews. See Economic organization, influence of Jews upon.
Jolly, Julius, 39, note 3.
Junius Brutus, 120; 120, note 2.
Jurisprudence, iv; 6; 9 seq.; 11; 385, note 2; 431 seq.; 448.
  and history, 208 seq.
  ethnological, 387 seq., 424.
Jus civile, xxv.
Jus naturæ. See Natural law.
Justice, 116; 117; 214; 411 seq.; 417 seq.
  and morality, 409 seq.; 452, seq.
Kakkadu, 34.
Kant, xi; xi, notes 2, 3; xii; xiii seq.; xiii, note 1; xv, note 1; xlvii, note; 17; 129; 129, note 1; 134; 134, note 6; 180–192; 195; 196; 199–200; 202; 221; 222, note 1; 229; 234; 235; 255; 286; 312; 314; 393; 408; 420; 428; 452; 460, note; 466; 477.
  conception of the State, 187; 188.
  ethics of, 181–184.
  philosophy of law, 184–187.
Kantian, xxi seq; 189–192.
Kaulla, 107, note.
Kautsky, K., 269, note 1; 279; 282.

INDEX

[The numbers refer to the pages.]

Kitzinger, 374, note 1.
Klassenstaat, 282; 473; 475; 476; 466 seq.; 473 seq.; 476 seq.
Klöppel, 328, note 2; 367.
Klotz, 373.
Knies, 375; 446, note 1.
Kohler, xvi; xvii seq; xvii, notes 1, 2, 3, 5; xviii, notes 1, 4; xix, note 2; xliii, note; xliv, note 3; 3, note; 10, note; 12; 13, note 1; 15, note 1; 17, note 1; 32, note 2; 53, notes 1, 3; 35, notes 1, 2; 55, note 4; 229; 230; 230, note; 387; 387, note 2; 389, note 1; 390; 422–427.
Krapotkin, 287, note; 291–292; 293, note 2; 294, note 4.
Krause, Karl Chr. Fr., 2, note; 240–244; 240, note 2; 246; 248; 443.
Krauss, A., 444, note.
Kuhlenbeck, 465–466.
Kuhn v. Fairmont Coal Co., v.
Kuhn, 36, note 3.
Kulturnormen, 10, note.
Kulturstaat, 183; 193; 200; 224; 231; 255; 268; 275; 300.
Laband, Paul, xxxix.
Labor, 172; 261; 266; 270 seq.
  and capital. See Capital.
  economics of, 270 seq.; 305; 471; 474 seq.
Labriola, 392, note; 395, note 3.
"Laisser faire," xiii; xlvii.
Lamarck, 230; 317; 465.
Lammasch, 374.
Lamprecht, K., 22, note; 107, note.
Landrecht. See Code, Prussian.
Landsberg, 124, note 4; 133, note 2.
Languet, Hubert, 120, note 2.
Lassalle, xlv, note 1; 48, note 2; 55, notes 3, 4; 56, notes 2, 3; 178; 232; 232, note 1; 233; 233, note 1; 274–276; 285; 471.
Lasson, xxii; 2, note; 67, note 2; 133, note 2; 194, note; 211, note 5; 217, note 2; 255–259.
Laurent, 105, note; 114, note.

Law. See also Legislation.
  and coercion, 405 seq.; 429.
  and economics, 20 seq.; 399 seq.; 418, 421. See also Economics, philosophy of.
  and society. See Social organization.
  and the human will, 217 seq.; 343.
  commerical —
    in Babylonia, 33.
    in Egypt, 33.
  comparative, 6; 12; 18; 387 seq.; 390 seq.
  constituted, 4; 98; 133; 411 seq.
  customary, 8.
  ecclesiastical, 4.
  Egyptian, 25 seq.
  ethical concepts in, 134; 157; 158; 160; 181–183; 198; 202; 203; 205–207; 236; 238 seq.; 248 seq.; 258; 259; 334 seq.; 336–337; 338 seq.; 359 seq.; 409 seq.; 412 seq.; 415; 422 seq.; 425, 427 seq.; 433 seq.; 446 seq.; 451 seq.; 454 seq.; 456 seq.
  historical school of, 6–7; 17; 21; 204 seq.; 254; 375.
  Mosaic, 35; 40 seq.
  natural. See Natural Law.
  Oriental. See Egyptian.
  origin of, 213; 320 seq.; 390.
  philosophy of, iv; xxiv seq.; xlvi; 8 seq.; 383; 422 seq.; 424; 441.
    conception of, 1–4; 180; 184 seq.; 216; 217; 447; 477.
    in Ahrens, 244 seq.
    in America, v seq.
    in Europe, vii.
    in Fichte, 194–198.
    in Germany, xxiii.
    in Greece, 46 seq.
    in Ihering, 350; 351.
    in Kant, 188 seq.
    in Krause, 240 seq.
    in Lasson, 255 seq.
    in Schelling, 204 seq.

INDEX

[The numbers refer to the pages.]

Law, philosophy of —(*continued*).
  method of, 16–20; 398 seq.
  or recent systems, 233 seq.
  psychological aspects of, 431 seq.; 442 seq.
  Roman, 7; 79 seq.; 156.
  æquitas in, 83 seq.
  and Christian ethics, 89 seq.
  justice in, 100.
  persona in, 86.
  precepts of, 99.
  Twelve Tables in, 78.
  statutory. See Law, constituted.
  Vedic Aryan, 36.
Le Bon, Gustave, 364, note.
Legislation —
  in Egypt, 28.
  Mosaic, 35.
Leibnitz, 126; 156–160; 180; 181; 314; 334.
Leist, B. W., 31, note 2; 36, note 2; 38, notes 1, 2; 39, notes 1, 2; 47, note 2; 48 notes 1, 2, 3; 83, notes 1, 2, 3; 84, note; 88, note 6; 391.
Leonardo da Vinci, 122, note 4.
Lepsius, C. R., 31, note 2.
Leroy, iv.
Letourneau, 364, note.
Lex. See Law.
Liberty. See Government and liberty.
Liepmann, 14, note 1; 120, note 1; 146, note 1; 147; 149, note 3; 450.
Lilienfeld, P. von, 364, note; 463, note 1.
Lilenthal, von, 373.
Lingg, 12, note 1; 17, note 1.
Lippert, 364, note.
Liszt, von, 15, note 2; 18, note 1; 372, and notes; 373; 373, note 3; 383, note.
Locke, 312, note 4; 134–137; 135, note 1; 136, note 1; 138.
Loening, Richard, 17, note 2; 68, note 2; 136, note 1; 215.
Lombroso, 443, note 4.

Loria, 303–304.
Lossen, 120, note 2.
Lupold v. Bebenburg, 109. See Bebenburg.
Luther, 113; 114; 114, note; 189; 284; 417.
Lyon, 34, note 4.
Ma, 31.
Macchiavelli, 110; 111.
Mackay, 287, note; 290, note; 294, notes 1, 3; 297, note 1; 322, note 2.
Maine, Sir Henry Sumner, xiv, note 5; 82, note; 86, note 1; 392, note.
Manchester School, 275; 275, note 1.
Manifesto of 1848, 283 seq ; 283, note.
Manu. See Code of Manu.
Marsilius of Padua, 109; 109, notes 1, 2, 3.
Marx, xiv; xlv, note 1; 20; 22; 178; 262; 269–274; 276; 277; 281; 282; 282, note; 283; 283, note; 285; 302; 410; 418; 465; 471; 474.
Masaryk, 269, note 2; 446, note 1.
Motzat, H., 462–463.
Maugras, G., 146, note 2; 150, note.
Mayer, Max Ernst, 10, note; 387.
McCulloch, 174, note 2.
Mediævelism, 93 seq.; 113; 120.
  and the Renaissance, 110.
Medici, Lorenzo de, 110.
Meili, F., 391, note 2.
Menger, Anton, 270, note; 272, note 1; 298–302.
Menger, Carl, 377.
Menzel, Ad., 132, note 1.
Mercantilists, 165 seq.; 170. See also Economics.
Merkel, Adolf, 7, note; 10; 10 note 3; 368; 382, note 2; 446–450.
Merkel, Rudolf, 446, note 2.
Metschnikoff, 323, note.
Meyer, Ed., 45, note 3.
Meyer, G., 14, note.

[The numbers refer to the pages.]

Michælis, Kurt, 41, note 1; 42, notes 1, 2, 3, 4; 43, notes 1, 2, 3, 4, 5; 44, notes 2, 4, 6, 7; 45, note 1; 462, note 1.
Mill, John Stuart, 68, note 2; 139–141; 139, note 3; 140, notes 1, 2, 3; 141, notes 1, 2.
Mirabeau, Victor Riquetti, 169; 170, note 1.
Miraglia, vii.
Mohl, R. von, 14, note; 95, note 2; 143, note 1; 167, note 1; 325.
Mollat, 156, note 2; 157, notes 2, 3; 158, notes 1, 2, 3, 4, 5; 159, note 2.
Monarchomach. See Tyranny, rebellion against.
Monism. See Evolution.
Monogamy. See Woman, position of.
Montaigne, 77, note 2.
Montesquieu, xliii, note 1; 3, note 1; 141–143; 141, note 5; 142, notes 1, 2; 143, note 1.
Morality. See Ethics, also Law, ethical concepts in.
Morgan, Lewis H., 276, note 2; 392, note.
Mosaic, 25; 35; 36; 40; 40 note 2; 41; 42; 43; 44.
   law. See Law, mosaic.
   religious view, 90.
Müller, David H., 35, notes 1, 2.
Müller, K. O. 48, note 3.
Müller, Max, 37, note 1.
Müller, Paul, 11, note 1.
Natorp, 393; 395–398; 395, note 3; 398.
Natural Law, xiv; xxii; 6; 21; 98; 115; 116; 120; 130; 133; 144; 167; 168; 174; 195; 197; 209; 247; 321; 413; 422.
Naville, 31, note 2.
Nemesis, 49.
Neo-Hegelian, xi; xv; xix; xxiv; xxxix.
Neo-Kantian, xi; xiii, xxi seq.; 8; 392 seq.
Neo-Platonists, 77.
Netter, 335.

Neukamp, 392, note.
Nicholaus Cusanus, 109.
Niebuhr, 212.
Nietzsche, xliv, note 2; 190; 290; 330; 334; 456–457.
Nordau, 459, note.
Norms, Theory of, 9; 381–384; 384–388; 412; 448. See also Binding.
Objectivism, 49 seq.
Œtker, 383, note.
Œttli, 35, note, 2; 42, note, 2; 44, note 5.
Oncken, Aug., 101, note 2; 107, note; 169, note 2.
Osiris, 31.
Ostwald, W., 323, note.
Ownership. See Property.
Pax. See Catholic Church, philosophy of, doctrines of.
Pachmann, 17, note.
Pantheism, xvi; 127.
Passow, 54, note 1.
Patersen, iv.
Paulsen, xii, note; 451–453; 461, note.
Peiser, 32, note 2; 33, notes 1, 3; 35, notes, 1, 2.
Penology, 17, note 2; 372 seq.
Persena, 224–227.
Peter de Andlo, 103; 103, note 2.
Pfleiderer, 48, note 3.
Philosophy —
   general, 313 seq;. 393; 402 seq.
      ethical concepts in, 128 seq; 393 seq.
   legal —
      in England, 134 seq.
      in France, 141 seq.
   post-Aristotelean. See Cynics, Cyrenaics, Stoics, Epicureans, Sceptics, Neo-Platonists.
   Roman —
      ethical concepts in, 79; 83; 85–87; 87–89; 90–91.
      in Cicero, 87 seq.
Phœnicia, 45.
Physis, 46; 47.
Physiocrats, 167 seq. See also Economics and Mercantilists.

INDEX

[The numbers refer to the pages.]

Pierret, 29, note 1; 30, notes 2, 3; 31, notes 1, 2.
Plato, xlvii, note; 28, note 1; 46; 57, notes 1, 2; 60 seq.; 63, notes 3, 4, 5; 64, notes 4, 5, 6, 7; 65, notes 1, 2, 3, 4, 5; 95; 239.
Platonism, 60 seq.
  ethical concepts in, 61; 62; 64; 65.
  Greek institutions in, 62; 65.
  ideas and ideals in, 63.
Plotinus, 77; 77, note 3.
Plutarch, 48, note 3; 76, note 1.
Politics, xlvii.
Polygamy. See Woman, position of.
Positive Law. See Law, constituted.
Positivism —
  and positivists, xi; xix seq.; 308 seq. See also Conite.
  and sociology, 133 seq.
Post, Alb. Herm., 12; 364, note; 390.
Pound, Roscoe, xiii, note 2; xiv, note 1; xvi, note 4; xx.
Pragmatism, xx.
Prins, 373.
Property, 226–228; 246; 322; 327.
Protagoras, 57.
Protection, 173.
Proudhon, 287–289; 289, note 2; 296, note 1.
Prutz, 108, note 1.
Ptolemies, 30.
Puchta, 6; 17; 212; 213.
Pufendorf, 118, note 1; 122–126; 126, note 1; 133; 157.
Punishment, 187; 203; 346; 382; 434; 442 seq.; 449–450. See also Penology.
  in Egypt, 26.
Pythagoras, 51; 52 seq.
  his philosophy, 51 seq.
  symbolism in, 52–54.
  justice in, 52, 53, 54.

Quasi-tutelle, 30.
Quesnay, F., 167; 168; 169, notes 1, 3; 170; 170, notes 1, 2; 172.

Ratio —
  legis, 4; 83; 84.
  naturalis, 97.
Rationalism, xvii.
Ratzenhofer, 358–364, and notes.
Rê, 26; 27.
Realism, 50.
Rechtsnormen, 10, note.
Rechtsstaat, 137; 186; 188; 189; 192 seq.; 200; 224; 268; 285; 466.
Reclus, Élisée, 287, note; 290, note; 293, note 1; 295; 297, note 1.
Reformation, 113; 114; 119.
Rehm, 14, note; 15, note 1; 103, note 2.
Religion, xliii.
  Egyptian, 26 seq.
Renaissance, 111.
Renan, 41, notes 3, 4.
Reuter, H., 95, note 1.
Revillout, Eugène, 25, note 1; 28, notes 1, 2; 29, notes 1, 2; 30, notes 1, 2, 4, 5; 31, notes 1, 3; 32, notes 1, 2; 33, notes 1, 2, 4, 5, 7; 34, notes 1, 2, 3.
Revillout, Victor, 25, note 1.
Ricardo, 22; 174–178; 290.
Richelieu, 166.
Ritter, 51, note 3; 53, note 2.
Rigveda, 36, note 1; 39, note 4.
Rita, 37; 38; 83; 97.
Rna, 40, note 1.
Roberty, 364, note.
Rodbertus–Jagetzow, 276–278.
Röder, 244.
Rohde, 48, note 3.
Roman dominion, 114.
Roman institutions. See Institutions, Roman.
Roman law. See Law, Roman.
Roman philosophy. See Philosophy, Roman.
Rossbach, 77, note 2.
Rousseau, J. J., 21; 120, note 1; 143–151, and notes; 186; 188; 199–201; 230; 285; 288, note 6; 298; 330; 351; 362; 408; 420; 466; 477.

INDEX

[The numbers refer to the pages]

Rousseau—(continued).
  origin of State, 147.
  social contract, 147–150; 148, note.
  social organization, 144–147.
Ruedemann, R., 444, note 1.
Ruppin, 462, note 1; 463.
Saint-Simon, 260–264; 309; 323.
Salzmann, 156, note 1.
Sandras de Courtilz, 167.
Sat-pati, 36.
Savigny, 6; 17; 84, note; 212; 213; 214.
Say, J. B., 178; 266.
Sâyana Akârya, 36, note 1.
Sceptics, 77.
Schäffle, 328, note 3; 354–356; 354, notes 7, 8; 364, note; 463, note 1.
Schallmeyer, 462, note 1.
Scheil, 34.
Schleiermacher, 354; 354, notes 2, 3, 4, 5, 6.
Schelling, 6; 17; 49, note 1; 55; 127; 204–211; 230; 234; 235; 243; 254; 285.
Schmidt, Kaspar. See Stirner.
Schmidt, Max, 392, note.
Schmidt, Rich., 15, note 1; 450–451.
Schmoller, 174, note 1; 377; 445, note 3.
Schoemann, 48, note 3.
Scholasticism, 16.
Schools —
  of philosophy of law, xxi seq.
Schopenhauer, xv, note 1; 117; 117, note 3; 143; 144; 190; 201–204.
Schreiter, 431; 456.
Schröder, L. von, 52, note 1; 54, note 1.
Schüller, Rich., 173, note 2; 377, note 2.
Schuppe, W., 12, note 3; 13, note 2; 17, note 1; 18, note 2; 386, note 4; 433, note 1; 454–456.
Schurtz, Heinrich, 364, note.
Scipio, K., 95, note 4; 96, note 1.
Seneca, 89; 115, note 3.

Shaftesbury, 336–337, 336, notes; 337, notes.
Shakespeare, 154; 470, note 2.
Sighele, Scipio, 373, 443; 444, note.
Simmel, George, 442.
Skarzynski, von, 171, note 2; 178, note 2.
Slavery, 145; 149; note 4; 319.
  in Babylonia and Assyria, 32.
  in Egypt, 28.
  in Greece, 62; 71; 71, note 1.
Smith, Adam, 170–174; 171, notes 1, 2; 178, note 2; 266; 275; 285; 290; 466. See also Ricardo.
Social aristocracy, 456 seq.
Social contract, 185; 186; 199.
Social democracy, 283 seq.; 472 seq., See also Socialism.
Social economics, 399 seq.
Social ethics, 331 seq.; 339 seq.; 347; 380.
Socialism, 267 seq.; 277 seq.; 298 seq.; 323; 461 seq.; 463 seq.; 472 seq.
  German, 269 seq.
  varieties of, 298 seq.
Social organization, xliii; 315 seq.; 318 seq.; 322 seq.; 325 seq.; 328 seq.; 341 seq.; 344; 367; 379; 399 seq.; 436 seq.
Social regulation, 342 seq.; 395 seq.
  in Middle Ages, 103 seq.
Society. See Social organization.
Sociological School, xxi; 308 seq.; 348; 351 seq.; 368 seq.
Sociology, 458 seq.
  and ethics, 349 seq.; 356; 361; 363; 366; 377 seq.
  and positivism, 313 seq.
  development of, 308 seq.; 352 seq. See also Comte, and Spencer.
  ideals in, 333 seq.
  legal, 6; 13–15; 15, notes 2, 3.
Socrates, iii; 28, note 1; 57 seq.; 60; 64.
  ethical concepts in, 58; 59.
  his philosophy, 57 seq.

INDEX

[The numbers refer to the pages.]

Solon, 28, note 1.
Sombart, 303–307; 365, note.
Sophists, 56; 59.
Sovereignty, 120; 121; 357; 438 seq.
 and the people, 121; 358.
Speck, J., 463, note 1.
Spencer, Herbert, xx; 56; 230; 317–323; 351 399.
Spinoza, 96; 127–132; 127, note 1; 129, note 1; 130, notes 2, 3; 131, note 2; 132, note 1; 158; 167; 185; 188; 235; 241; 314; 316; 363; 452; 461, note.
Stahl, 1, note; 6, note 1; 8, note; 95, note 1; 103, note 2; 130, note 2; 143, note 1; 211, note 5; 233–235; 281.
Stammler, xiv; xiv, notes 2, 3, 4; xv, note 1; 8; 21, note 2; 74, note 2; 115, note 1; 147; 147, notes 1, 2; 214, note 4; 393; 398–422.
State. See also Klassenstaat, Kulturstaat, Rechtsstaat, Zwangstaat.
 and contract, 125; 385.
 foundation of, 124–126; 135; 147; 161; 185; 186; 187; 188; 196; 197; 237; 451.
 nature of, 122 seq.; 136; 137; 210; 211; 223; 224; 252–254; 257; 258; 347 seq.; 357 seq.; 369; 378; 394 seq.; 436 seq.; 462 seq.; 466 seq.
 psychological motives, 128 seq.
 purpose of, xiii; 199; 266; 275.
Stein, Lorenz von, 325–331.
Stein, Ludwig, 294, note 2; 296, note 2; 333–335; 364, note; 435, note 4.
Steinmetz, S. R., 392, note.
Stern, Jacques, 215; 215, note 3.
St Hilaire, Geoffroy, 465.
Stintzing, 121, note 1.
Stirner, 130; 289–291; 296; 330; 456.
Stoics, 75; 87–89; 129; 130; 241; 434.

Stooss, Karl, 373; 373, notes 2, 6.
Subjectivism, 49 seq.
Sudra, 37.
Supply and demand, 175 seq.
Susa, 34.
Svadha, 38.
Tacitus, 154.
Tarde, 364, note; 442–443; 444; 444, note.
Tariff, xxv.
Theodorus, 75.
Themis, 38; 47.
Thomasius, 132–134; 132, note 5; 133, note 3; 169, note 2; 180.
Thompson, 270.
Thomsen, Andreas, 444, note.
Thon, 384.
Tille, Alex., 445, note 3; 458.
Timon, 77.
Tolstoi, 144; 297–298; 330.
Tönnies, Ferd., 328, note 2; 365–367; 464, note 2.
Treitschke, von, 325, note 2.
Trendelenburg, 238–240.
Tucker, Benj. R., 297.
Turgot, 167, note 4; 170.
Twesten, 28, note 1; 33, note 6; 37, notes 3, 4; 41, note 1; 45, note 2.
Two Swords. See Catholic Church, philosophy of, doctrines of.
Tyranny—
 rebellion against, 118–121, 148.
Tyrannomach, 286: 466. See Tyranny, rebellion against.
Uhlemann, 28, note 1; 30, note 2.
Uhlhorn, 332, note.
Utilitarianism, 138–141.
 and utility, 131.
 social, 336; 337.
Vanicek, 46, note 1; 47, note 2; 48, note 1.
Vaisya, 37.
Value. See Supply and demand.
Vanni, Icilio, xx.
Veda, 36; 36, note 1.
Vedic Aryans, 36; 47; 96.
Virchow, 463, note 3.
Voigt, Moritz, 84; 85.
Voltaire, 146, note 2.
Urata, 38.

INDEX

[The numbers refer to the pages.]

Vridanke, 102, note 1.
Wage, 177. See Labor.
Wahlberg, 443, note 4.
Wallon, 71, note 1.
War —
   legal relations of, 116–118.
Ward, Lester F., 364, note.
Warnkönig, 4, note 2.
Weber, A., 37, note 2.
Weber, Max, 365, note.
Weinrich, von, 383, note.
Weissmann, 465.
Wallhausen, J., 41, note 1.
Will. See Freedom and Free Will.
William of Occam, 108; 108, note 4.
Wilkinson, 26, note 1; 29, notes 2, 3; 30, note 1; 52, note 1.
Windelband, Wilh., xii, note, and note 2; xvi; xix, note 1.
Wolf, Jul., 281; 281, note 2.
Wolff, Chr. von, 126; 160–162, and notes; 180; 189; 285.
Wollstonecraft, Mary, 156.

Worms, 328, note 3; 364, note.
Woman —
   position of, 468 seq.
   in Babylonia and Assyria, 33.
   in Egypt, 30.
   in India, 37.
Wundt, 17, note 1; 23, note; 431–435.
Xenophon, 58, note; 59, note.
Zeno, 47; 48; 75.
Zeller, 77, notes 2, 3.
Zenker, 289, note 2; 294, note 2; 328, note 3; 364, note.
Ziegler, H. E., 462; 463.
Zimmer, 36, notes 2, 3; 37, notes 1, 2, 3 4; 40, note 1.
Zimmermann, R., 126, note 3.
Zimmern, Helen, 156, note 1.
Zitelmann, 383, note; 435; 454, note 3.
Zorn, 108, note 1.
Zwangstaat, 268.
Zweck im Recht. See Ihering.

www.ingramcontent.com/pod-product-compliance
Lightning Source LLC
Chambersburg PA
CBHW022054150426
43195CB00008B/133